SCOTT®

SPECIALIZED CATALOGUE OF UNITED STATES
ESSAYS AND PROOFS

EDITOR-IN-CHIEF	Jay Bigalke
EDITOR-AT-LARGE	Donna Houseman
CONTRIBUTING EDITOR	Charles Snee
EDITOR EMERITUS	James E. Kloetzel
SENIOR EDITOR/NEW ISSUES & VALUING	Martin J. Frankevicz
CATALOGUE COORDINATOR	Eric Wiessinger
SENIOR GRAPHIC DESIGNER	Cinda McAlexander
ADVERTISING/SALES	David Pistello, Eric Roth, Brenda Wyen, Julie Dalhstrom
PRESIDENT	Rick Amos

AMOS MEDIA

1660 Campbell Road, Suite A, Sidney, Ohio 45365

Publishers of
Linn's Stamp News, Scott Stamp Monthly, Coin World, and *Coin World Monthly*

ADVERTISING INDEX

ISBN: 978-0-89487-741-4

Additions, deletions and number changes

Number in 2024 Catalogue	Number in 2025 Catalogue
Essays and Proofs	
new	795-E1
new	795-E2
new	928-E1
new	3068-E1
new	3087-E1
new	3087-E2
new	3087-E3
new	3087-E4
new	3087-E5
new	3087-E6
new	3136-E1
new	3136-E2
new	3136-E3
new	3136-E4
new	3136-E5
new	3136-E6
new	3136-E7
new	3136-E8
new	3136-E9
new	3136-E10
new	3136-E11
new	BK294-E1
Trial Color, Die and Plate Proofs	
new	209TC6b
new	261ATC1de
new	795P1d
new	RO123TC1af

ESSAYS

An essay is a proposed design that differs in some way from the issued stamp.

During approximately 1845-1890, when private banknote engravers competed for contracts to print U.S. postage stamps, essays were produced primarily as examples of the quality of the firms' work and as suggestions as to what their finished product would look like. In most cases, dies were prepared, often with stock vignettes used in making banknotes. These dies were used to print essays for the Post Office Department. Rarely did the competitors go so far as to have essay plates made.

From 1894 onward, virtually all stamps were engraved and printed by the Bureau of Engraving and Printing (BEP). This usually required two types of essays. The first was a model design which was approved — or disapproved — by the Postmaster General. Sometimes preliminary drawings were made by the BEP designers, often in an enlarged size, subsequently photographically reduced to stamp size. An accepted stamp design usually became the engraver's model.

Occasionally during the course of engraving the die, a "progressive proof" was pulled to check the progress of the engraver's work. Because these were produced from an incompletely engraved die, they differ from the final design and are listed here as essays.

During approximately 1867-1870, various experiments were conducted to prevent the reuse of postage stamps. These included experimental grill types, safety papers, water-sensitive papers and inks, coupon essays, and others. These also differed in some way from issued stamps, even if the design was identical. A preliminary listing has been made here.

Because the essays in all their various colors have not been examined by the editors, traditional color names have been retained. Some color names have been taken from *Color Standards and Color Nomenclature,* by Robert Ridgway.

Only essays in private hands have been listed. Others exist but are not available to collectors.

Some essays were produced after the respective stamps were issued. Year dates are given where information is available. The most well known of these posthumous essays are those produced in 1903 for Ernest Schernikow, who purchased the original dies formerly controlled by Joseph R. Carpenter before his death. Schernikow arranged for a minimum of ten sets of die reprints to be made in a range of more than a dozen colors for each die in his possession. Fewer essay reprints were made on colored card, bond and pelure paper. Though the dies were originally engraved for approved stamp production, neither of the companies producing them had anything to do with these subsequent Schernikow reprints. Inasmuch as they are printed from authentic original dies they merit listing for study purposes, but they are not to be confused with original essays produced contemporaneously with stamp production. All of these unauthorized and unofficial essay reprints are presented here in their own sub-sections following Nos. 11-E17b, 72-E5c, 191-E2, 63-E2b, LO1-E1A and are footnoted in the Sanitary Fair section after No. WV13TC1.

Essay papers and cards are white, unless described otherwise.

Values for die essays are for essays showing full die sinkage, on intact card backing, where such are known. Measurements are given where such information is available. Cut-down or faulty examples sell for less, often much less. Examples on full-size original card command a premium. Plate essays are valued in the grade of very fine, where such exist. A number of essays are unique or are reported in very limited quantities. Such items are valued in the conditions in which they issued.

The listings are by manufacturer. Basic stamps may appear in two or more places.

This listing is not complete. Other designs, papers and colors exist. The editors would appreciate reports of unlisted items, as well as photos of items listed herein without illustrations.

POSTMASTERS' PROVISIONALS

NON-CONTIGUOUS LISTINGS

Because many listings are grouped by manufacturer, some catalogue numbers are separated.

No. 5-E1 to 5-E2	**follow 11-E16**
No. 11-E17 to 72-E5	**follow 5-E2**
No. 65-E5 to 72-E8	**follow 72-E5**
No. 63-E13 to 113-E2	**follow 72-E8**
No. 112-E2 to 129-E2	**follow 113-E2**
No. 120-E1 to 122-E5	**follow 129-E2**
No. 115-E3a to 129-E6	**follow 122-E5**
No. 115-E11 to 116-E8	**follow 129-E6**
No. 115-E17 to 148-E1	**follow 116-E8**
No. 145-E2 to 179-E3	**follow 148-E1**
No. 156-E2 to 191-E2	**follow 179-E3**
No. 184-E8	**follows 191-E2**
No. 182-E4 to 190-E3	**follow 184-E8**
No. 184-E17 to 293-E11	**follow 190-E3**
No. 285-E11 to 292-E9	**follow 293-E11**

Albany, N.Y.
Gavit & Co.

1Xa-E1

Design size: 23½x25½mm
Die size: 58x48mm

Benjamin Franklin. With crosshatching about 2mm outside border (usually cut off).

1847

1Xa-E1 5c

a. Die on India die sunk on large card, printed through a mat to eliminate cross-hatching

brownish black	*600.*
scarlet	*600.*
red brown	*600.*
blue	*600.*
green	*600.*

b. Die on India; some mounted on small card

bluish black	325.
scarlet	325.
brown	325.
yellow green	325.
gray blue	325.

c. Die on India cut close

black	300.
blue	300.
red brown	300.
scarlet	300.
green	300.
yellow green	300.
brown violet	300.
rose red	300.

d. Die on bond (1858)

bluish black	450.
scarlet	450.
brown	450.
blue	450.
blue green	450.
violet	450.

e. Die on ivory glazed paper (1905)

black	900.
dark brown	900.
scarlet	900.
blue	900.

New York, N.Y.
Rawdon, Wright & Hatch

9X1-E1

Design 22mm wide
Die size: 50x102mm

Vignette of Washington. Two transfers laid down vertically on the die 22mm apart; top one retouched, with frame around it (this is a proof). Values are for combined transfers. Vignette essay exists cut apart from proof, value $200 each.

1845

9X1-E1 5c

a. Die on India (1879)

black	450.
violet black	450.
gray black	450.

scarlet 450.
dull scarlet 450.
orange 450.
brown 450.
dull brown 450.
green 450.
dull green 450.
ultramarine 450.
dull blue 450.
red violet 450.

b. Die on white bond (1879)
gray black 550.
dull scarlet 550.
dull brown 550.
dull green 550.
dull blue 550.

c. Die on white glazed paper, die sunk (1879)
gray black 700.

POSTAGE STAMPS

1847 ISSUE
Rawdon, Wright, Hatch & Edson

The original model for No. 1 exists, engraved vignette of Franklin mounted on frame, part of frame engraved, rest in pencil, ink and a gray wash. Formerly No. 1-E1, now in the National Postal Museum collection.

Engraved vignette only, matted.

1-E2 5c Die on India (1895), brown *2,500.*

1-E3

Engraved frame only, matted from complete die.

1-E3 5c Die on India (1895), brown 2,500.

The 1895 dates are suppositional.

The original model for No. 2 exists, engraved vignette of Washington mounted (replaced) on frame, "POST OFFICE" and "FIVE CENTS" engraved on former No. 1-E1, "U" and "S" at top and "X" in bottom corners in black ink, rest in pencil and a gray wash. Formerly No. 2-E1, now in the National Postal Museum collection.

2-E1

Incomplete engraving of entire design, area around vignette incomplete, frame lines and "RWH&E" printer's initials not yet added.

2-E1 10c Die on proof paper, affixed to stiff blue laid paper backing, black —

2-E2

Engraved vignette only.

2-E2 10c Die on India (1895)
black *2,500.*
brownish black *2,500.*
brown *2,500.*

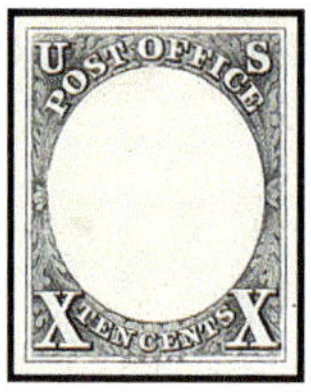

2-E3

Engraved frame only.

2-E3 10c Die on India (1895)
black *4,750.*
brown orange *4,750.*

The 1895 dates are suppositional.

1851 ISSUE
Submitted in Competition for the 1851 Issue Contract
Rawdon, Wright, Hatch & Edson, New York, N.Y.

11-E1

Design size: 18½x23mm
Large 3 in vignette.

11-E1 3c Die on India
black *7,000.*
blue *10,000.*

Submitted in Competition for the 1851 Issue Contract
Henry Benner, Washington, D.C.

11-E2

Design size: 19x24mm
Vignette of Washington.

11-E2 3c
a. Die on India
black *4,000.*
b. Die on proof paper, die sunk on 40x51mm card
black *4,000.*

Submitted in Competition for the 1851 Issue Contract
(Nos. 11-E3 and 11-E4)
John E. Gavit & Co., Albany, N.Y.

11-E3

Design size: 19x23mm
Vignette of Franklin. Three states of die. Second state has double line dash above P of POSTAGE, third state has single dash above P and dot in O of POSTAGE.

11-E3 3c
a. Die on India, die sunk on card
warm black *800.*
scarlet *800.*
red brown *800.*
blue green *800.*
b. Die on India, 41x43mm or smaller
black 300.
greenish black 300.
carmine 300.
scarlet 300.
yellow green 300.
brown 300.
blue green 300.
dull blue 300.
dark blue 300.
c. Die on India, cut to shape
warm black 250.
cool black 250.
black 250.
carmine 250.
orange 250.
brown 250.
dark green 250.
yellow green 250.
olive 250.
light blue 250.
dark blue 250.
violet 250.
scarlet 250.
d. Die on bond
cool black 250.
scarlet 250.
orange brown 250.
brown 250.
green 250.
blue 250.
e. Die on ivory glazed paper
black *700.*
dark brown *700.*
scarlet *700.*
blue *700.*
f. Die on thin card, dusky blue, cut to shape *200.*

11-E3g

g. Die on Francis Patent experimental paper with trial cancel
black *1,250.*
dark blue *1,250.*
brown *1,250.*

11-E4

Design size: 19x22mm
Die size: 47x75mm
Vignette of Washington. Two states of die. Second state has small diagonal dash in top of left vertical border below arch.

11-E4 3c
a. Die on India, die sunk on card
black *750.*
scarlet *750.*
brown red *750.*
blue green *750.*
b. Die on India, about 30x40mm or smaller
orange 400.
orange brown 400.
brown 400.
dusky yellow brown 400.
yellow green 400.
blue green 400.
dull blue 400.
red violet 400.
deep red orange 400.
black 400.
c. Die on bond (1858)
black 400.
scarlet 400.
brown 400.
green 400.
blue 400.
d. Die on ivory glazed paper (1858)
black *850.*
dark brown *850.*
scarlet *850.*
blue *850.*
e. Die on proof paper (1858)
cool black *475.*
dull red *475.*
dull brown *475.*
dull blue green *475.*
dull blue *475.*

Bradbury, Wilkinson & Co., England

11-E5

Design size: 20½x23½mm
Vignette of Washington.

11-E5 3c
- ***a.*** On stiff stamp paper about stamp size
  - black *1,250.*
  - violet red *1,250.*
  - deep carmine *1,250.*
  - dusky carmine *1,250.*
  - deep scarlet *1,250.*
  - orange brown *1,250.*
  - deep green *1,250.*
  - blue *1,250.*
  - ultramarine *1,250.*
  - brown *1,250.*
- ***b.*** On card
  - violet black *1,250.*
  - dull scarlet *1,250.*
  - blue *1,250.*
  - green *1,250.*
  - brown *1,250.*
- ***c.*** On stiff bond
  - brown *1,250.*
  - blue *1,250.*
  - violet black *1,250.*

Draper, Welsh & Co.

11-E6

Design size: 18x23mm
Vignette of Washington.

11-E6 3c Surface printed on card, black *700.*

11-E7

Design size: 17½x24mm
Die size: 44x106mm
Engraved vignette of Washington.

11-E7 3c
- ***a.*** Die on India, about 44x105mm, die sunk on card, in vert. pair with No. 11-E8
  - black *1,500.*
  - scarlet *1,500.*
  - brown red *1,500.*
  - green *1,500.*
- ***b.*** Die on India, about 40x45mm or smaller
  - warm black *400.*
  - cool black *400.*
  - dark carmine *400.*
  - scarlet *400.*
  - brown red *400.*
  - orange brown *400.*
  - brown *400.*
  - yellow green *400.*
  - blue green *400.*
  - blue *400.*
  - dull blue *400.*
  - brown violet *400.*
- ***c.*** Die on India, stamp size
  - rose 350.
  - scarlet 350.
  - red brown 350.
  - brown 350.
  - green 350.
  - cool black 350.
  - warm black 350.
  - yellow green 350.
  - brown violet 350.
  - ultramarine blue 350.
- ***d.*** Die on bond
  - black 400.
  - scarlet 400.
  - brown 400.
  - blue green 400.
  - blue 400.
- ***e.*** Die on ivory glazed paper
  - black *700.*
  - dark brown *700.*
  - scarlet *700.*
  - blue *700.*

Submitted in Competition for the 1851 Issue Contract
Draper, Welsh & Co., Philadelphia, Pa.

11-E8

Design size: 19½x24mm
Die size: 44x106mm
On same die 30mm below No. 11-E7
Vignette of Washington.

11-E8 3c
- ***a.*** Die on India, 28x32mm or smaller
  - black *300.*
  - dark carmine *300.*
  - scarlet *300.*
  - brown red *300.*
  - red brown *300.*
  - orange brown *300.*
  - brown *300.*
  - yellow green *300.*
  - green *300.*
  - blue green *300.*
  - blue *300.*
- ***b.*** Die on bond, about 32x40mm
  - black 300.
  - scarlet 300.
  - brown 300.
  - green 300.
  - blue 300.
- ***c.*** Die on ivory glazed paper
  - black *700.*
  - dark brown *700.*
  - scarlet *700.*
  - blue *700.*

11-E8D

Design size: 18x23mm
Vignette of Washington.
Washington vignette only. Same head as No. 11-E6 through 11-E8, but with more bust. No gridwork in background.

11-E8D 3c Die on proof paper, mounted on card, black *750.*

11-E9c

Design size (No. 11-E9a): 18x33mm
Vignette design size (Nos. 11-E9b, 11-E9c): 18x22mm
As No. 11-E8D, gridwork added to background oval.

11-E9 3c
- ***a.*** Die on India
  - black 350.
  - scarlet 350.
- ***b.*** Die on India, single line frame
  - black 300.
  - blue 300.
  - dark carmine 300.
  - orange red 300.
  - lilac 300.
  - brown 300.
  - scarlet 300.
  - rose violet 300.
  - deep yellow green 300.
- ***c.*** Die on India, imprint of Jocelyn, Draper, Welsh & Co., New York
  - black 300.
  - blue 300.
  - dark carmine 300.
  - orange red 300.
  - lilac 300.
  - brown 300.
  - scarlet 300.
  - rose violet 300.
  - deep yellow green 300.

Danforth, Bald & Co.

11-E10

Vignette size: 18x22mm
Design size: 20x26mm
Die size: 57x74mm
Vignette of Washington. Double line frame.

11-E10 3c
- ***a.*** Die on India, die sunk on card
  - black *750.*
  - scarlet *750.*
  - red brown *750.*
  - green *750.*
- ***b.*** Die on India, off card, about 33x38mm
  - black *200.*
  - scarlet *200.*
  - brown *200.*
  - blue *200.*
  - green *200.*
  - dull violet *200.*
  - dull blue *200.*
  - red brown *200.*
  - rose *200.*
- ***c.*** Die on bond, black *350.*
- ***d.*** Die on ivory glazed paper
  - black *750.*
  - dark brown *750.*
  - scarlet *750.*
  - blue *750.*

11-E11

Washington vignette only.

11-E11 3c Die on India
- black 325.
- dull rose 325.
- scarlet 325.
- orange 325.
- brown orange 325.
- brown 325.
- green 325.
- dark blue 325.
- dull violet 325.
- rose violet 325.

Submitted in Competition for the 1851 Issue Contract
Danforth, Bald & Co., Philadelphia, Pa.

11-E12

Design size: 20x26mm
Die size: 62x66mm
Vignette of Washington. Single line frame. Two states of die. Second state shows scars in lathe lines in front of neck over T, and small dot below design. A third printing has more scars in front of neck.

11-E12 3c
- ***a.*** Die on India, die sunk on card
  - black *750.*
  - scarlet *750.*
  - brown red *750.*
  - dusky brown yellow *750.*
  - brown *750.*
  - green *750.*
  - blue *750.*
  - dull blue *750.*
- ***b.*** Die on India, about 43x45mm
  - black *300.*
  - scarlet *300.*

deep scarlet 300.
brown 300.
yellow brown 300.
green 300.
yellow green 300.
blue 300.
dull blue 300.
dark blue 300.
ultramarine blue 300.
orange 300.
red 300.

c. Die on bond
dusky brown yellow 275.
blue 275.

d. Die on ivory glazed paper
black 700.
dark brown 700.
scarlet 700.
blue 700.

e. Plate on thick buff wove
rose 125.
violet brown 125.
orange 125.
dark orange 125.
pink orange 125.

f. Plate on India, dark red orange 150.

g. Plate on ivory wove (head more completely engraved, ruled lines between designs)
black 125.
dark carmine 125.
yellow 125.
blue 125.

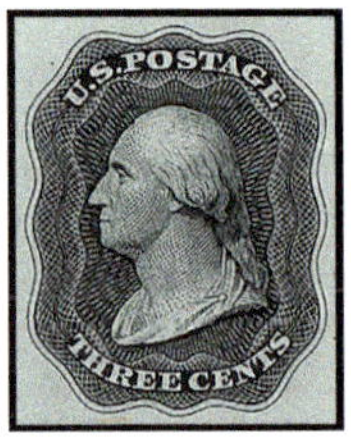

11-E13

Design size: 20x26mm
Die size: 62x66mm
Vignette of Washington. No. 11-E12 reengraved: more dark dots in forehead next to hair, thus line between forehead and hair more distinct.

11-E13 3c

a. Die on India, die sunk on card
black 750.
scarlet 750.
brown red 750.
brown 750.
green 750.

b. Die on ivory glazed paper
black 700.
dark brown 700.
scarlet 700.
blue 700.

Bald, Cousland & Co.

11-E14, 11-E14A, 11-E16

Design size: 22x28mm.
Incomplete design, tablets at top and bottom blank. See No. 11-E14A for listings.

11-E14 3c

Design size: 22x28mm
Die size: 95x43mm
Vignette of Washington. On same die with Nos. 11-E16 and 11-E14. Listings are for the complete triple die essay.

11-E14A 3c

b. Die on India
black 1,000.
scarlet 1,000.
red brown 1,000.
brown 1,000.
yellow green 1,000.
green 1,000.
blue green 1,000.
orange brown 1,000.
rose pink 1,000.
dull blue 1,000.
violet 1,000.

c. Die on bond
black 1,000.
scarlet 1,000.
brown 1,000.
blue green 1,000.
blue 1,000.

d. Die on white glazed paper
black 1,150.

11-E15

Design size: 28x22½mm
POSTAGE / 3 / CENTS in scalloped frame.

11-E15 3c

a. Die on India, die sunk on card
black 750.
scarlet 750.
red brown 750.
green 750.
slate 750.

b. Die on bond, about 40x30mm
black 175.
scarlet 175.
brown 175.
green 175.
blue 175.
slate 275.

c. Die on ivory glazed paper
black 700.
dark brown 750.
scarlet 750.
blue 750.

11-E16

Design size: 28x22½mm
U.S. at sides of 3.

11-E16 3c

a. Die on India, cut small
black 275.
light red 275.
red brown 275.
brown 275.
yellow green 275.
blue green 275.
green 275.
blue 275.
red violet 275.

b. Die on bond, about 40x30mm
black 175.
scarlet 175.
brown 175.
red brown 175.
green 175.
blue green 175.
blue 175.
violet 175.
slate 175.

c. Die on India, Nos. 11-E14A and 11-E16 with albino 11-E14
black 1,000.
scarlet 1,000.
brown 1,000.
green 1,000.
blue green 1,000.
blue 1,000.
red violet 1,000.

d. As "c," die on bond
black 750.
scarlet 750.
brown 750.
green 750.
blue green 750.
gray blue 750.

e. As "c," die on ivory glazed paper, 64x78mm, black 1,150.

f. Die on India, die sunk on card
black 900.
scarlet 900.

Toppan, Carpenter, Casilear & Co.

5-E1

Design size: 20½x26mm
Franklin vignette.

5-E1 1c

a. Die on old proof paper, master die shortened to 18½x22½mm, black 1,250.

b. Die on thick old proof paper, black 1,500.

c. Pair, Nos. 5-E1b, 11-E23, black 2,000.

5-E1E

5-E1Ef

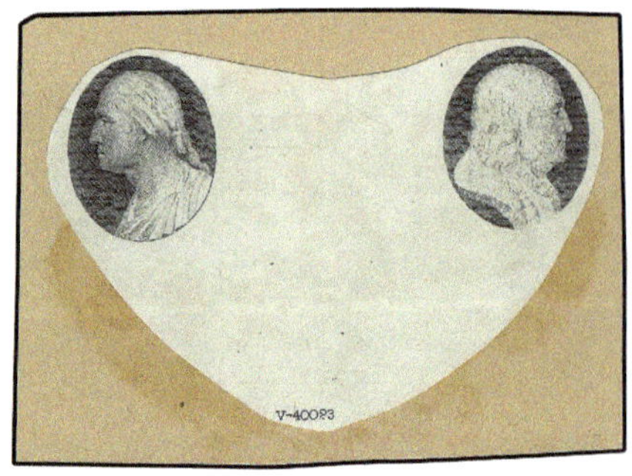

5-E1Eg

Design size: 20x24mm
Similar to No. 5-E1 but with no additional shaded oval border.

5-E1E 1c Die on thin card, black blue —

f. Block of 4 in combination with pair of No. 11-E23, on old proof paper, black 3,500.

g. Pair, No. 5-E1E in combination with No. 11-E23, on old proof paper, die V-40023, cut to shape to show die number and mounted on 75x54mm card 575.

h. Pair, No. 5-E1E in combination with No. 11-E23, die on India, die sunk on card, die V-40023 beneath images, black 5,000.

Nos. 5-E1Eg and 5-E1Eh are essays made by the American Bank Note Co. from the die acquired from Toppan, Carpenter and Company. The die number V-40023 is the new ABNCo. die number. While the essays were produced posthumously, this could prove to be the original die block from which transfers were taken up to be added to bank note designs and later to become the central vignettes for the 1851 postage stamps.

5-E2

Complete design, but with SIX CENTS in value tablet.

5-E2 1c Die on India, black, cut to shape 2,500.

Submitted in Competition for the 1851 Issue Contract (Nos. 11-E17a, 11-E17b, and 11-E18 to 11-E21) Toppan, Carpenter, Casilear & Co., Philadelphia, Pa.

11-E17

Design size: 21½x25mm
Die size: 50½x60mm
Vignette of Washington.

11-E17 3c
- ***a.*** Die on India, die sunk on card, penciled 'By Casilear at lower left, rose carmine 5,000.
- ***b.*** Die on old ivory paper
  - rose carmine *7,250.*
  - bluish-black *7,250.*

Essay reprints by Schernikow in 1903 from original die (See paragraph eight of the Essay section introduction)

11-E17 3c
- ***c.*** Die on proof paper, printed through a mat (1903)
  - black 175.
  - bright carmine 175.
  - dull carmine 175.
  - dark violet red 175.
  - dull scarlet 175.
  - dull violet 175.
  - dull red violet 175.
  - deep yellow 175.
  - deep orange 175.
  - orange brown 175.
  - dull brown olive 175.
  - deep green 175.
  - dark blue green 175.
  - ultramarine 175.
  - dark blue 175.
  - brown 175.
- ***d.*** Die on colored card (1903)
  - deep orange, *ivory* 300.
  - dark blue, *pale green* 300.
  - orange brown, *light blue* 300.

Toppan, Carpenter, Casilear & Co., Philadelphia, Pa.

11-E18

Design size: 20½x22½mm
Washington. Vignette has solid color background. Crack between N and T of CENTS.

11-E18 3c Die on India, card mounted, 24½x25mm
- black *2,000.*
- carmine *2,000.*

No. 11-E18A

Design size: 20½x22½mm
Washington. Like No. 11-E18 except background of vignette is clearly engraved horizontal and vertical lines. Crack between N and T of CENTS.

11-E18A 3c Die on India, die sunk on 60x50mm card, carmine *7,000.*
- ***b.*** As No. 11-E18A, cut down to stamp's size, black *7,000.*
- ***c.*** As No. 11-E18A, on old ivory paper, cut down to stamp size, rose carmine *7,000.*

No. 11-E19 On Left, No. 11-E20 On Right

No. 11-E19
Design size: 20½x22½mm
Similar to No. 11-E18, with a slightly modified design, vignette background engraved horiz. and vert. lines. In pair with No. 11-E20.

No. 11-E20
Design size: 20x22½mm
Blank curved top and bottom labels. In pair with 11-E19. Also found in pair with 11-E21.

11-E19 3c Die on India, Nos. 11-E19, 11-E20 mounted on card, black *16,500.*

11-E21

Straight labels. Similar to No. 11-E19 but labels erased and vignette cut out. In pair with No. 11-E20.

11-E21 3c Die on India, Nos. 11-E20, 11-E21 mounted on card, black *4,500.*

11-E22

Die size: 37½x46mm

Similar to issued stamp except lathework impinges on colorless oval.

11-E22 3c Die on India
- dusky blue *5,000.*
- black *5,000.*
- With layout lines *10,000.*

Some students consider No. 11-E22 to be proof strikes of the die used to make the "Roosevelt" and Panama-Pacific small die proofs, as the lathework impinges on the colorless oval of Nos. 11P2 and 11P2a as well.

11-E23

Design size: 18x22mm
Washington vignette only. From master die (21½mm high) with more robe and dark background.

11-E23 3c
- ***a.*** Master die impression, old proof paper, black *900.*
- ***b.*** Block of 4, 2mm between ovals, thick old ivory paper, black *3,000.*

11-E24

Washington vignette only, as No. 11-E23, with outer frame added.

11-E24 3c Die on old proof paper, die v 37991, cut to shape to show die number and mounted on 27x37mm card, black *700.*

No. 11-E24 is an essay made by the American Bank Note Co. from a die acquired from Toppan, Carpenter and Company. The die number V 37991 is the new ABNCo. die number.

13-E1

Design as adopted but top label has pencil lettering only, also no lines in leaf ornaments around Xs in top corners.

13-E1 10c Die on India, black *3,000.*

13-E2

Similar to No. 13-E1 but vert. shading around Xs and lines added in leaf ornaments. No lettering in top label.

13-E2 10c Die on India, black *3,000.*

17-E1

Design size: 19x21½mm
Block sinkage size: 57x49mm
Engine engraved frame without labels or interior shadow lines from straight bands and left side rosettes. No small equilateral crosses in central row of diamonds. Original vignette cut out and replaced by engraved vignette of Washington as adopted.

17-E1 12c Die on India, cut close, mounted on block sunk card, 77x57mm, black *10,000.*

17-E2

Similar to adopted design but no small vertical equilateral crosses in center rows of diamond networks at top, sides and bottom.

17-E2 12c Die on India, brown violet, cut close *900.*
17-E3 12c As No. 17-E2, die on wove, brown violet, cut close *750.*

37-E1

Design size: 19½x25½mm
Die size: 46x49mm or larger
Probably not the die used to make the plates. No exterior layout lines. Oval outline recut at bottom of jabot and vignette background etched much darker. Light horizontal lines on stock below chin.

37-E1 24c Die on India, black *2,500.*

37-E2

Incomplete essay for frame only as adopted: no outer frameline and lathework not retouched.

37-E2 24c Die on India, black *3,500.*

38-E1

Incomplete engraving of entire design, lacking text and numerals at top, bottom and sides.

38-E1 30c Die on India, on 37x45mm card, black *7,000.*

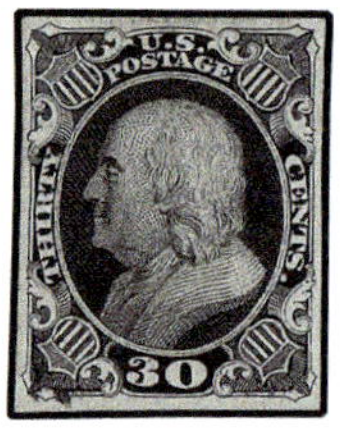

38-E2

Design size: 19x24mm
Incomplete engraving of entire design. Scrolls at each side of 30 have only one outer shading line.

38-E2 30c Die on India, black *2,250.*

39-E1

Design size: 19x24mm
Incomplete engraving of entire design, lacking "U.S. POSTAGE" at top and "NINETY CENTS" at bottom, incomplete curvature lines in top scroll, signed by engraver on card.

39-E1 90c Die on India (45x52mm), mounted on large card (150x215mm), black *4,500.*

1861 ISSUE
Toppan, Carpenter & Co.

For the 1903 Schernikow private reprint essays see section following No. 72-E5.

63-E2b

Franklin vignette with U S POSTAGE at top and ONE CENT at bottom.

63-E2 1c
b. Die on old proof paper, outer line at sides of oval missing (1861), black *1,000.*

63-E3

Side ornaments added.

63-E3 1c
a. Die on old proof paper (1861)
black *1,250.*
blue *1,250.*
b. Die on stiff old ivory paper (1861)
black *1,250.*
blue *1,750.*
f. Die on glazed card, black —

63-E4

With upper and lower right corners incomplete. Serifs of 1s point to right.

63-E4 1c Die on old proof paper (1861), black *2,250.*

63-E4E

As No. 63-E4 but with pencil shading in upper right corner around the "1".

63-E4E 1c Die on old proof paper (1861), black *2,750.*

63-E5

With four corners and numerals in pencil (ornaments differ in each corner).

63-E5 1c Die on old proof paper (1861), blue *2,750.*

63-E5A

As No. 63-E5 but ornaments different.

63-E5A 1c Die on old paper (1861), blue *2,750.*

63-E6

As No. 63-E5 but ornaments different.

63-E6 1c Die on old proof paper (1861), blue *3,500.*

63-E7

As Nos. 63-E5 and 63-E6 but ornaments different.

63-E7 1c Die on old proof paper (1861), blue *3,250.*

63-E8

Die proof of No. 5 with lower corners cut out of India paper and resketched in pencil on card beneath.

63-E8 1c Die on India, on card (1861), black *2,000.*

63-E9

Completely engraved design.

63-E9 1c
- ***a.*** Die on India, cut to shape (1861)
  - black, on brown toned paper *1,000.*
  - blue *600.*
- ***b.*** Die on India, about 58x57mm, die sunk on card (1861)
  - blue *2,000.*
- ***c.*** Die on old proof paper, about 48x55mm (1861)
  - black *2,000.*
- ***d.*** Die on large old white ivory paper (1861)
  - black *2,000.*
  - blue *2,000.*

65-E2

With tessellated frame, bottom label and diamond blocks. Without rosettes, top label and diamond blocks.

65-E2 3c
- ***a.*** Die on old proof paper (1861)
  - black *1,000.*
  - red *1,000.*
- ***f.*** Die on India
  - black —
  - rose —

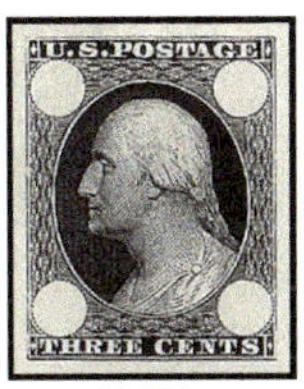

65-E3a

65-E3b

With top label and diamond blocks.

65-E3 3c
- ***a.*** Die on old proof paper (1861)
  - brown red *2,500.*
  - black *2,500.*
- ***b.*** Same as No. 65-E3 with numerals in pencil, Die on old proof paper (1861), black *6,000.*

65-E4

Complete die, with numerals in rosette circles.

65-E4 3c
- ***a.*** Die on India, 75x76mm die sinkage (1861)
  - black *1,500.*
  - carmine *1,500.*
- ***b.*** Die on old proof paper (1861)
  - black *1,500.*
  - dark red *1,500.*
- ***c.*** Die on India, cut to shape (1861)
  - black *1,000.*
  - carmine *1,000.*

67-E1a, Die I

67-E1b, Die II

Vignette size: 13½x16mm

Jefferson vignette only. Two dies: die I incomplete, light background in vignette; die II background essentially complete.

67-E1 5c
- ***a.*** Die I on old proof paper, black (1861) *750.*
- ***f.*** Die I on old thin ivory paper (1861), dark blue *1,000.*
- ***g.*** Die I on old proof paper (1861), dusky ultramarine *1,500.*
- ***h.*** Die II on old ivory paper (1861), navy blue *750.*

67-E2

Vignette die I framed, with spaces for numerals.

67-E2 5c
- ***d.*** Die I on old proof paper (1861), black *2,000.*

67-E3

67-E3c

With numerals.

67-E3 5c
- ***b.*** Die I on soft laid paper (1861)
  - black *750.*
  - dark brown *750.*
  - orange brown *750.*
- ***c.*** Die II on old proof paper, pencil designs drawn in corners (1861), black *2,500.*
- ***d.*** Die I on old proof paper, outer lines on corner curves missing (1861), black *500.*

67-E4b

67-E4e

Complete die II design with corner ornaments.

67-E4 5c
- ***a.*** Die II on India, cut to shape (1861), black *500.*
- ***b.*** Die II on brown toned paper (1861), cut to shape
  - black *900.*
  - brown *900.*
- ***c.*** Die II on old proof paper (1861)
  - orange brown *1,500.*
  - black *1,500.*
- ***d.*** Die II on old ivory paper (1861), black *1,500.*
- ***e.*** Die II on old proof paper, additional frameline drawn on curved corners and small circle drawn in each corner (1861), black *2,500.*

69-E1

Vignette size: 15x17mm

Washington vignette only. Die II with more engraving on face, horiz. background lines regularly spaced, outer oval border smudged. Die II known only as 1851 master die.

69-E1 12c
- ***a.*** Die II on old proof paper (1851), black 650.

69-E2b

Curved labels at top and bottom.

69-E2 12c
- ***b.*** Die I on old proof paper (1861)
  - dim red violet *500.*
  - red violet *500.*

69-E3b

69-E3d

69-E3g

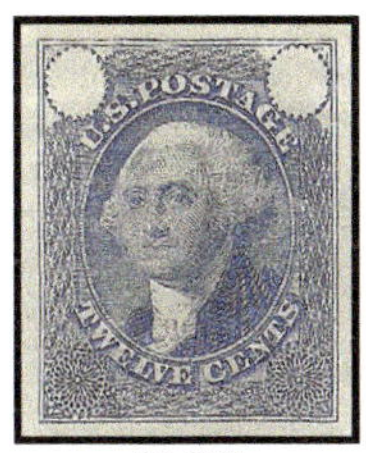
69-E3i

Frame incomplete: all four rosettes blank.

69-E3 12c
- ***b.*** Die on old proof paper (1861)
  - black *1,000.*
  - olive gray *1,000.*
- ***c.*** Die on old ivory, top border and half of rosettes missing (1861), black *1,000.*
- ***d.*** Die on stiff old ivory, top border missing (1861), bluish black *1,000.*
- ***g.*** Die on old proof paper, 1851 die with border lines complete, upper right rosette blank (1861)
  - orange *1,000.*
  - dark green *1,000.*
  - ultramarine *1,000.*
  - violet *1,000.*
- ***h.*** Die I on old proof paper, vignette background incomplete or worn, stock on neck unfinished (1861) —
- ***i.*** Die I on old proof paper, as 69-E3h but both upper rosettes blank (1861), ultramarine *1,000.*

69-E3j

69-E3k

69-E3l

- ***j.*** Die I on old proof paper, as No. 69-E3h but both upper plus lower left rosettes blank (1861), ultramarine *1,000.*
- ***k.*** Die I on old proof paper, as No. 69-E3h but both lower plus upper left rosettes blank, corner borders removed around blank rosettes (1861), ultramarine *1,000.*
- ***l.*** Die I on old proof paper, as No. 69-E3h but all rosettes blank, border lines complete (1861)
  - dim scarlet *750.*
  - orange *750.*
  - green *750.*
  - ultramarine *750.*
  - violet *750.*
- ***m.*** Die I on white wove, as No. 69-E3l (1861), scarlet *750.*
- ***n.*** Die I on old proof paper, complete design (1861)
  - orange *1,000.*
  - dark red *1,000.*
  - orange red *1,000.*
  - ultramarine *1,000.*

69-E4

69-E4d

69-E4e

Original complete design with numerals in corners.

69-E4 12c
- ***a.*** Die on India, card mounted (1861)
  - black *800.*
  - gray black *800.*
- ***b.*** Die on India, cut to shape (1861), black *500.*
- ***c.*** Die on old proof paper (1861), black *500.*
- ***d.*** Die on old proof paper, corners drawn in pencil (1861), black *2,750.*
- ***e.*** Die on old proof paper, as No. 69-E3a but numerals sketched in diagonally and vert. (1861), black *3,500.*
- ***f.*** Die on stiff old ivory paper, as No. 69-E4e but without top border (1861), bluish black *1,500.*
- ***g.*** Die on thin card, black —

70-E2

Washington vignette with oval label. Background complete, eyes retouched.

70-E2 24c
- ***b.*** Die I on old proof paper, background lines incomplete (1861)
  - black *750.*
  - dim red violet *750.*

70-E3b

With frame. Blank areas in corners for numerals.

70-E3 24c
- ***b.*** Die on old proof paper (1861), dusky red violet *1,000.*

70-E4

Complete design with numerals in corners.

70-E4 24c
- ***a.*** Die on old proof paper, cut to shape (1861)
  - lilac *400.*
  - black *400.*
  - red violet *400.*
- ***b.*** Die on India, cut close (1861)
  - black *400.*
  - lilac *400.*
  - brown lilac *400.*
- ***c.*** Die on India (1861), dark blue *750.*
- ***d.*** Die on India, mounted on 80x115mm card (1861), lilac *750.*
- ***e.*** On stiff old ivory paper (1861)
  - black *1,000.*
  - lilac *1,000.*

Lower corners of vignette cut out, "NINETY 90 CENTS" in pencil in bottom label.

72-E4 90c Die on India (1861), black *2,000.*

72-E5

Complete design.

72-E5 90c
- ***a.*** Die on India, cut to shape (1861)
  - black *350.*
  - dark blue *350.*
- ***b.*** Die on India, die sunk on card (1861), blue *2,500.*
- ***c.*** Die on India, cut close (1861)
  - black *350.*
  - blue *350.*

Essay reprints by Schernikow in 1903 from original dies (See paragraph eight of the Essay section introduction)

63-E1b

Vignette size: 18½x21½mm
Die size: 49x51mm
Franklin vignette only.

63-E1 1c
- ***a.*** Die on proof paper (1903)
  - black 75.
  - carmine 75.
  - dark carmine 75.
  - scarlet 75.
  - red brown 75.
  - orange 75.
  - yellow brown 75.
  - dark brown 75.
  - violet brown 75.
  - light green 75.
  - green 75.
  - dark blue 75.
  - ultramarine 75.
  - red violet 75.
  - dark violet 75.
  - dusky olive green 75.
- ***b.*** Die on colored card (1903)
  - orange red, *pale yellow* *125.*
  - orange, *pale pink* *125.*
  - yellow brown, *buff* *125.*
  - dark blue, *pink* *125.*
  - dark violet, *pale olive* *125.*
  - dull violet, *blue* *125.*
  - deep green, *pale blue* *125.*
  - violet, *light green* *125.*
- ***c.*** Die on green bond (1903)
  - black *125.*
  - dismal red *125.*
  - green *125.*

63-E2b

Franklin vignette with U S POSTAGE at top and ONE CENT at bottom.

63-E2 1c
- ***a.*** Die on proof paper (1903)
  - black 100.
  - carmine 100.
  - dark carmine 100.
  - scarlet 100.
  - red brown 100.
  - orange 100.
  - yellow brown 100.
  - violet brown 100.
  - gray brown 100.
  - light green 100.
  - green 100.
  - blue 100.
  - red violet 100.
  - ultramarine 100.
  - dusky olive 100.
- ***c.*** Die on green bond (1903)
  - orange *150.*
  - orange brown *150.*
  - violet *150.*
- ***d.*** Die on colored card (1903)
  - deep green, *pale blue* *150.*
  - violet, *light green* *150.*
  - dark orange red, *pale dull green* *150.*
  - olive, *ivory* *150.*
  - brown, *pink* *150.*
  - scarlet, *yellow* *150.*

63-E3

Side ornaments added.

63-E3 1c

c. Die on colored card (1903)

black, *ivory*	*150.*
brown, *pale pink*	*150.*
blue, *blue*	*150.*
orange brown, *pale pink*	*150.*
gray olive, *ivory*	*150.*
gray olive, *buff*	*150.*
scarlet, *pale yellow*	*150.*

d. Die on proof paper (1903)

black	85.
carmine	85.
dark carmine	85.
scarlet	85.
red brown	85.
orange	85.
yellow brown	85.
violet brown	85.
light green	85.
green	85.
blue	85.
violet	85.
red violet	85.
orange brown	85.
dusky olive	85.
ultramarine	85.

e. Die on green bond (1903)

carmine	*150.*
orange	*150.*
violet	*150.*

63-E9

Completely engraved design.

63-E9 1c

e. Die on proof paper, printed through mat (1903)

black	100.
carmine	100.
dark carmine	100.
scarlet	100.
orange	100.
orange brown	100.
yellow brown	100.
light green	100.
green	100.
black blue	100.
violet	100.
red violet	100.
violet brown	100.
gray	100.
blue	100.
ultramarine	100.

f. Die on bond (1903)

orange	*125.*
dismal blue green	*125.*

g. Die on bond, Walls of Troy wmk. (1903)

carmine	*200.*
orange red	*200.*
orange	*200.*
orange brown	*200.*
dark green	*200.*
light ultramarine	*200.*

h. Die on bond, double line of scallops wmk. (1903)

orange red	*200.*
dark green	*200.*

i. Die on green bond (1903)

dismal carmine	*125.*
dismal violet brown	*125.*
dull dark green	*125.*

j. Die on pinkish pelure (1903)

orange red	*300.*
brown red	*300.*
brown orange	*300.*
dull blue green	*300.*
violet	*300.*

k. Die on colored card (1903)

black, *pale blue*	*225.*
carmine, *pale yellow*	*225.*
carmine, *pale pink*	*225.*
brown red, *pale pink*	*225.*
chestnut, *pale olive*	*225.*
dismal olive, *buff*	*225.*
ultramarine, *ivory*	*225.*

l. Die on stiff card (1903), green	*250.*

65-E1

Vignette size: 16½x19mm
Die size: 49x50mm
1851 master die of Washington vignette only.

65-E1 3c

a. Die on proof paper (1903)

black	75.
carmine	75.
dark carmine	75.
scarlet	75.
red brown	75.
orange	75.
brown orange	75.
violet brown	75.
dusky olive	75.
light green	75.
green	75.
dark blue	75.
ultramarine	75.
lilac	75.
red violet	75.

b. Die on green bond (1903)

red	*125.*
brown	*125.*
blue	*125.*
olive	*125.*

c. Die on colored card (1903)

carmine, *pale green*	*125.*
scarlet, *yellow*	*125.*
orange, *ivory*	*125.*
olive brown, *blue*	*125.*
dark blue, *pink*	*125.*
violet, *buff*	*125.*
dark green, *pink*	*125.*

65-E2

With tessellated frame, bottom label and diamond blocks. Without rosettes, top label and diamond blocks.

65-E2 3c

b. Die on proof paper, printed through a mat (1903)

black	*85.*
carmine	*85.*
dark carmine	*85.*
scarlet	*85.*
orange	*85.*
yellow	*85.*
yellow brown	*85.*
dusky gray	*85.*
light green	*85.*
green	*85.*
black blue	*85.*
ultramarine	*85.*
lilac	*85.*
dark lilac	*85.*
red violet	*85.*

c. Die on green bond (1903)

black	*150.*
dull orange red	*150.*
orange	*150.*
orange brown	*150.*
blue violet	*150.*
black blue	*150.*
dusky green	*150.*

d. Die on dull pale gray blue thin wove (1903)

dull red	*300.*
orange	*300.*
yellow brown	*300.*
dusky green	*300.*
black blue	*300.*

e. Die on colored card (1903)

black, *light blue*	*150.*
orange red, *yellow*	*150.*
red brown, *ivory*	*150.*
light green, *pink*	*150.*
green, *light green*	*150.*
blue, *buff*	*150.*

65-E3a

65-E3b

With top label and diamond blocks.

65-E3 3c

c. Die on proof paper, no numerals, printed through a mat (1903)

black	90.
carmine	90.
dark carmine	90.
scarlet	90.
orange	90.
yellow	90.
yellow brown	90.
dusky olive	90.
light green	90.
green	90.
black blue	90.
violet blue	90.
violet brown	90.
lilac	90.
red violet	90.

d. Die on green bond (1903)

dull scarlet	*150.*
dim red	*150.*
orange	*150.*
yellow brown	*150.*
green	*150.*
dusky blue	*150.*
violet	*150.*
black	*150.*

e. Die on colored card (1903)

black, *buff*	*150.*
scarlet, *ivory*	*150.*
orange, *light yellow*	*150.*
brown, *light blue*	*150.*
violet blue, *light pink*	*150.*
violet, *light green*	*150.*

f. Die on pink thin wove (1903)

dull yellow	*300.*
dismal red	*300.*
yellow brown	*300.*
dusky blue green	*300.*
dusky blue	*300.*

67-E1, Die II

Vignette size: 13½x16mm
Jefferson vignette only, Die II, background essentially complete.

67-E1 5c

b. Die II on proof paper (1903)

black	75.
carmine	75.
dark carmine	75.
scarlet	75.
red brown	75.
orange brown	75.
brown	75.
dusky olive	75.
green	75.
dark green	75.
black blue	75.
ultramarine	75.
violet brown	75.
red violet	75.
lilac	75.

c. Die II on colored card (1903)

olive, *buff*	*150.*
carmine, *pale yellow*	*150.*
scarlet, *green*	*150.*
brown, *pink*	*150.*
black, *ivory*	*150.*
ultramarine, *pale blue*	*150.*

d. Die II on green bond (1903)

orange brown	*150.*
dismal red brown	*150.*
dark green	*150.*
violet	*150.*
black blue	*150.*

e. Die II on old thin ivory paper (1903)

green	175.
dark carmine	175.

i. Die II on laid proof paper (1903)	—

67-E2

Vignette die II framed, with spaces for numerals.

67-E2 5c
a. Die II on proof paper (1903)
black 95.
carmine 95.
dark carmine 95.
scarlet 95.
red brown 95.
orange 95.
yellow brown 95.
dusky olive 95.
violet brown 95.
light green 95.
dark green 95.
dark blue 95.
ultramarine 95.
red violet 95.
lilac 95.
b. Die II on colored card (1903)
orange brown, *light yellow* *175.*
deep blue, *light pink* *175.*
dusky olive, *light buff* *175.*
dark green, *pale blue* *175.*
red violet, *ivory* *175.*
c. Die II on green bond (1903)
orange brown *160.*
olive green *160.*
violet *160.*
blue *160.*
ultramarine *160.*

67-E3

67-E3 5c
a. Die I on proof paper, printed through a mat (1903)
black 125.
carmine 125.
dark carmine 125.
scarlet 125.
red brown 125.
yellow brown 125.
dark brown 125.
violet brown 125.
light green 125.
green 125.
dark blue 125.
lilac 125.
ultramarine 125.
red violet 125.
dusky olive 125.
e. Die I on colored card (1903)
orange red, *buff* *175.*
orange red, *light yellow* *175.*
olive green, *pale green* *175.*
deep green, *ivory* *175.*
dark blue, *light pink* *175.*
violet brown, *light blue* *175.*
f. Die I on green bond (1903)
black *160.*
scarlet *160.*
brown *160.*
green *160.*
g. Die I on yellow pelure (1903)
scarlet *350.*
brown red *350.*
brown *350.*
dark green *350.*
violet *350.*
blue *350.*
h. Die I on bond, Walls of Troy wmk. (1903)
dark orange *250.*
blue *250.*
carmine *250.*
i. Die I on bond, two line scalloped border wmk. (1903)
dark blue green *250.*
scarlet *250.*

67-E4j

Complete die II design with corner ornaments.

67-E4 5c
f. Die II on proof paper, printed through a mat (1903)
black 125.
carmine 125.
dark carmine 125.
scarlet 125.
orange 125.
brown 125.
yellow brown 125.
dusky olive 125.
light green 125.
green 125.
blue 125.
black blue 125.
violet brown 125.
red violet 125.
lilac 125.
ultramarine 125.
g. Die II on colored card (1903)
red, *light yellow* *150.*
brown, *buff* *150.*
olive green, *light pink* *150.*
dark violet *150.*
violet brown, *pale green* *150.*
dusky yellow green, *dull pale blue green* *150.*
brown, *ivory* *150.*
h. Die II on green bond (1903)
black *125.*
dull dark orange *125.*
violet *125.*
i. Die II on bond, Walls of Troy wmk. (1903)
scarlet *250.*
deep red *250.*
dark green *250.*
j. Die II on bond, two-line scalloped border wmk. (1903)
deep orange *250.*
blue *250.*
k. Die II on greenish pelure (1903)
orange *350.*
olive brown *350.*
dark green *350.*
l. Die II on bluish pelure (1903), red brown *450.*

69-E1

Vignette size: 15x17mm
Washington vignette only. Die I incomplete, horiz. background lines irregularly spaced, space occurring about every 2mm. Die I known only on Schernikow reprints.

69-E1 12c
b. Die I on proof paper (1903)
black 60.
carmine 60.
dark carmine 60.
scarlet 60.
red brown 60.
orange 60.
yellow brown 60.
violet brown 60.
gray brown 60.
light green 60.
green 60.
blue 60.
black blue 60.
red violet 60.
lilac 60.
ultramarine 60.
c. Die I on green bond (1903)
black *150.*
red brown *150.*
brown *150.*
d. Die I on colored card (1903)
dark carmine, *ivory* *150.*
dark carmine, *light blue* *150.*
dark olive, *buff* *150.*
dark green, *light yellow* *150.*
dark blue, *pale green* *150.*
violet brown, *light pink* *150.*

69-E2

Curved labels at top and bottom.

69-E2 12c
a. Die II on proof paper, some printed through a mat (1903)
black 75.
carmine 75.
dark carmine 75.
scarlet 75.
orange 75.
yellow 75.
yellow brown 75.
violet brown 75.
gray brown 75.
light green 75.
green 75.
light blue 75.
black blue 75.
red violet 75.
lilac 75.
ultramarine 75.
c. Die I on dull light green bond (1903)
black *150.*
dull red *150.*
dim orange *150.*
yellow brown *150.*
dusky green *150.*
dusky blue *150.*
red violet *150.*
d. Die I on pale yellow thin wove (1903)
dim red *200.*
deep orange red *200.*
yellow brown *200.*
dusky blue *200.*
red violet *200.*
e. Die I on colored card (1903)
dull red, *light pink* *150.*
orange red, *buff* *150.*
brown, *light blue* *150.*
dark olive, *light yellow* *150.*
dull dark blue, *ivory* *150.*
violet, *pale green* *150.*

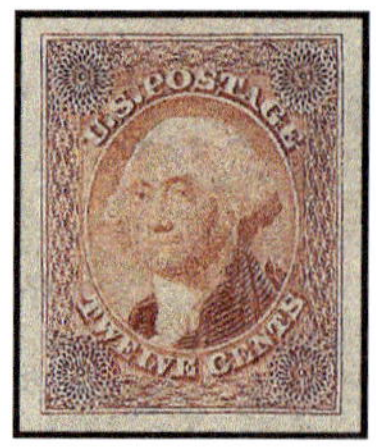
69-E3o

Frame incomplete: all four rosettes blank.

69-E3 12c
a. Die on proof paper (1903)
black 125.
carmine 125.
dark carmine 125.
scarlet 125.
red brown 125.
orange 125.
orange brown 125.
violet brown 125.
light green 125.
green 125.
light blue 125.
black blue 125.
red violet 125.
lilac 125.
ultramarine 125.
e. Die on colored card, top border missing (1903)
orange brown, *light blue* *175.*
deep green, *light yellow* *175.*
deep blue, *light pink* *175.*
violet, *ivory* *175.*
deep yellow orange, *pale yellow green* *175.*
brown, *buff* *175.*
f. Die on green bond, top border missing (1903)
orange *175.*
green *175.*
violet *175.*
o. Die I on pale yellow thin wove (1903), dark red *500.*
p. Die I on pink thin wove (1903), blue *500.*
q. Die I on pale pink (1903), blue *500.*

70-E1

Vignette size: 7x16mm

Washington die II vignette only.

70-E1 24c
a. Die II on proof paper (1903)
black 60.
carmine 60.
dark carmine 60.
scarlet 60.
orange 60.
yellow 60.
yellow brown 60.
violet brown 60.
gray olive 60.
light green 60.
green 60.
light blue 60.
black blue 60.
red violet 60.
lilac 60.
b. Die II on green bond (1903)
black *150.*
red brown *150.*
violet *150.*
orange *150.*
c. Die II on colored card (1903)
dull red, *ivory* *150.*
brown red, *buff* *150.*
brown orange, *light pink* *150.*
dark green, *light yellow* *150.*
blue, *pale green* *150.*
violet, *blue* *150.*

70-E2

Washington vignette with oval label. Background complete, eyes retouched.

70-E2 24c
a. Die II on proof paper (1903)
black 60.
carmine 60.
dark carmine 60.
scarlet 60.
orange 60.
yellow 60.
yellow brown 60.
violet brown 60.
light green 60.
green 60.
light blue 60.
black blue 60.
red violet 60.
lilac 60.
gray olive 60.
ultramarine 60.
c. Die I on colored card (1903)
black, *light pink* *150.*
orange, *buff* *150.*
orange, *light blue* *150.*
dark green, *pale green* *150.*
violet blue, *light yellow* *150.*
violet, *ivory* *150.*
d. Die I on green bond (1903), brown *150.*
e. Die I on dull light blue green bond (1903)
black *150.*
orange red *150.*
orange *150.*
yellow brown *150.*
dusky green *150.*
dull blue *150.*
red violet *150.*
f. Die I on dull pale green blue thin wove (1903)
orange red *300.*
orange *300.*
yellow brown *300.*
dusky green *300.*
dull blue *300.*

70-EA3

With frame. Blank areas in corners for numerals.

70-E3 24c
a. Die on proof paper (1903)
black 100.
carmine 100.
dark carmine 100.
scarlet 100.
orange 100.
yellow brown 100.
orange brown 100.
violet brown 100.
gray olive 100.
light green 100.
green 100.
light blue 100.
black blue 100.
red violet 100.
lilac 100.
ultramarine 100.
c. Die on colored card (1903)
carmine, *light blue* *175.*
blue, *pale green* *175.*
scarlet, *buff* *175.*
yellow brown, *cream* *175.*
dull violet, *pink* *175.*
dusky green, *light yellow* *175.*
gray olive, *ivory* *175.*
d. Die on green bond (1903)
black *175.*
orange brown *175.*
green *175.*

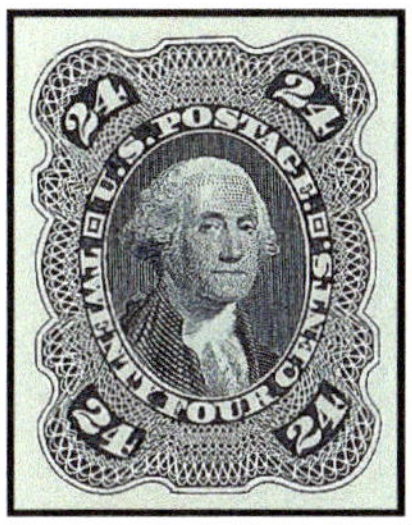
70-E4

Complete design with numerals in corners.

70-E4 24c
f. Die on proof paper, printed through a mat (1903)
black 125.
carmine 125.
dark carmine 125.
scarlet 125.
red brown 125.
yellow brown 125.
brown 125.
violet brown 125.
gray olive 125.
light green 125.
green 125.
light blue 125.
black blue 125.
red violet 125.
lilac 125.
ultramarine 125.
g. Die on blue pelure (1903)
dark carmine *300.*
scarlet *300.*
orange *300.*
brown *300.*
dusky green *300.*
h. Die on bond (1903)
black *175.*
scarlet *175.*
orange *175.*
dark green *175.*
blue *175.*
i. Die on green bond (1903)
black *250.*
dark red *250.*
green *250.*
j. Die on bond, Walls of Troy wmk. (1903), dark green *300.*
k. Die on bond, double line of scallops wmk. (1903)
deep orange red *300.*
scarlet *300.*
orange *300.*
light blue *300.*
l. Die on colored card, printed through a mat (1903)
dark orange, *ivory* *150.*
dark orange, *light pink* *150.*
brown, *light blue* *150.*
dull dark blue, *pale green* *150.*
violet, *light yellow* *150.*
violet brown, *buff* *150.*

72-E1

Vignette size: 16x17½mm
Washington vignette only.

72-E1 90c
a. Die on proof paper (1903)
black 100.
carmine 100.
dark carmine 100.
scarlet 100.
red brown 100.
orange 100.
orange brown 100.
violet brown 100.
gray olive 100.
light green 100.
green 100.
dark blue 100.
lilac 100.
red violet 100.
yellow brown 100.
ultramarine 100.
b. Die on colored card (1903)
black, *light yellow* *165.*
red brown, *light pink* *165.*
carmine, *buff* *165.*
brown, *pale green* *165.*
dark brown, *light blue* *165.*
ultramarine, *ivory* *165.*
c. Die on dull light blue green bond (1903)
violet brown *165.*
dusky green *165.*
dusky blue *165.*
red violet *165.*

72-E2

Vignette with blank top and bottom labels.

72-E2 90c
a. Die on proof paper (1903)
black 100.
carmine 100.
dark carmine 100.
scarlet 100.
orange 100.
yellow brown 100.
brown 100.
violet brown 100.
gray olive 100.
light green 100.
green 100.
dark blue 100.
red violet 100.
lilac 100.
ultramarine 100.
b. Die on green bond (1903)
dull orange *150.*
dull orange brown *150.*
red violet *150.*
c. Die on colored card (1903)
black, *buff* *185.*
orange red, *light yellow* *185.*
brown, *ivory* *185.*
olive green, *light pink* *185.*
green, *light blue* *185.*
violet brown, *pale green* *185.*

72-E3

U.S. POSTAGE in top label.

72-E3 90c
a. Die on proof paper (1903)
black 125.
carmine 125.
dark carmine 125.
scarlet 125.
orange 125.
yellow 125.
yellow brown 125.
brown 125.
violet brown 125.
gray olive 125.
light green 125.
green 125.
dark blue 125.
lilac 125.
red violet 125.
ultramarine 125.
b. Die on colored card (1903)
orange, *light blue* *185.*
orange red, *light yellow* *185.*
dark blue, *buff* *185.*
violet, *pale green* *185.*
violet brown, *ivory* *185.*
orange brown, *pale pink* *185.*
c. Die on green bond (1903)
black *175.*
brown *175.*
green *175.*
gray olive *175.*

72-E5

Complete design.

72-E5 90c
- ***d.*** Die on proof paper, printed through a mat (1903)
  - black 175.
  - carmine 175.
  - dark carmine 175.
  - scarlet 175.
  - orange 175.
  - orange brown 175.
  - yellow brown 175.
  - brown 175.
  - violet brown 175.
  - gray olive 175.
  - light green 175.
  - green 175.
  - dark blue 175.
  - lilac 175.
  - red violet 175.
  - ultramarine 175.
- ***e.*** Die on colored card (1903)
  - carmine, *light blue* *250.*
  - dismal brown, *light pink* *250.*
  - orange brown, *buff* *250.*
  - blue, *ivory* *250.*
  - violet, *pale green* *250.*
  - green, *pale yellow* *250.*
- ***f.*** Die on green bond (1903)
  - dark carmine *225.*
  - red brown *225.*
  - green *225.*
- ***g.*** Die on bond (1903)
  - brown *250.*
  - orange brown *250.*
  - dark green *250.*
- ***h.*** Die on bond, "Bond No. 1" wmk. (1903), orange brown *350.*
- ***i.*** Die on bond, "Bond No 2" wmk. (1903), orange brown *350.*
- ***j.*** Die on bond, Walls of Troy wmk. (1903)
  - carmine *300.*
  - scarlet *300.*
  - orange *300.*
  - dark green *300.*
  - ultramarine *300.*
- ***k.*** Die on pink pelure (1903)
  - brown red *350.*
  - dull yellow *350.*
  - very dark green *350.*
  - dark blue *350.*
  - dull violet *350.*
- ***l.*** Die on bond, Double Scallops wmk. (1903), scarlet *300.*

American Bank Note Co.

65-E5

Design size: 19x23½mm
Engraved frame with pencil border, center cut out, mounted over 22x27mm engraved vignette of Washington.

65-E5 3c Die on India, black *3,000.*

65-E6

Design size: 19x24½mm
Engraved frame with pencil border, center cut out, mounted over engraved ruled background with engraved Washington vignette mounted on it.

65-E6 Three Cents Die on India, on card about 23x27½mm, black *2,500.*

65-E7

Master die No. 80 of frame only.

65-E7 3c Die on India, card mounted
- deep orange *2,000.*
- dark brown *2,000.*
- green *2,000.*
- dark blue *2,000.*
- black *2,000.*

65-E7Aa

65-E7Ab

Design size: 19½x24½mm
Engraved lathework frame with Bauld, Cousland & Co. engraved Washington vignette. No denomination.

65-E7A (3c)
- ***a.*** Die on India (29x35 mm). Engraved frame with pencil border. Blank labels *1,000.*
- ***b.*** Die on India (53x62 mm), die sunk on card. Blank labels and corner tablets
  - black *1,000.*
  - green *1,000.*
  - brown purple *1,000.*
- ***c.*** As 65-E7Ab, die sunk on card. Top label: American Bank Note. Bottom label: Company. New York. Corner tablets: A, B, N, C. Exists in various states of wear outside the design and off the card, cut down on India
  - black *1,000.*
  - blue *1,000.*
  - brown *1,000.*
  - brown red *1,000.*
  - red brown *1,000.*
  - orange brown *1,000.*
  - scarlet *1,000.*
  - dark green *1,000.*
  - dull purple *1,000.*
- ***d.*** As No. 65-E7Ac, plate essay, imperf, ungummed. Green on white wove. Complete bottom row of 4 (one recorded) —
- ***e.*** As No. 65-E7Ac. Loewenberg decal essay, blue (one recorded) —

65-E8

Design size: 19½x24½mm
Engraved lathework frame with Bald, Cousland & Co. engraved Washington vignette and engraved lettered labels and numerals mounted on it.

65-E8 3c Die on India, on 22x27mm card, black *11,000.*

65-E9

Master die No. 81 of frame only.

65-E9 3c Die on India
- black *2,750.*
- brown yellow *2,750.*
- dark green *2,750.*
- orange red *2,750.*

65-E10

Engraved lathework frame with Bald, Cousland & Co. engraved Washington vignette and engraved lettered labels and numerals mounted on it.

65-E10 3c Die on India, on 28x35mm card, black *7,000.*

67-E5

Design size: 21x25mm
Engraved frame used for the 1860 Nova Scotia 5c stamp cut to shape, with engraved lettered labels and Washington vignette No. 209-E7 mounted on it.

67-E5 Five Cents Die on India, on 23x27mm card, black *2,500.*

67-E6

Design size: 19x24
Engraved lathework background with Bald, Cousland & Co. engraved Washington vignette and engraved lettered labels and numerals mounted on it.

67-E6 5c Die on India, mounted on 22x26mm card, black *7,000.*

67-E7

Design size: 19x24mm
Engraved lathework background with Bald, Cousland & Co. engraved Washington vignette and engraved lettered labels and numerals mounted on it.

67-E7 5c Die on India, mounted on 21x26½mm card, black *7,000.*

National Bank Note Co.

The following essays include those formerly listed as Nos. 55-57, 59 and 62 in the Postage section, and the corresponding die and plate essays formerly listed in the Proof section. Former No. 58 is now No. 62B. Former Nos. 60 and 61 are now Nos. 70eTC and 71bTC in the Trial Color Proofs section.

Small die essays from the 1903 Roosevelt albums have "RA" as part of the listing description. Small die essays from the special Panama-Pacific Exposition printings have "PP" as part of the listing description.

63-E10

Frame essay with blank areas for Franklin vignette, labels, numerals, U and S.

63-E10 1c Die on India, black *6,000.*

63-E11

Die size: 58x56mm
"Premiere Gravure" die No. 440.

63-E11 1c
- ***a.*** "Premiere Gravure" die essay on India (formerly Nos. 55P1, 55TC1)
  - black *5,500.*
  - indigo *1,500.*
  - ultramarine *2,750.*
- ***b.*** RA "Premiere Gravure" small die essay on white wove, 28x31mm (**formerly No. 55P2**), indigo *325.*
- ***c.*** "Premiere Gravure" plate essay on India (**formerly Nos. 55P3, 55TC3**)
  - indigo *300.*
  - blue —
  - ultramarine *300.*
  - violet ultramarine —
- ***d.*** "Premiere Gravure" plate essay on semitransparent stamp paper (**formerly No. 55TC4**), ultramarine *450.*

63-E11e

- ***e.*** Finished "Premiere Gravure" plate essay on semitransparent stamp paper, perf. 12, gummed (**formerly No. 55**), indigo *55,000.*

No. 63-E11e is valued with perfs cutting slightly into design at top.

63-E12

Die size: 47x55mm
Apparently complete die except value numerals have been cut out.

63-E12 1c Die on India, die sunk on card, black *1,500.*

65-E11

Die size: 64x76½mm
Washington head only. No die number. NBNC imprint 24 mm below the base of the bust. Vignette similar to No. 65-E14.

65-E11 3c
- ***a.*** Die on India, on card, carmine (two recorded) *750.*
- ***b.*** Die on white glazed paper
  - black (five recorded) *750.*
  - scarlet (four recorded) *750.*
  - brown violet *750.*

65-E12

Die size: 78x55mm
Incomplete engraved design, no scrolls outside framelines, no ornaments on 3s, U and S. Vignette: no imprint. No silhouette on top of the head. Thin wispy hair. No gash in the hair around the ear. Well defined chin and lines at the base of the bust.

65-E12 3c Die on India, die sunk on card
- black *1,000.*
- blue *1,000.*

65-E13

As No. 65-E12 but ornaments on 3s, U and S. Shows traces of first border design erased. With imprint and No. 441 below design.

65-E13 3c Die on India, card mounted
- scarlet *1,000.*
- brown red *1,000.*
- ultramarine *1,000.*

65-E14

Die size: 59x55mm
Frame as No. 65-E13 but with scrolls added outside the frame. Vignette: top of head silhouetted. Thick hair lines. Gash in the hair around the ear. Poor definition around the chin and at the base of the bust. No imprint.

65-E14 3c Die on India, die sunk on card
- ***a.*** Die on India (62 x 74 mm), die sunk on card
  - black *750.*
  - scarlet *750.*
  - pink *1,250.*
  - brown orange *750.*
  - deep orange red *750.*
  - deep red *1,500.*
- ***b.*** Die on pelure paper, dim deep red (one recorded) —

65-E15

Washington vignette as No. 65-E12: no silhouette on top of the head, no gash around the ear, well defined lines at the base of the bust; frame as No. 65-E14.

65-E15 3c
- ***a.*** Die on India, card mounted, deep orange red *1,000.*
- ***b.*** "Premiere Gravure" die essay on semitransparent stamp paper, 20x25mm-30x37mm
  - deep orange red *750.*
  - deep red orange *750.*
  - dim red *750.*
  - dim deep red *750.*
  - dim orange red *750.*
  - dull pink *750.*
  - dull violet red *750.*
- ***c.*** "Premiere Gravure" small die on India (59x55 mm), die sunk on card. Die 441 with NBNC imprint, became the basis of the issued stamp after corner ornaments added (eleven recorded)
  - red *1,350.*
  - black *1,750.*
  - scarlet *1,750.*
  - pink *2,850.*
  - orange red *2,000.*
  - dark orange red *2,000.*
- ***d.*** RA Small die essay on white wove, 28x31mm altered laydown die of complete design but with outer scrolls removed and replaced by ones similar to "Premiere Gravure" design (1903) (**formerly No. 56P2**), dim deep red *500.*
- ***e.*** As "c," PP small die essay on pale cream soft wove, 24x29mm (1915) (**formerly No. 56P2a**), deep red *1,250.*
- ***f.*** "Premiere Gravure" plate No. 2 essay on India (**formerly Nos. 56P3, 56TC3**)
  - red *250.*
  - scarlet *350.*
- ***g.*** "Premiere Gravure" plate essay on semitransparent stamp paper (**formerly Nos. 56aP4, 56TC4**)
  - red, pair with gum *1,750.*
  - black *400.*

65-E15h

- ***h.*** Finished "Premiere Gravure" plate essay on semitransparent stamp paper, perf. 12, gummed (**formerly No. 56**)
  - brown rose *600.*
  - orange red *475.*
  - bright orange red *475.*
  - dark orange red *475.*
  - dim deep red *475.*
  - pink *475.*
  - deep pink *475.*
  - P# block of 8, Impt. (any shade) *20,000.*

67-E8

Incomplete impression from die No. 442, border lines and corner scrolls missing.

67-E8 5c Die on India, mounted on 34x50mm card, black *1,750.*

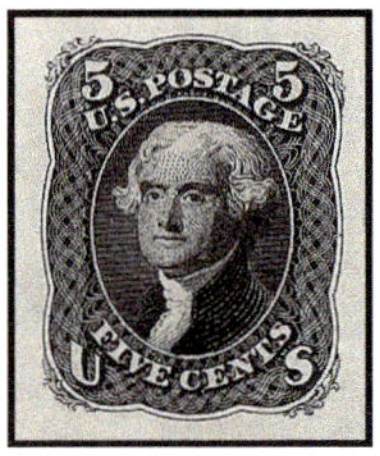

67-E9

Size of die: 58x59mm
"Premiere Gravure" design, with corner scrolls but without leaflets.

67-E9 5c
a. "Premiere Gravure" die essay on India, card mounted (formerly No. 57TC1)
black *2,500.*
scarlet *2,500.*
b. RA Small die essay on white wove, 28x31mm, altered laydown die of complete design but with scrolls removed from corners to resemble "Premiere Gravure" (1903) (**formerly No. 57P2), brown** 400.
c. As "b," PP die essay on pale cream soft wove, 24x29mm (1915) (**formerly No. 57P2a**), brown *1,750.*
d. "Premiere Gravure" plate No. 3 essay on India (**formerly Nos. 57P3, 57TC3)**
brown *350.*
light brown *300.*
dark brown *300.*
red brown *300.*

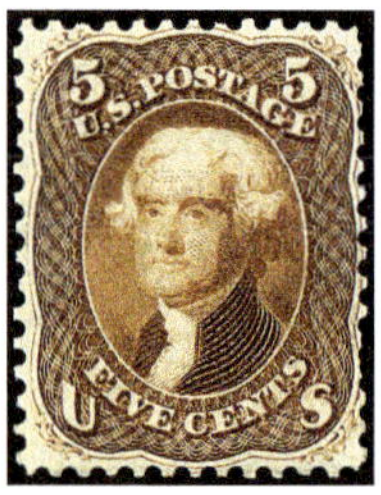

67-E9e

e. Finished "Premiere Gravure" plate essay on semitransparent stamp paper, perf. 12, gummed (**formerly No. 57**), brown *25,000.*

One example is recorded of No. 67-E9e postally used. It has small faults and a circular datestamp in black, and it is valued thus. Value, $30,000.

68-E1

Design size: 14x17½mm
Die size: 26x31mm
Washington vignette only.

68-E1 10c
a. Die on ivory paper, black *1,000.*
b. Die on India *1,000.*

68-E2

Incomplete die No. 443.

68-E2 10c Die on India, 22x26mm, dark green *2,500.*

68-E3

Incomplete die of No. 68P1, thin lines missing on top of frame.

68-E3 10c Die on India
yellowish green *1,100.*
dark green *1,000.*

69-E5

Design size: 12½x16mm
Die size: about 62x65mm
Washington vignette only.

69-E5 12c
a. Die on India, die sunk on card
black *400.*
dark red *400.*
orange red *400.*
b. Die on ivory paper, about 24x28mm
black *500.*
scarlet *500.*
black brown *500.*
blue *500.*

69-E6

Incomplete die No. 444, without corner ornaments.

69-E6 12c
a. "Premiere Gravure" die essay on India, mounted on card (**formerly Nos. 59P1, 59TC1**)
black *2,500.*
scarlet *2,500.*
dark green *2,500.*
b. RA Small die essay on white wove, 29x31mm, altered laydown die of complete design but with scrolls removed from corners to resemble the "Premiere Gravure" (1903) (formerly Nos. 59P2), black *450.*
c. PP "Premiere Gravure" small die essay on pale cream soft wove, 24x29mm (1915) (**formerly No. 59P2a**), black *1,750.*
d. "Premiere Gravure" plate No. 5 essay on India (**formerly No. 59P3**), black *300.*

69-E6e

e. Finished "Premiere Gravure" plate essay on semitransparent stamp paper, perf. 12, gummed (**formerly No. 59**), black *80,000.*

70-E5

Washington vignette in incomplete frame.

70-E5 24c Die on India, black *3,250.*

70-E6

Die size: 56½x56mm
Incomplete die (No. 445): silhouette unfinished, especially scrolls around numerals; shadows over numerals not acid etched.

70-E6 24c Die on India, die sunk on card
black *900.*
violet *900.*
gray violet *900.*
dark violet *900.*
scarlet *900.*
green *900.*
orange *900.*
red brown *900.*
orange brown *900.*
orange yellow *900.*
rose red *900.*
gray *900.*
steel blue *900.*
blue *900.*

For finished "Premiere Gravure" trial color plate proof on semitransparent stamp paper, perf 12, gummed (formerly No. 60), see 70TC6 in the Trial Color, Die and Plate Proof section.

71-E1

Die size: 46x60mm
Incomplete die (No. 446): additional ornaments at top and bottom in pencil, as later engraved.

71-E1 30c Die on India, black *1,750.*

71-E2

"Premiere Gravure" die: left side of frame and silhouette at lower right unfinished.

71-E2 30c
a. "Premiere Gravure" die essay on India, die sunk on card (**formerly No. 61TC1**)
black *1,500.*
green *1,500.*
dull gray blue *1,500.*
violet brown *1,500.*
scarlet *1,500.*
dull rose *1,500.*
b. "Premiere Gravure" plate essay on India (**formerly No. 61P3**), deep red orange *600.*
c. "Premiere Gravure" plate essay on card
black (split thin) *500.*
blue *750.*
d. "Premiere Gravure" plate essay on card, black 12x2mm SPECIMEN overprint, blue *750.*
e. "Premiere Gravure" plate essay on semitransparent stamp paper
deep red orange *1,250.*
yellow orange *1,250.*
lemon yellow *1,250.*
dark orange yellow *1,250.*
dull orange yellow *1,250.*

For finished "Premiere Gravure" trial color proof on semitransparent stamp paper, perf 12, gummed (formerly No. 61), see No. 71TC6 in the Trial Color, Die and Plate Proof section.

72-E6

Die size: 54x63mm
Incomplete die: without thin lines at bottom of frame and in upper left triangle between label and frame, and without leaves at left of U and right of S.

72-E6 90c Die on India, blue (shades) *1,000.*

72-E7

Similar to 72-E6 but lines added in upper left triangle, leaves added at left of U and at right of S. Exists with and without imprint and Die No. 447 added below design.

72-E7 90c
a. Die on India, die sunk on card, black 1,750.
b. "Premiere Gravure" die essay on India, thin line under bottom center frame (**formerly Nos. 62P1, 62TC1**)
blue 1,350.
black 1,500.
d. PP "Premiere Gravure" small die essay on pale cream soft wove, 24x29mm (1915) (**formerly No. 62P2a**), blue 1,750.
e. "Premiere Gravure" plate essay on India, blue 500.
f. "Premiere Gravure" plate essay on card, black (split thin) 500.
g. "Premiere Gravure" plate essay on semi-transparent stamp paper (**formerly Nos. 62aP4, 62TC4**)
blue, pair, gummed 5,500.
blue green 275.

72-E7h

h. Finished "Premiere Gravure" plate essay on semitransparent stamp paper, perf. 12, gummed (**formerly No. 62**), blue 40,000.

Die size: 54x63mm
Similar to Nos. 72-E6 and 72-E7 but leaf at left of "U" only, no shading around "U" and "S," leaf and some shading missing at bottom right above "S," shading missing in top label, etc., faint ms. "8" at bottom of backing card.

72-E8 90c Die on India, die sunk on 3¼x3½-inch card, dark blue —

63-E13b

63-E13g

Design size: 20x47mm
Die size: 57x95mm
Bowlsby patent coupon at top of 1c stamp design.

63-E13 1c
a. Die on India, die sunk on card
black 1,750.
red 1,750.
scarlet 1,750.
orange 1,750.
orange brown 1,750.
brown 1,750.
yellow brown 1,750.
blue green 1,750.
olive green 1,750.
olive 1,750.
blue 1,750.
violet 1,750.
red violet 1,750.
gray 1,750.
gray brown 1,750.
dull orange yellow 1,750.
b. Die on white glazed paper
black 1,750.
dark brown 1,750.
scarlet 1,750.
blue 1,750.
c. Plate on pelure paper, gummed, red 300.
d. Plate on white paper, red 250.
e. Plate on white paper, with 13x16mm points-up grill, red 350.
Split grill 750.
f. Plate on white paper, perf. all around and between stamp and coupon
red 200.
blue 200.
g. Plate on white paper, perf. all around, imperf. between stamp and coupon
red 250.
blue 250.
h. Plate on white paper, perf. all around, rouletted between stamp and coupon
red 300.
blue 300.
i. Plate on India paper, black 750.

1861-66 Essays
Authors Unknown

73-E2

Design size: 21x26mm

73-E2 2c Pencil and watercolor on thick card, bright green 3,750.

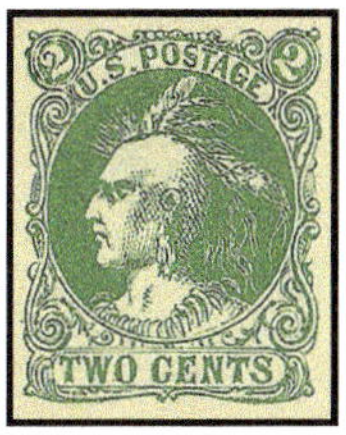

73-E3

Design size: 21x26mm
Indian vignette. Typographed printings from woodcuts. Plates of three rows of three, one row each of Nos. 73-E3, 73-E4, 73-E5. Listings are of singles.

73-E3 2c
a. Plate on white wove
red 30.
scarlet 30.
violet 30.
black 30.
blue 30.
green 30.
b. Plate on mauve wove
red 50.
violet 50.
black 50.
blue 50.
green 50.
c. Plate on yellow wove
red 50.
violet 50.
black 50.
blue 50.
green 50.
d. Plate on yellow laid
red 50.
violet 50.
black 50.
blue 50.
green 50.
e. Plate on pink laid
red 50.
violet 50.
black 50.
blue 50.
green 50.
f. Plate on green laid
red 50.
violet 50.
black 50.
blue 50.
green 50.
g. Plate on cream laid
red 50.
violet 50.
black 50.
blue 50.
green 50.
h. Plate on pale yellow wove
red 50.
green 50.
blue 50.
i. Plate on yellow-surfaced card, violet 50.
j. Plate on fawn wove, green 50.

73-E4

Design size: 23x26½mm
Small head of Liberty in shield. Typographed printings from woodcuts. On plate with Nos. 73-E3 and 73-E5. Listings are of singles.

73-E4 3c
a. Plate on white wove
red 30.
scarlet 30.
violet 30.
black 30.
blue 30.
green 30.
b. Plate on mauve wove, violet 50.
c. Plate on yellow wove
red 50.
violet 50.
black 50.
blue 50.
green 50.
d. Plate on yellow laid
red 50.
violet 50.
black 50.
blue 50.
green 50.
e. Plate on pink laid
carmine 50.
violet 50.
black 50.
blue 50.
green 50.
f. Plate on green laid
carmine 50.
green 50.
dull violet 50.
blue 50.
g. Plate on cream laid
red 50.
violet 50.
black 50.
blue 50.
green 50.
h. Plate on pale yellow wove
red 50.
green 50.
blue 50.
i. Plate on yellow-surfaced card, violet 50.
j. Plate on fawn wove, green 50.

73-E5

Design size: 22½x25½mm
Large head of Liberty. Typographed impressions from woodcut. On plate with Nos. 73-E3 and 73-E4. Listings are of singles.

73-E5 5c
a. Plate on white wove
red 30.
scarlet 30.
violet 30.
black 30.
blue 30.
green 30.
b. Plate on mauve wove, violet 50.
c. Plate on yellow wove
red 50.
violet 50.
black 50.
blue 50.
green 50.
d. Plate on yellow laid
red 50.
violet 50.
black 50.
blue 50.
green 50.
e. Plate on pink laid
red 50.
black 50.
blue 50.
green 50.
f. Plate on green laid
red 50.
violet 50.
black 50.
blue 50.
green 50.
g. Plate on cream laid
red 50.
black 50.
blue 50.

green 50.
h. Plate on pale yellow wove
red 50.
blue 50.
green 50.
i. Plate on yellow-surfaced card, violet 50.
j. Plate on fawn wove, green 50.

73-E6

Size of design: 21x27mm
Indian vignette. Typographed impressions from woodcut.

73-E6 10c
a. Die on proof paper
black 200.
gray black 200.
carmine 200.
dusky red 200.
brown 200.
green 200.
blue 200.
violet 200.
b. Plate on white paper (pane of 4)
red 600.
violet 600.
brown 600.
black 600.
blue 600.
green 600.
c. Plate on soft cream card (pane of 4)
black 600.
red 600.
blue 600.
green 600.
red violet 600.

1863-64
Henry Loewenberg
Decalcomania and Coated Paper Essays

79-EP

Decalcomania essay pasted to the back of a letter dated Mar. 23, 1863. Written by James MacDonough of the NBNC to the PO's Anthony Zevely. Illustrates Loewenberg's patent 40,489 (granted Nov. 3, 1863). Printed on goldbeaters' skin paper and gummed over the printing. Bottom left corner folded back to prove the concept i.e. that attempts to remove a stamp from an envelope should leave the design behind.

79-EP Shield design. Block of 8, black (one recorded) —

79-E65P5

79-E65P6

79-E66P5

79-E67P5

79-E71P5

79-E72P5

79-E73P5

Plate proofs of the 1861 issue printed on goldbeaters' skin paper (Loewenberg patent 40,489). Letters dated Nov. 6 and 28, 1863, in the Brazer archive, indicate that there were at least two printings. The first, before Nov. 6, was mistakenly gummed with NBNC gum. The second was printed between Nov. 6 and 28, and was abandoned half-finished; i.e. probably ungummed.

Values are for essentially sound examples with a very minimal amount of flaking or creasing.

No. 79-E65P6: Based on Loewenberg patent 42,207 (April 5, 1864) for printing on starch-coated paper. Attempts to clean the stamp should result in the coating and the design being wiped from the paper.

79-E65P5 3c
a. Imperforate
rose 50.00
brown lake 50.00
blue 150.00
b. Lake on pale blue 300.00
79-E65P6 3c 3c perforated, rose 75.00
79-E66P5 3c
a. Lake 100.00
b. Lake on pale green 150.00
79-E67P5 5c
brown 75.00
79-E68P5 10c
a. Green 150.00
b. Green on pale rose 250.00
79-E69P5 12c
black 300.00
79-E70P5 24c
a. Lilac 75.00
b. Lilac on pale green 250.00
79-E71P5 30c
a. Orange 100.00
b. Orange on blue-green 250.00
79-E72P5 90c
dark blue 75.00
79-E73P5 2c
a. Black 75.00
b. Black on pale rose 250.00

1867 Essays
Re-use Prevention
Authors Unknown

Unfolded — 79-E1

Folded — 79-E1

Design size (folded): 18x23mm
Design size (unfolded): 18x58mm
Folded and scored four times, horiz. crease at center. Bronze overprint U 2 S, (2 punched out). Lower ⅔ gummed below second fold so top ⅓ could be torn off for canceling.

79-E1 2c On white paper, dull red violet 5,000.

79-E2

Similar to No. 79-E1 but larger and not folded. Pierced with S-shaped cuts as well as punched out 2.

79-E2 2c
a. On white paper, US 7½mm high, bronze, US in dull black 5,000.
b. On white paper, US 10mm high, bronze, US in violet 5,000.

79-E3

Cuts as on back

U.S. No. 73 as issued but pierced with S-shaped cuts, ovptd. in metallic color.

79-E3 2c Essay on 2c stamp, gold overprint 7,500.

79-E4a

79-E4b

Similar to No. 79-E1 but with punched out 3.

79-E4 3c
- ***a.*** On white paper, U 3 S black above, bronze below and on face beneath folds — *5,000.*
- ***b.*** On green paper, 3 not punched out, 3 black, POSTAGE blue — *5,000.*

79-E5

Similar to No. 79-E4, with "3 U.S. 3 / Three Cents / Void if detached."

79-E5 3c On green paper, black — *3,000.*

79-E6

Similar to No. 79-E2 but with punched out 3, gummed.

79-E6 3c
- ***a.*** On white paper, bronze over violet — *3,000.*
- ***b.*** On white paper, U S black, rest bronze — *3,000.*

79-E7

Vignette map of U.S.

79-E7 3c On thick white paper, rouletted, green, gold 3 on map — *8,500.*

79-E7A

Similar to 79-E7, without "3" on map.

79-E7A 3c On thick white paper, imperforate block of 9 (unique), black — —

1865-66 Essays
Henry Loewenberg

79-E8

Design created by The Loewenberg Stamp Company in 1864. Washington vignette flanked by rod and axe. Printed in reverse on the back of transparent paper, reads correctly from the front. Based on two patents: 40,489 (print first and then gum); and 45,057 (gum first and then print). It is impossible to distinguish between the two without damaging the stamps. Plate essays are from sheets of 25.

79-E8 3c
- ***a.*** Plate on onionskin paper, imperf., gummed
  - brown — *10.*
  - orange brown — *10.*
  - deep orange brown — *10.*
  - orange — *10.*
  - green — *10.*
  - light green — *10.*
  - blue green — *10.*
  - pale green — *10.*
  - red — *10.*
  - light red — *10.*
  - dark red — *10.*
  - violet red — *10.*
  - violet — *10.*
  - light violet — *10.*
  - dull pale violet — *10.*
  - blue — *10.*
  - dark blue — *10.*
  - deep blue — *10.*
  - pale blue — *10.*
  - dull blue — *10.*
  - gold — *50.*
  - gray — *7.*
  - black — *7.*
  - carmine — *7.*
- ***b.*** Plate on onionskin paper, perf. 12, gummed
  - gray black — *25.*
  - gray — *25.*
  - gray violet — *25.*
  - dull violet — *25.*
  - brown red — *25.*
- ***c.*** Plate on more opaque onionskin paper, imperf.
  - black — *25.*
  - red violet — *25.*
  - dull violet — *25.*
- ***d.*** Plate on thick transparent paper
  - gray — *25.*
  - black — *25.*

79-E9

As 79-E8 but printed on the front of the paper. Plate essays are from sheets of 25.

79-E9 3c
- ***a.*** Plate on white wove, imperf., gummed
  - blue — *10.*
  - red — *10.*
  - gray — *10.*
  - brown — *10.*
  - orange — *10.*
  - green — *10.*
  - yellow green — *10.*
- ***b.*** Plate on clear white paper, imperf.
  - orange — *10.*
  - blue — *10.*
  - gray — *10.*
  - dark gray — *10.*
- ***c.*** Plate on thick wove, fugitive ink, perf., gummed
  - carmine — *10.*
  - violet carmine — *10.*
  - pale dull red — *10.*
  - gray — *10.*
  - pale gray — *10.*
  - pale dull tan — *10.*
  - green — *10.*
- ***d.*** As "c," strip of 3, signed Henry Lowenberg, pale tan — *400.*

79-E9e

- ***e.*** Plate on white paper treated with prussiate of potash (Loewenberg patent 53,081, March 6, 1866). The paper turns blue when wet
  - carmine — *10.*
  - Prussian blue — *10.*
  - orange — *10.*
  - green — *10.*
  - brown — *10.*
  - black — *10.*
- ***f.*** As "e," perf.
  - carmine — *10.*
  - scarlet — *10.*
  - orange — *10.*
  - blue — *10.*
  - green — *10.*
  - brown — *10.*
- ***g.*** Plate on India
  - violet brown — *10.*
  - green — *10.*
  - blue — *10.*
  - dark blue — *10.*
- ***h.*** Plate on India, signed D.H. Craig, red — *350.*
- ***i.*** On white card, 62x72mm, design deeply indented, green — *15.*
- ***j.*** On blue wove, red — *15.*
- ***k.*** On orange laid
  - black — *15.*
  - gray — *15.*
- ***l.*** On blue laid, scarlet — *15.*
- ***m.*** On white laid, blue — *15.*
- ***n.*** On pink laid, blue — *15.*
- ***o.*** On linen cloth. Possibly based on patent 45,468 (Feb. 28, 1865) for embossing linen
  - green — *50.*
  - red — *50.*
  - blue — *50.*
- ***p.*** On glazed white paper, blue — *20.*

1867 Essays
John M. Sturgeon

79-E10

Liberty vignette. Curved labels top and bottom. Self-canceling: CANCELLED in colorless sensitive ink, becomes colored when wet. Patented 1867, 1868.

79-E10 10c
- ***a.*** Die on stiff card, cut close, clearly engraved, not canceled, both labels completely blank, dark carmine — *350.*
- ***b.*** Die on wove, rough impression, CANCELLED diagonally each way, dark carmine — *450.*
- ***c.*** Die on thick white or tinted paper, gummed, rough impression, about 21x26mm, two lines in upper label, one line in lower label
  - carmine — *200.*
  - dark carmine — *200.*
  - very dark carmine — *200.*
  - green — *200.*
  - dark green — *200.*
  - dull red violet — *200.*
- ***d.*** As "c," on thick pinkish paper, dark green — *250.*
- ***g.*** Single centered in 6-inch wide strip of thick white paper, almost always cut in at top and bottom, dark carmine — *400.*
- ***h.*** Horiz. row of five designs on thick white paper, 10mm apart
  - dark carmine — *1,200.*
  - dark purple — *1,200.*

black 1,200.
i. Single on blue card, ovptd. seal BRITISH CONSULATE, V.R. in center, black 1,250.

American Bank Note Co.

79-E11a

Design size: 16x22mm
Vignette of Columbia. Probably submitted by Charles F. Steel.

79-E11 2c and 3c
a. Engraved die on thick yellowish wove, black —

79-E11b

Design size: 18x22mm
Engraving of frame lines, horiz. shading lines and "3" and "2" added to Columbia vignette, black

b. Engraved die on thick yellowish wove, black —
c. Engraved plate on thick yellowish wove, imperf. (usually found in upper left margin blocks)

rose scarlet	300.
Block of 4	1,250.
blue green	300.
Block of 4	1,250.

79-E11d

d. Engraved plate on stamp paper, perf. 12, gummed

black	175.
rose scarlet	175.
blue green	175.
blue	175.

Author Unknown

79-E12

Design size: 20x26mm
Vignette of Liberty in circle of stars. Vertical color lines outside design to 24x28mm. Curved labels blank. Lithographed.

79-E12 No denomination
a. Die on white paper, dull violet 2,750.
b. Die on bluish paper, blue 2,750.

1865-67 Grill Essays
National Bank Note Co.

79-E13a

Correspondence in the Brazer archive proves that Charles Steel had produced the first "grill" experiments by late 1865. His patent was registered in 1867.

79-E13
a. Wove paper, 80x140mm, impressed with four diff. seals, crossed lines and flat-bottom square grill, points down, circles 11 or 12mm (two recorded) 9,000.

b. Grills in odd shapes produced by a scratch-like process on white wove, each about 20x25mm (only one of each recorded—do not conform to Steel patent)

cross	1,500.
star in square	1,500.
horizontal lined oval in square	1,500.
diagonal lined oval in square	1,500.

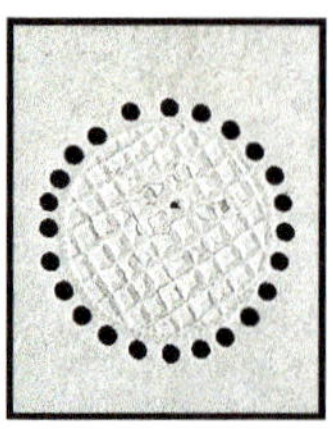
79-E13c

c. White wove, gummed, 15mm circle with points down, flat-bottom square grill, surrounded by 24 perforated holes 1,000.
d. White wove, quadrille batonne watermark, 12mm colored circle with points down grill around 3, roughly grilled colorless 3 below 1,250.

79-E13e

e. White wove, 12mm circle points down, flat-bottom square grill around 3. Grill lines and 3 colored carmine (two recorded) 750.
f. Colorless 15mm points down, flat-bottom square grilled circle on white wove, gummed, perf. 12 500.

79-E14a

79-E14c

79-E14d

Allover pyramid shaped grill with varying degrees of flattening after grilling as called for by Steel↔s patent.

79-E14
a. White wove, about 47x26mm, points down pyramid grill, stamped with red 6-digit number, probably to test printing numbers on a grill 750.
b. As "a" but with black scribbles in pen and ink around the number, probably to test pen and ink cancellation on a grill (one recorded) 750.
c. Wove paper with 144x28mm all-over grill with points up as adopted, with manuscript "Ten Thousand Dollars" written across grill area, probably to test ink absorption 1,000.
d. Wove paper in various colors, about 85x40mm, points up grill as adopted

white	200.
pale pink	200.
salmon	200.
light yellow	200.
light gray green	200.
light blue	200.
pale lilac	200.
light gray	200.

79-E14e, Type I

e.
Type I. As "d". Allover grill. Four blocks stuck to white card (152x228 mm). Signed: Steel, Duke, MacDonough, Dougherty. The essay records Steel's claim to the grill patent *5,000.*
Type II. As "d". Allover grill. Three large blocks stuck to white card. Only signed by Steel. *3,000.*

79-E14f

f. Colorless 12mm "3" in pyramid grill circle on tan white wove, gummed, perf. 12 *200.*
g. As "f," yellow wove *200.*
h. As "f," white wove, block of 6 with ms. "Subject to a half hour pressure after embossing" *3,500.*

79-E15

79-E15a

Square Flat Grill

Experimental grills on perf. or imperf. stamps or stamp-size pieces of paper.

Numbers "a" and "b" are allover grills with the square flat shape of the 1865 grill experiments.

No. 79-E15a shows the distinctive square flat grill, enlarged.

79-E15
a. Allover grill of small, flat-bottom squares on stamp paper, points down, 3c rose, imperf, gummed 350.
perf. 12, gummed 250.
perf. 12, cancelled by New York "biscuit" cancel, ungummed (15 recorded) —
b. As "a" but points up, on 3c stamp, perf. 12, gummed
rose *200.*
with black handstamp cancel *600.*
black *200.*
rose, imperf.— various tests of pen and ink cancels *400.*

79-E15c

Pyramid Grill

No. 79-E15c has the flattened, pyramid shape that was used for the A grill stamps.

c. points up, imperf. pairs, gummed
3c rose (**formerly No. 79P4**) *750.*
3c lake (**formerly No. 66aP4**) *750.*

79-E15d

79-E15e, Type I irregular

79-E15e, Type II regular

Nos. 79-E15d to 79-E15f are allover pinpoint grills (the so-called "Music Box" grill) on various plates.

d. Type I. Points up, irregular pattern, (on plates 11, 34, 52) *75.*
Type II. Points up, regular pattern (on plates 11, 34, 52) *75.*
Type III. Points up, canceled on piece (two recorded) —
e. Type I. Points down, irregular pattern (on plate 11) *125.*
Type II. Points down, regular pattern (on plate 11) *125.*
f. 15x16mm grill on stamp size white wove paper, perf. 12, gummed *125.*

The C grill dates from late 1867 and was required by the Post Office because the allover A pyramid grill, proved too fragile for postal use. The following essays are all C grill experiments.

g. C grill, 13x16mm, points down on stamp size wove paper, perf. 12, gummed
white *100.*
yellowish *100.*
pinkish *100.*
blue *100.*
h. As "g" but points up, on white wove *100.*

Nos. 79-E15i through 79-E15n test the C grill on stamps of the 1861 issue. They originate from the archive of papers and stamps retained by Charles F. Steel.

i. C grill on 1c stamp (No. 63), points down (two recorded) —
j. C grill on 3c stamp (No. 65)
points up (one recorded) —
points down (one recorded) —

The 3c C grill essay is almost identical to the issued stamp. There are slight differences in the essay grill which match those on No. 79-E15i and Nos. 79-E15k through 79-E15n.

k. C grill on 5c stamp (No. 76)
points up (one recorded) —
points down (one recorded) —
l. C grill on 10c stamp (No. 68)
points up (one recorded) —
points down (one recorded) —
m. C grill on 12c stamp (No. 69)
points up (one recorded) —
points down (one recorded) —
n. C grill on 30c stamp (No. 71)
points up (one recorded) —
points down (one recorded) —
o. C-grill sheet of 100 stamps on stamp paper, imperf., gummed —
p. Type I. C grill permeability test, "No 1." in pen and ink. Block of 6, imperf., gummed, unflattened —
Type II. C grill permeability test, "No 2" in pen and ink. Block of 6. Perf. 12, gummed, flattened —
Type III. C grill block of 6. Flattened, perf. 12, gummed, Signed: MacDonough and Duke —

The E grill dates from 1868. The following are E grill essays, 11x13mm on white wove stamp paper, perf 12, gummed.

q. Points up *100.*
r. Points down *100.*

1867 "Z" grill Experimental Essays

85C-E1

85C-E1 Sheet of white wove stamp paper, imperf., gummed, with experimental "Z" grill impressions, 11x14mm, points down 175.

85C-E2

85C-E2 Z grill, 11x14mm, points down on stamp size wove paper, perf. 12, partly gummed
white *200.*
salmon *200.*
yellow *200.*
greenish *200.*
dull violet *200.*
pale lilac *200.*

These were made on fully perforated sheet selvage from the 3c and 12c essay panes.

85E-E1 12c Experimental "Z" grill essay, 11x14mm, on heavily horizontally laid paper, gummed, perforated 12
a. On thin transparent paper white paper (not laid), blue *250.*
b. On salmon paper
black *250.*
brown *250.*
green *250.*
blue *250.*
c. On deep orange paper
black *250.*
scarlet *250.*
brown *250.*
green *250.*
blue *250.*
d. On yellow paper
black *250.*
brown *250.*
e. On straw paper
brown *250.*
green *250.*
f. On green paper
black *250.*
scarlet *250.*
brown *250.*
green *250.*
blue *250.*
g. On lilac paper
black *250.*
scarlet *250.*
brown *250.*
green *250.*
blue *250.*
h. On pale rose paper
black *250.*
scarlet *250.*
brown *250.*
green *250.*
blue *250.*

Continental Bank Note Co.

White wove paper about 6x9 inches with 7x9½mm grills spaced as they would fall on centers of stamps in a sheet.

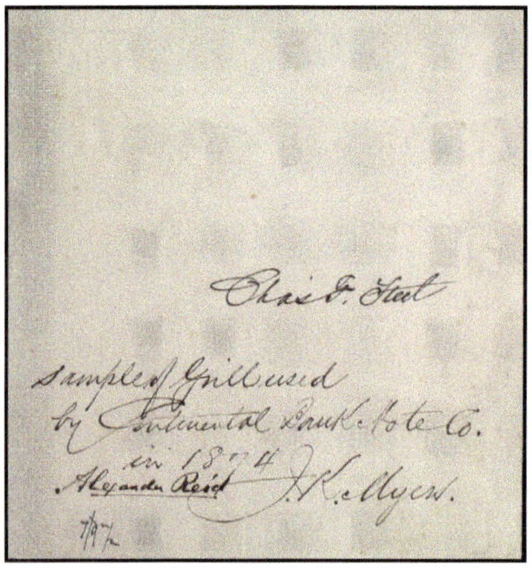
79-E16a

79-E16d

79-E16
- *a.* End roller grill at left, ms. "Chas. F. Steel-Sample of Grill used by Continental Bank Note Co. in 1874. Alexander Reid. J.K. Myers." — *3,000.*
- *b.* Without end roller grill, ms. "Grill of Continental Bank Note Co. Chas. F. Steel." — *3,000.*
- *c.* End roller grill at right, same inscription as "b" — *3,000.*
- *d.* On soft card, six grills — *600.*

Wilbur I. Trafton

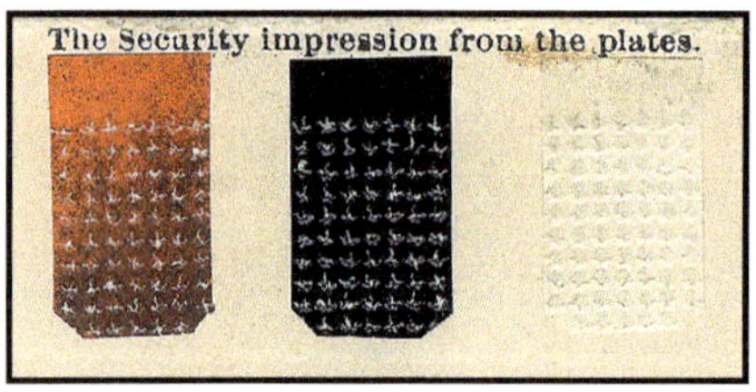

79-E17

Coarse grill in 15mm circle with 7 points up in 11mm, found on 1873 1c, some with 18mm circular cancel, stuck down on printed ad circular along with black, red and albino grill impressions (two each) on paper labeled "The Security Impression from the plates."

79-E17 Entire ad circular with grill examples — *750.*

National Bank Note Co.

On Nov. 6, 1867, MacDonough wrote a letter to Steel in which he asked Steel to bring the design for a "stamp you wish to have made." The following essays almost certainly date from this period. They come closest to what Steel described in his patent as "the ideal stamp."

79-E18

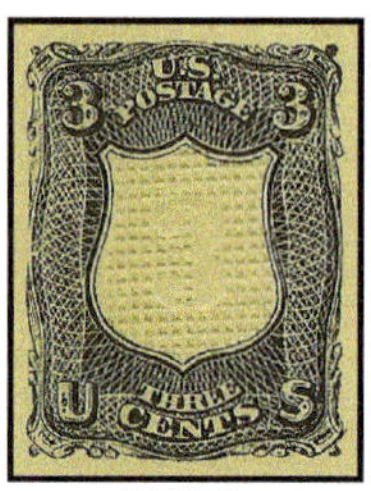
79-E18c

79-E18h

Albino 3 in points down shield-shaped grill in lithographed frame of 3c 1861 stamp.

79-E18 3c
- *a.* Die on thick white paper, gummed
  - black — *1,000.*
  - deep pink — *1,000.*
- *b.* As "a," with Washington, D.C. Feb. 21 pmk.
  - black — *1,750.*
  - deep pink — *1,750.*
- *c.* As "a" but grill with points up, black — *1,000.*
- *d.* As "a," perf. 12, gummed, black — *1,000.*
- *e.* Die on yellow wove, gummed
  - black — *1,000.*
  - red — *1,000.*
- *f.* Die on orange wove
  - black — *1,000.*
  - carmine — *1,000.*
- *g.* Die on yellow laid, black — *1,000.*
- *h.* Numeral handcolored, dull carmine — *1,500.*
- *i.* Frame only, no grill, on grayish wove with pencil "McDonald P.O. Dept. Steel Nature(?)", pale orange brown — *1,500.*

79-E18j

79-E18k

Albino 3 in 13x14mm shield made up of embossed narrow spaced horiz. lines.

- *j.* White wove stamp paper, 22x27mm, perf. 12, gummed — 450.

Albino 3 in 13x14mm shield slightly different from No. 79-E18j.

- *k.* As "j," different shield — 350.

79-E19a

Illustration reduced.

Typographed impression of frame, lettering and numerals of 3c 1861 stamp with 3 in double lined shield in center. In strip of three about 20mm apart, impression of 3 and shield progressively lighter on impressions two and three.

79-E19 3c
- *a.* Engraved (die No. 1570) — *2,500.*
  - green — *2,500.*
  - brown — *2,500.*
  - black — *2,500.*
- *b.* Typographed in color on white paper
  - blue green — *2,750.*
  - dark red brown — *2,750.*
- *c.* As "b," colored and colorless parts interchanged, on thick paper
  - blue green — *2,750.*
  - dark red brown — *2,750.*

79-E20

Embossed albino shield, uncleared purple ink on rest of die.

79-E20 Shield design, die on card —

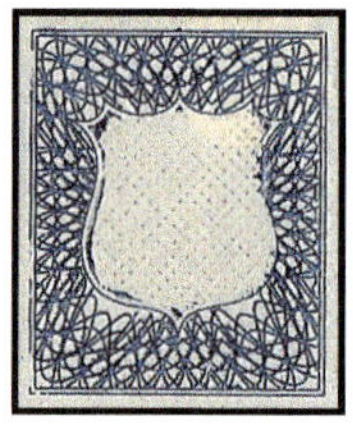
79-E21

Lathework frame with shield shaped vignette cut out, albino 3 in circular grill in center.

79-E21 3c
- *a.* Thick paper, perf. 12
  - blue — *500.*
  - carmine — *500.*
- *b.* At left in strip of 3 with 2 No. 79-E14e, latter black cancels, carmine — *3,500.*
- *c.* Lathework frame on thin wove, allover diagonal grill, imperf., gummed, blue — *1,000.*

79-E22

Lathework frame similar to No. 79-E21 but vignette of 6 horiz. bars with 3 in center printed in glossy ink.

79-E22 3c On pink lilac paper, blue — 2,000.

79-E23

Design of 3c 1861 stamp typographed in relief for surface printing. Single impression lightly block sunk 63x62mm in color. Design has 21x26½mm border inside 23x28½mm colorless rectangle.

79-E23 3c
- *a.* Die on 64x75mm ivory paper, black — *400.*
- *b.* Die on India, dull violet-red-red — *325.*
- *c.* Die on 59x54mm stiff white card, color about 40mm wide (not extending to edges)
  - light red violet — *325.*
  - carmine — *325.*
  - blue — *325.*
- *d.* Washington head only, lines on face around eye, on soft card
  - dim blue-green blue — *250.*
  - dim orange-orange red — *250.*

On 17x21mm plain colored rectangle printed through a mat, surrounded by 55x62mm colorless rectangle, vert. 4½mm wide color bands at sides inside 64x62mm die sinkage.

- *e.* Washington head with dots around eye, on 17x42mm solid color, on 77x45mm stiff white paper, dull violet-red — *250.*
- *f.* India paper on soft white card block sunk 63x62mm, dull violet-red-red with solid color margins — *250.*

Colored India generally cut away outside colorless rectangle 23x28½mm, design heavily embossed through to card beneath.

- *g.* As "f," trimmed to shape
  - dark carmine — *350.*
  - orange — *350.*
  - blue green — *350.*
  - red violet — *350.*

h. Complete design on India, sunk on card, trimmed to shape
blue 100.
dull green blue 100.
i. Plate typographed on white wove, imperf., gummed
dim red 50.
dim light orange red 50.
dim blue green 50.
dim pale blue 50.
dim dark blue 50.
dusky violet red 50.

Color outside design generally fills rectangle, design impression shows on back.

j. Complete design on glossy sticky paper, deep violet red 150.
k. As "j," on pelure, perf. 12, gummed, rose 175.
l. As "k," allover grill, dim red 150.
m. As "k," 13x16mm grill, gray black 150.

79-E24

79-E24c

Block sinkage: 65x76mm
Washington head only.

79-E24 3c
a. Lithographed, face dotted, on 65x76mm solid color background
black 750.
red violet 750.
olive black 750.
b. Typographed, background irregular edge, on card, gray black 1,500.
c. Face lined, on 64x72mm solid color background
black 750.
scarlet 750.

Lithographic Essays Derived from the 1861 3c die: Scott 79-E25c-r

79-E25

Plate essays of complete 1861 3c design.

79-E25 3c
a. Plate on hard white transparent wove, dark red 50.
b. Plate on more opaque white wove, dim red 50.

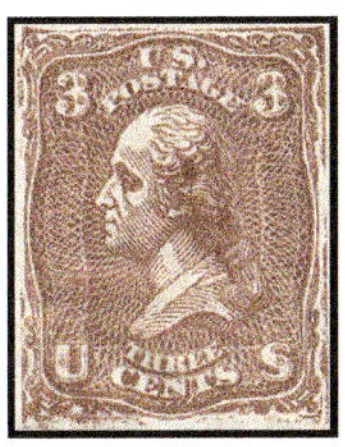
79-E25c

Under Magnification, Surface Cracks Show the Starch Coating

c. Plate on Loewenberg starch coated paper (patent 42,207 of April 5, 1864), generally crinkled. Under magnification, the printed surface can be seen to be cracking
light pink 25.
pink 25.
yellow 25.
yellow orange 25.
orange 25.
brown 25.
green 25.
blue 25.
dark blue 25.
very light gray 25.
gray 25.
black 25.

79-E25d

d. Plate printed with MacDonough fugitive ink (patent 52,869 of Feb. 27, 1866). Glistens in the light. Poorly printed with signs of the ink running during and after printing
light yellow 20.
dull olive yellow 20.
dark olive yellow 20.
light yellow orange 20.
yellow orange 20.
dark yellow orange 20.
light orange red 20.
orange red 20.
dusky violet red 20.

79-E25e

No Surface Cracks Under Magnification

e. Plate on semi-transparent paper. Wyckoff coated paper (patent 53,723 of April 3, 1866). Good quality printing. No cracking to the printed surface
dull pale blue 25.
green 25.
dull orange yellow 25.
dull orange red 25.
f. Plate on pale green paper, clearly printed, dark g-b green 40.
g. Plate on white wove, 13x16mm points down grill, gummed, dark blue 40.
h. Plate on lilac gray paper, 13x16mm grill, gummed
dark blue 40.
dull red 40.
black 40.
i. Plate on white paper (ungrilled), perf. 12, gummed
red 25.
light red 25.
pale red 25.
light orange red 25.
deep yellow orange 25.
brown 25.
dark green 25.
deep blue 25.
dull g-b blue 25.
gray black 25.
j. As "h," ms. A or B in UL corner, red 50.
k. Plate on white paper, 13x16mm points down grill, perf. 12, gummed
black 25.
gray black 25.
pale red 25.
light red 25.
orange red 25.
deep orange yellow 25.
brown 25.
dark brown 25.
green 25.
blue 25.
dark blue 25.
l. As "j," ms. "s No. 6" on back
red 50.
gray black 50.
dark blue 50.
m. As "j," but grill points up
red 40.
pink 40.
pale rose 40.
brown 40.
orange yellow 40.
deep red orange 40.
green 40.
dull blue 40.
dull light blue 40.
n. As "l," pair with blue oval "American Bank Note Co. April 17, '79", pink 150.
o. Plate on greenish gray chemical paper, 13x16mm grill, perf. 12
black 50.
green 50.
dark blue 50.
orange red 50.
light yellow gray 50.
light red gray 50.
p. As "n," without grill
red 50.
rose 50.
q. Plate on pelure, without grill, imperf., gummed, dim red 50.
r. As "p," perf. 12, dim red 50.

Gibson and Harmon Safety Design Overprints: Scott 79-E26

79-E26c

Illustration Reduced.
Plate impressions of 1861 3c stamp overprinted with various safety network designs.

79-E26 3c
a. Vert. pair on 58x80mm India, overprint die 54x71mm or more, small ONE repeated in 41 vert. lines per 40mm, rose pink, overprint deep orange yellow 2,000.
b. As "a," block of 6 inscribed "J. Sangster Pat. 190376, Jan. 6, 1877" 3,500.
c. 65TC3, "VEINTE" overprint, in miniature sheet of 12, perf. 12, black, overprint orange 7,500.

79-E26d

3c 1861 printed in various colors in miniature sheets of 12 with safety overprints based on Gibson's patent 41,118 dated Jan. 5, 1864, for a network overprint in fugitive ink.

Type 1: Big waves. Wavelength = 3.32mm. Amplitude = 3.32mm. Each wave is as high as it is wide.

Two sets of vertical rows. The waves of the second set lie between those of the first, but slightly offset to be higher/lower.

The pattern of the wave is illustrated with black dotted lines.

The left hand margin of each sheet has an additional row of waves which lies between the main rows (illustrated in red).

d. Type 1: perforated stamps are gummed, imperf are ungummed
perf. 12, green, overprint gray tan 550.
perf. 12, violet, overprint gray tan 550.
perf. 12, rose red, overprint dull blue 550.
perf. 12, light red brown, overprint light brown 550.
imperf., green, overprint greenish tan 550.
imperf., violet, overprint gray tan 550.
imperf., rose red, overprint dull blue 550.
imperf., yellow brown, overprint tan 550.

79-E26e

Type 2: Medium size waves. Wavelength = 3.32mm. Amplitude = 1.66mm. Each wave is half as high as it is wide.

Two sets of vertical rows. The waves of the second set lie between those of the first, but with an approximate 1 mm offset. The two set pattern is illustrated with black dotted lines.

The right hand margin of each sheet has an additional row of waves which lies to the right and above the main pattern (illustrated in red).

e. Type 2: perforated stamps are gummed, imperf are ungummed	
perf. 12, dark green, overprinted dull blue	*425.*
perf. 12, violet, overprint gray	*425.*
perf. 12, violet, overprinted gray green	*425.*
perf. 12, violet, overprinted dull blue	*425.*
perf. 12, rose red, overprinted gray blue	*425.*
perf. 12, dull brown red, overprinted olive tan	*425.*
imperf: ultramarine, overprinted tan	*425.*
imperf: violet, overprinted dull blue	*425.*
imperf: violet, overprinted greenish gray	*425.*
imperf: dull rose red, overprinted gray blue	*425.*
imperf: light brown, overprinted light brown	*425.*

Type 3

Type 3: Mesh of waves. Wavelength = 3.32mm. Amplitude = 0.83mm. Each wave is a quarter as high as it is wide.

Three identical sets of waves. One horizontal, two vertical.

The waves in the horizontal set are about 0.41mm apart.

Each wave in the vertical sets is about 0.83mm apart. The second set lies between the first with an approximate 0.5mm offset. Black dotted lines illustrate the pattern.

f. Type 3	
perf. 12, violet, overprint olive gray	*550.*
perf. 12, violet, overprint greenish gray	*550.*
perf. 12, rose red, overprint gray	*550.*
perf. 12, dull red brown, overprint yellowish tan	*550.*
perf. 12, dull red brown, overprint light brown	*550.*
imperf., violet, overprint olive gray	*550.*
imperf., rose red, overprint gray	*550.*
imperf., rose red, overprint yellowish tan	*550.*
imperf., light brown red, overprint light brown	*550.*

79-E26g

1c blue and 3c rose of 1861 overprinted by a safety network based Harmon's patent 41,105 of Feb. 9, 1864. Overprinted in interlocking circles in colors used for conventional cancellations.

g. 1c blue, perf 12, gummed red overprint	*2,000.*
h. 3c rose, perf. 12, gummed. Overprinted as #79-E26g	
black overprint	*2,000.*
red overprint	*2,000.*
blue overprint	*2,000.*
i. 3c rose, perf. 12, canceled, ungummed Buffalo patent cancel used from 1863-65, black overprint (two recorded)	*2,000.*
On piece. Washington, DC (March 14). Black overprint (one recorded)	*2,000.*

79-E27

79-E27c

Design size: 20½x26½mm

Engraved in relief for surface printing, large 2 vignette, on same die with No. 79-E28, 20mm apart. Also essayed for envelopes on thick papers.

79-E27 2c	
a. Untrimmed die, 30x42mm, on paper with "US" monogram, pale rose	*850.*
b. Die on stiff glazed paper, 63x50mm, black	*600.*
c. Trimmed die on India, on thick soft card, colorless parts in relief	
black	*450.*
red	*450.*
orange	*450.*
violet red	*450.*
d. Die on 35x40mm white wove, imperf., gummed	
blue	*450.*
albino	*450.*
e. Die on white wove, perf. 12, gummed, smoky violet red	*450.*
f. Untrimmed die on white wove, 61x42mm, black	*550.*

79-E28b

79-E28c

79-E28g

79-E28i

Design size: 21x25½mm

Engraved in relief for surface printing, large 3 in shield vignette, on same die with No. 79-E27, 20mm apart. Also essayed for envelopes on thick papers.

79-E28 3c	
a. Untrimmed die on stiff ivory paper, showing color 30x42mm	
black	*700.*
rose	*700.*
orange	*700.*
blue	*700.*
b. Untrimmed die on India with No. 79-E27, both embossed, yellow orange	*1,300.*
c. Trimmed die heavily struck on India, card mounted, colorless parts in relief	
black	*500.*
red	*500.*
orange	*500.*
d. Die on wide laid paper, "US" monogram, perf. 12, gummed	
pale rose	*250.*
dull brown yellow	*250.*
e. Die on greenish wove, 10x12mm points down grill, imperf., gummed, dull brown	*250.*
f. Die on white paper, perf. 12, gummed	
smoky violet red	*250.*
green	*250.*
g. Underprinted design only on thin white wove	
light blue	*350.*
albino	*350.*
i. "3" within shield, similar to No. 79-E28 but with wide printed margins, paper with vertical scoring, design 30x35mm	*300.*

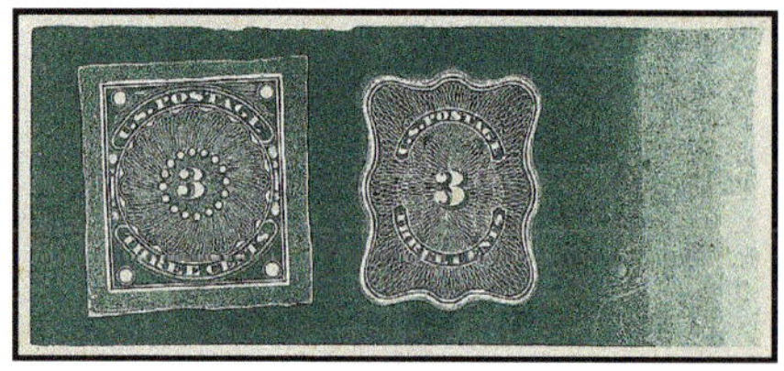

79-E28H

Illustration reduced.

Design size: 68x38mm

Two compound surface-printed designs, "3" within ornate frame.

79-E28H 3c Untrimmed die on wove paper, green	*2,500.*

79-E29

1861 1c frame only.

79-E29 1c	
a. Die on thin crisp paper, safety design underprint, black on dull olive green	*2,750.*
b. Die on pink paper, 18x13mm points down grill, imperf., gummed, red brown	*1,750.*
c. Die on pink "laid" paper, red	*1,750.*
d. Die on pale pink paper, red brown	*1,750.*
e. Die on transparent white paper, red brown	*1,750.*
f. Die on thick yellow paper, red brown	*1,750.*
g. Die on thin transparent white paper, 11x13mm points down grill, perf. 12, gummed, red brown	*1,750.*
h. As "g," imperf.	*2,000.*
i. As "f," with 14x16 points E grill, gummed, red brown	*1,750.*

79-E29j

As No. 79-E29 but with monogram in vignette.

j. Die on transparent white stamp paper, perf. 12, gummed, red brown 11,000.

79-E29Xa

No. 79-E29Xb

Similar to frame design of No. 79-E32, with colors reversed on No. 79-E29Xa, but "normal" on No. 79-E29Xb. "EXPERIMENT" in top label, "THREE 3 ESSAY" in bottom label, blank vignette area, "25868" die number and "EXPERIMENT No. 1" in paper above design on No. 79-E29a, essay cut to shape on No. 79-E29Xb. Each of the listings believed to be unique. American Bank Note Co. essay model.

79-E29X 3c Die on wove, black

a. Colors reversed from "normal" with black lettering and a black outer frame, affixed to tan paper 2,500.

b. Colors "normal" with white lettering and a white outer frame, affixed to black card 2,500.

79-E30

Design size: 20x26mm
Block size: 64x76½mm
Vignette of Liberty. Typographed.

79-E30 3c

a. Colors reversed from "normal" with black lettering and a black outer frame, affixed to tan paper 2,500.
black 850.
blue green 850.

b. Vignette only, on 66x100mm card
black 750.
blue green 750.
blue 750.

c. Vignette only, on proof paper
bright blue 600.
blue green 600.
black 600.

d. Complete design, untrimmed block, colorless 22x27 rectangle around design, broad outer edge in color, on stiff yellowish wove
black 750.
blue green 750.
violet brown 750.
bright violet red 750.
red violet 750.
buff 750.

e. As "d," on proof paper
buff 750.
deep blue green 750.
red brown 750.
carmine 750.
black 750.

f. Die on proof paper, perf. 12, vignette oval perf. 16, carmine 200.

g. Die on stiff ivory paper about 28x32mm
black 175.
carmine 175.
yellow 175.
dark blue green 175.
rose violet 175.

h. Die on stiff ivory paper, no color outside design, block of 4, carmine 500.
Block of 8 with vert. pairs in orange, dull yellow green, dark green and dark violet 900.

79-E30i

i. Die with outer color removed, on 64x90mm white wove stamp paper with imprint below, imperf., gummed
carmine 175.
scarlet 175.
dim orange red 175.
orange 175.
dull yellow orange 175.
pale dull yellow 175.
brown 175.
lemon 175.
yellow green 175.
dull olive green 175.
dull greenish gray 175.
dim blue green 175.
dull blue 175.
dull red violet 175.
pale red violet 175.

j. As "i," tete-beche pairs, each with imprint
carmine, orange 350.
buff, pale lilac 350.
dark orange brown, yellow 350.
dull green gray 350.

79-E30k

k. As "i," perf. 12, vignette oval perf. 16 (also found without paper outside perfs.
carmine 150.
pale rose 150.
dim scarlet 150.
dull scarlet 150.
dim orange red 150.
light red brown 150.
dark brown 150.
orange 150.
dull orange 150.
dismal orange 150.
dull brown orange 150.
pale dull yellow 150.
dull brown 150.
yellow brown 150.
dull olive green 150.
dim dark yellow orange 150.
light yellow green 150.
green 150.
dim blue green 150.
dark blue green 150.
dull greenish gray 150.
dull yellowish gray 150.
dull blue 150.
dim red violet 150.
dull red violet 150.
pale red violet 150.
red violet 150.

79-E30l

l. Plate essay on wove, apparently in vertical pairs of designs 7mm apart, in two colors shading into each other, imperf.
red brown to dark orange 150.
dark orange to brown red 150.
brown olive to red brown 150.
red brown to yellow green 150.
yellow green to dull carmine 150.
dull carmine to yellow green 150.
blue green to dull carmine 150.
dull carmine to deep blue 150.
dull carmine to brown olive 150.
brown olive to dull carmine 150.
dull carmine to orange 150.
orange to deep blue 150.
deep blue to orange brown 150.
orange brown to dull orange 150.

79-E30m Block

Illustration reduced.

m. As "l," on transparent wove, imperf.
red violet to deep violet 150.
deep violet to carmine 150.
dull scarlet to gold 150.
gold to carmine 150.
dark violet to blue green 150.
blue green to dark violet red 150.
violet to yellow green 150.
yellow green to red violet 150.

n. As "l," plate on stiff yellowish wove, imperf.
dull carmine to orange 150.
orange to deep blue 150.
brown olive to brown red 150.
brown red to yellow green 150.
blue green to dull carmine 150.
dull carmine to deep blue 150.
deep blue to dark brown 150.
dark brown to orange 150.

o. As "n," outside edge perf. 12
blue green to dull carmine 150.
dull carmine to deep blue 150.
deep blue to dark brown 150.
dark brown to dull orange 150.
dull carmine to dull orange 150.
dull orange to deep blue 150.
yellow green to dull carmine 150.
dull carmine to yellow green 150.
brown olive to brown red 150.
brown red to yellow green 150.

p. As "o," plate in single color, outside edge perf. 12, gummed
carmine 150.
dull orange 150.
orange brown 150.
dark brown 150.
brown olive 150.
dark blue green 150.
violet 150.

q. As "p," imperf., gummed
brown 125.
brown orange 125.
dull blue green 125.
deep blue 125.
carmine 125.

r. As "b," heavily stamped on white card, only faint traces of vignette, albino 125.

s. As "r," printed design at right, very dark blue green 250.

Thorpe Patent Essays

79-E31a

79-E31b

79-E31c

79-E31d

79-E31e

79-E31f

79-E31g

Thorpe's patent 95,624 for double printing was granted on Oct. 5, 1869. His idea was to print every stamp in two inks. Both inks should be insoluble in water. One should be resistant to alkalis and the other to acids. The two printings should be overlaid. Trying to erase a cancel with either an acidic or alkaline solvent, should erase one of the printings, leaving the other exposed.

79-E31 3c Same design as No. 79-E30, black green on white wove paper, underprinted with different designs in various colors, imperf.
- ***a.*** Red horiz. diamonds *1,400.*
- ***b.*** Dull yellow green with ONE repeated *1,400.*
- ***c.*** Red with 2 in circular stars *1,400.*
- ***d.*** Red with 2 in ovals *1,400.*
- ***e.*** Red with 3 in diamonds *1,400.*
- ***f.*** Black with 5 in hexagons *1,400.*
- ***g.*** Red with X repeated *1,400.*

79-E31i

79-E31j

79-E31k

- ***h.*** Die on deep orange-surfaced white paper, carmine *150.*
- ***i.*** As "h," perf. 12, gummed, carmine *150.*
- ***j.*** Die on tinted wove paper, imperf., carmine
  - yellow surfaced paper (two blocks of 4 recorded) *150.*
  - green surfaced paper (one block of 8 recorded) *150.*
- ***k.*** die on white wove, one color directly over another (gives effect of one color)
  - black on scarlet *275.*
  - brown on scarlet *275.*

79-E32

Similar to No. 79-E30f, but perf. vignette removed and frame mounted over 18x23mm Washington vignette.

79-E32 3c Die on 34x40mm white wove, black vignette, blue frame *8,000.*

1868 Essays
Experiments for bicolor printing

79-E33

1c 1861 design, color reversed as adopted. Typographed frame with 43x60mm untrimmed solid color border.

79-E33 1c Die on thin white paper, frame pink, vignette dark blue over pink *1,500.*

79-E35a

79-E35c

79-E35e

79-E35f

Frame lithographed, colored and colorless parts interchanged, vignette engraved and printed in another color.
Die I: colorless vignette oval (Nos. 79-E35a, 79-E35b)
Die II: vignette with horiz. lines (Nos. 79-E35d through 79-E35f)

79-E35 5c
- ***a.*** Untrimmed die on thin white paper, 40x60mm (values for cut to stamp size)
  - frame buff, vignette black *2,000.*
  - frame buff, vignette blue *2,000.*
  - frame buff, vignette red brown *2,000.*
  - frame buff, vignette dark brown *2,000.*
  - frame buff, vignette orange *2,000.*
  - frame buff, vignette carmine *2,000.*
  - frame blue green, vignette dark brown *2,000.*
  - frame blue green, vignette red brown *2,000.*
  - frame blue green, vignette orange *2,000.*
  - frame carmine, vignette blue *2,000.*
  - frame carmine, vignette red brown *2,000.*
  - frame violet, vignette orange *2,000.*
  - frame light red, vignette deep orange red *2,000.*
  - frame light red, vignette yellow orange *2,000.*
- ***b.*** Die on stiff wove, frame brown, vignette scarlet *2,000.*
- ***c.*** 45x65mm die impression of lithographed frame only, on ivory paper
  - black *2,000.*
  - blue green *2,000.*
- ***d.*** Die on thin white paper
  - frame violet, vignette carmine *2,000.*
  - frame violet, vignette brown *2,000.*
  - frame violet, vignette red brown *2,000.*
  - frame carmine, vignette black *2,000.*
- ***e.*** Vignette only on white glazed paper
  - black *2,000.*
  - blue *2,000.*
  - scarlet *2,000.*
  - dark brown *2,000.*
- ***f.*** As "e," without thin outer frameline, on India
  - lake *2,000.*
  - red *2,000.*
  - deep red orange *2,000.*
  - scarlet *2,000.*
  - deep green *2,000.*
  - ultramarine *2,000.*
  - black *2,000.*

79-E36

Die II vignette as No. 79-E35e, with gothic "United States" above.

79-E36 5c
- ***a.*** Die on white glazed paper
  - black *450.*
  - scarlet *450.*
  - dark brown *450.*
  - green *450.*
  - blue *450.*

No. 79-E36 may be a revenue essay.

79-E37

79-E37a

Die size: 51x63½

5c 1861 design, color reversed as adopted, vignette mounted on typographed frame.

79-E37 5c
- ***a.*** Die on white card, frame light blue, vignette black *1,000.*
- ***b.*** Vignette only, die on India, black *350.*
- ***c.*** Vignette only, die on white glazed paper
  - blue *350.*
  - black *350.*
  - green *350.*

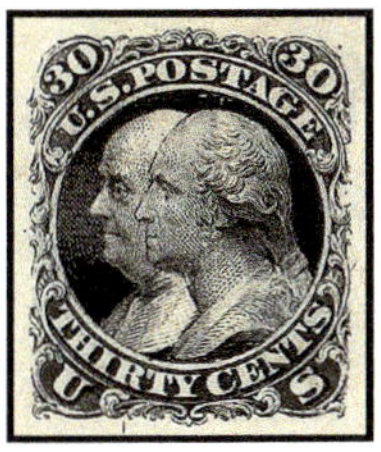
100-E1

Design size: 20½x24½mm
Engraved circular Franklin vignette mounted on 43x75mm white card, engraved Washington head mounted thereon; background, silhouette, etc., retouched in black ink. With engraved frame of No. 71-E1 (vignette cut out) mounted over the double vignette.

100-E1 30c Die on India, 30x34mm, black *16,000.*

1869 ISSUE
George T. Jones

112-E1a

112-E1b

Design size: 24x30mm
U.S. Grant vignette in frame with blank labels, ovals, etc. Paper overprinted with network of fine colored wavy lines in fugitive inks as on beer stamps.

112-E1 No Denomination
- ***a.*** Die on India cut to stamp size, 1 color
  - black *2,250.*
  - blue *2,250.*
- ***b.*** Die on India cut to stamp size, 2 colors (head in black)
  - blue, light gray overprint *3,250.*
  - red, light gray overprint *3,250.*
  - black, light violet overprint *3,250.*
  - ocher, pale red violet ovpt. *3,250.*
  - carmine, gray overprint *3,250.*
  - blue, yellow overprint *3,250.*

113-E1

Design size: 24x30mm
U.S. Treasury Dept. seal in vignette oval.

113-E1 2c
- ***a.*** Die on India cut to stamp size, 1 color
  - carmine *2,500.*
  - blue *2,500.*
- ***b.*** Die on India cut to stamp size, 3 colors, black on pale red violet wavy lines and blue green lined vignette *3,750.*

Frame as 112-E1 but with Washington vignette and 2c denomination. Another Washington vignette below but in horiz. lined oval frame.

113-E2 2c Die on 1⅝x3½inch India, black *5,000.*

National Bank Note Co.

All values originally essayed with numerals smaller than adopted. All designs are same size as issued stamps. Sheets of 150 of 1c-12c, sheets of 50 of 24c-90c. Many colors of plate essays exist from one sheet only, some colors from two sheets and a few from three. Some plate essays exist privately perforated.

112-E2

Die size: 40x65mm
Vignette size: 17mm diameter
Vignette of Franklin.

112-E2 1c Die of vignette only on India
- orange *900.*
- violet brown *900.*
- black *900.*

112-E3

Circle of pearls added to vignette, suggestion for frame and 1 in circle at bottom penciled in.

112-E3 1c Die on India, black *1,500.*

112-E4

Complete design as issued but with small value numeral.

112-E4 1c
- ***a.*** Die on India, die sunk on card
  - black *1,250.*
  - violet brown *1,250.*
  - dark brown *1,250.*
  - yellow brown *1,250.*
  - scarlet *1,250.*
  - carmine *1,250.*
  - deep violet *1,250.*
  - blue *1,250.*
  - green *1,250.*
  - yellow *1,250.*
- ***b.*** Plate on stamp paper, imperf., gummed
  - buff *100.*
  - deep orange brown *100.*
  - orange brown *100.*
- ***c.*** Plate on stamp paper, perf. 12, gummed
  - buff *100.*
  - orange brown *100.*
  - orange *125.*
- ***d.*** As "c," with 9x9mm grill
  - buff *110.*
  - orange brown *110.*
  - red brown *110.*
  - chocolate *110.*
  - black brown *110.*
  - dull red *110.*
  - violet *110.*
  - dark violet *110.*
  - blue *110.*
  - deep blue *110.*
  - green *110.*
  - yellow *110.*
  - orange *110.*
  - rose red *110.*
- ***e.*** Horiz. pair, one #112-E4c, one #112-E4d *400.*

112-E5

Design size: 23x31mm
Die size: 51x55mm
Design as issued but surrounded by fancy frame with flags and shield. Also essayed for envelopes and wrappers on thick paper.

112-E5 1c
- ***a.*** Die on stamp paper, perf. 12, gummed, gray *3,000.*
- ***b.*** Die on white ivory paper
  - black *2,000.*
  - black brown *2,000.*
  - scarlet *2,000.*
  - blue *2,000.*
- ***c.*** Die on India
  - blue *2,000.*
  - blue green *2,000.*
- ***d.*** Die on India, cut to shape
  - carmine *750.*
  - yellow *750.*

113-E3b

113-E3c

Die size: 41x50mm
Design as issued but with small value numeral. Nos. 113-E3a and 113-Eb have incomplete shading around "UNITED STATES."

113-E3 2c
- ***a.*** Die on India, die sunk on card
  - black *1,500.*
  - yellow *1,500.*
  - red orange *1,500.*
  - deep scarlet *1,500.*
  - brown *1,500.*
  - green *1,500.*
  - dusky blue *1,500.*
  - deep blue *1,500.*
- ***b.*** Die on India, cut to stamp size
  - deep orange red *400.*
  - deep orange yellow *400.*
  - blue green *400.*
  - gray black *400.*
  - light blue *400.*
  - rose *400.*
- ***c.*** Complete die on India, die sunk on card
  - brown *1,500.*
  - rose *1,500.*
  - mauve *1,500.*
  - green *1,500.*
  - dark chocolate *1,500.*
  - red brown *1,500.*
- ***d.*** Plate on stamp paper, perf. 12, gummed
  - brown *425.*
  - dark brown *425.*
  - yellow *425.*
- ***e.*** As "d," with 9x9mm grill
  - brown *80.*
  - dark brown *80.*
  - orange brown *80.*
  - dark orange brown *80.*
  - rose *80.*
  - brown rose *80.*
  - copper red *80.*
  - deep copper red *80.*
  - green *80.*
  - deep green *80.*
  - blue green *80.*
  - yellow *80.*
  - orange *80.*
  - dull yellow orange *80.*
  - blue *80.*
  - light violet *80.*
  - violet *80.*
  - dark violet *80.*
- ***f.*** As "e," double grill, orange *300.*
- ***g.*** Horiz. pair, one #113-E3d, one #113-E3e *1,000.*

113-E4

Original sketch of postrider, printed "NATIONAL BANK NOTE COMPANY. BUSINESS DEPARTMENT. 1868" at top, pencil instructions at bottom, "Reduce to this length" and "2 copies on one plate. Daguerrotype."

113-E4 2c Drawing on paper, black —

114-E3

Die size: 53x47mm

Design nearly as issued: larger motive above and below "POSTAGE" erased, no shading on numeral shield, top leaves and corner leaves do not touch, no dots in lower corners or scrolls beside bottom of shield, no vert. shading lines in "POSTAGE" label. Small value numeral.

114-E3 3c Die on 30x30mm ivory paper, black *1,500.*

114-E4

Similar to 114-E3, but smaller motive around "POSTAGE," shield shaded.

114-E4 3c
- ***a.*** Die on India, die sunk on card
  - black *1,500.*
  - carmine *1,500.*
  - scarlet *1,500.*
  - orange red *1,500.*
  - yellow orange *1,500.*
  - dull yellow *1,500.*
  - red sepia *1,500.*
  - blue green *1,500.*
  - blue *2,000.*
  - dull red *1,500.*
  - orange brown *1,500.*
- ***b.*** Die on India, cut to stamp size
  - black *500.*
  - rose *500.*
  - scarlet *500.*
  - chocolate *500.*
  - dull dusky orange *500.*
  - red violet *500.*
  - blackish slate *500.*

114-E5

Similar to No. 114-E4 but vert. shading lines added to "POSTAGE" frame.

114-E5 3c Die on India
- chocolate *1,500.*
- dusky yellow orange *1,500.*

114-E6

Completed small numeral die essay: leaves at top and sides touch, dots in lower corners added, vert. shading lines in frame around "POSTAGE," shield shaded darker at bottom, scrolls added to bottom of shield.

114-E6 3c
- ***a.*** Die on India, card mounted
  - black *1,750.*
  - blue *1,750.*
  - deep orange red *1,750.*
- ***b.*** Plate on stamp paper, imperf., gummed
  - ultramarine *125.*
  - dark ultramarine *125.*
  - light brown *85.*
  - red brown *85.*
  - dark red brown *85.*
  - pale rose *85.*
  - rose *85.*
  - brown rose *85.*
- ***c.*** Plate on stamp paper, perf. 12, gummed
  - ultramarine *500.*
  - dark ultramarine *500.*
- ***d.*** As "c," with 9x9mm grill
  - blue *80.*
  - deep blue *80.*
  - orange brown *80.*
  - black brown *80.*
  - deep black brown *80.*
  - rose red *80.*
  - green *80.*
  - yellow *80.*
  - orange *80.*
  - deep orange *80.*
  - dull violet *80.*
  - deep violet *80.*
  - red violet *80.*

114-E7

Same design and color as issued stamp, but with allover essay grill of squares up.

114-E7 3c
- ***a.*** Imperf., gummed, ultramarine *700.*
- ***b.*** As "a," 23mm "NATIONAL BANK NOTE CO. N.Y. SEP 27, 1869" circular pmk., ultramarine *1,100.*
- ***c.*** On thick paper, imperf., gummed, horiz. line defacement, ultramarine *700.*
- ***d.*** Perf. 12, horiz. line defacement, ultramarine *700.*

115-E1

Die size: 40x60mm

Vignette of Washington. Design as issued 6c stamp but with 5c denomination. Large lettering, large U and S in corners. Also essayed for envelopes on thick paper.

115-E1 6c
- ***a.*** Die on India, no frameline, solid vignette background, corner spandrels short at centers
  - black *700.*
  - carmine *700.*
  - dismal red brown *700.*
  - smoky dusky brown *700.*
  - gray violet *700.*
- ***b.*** Completed die on India, die sunk on card
  - black *600.*
  - carmine *600.*
  - deep rose *600.*
  - red violet *600.*
  - red brown *600.*
  - deep yellow brown *600.*
  - black brown *600.*
  - dull yellow *600.*
  - orange *600.*
  - dusky blue *600.*
  - dusky slate blue *600.*
  - green *600.*
  - blue green *600.*
  - scarlet *600.*
- ***c.*** Die on proof paper, about 40x65mm
  - black *600.*
  - carmine *600.*
  - scarlet *600.*
  - red orange *600.*
  - orange *600.*
  - dull yellow *600.*
  - orange brown *600.*
  - olive brown *600.*
  - dusky green *600.*
  - dusky yellow green *600.*
  - light blue *600.*
  - deep blue *600.*
  - red violet *600.*
- ***d.*** Die on pink bond
  - orange *600.*
  - brown *600.*
  - blue *600.*
- ***e.*** Die on light yellow green bond, black *600.*
- ***f.*** Die on pale olive buff bond
  - black *600.*
  - carmine *600.*
  - orange *600.*
  - red orange *600.*
  - brown *600.*
- ***g.*** Die on cream wove
  - black *600.*
  - orange *600.*
  - brown *600.*
  - blue *600.*
- ***h.*** Die on clear white bond
  - black *600.*
  - blue *600.*
  - orange *600.*
  - red orange brown *600.*
- ***i.*** Die on thick cloudy bond
  - black *600.*
  - red *600.*
  - orange *600.*
  - orange brown *600.*
  - blue *600.*
  - reddish brown *600.*
- ***j.*** Die on pale lilac bond
  - dark red orange *700.*
  - orange *700.*
  - blue *700.*
- ***k.*** Die on glazed paper
  - black *550.*
  - scarlet *550.*
  - yellow *550.*
  - dark brown *550.*
  - blue *550.*
- ***l.*** Die on marbled white card
  - green on red violet veined *1,750.*
  - black on green veined *1,750.*
  - red violet on green veined *1,750.*
- ***m.*** Die on ivory card
  - black *1,500.*
  - blue *1,500.*
- ***n.*** Die on white card, cut to stamp size, red orange *250.*

115-E2

Die size: 43x63mm

Similar to No. 115-E1 but lettering, U and S smaller.

115-E2 6c
- ***a.*** Incomplete die on India (incomplete spandrel points, hair on top of head, etc.)
  - black *750.*
  - dull red brown *750.*
- ***b.*** Complete die on India, die sunk on card
  - black *750.*
  - blue *750.*
  - dull dusky violet *750.*
  - scarlet *750.*
  - dark orange red *750.*
  - dim dusky red orange *750.*
  - dusky green *750.*
  - dusky green blue green *750.*
  - dusky blue green *750.*
- ***c.*** Plate essay on wove, imperf., gummed
  - deep ultramarine *150.*
  - orange *150.*
  - dull red violet *80.*
  - deep red violet *80.*
  - red brown *80.*
  - dull red brown *80.*
  - buff *80.*
  - green *80.*
- ***d.*** Plate essay on wove, perf. 12, gummed
  - orange *200.*
  - blue *200.*

115-E3D

Vignette of Washington as used on stamp but with shorter shirt front.

115-E3D 6c Die on India, affixed to card, 35x37mm, black —

115-E3E

As No. 115-E3D, with circle of pearls added around vignette.

115-E3E 6c Die on India, affixed to card, 59x85mm, black *3,000.*

116-E1

Oval vignette of Lincoln as on No. 77, but surrounded by double frame line.

116-E1 10c Die on India, 24x24mm, black *1,500.*

116-E1D

Die size: 14x18mm

Vignette of Lincoln as on No. 77. As No. 116-E1, but double frame lines removed.

116-E1D 10c Die on India, on card, black *1,150.*

116-E1a

Design size:14x14½mm
Round vignette of Lincoln as on No. 77, reduced at bottom.

116-E1a Die on India, on card, black *1,700.*

116-E1b

Design size: about 19½x19½mm
Die size: 64x68½mm
Head as on No. 77 but less bust, large unshaded collar, no cross shading in triangles between labels and fasces, no shading on diamonds at end of value label.

116-E1b Incomplete die on India, on card, black *6,000.*

116-E1c

Small collar, shading on diamonds at end of value label. Also essayed for envelopes on yellow laid paper.

116-E1c Complete die on India, die sunk on card
black *1,100.*
brown black *1,100.*
gray black *1,100.*
carmine *1,100.*
scarlet *1,100.*
brown red *1,100.*
orange *1,100.*
deep orange *1,100.*
deep red *1,100.*
yellow brown *1,100.*
yellow *1,100.*
green *1,100.*
blue green *1,100.*
deep blue *1,100.*
red violet *1,100.*
brown *1,100.*

d. Die on proof paper
black *1,000.*
carmine *1,000.*
bright red *1,000.*
orange red *1,000.*
orange *1,000.*
dark chocolate *1,000.*
dusky yellow brown *1,000.*
green *1,000.*
blue *1,000.*
red violet *1,000.*

e. Die on ivory paper
black *1,000.*
scarlet *1,000.*
black brown *1,000.*
blue *1,000.*

f. Die on clear white thin bond, about 30x35mm
black *1,000.*
red orange *1,000.*
red brown *1,000.*
orange *1,000.*
yellow *1,000.*
blue *1,000.*

g. Die on cloudy cream bond, about 30x35mm
black *1,100.*
light red brown *1,100.*
red orange *1,100.*
blue *1,100.*

h. Die on pink bond, about 39x45mm
red orange *1,000.*
red brown *1,000.*
yellow *1,000.*

i. Die on pale greenish gray bond, about 33x37mm
black *1,050.*
deep carmine *1,050.*
dull scarlet *1,050.*
dark brown *1,050.*
blue *1,050.*

j. Die on marbled white ivory card, about 38x62mm
black on green veined *3,000.*
orange red on green veined *3,000.*
red orange on green veined *3,000.*
dark orange brown on red violet veined *3,000.*

k. Plate on stamp paper, imperf., gummed
deep green *150.*
blue *125.*
ultramarine *125.*
dark ultramarine *125.*
light ultramarine *125.*

l. Plate on stamp paper, perf. 12, gummed
black *1,000.*
orange *200.*

116-E2

Die size: 101x62mm
Vignette of signing the Declaration of Independence as adopted for 24c.

116-E2 10c

a. Die on India, die sunk on card
black *4,250.*
carmine *4,250.*
dim rose *4,250.*
dull scarlet *4,250.*
red orange *4,250.*
orange yellow *4,250.*
red brown *4,250.*
orange brown *4,250.*
green *4,250.*
blue *4,250.*
gray *4,250.*

b. Die on India, cut to stamp size
black *1,500.*
red orange *1,500.*
blue green *1,500.*
dim rose *1,500.*
brown *1,500.*
buff *1,500.*
dull scarlet *1,500.*

Other colors reported to exist.

116-E3

Die size: 63x75mm
Design as adopted for issued stamp, but incomplete shading on bottom ribbon, thin shading lines behind "States," and center of "0" of "10" not filled in.

116-E3 10c Die on India on 61x53mm card, black *2,500.*

116-E4

Similar to No. 116-E3 except shading lines added behind "Ten Cents" and center of "0" of "10" filled in.

116-E4 10c Die on India, die sunk on card
black *2,500.*
orange *2,500.*
blue *2,500.*

117-E1

Die size: 47x51 mm

Similar to No. 117 but with smaller value numerals and blunt tip on arrowhead in triangular element to left of "UNITED STATES POSTAGE". Other subtle differences exist.

117-E1 12c

a. Incomplete die on India, on card, black —

117-E2

Die size: 47x51mm
Design as issued but with smaller value numerals. Sharp tip on arrowhead in triangular element to left of "UNITED STATES POSTAGE". Solid line above dashed line at top of value tablet and curved line added to top-left edge of value tablet. Other subtle differences exist between Nos. 117-E2 and 117-E1.

117-E2 12c

a. Die on card, black *1,600.*

b. Vignette die on India, pencil "Adriatic", black *1,600.*

c. Complete die on India, die sunk on card
black *1,350.*
rose *1,350.*
yellow *1,350.*
scarlet *1,350.*
dark red brown *1,350.*
blue green *1,350.*
blue *1,350.*
dull violet *1,350.*
gray black *1,350.*
orange brown *1,350.*
yellow brown *1,350.*
dull orange red *1,350.*

d. Die on India, cut to stamp size
black *600.*
dusky red orange *600.*
deep orange red *600.*
dim blue *600.*

e. Plate on stamp paper, 9x9mm grill, perf. 12, gummed
green *125.*
rose red *125.*
pale rose red *125.*
yellow brown *125.*
red brown *125.*
orange *125.*
blue *125.*
dull violet *125.*
dull red violet *125.*
yellow orange *125.*

117-E2F

Similar to No. 117-E2, but small numeral not printed, large 12 drawn in pencil.

117-E2F 12c Die on India, black *2,750.*

117-E3

Typographed small numeral design similar to No. 117-E1, relief engraved for surface printing. Heavier lines, upper label with solid background, letters of "UNITED STATES POSTAGE" colorless. Nos. 117-E3a through 117-E3c from untrimmed die, heavily struck with uncolored areas in relief, color covering borders beyond white line exterior of frame. Untrimmed die size: 58x45mm.

117-E3 12c

a. Untrimmed die on card
brown red *750.*
green *750.*
black *750.*
red brown *750.*

b. Untrimmed die on thin pinkish wove
gray black *450.*
dull deep red orange *450.*
dark red orange *450.*

c. Untrimmed die on thick white wove
carmine *600.*
green *600.*

d. Die on white paper, stamp size
carmine *400.*
orange *400.*
brown *400.*
lilac *400.*
green *400.*

e. Die on thin white wove

carmine 400.
gray black 400.
dull deep red orange 400.
deep orange red 400.
g. Die on pinkish wove, perf. 12, gummed, red brown 400.
h. Die on yellow wove, imperf.
gray black 400.
carmine 400.
red brown 400.
dark red violet 400.
i. Die on yellow wove, 11x13mm grill, imperf., red brown 400.
j. Die on white laid
gray 400.
gray black 400.
brown 400.
red brown 400.
k. Die on yellow laid
red brown 400.
brown 400.
dull red violet 400.
carmine 400.
l. Die on salmon laid, red brown 400.
m. Die on pinkish laid
red brown 400.
gray 400.
n. Die on pinkish laid, 11x13mm grill, gummed, red brown 400.
o. Die on dull red violet laid, gray 400.

117-E4

Vignette size: 15x11mm
Untrimmed die size: 63x32mm
Vignette only, similar to No. 117-E3 but lithographed instead of typographed.

117-E4 12c
a. Die on white ivory paper, black 1,000.
b. Complete impression from untrimmed stone in solid color about 63x63mm, on white ivory paper, black 750.
c. Die on glossy-surfaced thin white wove, trimmed to stamp size
carmine 750.
rose pink 750.
yellow 750.
blue green 750.
dim red violet 750.
pale red violet 750.
deep red orange 750.
dull dark red orange 750.
dull dark yellow orange 750.
dark violet red 750.
pale gray 750.
d. Die on thick white wove
yellow 750.
violet red 750.
deep red violet 750.

118-E1

118-E1a

118-E1 15c Die of vignette only on India, mounted on 62x62mm India, die sunk on card, dark blue 3,500.
a. As No. 118-E1, but vignette cut from a plate proof on India, showing framelines on plate, mounted on India, die sunk on card, dark blue —

Type I design but with smaller value numerals.

118-E2 15c Incomplete die (no outer frameline or shading outside frame scrolls) on India, black 4,500.

118-E3

Die size: 62x49mm
Type I design as issued but with smaller value numerals.

118-E3 15c Complete die on India, die sunk on card
black 5,000.
scarlet 5,000.
orange brown 5,000.
green 5,000.
dull violet 5,000.
red brown 5,000.
blue 5,000.

118-E4

Types I and III frame only.

118-E4 15c
a. Die on India, red brown 2,750.
b. Die on India, with vignette mounted in place, blue frame, yellow vignette 3,750.
c. Die on India, with vignette mounted in place, red brown frame, blue vignette 3,500.

118-E5

Type III frame only.

118-E5 15c Die on pink-tinted paper, perforated 3,750.

The type I frame also was used to produce type III stamps, No. 129. On No. 118, the brown fringe lines placed at the sides of the vignette were entered onto the plate one at a time. The lines were not on the die. All positions of the resulting stamp, No. 118, will differ slightly upon close examination.

119-E1a

119-E1c

Type II design with large value numerals as issued.

119-E1 15c
a. Type II frame only, die on India
black 3,500.
red brown 3,500.
b. Vignette only, die on India, blue —
c. Type II frame with vignette mounted in place, die on India, red brown frame, blue vignette 7,500.
d. Type II frame with vignette mounted at right, die on India, red brown frame, blue vignette —

129-E1

Die size: 65x49
Type III design as adopted, except in various single colors, large "15" overprint in diff. color.

129-E1 15c
a. Die on India, die sunk on card
orange brown, red overprint 3,500.
blue green, red overprint 3,500.
ultramarine, red overprint 3,500.
violet, red overprint 3,500.
red brown, red overprint 3,500.
b. Die on India, die sunk on card
rose red, ultramarine overprint 3,500.
dull scarlet, ultramarine overprint 3,500.
dark red brown, ultramarine ovpt. 3,500.
c. Die on India, die sunk on card
scarlet, blue green overprint 3,500.
orange brown, blue green overprint 3,500.
dark red brown, blue green overprint 3,500.

129-E2

Similar to No. 129-E1 but without the "15" overprint.

129-E2 Die on India, 34x30mm, dark blue 10,000.

120-E1

Die size: 102x63mm
Design nearly as issued, but shading under leaves at top of frame and ribbon over "TWENTY" are unfinished. Small value numerals. Single color.

120-E1 24c Die on India, black 4,000.

120-E2a

120-E2b

Completed small numeral design in single color. No. 120-E2a has 8mm-high bands of shaded colored lines 31mm long overprinted above and below vignette, printed in various single colors with bands in contrasting color.

120-E2 24c
a. Die on India
black with carmine bands 8,000.
black with violet brown bands 8,000.
black with brown orange bands 8,000.
orange brown with deep dull violet bands 8,000.
orange brown with blue green bands 8,000.
b. Die on India
black 6,500.
scarlet 6,500.
dark red brown 6,500.
blue 6,500.
violet 6,500.
c. Plate on red salmon tinted paper, black 200.
d. Plate on orange buff tinted paper, black 250.
e. Plate on dull yellowish tinted paper, black 250.
f. Plate on blue tinted paper, black 600.
g. Plate on gray tinted paper, black 500.
h. Plate on India, black 300.
j. Plate on card, imperf., black 350.
k. Hybrid die essay on India, small numeral frame, in violet, die sunk on card, red vignette mounted in place, "National Bank Note Co., N.Y." on the India paper at bottom 6,500.

120-E3a

120-E3b

120-E3d

No. 120-E3a bicolor design as issued, except vignette printed separately and mounted in place; No. 120-E3b frame only with

3 border lines around vignette space; No. 120-E3c frame only with 2 border lines around vignette space as issued.

120-E3 24c
a. Die on India, card mounted
dull violet frame, green vignette *4,500.*
violet frame, red vignette *4,500.*
green frame, violet vignette *4,500.*
rose frame, green vignette *4,500.*
b. Frame die on India, card mounted
black *5,000.*
light green *5,000.*
dark green *5,000.*
c. Frame die on India, block sunk on India, green *5,000.*
d. As "b," but frame perforated, and with violet vignette removed and separately die sunk to the right, 108x58mm card *2,000.*
e. As "c," but with violet vignette removed from frame and separately die sunk to the right, 88x46mm card. *5,000.*

121-E1

Design size: 21½x22mm
Die Size: 71x51mm
Vignette of Surrender of Gen. Burgoyne in ornate frame.

121-E1 30c
a. Die on India, die sunk on card
black *800.*
carmine *800.*
rose red *800.*
light brown red *800.*
red brown *800.*
brown orange *800.*
orange *800.*
red orange *800.*
yellow green *800.*
blue *800.*
dull dark violet *800.*
yellow brown *800.*
scarlet *800.*
b. Die on stiff ivory paper
black *650.*
c. Die on India, cut to stamp size
dim deep orange red *250.*
deep yellow orange *250.*
dim deep blue green *250.*
dim dusky blue *250.*
d. Die on India die sunk on 78x58mm white card
dusky blue *1,000.*
e. Die on white card, cut to stamp size
dim orange *500.*
f. Die on proof paper, about 70x50mm
black *500.*
carmine *500.*
scarlet *500.*
red orange *500.*
green *500.*
violet *500.*
g. Die on ivory paper, about 64x50mm
black *1,000.*
dark brown *1,000.*
scarlet *1,000.*
blue *1,000.*
h. Die on ivory card
black *1,000.*
carmine *1,000.*
i. Die on clear white bond, about 33x33mm
black *600.*
blue *600.*
light red brown *600.*
orange *600.*
j. Die on yellowish cloudy bond, about 34x34mm
black *600.*
orange *600.*
light red brown *600.*
blue *600.*
k. Die on smoky yellow greenish bond
black *600.*
carmine *600.*
orange *600.*
l. Die on pink bond, about 40x40mm
blue *600.*
dim orange red *600.*
orange *600.*
m. Die on pale olive buff paper
black *600.*
dim orange red *600.*
orange *600.*
n. Die on thick yellowish wove, dim green blue *600.*
o. Die on marbled white ivory card, about 40x60mm
black on green veined *2,500.*
black on red violet veined *2,500.*
p. Plate essay in black on thin surface-tinted paper
pale gray *275.*
salmon red *175.*
yellow *175.*
orange *275.*
orange buff *275.*
pink *275.*
pale pink *275.*
blue *275.*
light blue *275.*
pale green *275.*
brown violet *275.*
q. Plate essay in black on India *300.*
r. Plate on thick rough pitted card, black *300.*

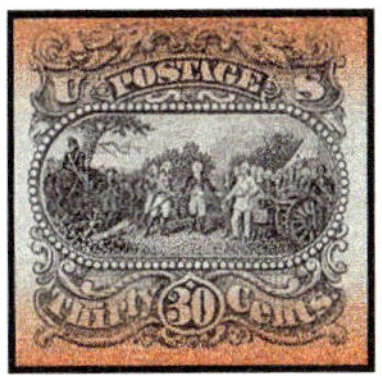
121-E1s

s. Plate on bond, red bands overprinted top and bottom as on No. 120-E2a, dull red violet *350.*

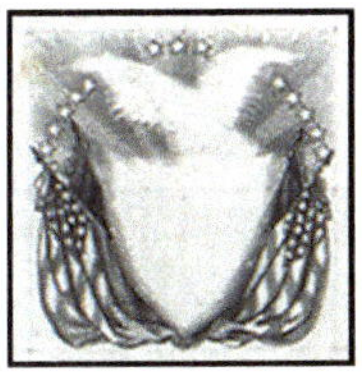
121-E2

Flags, stars and rays only as adopted for issued stamp. Black essay shows traces of vignette also.

121-E2 30c Die on India, mounted on India, block sunk on card
black *7,500.*
light ultramarine *6,000.*
dark blue *6,000.*

121-E3

Eagle, shield and value only as adopted for issued stamp.

121-E3 30c Die on India, card mounted, black *8,500.*

122-E1

Die size: 62x69mm
Vignette of Washington in frame similar to that of issued stamp but no shading over U and S in lower corners, small value numerals.

122-E1 90c Die on India, black *3,250.*

122-E2

Similar to No. 122-E1 but shading over U and S.

122-E2 90c
a. Die on India, die sunk on card
black *2,500.*
carmine *2,500.*
scarlet *2,500.*
red brown *2,500.*
blue green *2,500.*
violet *2,500.*
b. Plate essay with black vignette on stamp paper, imperf.
dull violet *275.*
red brown *275.*
orange red *275.*
pale orange red *275.*
blue *275.*

122-E3

Frame as No. 122-E2, vignette oval with narrow-spaced horiz. lines in same color as frame, but no head.

122-E3 90c Plate on medium India paper, imperf.
red brown *225.*
blue *225.*
dark blue *225.*
red violet *225.*
dull violet *225.*
dark violet *225.*
rose red *225.*
deep rose red *225.*
yellow *225.*
orange brown *225.*
dark navy blue *225.*
blue green *225.*
deep blue green *225.*
dark blue green *225.*
orange *225.*

122-E4

122-E4b

Small numeral frame but with black cut down Lincoln vignette on India from No. 77 mounted in place.

122-E4 90c
a. Die on medium India
yellow *3,000.*
red brown *3,000.*
rose red *3,000.*
deep blue green *3,000.*
dark navy blue *3,000.*
steel blue *3,000.*
dull violet *3,000.*
b. Plate of Lincoln vignette only, on rough pitted thick gray paper, black *500.*
Block of 4 *2,250.*
c. Die on India, Lincoln vignette as used on No. 77, black *2,500.*

122-E5

Similar to No. 122-E1, with Washington vignette but with large numerals as on issued stamp.

122-E5 90c
a. Die on India, die sunk on card
black *5,000.*
carmine *5,000.*
b. Plate of frame only, 2 lines at top, 3 lines at bottom, on India, mounted on block sunk card, rose red *1,250.*
c. As "b," 3 lines at top, 2 lines at bottom
rose red *7,750.*
red brown *1,250.*

Safety paper essays, circa 1868-69, on India paper, overprinted or underprinted with a stable ink with various engraved safety paper designs in another color.

26 different designs found on 5c (No. 115-E), 10c (No. 116-E), 15c (No. 118-E) and 30c (No. 121-E). The number following the "E" in the listing corresponds to the design numbers identified and illustrated, e.g., No. 115-ESP1 identifies the 5c stamp with safety paper design 1, etc. Stamp color given first.

115-ESP1

Design 1: wavy lines

115-ESP1 5c
carmine, safety design in scarlet 3,250.
orange, safety design in scarlet 3,250.
116-ESP1 10c blue, safety design in scarlet 5,000.
121-ESP1 30c carmine, safety design in scarlet 3,500.

121-ESP2

Design 2: banknote type

115-ESP2 5c
carmine, safety design in violet 3,250.
orange, safety design in violet 3,250.
116-ESP2 10c carmine, safety design in violet 5,000.
121-ESP2 30c
carmine, safety design in violet 3,500.
orange, safety design in violet 3,500.
orange, safety design in gray 3,500.

115-ESP3

Design 3: banknote type

115-ESP3 5c
carmine, safety design in orange red 3,250.
carmine, safety design in brown 3,250.
orange, safety design in brown 3,250.
116-ESP3 10c
carmine, safety design in orange red 5,000.
blue, safety design in orange and red 5,000.
121-ESP3 30c
carmine, safety design in orange red 3,500.
orange, safety design in brown 3,500.

116-ESP4

Design 4: continuous wavy lines

115-ESP4 5c orange, safety design in scarlet 3,250.
116-ESP4 10c
blue, safety design in scarlet 5,000.
carmine, safety design in scarlet 5,000.
121-ESP4 30c black, safety design in scarlet 3,500.

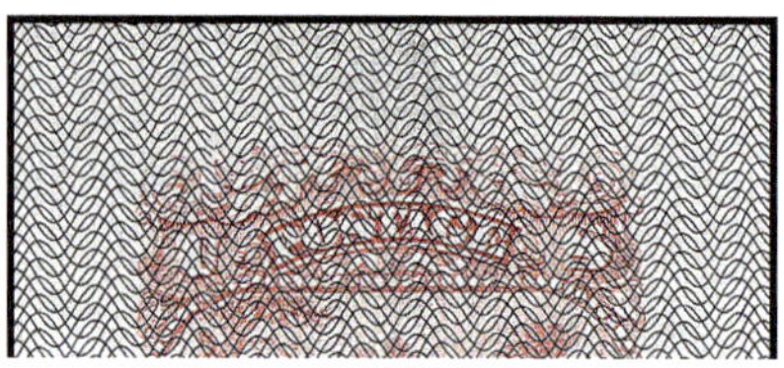

121-ESP5

Design 5: wavy lines

115-ESP5 5c
orange, safety design in orange 3,250.
orange, safety design in black 3,250.
116-ESP5 10c
dark brown, safety design in black 5,000.
orange red, safety design in black 5,000.
carmine, safety design in scarlet 5,000.
121-ESP5 30c
carmine, safety design in black 3,500.
carmine, safety design in scarlet 3,500.

121-ESP6

Design 6: wavy lines

115-ESP6 5c orange, safety design in black 3,250.
116-ESP6 10c blue, safety design in black 5,000.
121-ESP6 30c
carmine, safety design in black 3,500.
orange, safety design in black 3,500.

115-ESP7

Design 7: crossed wavy lines

115-ESP7 5c
carmine, safety design in black 3,250.
orange, safety design in black 3,250.
116-ESP7 10c blue, safety design in black 5,000.
121-ESP7 30c orange, safety design in black 3,500.

116-ESP8

Design 8: wavy lines

115-ESP8 5c carmine, safety design in scarlet 3,250.
116-ESP8 10c
blue, safety design in scarlet 5,000.
carmine, safety design in scarlet 5,000.
orange red, safety design in scarlet 5,000.

118-ESP9

Design 9: wavy lines

118-ESP9 15c
orange brown, safety design in orange 3,500.
blue green, safety design in orange 3,500.
dark blue, safety design in orange 3,500.

118-ESP10

Design 10: continuous whorls

118-ESP10 15c
orange brown, safety design in scarlet, horiz. 3,500.
blue green, safety design in scarlet, horiz. 3,500.
dark blue, safety design in scarlet, vert. 3,500.

118-ESP11

Design 11: banknote type

118-ESP11 15c
orange brown, safety design in light scarlet, horiz. 3,500.
blue green, safety design in light scarlet, vert. 3,500.
dark blue, safety design in light scarlet, horiz. 3,500.

118-ESP12

Design 12: banknote type

118-ESP12 15c
orange brown, safety design in deep scarlet 3,500.
blue green, safety design in deep scarlet 3,500.
dark blue, safety design in deep scarlet 3,500.

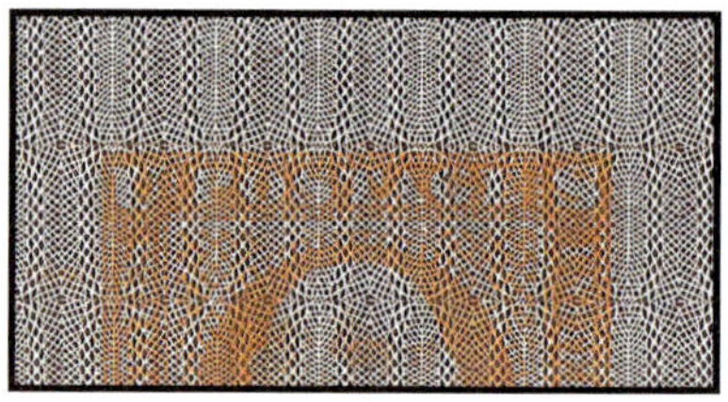

115-ESP13

Design 13: banknote type

115-ESP13 5c orange, safety design in brown 3,250.
116-ESP13 10c
carmine, safety design in brown 5,500.
orange red, safety design in brown 5,500.
blue, safety design in brown 5,500.
121-ESP13 30c carmine, safety design in brown 3,500.

115-ESP14

Design 14: banknote type

115-ESP14 5c
carmine, safety design in scarlet 4,500.
black, safety design in scarlet 4,500.
116-ESP14 10c
carmine, safety design in scarlet 5,500.
orange, safety design in scarlet 5,500.
sepia, safety design in scarlet 5,500.
blue, safety design in scarlet 5,500.
121-ESP14 30c black, safety design in scarlet 3,500.

115-ESP15

Design 15: banknote type

115-ESP15 5c carmine, safety design in orange brown — *3,250.*
121-ESP15 30c carmine, safety design in deep orange — *3,500.*

116-ESP16

Design 16: multiple rosettes

115-ESP16 5c orange, safety design in scarlet — *3,250.*
116-ESP16 10c
carmine, safety design in scarlet — *5,000.*
orange red, safety design in scarlet — *5,000.*
sepia, safety design in scarlet — *5,000.*
blue, safety design in scarlet — *5,000.*

115-ESP17

Design 17: multiple oval rosettes

115-ESP17 5c carmine, safety design in scarlet — *3,250.*
121-ESP17 30c
carmine, safety design in scarlet — *3,500.*
orange, safety design in scarlet — *3,500.*

115-ESP18

Design 18: negative stars in diagonal lines

115-ESP18 5c
black, safety design in scarlet — *3,250.*
carmine, safety design in scarlet — *3,250.*
116-ESP18 10c
carmine, safety design in scarlet — *5,500.*
sepia, safety design in scarlet — *5,500.*
121-ESP18 30c carmine, safety design in scarlet — *3,500.*

116-ESP19

Design 19: multiple 6-point stars in lathework

116-ESP19 10c blue, safety design in blue green — *7,500.*
121-ESP19 30c carmine, safety design in blue green — *3,500.*

116-ESP20

Design 20: banknote type

116-ESP20 10c
brown, safety design in orange — *5,500.*
blue, safety design in orange — *5,500.*

116-ESP21

Design 21: multiple "ONE"

116-ESP21 10c blue, safety design in scarlet — *5,500.*

115-ESP22

Design 22: multiple "TWO"

115-ESP22 5c orange, safety design in scarlet — *3,250.*
116-ESP22 10c carmine, safety design in scarlet — *5,500.*

115-ESP23

Design 23: multiple "5"s in oval rosettes

115-ESP23 5c black, safety design in carmine — *3,250.*

116-ESP24

Design 24: multiple "TEN 10" with gap between rows of arches

116-ESP24 10c
carmine, safety design in scarlet — *5,500.*
orange red, safety design in scarlet — *5,500.*
brown, safety design in scarlet — *5,500.*
blue, safety design in scarlet — *5,750.*

116-ESP25

Design 25: multiple "TEN 10" with rows of arches touching

115-ESP25 5c
orange, safety design in scarlet — *3,750.*
carmine, safety design in scarlet — *3,750.*
116-ESP25 10c
blue, safety design in scarlet — *5,500.*
carmine, safety design in scarlet — *5,500.*

115-ESP26

Design 26: multiple "50"

115-ESP26 5c
black, safety design in black — *3,250.*
orange, safety design in black — *3,250.*

1870 ISSUE
Continental Banknote Co.
Series 1: Designs derived from concurrent tax paid revenue stamps and essays

145-E1

Vignette of Washington in large ornate "1." Labels and side ornaments not yet engraved.

145-E1 1c engraved die on India, black — *1,850.*

145-E1C

Continental Bank Note Co. Imprint

Design size: 21x24mm.
Die size: 52x52mm
Vignette of Washington in large ornate "1." Die proofs exist on full size 148x231mm card bearing a handstamped imprint as illustrated. These sell for much more.

145-E1C One Cent
d. Engraved die on India, die sunk on card reduced to about die size
black — *1,500.*
scarlet — *1,500.*
green — *1,500.*
ultramarine — *1,500.*
blue — *1,500.*
e. Engraved die essay on India cut close and block sunk on card (about 45x45mm)
scarlet — *1,500.*

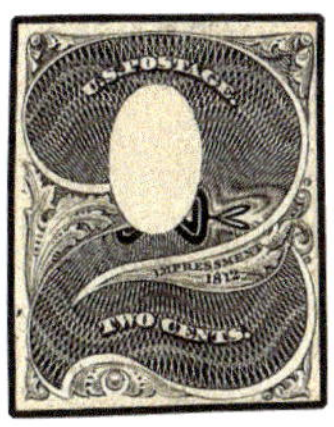

146-E1

Design size: 21x25mm
Die size: 46x45mm
Blank vignette in large ornate "2." Die proofs exist on full size 148x231mm card bearing a handstamped imprint as illustrated with No. 145-E1C.

146-E1 Two cent
a. Engraved die on India, die sunk on card reduced to about die size
black — *1,500.*
scarlet — *1,500.*
green — *1,500.*
ultramarine — *1,500.*

blue — *1,500.*

b. Die essay on India cut close and block sunk on card (about 45x45mm)
scarlet — *1,500.*
green — *1,500.*
blue — *1,500.*

147-E1

Design size: 20x25mm
Die size: 43x48mm
Vignette of Lincoln in large ornate "3" with rounded top. Die proofs exist on full size 148x231mm card bearing a hand-stamped imprint as illustrated with 145-E1C.

147-E1 Three Cent
a. Engraved die on India, die sunk on card reduced to about die size
black — *2,250.*
scarlet — *2,250.*
green — *2,250.*
blue — *2,250.*
b. Die sunk on proof paper 62x68mm
ultramarine — *2,500.*
black (stamp size) — *1,000.*
c. Engraved die on India, cut close and block sunk on card (about 45x45mm)
scarlet — *1,500.*
green — *1,500.*
blue — *1,500.*

148-E1

Design size: 21½x22½mm
Die size: approx. 51x53mm
Blank vignette in large ornate "6."

148-E1 Six Cent
a. Engraved die on India, die sunk on card reduced to about die size
black — *1,500.*
scarlet — *1,500.*
green — *1,500.*
blue — *1,500.*
ultramarine — *1,500.*
b. Die essay on India cut close and block sunk on card (about 45x45mm)
scarlet — *1,650.*
green — *1,650.*
blue — *1,650.*

Series 2: Variations on a three-cent frame pertaining to a vignette of Columbia

147-E2

Design size: 11½x15½mm
Die size: 47x51mm
Vignette only of Columbia. Continental imprint and die number below design. All known examples have the original die number crossed out by three lines and replaced with V48134 from a reworked die by the American Bank Note Co. Items on Kraft paper are from the archives of the ABNCo.

147-E2
a. Engraved die on India, die sunk on card
black — *1,450.*
b. Die on India reduced and mounted on Kraft paper (from ABNCo. archives)
black — —

Type I: "Flat topped" numeral "3," foliate frame around; 10½x14½ mm oval vignette frame

147-E3

Die State 1: blank panels within, no vignette.

147-E3 3c Engraved die on India cut close to design, mounted on India and block sunk on card
black — *2,500.*
green — *2,500.*

147-E3B

No. 147-E2, Columbia vignette in black, cut to shape and mounted in oval.

147-E3B 3c Engraved die on India on card, reduced to approx. 35x41mm
black — *2,750.*
green — *2,750.*

147-E4

Die State 2: As Die State 1 with panels engraved, "THREE CENTS" above, "UNITED STATES POSTAGE" below. Columbia vignette cut to oval shape and pasted in.

147-E4 3c Engraved die on India, die sunk on card
black — *2,250.*
green — *2,000.*

Type II: "Flat topped" numeral; finished panel lettering, 10x14½mm oval vignette frame.

147-E5

Die State 1: numeral only, surrounded by a lined frame 21x25mm without ornamentation.

147-E5 3c Engraved die on India cut close and mounted on card
black — *2,250.*

147-E6A

Die State 2: numeral surrounded by scrolled ornamentation, no vignette.

147-E6A 3c Engraved die on India on card, reduced to approx 35x41mm
black — *2,250.*
green — *2,000.*

147-E6B

No. 147-E6A with black Columbia vignette cut to oval and pasted in.

147-E6B 3c Engraved die on India on card, reduced to approx 35x41mm
black — *2,650.*
green — *2,650.*

147-E6C

Die State 3: As Die State 2, but die number "560" added and corrosion marks in vignette frame.

147-E6C 3c Engraved
d. On proof paper reduced to stamp size
black — *1,000.*
e. On India paper reduced to stamp size, on card
green — *2,000.*
f. On India paper, stamp size
green — *750.*

National Banknote Co.

145-E2

Die size: 64x74mm
Engraved vignette of Franklin facing right.

145-E2 1c Die on India, die sunk on card
black (with pencil lines on bust) — *700.*
dull dark orange — *700.*

145-E3

Engraved incomplete Franklin vignette facing right mounted over pencil sketch of frame.

145-E3 1c Die on thin white card, 55x66mm, black — *2,850.*

145-E4

Incomplete Franklin vignette mounted on more complete pencil sketch of frame.

145-E4 1c Die on thin white card, orange brown — *2,000.*

145-E5

Design size: 20x26mm
Engraved vignette mounted on pencil and watercolor frame design, "U.S. POSTAGE" and "ONE CENT" penciled on card.

145-E5 1c Die on thin white card, 45x51mm, dull dark orange *5,750.*

145-E6

Incomplete engraving of entire design; lower edge of bust vert. shading only.

145-E6 1c
a. Die on 64x71mm India, die sunk on card
- ultramarine *475.*
- red *475.*
- orange brown *475.*
- red brown *475.*
- blue green *475.*
- mauve *475.*
- dull lilac *475.*
- black *475.*
- gray *475.*
- carmine *475.*
- carmine rose *475.*
- dull rose *475.*
- dull yellow brown *475.*
- brown violet *475.*
- light green *475.*
- green *475.*
- gray olive *475.*
- yellow *475.*

b. Die on bond, die sunk on card, dark yellow *750.*

145-E8

Completed die: additional shading lines in background, four horiz. shading lines at top of lower edge of bust.

145-E8 1c
a. Die on India, die sunk on card
- black *475.*
- blue green *475.*
- carmine *475.*
- yellow *475.*
- orange brown *475.*
- orange *475.*
- gray green *475.*
- dull red violet *475.*
- dark blue *475.*

b. Die on ivory glazed paper, 65x72mm
- black *425.*
- black brown *425.*
- scarlet *425.*
- blue *425.*

c. Completed die on thick wove, dismal dusky yellow *425.*

145-E9

Die size: 50½x64mm
Engraved vignette of Franklin facing left, no shading lines at top of bust, etc.

145-E9 1c
a. Die on white glazed paper, black *475.*
b. Die on India, mounted on card stamped "J.I. PEASE.", black *450.*

146-E2

Die size: 62x76mm
Vignette only of Jackson in high stiff collar.

146-E2 2c Die on India, die sunk on card
- black *900.*
- orange brown *900.*

146-E3

Engraved Jackson vignette mounted on watercolor frame.

146-E3 2c Die on thin white card, 46x89mm, black vignette, dark gray frame *5,000.*

146-E4

Engraved Jackson vignette, mounted on watercolor frame (diff. from No. 146-E3).

146-E4 2c Die on thin white card, 46x89mm, black vignette, gray frame *5,000.*

146-E5

Similar to No. 146-E4 but with pencil border around frame.

146-E5 2c Die on thin white card, 45x50mm, dark orange *5,000.*

146-E6

Incomplete die: without shading lines under value ribbon, vert. lines in colorless strips, and broken horiz. lines at top and bottom of frame.

146-E6 2c Die on thin white card, dark orange *2,500.*

146-E7

Die size: 64½x73mm
Completed die of unadopted design.

146-E7 2c
a. Die on India
- carmine *1,000.*
- deep rose *1,000.*
- scarlet *1,000.*
- dim dusky orange orange red *1,000.*
- deep yellow orange *1,000.*
- bone brown *1,000.*
- orange brown *1,000.*
- brown *1,000.*
- canary yellow *1,000.*
- yellow brown *1,000.*
- dark olive green *1,000.*
- green *1,000.*
- dim dusky blue green *1,000.*
- dark blue *1,000.*
- deep ultramarine *1,000.*
- bright blue *1,000.*
- dull violet *1,000.*
- smoky deep red violet red *1,000.*
- gray *1,000.*
- black *1,000.*

b. Die on ivory glazed paper, about 64x77mm
- black *1,000.*
- brown black *1,000.*
- scarlet *1,000.*
- blue *1,000.*

c. Die on thin wove, dark yellow *1,000.*

146-E9

Die size: 62x76mm
Incomplete vignette of Jackson as on issued stamp: incomplete shading in eye and hair in front of ear, right neck tendon on chest not shaded.

146-E9 2c
a. Die on India, on 55x66mm card
- black *750.*
- orange *750.*
- deep yellow orange *750.*
- red brown *750.*
- orange brown *750.*
- dark blue green *750.*
- red violet *750.*

Also known on 87x143mm card showing full die sinkage, pencil inscribed "2c" above and "Jackson" below sinkage area. Value, *$750.*

The red violet shade also is known cut to shape and mounted on card, presumably as a template for a hand-drawn essay for the frame. Value $1,000.

b. Die on glazed paper, die sinkage 50x63mm, black *1,000.*

146-E10

Completed Jackson vignette.

146-E10 2c Die on glazed paper, black *750.*

146-E11

Engraved vignette with pencil and watercolor frame design, labels blank.

146-E11 2c Die on thin white card, 50x60mm, dim dusky bright blue green vignette, dark green frame *6,250.*

146-E12

Die size: 62x75mm
Incomplete engraving of entire design: no leaves on wide bands at sides below vignette, neck tendon and hair in front of ear changed, top of head incomplete, ear hole too dark. This design essayed for envelopes on thick papers.

146-E12 2c Die on India, die sunk on card

carmine	*1,250.*
orange	*1,250.*
brown orange	*1,250.*
brown	*1,250.*
blue	*1,250.*
violet	*1,250.*
green	*1,250.*

147-E7

Incomplete engraved vignette of Lincoln (horiz. line background), mounted on pencil and watercolor frame design.

147-E7 3c Die on thin white card, black vignette, gray black frame *4,000.*

147-E8

Design size: 11x18mm
Incomplete engraving of head only of Washington.

147-E8 3c Die on white glazed paper, black *550.*

147-E9

Die size: 16x20mm
Engraved Washington vignette only as adopted.

147-E9 3c Die on white glazed paper, black *650.*

Nos. 147-E8 and 147-E9 may have been made from completed dies of No. 147 to produce Nos. 184-E9 and 184-E10.

147-E11

Design size: 20x25½mm
Incomplete engraved vignette (horiz. lined background), mounted on pencil and watercolor frame design.

147-E11 3c Die on thin white card, 45x54mm, carmine vignette, dim light red violet red frame *5,000.*

147-E12

Incomplete engraving of entire design: no horizontal lines on nose, parts of hair, chin, collar, forehead unfinished.

147-E12 3c Die on India, die sunk on card

black	*575.*
deep red	*575.*
carmine	*575.*
yellow orange	*575.*
brown	*575.*
red brown	*575.*
dark red brown	*575.*
yellow brown	*575.*
ultramarine	*575.*
dark blue	*575.*
dark violet blue	*575.*
blue green	*575.*
dark red violet	*575.*

147-E12A

Similar to No. 147-E12 but two sets of horizontal lines in collar area have been lengthened and strengthened; also 11 scored lines cut across thick ink lines of the shoulder cut of vignette.

147-E12A Die on India, dull grayish red —

147-E13

Issued stamp, No. 147, in trial colors, underprinted network in fugitive ink.

147-E13 3c

a. On thick paper, perf. 12, gummed	
gray blue, underprinting gray brown	*150.*
gray blue, underprinting olive gray	*150.*
green, underprinting olive gray	*150.*
dim red, underprinting olive gray	*150.*
dull orange, underprinting olive gray	*150.*
brown, underprinting olive gray	*150.*
b. As "a," faint 6mm-high horiz. bar trial cancel	
dim red	*450.*
dull orange	*450.*
c. As "a," underprinting omitted	
gray blue	—
dim red	—
dull orange	—
brown	—
d. As "a," imperf, green, underprinting olive gray	325.
Pair	*700.*
e. As "d," underprinting omitted	325.
Pair	*700.*
P# block of 10	—

Multiples of the No. 147-E13 varieties can be found with fully or partially underprinted stamps in conjunction with underprinting-omitted stamps.

148-E2

Design size: 19½x25½mm
Die size: 63x76mm
Engraved Lincoln vignette only, hair brushed back, horiz. line background.

148-E2 6c Die on India, die sunk on card

black	*1,000.*
blue	*1,000.*

148-E3

Incomplete engraved Lincoln vignette (horiz. lined background) mounted on pencil and watercolor frame with blank labels. Unique.

148-E3 6c Die on thin white card, 45x52mm, dim blue vignette, dim dark blue frame *14,000.*

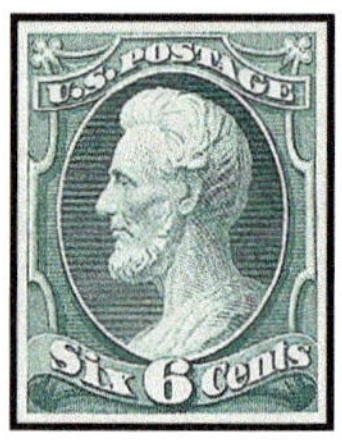

148-E4

Incomplete engraving of entire design: horiz. line background in vignette, lines on cheek and hair unfinished, capital "S" and dotted "i" in "Six" and capital "C" in "Cents," plus ornaments in top corners.

148-E4 6c Die on India, on card, about 50x52mm

carmine	*700.*
rose	*700.*
dull rose	*700.*
red violet	*700.*
dull violet	*700.*
deep ultramarine	*700.*
dark black blue	*700.*
yellow	*700.*
green	*700.*
dark green	*700.*
dark red brown	*700.*
deep yellow brown	*700.*
yellow brown	*700.*
orange brown	*700.*

Incomplete engraving of entire design: horiz. line background in vignette, no shading directly under value label, shadows on "SIX CENTS" and shading on ornaments in upper corners unfinished, capital "S" and dotted "i" in "Six" and capital "C" in "Cents," plus ornaments in top corners.

148-E5 6c Die on India, on card

ultramarine	*1,000.*
carmine	*1,250.*

148-E6

Similar to No. 148-E5 but with diagonal lines added to vignette background, capital "S" and dotted "i" in "Six" and capital "C" in "Cents," plus ornaments in top corners. (Essay in orange brown has pencil notations for changes.)

148-E6	6c Die on India, die sunk on card	
	black	*1,000.*
	dull carmine	*1,000.*
	dark rose	*1,000.*
	yellowish black	*1,000.*
	brown	*1,000.*
	gray brown	*1,000.*
	black brown	*1,000.*
	yellow	*1,000.*
	gray olive green	*1,000.*
	dark green	*1,000.*
	ultramarine	*1,000.*
	deep ultramarine	*1,000.*
	dull ultramarine	*1,000.*
	violet	*1,000.*
	dark violet	*1,000.*
	red violet	*1,000.*
	orange brown	*1,000.*

148-E7

Similar to No. 148-E6 but with dots added to top of hair, capital "S" and dotted "i" in "Six" and capital "C" in "Cents," plus ornaments in top corners.

148-E7	6c Die on India, on card	
	dark carmine	*1,000.*
	dull rose	*1,000.*
	orange	*1,000.*
	yellow brown	*1,000.*
	dark brown	*1,000.*
	black brown	*1,000.*
	yellow green	*1,000.*
	blue green	*1,000.*
	ultramarine	*1,000.*
	dark red violet	*1,000.*

148-E8

Similar to No. 148-E7 but die with lines on cheek softened to dots only, capital "S" and dotted "i" in "Six" and capital "C" in "Cents," plus ornaments in top corners.

148-E8	6c Die on India	
	yellow green	*250.*
	brown	*250.*
	rose	*250.*

All known examples are much reduced.

148-E9

Incomplete engraving of entire design, similar to No. 148-E10 but with hair brushed forward as on adopted design but shadow under hair in front of ear is round at bottom, not pointed as on approved design. Shading on cheek behind nostril is dotted instead of lined on completed design, undotted "I" in "SIX" and lower case "c" in "cents," plus no ornaments in top corners. Shading extended at sides.

148-E9 6c Die on India, on card, red violet *1,200.*

148-E9A

Similar to No. 148-E9, except recessed shadow sections do not continue above "U.S. POSTAGE" label or at sides.

148-E9A 6c Die on India, on card *2,500.*

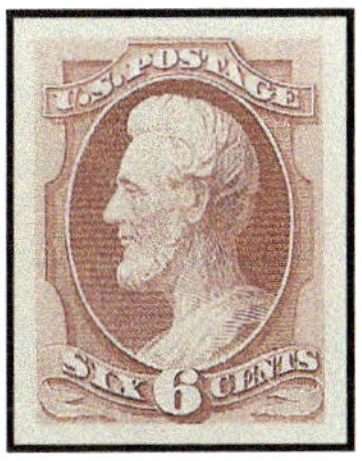

148-E10

Die size: 64x75mm

Frame as adopted, vignette similar to No. 148-E9 but with hair brushed back; lines on cheek. Undotted "I" in "Six" and lower case "c" in "cents," plus no ornaments in top corners. Shading extended at sides.

148-E10 6c

a. Die on India, die sunk on card, deep blue *850.*

b. Die on India, about 30x35mm, carmine *700.*

c. As "a," but no panels above top label, carmine *2,500.*

148-E11

Similar to No. 148-E10a but dots (not lines) on cheek and on lower lip. Shadow under hair in front of ear is rounded at bottom, not pointed as on approved design. Undotted "I" in "Six" and lower case "c" in "cents," plus no ornaments in top corners. Shading extended at sides.

148-E11	6c Die on India, on card	
	rose pink	*700.*
	deep rose	*700.*
	pale rose	*700.*
	brown rose	*700.*
	rose carmine	*700.*
	deep carmine	*700.*
	brown	*700.*
	yellow brown	*700.*
	blue	*700.*
	red violet	*700.*

Die of completed vignette only with hair brushed forward.

148-E12 6c Die on white glazed paper, black *1,500.*

149-E4

Die size: 62x75mm

Vignette of Stanton.

149-E4 7c Die on India, on card, black *1,000.*

149-E4a

Engraved frame of adopted 30c design but with vignette cut out and mounted over Stanton vignette on India No. 149-E4.

149-E4a Stanton vignette with 30c frame on thin, stiff paper mounted on top, black *500.*

The status of No. 149-E4a has been questioned.

149-E6

Design as issued but shading under ear incomplete.

149-E6	7c Die on India, die sunk on card	
	black	*500.*
	dark red	*500.*
	light red	*500.*
	gray green	*500.*
	gray black	*500.*
	yellow brown	*500.*
	dark brown	*500.*
	dull yellow brown	*500.*
	dull red brown	*500.*
	blue green	*500.*
	ultramarine	*500.*
	dim blue	*500.*
	lilac	*500.*
	red orange	*500.*
	yellow orange	*500.*

Similar to No. 149-E6 but with dots added on forehead.

149-E7 7c Die on India, brown *1,250.*

150-E1

Design size: 20x25½mm

Incomplete engraved vignette of Jefferson (horiz. line background) mounted on pencil and watercolor frame design with blank labels.

150-E1 10c Die on thin white card, 45x51mm, black vignette, gray frame *3,000.*

150-E2

Design size: 19½x25½mm

Die size: 62x75mm

Jefferson vignette with incomplete engraving of frame: unfinished shading under "TEN" ribbon, under oval at ends of "U.S. POSTAGE," and under shield over ends of value label ribbons.

150-E2 10c Die on India, on card, deep blue green *2,500.*

Similar to No. 150-E2 but showing horizontal shading lines only.

150-E2A	10c Die on India, die sunk on 152x225mm card	
	blue green	*750.*
	red violet	*750.*

150-E3

Completed engraving of unadopted design.

150-E3 10c

a. Die on India, die sunk on card

carmine	*750.*
rose	*750.*
gray brown rose	*750.*
yellow	*750.*
yellow brown	*750.*
orange	*750.*
orange brown	*750.*
brown	*750.*
chocolate	*750.*
green	*750.*
blue green	*750.*
greenish gray	*750.*
blue	*750.*
dull violet	*750.*
dull red violet	*750.*
dark navy blue	*750.*
ultramarine	*750.*
deep ultramarine	*750.*
dull dusky blue	*750.*
navy blue	*750.*
slate	*750.*

b. Die on bond

dull dusky brown	*500.*
brown gray	*500.*

All known examples of No. 153-E3b are reduced.

150-E4

Three separate designs. Left one dark blue green, similar to No. 150-E3 but shows engraved attempt to remove coat collar to obtain nude neck (some coat still shows under chin). Middle one brown orange (No. 150-E2) with coat collar and top of hair cut out, neck and bust drawn in. Right one black vignette of head finally adopted (No. 150-E7).

150-E4 10c Dies on India, on card *2,500.*

150-E5

Design size: 19½x25½mm
Same frame as No. 150-E2, but Jefferson vignette has hair arranged differently and bust has no clothing.

150-E5 10c

a. Die on India, die sunk on card

black	*600.*
scarlet	*600.*
brown	*600.*
blue	*600.*
green	*600.*

b. Die on ivory glazed paper, 66x75mm

black	*500.*
black brown	*500.*
scarlet	*500.*
blue	*500.*

c. Die on thin wove, dark yellow *500.*

150-E6

Frame of No. 150-E5 with vignette cut out and replaced by black vignette as adopted.

150-E6 10c Die on India

deep orange brown	*1,750.*
black	*1,500.*

150-E7

Die size: 62x76mm
Vignette of Jefferson as adopted.

150-E7 10c Die on India, die sunk on card

dark ultramarine	*700.*
yellow	*700.*
brown	*700.*

151-E1

Design size: 20x25½mm
Engraved vignette of Washington (No. 79-E37b) mounted on incomplete pencil drawing of frame design.

151-E1 12c Die on India, on 38x47½mm card, black vignette, pencil frame *2,500.*

151-E2

Design size: 20x25½mm
Engraved vignette of Washington (No. 79-E37b) mounted on pencil and watercolor frame design with blank labels.

151-E2 12c Die on card, 46x89mm, black vignette, gray frame *3,000.*

151-E3

Design size: 20x25½mm
Engraved vignette of Washington (No. 79-E37b) mounted on pencil and watercolor frame design with ribbons and blank labels.

151-E3 12c Die on card, 46x89mm, black vignette, gray frame *3,000.*

151-E4

Design size: 20x25½mm
Engraved vignette of Washington (No. 79-E37b) mounted on pencil and watercolor frame design with "U, S, 12" and blank labels.

151-E4 12c Die on card, 46x89mm, black vignette, gray frame *3,000.*

151-E5

Design size: 19½x25½mm
Die size: 62x74mm
Vignette of Henry Clay only.

151-E5 12c Die on India, die sunk on card

black	*600.*
deep carmine	*600.*
yellow	*600.*
yellow brown	*600.*
brown orange	*600.*
dark orange brown	*600.*
black brown	*600.*
ultramarine	*600.*
dark blue green	*600.*
red violet	*600.*

151-E6

Incomplete Clay vignette mounted on watercolor shield-like frame design on gray background, pencil notation "background of stars to be grey."

151-E6 12c Die on card, 53x75mm, blue black vignette, blue frame *4,000.*

151-E7

Die sinkage size: 63x77mm
Completed die of unadopted design similar to No. 151-E6. This design essayed for envelopes on thick paper.

151-E7 12c
a. Die on India, on card

deep orange brown	*900.*
green	*900.*
deep ultramarine	*900.*
violet	*900.*
deep red	*900.*
deep orange red	*900.*
orange	*900.*
dusky red	*900.*

b. Die on wove

carmine	*700.*
orange	*700.*
brown	*700.*
orange brown	*700.*
ultramarine	*700.*

c. Die on card colored yellow, black *700.*

151-E8

Engraved vignette of Washington mounted on partly complete pencil drawing of frame, pencil notation "new border for clay 12c."

151-E8 12c Die on card, black, pencil frame *2,750.*

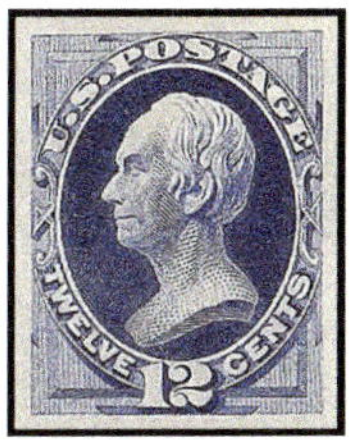

151-E9

Die size: 55x63mm
Incomplete engraving of entire adopted design, without 3 vert. shading lines at left side of lower triangle.

151-E9 12c
a. Die on India, die sunk on card

black	*650.*
carmine	*650.*
blue green	*650.*
blue	*650.*
light blue	*650.*
orange	*650.*
orange brown	*650.*
dull red	*650.*
brown red	*650.*

b. Die on proof paper, about 38x45mm

carmine	*650.*
dull carmine	*650.*
orange brown	*650.*
dull red	*650.*
ultramarine	*650.*

c. Die on India, on card, about 30x35mm, dark blue *650.*

152-E1

Design size: 19½x25mm
Incomplete vignette of Webster with side whiskers bolder than as adopted, mounted on watercolor frame design with 15 and blank labels.

152-E1 15c Die on white card, 40x61mm, dim red vignette, light red violet frame *2,250.*

152-E2

Design size: 19½x25mm
Die size: 63x76mm
Incomplete engraving of vignette only: missing shading under ear and at back of neck.

152-E2 15c Die on India, die sunk on card, black *750.*

152-E3

Vignette similar to No. 152-E2 but with shading under ear, more shading at back of neck.

152-E3 15c Die on India, die sunk on card

black	*700.*
dark orange	*700.*
orange	*700.*
yellow	*700.*
red violet	*700.*
ultramarine	*700.*
brown	*700.*

152-E5

Incomplete engraved design: shading on corner panel bevels incomplete, side whiskers bolder than as adopted. Also essayed for envelopes on thick paper.

152-E5 15c Die on India, die sunk on card, orange brown *750.*

Similar to No. 152-E5 but with pencil marks suggesting shading on corner panels.

152-E6 15c Die on India, orange brown *750.*

152-E7

Similar to No. 152-E5 with engraved shading added to corner panels but white areas incomplete.

152-E7 15c Die on India

orange	*650.*
orange yellow	*650.*
orange brown	*650.*
green	*650.*
red violet	*650.*
rose carmine	*650.*

152-E8

Similar to No. 152-E7 but shading on corner panels complete.

152-E8 15c Die on India, on card, black *1,000.*

153-E1

Design size: 18x23mm
Incomplete engraved vignette of Scott mounted on pencil sketch of partial frame design.

153-E1 24c Die on white card, 33x39mm, dull red violet vignette, pencil frame *1,750.*

153-E2

Design size: 19½x25mm
Complete engraved vignette mounted on pencil and watercolor frame design with "U.S. POSTAGE" in ink.

153-E2 24c Die on white card, 73x110mm, dim blue green *3,250.*

153-E3

Die size: 62x76mm
Incomplete engraved vignette only.

153-E3 24c Die on India, die sunk on card

black	*600.*
yellow	*600.*
yellow brown	*600.*
dark orange brown	*600.*

ultramarine	*600.*
dark ultramarine	*600.*
red violet	*600.*

153-E4

Die size: 62x77mm
Incomplete design as adopted: upper corners not squared outside scrolls, no periods after U and S in stars.

153-E4 24c Die on India, die sunk on card

carmine	*650.*
orange	*650.*
brown orange	*650.*
yellow brown	*650.*
deep brown	*650.*
ultramarine	*650.*
dark red violet	*650.*
green	*650.*

Value off card, cut down, $275.

Previous No. 154-E1 is now No. 149-E4a.

154-E2

Pencil drawing of entire design, labeled "Scott."

154-E2 30c Pencil drawing on white card, 53x92mm *2,400.*

Engraved vignette of Hamilton mounted on pencil drawing of frame.

154-E3 30c Die on card, yellow brown vignette, pencil frame *1,500.*

154-E4

Incomplete engraved vignette of Hamilton.

154-E4 30c Die on India, die sunk on card

yellow brown	*700.*
dark ultramarine blue	*700.*
orange	*700.*
red violet	*700.*

154-E5

Vignette of Hamilton with more engraving on forehead, nose, neck, etc.

154-E5 30c Die on India, die sunk on card

dark red brown	*700.*
dull carmine	*700.*
ultramarine	*700.*
green	*700.*

155-E1

Pencil drawing of entire design, labeled "Perry."

155-E1 90c Pencil drawing on white card, 53x92mm *3,000.*

155-E2

Design size: 19½x25mm
Engraved vignette of Perry mounted on pencil and watercolor frame design.

155-E2 90c Die on white card, 73x110mm, dull dark violet vignette, dull red violet frame *3,250.*

155-E3

Die size: 58x79mm
Incomplete engraving of Perry vignette as adopted.

155-E3 90c

a. Die on India, die sunk on card

black	*1,500.*
deep yellow orange	*600.*
orange brown	*600.*
dark brown	*600.*
dull carmine	*600.*
ultramarine blue	*600.*
dark blue green	*600.*
dark red violet	*600.*
b. Die on white ivory paper, black	*600.*
c. Die on card, carmine	*750.*

155-E4

Similar to No. 155-E3 but more lines in hair above forehead.

155-E4 90c Die on India, on card, black *600.*

155-E5

Incomplete engraving of design as adopted: rope above vignette unfinished. Known in black with pencil drawing of rope beneath on the card; value thus, $3,000. Also essayed for envelopes on thick paper.

155-E5 90c Die on India, die sunk on card

black	*750.*
carmine, off card	*325.*
orange	*750.*
dark orange	*750.*
yellow brown	*750.*
brown	*750.*
deep orange brown	*750.*
deep ultramarine	*750.*
blue green	*750.*
red violet	*750.*

Value off card, cut down, $250.

1873 ISSUE
Continental Bank Note Co.

179-E1

Die size: 20x25mm
Vignette of Taylor by Bureau of Engraving and Printing, in engraved frame.

179-E1 Five Cents, Die on India

black	*4,500.*
blue	*4,500.*

179-E2

Design size: 24x29mm
Vignette of Taylor by Bureau of Engraving and Printing, in ornate wash drawing of frame ("FIVE CENTS" black, on shaded ribbon).

179-E2 5c Die on card, black *4,000.*

179-E3

Incomplete vignette: hair, coat, background, etc., unfinished.

179-E3 5c Die on India, violet *2,000.*

George Bowlsby patent

George W. Bowlsby 1873 essay similar in concept to his No. 63-E13 but without coupon attached. It consisted of an unused 1c stamp (No. 156) with horiz. sewing machine perfs. through center, gummed on upper half only, as described in his Dec. 26, 1865 patent. Stamp was meant to be torn in half by postal clerk as cancellation, to prevent reuse.

156-E1 1c blue *250.*
Block of 4 with plate number *1,500.*

1876 - National Safety Paper

Plate designs of 1873-75 issues in normal colors, printed by Continental Bank Note Co. on tinted, thick "pseudo-laid" paper produced by Campbell, Hall and Co. under direction of Samuel Francis. Three paper colors are recorded.

156-E2 1c Blue on:

pale rose	*150.*
pale yellow	*150.*
pale violet	*150.*

158-E1 3c Green on:

pale rose	*150.*
pale yellow	*150.*
pale violet	*150.*

161-E1

161-E1 10c Brown on:
pale rose 150.
pale yellow 150.
pale violet 150.

163-E1 15c Yellow orange on:
pale rose 200.
pale yellow 200.
pale violet 200.

178-E1

178-E1 2c Vermilion on:
pale rose 150.
pale yellow 150.
pale violet 150.

179-E4

179-E4 5c Blue on:
pale rose 300.
pale yellow 300.
pale violet 300.

See No. 147-E13.

The following four listings are known or believed to exist, but they are not on "pseudo-laid" paper and therefore they are not likely on National Safety Paper.

160-E1 7c scarlet vermilion on deep yellow wove —
161-E2 10c brown on deep yellow wove —

165-E1 30c Gray black on:
pale rose —
deep yellow —
pale violet —

166-E1 90c Rose carmine on:
pale rose —
deep yellow —
pale violet —

The editors would like to see evidence of the existence of Nos. 165-E1 and 166-E1.

1876 Joseph Schnoble Patent #171871, Jan 4, 1876

Prior to printing, specially sized paper was top coated on the printing side with an albumin and flycerine "varnish" and allowed to harden. Upon this prepared surface the stamp designs were intaglio printed as usual. Attempts to wash off a cancellation would cause the design to wash off from the layered colored ground.

156-E3

156-E3 1c ultra on dull rose, imperf. 100.
156-E4 1c ultramarine on deep carmine, perf. 12 100.
ultramarine on dull rose, pair, P#229 250.
a. Wash-tested strip of 3, ultramarine on dull rose, P#229 —

158-E2

158-E2 3c green on deep carmine, imperf. 100.
green on pale rose, imperf. 100.
green on faint rose, imperf. 100.
158-E3 3c green on deep carmine, perf. 12 100.
green on bright rose, perf. 12 100.
green on pale rose, perf. 12 100.
green on faint rose, perf. 12 100.
a. Wash-tested strip of 4, green on deep carmine, P#257 —
b. Crayon-tested, green on bright rose —

1877 Essays
Philadelphia Bank Note Co.

Die essays for this section were all engraved. The frame-only dies for all values of this series were engraved with two values appearing per die, except the 3c (No. 184-E1) which was engraved alone. In each case the listing is under the lower denomination. The Washington vignette associated with each value of the frames is from engraved master die No. 14. (No. 182-E1).

Except as noted, plate essays in this section are all lithographed from a composite stone plate of two panes. The left pane ("plate 1") consists of horiz. rows of four of the 1c, 3c, 7c, 24c and 90c. The right pane ("plate 2") consists of horiz. rows of four 2c, 6c, 12c and 30c. "Printed by Philadelphia Bank Note Co. Patented June 16, 1876" imprint below 2nd and 3rd designs on each row.

For the 1903 Schernikow private reprint essays see section following No. 191-E2.

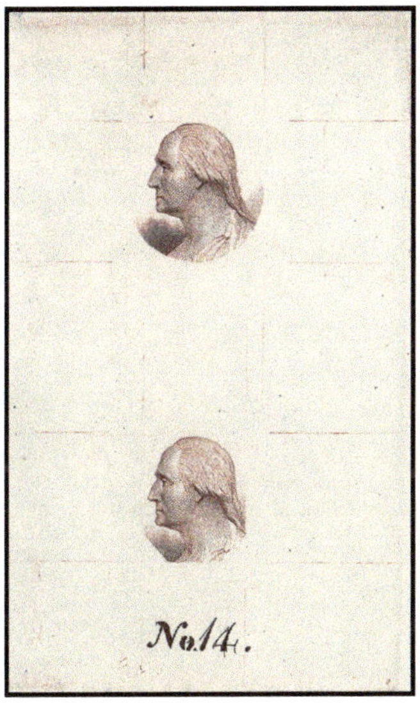

182-E1

Vignette master die "No. 14": two slightly diff. vignettes of Washington, one above the other, bottom one with truncated queue, bust and shading in front of neck.

182-E1
a. Die on old white glazed paper, black 500.

182-E2b

Design size: 20x25mm
Die size: 98x53mm
Frames of 1c and 2c side by side.

182-E2 1c + 2c
a. Die on white pelure
dark carmine 250.
orange 250.
brown 250.
blue green 250.
blue 250.
b. Die with vertical line between designs (die size 85x54mm), on India, die sunk on card
dusky red 400.
deep orange 400.
orange brown 400.
dark green 400.
dark blue 400.
c. Die on stiff glazed paper, black 400.
e. Plate sheet of 1c, 2c, 3c, 12c, 24c, 30c, 90c frames only, on card, pale green blue 1,500.

182-E3b

Complete 1c design, lithographed.

182-E3 1c
a. Plate on stamp paper, imperf., gummed
black 75.
blue green 75.
bright ultramarine 75.
yellow 75.
b. Plate on stamp paper, perf. 12, gummed
dark red orange 50.
orange brown 50.
red brown 50.
red violet 50.
violet blue 50.
ultramarine 50.
c. Plate 1 "sheet" of 20, complete designs, without imprint, on old glazed paper, imperf., deep brown orange 800.
d. As "c," with imprint, on old glazed paper, imperf., gummed
black 800.
dull deep violet red 800.
ultramarine 800.
scarlet 800.
orange 800.
carmine 800.
dark carmine 800.
green 800.
bluish green 800.
e. As "d," perf. 12, gummed
dull deep violet red 700.
ultramarine 700.
red brown 700.
violet blue 700.

Concerning plate 1 sheets of 20, note that composite stone plates also contained the plate 2 sheets of 16 listed as Nos. 183-E2c to 183-E2e. Many such composite sheets remain intact. All separated plate 1 or plate 2 sheets originally were part of a composite sheet.

183-E2b

Complete 2c design, lithographed.

183-E2 2c
a. Plate on stamp paper, imperf.
blue green 60.
bright ultramarine 60.
brown 60.
b. Plate on stamp paper, perf. 12, gummed
bright red orange 35.
dull red orange 35.
dark red orange 35.
red brown 35.
dark red brown 35.
dark orange brown 35.
yellow brown 35.
dull yellow green 35.
green 35.
dull ultramarine 35.
bright ultramarine 35.
blue violet 35.
red violet 35.
light red violet 35.
violet red 35.
c. Plate 2 "sheet" of 16, complete designs, without imprint, on old glazed paper, imperf., deep brown orange 600.
d. As "c," with imprint, on old glazed paper, imperf., gummed
black 600.
dull deep violet red 600.
e. As "d," perf. 12, gummed
dull deep violet red 500.
deep brown orange 500.

See note following No. 182-E3e.

184-E1

Design size: 20x25mm
Die size: 54x55mm
Engraved frame of 3c alone on die.

184-E1 3c

a. Die on pelure paper	
dark carmine	*250.*
dark orange	*250.*
orange brown	*250.*
bright blue	*250.*
green	*250.*
dark green	*250.*

184-E2a

184-E2a Variety

Built-up model of engraved frame cut to shape inside and out, mounted atop engraved vignette of the same or different color. Warning: fraudulent models combining engraved and lithographed materials exist.

184-E2 3c

a. Die on proof paper	
dark scarlet, cut close	*250.*
blue green, cut close	*250.*
deep blue, cut close	*250.*
deep blue frame, dark scarlet vignette	*500.*
blue green frame, dark scarlet vignette	*500.*
b. Four examples mounted 2½mm apart on stiff white card, 80x87mm	
red	*1,000.*
orange brown	*1,000.*
green	*1,000.*
blue	*1,000.*
violet	*1,000.*
green frame, light blue vignette	*1,000.*

Built-up model as No. 184-E2, vignette as No. 184-E5 with dark background.

184-E3 3c Die on proof paper, scarlet *250.*

184-E4

Complete 3c design, vignette with light background.

184-E4 3c

c. Plate lithographed on stamp paper, imperf.	
black	*75.*
carmine	*75.*
green	*75.*
dark green	*75.*
bright ultramarine	*75.*
orange	*75.*

No. 184-E4c exists in two plates of 9 tete-beche, in diff. colors, on same piece of paper. Value, $1,400 sheet of 18.

d. Plate lithographed on stamp paper, perf. 12, gummed	
dark red orange	*50.*
red brown	*50.*
red voilet	*50.*
brown orange	*50.*
ultramarine	*50.*
violet blue	*50.*
e. Plate sheet of 9 (3x3), imprint below, on stiff white wove	
carmine	*300.*
blue green	*300.*
f. Plate sheet of 9 (3x3), on glazed thin wove	
carmine	*300.*
blue green	*300.*
blue	*300.*
orange	*300.*
g. Plate sheet of 9 (3x3), on yellowish wove	
carmine	*300.*
blue green	*300.*
blue	*300.*
h. Die of complete design on old stiff glazed paper (die size: 55x66mm), black	*350.*
i. Complete die on glazed wove	
deep carmine	*200.*
scarlet	*200.*
ultramarine	*200.*
j. Complete die on India, light orange red	*200.*

184-E5

Design size: 19x24½mm
Die No. 1 size: about 63x94mm Vignette of Washington slightly diff. from rest of series but with quite diff. frame design.

184-E5 3c

a. Die on glazed paper, about 50x75mm, black	*350.*
d. Engraved plate of 25 on India, mounted on large card, red brown	*750.*
f. Plate on proof paper, perf. 12, lithographed	
carmine	*100.*
rose lilac	*100.*
red orange	*100.*
h. Plate (printed before plate crack developed) on semiglazed yellowish wove, laid watermark	
carmine	*30.*
dull red	*30.*
bright orange red	*30.*
deep orange red	*30.*
scarlet	*30.*
deep orange	*30.*
yellow orange	*30.*
orange brown	*30.*
orange yellow	*30.*
dark yellow green	*30.*
dusky blue green	*30.*
dull green blue	*30.*
violet blue	*30.*
red violet	*30.*
black	*30.*
i. Plate single from sheets of 100 with imprint on yellowish glazed chemically prepared wove, lithographed	
black	*20.*
brown	*20.*
scarlet	*20.*
light red	*20.*
rose pink	*20.*
carmine	*20.*
deep carmine	*20.*
violet rose	*20.*
deep violet rose	*20.*
violet red	*20.*
red violet	*20.*
violet	*20.*
blue	*20.*
pale blue	*20.*
pale dull blue	*20.*
yellow	*20.*
dull brown yellow	*20.*
orange	*20.*
red orange	*20.*

184-E6

Illustration with card margins reduced.

Similar to No. 184-E1 but engraved vignette of Lincoln on India facing ¾ to right. Each design has vignette attached to frame from behind.

184-E6 3c Four examples mounted on 80x89mm card to resemble block of 4

blue	*3,000.*
green	*3,000.*

Frame of No. 184-E5 with engraved vignette of Lincoln mounted in place.

184-E7 3c Die on card, brown —

There is some doubt whether No. 184-E7 exists as a genuine essay. The editors would like to see authenticated evidence of its existence.

186-E1a

Design size: 20x25mm
Die size: 92x50mm
Frames of 6c and 7c side by side (6c at right).

186-E1 6c + 7c

a. Die on white pelure, orange	*375.*
c. Die on white pelure, both 7s reversed on 7c frame, orange	*750.*
d. Die on old stiff glazed, black	*400.*

186-E2a

Complete 6c design, lithographed.

186-E2 6c

a. Plate on stamp paper, perf. 12, gummed	
bright red orange	*35.*
dull red orange	*35.*
dark red orange	*35.*
red brown	*35.*
dark red brown	*35.*
dark orange brown	*35.*
yellow brown	*35.*
dull yellow green	*35.*
green	*35.*
dull ultramarine	*35.*
bright ultramarine	*35.*
blue violet	*35.*
red violet	*35.*
light violet red	*35.*
violet red	*35.*
b. Plate on stamp paper, gummed	
ultramarine	*60.*
lilac	*60.*
scarlet	*60.*
orange	*60.*
carmine	*60.*
dark carmine	*60.*
blue green	*60.*

186a-E2b

Complete 7c design, lithographed.

186a-E2 7c

a. Plate on stamp paper, imperf.	
black	*75.*
carmine	*75.*
red orange	*75.*
yellow orange	*75.*
green	*75.*
dark green	*75.*
dark blue	*75.*
b. Plate on stamp paper, perf. 12, gummed	

red brown 50.
dark red orange 50.
brown orange 50.
red violet 50.
ultramarine 50.
violet blue 50.

188a-E1

Design size: 20x25mm
Die size: 78½x64mm
Frames of 12c and 24c side by side (12c on right).

188a-E1 12c + 24c
a. Die on white pelure
deep carmine 300.
brown orange 300.
orange brown 300.
blue green 300.
blue 300.
c. Die on old stiff glazed, black 400.

188a-E2a

Complete 12c design, lithographed.

188a-E2 12c
a. Plate on stamp paper, perf. 12, gummed
bright red orange 35.
dull red orange 35.
dark red orange 35.
red brown 35.
dark red brown 35.
dark orange brown 35.
yellow brown 35.
dull yellow green 35.
green 35.
dull ultramarine 35.
bright ultramarine 35.
blue violet 35.
red violet 35.
light red violet 35.
violet red 35.
b. Plate on stamp paper, gummed
ultramarine 60.
lilac 60.
scarlet 60.
orange 60.
carmine 60.
dark carmine 60.
blue green 60.

189a-E2a

Complete 24c design, lithographed.

189a-E2 24c
a. Plate on stamp paper, perf. 12, gummed
red brown 50.
dark red orange 50.
brown orange 50.
ultramarine 50.
violet blue 50.
red violet 50.
b. Plate on stamp paper, gummed
ultramarine 75.
lilac 75.
scarlet 75.
orange 75.
carmine 75.
dark carmine 75.
green 75.

190-E1c

Design size: 20x25mm
Die size: 79x64mm
Frames of 30c and 90c side by side.

190-E1 30c + 90c
a. Die on white pelure
dark carmine 300.
dark red orange 300.
dark orange brown 300.
brown 300.
blue green 300.
bright blue 300.
b. Die on stiff glazed paper, blue black 500.

190-E2a

Complete 30c design, lithographed.

190-E2 30c
a. Plate on stamp paper, perf. 12, gummed
bright red orange 35.
dull red orange 35.
dark red orange 35.
red brown 35.
dark red brown 35.
dark orange brown 35.
yellow brown 35.
dull yellow green 35.
green 35.
dull ultramarine 35.
bright ultramarine 35.
blue violet 35.
red violet 35.
light red violet 35.
violet red 35.
b. Plate on stamp paper, gummed
ultramarine 60.
lilac 60.
scarlet 60.
orange 60.
carmine 60.
dark carmine 60.
blue green 60.

191-E2

Complete 90c design, lithographed.

191-E2 90c
a. Plate on stamp paper, perf. 12, gummed
black 50.
red brown 50.
dark red orange 50.
brown orange 50.
ultramarine 50.
violet blue 50.
red violet 50.
violet red 50.
dark blue green 50.
orange brown 50.
b. Plate on stamp paper, gummed
ultramarine 75.
lilac 75.
scarlet 75.
orange 75.
carmine 75.
dark carmine 75.
green 75.

Essay reprints by Schernikow in 1903 from original dies (See paragraph eight of the Essay section introduction)

182-E1

Vignette master die "No. 14": two slightly diff. vignettes of Washington, one above the other, bottom one with truncated queue, bust and shading in front of neck.

182-E1
b. Die on proof paper (1903)
black 100.
carmine 100.
dull carmine 100.
dusky carmine 100.
yellow 100.
dull scarlet 100.
dull orange 100.
brown orange 100.
brown 100.
gray olive 100.
blue green 100.
dark green 100.
black blue 100.
ultramarine 100.
violet 100.
red violet 100.

182-E2

Design size: 20x25mm
Die size: 98x53mm
Frames of 1c and 2c side by side.

182-E2 1c + 2c
d. Die on proof paper, printed through a mat (1903)
black 100.
bright carmine 100.
dull carmine 100.
dim scarlet 100.
dark orange 100.
dull yellow 100.
dark orange brown 100.
black olive 100.
dark blue green 100.
dark blue 100.
ultramarine 100.
dark navy blue 100.
blue violet 100.
dull violet 100.
red violet 100.

184-E1

Design size: 20x25mm
Die size: 54x55mm

Engraved frame of 3c alone on die.

184-E1 3c
b. Die on proof paper (1903)
black 100.
bright carmine 100.
dull carmine 100.
dim scarlet 100.
dark orange 100.
dull yellow 100.
dark orange brown 100.
black olive 100.
dark rose 100.
green 100.
yellow green 100.
dark blue green 100.
dark blue 100.
deep ultramarine 100.
dark navy blue 100.
blue violet 100.
dull violet 100.
red violet 100.

184-E4

Complete 3c design, vignette with light background.

184-E4 3c
k. Complete die on proof paper (1903)
black 75.
bright carmine 75.
dull carmine 75.
dim scarlet 75.
dark orange 75.
dull yellow 75.
dark orange brown 75.
black olive 75.
green 75.
dark blue green 75.
deep ultramarine 75.
dark navy blue 75.
blue violet 75.
dull violet 75.
red violet 75.
l. Complete die on large colored card (1903)
black, *light green* 150.
deep scarlet, *ivory* 150.
red violet, *light blue* 150.
carmine, *pink* 150.

184-E5

Design size: 19x24 ½mm
Die No. 1 size: about 63x94mm Vignette of Washington slightly diff. from rest of series but with quite diff. frame design.

184-E5 3c
b. Die on proof paper (with and without printing through mats) (1903)
black 100.
dark carmine 100.
carmine 100.
bright carmine 100.
brown 100.
red brown 100.
yellow 100.
orange 100.
violet 100.
red violet 100.
violet brown 100.
blue 100.
steel blue 100.
light green 100.
dark green 100.
dull olive 100.
c. Die on colored card, 61x93mm (1903)
scarlet, *yellow* 150.
olive gray, *pale pink* 150.
dull violet, *buff* 150.

Plate proofs printed in sheets of 25 (plate size: 140x164mm). A horiz. crack extends through upper 3s from 2mm back of head on position 11 to vignette on position 12.
All plate essay items valued as singles except No. 184-E5d.

e. Plate on proof paper (1903)
black 15.
blue black 15.
greenish black 15.
dull red violet 15.
dark red violet 15.
dull violet 15.
violet brown 15.
light red brown 15.
orange brown 15.
brown carmine 15.
brown 15.
dim orange 15.
yellow 15.
dull yellow 15.
carmine 15.
light carmine 15.
dark carmine 15.
dull carmine 15.
dull scarlet 15.
dark green 15.
light green 15.
dull olive green 15.
deep ultramarine 15.
g. Plate on green bond, "Crane & Co. 1887" wmk. (1903)
black 25.
carmine 25.
dull carmine 25.
scarlet 25.
brown 25.
brown red 25.
orange brown 25.
red violet 25.
yellow 25.
orange 25.
dark green 25.
light green 25.
yellow green 25.
deep ultramarine 25.
dark navy blue 25.

186-E1

Design size: 20x25mm
Die size: 92x50mm
Frames of 6c and 7c side by side (6c at right).

186-E1 6c + 7c
b. Die on proof paper, printed through a mat (1903)
black 100.
bright carmine 100.
dull carmine 100.
dim scarlet 100.
dark orange 100.
dull yellow 100.
dark orange brown 100.
black olive 100.
green 100.
dark blue green 100.
dark blue 100.
deep ultramarine 100.
dark navy blue 100.
blue violet 100.
dull violet 100.
red violet 100.

188a-E1

Design size: 20x25mm
Die size: 78 ½x64mm
Frames of 12c and 24c side by side (12c on right).

188a-E1 12c + 24c
b. Die on proof paper, printed through a mat (1903)
black 100.
bright carmine 100.
dull carmine 100.
dim scarlet 100.
dark orange 100.
dull yellow 100.
dark orange brown 100.
black olive 100.
green 100.
dark blue green 100.
dark blue 100.
deep ultramarine 100.
dark navy blue 100.
blue violet 100.
dull violet 100.
red violet 100.

190-E1

Design size: 20x25mm
Die size: 79x64mm
Frames of 30c and 90c side by side.

190-E1 30c + 90c
c. Die on proof paper, printed through a mat (1903)
black 100.
bright carmine 100.
dull carmine 100.
dim scarlet 100.
dark orange 100.
dull yellow 100.
dark orange brown 100.
black olive 100.
green 100.
dark blue green 100.
dark blue 100.
deep ultramarine 100.
dark navy blue 100.
blue violet 100.
dull violet 100.
red violet 100.

1879 Coupon Essay
Azariah B. Harris

184-E8a

Size of coupon design: 25x7 ½mm
A proposed $300 30-year Postal Revenue Bond with 3.65% interest. Daily coupons 3c each, "Receivable for Postage in all parts of the U.S." after date thereon. Entire bond contained six pages of coupons with 16 rows of four (one for each day of two months); 20% bear month and day, others blank.

184-E8 3c
a. Coupon on bond (dated Jan. or Feb.), imperf., black 350.
b. Engraved die on old ivory paper (undated), black 1,000.
c. Single coupon on bond (dated), perf. 12, gummed, blue green 125.
d. Single coupon on bond (undated), perf. 12, gummed, blue green 50.

Continental Bank Note Co.

182-E4

Design size: 18x22mm
Die size: 59x67mm
Engraved vignette of Franklin on white background in unadopted frame.

182-E4 1c
a. Die on India, blue 575.
b. Die on proof paper
black 500.
dull scarlet 500.
dull brown 500.
dull green 500.
dull blue 500.
c. Die on ivory glazed paper
black 750.
black brown 750.
scarlet 750.
blue 750.

All known examples of "b" have reduced margins.

184-E9

Die size: 61½x76½mm
Vignette of Washington on white background in incomplete frame as adopted: no veins in trifoliate ornaments in upper corners.

184-E9 3c Die on India, on card
black 750.
green 750.

184-E10

Similar to No. 184-E9 but completed frame with veins in trifoliate ornaments.

184-E10 3c
a. Die on India, die sunk on card, green 750.
b. Die on proof paper, about 35x40mm
gray black 350.
dull red 350.
dull blue 350.
dull green 350.
dull brown 350.
c. Die on ivory glazed paper
black 600.
black brown 600.
scarlet 600.
blue 600.

Nos. 147-E8 and 147-E9 may have been made from completed dies of No. 147 to produce Nos. 184-E9 and 184-E10.

184-E11

Design size: 17½x21½mm
Die size: 60x75mm
Complete unadopted design with vignette of Liberty on white background.

184-E11 3c
a. Die on India
black 350.
brown red 350.
orange 350.
green 350.
blue 350.
scarlet 350.
b. Die on proof paper
brown 350.
green 350.
gray black 350.
dull red 350.
dull blue 350.
c. Die on ivory glazed paper
black 750.
black brown 750.
scarlet 750.
blue 750.

All known examples of Nos. 184-E11a, 184-E11b have reduced margins.

184-E12

Design size: 19½x24½mm
Die size: 61x71mm
Complete unadopted design with vignette of Washington on white background in frame similar to No. 184-E11 but with numerals of value.

184-E12 3c
a. Die on India, die sunk on card
black 650.
dull scarlet 650.
brown 650.
green 650.
b. Die on white glazed paper
black 500.
black brown 500.
scarlet 500.
blue 500.
c. Plate on India (some adhering to original card backing), imperf.
black 100.
scarlet 100.
orange red 100.
green 100.
d. Plate on white paper, perf. 12, gummed
black 75.
green 75.
blue 75.
brown 75.
red brown 75.
orange 75.
dull scarlet 75.
orange brown 75.
e. Plate on Francis Patent bluish chemical paper, perf. 12, gummed
black 150.
scarlet 150.
red brown 150.
brown 150.
yellow 150.
green 150.
gray 150.
f. Plate on brown chemical paper, perf. 12, gummed
blue 150.
ultramarine 150.
g. Hybrid die on India, mounted on India, block sunk on card, green 400.

184-E13

Design size: 18x22mm
Die size: about 61x62mm
Similar to No. 184-E12 but slightly different frame.

184-E13 3c
a. Die on India, die sunk on card
black 650.
scarlet 650.
green 650.
blue 650.
black brown 650.
blue green 650.
b. Die on ivory glazed paper
black 750.
black brown 750.
scarlet 750.
blue 750.
c. Plate on India, imperf.
black 100.
deep scarlet 100.
green 100.
dark green 100.
dark yellow brown 100.
olive brown 100.
violet brown 100.
orange 100.
d. Plate on stamp paper, perf. 12, gummed
black 75.
dull scarlet 75.
blue green 75.
brown 75.
red brown 75.
dull blue 75.
dark blue 75.
orange 75.
yellow 75.
yellow brown 75.
gray 75.

184-E14

Design size: 19x24½mm
Die size: about 67x71mm
Similar to No. 184-E13 but value label with "THREE" above "CENTS."

184-E14 3c
a. Hybrid die on India mounted on India, block sunk on card
brown red 400.
green 400.
b. Die on ivory glazed paper
black 500.
black brown 500.
scarlet 500.
blue 500.
c. Die on proof paper, about 35x35mm
black 300.
dull scarlet 300.
dull brown 300.
dull green 300.
dull blue 300.
brown red 300.
red brown 300.

184-E15

Design size: 20x25½mm
Die size: 60x73mm
Vignette of Indian maiden in headdress, "PORTAGE" error in top label.

184-E15 3c
a. Hybrid die on India, cut close, mounted on India, block sunk on card
black 900.
dark green 900.
b. Die on proof paper, about 28x35mm
black 600.
dull scarlet 500.
dull brown 500.
dull blue 500.
dull green 500.
c. Die on ivory glazed paper
black 750.
black brown 750.
scarlet 750.
blue 750.
d. Die on India, scarlet —

184-E16

Similar to No. 184-E15 but with spelling corrected to "POSTAGE."

184-E16 3c Die on India, cut close, mounted on India, block sunk on card
black 1,250.
blue 1,250.
steel blue 1,250.
carmine 1,250.
scarlet 1,250.
brown 1,250.
dark green 1,250.

190-E3

Die size: 44½x71½mm
Vignette of Hamilton on white background in frame as adopted.

190-E3 30c
a. Die on proof paper, about 35x48mm
gray black 500.
dull red 500.
dull green 500.
dull brown 500.
dull blue 500.
b. Die on ivory glazed paper
black 750.
black brown 750.
scarlet 750.
blue 750.

American Bank Note Co.

184-E17a

184-E17b

Design size: 22x30mm
Silver photo print of engraved vignette of Washington mounted on pencil and ink frame design.

184-E17 3c
- ***a.*** Die on white card, 38x49mm
  light brown vignette, black frame — *1,250.*
- ***b.*** Die on white card, 38x50mm
  light brown vignette, black frame — *1,250.*

On No. 184-E17b, the oval frame lines at the sides and the ornaments at top and bottom extend beyond the rectangular frame lines, and the lettering is less complete than on No. 184-E17a.

1881-82 ISSUE
American Bank Note Co.

205-E1

Die size: 59x74mm
Vignette of Garfield in lined oval.

205-E1 5c Die on India, die sunk on card, black — *500.*

205-E2

Die No. C-47 size: 70x83mm
Vignette of Garfield in beaded oval, in plain border of horiz. lines. Found with and without imprint and die number.

205-E2 5c Die on India, die sunk on card
- gray brown — *250.*
- gray black — *250.*

No. 205-E2 may not be a stamp essay.

205-E3a

205-E3c

Die size: 78x78mm

Vignette of Garfield in beaded oval with cutout at bottom for top of star.

205-E3 5c
- ***a.*** Die on India, die sunk on card
  - black — *750.*
  - deep red orange — *750.*
  - red brown — *750.*
  - blue — *750.*
  - green — *750.*
- ***b.*** Die on ivory glazed paper
  - black — *750.*
  - green — *750.*
  - blue — *750.*
  - scarlet — *750.*
  - red brown — *750.*
- ***c.*** Negative impression, solid color outside design, die on India, bright red orange — *1,000.*

205-E4

Vignette of Garfield as No. 205-E1 in lined oval and finished frame as adopted.

205-E4 5c Die on India, 24x30mm, black — *900.*

206-E1

Image of unadopted frame, printed on 40x60mm India paper with text and right "1" cut out.

206-E1 1c Black on India — *2,500.*

206-E1B

Image of frame with "DOS CENTAVOS" in upper label and "ONE CENT" pasted on bottom label, affixed to 57x71mm card with additional pencil sketch at right.

206-E1B 1c Black image affixed to card — *2,500.*

206-E1C

Design size: 21x26mm
Engraved frame of unadopted design.

206-E1C 1c
- ***a.*** Die on white glazed paper, 42x74mm, black — *1,000.*
- ***b.*** Die on surface-tinted glazed paper, cut close
  - green, *buff* — *600.*
  - black, *orange* — *600.*
  - brown orange, *blue* — *600.*

206-E2

Engraved frame almost identical to No. 206-E1C with small typographed vignette of Peace.

206-E2 1c Die on blue surface-tinted ivory paper, cut close, buff vignette, carmine frame — *800.*

206-E3

206-E3c

Vignette of Peace only.

206-E3 1c
- ***a.*** Engraved vignette
  - black — *350.*
  - dull red violet — *350.*
- ***b.*** Typographed vignette — *350.*
- ***c.*** Die on old proof paper, cut to shape to show AMERICAN BANK NOTE CO. and die number V46742, with die number 340 crossed out by etched lines, mounted on card, black — *350.*

Nos. 206-E3a and 206-E3c are essays made by the American Bank Note. Co. from a die acquired from Toppan, Carpenter and Company. The die number V46742 is the new ABNCo. die number.

206-E4

Engraved frame (No. 206-E1C) with typographed vignette of Lincoln mounted on it. Four diff. colors (dull carmine, dull scarlet, dark brown, green) on cream white ivory paper, 22x27mm each, mounted together on 92x114mm thick white card, ms. "American Bank Note Co. N.Y." at lower right.

206-E4 1c Four designs on cream white ivory on card *2,250.*

206-E5

Design size: 18x23½mm

Typographed vignette of Lincoln only.

206-E5 1c Die on white ivory paper
- dull carmine *450.*
- dark yellowish brown *450.*
- dull purple *450.*
- dull dark blue *450.*
- orange *450.*

Do not confuse the listed Lincoln vignette, No. 206-E5, with somewhat similar engravings ca. 1894 by Schlecht for currency.

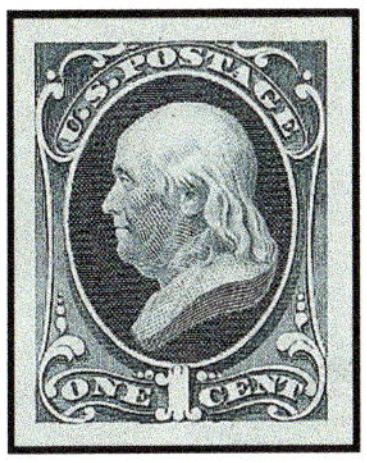
206-E6

Incomplete engraving of complete design as issued: no shading in upper arabesques.

206-E6 1c
- ***a.*** Die on India
  - gray blue *750.*
  - green blue *750.*
- ***b.*** Die on India, cut close, on India block sunk on card, deep gray blue *350.*

207-E1

Design size: 20½x25½mm

Die size: 49x54½mm

Engraved unadopted frame design with 3's at sides and large 3 at top.

207-E1 3c
- ***a.*** Die on India
  - yellow brown *750.*
  - dull brown *750.*
  - dull blue *750.*
  - green *750.*
- ***b.*** Die on white glazed paper, 32x38mm
  - black *650.*
  - dull dark yellow *650.*
- ***c.*** Die on surface-tinted ivory paper, cut close
  - black, *orange* *500.*
  - green, *buff* *500.*
  - violet blue, *orange* *500.*

207-E2

Engraved frame as No. 207-E1, with typographed vignette of Peace.

207-E2 3c Die on blue surface-tinted ivory paper, cut close, buff vignette, carmine frame *850.*

207-E3

Engraved frame (No. 207-E1) with typographed vignette of Peace mounted on it. Four diff. color combinations (orange red vignette, dull carmine frame; dull carmine vignette, dull red brown frame; yellow brown vignette and frame; blue green vignette and frame) on cream white ivory paper, 22x27mm each, mounted together on 92x114mm thick white card, ms. "American Bank Note Co. N.Y." at lower right.

207-E3 3c 4 designs on cream white ivory on card *2,500.*

208-E1

Incomplete engraving of design as adopted: unfinished shading on top label and bottom ribbon, four lines between frame sinkage at right and left edges, horiz. line at bottom.

This is a new die engraved by the Bureau of Engraving & Printing for "Roosevelt" proof albums.

208-E1 6c Die on India, on card, black *2,400.*

209-E1

Design size: 20x25mm

Die size: 58x76mm

Engraving of unadopted frame only, no horiz. lines in background.

209-E1 10c Die on thick white card, about 25x33mm
- blue *800.*
- green *800.*

209-E2

Similar to No. 209-E1 but with horiz. lines added to background.

209-E2 10c
- ***a.*** Die on thick white card
  - black *700.*
  - red *700.*
  - green *700.*
  - blue *700.*
- ***b.*** Die on India, on 50x70mm card, black *800.*
- ***c.*** Die on white glazed paper, black *800.*

209-E3

Engraved frame similar to No. 209-E2 with typographed vignette of Peace.

209-E3 10c
- ***a.*** Die on blue surface-tinted glazed paper, cut close, buff vignette, carmine frame *650.*
- ***b.*** Die on orange surface-tinted glazed paper
  - dull carmine vignette, violet frame *650.*
  - dull yellow vignette, violet frame *650.*
  - yellow vignette, green frame *650.*

209-E4

Vignette diameter: 17mm

Engraved Franklin vignette.

209-E4 10c
- ***a.*** Die on India
  - black *575.*
  - dusky carmine *575.*
  - dull scarlet *575.*
  - dim orange *575.*
  - orange brown *575.*
  - yellow green *575.*
  - dim blue green *575.*
  - deep blue *575.*
  - red brown on blue ground *575.*
  - dark red violet *575.*
- ***b.*** Die sunk on glazed paper, approx. 51x69mm
  - dusky carmine *775.*
  - dim scarlet *775.*
  - dim orange *775.*
  - deep blue *775.*
  - dim blue green *775.*
  - dim brown *775.*

209-E5

Design size: 21x26mm

Engraved frame with typographed vignette mounted on it. Four diff. color combinations (dull scarlet vignette, dull carmine frame; dull orange vignette, brown orange frame; yellow brown vignette, dark brown frame; blue green vignette and frame) on cream white ivory paper, 22x27mm each, mounted together on 92x114mm thick white card, ms. "American Bank Note Co. N.Y." at lower right.

209-E5 10c Four designs on cream white ivory on card *2,500.*

209-E6

Vignette diameter: 18mm

Engraved Washington vignette.

209-E6 10c
- ***a.*** Die on India
  - black *600.*
  - dim deep carmine *600.*
  - dim deep scarlet *600.*
  - dull orange *600.*
  - dull brown *600.*
  - dim blue green *600.*
  - blue *600.*
  - dusky red violet *600.*
- ***b.*** Die sunk on white ivory paper, 55x67mm
  - dusky carmine *800.*
  - dull orange *800.*
  - dull blue green *800.*
  - scarlet *800.*
  - dull brown *800.*
  - red violet *800.*

209-E7

Design size: 21x26mm
Engraved frame with typographed vignette mounted on it. Four diff. color combinations (dull carmine vignette and frame; dull orange vignette, brown orange frame; yellow brown vignette, dark brown frame; blue green vignette and frame) on cream white ivory paper, 22x27mm each, mounted together on 92x114mm thick white card, ms. "American Bank Note Co. N.Y." at lower right.

209-E7 10c
- ***a.*** Four designs on cream white ivory on card *2,500.*
- ***b.*** Single composite off card, dull carmine vignette, blue green frame *400.*

Issued stamp, No. 209, in trial color, overprinted network in fugitive ink.

209-E8 10c On thick paper, perf. 12, gummed, sepia, overprint olive gray *150.*

1883 ISSUE
American Bank Note Co.

210-E1

Design size: 20x25½mm
Engraved vignette of Washington (from proof on India of No. 207) with watercolor frame design nearly as adopted but with "TWO" and "CENTS" at an angle, rubber stamp "Feb. 17, 1883" on back.

210-E1 2c Die on white card, 80x90mm, black vignette, gray and white frame *3,000.*

210-E2

Design size: 20x25mm
Engraved vignette of Washington (from proof on India of No. 207) mounted on unadopted watercolor and ink frame design. backstamped "American Bank Note Co. Feb. 27, 1883."

210-E2 2c Die on thick white card, 87x100mm, black and white *3,000.*

210-E3

Design size: 20x25½mm
Engraved vignette of Washington (from proof on India of No. 207) mounted on watercolor frame design as adopted, ms. "2 March 1883 No. 1."

210-E3 2c Die on white card, 80x90mm, black vignette, gray & white frame *6,000.*

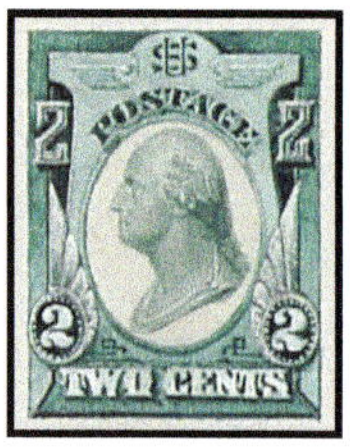
210-E4

Design size: 20x25mm
Engraved vignette of Washington on white background mounted on a brush and pen watercolor drawing of unadopted fancy frame design, backstamped "American Bank Note Co. Mar. 2, 1883" and pencil "No. 2."

210-E4 2c Die on white card, 88x101mm, dusky blue green *5,500.*

210-E5

Design size: 20x25mm
Engraved vignette of Washington (from revenue stamp No. RB17) mounted on wash drawing of unadopted ornate frame design, backstamped "American Bank Note Co. Mar. 2, 1883" and pencil "No. 3."

210-E5 2c Die on white card, 88x101mm, blue violet vignette, black frame *2,500.*

211-E1

Design size: 20x25½mm
Engraved vignette of Jackson mounted on unadopted watercolor frame design.

211-E1 4c Die on white card, 70x70mm, blue green vignette and frame *3,500.*

211-E2

Engraved head of Jackson only.

211-E2 4c Die on India, die sunk on card, black *2,500.*

211-E3

Incomplete engraved vignette of Jackson: lower edge of bust incomplete.

211-E3 4c Die on India, die sunk on card
- black *2,500.*
- green *2,500.*
- red brown *2,500.*

Complete engraved vignette of Jackson.

211-E4 4c Die on India, die sunk on card, blue green *2,500.*

Die size: 60x62mm
Complete design as adopted but with pencil sketch of pedestal top under bust.

211-E5 4c Die on India, die sunk on card, gray black *5,750.*

211-E6

Similar to No. 211-E5 but with incomplete shading engraved on pedestal.

211-E6 4c Die on India, die sunk on card, blue green *2,500.*

1887 ISSUE
American Bank Note Co.

212-E1

Die I, State 1
Die size: 62.5x62.5mm
Incomplete engraved vignette of Franklin facing right; horiz. background lines only.

212-E1 1c Die on 32½x35mm card, India mounted, die sunk on card, black *1,000.*

212-E2

Die 1, State 2
Die size: 62.5x62.5mm
Franklin vignette as on No. 212-E1 but with diagonal lines added to the background shading, sloping downward from right to left.

212-E2 1c Die on India, die sunk on card
- black *600.*
- ultramarine *600.*

212-E2A

Die II, State 1
Die size: 55x64mm
Incomplete engraved vignette almost exactly like on No. 212-E2, but on a new size die block.

212-E2A 1c Die on India, die sunk on card
- black *600.*
- ultramarine *600.*

212-E2B

Die II, State 1, marked in pencil
Die size: 55x64mm
As No. 212-E2A, with pencil shading added to mark need for revision.

212-E2B 1c Die on India, die sunk on card, black *850.*

212-E3

Die II, State 2
Die size: 55x64mm
Similar to No. 212-E2A, diagonal shading unchanged, shadows deepened by deeper cut lines per changes suggested by pencil shading on No. 212-E2B.

212-E3 1c Die on India, die sunk on card
black *600.*
ultramarine *600.*

212-E4

Die II, State 3
Die size: 55x64mm
Frame added, very small changes to the vignette, earliest full frame design.

212-E4 1c Die on India, die sunk on card
a. Die on India, die sunk on card, brown (full size) *1,000.*
black *600.*
ultramarine *600.*
b. Die on ivory glazed paper (c. 1893)
black *750.*
black brown *750.*
scarlet *750.*
blue *750.*

212-E5

Die III
Die size: 62.5x62.5mm
New engraving of Franklin vignette facing left; background shading as on No. 212-E2 with diagonal lines sloping downward from right to left.

212-E5 1c Die on India, die sunk on card, ultramarine *600.*

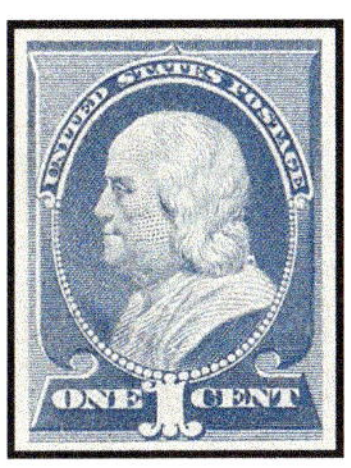

212-E6

Die IV, State 1
Die size: 57x65mm
Frame added as on No. 212-E4, but a few frame elements differ.

212-E6 1c Die on India, die sunk on card, ultramarine 850.

212-E7

Die IV, State 1, marked in pencil
Die size: 57x65mm
Similar to No. 212-E6, with pencil shading added to mark need for revision.

212-E7 1c Die on India, die sunk on card, ultramarine *850.*

212-E8

Die IV, State 2a
Die size: 57x65mm
Similar to No. 212-E6, with some vignette shading lines strenghtened in accordance with pencil markings on No. 212-E7; arc lines on bottom of vignette frame extended from numeral to 8th pearl on right and 13th pearl on left; tablet is unchanged.

212-E8 1c Die on India, die sunk on card
ultramarine *750.*
green *750.*

212-E9

Die 4, State 2b
Die size: 57x65mm
As No. 212-E8 but vignette frame shading lines extend to 21st pearl on right and 22nd pearl on left; deeper shading outside lower right of shield; tablet shading per changes suggested by pencil shading on No. 212-E7.

212-E9 1c Die on India, die sunk on card, ultramarine *750.*

212-E10

Die IV, State 3
Die size: 57x65mm
Deeply cut left background shading extended; pencil lines and notation: "Mr. Jones, Don't you think it would be well to tone off a little of the hard edge of your cut line — This in printing will fill up WMS."

212-E10 1c Die on India, die sunk on card, ultramarine *750.*

1890 ISSUE
American Bank Note Co.

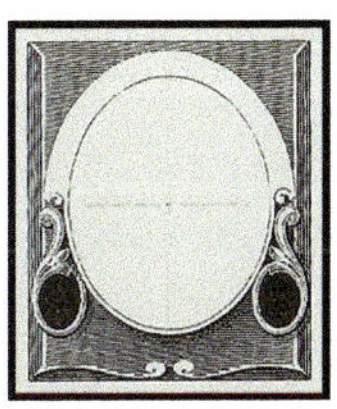

219-E1

Design size: 19x22½mm

Die size: 58x64mm
Engraved die of frame only with blank labels quite similar to adopted design.

219-E1 1c Die on ivory paper, 64x72mm, black *1,250.*

219-E2

Design size: 19x22mm
Engraved Franklin vignette cut down from 1887 1c stamp (No. 212) mounted on watercolor frame design.

219-E2 1c Die on thick light buff card, ultramarine frame *6,000.*

219-E3

Die size: 62x62mm
Engraved Franklin vignette with lettered label above.

219-E3 1c Die on India, die sunk on card, blue *2,000.*

219-E4

Engraved die of vignette only with outer line around the oval.

219-E4 1c Die on India, die sunk on card, 71x70mm, ultramarine *800.*

220-E1

Design size: 19x22mm
Engraved Washington vignette from 3c stamp (from proof on India of No. 184) mounted on watercolor frame design.

220-E1 2c Die on thick white card, 62x66mm, light carmine frame *3,750.*

220-E2

Design size: 19x23mm
Engraved Washington vignette cut from 1887 2c stamp (No. 213) mounted on shield-like watercolor frame design.

220-E2 2c Die on thick light buff card, gray frame *3,000.*

220-E3

Design size: 19x23mm
Engraved Washington vignette cut from 1887 2c stamp (No. 213) mounted on watercolor frame design.

220-E3 2c Die on white card, 105x135mm, gray black frame *6,000.*

220-E4

Design size: 19x22mm
Die size: 56x63mm
Engraved unadopted frame only.

220-E4 2c Die on white ivory paper, black *1,750.*

220-E5

Die size: 61x62mm
Engraved vignette of Washington in oval line frame. Issue 1890 at bottom.

220-E5 2c Die on India, die sunk on card, dark carmine *2,000.*

220-E6

Engraved Washington vignette with lettered label above.

220-E6 2c Die on India, dusky carmine *1,250.*

220-E7

Design size: 19x22½mm
Engraved Washington vignette and lettered top label mounted on pencil drawing of frame design adopted, ms. "J.J.M. — engraved background only without figures or words;" backstamped "Nov. 15, 1889 American Bank Note Co."

220-E7 2c Die on 50x55mm white card, mounted on thick white card, 119x122mm, black vignette, pencil frame *3,000.*

220-E8

Design size: 19x22mm
Die size: 56x63mm
Engraved frame only as adopted with numerals, blank curved top label.

220-E8 2c

a. Die on ivory paper, 64x71mm, black	*1,500.*
b. Die on India, 51x62mm	
black	*1,500.*
brown black	*1,500.*
dark brown	*1,500.*
dull scarlet	*1,500.*
dark blue green	*1,500.*
dark blue	*1,500.*
red violet	*1,500.*
red orange	*1,500.*

220-E9

Incomplete engraving of entire design as adopted: no dots in rectangular spaces between shading lines on cheek under hair in front of ear and on back of neck.

220-E9 2c Die on India, die sunk on card, lake *1,250.*

(Probably by) The Times, Philadelphia

220-E11

Surface-printed essay for proposed business advertising on stamps.

220-E11 2c Die on India, on card, bright green blue —

American Bank Note Co.

221-E1

Engraved 3c frame as adopted with vignette cut out, mounted over photo of James Madison.

221-E1 3c Die on India, cut close, dark green *2,500.*

221-E2

Engraved vignette of Jackson with lettered label above.

221-E2 3c Die on India, die sunk on card, purple *1,250.*

Design size: 19x22mm
Incomplete engraved design as adopted except Lincoln facing ¾ left: unfinished shading under collar.

222-E1 4c Die on India, die sunk on card, black brown *1,250.*

222-E2

Die No. C-226 size: 62½x62½mm
Completed design with die no. and impt., Lincoln facing ¾ left.

222-E2 4c Die on India, on 25x32mm card, black brown *2,000.*
a. Die number and impt. erased, die sunk on card *2,250.*

222-E3

Incomplete engraving as adopted: no wart on face, no lines on shirt.

222-E3 4c Die on India, die sunk on card, black brown *1,500.*

223-E1

Design size: 19x21½mm
Photo of Seward vignette mounted on watercolor frame design.

223-E1 5c Gray and white on light buff paper in upper right corner of short envelope *7,000.*

223-E2

Design size: 19x22mm
Die size: 63x62mm
Incomplete engraved design as adopted except Grant facing ¾ left: hair neatly combed.

223-E2 5c Die on India, die sunk on card

black	*1,750.*
orange brown	*1,750.*

223-E3

Design size: 19x22mm
Die size: 63x62mm
Incomplete engraving of complete bearded left-facing design: eye pupils not solid color, light shading on right side of face, only one diagonal shading line on left coat shoulder.

223-E3 5c Die on India, die sunk on card, chocolate *1,750.*

Similar to No. 223-E3 but more complete. Left beard has no diagonal lines and is light at top center.

223-E4 5c Die on India, die sunk on card, chocolate *1,750.*

223-E5

Third state of die: no horiz. lines on left moustache or under lower lip.

223-E5 5c Die on India, die sunk on card, chocolate *1,750.*

223-E6

Completed left-facing design: shows lines omitted from No. 223-E5, several diagonal shading lines on left shoulder of coat.

223-E6 5c Die on India, die sunk on card

black	*700.*
chocolate	*700.*

223-E7

Design size: 19x22mm
Die size: 62x62mm
Left-facing design with slightly diff. portrait, hair neatly combed. Horiz. shading lines on left coat shoulder, no wash-etched shadows on coat, beard and tie.

223-E7 5c

a. Die on India, die sunk on card

black	*700.*
dark brown	*700.*

b. Die on glazed paper, impt. and "ESSAY MARCH 1890"

black	*750.*
black brown	*750.*
scarlet	*750.*
blue	*750.*

Design size: 19x22mm
Die similar to No. 223-E7 but diagonal shading lines on left coat shoulder, wash-etched shadows on coat, beard and tie.

223-E8 5c Die on India, on card, brown *700.*

223-E9

Die size: 62x63mm
Engraving of right-facing Grant design diff. than adopted: light oval line around vignette, three diagonal lines on shirtfront under tie. Incomplete engraving: right collar unshaded.

223-E9 5c Die on India, dark orange brown *700.*

223-E10

Similar to No. 223-E9 but engraving completed: right collar shaded.

223-E10 5c

a. Die on India, die sunk on card, dark orange brown *700.*

b. Die on ivory paper, impt. and "ESSAY MARCH 1890"

black	*750.*
black brown	*750.*
scarlet	*750.*
blue	*750.*

Ferrotype plate 39x51mm of Grant facing ¾ left, outlines engraved, filled with red.

223-E11 5c Metal plate *2,000.*

223-E12

Printing from ferrotype plate, No. 223-E11.

223-E12 5c Die on card, 43x56mm, red *3,000.*

226-E1

Design size: 19x22½mm
Incomplete engraved vignette of Webster with curved label above, mounted on pencil drawing of frame design (includes additional pencil drawings of lower part of frame, value lettering), backstamped "D.S. Ronaldson," frame engraver.

226-E1 10c Die on white card, 51x55mm, black *13,500.*

226-E2

Design size: 19x22½mm
Engraving of unadopted frame design.

226-E2 10c Die on white glazed paper, black *1,000.*

226-E3

Design size: 19x22mm
Engraved 10c frame as adopted, vignette cut out and mounted over photo of John Adams.

226-E3 10c Die on India, cut close, dark green *2,500.*

226-E4

Design size: 19x22mm
Engraved 10c frame as adopted, vignette cut out and mounted over photo of William T. Sherman.

226-E4 10c Die on India, cut close, dark green *2,500.*

227-E1

Design size: 19x22 ½mm
Engraved vignette of Henry Clay with curved label above, mounted on wash drawing of frame design (includes additional enlarged pencil and wash drawing of frame).

227-E1 15c Die on white card, mounted at left on light buff card, 110x123mm (frame drawing at right), black *7,500.*

228-E1

Design size: 17x18 ½ mm
Die size: 62x61mm
Incomplete engraved vignette of Jefferson with curved lettered label at top: hair shading incomplete.

228-E1 30c Die on India, die sunk on card, black *750.*

228-E2

Design size: 17x18 ½mm
Similar to No. 228-E1 but more shading on hair, vert. shading lines on chin.

228-E2 30c Die on India, die sunk on card, black *2,500.*

229-E1

Design size: 17x18 ½ mm
Die size: 62x62mm
Engraved vignette of Perry with curved lettered label at top.

229-E1 90c Die on India, die sunk on card, red orange *2,500.*

COLUMBIAN ISSUE

Lyman H. Bagg

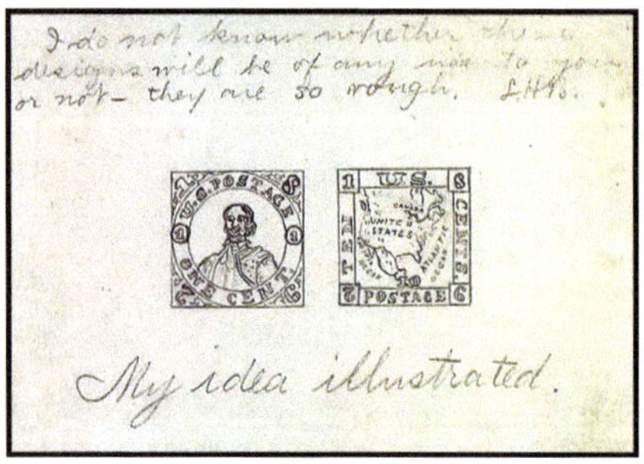

230-E1

Design sizes: 22x22mm
Left: No. 230-E1 — pencil drawing of Columbus in armor, on paper. "I do not know whether these designs will be of any use to you or not — they are so rough. L.H.B." written at top, "My idea illustrated" at bottom.
Right: No. 237-E1 — pencil drawing of North American continent, on paper.

230-E1 One Cent, Ten Cents, Drawings on 114x72mm white wove, Nos. 230-E1, 237-E1 *6,000.*

American Bank Note Co.

230-E2

230-E3

230-E4

Design size: 33x22mm
Silver print photo vignette of Columbus head mounted on watercolor drawing of unadopted frame design.

230-E2 1c Red violet on stiff white drawing paper *4,500.*
230-E3 1c Blue green on stiff white drawing paper *4,500.*
230-E4 1c Light red on stiff white drawing paper *4,500.*

230-E5

Die size: 57x38mm
Ferrotype metal plate with outline of adopted vignette (reversed) and drawings of Indian man and woman at sides in single line frame 39mm long.

230-E5 1c Metal plate 1,250.

230-E6

Vignette size: 16x15mm
Engraved vignette only as adopted.

230-E6 1c Die on 53x39mm India, on card
yellow brown *2,000.*
black *2,000.*

230-E7

Incomplete engraving of vignette, lettering, value numerals and tablet as issued: without palm tree, incomplete shading on and behind Indian and maiden, on Columbus' head, no shading on scrollwork, etc.

230-E7 1c Die on 39x28mm stiff wove, deep blue *2,000.*

230-E8

Incomplete engraving of entire design as issued: maiden's skirt only lightly engraved, chief's torso and shoulder incompletely engraved, incomplete shading in frame design at top, etc.

230-E8 1c Die on India, die sunk on 99x84mm card, deep blue *1,500.*

231-E1

Design size: 34x22mm
Silver print photo of vignette as adopted, mounted on watercolor drawing of unadopted frame design.

231-E1 2c Die on stiff white drawing paper, red violet *8,500.*

Die size: 74x61 ½mm
Incomplete engraving of adopted vignette only.

231-E2 2c Die on India, die sunk on card
black *1,500.*
sepia *1,500.*

231-E3

Design size: 35 ½x22mm
Engraved vignette of Columbus asking aid of Isabella as adopted for 5c, mounted on watercolor drawing of frame design similar to that adopted for 2c.

231-E3 2c Die on stiff white drawing paper, dark brown *4,000.*

231-E4

Vignette size: 29x15mm
Die size: 74x61 ½mm
Incomplete engraving of vignette as adopted (probably first state of die): cape on back of central figure incomplete, etc.

231-E4 2c Die on India, die sunk on card, black *2,500.*

231-E5

Incomplete engraving of vignette as adopted (probably second state of die): more shading on top right face, etc.; also pencil sketches for lengthening vignette.

231-E5 2c Die on India, die sunk on card, black *3,250.*

231-E6

Vignette size: 31½x15mm
Die size: 74x61½mm
Incomplete engraving of vignette, longer than Nos. 231-E4 and 231-E5, later shortened as adopted: Columbus' legs, central figure's cape, etc., are incomplete.

231-E6 2c Die on India, die sunk on card, black *2,500.*

231-E7

Design size: 33x22mm
Die size: 74x61½mm
Incomplete engraving of entire design almost as adopted: figures of value narrower, unfinished crosset shadows in lower corners.

Ridgway numbers used for colors of No. 231-E7.

231-E7 2c
a. Die on India, die sunk on card
13m/4 smoky dusky o-yellow-orange *1,250.*
b. Die on thin white wove card
69o/5 black *800.*
1m/0 dusky red *800.*
3k/2 dull dark orange-red *800.*
5i/0 deep o-orange-red *800.*
5j/1 deep v-deep o-orange-red *800.*
6i/0 deep m. red-orange *800.*
9i/0 deep o-yellow-orange *800.*
9m/0 dusky o-red-orange *800.*
9m/3 dismal dusky o-red-orange *800.*
9m/4 smoky dusky o-red-orange *800.*
9n/2 dull v. dusky o-red-orange *800.*
10k/0 m. dark orange *800.*
11i/0 deep orange *800.*
11k/1 dim dark orange *800.*
13m/1 dim dusky o-yellow-orange *800.*
13m/4 smoky dusky o-yellow-orange *800.*
33m/2 dull dusky g-yellow-green *800.*
37m/1 dim dusky g-blue-green *800.*
43m/2 dull dusky green-blue *800.*
49m/0 dusky blue *800.*
49m/1 dim dusky blue *800.*
55m/2 dull dusky blue-violet *800.*
59m/2 dull dusky violet *800.*
65m/2 dull dusky r-red-violet *800.*
70i/0 deep violet-red-red *800.*

231-E8

Design size: 33x22mm
Incomplete engraving of entire design as adopted: value numerals same as on issued stamp but without thick shading bars at ends of outer frame rectangles, etc.

231-E8 2c Die on India, card mounted, sepia *1,500.*

232-E1

Design size: 33½x22mm
Silver print photo of vignette unadopted for any value (Columbus embarking on voyage of discovery), mounted on watercolor drawing of unadopted frame design.

232-E1 3c Die on stiff white drawing paper, 41x29mm, orange brown *4,000.*

Ferrotype metal plate showing 19x15mm outline of *Santa Maria* (reversed) in 33x15mm vignette frame, outline engraved and filled with red ink.

232-E2 3c Metal plate, 51x30mm *1,250.*

232-E3

Printing from ferrotype plate No. 232-E3.

232-E3 3c Die on stiff white card with rounded corners, 55x42mm, red *1,250.*

232-E4

Vignette size: 30x15mm
Die size: 74x61mm
Incomplete engraving of vignette as adopted: sky composed of horiz. ruled lines, no clouds.

232-E4 3c Die on India, die sunk on card
black *1,250.*
dark yellow-orange *1,250.*
sepia *1,750.*

232-E5

Engraved vignette similar to No. 232-E4 but with "1492 UNITED STATES OF AMERICA 1892" and scrolls around numerals engraved in outline only, pencil outline of frame.

232-E5 3c Die on thick artist's card with beveled edges, 50x38mm, black brown *3,000.*

233-E1

Design size: 33½x22mm
Silver print photo of wash drawing of vignette as adopted, mounted on watercolor drawing of frame design as adopted but titled "COLUMBUS ON VOYAGE OF DISCOVERY. SHIPS AT SEA."

233-E1 4c Die on stiff white drawing paper, 41x29mm, brown red *4,750.*

233-E2

Design size: 33x22mm
Die size: 74x61½mm
Incomplete engraving of complete design as adopted: unfinished crosset shadows in lower corners.

Ridgway numbers used for some colors of No. 233-E2.

233-E2 4c
a. Die on India, die sunk on card
black *1,250.*
dark yellow orange *1,250.*
b. Die on thin white wove card, die sunk on card
1m/0 dusky red *800.*
3i/1 dim deep orange-red *800.*
3k/2 dull dark orange-red *800.*
5i/0 deep o-orange-red *800.*
9i/0 deep o-red-orange *800.*
9m/1 dim dusky o-red-orange *800.*
11i/0 deep orange *800.*
11k/1 dim dark orange *800.*
11m/2 dull dusky orange *800.*
13k/1 dim dark o-yellow-orange *800.*
13m/2 dull dusky o-yellow-orange *800.*
13k/3 dismal dark o-yellow-orange *800.*
13k/4 smoky dark o-yellow-orange *800.*
13m/4 smoky dusky o-yellow-orange *800.*
15m/2 dull dusky yellow-orange *800.*
33m/2 dull dusky g-yellow-green *800.*
35m/5 gloomy dusky green *800.*
37m/1 dim dusky g-blue-green *800.*
39m/1 dim dusky blue-green *800.*
41m/1 dim dusky b-blue-green *800.*
47m/0 dusky green-blue-blue *800.*
55m/2 dull dusky blue-violet *800.*
63m/2 dull dusky red-violet *800.*
69m/1 dull dusky red-violet-red *800.*
69k/3 dismal dark red-violet-red *800.*
71i/0 deep violet-red-red *800.*
71m/0 dusky violet-red-red *800.*
71o/5 black *800.*
ultramarine *800.*
violet *800.*
red violet *800.*
brown violet *800.*
orange brown *800.*
dark brown *800.*

234-E1

Design size: 38½x22mm
Engraved vignette as adopted, mounted on watercolor drawing of frame design similar to but longer than adopted. Vignette also used on No. 231-E3.

234-E1 5c Die on thick artist's card, block sunk as die essay, black brown *8,500.*

234-E2

Design size: 34x22½mm
Die size: 67x63mm
Engraved vignette as adopted, mounted on watercolor drawing of frame design as adopted, pencil "Oct. 5/92," approval monogram of J.D. Macdonough and $\frac{7}{8}$x1$\frac{1}{32}$ inches. Vignette also used on No. 231-E3.

234-E2 5c Die on thick artist's card, die sunk, black brown & white *4,000.*

234-E3

Vignette size: 29½x15mm
Die size: 74x61½mm
Engraved vignette only as adopted.

234-E3 5c Die on India, die sunk on card, sepia *1,250.*

234-E4

Incomplete engraving of entire design: bench at left has horiz. shading only, incomplete shading in Columbus' face, etc.

234-E4 5c Die on 74x60mm India, on card
sepia *1,000.*
blue *1,000.*

235-E1

Ferrotype metal plate with engraved outline design (reversed) of vignette as used on 6c, engraved lines filled with red ink.

235-E1 6c Metal plate, 38x38mm *1,100.*

235-E2

Printing from ferrotype plate No. 235-E1.

235-E2 6c Die on stiff white card with rounded corners, 55x42mm, red *1,250.*

235-E3

Incomplete engraving of frame as adopted: unfinished crosset shadows in lower corners.

235-E3 6c Die on India, black *2,000.*

235-E4

Design size: 34x22mm
Die size: 73x60mm
Incomplete engraving of entire design as adopted: neck and shoulder of horse, side figures in niches, crosset shadows in lower corners all unfinished.

235-E4 6c Die on India, die sunk on card, blue violet *1,500.*

236-E1

Design size: 33½x22mm
Die size: 73x62mm
Design as adopted but frame incompletely engraved: unfinished crosset shadows in lower corners.

236-E1 8c Die on India, on card, black *2,500.*

236-E2

Design as adopted but frame incompletely engraved: unfinished crosset shadows in lower corners, incomplete gown at left and faces at right.

236-E2 8c Die on India, on card, black *1,000.*

237-E2

Ferrotype metal plate with engraved outline design (reversed) of vignette as used on 10c, engraved lines filled with red ink.

237-E2 10c Metal plate, 43x28mm *1,200.*

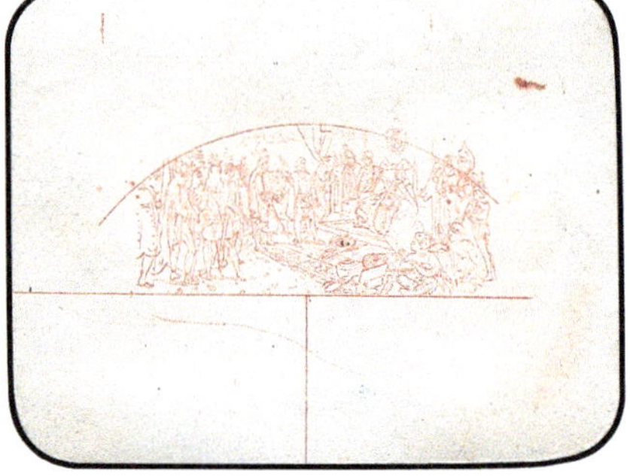

237-E3

Printing from ferrotype plate No. 237-E2.

237-E3 10c Die on stiff white card with rounded corners, 55x42mm, red *1,200.*

237-E4

Design size: 33x22mm
Die size: 74x62mm
Incomplete engraving of entire design as adopted: surroundings of Columbus, floor, etc., three figures behind King Ferdinand, crosset shadows in lower corners all unfinished.

237-E4 10c Die on India, card mounted
black brown *1,000.*
rose carmine *1,000.*

237-E5

Similar to No. 237-E4 but more completely engraved: missing lines on ankle bracelet of Indian, many details in vignette and crosset shadows in lower corners.

237-E5 10c Die on India, die sunk on card
black brown *1,500.*
carmine *1,500.*

238-E1

Design size: 33½x22mm
Silver print photo of vignette unadopted for any value (Columbus relating incidents of voyage to Ferdinand and Isabella), mounted on watercolor drawing of frame design similar to that adopted.

238-E1 15c Die on stiff white drawing paper, 42x30mm, bright ultramarine *5,000.*

238-E2

Vignette size: 30x15mm
Die size: 71x59mm
Incomplete engraving of vignette only as adopted: shading on Columbus' tunic and arms, Isabella's sholder, Ferdinand's robe, seated Indian's robe, robe of kneeling figure in lower left corner, etc., all unfinished.

238-E2 15c Die on India, die sunk on card, black brown *1,500.*

238-E3

Complete engraving of vignette adopted.

238-E3 15c Die on India, black brown *1,500.*

238-E4

Design size: 33½x22mm
Die size: 73½x62mm
Incomplete engraving of complete design as adopted: shading on Isabella's shoulder, Ferdinand's robe, seated Indian's blanket and crosset shadows in lower corners all unfinished.

238-E4 15c Die on India, on card
black brown 1,500.
blue green 1,500.

239-E1

Design size: 34½x22½mm
Silver print photo of vignette adopted for 15c, mounted on watercolor and ink drawing of unadopted frame design, titled "COLUMBUS PRESENTING NATIVES TO FERDINAND AND ISABELLA."

239-E1 30c Bluish gray on stiff white drawing paper, 42x30mm 5,000.

239-E2

Ferrotype metal plate with engraved outline design (reversed) of vignette as used on 30c, engraved lines filled with red ink.

239-E2 30c Metal plate, 39x29mm 1,200.

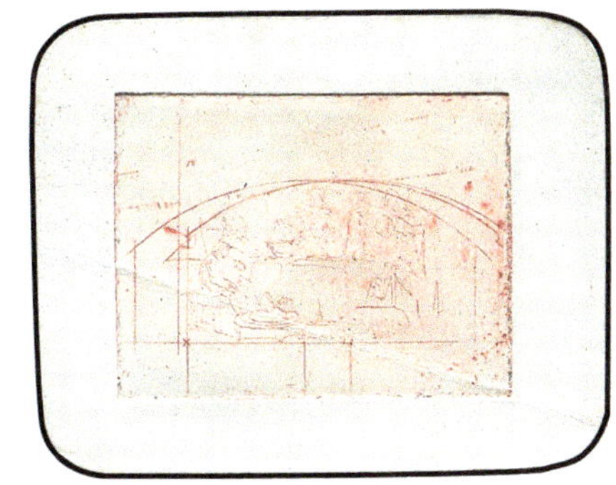
239-E3

Printing from ferrotype plate No. 239-E2.

239-E3 30c Die on stiff white card with rounded corners, 55x43mm, red 1,200.

239-E4

Vignette size: 30x15mm
Die size: 74x62mm
Incomplete engraving of adopted vignette only: table cloth dark at top; horiz. lines on front edge of octagonal footstool, horiz. dots in shadow below windowsill at left, dots on top of head of man standing next to Columbus, etc., all missing.

239-E4 30c Die on India, die sunk on card, black 1,750.

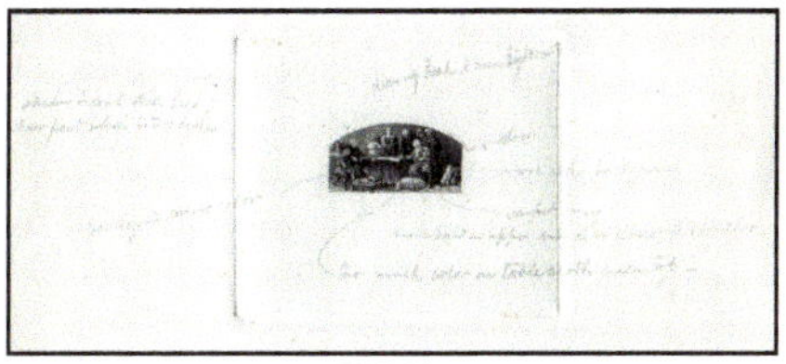
239-E5

Similar to No. 239-E4 but further engraved: has horiz. lines on front of footstool, etc. Eight pencil instructions for finishing vignette engraving written on large card backing, e.g., "Too much color on table cloth near top."

239-E5 30c Die on India, die sunk on 177x117mm card
black 2,000.
black brown 2,000.

239-E6

Design size: 33½x22mm
Die size: 74x63mm
Incomplete engraving of entire design as adopted: table cloth dark at top, diagonal dashes in one direction only between horiz. lines at lower left of vignette, etc.

239-E6 30c Die on India, die sunk on card
black 2,000.
black brown 2,000.

239-E7

Similar to No. 239-E6 but diagonal dashes in two directions, more dots on head and hand of man seated at near end of table.

239-E7 30c Die on India, die sunk on card
black brown 1,750.
orange 1,750.

239-E8

Incomplete engraving of entire design: window frame, horiz. shading lines on shoulder of man at right, vert. lines on front of table cloth below Columbus all missing. Lighter shading at top of table cloth as on issued stamp.

239-E8 30c Die on India, on card, orange 2,500.

240-E1

Design size: 34x22mm
Die size: Incomplete engraving of entire design as adopted: unfinished shadows between right arm and body of man on donkey, distant object in front of bowing man's head darker than on issued stamp.

240-E1 50c Die on India, on card, slate blue 1,500.

240-E2

Incomplete engraving of entire design: missing dots on donkey's flank and long lines on wrist of bowing man, no etching on two riders or their mounts.

240-E2 50c Die on India, on card, slate blue 1,500.

240-E3

Incomplete engraving of entire design: additional engraving on donkey's hindquarters and face of figure to left of Columbus.

240-E3 50c Die on India, on card, slate blue 1,500.

241-E1

Ferrotype metal plate with engraved outline design (reversed) of vignette as used on $1, engraved lines filled with red ink.

241-E1 $1 Metal plate, 45x29mm 1,200.

241-E2

Printing from ferrotype plate No. 241-E1.

241-E2 $1 Die on stiff white card with rounded corners, 55½x43mm, red 1,200.

241-E3

Vignette size: 31x15mm
Die size: 72x59mm
Incomplete engraving of vignette only as adopted (very early state of die): very little shading on Isabella, floor, walls, etc.

241-E3 $1 Die on India, die sunk on card, black brown 2,000.

241-E4

Incomplete engraving of entire design as adopted: shadow on table cloth, woman in front of table, crosslet shadows at lower corners all unfinished.

241-E4 $1 Die on India, on card, black brown *2,000.*

241-E5

Later state of complete design: horiz. lines in rectangle above Isabella missing.

241-E5 $1 Die on India, die sunk on 86x69mm card, black brown *2,000.*

242-E1

Design size: 33½x22mm
Die size: 75x62mm
Incomplete engraving of entire design as adopted: about 12 horiz. lines missing on back of cape of tall man at right, some vert. dashes missing on corselet of soldier at right, incomplete foliage over "C" of "COLUMBUS," etc.

242-E1 $2 Die on India, die sunk on card
dull yellow orange *2,000.*
olive brown *2,000.*

243-E1

Ferrotype metal plate with engraved outline design (reversed) of vignette as used on $3, engraved lines filled with red wax.

243-E1 $3 Metal plate, 45x29mm *1,250.*

243-E2

Printing from ferrotype plate No. 243-E1.

243-E2 $3 Die on stiff white card with rounded corners, 55x43mm, red *1,250.*

243-E3

Design size: 33½x22mm
Incomplete engraving of entire design as adopted: unshaded crossets in lower corners, shading lines on crossets and frame above title label too light. Pencil marks correct these.

243-E3 $3 Die on India, die sunk on card, dark yellow green *1,500.*

243-E4

Incomplete engraving of entire design as adopted, before etching of shadows on Columbus, Ferdinand, backs of chairs, etc.

243-E4 $3 Die on India, on card, dark red *2,000.*

244-E1 $4 Metal plate, 33x44mm *1,500.*

Ferrotype metal plate with engraved outline design (reversed) of Queen Isabella vignette as used on $4, engraved lines filled with red wax.

— 244-E1 — 244-E2

Printing from ferrotype plate No. 244-E1.

244-E2 $4 Die on stiff white card with rounded corners, 43x55mm, red *1,500.*

244-E3

Vignette diameter: 14mm
Incomplete engraving of Isabella head with background of uniform ruled horiz. lines only, blank circle for Columbus vignette at right adjoining.

244-E3 $4 Die on India, on card, black *3,000.*

Similar to No. 244-E3 but background has diagonal shading also.

244-E4 $4 Die on India, on card, black *3,000.*

244-E5

Design size: about 34x21½mm
Die size: 74½x61½mm
Incomplete engraving of vignettes and lettering only: no diagonal shading lines in background of Columbus vignette.

244-E5 $4 Die on India, die sunk on card
black *3,500.*
dark red *4,000.*

244-E6

Design size: 34x22mm
Same engraving as No. 244-E5 but with wash drawing of frame design as adopted.

244-E6 $4 Die on thick artist's card with beveled edges, 50x39mm, gray black *32,000.*

244-E7

Incomplete engraving of entire design as adopted: shadow at top of vert. bar and lines on leaves at bottom between vignettes unfinished; no circular line bordering vignette at Isabella's right shoulder.

244-E7 $4 Die on India, on card, black brown *2,000.*

244-E8

More complete engraving than No. 244-E7 but still missing circular line at Isabella's shoulder; only light shading on Columbus' collar.

244-E8 $4 Die on India, on card
black brown *2,000.*
dark red —

245-E1

Design size: 34½x22½mm
Incomplete engraved vignette as adopted for 1c: missing sky, etc., with pencil drawing of part of frame design.

245-E1 $5 Die on 50x38mm artist's card-board, on thicker card, 55x43mm, black *4,000.*

245-E2

Design size: 34x22½mm
Die size: 74½x61½mm
Incomplete engraving of vignette, lettering and frame as adopted (side panels blank): shading unfinished on Columbus' neck, hair and background, and with white and black wash touches.

245-E2 $5 Die on India, die sunk on card, black *3,000.*

245-E3

Similar to No. 245-E2 but further engraved: shading lines on neck, diagonal lines in background, etc.

245-E3 $5 Die on India, on card, 65x54mm, black *3,000.*

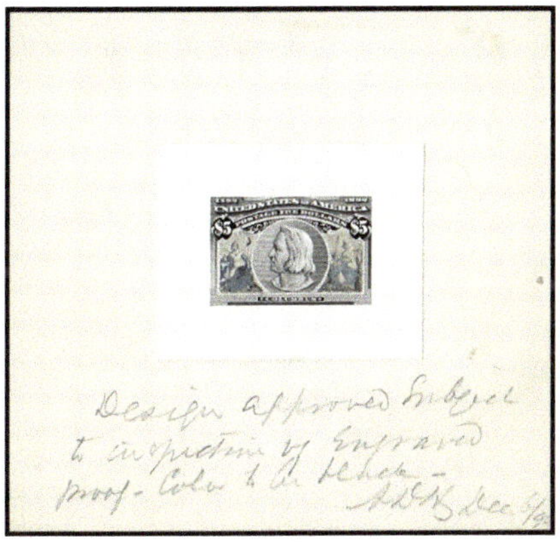

245-E4

Model with photos of female figures mounted each side of vignette, pencil "Design approved subject to inspection of engraved proof, color to be black. A.D.H. Dec. 6 '92" (A.D. Hazen, 3rd asst. PMG).

245-E4 $5 Die on thick white card, on 117x116mm card, black *3,750.*

245-E5

Engraving of No. 245-E3 with retouched photos of side subjects mounted in place.

245-E5 $5 Die on white artist's cardboard, 56½x46mm, die sunk on card, black *2,000.*

245-E6

Design size: 33½x22mm
Incomplete engraving of entire design: one line under "POSTAGE FIVE DOLLARS", no lines outside and no diagonal lines in sky to upper right and upper left of vignette, etc.

245-E6 $5 Die on India, on card, black *2,000.*

245-E7

Similar to No. 245-E2 but with pencil marks to show engraver where to place diagonal shading lines behind head and in front of bust.

245-E7 $5 Die on 65x55mm India, card mounted, black *3,000.*

245-E8

Similar to No. 245-E6 but with pencil marks and white ink suggestions for further engraving.

245-E8 $5 Die on India, die sunk on 83x68mm card, black *2,000.*

245-E9

Similar to No. 245-E6 but further engraved: with diagonal shading above side figures, below numerals and around vignette circle, but still incomplete in arched band above vignette.

245-E9 $5 Die on India, die sunk on 110x83mm card, black *2,000.*

245-E10

Similar to No. 245-E9 but further engraved: with shading lines in arched band above vignette but no shading on pole of liberty cap, object below shield has dotted shading only, spear tip shading incomplete.

245-E10 $5 Die on India, die sunk on 85x70mm card, black *2,000.*

1894 ISSUE
Bureau of Engraving and Printing

The 1c-15c designs of the 1890 issue engraved by the American Bank Note Co. were worked over by the BEP, including the addition of triangles in the upper corners. The 1890 30c was changed to a 50c and the 90c to a $1. Some 1894 essays have American Bank Note Co. imprints below the design.

247-E1

Design size: 18½x22mm
Die size: 61x62mm
Large die engraving of 1890 1c with pencil drawing of UL triangle 3½mm high with straight side next to curved upper label, freehand horiz. ink line at UR.

247-E1 1c Die on India, die sunk on card, black *3,000.*

247-E2a

Experimental laydown die with 1890 1c proof 4mm to left of similar design with 15-line high type I triangle in UR corner. Same laydown die also contains two 2c designs 18mm below, 5½mm apart, either uninked or lightly inked in color of 1c (sometimes found separated from 1c designs). No. 247-E2b nearly always found cracked horiz. through designs.

247-E2 1c
a. Die on semiglazed white wove with pencil notations

blue	*1,850.*
ultramarine	*1,850.*

247-E2b

b. Die on white card with pencil notations re color

"1-1 Antwerp, 4 Ultra."	*1,000.*
"2--little lighter--"	*1,000.*
"1 Antwerp blue, 1 Ultra." (not cracked)	*1,400.*
"3 Ul. Blue, 1 Chinese Blue, 2 white"	*1,000.*
"4 Cobalt and Indigo"	*1,000.*
"No 5"	*1,000.*
"No. 6--Antwerp blue"	*1,000.*
"No. 6--with little Antwerp blue"	*1,000.*

247-E3

Die impression of 1890 1c with 15-line high type I triangle in UR corner.

247-E3 1c Die on India, 50x52mm, dusky green *2,500.*

247-E4

Experimental die impression of single 1890 1c with 2c 18mm below, triangles added in ink to upper corners of both designs, ms. "Approved" notations.

247-E4 1c +2c, Die on India, mounted on 57x102mm card, mounted on another card, 144x195mm

green	*4,250.*
dull violet (without added triangles)	*4,000.*

247-E5

Large die engraving of 1890 1c with 18-line high triangle in UL corner (inner lines very thick).

247-E5 1c Die on India, die sunk on card, dusky blue green *1,500.*

247-E6

Similar to No. 247-E5 but inner line of triangle almost as thin as outer line.

247-E6 1c Die on India, die sunk on card, dusky blue green *1,500.*

247-E7

Similar to No. 247-E6 but inner line of triangle same thickness as adopted.

247-E7 1c Die on India, die sunk on card, dusky blue green *1,250.*

247-E8

Incomplete engraving of entire design as adopted including triangles: coat collar, scroll under "U," horiz. lines on frame, oval line of vignette, etc., all unfinished; vignette background not re-etched.

247-E8 1c Die on India, die sunk on card

ultramarine	*1,000.*
blue ("Cobalt 2--Indigo 4")	*1,250.*
dusky blue green	*1,000.*

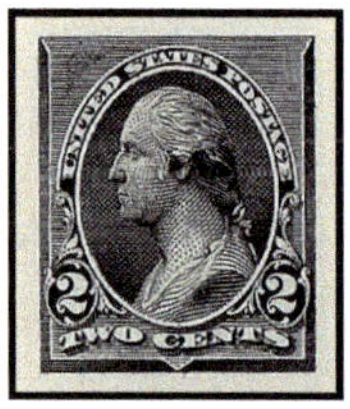

250-E1

Design size: 18½x22mm
Die size: 61x62½mm
Large die engraving of 1890 2c with pencil drawing of UL triangle 2½mm high.

250-E1 2c Die on India, die sunk on card, black *2,300.*

250-E2

Die width: 92mm
Experimental laydown die with 1890 2c proof 5½mm to left of similar design with 14-line high type I triangles in upper corners (found cut apart from No. 247-E2 and used for trial colors as noted thereon in pencil).

250-E2 2c Die on white card

"1 R&D Lake, 1½P. white"	*2,000.*
"M3 1 white, 7 Gem Lake, ¼ Car. Lake"	*2,000.*
"2 White, 4 Ger. Lake No. 1, ½ R&D Lake"	*2,000.*
"Opal Red"	*2,000.*
"Opal Orange"	*2,000.*
"Opal Maroon"	*2,000.*

250-E3

Die size: 61½x62½mm
American Banknote Co. die No. C-224 annealed, with 18-line high type I triangles engraved in upper corners, ms "No. 1" at lower left of card backing.

250-E3 2c Die on India, die sunk on card

medium deep red	*1,250.*
deep red	*1,250.*
dusky red	*1,250.*
dim red	*1,250.*
medium deep orange-red	*1,250.*
deep o-orange-red	*1,250.*
dusky g-blue-green	*1,250.*
dark medium violet-red-red	*1,250.*

250-E4

Incomplete engraving of entire design: shadows on frame not etched; lines on foliage, front collar and oval line at vignette bottom not recut; dots instead of lines over corner of eye; only one line on truncated scroll at left of right 2 and no line on similar scroll at right of left 2; shadows of TWO CENTS not etched.

250-E4 2c Die on India, die sunk on card

bright red	*1,250.*
light red	*1,250.*
dark red	*1,250.*
deep orange red	*1,250.*

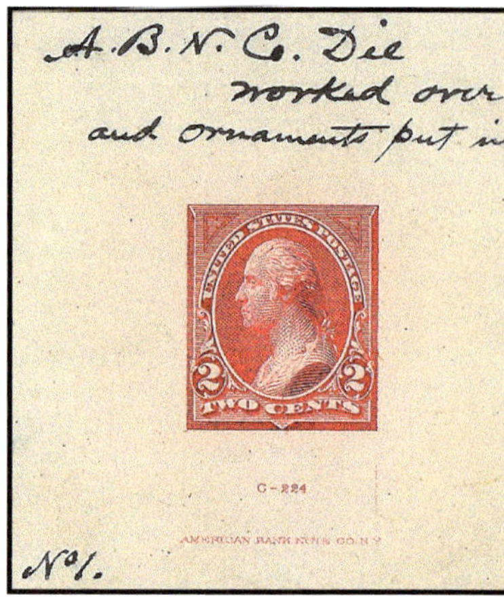

250-E5

Similar to No. 250-E4 but line added to scroll at right of left 2, ms. "A.B.N.Co. Die worked over and ornaments put in" at top, ms. "No. 1" at lower left.

250-E5 2c medium deep red *1,250.*

250-E6

Incomplete engraving of entire design: two lines on truncated scroll at left of right 2 (one later removed), scroll at left of right 2 unfinished, profile of nose and forehead darker than on issued stamp, shadows of "TWO CENTS" not etched, short dashes on inside of outer edge of white oval at lower right, veins on scrolls around 2s not recut. Pencil notations incl. "Old A.B.N.Co. annealed & triangles engraved and rehardened to take up roll for plate."

250-E6 2c Die on India, die sunk on card, medium deep red *1,250.*

250-E7

Incomplete engraving of entire design: bottom of ear still angular and not yet rounded, dots on lobe not yet gathered into two lines, dot shading under corner of eye not yet gathered into four lines, shadows of "TWO CENTS" have been etched.

250-E7 2c Die on India, die sunk on card, medium deep red *1,000.*

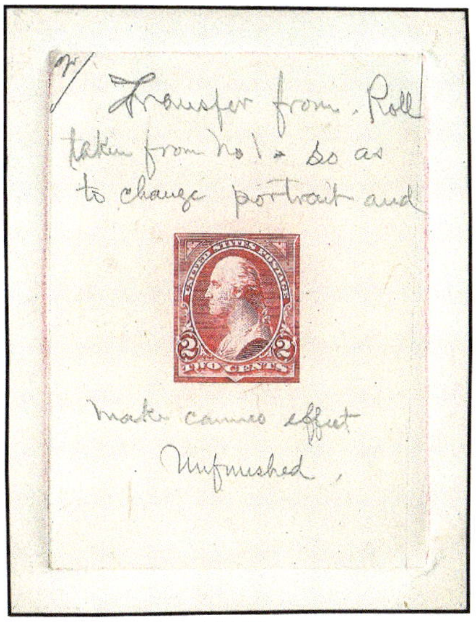

251-E1

Die size: 57x76mm

Incomplete engraving of entire design with type II triangles: top of head not silhouetted. Pencil notation "2/ Transfer from roll taken from No. 1 so as to change portrait and make cameo effect. Unfinished."

251-E1 2c Die on India, die sunk on card
- dark violet red *750.*
- light carmine *750.*

251-E2

Similar to No. 251-E1 but hair in front of ear unfinished, forehead and hair lightened.

251-E2 2c Die on India, die sunk on card, dusky gray *1,250.*

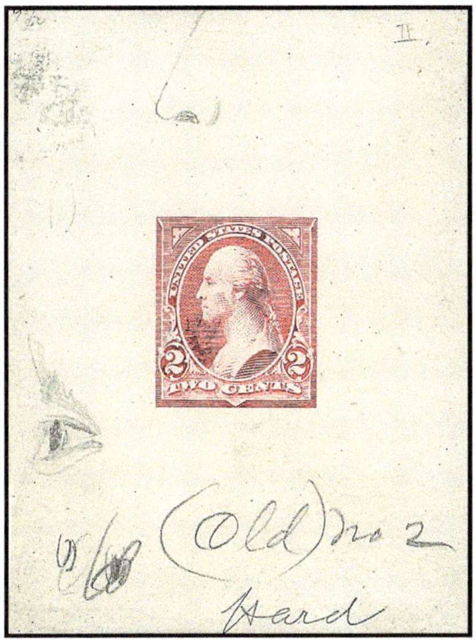

251-E3

Similar to No. 251-E1, made from hardened die, penciled "(Old) No. 2 / Hard" plus suggestions for strengthening design - drawings of nose and eye.

251-E3 2c Die on India, on 55x73mm card, light carmine *1,000.*

252-E1

Die size: 57x81mm

Incomplete engraving of entire design with type III triangles: top of head not silhouetted, unfinished shadow over eye, etc.

252-E1 2c Die on India, die sunk on card, medium deep red *1,000.*

252-E2

Incomplete engraving of entire design with type III triangles: unfinished shadow over eye, etc.

252-E2 2c Die on India, die sunk on card
- dusky blue green *2,000.*
- dark violet red *1,000.*

252-E3

Design size: 19x22mm

Die size: 56x80½mm

Discarded die, vignette overengraved: too much shading on front hair, cheek, nose, below eye; background too dark; hair in front of ear very prominent.

252-E3 2c Die on India, die sunk on card
- light carmine *3,000.*
- green, not on card (unique) *3,750.*

253-E1

Die size: 60x63mm

Complete engraved design as adopted but with type II triangles.

253-E1 3c
- ***a.*** Die on India, die sunk on card
  - dusky blue green *1,250.*
  - dark red violet *1,000.*
  - dusky red violet *1,000.*
- ***b.*** Die printed directly on card, die sunk on card, violet *1,250.*

254-E1

Design size: about 19x22mm

Die size: 61x63mm

Incomplete engraving of entire design: line under collar wings missing, oval line around vignette not recut; hair, beard, forehead, neck, collar, shirt, etc., all incomplete.

254-E1 4c Die on India, die sunk on card, dark yellow brown *1,500.*

Entire design engraved further than No. 254-E1 but still incomplete: shadows in lettering, etc., not etched, faint lines under collar incomplete, oval around vignette not recut.

254-E2 4c Die on India, die sunk on card, dark yellow brown *1,500.*

254-E3

Entire design engraved further than No. 254-E2 but still incomplete: beard, collar and necktie, etc., unfinished. Some veins recut on foliage under oval label.

254-E3 4c Die on India, die sunk on card, black brown *1,500.*

255-E1

Design size: 19x22mm

Engraved frame of American Bank Note Co. die No. C-227 with triangles, vignette cut out, mounted over engraved vignette of Washington.

255-E1 5c Die on 41x53mm India, on white wove, 48x75mm, black *2,750.*

255-E2

Washington vignette only as on No. 255-E1.

255-E2 5c Die on India, 56-69mm, green *2,000.*

255-E3

Design size: 19x22mm
Engraved frame as adopted with William H. Seward photo mounted on it.

255-E3 5c Die on India, cut close, mounted on 74x84mm white card, black *5,000.*

255-E4

Design size: about 19x22mm
Die size: 62½x75mm
Incomplete engraving of entire design as adopted: no oval border line around vignette.

255-E4 5c Die on India, die sunk on card, orange brown *1,000.*

256-E1

Design size: about 19x22mm
Die size: 62x61½mm
Incomplete engraving of entire design as adopted: white spot on eye and shadows not darkened, diagonal lines missing on beard under mouth, lines on coat unfinished, pencil notations and date "1894" below design.

256-E1 6c Die on India, die sunk on card, dark red *1,250.*

256-E2

Entire design engraved further than No. 256-E1 but still incomplete: diagonal lines on beard under mouth incomplete, lines on coat not as dark as on issued stamp.

256-E2 6c Die on India, die sunk on card, dim dusky red *1,000.*

257-E1

Design size: about 19x22mm
Die size: 58½x60mm
Incomplete engraving of entire design as adopted: lines on coat not recut darker, vignette background not etched darker.

257-E1 8c Die on India, die sunk on card, dusky red violet *1,000.*

258-E1

Design size: about 19x22mm
Die size: 61½x61½mm
Incomplete engraving of entire design as adopted: shading unfinished on cheek, in ear, etc.

258-E1 10c Die on India, die sunk on card, dark brown *1,500.*

Entire design engraved further than No. 258-E1 but still incomplete: unfinished shading on cheek under eye.

258-E2 10c Die on India, die sunk on card, red brown *1,500.*

260-E1

Die impression of 30c No. 228 with "THIRTY CENTS" crossed out by ink, ms "On roll without the head take out ornament."

260-E1 (50c) Die on India (torn before affixing), on 77x77mm card, black *1,500.*

260-E2

Entire design engraved, but without triangles at top corners.

260-E2 50c Die on India, die sunk on 70x115mm card, dark green *2,400.*

261-E1

Design size: 19x22mm
Die size: 50x101mm
Large die engraving of 1890 90c with value label and figure circles blank, no triangles.

261-E1 $1 Die on India, die sunk on card, black *2,250.*

261-E2

Similar to No. 261-E1 but head further re-engraved and background shadows etched deeper.

261-E2 $1 Die on India, die sunk on card, blue green *2,250.*

261-E3

Design size: 19x22mm
Model of engraved Perry vignette mounted on 1890 engraved frame with penciled in triangles, values painted in white and black. Ms. "O.K. July 14/94 TFM" below.

261-E3 $1 Die on India, cut close, mounted on 63x101mm white card, green vignette, black frame *2,000.*

261-E4

Similar to No. 261-E3 but with value lettering and circles added, background of circles unfinished, no triangles.

261-E4 $1 Die on India, die sunk on card, dark indigo blue *2,000.*

261-E4A

Similar to No. 261-E4 but with engraved triangles added, tiny white space above each numeral.

261-E4A $1 Die on India, die sunk on 67x122mm card, deep blue green *3,500.*

261-E5

Incomplete engraving of entire design: hair on top and back of head, whiskers and back of neck, and shading in value circles all unfinished. Triangles are engraved.

261-E5 $1 Die on India, die sunk on card
black *2,000.*
orange *2,000.*

261-E6

Similar to No. 261-E5 but hair at back of head and whiskers darker, face in front of whiskers darker as on issued stamp. Circular lines extend into colorless vignette oval.

261-E6 $1 Die on India, die sunk on card
black *2,000.*
blue green *2,000.*

261-E7

Design size: 19x21½mm
Die size: 49x100mm
Incomplete engraving of unadopted dollar value design with portrait of Sen. James B. Beck: value label and numerals blank.

261-E7 $1 Die on India, die sunk on card, black *4,000.*

262-E1

Design size: 19x22mm
Die size: 50x101mm
Incomplete engraving of frame only nearly as adopted: smaller $2's.

262-E1 $2 Die on India, die sunk on card, blue green *3,000.*

262-E2

Design size: 19x22mm
Die size: 51x112mm
Incomplete engraving of entire design: left value circle blank, right circle engraved $2 outline only, signed by engraver "Lyman F. Ellis."

262-E2 $2 Die on India, die sunk on card, black *3,000.*

262-E3

Die size: 51x112mm
Incomplete engraving of entire design: vignette shading unfinished, no veins in leaves around value circles.

262-E3 $2 Die on India, die sunk on card, black *2,500.*

262-E4

Incomplete engraving of entire design: inside of right border line above $2 unfinished, with pencil "line" instruction for border line strengthening, plus penciled "Then O.K./Blue/Lake/Green/Vermilion/Brown/Purple."

262-E4 $2 Die on India, die sunk on 62x128mm card, black *2,500.*

Similar to No. 262-E4 but border line complete.

262-E5 $2 Die on India, die sunk on card, black *2,500.*

263-E1

263-E1a

Die size: 50x112½mm
Incomplete engraving of entire design: only one line in each scroll at right and left of $5, inner line of right border above $5 unfinished, etc., veins on leaves around right value circle unfinished.

263-E1 $5 Die on India, die sunk on card, black *3,000.*
a. With photographic portrait of Marshall affixed as vignette with paper hinge *2,500.*

263-E2

Similar to No. 263-E1 but horiz. lines cut into oval line at top and inner oval line above L and R of DOLLARS required retouching as indicated by pencil instructions. Two lines in scrolls around value circles as adopted.

263-E2 $5 Die on India, die sunk on card, black *3,000.*

The bicolored essays commonly offered as No. 285-293 bicolored proofs can be found under the following listings: Nos. 285-E8, 286-E8, 287-E9, 288-E5, 289-E4, 290-E4, 291-E8, 292-E6, 293-E7. Values are for full-size cards (approximately 8x6 inches).

TRANS-MISSISSIPPI ISSUE

285-E1

Die size: 79x68mm
Incomplete engraving of vignette only: initial state of die, no lines in sky or water.

285-E1 1c Die on India, die sunk on 151x97mm card, black *2,500.*

285-E2

Vignette further engraved: lines in sky and water. Additional shading to clothing, most noticeable on legging of Native American at bottom of vignette. Shading still incomplete.

285-E2 1c Die on India, die sunk on card, black *2,500.*

285-E3

Vignette further engraved: shading added to chief's headdress and bracelet, woman's neck and oarman's hand. Shading still incomplete.

285-E3 1c Die on India, die sunk on card, black *2,500.*

285-E4

Vignette further engraved: crosshatching added to bottom of chief's nose, Marquette's hair is larger and darker, incomplete shading on background shore.

285-E4 1c Die on India, die sunk on card, black *2,500.*

285-E5

Vignette further engraved: additional shading on rocky shoreline behind Marquette's arm, shading missing on grass in foreground.

285-E5 1c Die on India, die sunk on card, black *2,500.*

285-E6

Incomplete bi-color engraving of entire design, shading added to grass in foreground and around woman's left side, tree branches not cut away (extend into upper left frame), no inner line on numeral "1" in frame.

285-E6 1c Die on India, die sunk on card, deep brown red & black *2,500.*

285-E6A

Design size: 34x22mm
Die size: 73x62mm
Incomplete bicolor engraving of entire design: no inner line on numerals "1" in frame.

285-E6A 1c Die on India, die sunk on card, orange & black *2,500.*

Die size: 83x68mm
Incomplete engraving of entire design,vignette is unfinished but has unshaded inner line in numeral "1"in frame.

285-E7 1c Die on India, die sunk on card, black *3,500.*
a. As No. 285-E7 but with pencil modeling applied 3,500.

285-E8

Die size: 63x51mm
Complete bicolor engraving of entire design.

285-E8 1c Die with black vignette on India, die sunk on card
dark yellow green ("normal" bicolor) *700.*
dusky green *2,000.*
dusky blue green *2,000.*
brown *2,000.*

285-E9

Die size: 88x70mm
Incomplete engraving of entire design, corn, corn husks and panels in frame incomplete, shading in inner line on numeral "1" in frame.

285-E9 1c Die on India, die sunk on card, dusky green *2,500.*

285-E10

Unfinished frame in red brown missing second inner line in numerals, with black unfinished "Cattle in the Storm" vignette as used on the $1 value, foreground snow at left incomplete.

285-E10 1c Die on India, red brown & black 3,500.

286-E1

Die size: 78x68mm
Incomplete engraving of Mississippi River Bridge vignette (originally intended for 2c but eventually used on $2): initial state of die, very lightly engraved with missing lines on center arch of the bridge.

286-E1 2c Die on India, die sunk on card, black *3,750.*

286-E2

Vignette further engraved: lines added to center arch, shading added to windows, road, water and city skyline, no crosshatching on lower shore.

286-E2 2c Die on India, die sunk on card, black *5,000.*

286-E3

Vignette further engraved: crosshatching on shore at bottom, paddlewheels on boats engraved, horse cart faintly visible on lower shore (later removed).

286-E3 2c Die on India, die sunk on card, black *3,000.*

Complete engraving of vignette only.

286-E4 2c Die on India, die sunk on card, black *3,000.*

286-E5

Design size: 137x88½mm
Pencil sketch by R. Ostrander Smith of 2c frame design with left half adopted and right half without wheat at top, titled "ST. LOUIS BRIDGE."

286-E5 2c Sketch on tracing paper, 178x120mm *1,500.*

286-E6

Design size: 137x89mm
Complete pencil drawing ("P" of "POSTAGE" in ink) by R. O. Smith of frame design as adopted except titled "ST. LOUIS BRIDGE."

286-E6 2c Drawing on Whatman drawing board, 1889 wmk., 217x163mm *1,500.*

286-E7

Pencil drawing by R.O. Smith, no title, no corn or wheat in frame.

286-E7 2c Drawing on 72x61mm tracing paper *1,500.*

286-E7A

Ink and wash drawing of frame, stamp size, similar to adopted design, but with no corn or wheat.

286-E7A 2c Drawing on hard, thick paper, black *11,000.*

286-E7B

Photo essay of No. 286-E7A with blades of wheat painted over side columns.

286-E7B 2c black —

286-E7C

Photo essay of No. 286-E7A with 7 ears of corn and blades of wheat painted over side columns.

286-E7C 2c black —

286-E7D

Photo essay of No. 286-E7A with 4 ears of corn and blades of wheat painted over side columns.

286-E7D 2c black —

286-E7E

Photo essay of No. 286-E7A with ears of corn painted over left column and blades of wheat over right column.

286-E7E 2c black —

286-E7F

Photo essay of frame as adopted with center cut away.

286-E7F 2c black —

286-E8

Die size: 63x51mm
Complete bicolor engraving of 2c design but with Mississippi River Bridge vignette as used on $2.

Ridgway numbers used for colors of No. 286-E8.

286-E8 2c Die with black vignette on India, die sunk on card

dark red ("normal" bicolor)	*700.*
3k/0 dark orange red	*2,000.*
5k/0 dark o-orange-red	*2,000.*
5m/1 dim dusky o-orange-red	*2,000.*
7i/0 deep red orange	*2,000.*
7m/0 dusky red orange	*2,000.*
9m/0 dusky o-red-orange	*2,000.*
9k/2 dull dark o-red-orange	*2,000.*
13m/3 dismal dusky o-yellow-orange	*2,000.*
35m/1 dim dusky green	*2,000.*
49m/1 dim v. dusky blue	*2,000.*
63m/1 dim dusky red violet	*2,000.*
71-/0 deep violet-red-red	*2,000.*

286-E8A

Composite model of 2c "MISSISSIPPI RIVER BRIDGE" frame in copper red with cut No. 293-E6 vignette pasted over top, signed by Baldwin.

286-E8A 2c copper red & black —

286-E8B

Composite model of 2c "MISSISSIPPI RIVER BRIDGE" frame in red orange with cut No. 286-E3 vignette pasted over top, signed by Baldwin.

286-E8B 2c red orange & black —

286-E9

Complete engraved "FARMING IN THE WEST" design with unfinished engraving around title and at edges where vignette connects to frame.

286-E9 2c Die with black vignette on India, die sunk on card —

286-E10

Complete engraved "FARMING IN THE WEST" design with additional engraving connecting vignette to frame, missing furrow in field near right frame.

286-E10 2c Die on India, die sunk on card, red —

287-E1

Design size: 28x16.5mm
Die No. 259 size: 77x70mm
Initial state of vignette die, very lightly engraved, no engraving lines in sky.

287-E1 4c Die on India, die sunk on card, black *3,000.*

287-E2

Vignette further engraved: sky lines ruled in, additional shading on buffalo and back leg of horse.

287-E2 4c Die on India, die sunk on card, black *3,000.*

287-E2A

Vignette further engraded: additional engraving on saddle, pencil modeling on buffalo and shadow.

287-E2A 4c Die on India, die sunk on card, black —

287-E3

Vignette further engraved on hunter's clothing, horse's head and legs, buffalo's fur, no significant shadows on right forefoot under buffalo.

287-E3 4c Die on India, die sunk on card, black *4,500.*

287-E4

Vignette further engraved: engraving darkened overall, no significant shadows on right forefoot under buffalo.

287-E4 4c Die on India, die sunk on card, black *3,750.*

287-E5

Vignette further engraved on hunter's clothes, bow and horse, pencil shading under buffalo and in grass at bottom of vignette.

287-E5 4c Die on India, die sunk on card, black *3,750.*

287-E6

Vignette further engraved: buffalo's right foot now added, shadow under buffalo engraved but not complete.

287-E6 4c Die on India, die sunk on card, black *3,750.*

287-E7

Die size: 83x67mm
Incomplete engraving of entire design, buffalo and shadows fully engraved but with no lines in the sky.

287-E7 4c Die on India, die sunk on card
black *3,500.*
deep orange *3,500.*

287-E8

Die size: 63x51mm
Incomplete engraving of entire design: corn husks at lower sides of frame unfinished.

Ridgway numbers used for colors of No. 287-E8.

287-E8 4c Die with black vignette on India, die sunk on card
5k/0 dark o-orange-red *2,000.*
5m/0 dusky o-orange-red *2,000.*
7m/0 dusky red orange *2,000.*
11o/2 dull v. dusky orange *2,000.*
13m/3 dismal dusky o-yellow-orange *2,000.*
35m/1 dim dusky green *2,000.*
39m/1 dim dusky blue green *2,000.*
49o/1 dim v. dusky blue *2,000.*
61k/1 dim dark violet-red violet *2,000.*
63m/1 dim dusky red violet *2,000.*
71m/0 dusky violet-red-red *2,000.*

287-E9

Die size: 62x51mm
Complete bicolor engraving.

287-E9 4c Die with black vignette on India, die sunk on card
red orange ("normal" bicolor) *500.*
deep red orange ("normal" bicolor) *500.*

288-E1

Die size: 75x68mm
Initial state of vignette die, very lightly engraved.

288-E1 5c Die on India, die sunk on card, black *3,500.*

288-E2

Vignette further engraved: engraving added to mountainsides, clouds at right and torsos of waving men.

288-E2 5c Die on India, die sunk on card, black *5,500.*

288-E3

Vignette further engraved: more engraving added to mountainsides and waving man at right.

288-E3 5c Die on India, die sunk on card, black *3,750.*

288-E4

Engraving missing in sky to left of flag, pencil modeling added to the mountainsides.

288-E4 5c Die on India, die sunk on card, black *3,750.*

288-E5

Design size: 34x22mm
Die size: 63x51mm
Incomplete bicolor engraving of entire design: unfinished crosshatching at left of "FREMONT," lines against bottom label and frame unfinished, no etching on flag.

Ridgway numbers used for colors of No. 288-E5.

288-E5 5c Die with black vignette on India, die sunk on card
49m/1 dim dusky blue ("normal" bicolor) *700.*
49k/1 dim dark blue ("normal" bicolor) *700.*
3k/0 dark orange red *2,000.*
3m/0 dusky orange red *2,000.*
7m/0 dusky red orange *2,000.*
7m/1 dim dusky red orange *2,000.*
9m/0 dusky o-red-orange *2,000.*
11o/2 dull v. dusky orange *2,000.*
37m/1 dim dusky g-blue-green *2,000.*
39m/1 dim dusky blue green *2,000.*
49o/1 dim v. dusky blue *2,000.*
63m/1 dim dusky red violet *2,000.*
71n/0 medium deep violet-red-red *2,000.*
35m/1 dim dusky green *2,000.*

288-E7

Die size: 82x68½mm
Incomplete engraving of entire design, corn husks on frame unfinished, engraving on vignette near edges of frame and shading on mountain and rock in foreground unfinished.

288-E7 5c Die on India, die sunk on card, black *3,250.*

Incomplete engraving of vignette: no dots on mountain tops next to right border, unfinished crosshatching at left end of title label.

288-E8 5c Die on India, die sunk on card, black *3,750.*

288-E10

Nearly complete engraving of entire design with area on mountain face unfinished.

288-E10 5c Die on India, die sunk on card, brown —

289-E1

Engraved vignette only of mounted Indian, not used for any value.

289-E1 8c Die on India, on card, black *7,500.*

289-E2

Incomplete engraving of vignette only as adopted: blank area for label wider than completed bicolor vignette, knee of kneeling soldier at right and vegetation at left unfinsihed.

289-E2 8c Die on India, die sunk on card, black *3,000.*

289-E3

Design size: about 33½x21½mm
Incomplete engraving of frame only: shading of sunken center of cartouche at right of vignette unfinished.

289-E3 8c Die on India, 37x26mm, black *3,000.*

289-E4

Incomplete engraving of entire design: top row of distant shrubbery under "ERICA" missing, crosshatching on distant mountains at left, blades of grass at left end of label, some dots against top label all unfinished.

Ridgway numbers used for colors of No. 289-E4.

289-E4 8c Die with black vignette on India, die sunk on card

dark red ("normal" bicolor)	*700.*
dusky red ("normal" bicolor)	*700.*
3m/0 dusky orange red	*2,750.*
5m/0 dusky o-orange-red	*2,750.*
7i/0 deep red orange	*2,750.*
7m/0 dusky red orange	*2,750.*
9m/0 dusky o-red-orange	*2,750.*
11o/2 dull v. dusky orange	*2,750.*
35m/1 dim dusky green	*2,750.*
39m/1 dim dusky blue-green	*2,750.*
49o/1 dim v. dusky blue	*2,750.*
63m/1 dim dusky red violet	*2,750.*
71-/0 deep violet-red-red	*2,750.*

290-E1

Die size: 77x64mm
Incomplete engraving of vignette only: two rows of dots in sky over wagon.

290-E1 10c Die on India, die sunk on card, black *8,500.*

290-E1A

Die size: 77x64mm
No. 290-E1 with additional shading penciled in.

290-E1A 10c Die on India, die sunk on card, black —

290-E2

Vignette further engraved: three rows of dots in sky over wagon, shading added on and under body of horse.

290-E2 10c Die on India, die sunk on card, black *3,750.*

290-E3

Vignette further engraved: front of wagon canvas crosshatched, additional shadows on ground, engraving on shrubs near edges incomplete.

290-E3 10c Die on India, die sunk on card, black *3,750.*

290-E4

Incomplete bicolor engraving of entire design: cornhusks unfinished, blades of grass to right of girl's feet and some to right of dark horse's feet are missing. Five lines of dots in sky over wagon.

Ridgway numbers used for colors of No. 290-E4.

290-E4 10c Die with black vignette on India, die sunk on card

dull dusky violet blue ("normal" bicolor)	*700.*
dusky blue violet ("normal" bicolor)	*700.*
1i/0 deep red	*2,500.*
3k/0 dark orange red	*2,500.*
5k/0 dark o-orange-red	*2,500.*
5m/0 dusky o-orange-red	*2,500.*
7i/0 deep red orange	*2,500.*
9m/0 dusky o-red-orange	*2,500.*
11o/2 dull v. dusky orange	*2,500.*
35m/1 dim dusky green	*2,500.*
39m/1 dim dusky blue green	*2,500.*
49o/1 dim v. dusky blue	*2,500.*
55m/2 smoky dark v.-blue violet	*2,500.*
63m/1 dim dusky red violet	*2,500.*
71-/0 deep violet-red-red	*2,500.*

290-E6

Incomplete engraving of entire design: corn husks and side panels on frame unfinished, vignette from bicolor essay trimmed to fit frame.

290-E6 10c Die on India, die sunk on card, black brown *3,000.*

Incomplete engraving of entire design: cornhusks and panels at ends of cartouche and both sides and botton of vignette next to border unfinished.

290-E7 10c Die on India, die sunk on card, dull red violet *3,000.*

290-E8

Incomlete engraving of entire design: side panels on frame further engraved, but corn husks still unfinished, vignette unfinsihed at edges near frame border.

290-E8 10c Die on India, dull red violet *3,000.*

291-E1

Die size: 76x68mm
Incomplete engraving of vignette only, lightly engraved, no sky or mountains engraved in background.

291-E1 50c Die on India, die sunk on card, black *3,750.*

291-E2

Vignette further engraved: hills and sky added to background, additional engraving on miner's pants, mountains at upper right only lightly engraved.

291-E2 50c Die on India, die sunk on card, black *3,750.*

291-E3

Vignette further engraved: outline added to mountains at upper right, additional engraving on grass at base of hills and rocks at left side, shading on donkey still incomplete.

291-E3 50c Die on India, die sunk on card, black *3,750.*

291-E4

Vignette further engraved: engraving darkened overall, mountain in background missing some horizontal lines.

291-E4 50c Die on India, die sunk on card, black *3,750.*

291-E5

Vignette further engraved: horizontal lines added to mountains at upper right creating a V-shaped ridge, additional engraving on large rock to left of miner.

291-E5 50c Die on India, die sunk on card, black *3,750.*

291-E6

Vignette further engraved: shadows on miner's hat darker (etched).

291-E6 50c Die on India, die sunk on card, black *3,750.*

291-E7

Vignette further engraved: girth under donkey darkened.

291-E7 50c Die on India, die sunk on card, black *9,000.*

291-E8

Design size: 34x22mm
Die size: 89x71mm
Incomplete bicolor engraving of entire design: shading lines on scroll in LR corner of frame and shrubbery in UL corner of vignette unfinished, sky incomplete.

Ridgway numbers used for colors of No. 291-E8.

291-E8 50c Die with black vignette on India, die sunk on card

dull dusky b-blue-green ("normal" bicolor; die size: 63x51mm)	*700.*
dull dusky g-blue-green ("normal" bicolor; die size: 63x51mm)	*700.*
1i/0 deep red	*2,500.*
3k/0 dark orange red	*2,500.*
5m/0 dusky o-orange-red	*2,500.*
7m/0 dusky red orange	*2,500.*
9i/0 deep o-yellow-orange	*2,500.*
9m/0 dusky o-red-orange	*2,500.*

11m/2 dull dusky orange	2,500.
13m/3 dismal dusky o-yellow-orange	2,500.
35m/1 dim dusky green	2,500.
39m/1 dim dusky blue green	2,500.
47n/2 dull v. dusky green-blue blue	2,500.
49o/1 dim v. dusky blue	2,500.
61k/1 dim dark violet-red-violet	2,500.
71m/0 dusky violet-red-red	2,500.

291-E9

Incomplete engraving of entire design: vignette against top frame unfinished.

291-E9 50c Die on India, die sunk on card
black 3,000.
deep red orange 3,000.

291-E10

Incomplete engraving of entire design: engraving on bottom of miner's pan dots only, not lines as on issued stamp.

291-E10 50c Die on wove, dark green 3,000.

292-E1

Incomplete engraving of vignette only: initial state of die, lightly engraved.

292-E1 $1 Die on India, die sunk on card, black 6,500.

292-E2

Vignette further engraved: light shield-shaped vignette outline (later removed.)

292-E2 $1 Die on India, die sunk on card, black 7,500.

292-E3

Vignette further engraved: left front hoof of lead bull darker.

292-E3 $1 Die on India, die sunk on card, black 3,750.

Vignette similar to No. 292-E3 but with penciled modeling in snow and among cattle.

292-E4 $1 Die on India, die sunk on card, black 3,750.

292-E5

Vignette further engraved: foreground snow at left darkened, shield outline removed.

292-E5 $1 Die on India, die sunk on card, black 9,500.

292-E6

Incomplete engraving of entire bicolor design, in frame the shading on corn husks are unfinsihed, in vignette shading is missing in snow directly to the right of the title label.

Ridgway numbers used for colors of No. 292-E6, where available.

292-E6 $1 Die with black vignette, on India, die sunk on card

dull violet blue ("normal" bicolor)	700.
dull blue ("normal" bicolor)	700.
dull violet ("normal" bicolor)	3,000.
3k/0 dark orange red	3,000.
5m/0 dusky-o-orange-red	3,000.
7m/0 dusky red orange	3,000.
9m/0 dusky o-red-orange	3,000.
9n/3 dismal v. dusky o-red-orange	3,000.
13n/3 dismal v. dusky o-yellow-orange	3,000.
35m/1 dim dusky green	3,000.
43m/1 dim dusky green blue	3,000.
49m/1 dim dusky blue	3,000.
57k/4 smoky dark violet-blue violet	3,000.
63m/1 dim dusky red violet	3,000.
71-/0 violet-red-red	3,000.
47n/2 dull dusky green blue	3,000.
dark brown	3,000.

292-E7

Incomplete engraving of entire design: left frameline, cornhusks and shading in frame over cornhusks all unfinished.

292-E7 $1 Die on India, die sunk on card
black 3,000.
dusky orange red 3,000.

293-E1

Design size: 34x22mm
Die size: 73x63mm
Incomplete engraving of entire design with unadopted vignette, vignette of Western mining prospector as used on the 50c but labeled "HARVESTING IN THE WEST," frame shows $-sign same size as numeral "2."

293-E1 $2 Die on India, on card, dusky violet & black 3,500.

293-E2

Die size: 77x66mm
Incomplete engraving of Farming in the West vignette (originally intended for $2 but eventually used on 2c): initial state of die, very lightly engraved.

293-E2 $2 Die on India, die sunk on card, black 3,000.

293-E3

Vignette further engraved: four horses shaded, area at left still lightly engraved.

293-E3 $2 Die on India, die sunk on card, black 3,000.

293-E4

Vignette further engraved: background figures further engraved, pencil modeling added above and below half horse at left and on body of front right horse.

293-E4 $2 Die on India, die sunk on card, black 3,000.

293-E5

Vignette further engraved: engraving added to horses and to figures at left side of vignette.

293-E5 $2 Die on India, die sunk on card, black 3,000.

293-E6

Vignette further engraved: engraving added to harness at lead horse's shoulder, foreground in front of plow still unfinished.

293-E6 $2 Die on India, die sunk on card, black 3,000.

293-E7

Die size: 62x51mm
Incomplete engraving of entire bicolor design: only one plowshare shown, label longer, less foreground than on issued stamp.

Ridgway numbers used for colors of No. 293-E7.

293-E7 $2 Die with black vignette on India, die sunk on card

dusky orange red ("normal" bicolor; die size: 63x61mm)	700.
dark red orange ("normal" bicolor; die size: 63x61mm)	700.
1-/0 red	3,000.
3k/0 dark orange red	3,000.
7m/0 dusky red orange	3,000.
35m/1 dim dusky green	3,000.
39m/1 dim dusky blue green	3,000.
45o/1 dim v. dusky blue-green blue	3,000.
45m/2 dull dusky blue-green blue	3,000.
63m/1 dim dusky red violet	3,000.
71i/0 deep violet-red-red	3,000.
47n/2 dull dusky green blue	3,000.

The bicolored essays commonly offered as Nos. 285-293 "bicolored proofs" in "original colors," are Nos. 285-E8, 286-E8, 287-E9, 288-E5, 289-E4, 290-E4, 291-E8, 292-E6 and 293-E7. Value, set of nine $6,100.

293-E8

Die size: 82x68mm
Complete engraving with "HARVESTING IN THE WEST" $2 frame, vignette as adopted for 2c stamp but from a die not used for the stamp, horses at left vignette border engraved up to the border line.

293-E8 $2 Die on India, die sunk on card (marked "Proof from 1st die.")
black *2,500.*
dark orange red *2,500.*
blue *2,500.*

293-E8A

Complete engraving with "HARVESTING IN THE WEST" $2 frame, as No. 293-E8, but with engraving of vignette extended slightly toward frame border.

293-E8A $2 black *2,500.*

293-E9

Incomplete engraving of entire design: circles in upper corners of vignette next to value ovals, water next to right end of title label, corn husks in frame all unfinished. First state of the composite essay.

293-E9 $2 Die on India, die sunk on card, black *3,500.*

293-E10

Complete design, vignette further engraved: engraving completed between title and label, steamboat and frame, city next to right frame, near side of bridge and smoke shadow on water lighter than on issued stamp. Second state of the composite essay.

293-E10 $2 Die on India, die sunk on card, black *3,500.*

293-E11

Incomplete engraving of entire design as adopted: black wash over engraving on side of bridge and foreground (engraving under wash unfinished). Third state of the composite essay.

293-E11 $2 Die on India, die sunk on card, black *3,500.*

Edward Rosewater

Rosewater, of St. Louis, was asked by the Post Office Dept. in 1897 to submit proposed designs for the Trans-Mississippi Exposition issue. For that reason, they are listed here.

All are drawings on tracing paper, on 91x142mm buff card.

285-E11

Design size: 62x97mm
Wash drawing of cattle.

285-E11 1c dull orange *12,500.*

286-E11

Design size: 57x98mm
Wash drawing of mounted Indian saluting wagon train.

286-E11 2c deep orange red *12,500.*

288-E9

Design size: 61x100mm
Wash drawing of man plowing field.

288-E9 5c dark yellow green *12,500.*

290-E9

Design size: 62x99mm
Wash drawing of train coming around mountain.

290-E9 Ten Cents, dusky blue *12,500.*

292-E9

Design size: 60x98mm
Wash drawing of woman holding light, standing on globe.

292-E9 $1 deep orange yellow *12,500.*

PAN-AMERICAN ISSUE
Bureau of Engraving and Printing

294-E1

Design size: 114x82½mm
Preliminary pencil drawing for frame design as adopted.

294-E1 1c Drawing on tracing paper, black *1,750.*

Design size: 114x82½mm
Second state of ink drawing for frame design as adopted.

294-E2 1c Drawing on white card, about 6½x5 inches, black *1,750.*

294-E3

Second state of ink drawing for frame design reduced by Bureau of Engraving and Printing to stamp size.

294-E3 1c Reduced drawing on paper, mounted on 59x38mm black card, black —

294-E4

Similar to No. 294-E2, but design reduced to stamp size and with additional details added to columns and elsewhere, "1" denominations made wider (changed back to narrower on final frame engraving).

294-E4 1c Die on India, die sunk on 59x38mm black card, black 1,500.

294-E5

Engraving of vignette only, faint lines especially on the hull of the ship.

294-E5 1c 1c Die on India, die sunk on 107x88mm card, black *1,500.*

294-E6

Engraving of vignette only, various elements such as lines on hull of ship more deeply engraved.

294-E6 1c Die on India, die sunk on 94x78mm card, black 1,500.

294-E7

Engraving of vignette only, lines more deeply engraved than on Nos. 294-E5 and 294-E6, blue die number 10685 on back of card.

294-E7 1c Die on India, die sunk on 201x152mm card, black *1,500.*

294-E8

Die size: 87x68½mm
Engraving of vignette only, still more deeply engraved lines, more smoke from the funnel.

294-E8 1c Die on India, die sunk on card, black *1,500.*

294-E9

Engraving of both frame and vignette, on vignette long lines in the water, ship and sky unfinished

294-E9 1c Die on India, die sunk on 107x88mm card, green and black *1,750.*

295-E1

Design size: 108x82mm
Preliminary pencil drawing of frame similar to that adopted (side ornaments, etc., different); UR corner, etc., unfinished.

295-E1 2c Drawing on tracing paper, black *1,750.*

295-E2

Design size: 114x83mm
Preliminary pencil drawing of frame similar to No. 295-E1 (minor differences) but with UR corner complete.

295-E2 2c Drawing on tracing paper, black *1,500.*

295-E3

Design size: 108x82mm
Preliminary pencil drawing of frame design similar to No. 295-E2 but with minor differences at top, in lettering, etc.

295-E3 2c Drawing on tracing paper, black *1,750.*

295-E4

Design size: 95x70mm
Ink and wash drawing model of frame design as adopted, side torchbearers engraved on India as on U.S. Series of 1901 $10 note.

295-E4 2c Die on white card, about 108x82mm, black *1,750.*

295-E4A

Design size: 88x69mm
Incomplete engraving of vignette only.

295-E4A 2c Die on India, die sunk on card, black *3,500.*

295-E5

Design size: 27x19½mm
Die size: 88x68mm
Complete engraving of frame only as adopted.

295-E5 2c Die on India, die sunk on card, carmine *3,750.*

295-E6

Die size: 88½x69mm
Engraving of entire design with vignette incomplete near frame and on cars.

295-E6 2c Die on India, die sunk on card, carmine & black *2,250.*

296-E1

Preliminary pencil drawing of unadopted frame design.

296-E1 4c Drawing on tracing paper, black *1,750.*

296-E2

Design size: 114x82½mm
Final ink drawing for frame design as adopted.

296-E2 4c Drawing on white card, about 6½x5 inches, black *1,750.*

296-E3

Ink drawing of design in No. 296-E2 reduced by Bureau of Engraving and Printing to stamp size.

296-E3 4c Reduced drawing on paper, mounted on 59x38mm black card, black *750.*

296-E4

Design size: 27x19mm
Die size: 88x67mm
Incomplete engraving of entire design as adopted: lines missing at base of capitol dome, above driver's head.

296-E4 4c Die on India, die sunk on card, deep red brown & black *1,750.*

297-E1

Photo reproduction of pencil sketch of unadopted frame design on photosensitive tan paper, reduced to stamp size. Incomplete preliminary pencil drawing of frame design as adopted.

297-E1 5c Photo reproduction on tan paper *1,750.*

297-E2

Design size: 114x83mm
Incomplete preliminary pencil drawing of frame design as adopted.

297-E2 5c Drawing on tracing paper, black *1,750.*

297-E3

Design size: 114x82½mm
Final ink drawing for frame design as adopted.

297-E3 5c Drawing on white card, about 6½x5 inches, black *1,750.*

297-E4

Photo reproduction of sketch of adopted frame design on photosensitive paper, reduced to stamp size.

297-E4 5c Photo reproduction on tan paper *750.*

297-E5

Die size: 87x68mm
Incomplete engraving of vignette only.

297-E5 5c Die on India, die sunk on card, black *1,500.*

297-E6

Die size: 87x68mm
As No. 297-E5, but more completely engraved.

297-E6 5c Die on India, die sunk on card, black *1,500.*

297-E7

Design size: 27x19 ½mm
Die size: 87x68mm
Incomplete engraving of entire design as adopted: shading at bottom of battleaxes and scrolls at ends of title frame unfinished.

297-E7 5c Die on India, die sunk on card, blue & black *1,750.*

298-E1

Design size:108x82mm
Preliminary pencil drawing of unadopted frame design.

298-E1 8c Drawing on tracing paper, black *1,750.*

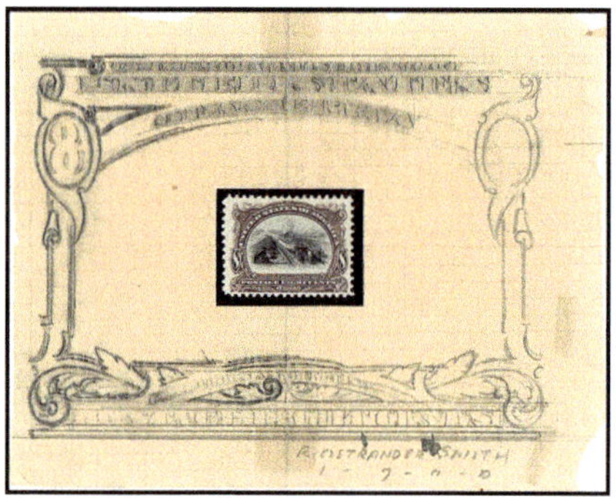

298-E2

Design size: 114x83mm
Incomplete preliminary pencil drawing of unadopted frame design.

298-E2 8c Drawing on tracing paper, black *1,750.*

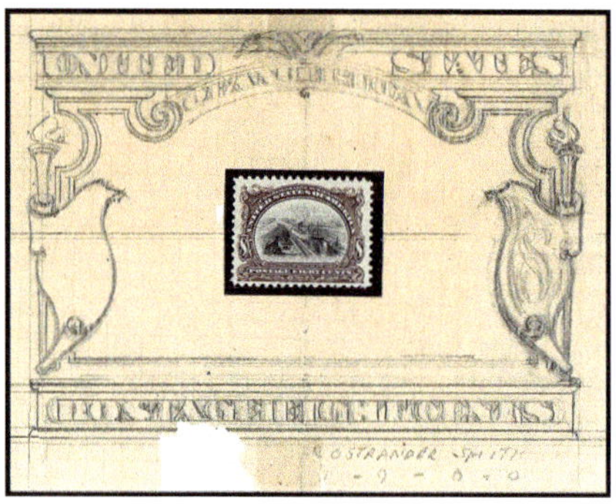

298-E3

Design size: 114x80mm
Preliminary pencil drawing of unadopted frame design.

298-E3 8c Drawing on tracing paper, black *1,500.*

298-E4

Design size: 114x83mm
Preliminary pencil drawing of frame design as adopted.

298-E4 8c Drawing on tracing paper, black *1,500.*

298-E5

Design size: 114x82 ½mm
Final ink drawing for frame design as adopted. No. 298-E5 has an example of No. 298 mounted in the vignette area.

298-E5 8c Drawing on white card, about 6 ½x5 inches, black *1,750.*

298-E6

Design size: 34x26mm
Photo reproduction of sketch of adopted frame design on photosensitive paper, reduced to stamp size.

298-E6 8c Photo reproduction on tan paper *1,250.*

298-E7

Design size: 27x20mm
Die size: 87x69mm
Incomplete engraving of entire design: shading lines of ornaments, scrolls and ribbons at top unfinished, vignette incomplete at right, no etching on building in left foreground.

298-E7 8c Die on India, die sunk on card, bi-colored *1,750.*

299-E1

Design size: 114x83mm
Preliminary pencil drawing of unadopted frame design (small blank oval at center).

299-E1 10c Drawing on tracing paper, black *1,750.*

299-E2

Design size: 114x82 ½mm
Similar to No. 299-E1 but with outline of eagle and shield in center oval.

299-E2 10c Drawing on tracing paper, black *1,750.*

299-E3

Design size: 114x83mm
Preliminary pencil drawing for frame design as adopted.

299-E3 10c Drawing on tracing paper, black *1,750.*

299-E4

Design size: 114x82 ½mm
Final ink drawing for frame design as adopted.

299-E4 10c Drawing on white card, about 6 ½x9 inches, black *1,750.*

299-E5

Photo reproduction of sketch of adopted frame design on photosensitive paper, reduced to stamp size.

299-E5 10c Photo reproduction on tan paper *750.*

299-E6

Die size: 87x68mm
Incomplete engraving of entire design: frame complete but lines later engraved in the mast, smokestack and sky.

299-E6 10c Die on India, die sunk on card, bi-colored *2,750.*

1902 ISSUE

300-E1

Incomplete engraving of vignette and lower part of frame.

300-E1 1c Die on India, die sunk on card, black *4,000.*

300-E2

Design size: 19x22mm
Die size: 74½x88½mm
Incomplete engraving of entire design: vignette background has horiz. lines only, neckpiece, men at sides, etc., all unfinished.

300-E2 1c Die on India, die sunk on card, black *3,500.*

300-E3

Design size: 136x190mm
Preliminary ink drawing for 5c frame design but later adopted for 1c.

300-E3 1c Drawing on manila paper, blue green, gray blue & black *2,000.*

No. 300-E3 is on the opposite side of the same piece of paper bearing No. 307-E1. Value is for both essays.

300-E4

Design size: 116x135mm
Preliminary pencil and ink drawing for frame design as adopted.

300-E4 1c Drawing on white card, black *3,000.*

301-E1

Design size: 162x188mm
Paper size: 169x214mm
Preliminary pencil drawing of frame design (Raymond Ostrander Smith). Not adopted.

301-E1 2c Drawing on yellowed transparent tracing paper, black *1,500.*

301-E1A

Preliminary pencil and ink drawing of unadopted frame design, on 77x82mm yellowish wove paper, folded vertically and with ink tracing of frame on reverse.

301-E1A 2c Drawing on woven paper, black *2,000.*

301-E1B

Design size: 145x168mm
Preliminary pencil drawing of frame design as adopted.

301-E1B 2c Drawing on tracing paper, black *3,500.*

301-E2

Model with vignette of Houdon bust of Washington, on wash drawing over photo reduced to stamp size for approval by PMG.

301-E2 2c Model mounted on card, black *750.*

301-E3

Design size: 19x22mm
Die size: 75x87½mm
Incomplete engraving of entire design: head unfinished, horiz. background lines only, frame unfinished, lettering either blank or unfinished.

301-E3 2c Die on India, die sunk on card, black *4,000.*

301-E4

Design size: 60x88mm
Preliminary pencil drawing of right numeral 2 design as adopted.

301-E4 2c Drawing on tracing paper, black *500.*

301-E5

Design size: 176x120mm
Preliminary pencil drawing of lower left and upper right design.

301-E5 2c Drawing on tracing paper, black *700.*

301-E6

Design size: 19x22mm
Die size: 74x89mm
Incomplete engraving of entire design: head unfinished, horiz. background lines only, frame almost finished, lettering complete. No. 62057 on back.

301-E6 2c Die on India, die sunk on 153x202mm card, black *3,000.*

302-E1

Design size: 19x22mm
Die size: 74½x88mm
Incomplete engraving of entire design: vignette unfinished, horiz. background lines only, atlantes at sides unfinished. No. 66218 on back.

302-E1 3c Die on India, die sunk on card, black *3,250.*

303-E1

Design size: 19x22mm
Die size: 75x88mm
Incomplete engraving of entire design: vignette unfinished on eyes, hair, beard, etc. No. 58920 on back.

303-E1 4c Die on India, die sunk on card, black *2,500.*

303-E2

Design size: 19x22mm
Incomplete engraving of entire design, shading lines in top of frame unfinished. No. 60085 on back.

303-E2 4c Die on India, die sunk on card, black *2,000.*

303-E3

Photograph of unaccepted design, stamp size, with white wash inside vignette and eagles in corners drawn in pen over portions of photo.

303-E3 4c Retouched photo-sensitive paper, black *900.*

303-E4

Photograph of unaccepted design with additional overlay photo of top portion of frame with eagles similar to those on No. 303-E3.

303-E4 4c Photo-sensitive paper mounted on paper, black *1,100.*

304-E1

Design size: 19x22mm
Die size: 74x87½mm
Rejected die: figure at right poorly draped, blank triangles below "UNITED STATES," no shading in frame around "POSTAGE/FIVE CENTS" except at extreme ends.

304-E1 5c Die on India, die sunk on card, blue *2,300.*

304-E2

Incomplete engraving of entire design: shading on side figures unfinished.

304-E2 5c Die on India, die sunk on card, blue *1,500.*

304-E3

Design size: 107x110mm
Paper size: 141x128mm
Preliminary pencil and ink drawing of unadopted frame design.

304-E3 5c Drawing on onion skin paper, black *1,500.*

Incomplete engraving of entire design as adopted.

305-E1 6c Die on India, lake *1,250.*

305-E2

Design size: 123x210mm
Preliminary ink drawing for unadopted frame design.

305-E2 6c Drawing on kraft paper, black & blue green *4,500.*

Nos. 305-E2, 306-E3 and 308-E2, are all on same piece of kraft paper, with No. 306-E3 on one side and the other two on the other side. Value is for the entire unit of three essays.

306-E1

Design size: 7x3½ inches
Preliminary pencil drawing of left side of frame design as adopted.

306-E1 8c Drawing on tracing paper, black *2,000.*

306-E2

Die size: 76x89mm
Incomplete engraving of vignette and numerals only: head drapery unfinished, horiz. background lines only.

306-E2 8c Die on India, die sunk on card, black *5,000.*

306-E3

Design size: 165x175mm
Preliminary ink drawing for unadopted frame design.

306-E3 8c Drawing on kraft paper, black, blue & green *4,500.*

See note after No. 305-E2.

307-E1

Design size: 135x174mm
Preliminary ink drawing for unadopted frame design.

307-E1 10c Drawing on kraft paper, gray blue *2,000.*

No. 307-E1 is on the opposite side of the same piece of paper bearing No. 300-E3. Value is for both essays.

308-E1

Design size: 19x22mm
Die size: 69x85½mm
Incomplete engraving of entire design: hair, beard, right cheek, eyes and right shoulder all unfinished, horiz. background lines only, name panel blank, ribbon shading unfinished, etc. No. 57796 on back.

308-E1 13c Die on India, die sunk on card, black *3,750.*

308-E2

Design size: 177x220mm
Preliminary ink drawing of 3c frame design but later adopted for 13c.

308-E2 13c Drawing on kraft paper, black & blue green *4,500.*

See note after No. 305-E2.

Design size: 19x22mm
Die size: 75x78mm
Incomplete engravng with complete portrait and initial lines of frame, blue "66439" handstamp on reverse.

309-E1 15c Die on India, die sunk on 153x204mm card, black *4,000.*

310-E1

Design size: 19x22mm
Die size: 74x87½mm
Incomplete engraving of entire design: hair and right cheek unfinished, horiz. background lines only, top of frame and eagles unfinished.

310-E1 50c Die on India, die sunk on card, black *4,000.*

310-E2

Incomplete engraving of entire design, further engraved than No. 310-E1: oval line outside top label thinner at bottom ends than on issued stamp.

310-E2 50c Die on India, die sunk on card, black *4,000.*

312-E1

Design size: 19x22mm
Die size: 76x88mm
Incomplete engraving of entire design: hair, neckpiece, etc., unfinished, horiz. background lines only; top of frame, leaves and numeral surrounds all unfinished.

312-E1 $2 Die on India, die sunk on card, black *4,500.*

313-E1

Design size: 19x22mm
Die size: 75½x87½mm
Incomplete engraving of entire design: eyes, cheeks, hair, neckpiece all unfinished, horiz. background lines only, frame engraved in outlines only.

313-E1 $5 Die on India, die sunk on card, dark green *12,000.*

319-E1

Design size: 19½x22mm
Die size: 75x87½mm
Incomplete engraving of entire design from rejected die (central star between UNITED and STATES, four lines above small lettering, bottom of shield curved): name and date ribbon blank.

319-E1 2c Die on India, die sunk on card, carmine *5,250.*

319-E2

Incomplete engraving of entire design from rejected die: shading on leaves and vignette completed, lettering added to bottom ribbon and started on label above vignette. Blue pencil note on card backing, "May 1903. This die was abandoned at this stage because of crowded condition of lettering above portrait. G.F.C.S." No. 83909 on back.

319-E2 2c Die on India, die sunk on card, carmine *5,250.*

319-E3

Design size: 19½x22mm
Die I size: 75½x88mm
Incomplete engraving of entire design as adopted (no star between UNITED and STATES, bottom of shield straight): small label above vignette is blank.

319-E3 2c Die on India, die sunk on card, black *5,250.*

LOUISIANA PURCHASE ISSUE

324-E1

Incomplete engraving of entire design: head, hair, eyes, chin, coat all unfinished, horiz. background lines only, bottom label and upper corner labels blank, frame shading unfinished.

324-E1 2c Die on India, die sunk on card, black *3,250.*

325-E1

Incomplete engraving of entire design: head only lightly engraved, horiz. background lines only, laurel leaves unshaded, leaves' background and numeral shields blank.

325-E1 3c Die on India, die sunk on card, black *3,250.*

326-E1

Incomplete engraving of entire design: vignette unfinished, horiz. background lines only, much of frame blank or incomplete.

326-E1 5c Die on India, die sunk on card, black blue *3,500.*

JAMESTOWN ISSUE

328-E1

Incomplete engraving of entire design: vignette, shading on heads in upper corners, numerals and numeral shields all unfinished.

328-E1 1c Die on pale cream soft wove, 30x24mm, dusky green *1,250.*

328-E2

Incomplete engraving of entire design: vignette, shading on heads in upper corners, and value tablets unfinished, pencil note "unfinished" at bottom of card.

328-E2 1c Die on India, die sunk on card, 109x94mm, green *2,400.*

330-E1

Incomplete engraving of vignette only: collar, hat, corselet, etc., unfinished. No. 245910 on back.

330-E1 5c Die on India, die sunk on card, 123x132mm, black *2,400.*

330-E2

Incomplete engraving of entire design: no shading in frame background.

330-E2 5c Die on India, die sunk on card, 109x95mm, blue *6,300.*

330-E3

Incomplete engraving of entire design: shading on corselet and arm of Pocahontas unfinished, horiz. background lines only, shading around date and name ribbon unfinished. No. 247606 on back.

330-E3 5c Die on card, 123x175mm, die sunk, blue *4,500.*

Incomplete engraving of entire design: shading on ribbons unfinished.

330-E4 5c Die on India, die sunk on card, 108x98mm, black *6,300.*

1908 ISSUE

331-E1

Photograph of wash drawing of entire design, head and vignette background retouched with black wash. Ms. "GVLM-Sept. 26th-1908" (PMG) in LR corner of backing card.

331-E1 1c Retouched photo on thick gray cardboard, 83x100mm, black *3,750.*

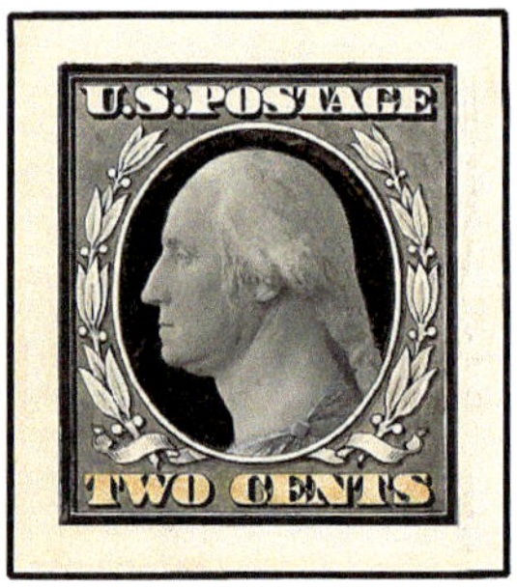

332-E1

Design size: 6⅛x7¼ inches
Wash drawing of frame design with vignette cut out, mounted over retouched glossy black photo of Houdon bust of Washington.

332-E1 Two Cents, Design on drawing paper, black *1,250.*

332-E1A

Design size: 19x22mm
Photograph of wash drawing of entire design, denomination blank, part of design hand-painted in black ink and wash.

332-E1A (2c) Retouched photo on 30x34mm card, black *3,250.*

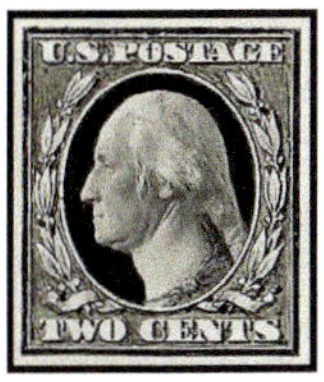
332-E2

Design size: 19x22mm
Photograph of wash drawing of entire design, almost completely retouched with black ink and wash. Pencil "GVLM" (PMG) at top of backing card.

332-E2 Two Cents, Retouched photo on thick gray cardboard, 81x100mm, black *2,000.*

332-E3

Design size: 19x22mm
Incomplete engraving of entire design: shading on leaves at right unfinished. Pencil "Oct 15 - 1908" at LR of backing card.

332-E3 Two Cents, Die on India, die sunk on card, carmine *1,250.*

333-E1

Design size: 18½x22mm
Engraving of design as adopted except "THREE CENTS" at bottom.

333-E1 Three Cents, Die printed directly on card, deep violet *1,250.*

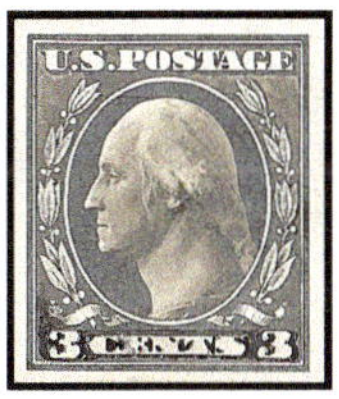
333-E2

Design size: 19x22mm
Photograph of wash drawing of entire design with "3 CENTS 3" drawn in black and white wash. Ms. "Nov. 24/08. J.E.R." (BEP director) in LR corner of backing card.

333-E2 3c Retouched photo on thick gray cardboard, 80x100mm, black *2,000.*

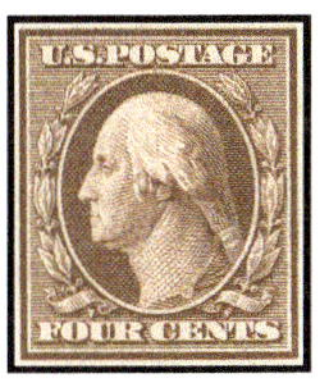
334-E1

Design size: 18½x22mm
Engraving of design as adopted except "FOUR CENTS" at bottom.

334-E1 Four Cents, Die printed directly on card, orange brown *1,250.*

334-E2

Design size: 19x22mm
Photograph of wash drawing of entire design with "4 CENTS 4" drawn in black and white wash. Ms. "Nov. 24/08. J.E.R." (BEP director) in LR corner of backing card.

334-E2 4c Retouched photo on thick gray cardboard, 80x100mm, black *2,000.*

335-E1

Design size: 18½x22mm
Engraving of design as adopted except "FIVE CENTS" at bottom.

335-E1 Five Cents, Die printed directly on card, blue *1,500.*

335-E2

Design size: 19x22mm
Photograph of wash drawing of entire design with "5 CENTS 5" drawn in black and white wash. Ms. "Nov. 24/08. J.E.R." (BEP director) in LR corner of backing card.

335-E2 5c Retouched photo on thick gray cardboard, 80x100mm, black *2,000.*

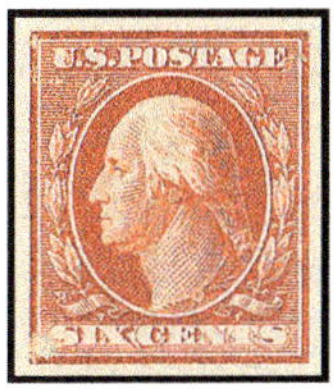
336-E1

Design size: 18½x22mm
Incomplete engraving of design with "SIX CENTS" at bottom.

336-E1 Six Cents, Die on India, on card, red orange *1,250.*

336-E2

Design size: 19x22mm
Photograph of wash drawing of entire design with "6 CENTS 6" drawn in black and white wash. Ms. "Nov. 24/08. J.E.R." (BEP director) in LR corner of backing card.

336-E2 6c Retouched photo on thick gray cardboard, 80x100mm, black *2,000.*

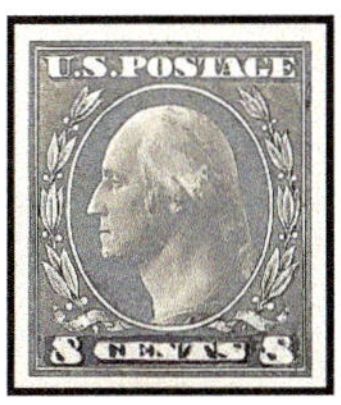
337-E1

Design size: 19x22mm
Photograph of wash drawing of entire design with "8 CENTS 8" drawn in black and white wash. Ms. "Nov. 24/08. J.E.R." (BEP director) in LR corner of backing card.

337-E1 8c Retouched photo on thick gray cardboard, 80x100mm, black *2,000.*

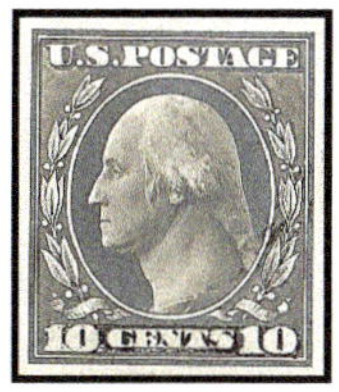
338-E1

Design size: 19x22mm
Photograph of wash drawing of entire design with "10 CENTS 10" drawn in black and white wash. Ms. "Nov. 24/08. J.E.R." (BEP director) in LR corner of backing card.

338-E1 10c Retouched photo on thick gray cardboard, 80x100mm, black *2,000.*

338a-E1

Design size: 18½x22mm
Complete engraving of entire adopted design but a value not issued: "12 CENTS 12" at bottom. Virtually all are stamp size, imperf.

Ridgway numbers used for colors of No. 338a-E1.

338a-E1 12c
- ***a.*** Die on bluish white wove
  - 41n/1 dim v. dusky b-blue-green *900.*
- ***b.*** Die on 1f/1 dim pale red wove
- ***c.*** Die on 7d/1 dim light red orange wove
  - 47m/1 dim dusky g-b. blue *900.*
- ***d.*** Die on 17b/1 dim bright o-y. yellow wove
  - 1i/0 deep red *900.*
  - 5i/0 deep o-orange-red *900.*
  - 27m/0 dusky green yellow *900.*
  - 37m/0 dusky g-blue-green *900.*
  - 41m/0 dusky b-blue-green *900.*
  - 55m/1 dim dusky blue violet *900.*
  - 59m/1 dim dusky violet *900.*
  - 69m/3 dismal dusky r-violet-red *900.*
- ***e.*** Die on 19f/0 pale y-orange yellow wove
  - 1i/0 deep red *900.*
  - 15i/1 dim deep yellow orange *900.*
  - 35m/0 dusky green *900.*
  - 43d/1 dim light green blue *900.*
  - 61m/3 dismal dusky v-red-violet *900.*
  - 69o/5 black *900.*
- ***f.*** Die on 31f/2 dull pale yellow green wove
  - 69o/5 black *900.*
- ***g.*** Die on 42d/1 dim bright green blue wove
  - 41m/1 dim dusky b-blue-green *900.*
- ***h.*** Die on 44-/1 dim medium green blue wove
  - 9k/2 dull dark o-r-orange *900.*
- ***i.*** Die on 45l/1 dim v. dark b-green-blue wove
  - 5i/0 deep o-orange-red *900.*
  - 27m/2 dull dusky green yellow *900.*
- ***j.*** Die on 69g/0 pale r-v. red wove *900.*
- ***k.*** Die on dark blue bond, 69o/5 black *900.*

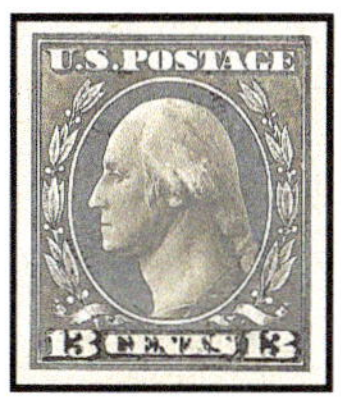
339-E1

Design size: 19x22mm
Photograph of wash drawing of entire design with "13 CENTS 13" drawn in black and white wash. Ms. "Oct. 7-08. J.E.R.-GVLM" (BEP director, PMG) in LL corner of backing card.

339-E1 13c Retouched photo on thick gray cardboard, 80x100mm, black *2,000.*

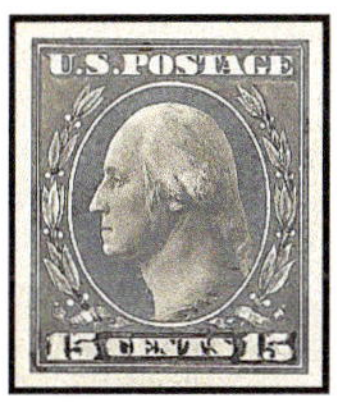
340-E1

Design size: 19x22mm

Photograph of wash drawing of entire design with "15 CENTS 15" drawn in black and white wash. Ms. "Oct. 7-08. J.E.R.-GVLM" (BEP director, PMG) at bottom of backing card.

340-E1 15c Retouched photo on thick gray cardboard, 80x100mm, black *2,000.*

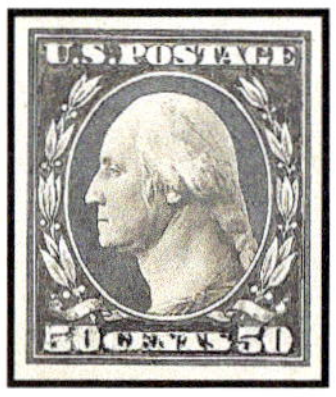

341-E1

Design size: 19x22mm
Photograph of wash drawing of entire design with "50 CENTS 50" drawn in black and white wash. Ms. "Oct. 7-08. J.E.R.-GVLM" (BEP director, PMG) at bottom of backing card.

341-E1 50c Retouched photo on thick gray cardboard, 80x100mm, black *2,000.*

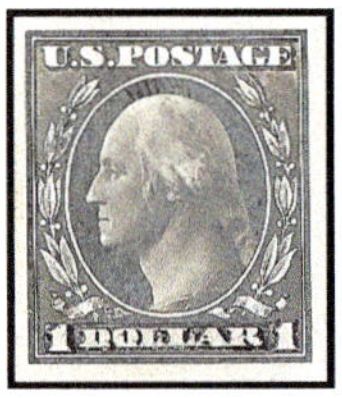

342-E1

Design size: 19x22mm
Photograph of wash drawing of entire design with "1 DOLLAR 1" drawn in black and white wash. Ms. "Oct. 7-08. J.E.R.-GVLM" (BEP director, PMG) at bottom of backing card.

342-E1 $1 Retouched photo on thick gray cardboard, 80x100mm, black *2,000.*

LINCOLN MEMORIAL ISSUE

Design size: 7x8 inches
Photostat of 1908 2c frame design with wash drawing of ribbons and vignette photo of Lincoln's head.

367-E1 Two Cents, Model of Lincoln design, black *1,500.*

367-E2

Photo of No. 367-E1 reduced to stamp size, retouched to highlight hair and beard, dates added.

367-E2 Two Cents, Retouched photo, black *1,350.*

367-E3

Design size: 19x22mm
Incomplete engraving of entire design: head, background, name/date ribbon all unfinished.

367-E3 Two Cents, Die on India, die sunk on card, 148x201mm, carmine *4,500.*

ALASKA-YUKON-PACIFIC EXPOSITION ISSUE

370-E1

Design size: 18½x22mm
Wash drawing of frame similar to 1908 2c design with photo of wash drawing of seal on ice cake as vignette. Ms. "#1" at top of backing card.

370-E1 2c Model on card, about 3x4 inches, black *1,500.*

370-E2

Design size: 18½x22mm
Engraved frame similar to 1908 2c but with wash drawing of "1870 1909" in ribbons and "2 CENTS 2" at bottom, vignette cut out, mounted over engraved vignette of Wm. H. Seward from snuff stamp. Ms. "#2" at UL corner of backing card.

370-E2 2c Model on card, about 3x4 inches, black *1,500.*

370-E3

Design size: 27½x20½mm
Photo of seal on ice cake vignette as originally approved, mounted on ink and wash drawing of frame design as approved. Ms. "#3" at UL corner of backing card, engraved Seward vignette pasted on at bottom, "Approved April 3, 1909 FH Hitchcock Postmaster-General" at right.

370-E3 2c Model on glazed card, 93x70mm, black, white and gray *6,000.*

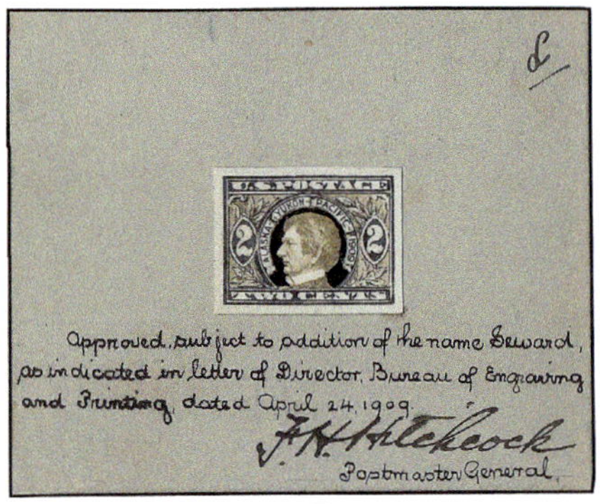

370-E4

Design size: 27½x20mm
Photo of wash drawing of frame and arched ribbon as adopted, vignette cut out, mounted over photo of engraved Seward vignette, background retouched with black wash. Ms. "Approved subject to addition of the name Seward, as indicated in letter of Director, Bureau of Engraving and Printing, dated April 24, 1909. F.H. Hitchcock Postmaster General."

370-E4 2c Model on 93x75mm thick gray card, black *2,250.*

370-E5

Design size: 27x20mm
Retouched photo of wash drawing of adopted frame with seal on ice cake vignette but pencil "WILLIAM H. SEWARD" on white wash ribbon below. Ms. "April 26/09 Approved J.E.R." (BEP director) at LR corner of backing card.

370-E5 2c Retouched photo and pencil on 94x66mm thick gray card, black *2,000.*

Incomplete engraving of entire design: no shading on head or vignette background, no shading lines on ribbons.

370-E6 2c Die on India, die sunk on 8x6 inch card, carmine *2,000.*

370-E7

Design size: 26½x19½mm
Similar to No. 370-E6 but further engraved: face and collar lightly engraved, horiz. background lines only, no shading lines on ribbons.

370-E7 2c Die on wove, 32x26½mm, carmine *2,000.*

372-E1

Wash drawing of adopted vignette design.

372-E1 2c Drawing on artist's cardboard, 11¼x6¾ inches, black *2,000.*

372-E2

Wash drawing of frame design as adopted except "HUDSON-FULTON CENTENARY" at top.

372-E2 2c Drawing on artist's cardboard, $7\frac{3}{4}$x$6\frac{3}{4}$ inches, black *3,000.*

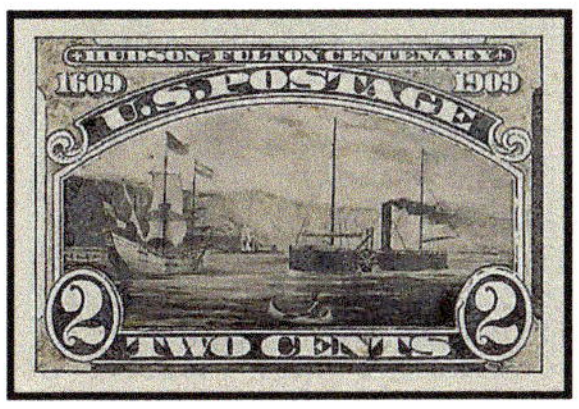

372-E3

Design size: 33x21½mm
Wash drawing of frame design as adopted with dates "1609-1807" and photo of No. 372-E1 reduced to fit and worked over with wash.

372-E3 2c Model on card, 4x3 inches, black *3,600.*

372-E4

Design size: 33x21½mm
Wash drawing of frame with vignette cut out, mounted over photo of No. 372-E1. Typed/ms. "Approved August 17, 1909 F.H. Hitchcock Postmaster General" and "August 19, 1909 Amend by substituting word 'Celebration' for 'Centenary.' F.H. Hitchcock Postmaster General." Pencil "P.O. 488" in LR corner.

372-E4 2c Model on white card, 126x100mm, black *4,750.*

372-E5

Incomplete engraving of entire design: lettering on flag at masthead of *Clermont* has "N" reversed and no "T."

372-E5 2c Die on wove, 38x27mm, carmine *2,000.*

PANAMA-PACIFIC ISSUE

397-E1

Design size: 27x20mm
Photo of incomplete frame with overlay of circular photo vignette as adopted, with wash drawing of palm trees on each side and "1 CENT 1" in wash. Ms. "Approved July 16, 1912 Frank H. Hitchcock Postmaster General" on backing card.

397-E1 1c Model on card, about 89x77mm, black *1,500.*

Design size: 27x20mm
Photo of incomplete frame with overlay circular photo vignette as adopted, with wash drawing of palm trees on each side and "1 CENT 1" in wash, with "Approved" and signed by the BEP Director J.E. Ralph, but "Opening of Panama Canal 1913" later changed for stamp to "San Francisco 1913."

397-E2 1c Model on thick gray card, 106x86mm, black *1,500.*

398-E1

Design size: about 29½x20mm
Ink and wash drawing of frame design longer than adopted with photo of wash drawing of Golden Gate as eventually used (reduced) on 5c. Backstamp "STAMP DIVISION FEB. 12, 1912 P.O. DEPT" on backing card.

398-E1 2c Model on card, about 4x3 inches, black *2,500.*

398-E2

Design size: 27x20mm
Photo of incomplete frame with photo of wash drawing of vignette as adopted with title "GATUN LOCKS," wash drawing of value numerals. Ms. "Approved Aug. 27, 1912 Frank H. Hitchcock Postmaster General" on backing card.

398-E2 2c Model on thick gray card, 99x72mm, black *1,500.*

Very similar to No. 398-E2 with slightly different wash touch-up and "2"s, with "Approved" and signed by BEP Director J.E. Ralph.

398-E2A 2c Model on thick gray card, 107x86mm, black *1,500.*

398-E3

Completely engraved design as adopted except titled "GATUN LOCKS" in error (design pictures Pedro Miguel locks).

398-E3 2c
- ***a.*** Large die on India, die sunk on card, 202x152mm, carmine *10,000.*
- ***b.*** Small die on India (formerly #398AP2), carmine *6,000.*

398-E4

Design size: 27x20mm
Photo of incomplete engraving (no sky in vignette) with "GATUN LOCKS" in error, ms. "Approved Dec. 17, 1912 Frank Hitchcock Postmaster General" on backing card.

398-E4 2c Model on thick gray card, 97x74mm, black *1,500.*

399-E1

Design size: 27x20mm
Photo of wash drawing of frame design as adopted with photo of wash drawing of adopted vignette mounted in place, with additional hand touch-up done in wash on vignette, ms. "Approved July 16, 1912 Frank H., Hitchcock Postmaster General" on backing card.

399-E1 5c Model on 30x22mm white paper, mounted on card, 97x73mm, black *1,500.*

Very similar to No. 399-E1 with slightly different wash touch-up and no steamship below sun, with "Approved" and signed by BEP Director J.E. Ralph.

399-E2 5c Model on thick gray card, 106x86mm, black *1,500.*

400-E1

Design size: 27x20mm
Photo of wash drawing of frame design as adopted with photo of painting adopted for vignette mounted in place, ms. printed "Approved" and dated and signed " Aug. 22, 1912, Frank H. Hitchcock Postmaster General" on backing card.

400-E1 10c Model on 31x34mm white paper, on thick gray card, 98x73mm, black *1,500.*

Very similar to No. 400-E1 with more extensive touching-up of the vignette and frame, with "Approved" and signed by BEP Director J.E. Ralph.

400-E1A 10c Model on thick gray card, 107x86mm, black *1,500.*

400-E2

Design size: 27x20mm
Photo of wash drawing of frame design as adopted with photo of wash drawing of two galleons at anchor in bay, titled "CABRILLO 1542" mounted in place. Backing card marked "II."

400-E2 10c Model on white paper, on 91x85mm thick gray card, black *1,500.*

400-E3

Design size: 27x20mm
Photo of wash drawing of frame design as adopted with photo of Liberty standing among palm fronds, wash touch-up on vignette and "10" denominations drawn in black and white wash, two battleships in bay. Backing card marked "III."

400-E3 10c Model on white paper, on thick gray card, 90x84mm, black *1,500.*

400-E4

Design size: 27x20mm
Similar to No. 400-E3 but steamships replace battleships. Backing card marked "IV."

400-E4 10c Model on white paper, on thick gray card, 90x83mm, black *1,500.*

400-E5

Design size: 27x20mm
Similar to No. 400-E2 but different hand drawn vignette picturing two galleons under full sail in front of snowclad mountains. Backing card marked "V."

400-E5 10c Model on white paper, on thick gray card, 89x83mm, black *1,500.*

1912 ISSUE

Incomplete engraving of entire design, except value tablet area which is '1 CENT 1' at bottom drawn in wash. Ms. "Approved. July 17, 1911 Frank H. Hitchcock. P.M. Gen." on backing card.

405-E1 1c Model on 3½x3¾-inch card, black *6,000.*

406-E1

Incomplete engraving of entire design, except value tablet area which is '2 CENTS 2' at bottom drawn in wash. Ms. "Approved. July 17, 1911 Frank H. Hitchcock P. M. Gen." on backing card.

406-E1 2c Model on 3⅜x3 11/16-inch card, black —

414-E1

Wash drawing of design as adopted, worked over partial photo with 8 in lower corners drawn in wash. Ms. "Approved. July 17, 1911 Frank H. Hitchcock Postmaster General" on backing card.

414-E1 8c Model on 3½x3¾-inch card, black *2,000.*

414-E2

Vignette of head only without background gridwork, control #490311 on back of card.

414-E2 8c Die on India, die sunk on 152x202mm, olive green *2,250.*

416-E1

Design size: 19x22mm
Photo of wash drawing of generic design with 10 in lower corners drawn in black ink. Ms. "July 17, 1911. (May, 1911 erased) Approved: Frank H. Hitchcock PM Gen" on backing card, backstamped "STAMP DIVISION P.O. DEPT. MAY 15, 1911."

416-E1 10c Model on 87x113mm thick gray card, black *2,000.*

418-E1

Design size: 19x22mm
Photo of wash drawing of generic design with background of frame between oval and outer colorless line in dark gray wash and some colorless retouching, 15 in lower corners drawn in black ink. Ms. "July 17, 1911. (May, 1911 erased) Approved: Frank H. Hitchcock PM Gen" on backing card, backstamped "STAMP DIVISION P.O. DEPT. MAY 15, 1911."

418-E1 15c Model on 87x113mm thick gray card, black *2,000.*

421-E1

Design size: 19x22mm
Photo of wash drawing of generic design with 50 in lower corners drawn in black ink. Ms. "July 17, 1911. (May, 1911 erased) Approved: Frank H. Hitchcock PM Gen" on backing card, backstamped "STAMP DIVISION P.O. DEPT. MAY 15, 1911."

421-E1 50c Model on 77x112mm thick gray card, black *2,000.*

423-E1

Design size: 19x22mm
Photo of wash drawing of generic design with entire value label drawn in black ink. Ms. "July 17, 1911. (May, 1911 erased) Approved: Frank H. Hitchcock PM Gen" on backing card, backstamped "STAMP DIVISION P.O. DEPT. MAY 15, 1911."

423-E1 $1 Model on 87x113mm thick gray card, black *2,000.*

1916 PRECANCEL ESSAYS

499-E1

Design size: 19x22mm
Die size: 90x88mm
"NEW YORK/N.Y." precancel engraved directly onto type I die, printed in one color. Ms. "8/16/22 J.S." in LR corner of backing card on No. 499-E1a. Although dated 1922, records indicate an original proof was pulled in 1916.

499-E1 2c
- ***a.*** Die on India, die sunk on card, lake —
- ***b.*** Die on bond paper, 33x36mm, dark carmine —

1918 ISSUE

Complete engraving of Franklin head only as on $2 and $5 values, no shading around head, control #834424 on back of card.

523-E2 $2 Die on India, die sunk on 151x103mm card, black *1,750.*

523-E3

Design size: 16x18¾mm
Complete engraving of vignette only including shading. Pencil control # "837660 May 1917" on back of India paper, pencil "Schofield" at bottom of backing card (#523-E3a), or control #837662 (1917) on back of card (No. 523-E3b).

523-E3 $2
- ***a.*** Die on 32x33mm India, card mounted, black 1,000.
- ***b.*** Die on wove, die sunk on card, 203x151mm, black 1,000.

PEACE ISSUE

537-E1

Design size: 21½x18½mm
Stamp never issued due to World War I.

537-E1 2c
- ***a.*** Die on India, die sunk on card, deep red 2,250.
- ***b.*** Die on wove, die sunk on card, 201x138mm, signed on card by Harry S. New 4,000.

537-E2

Die size: 22x19mm
Stamp never issued due to World War I.

537-E2 5c
- ***a.*** Die on India, die sunk on card, dim dusky g-b-blue 2,000.
- ***b.*** Die on wove, die sunk on card, 201x138mm, signed on card by Harry S. New 4,000.

SAMUEL F.B. MORSE ISSUE

537-E3

Design size: 21½x18½mm
Incomplete engraving of entire design: vignette and lettering finished but blank spaces beside vignette. Backstamped "932944" and "Jan. 1, 1919" or "932945" and "Jan. 7, 1919". Frame design subsequently used for 3c Victory issue, No. 537, though lettering and value numerals made slightly smaller.

537-E3 3c Die on India, die sunk on card, 141x173mm (#932944) or 151x202mm (#932945), black *3,000.*

VICTORY ISSUE

537-E4

Design size: 21½x18½mm
Die size: 85½x75½mm
Incomplete engraving of entire design: no shading in border and some flags unfinished. Backstamped "936356 Jan. 25, 1919."

537-E4 3c Die on India, die sunk on card, black *3,000.*

PILGRIM ISSUE

548-E1

Design size: 26x19mm
Incomplete engraving of entire design: sky blank, sails unshaded.

548-E1 1c Die on India, die sunk on card, 201x151mm, green *1,600.*

Almost complete engraving of entire design as adopted, but no crosshatching behind the "1" denominations.

548-E2 1c Die on India, die sunk on card, 203x151mm, green *1,600.*

549-E1

Incomplete engraving of frame only: "CENTS" engraved but numeral circles blank (probably an essay for the 2c and 5c).

549-E1 Die on India, die sunk on card
- black *1,600.*
- green *1,600.*

549-E2

Design size: 26x19mm
Incomplete engraving of entire design: vignette unfinished, control #1063097 on back of card.

549-E2 2c Die on India, die sunk on card, 202x151mm, black *1,600.*

549-E3

Incomplete engraving of entire design, virtually complete but no crosshatching behind the numeral "2" denominations.

549-E3 2c
- ***a.*** Die on India, die sunk on card, 202x151mm, control #1063875 on back, black 1,600.
- ***b.*** Die on India, die sunk on card, 202x151mm, control #1064174 or #1064271 on back, carmine rose 1,600.

1922 ISSUE

551-E1

Design size: 19x22mm
Incomplete engraving of entire design as adopted: name label blank, vignette unfinished. Ms. "Approved--Harry S. New" on backing card on olive brown essay; others not signed but with notation of denomination of stamp for color used ("1c" for green, etc.)

551-E1 ½c Die on India, die sunk on 151x202mm card

olive brown	*3,000.*
green	*2,500.*
carmine	*2,500.*
orange	*2,500.*
rose	*2,500.*
yellow	*2,500.*
blue green	*2,500.*
yellow green	*2,500.*
carmine rose	*2,500.*

Incomplete engraving of entire design but further engraved than No. 551-E1: no lines in white oval over ends of title ribbon and ribbon foldunders not etched as darkly as on issued stamp.

551-E2 ½c Die on India, die sunk on 149x201mm card, olive brown *1,500.*

Nos. 555-E1 Thru 571-E1 Are For Pencil Drawings Of Unadopted Frame Designs, Each On Thin Tissue Paper

555-E1

557-E1

555-E1 3c black 1,150.
557-E1 5c black 1,150.
557-E2 5c black 1,150.
566-E1 15c black 1,150.
571-E1 $1 black 1,150.

555-E2

Incomplete engraving, no engraving around bust of Lincoln, no denomination.

555-E2 (3c) Die on India, affixed to 5x6¾inch card, black *3,000.*

555-E3

Complete engraving with cross-hatched lines surrounding bust of Lincoln.

555-E3 3c Die on India, affixed to card, 26x30mm, violet *3,250.*

560-E1

Complete engraving with background of cross-hatched lines surrounding slightly larger bust of Grant.

560-E1 8c Die on India, die sunk on 97x111mm card, dark olive green *2,000.*

567-E2

Design size: 19x22mm
Engraving of unadopted vignette with unadopted engraved frame cut away.

567-E2 20c Die on India, die sunk on 151x201mm card, cobalt blue *1,750.*

568-E2

Design size: 19x15mm
Die size: 88x75mm
Engraving of adopted vignette with engraved frame cut away.

568-E2 25c Die on India, die sunk on 202x151mm card, green *1,750.*

573-E1

Engraving of accepted vignette.

573-E1 $5 Die on India, affixed to card, 73x87mm, blue *3,750.*

HUGUENOT-WALLOON TERCENTENARY ISSUE

614-E1

Design size: 8½x7¼ inches
Preliminary pencil drawing of *Nieu Nederland* in circular frame. Pencil note: "Reverse — Sailing to America, not away from America — J. B. Stoudt" originally on drawing has been removed.

614-E1 1c black *1,000.*

615-E1

Incomplete engraving of entire design, background of vignette incomplete and central figures only roughed in.

615-E1 2c Die on India, 82x69mm, black *4,500.*

616-E1

Design size: 5½x3⅛ inches
Wash drawing of design adopted for vignette.

616-E1 5c black *1,500.*

617-E1

Almost complete engraving of entire design, lacking strong shading in the foreground of the vignette.

617-E1 1c Die on India, die sunk on card, 126x115mm, green *1,500.*

618-E1

Design size: 36x21mm
Incomplete engraving of entire design as adopted: spaces between letters of "BIRTH OF LIBERTY" not solid color.

618-E1 2c Die on India, die sunk on card, black *1,250.*

618-E2

Design size: 36x21mm
Incomplete engraving of entire design as adopted: numeral circles blank, many shading lines missing in vignette, no shading around "TWO CENTS," etc.

618-E2 2c Die on India, die sunk on 91x71mm card, black *1,500.*

618-E3

Design size: 36x21mm
Engraving of frame only, without vignette or value tablets, control #1317765 on back of card.

618-E3 2c Die on India, die sunk on card, 202x118mm, carmine *1,500.*

NORSE-AMERICAN ISSUE

620-E1

Design size: 21½x19mm
Die essay on wove, vignette complete, frame with blank ribbon and without dates and "CENTENNIAL," hinged onto a 3½ inch square matboard.

620-E1 2c Die essay with frame incomplete, carmine and black *2,500.*

621-E1

Design size: 21½x19mm
Engraving of frame only.

621-E1 5c Die on India, die sunk on card, dark blue *3,000.*

ERICSSON MEMORIAL ISSUE

Wash drawing of design as adopted, stamp size.

628-E1 5c black *750.*

BATTLE OF WHITE PLAINS ISSUE

629-E1

Design size: 8⅜x9 inches
Preliminary ink and watercolor drawing of entire design quite similar to that adopted.

629-E1 2c black & red *750.*

629-E2

Design size: 22x19mm
Card size: 94x66mm
Unfinished engraving of design, vignette, background, foreground, flags and ribbons incomplete, "70010" control number on back.

629-E2 2c Die on India, mounted on card, carmine rose *1,500.*

BURGOYNE CAMPAIGN ISSUE

644-E1

Design size: 22x19mm
Essay size: 25x22mm
Card size: 78x98mm
Photo of wash drawing of unadopted design, on white paper mounted on thick gray card with "Approved" in ink and "May 7, 1927" in pencil subsequently crossed out with "X's."

644-E1 2c black *1,500.*

683-E1

Design size: 13x17 inches
Preliminary ink drawing of design nearly as adopted.

683-E1 2c Drawing on artist's cardboard, black *500.*

American flag and pencil touch-up of outer frame on photo of artist's model with vignette as adopted but entirely different frame.

690-E1 2c black *400.*

702-E1

Engraving of entire design without red cross, engraved cross shows faintly, control #70015 on back of card.

702-E1 2c Die on India, die sunk on 120x142mm card, black *5,000.*

704-E1

Design size: 119x150mm
Preliminary pencil sketch of unadopted ½c design.

704-E1 ½c Drawing on tracing paper, mounted on 195x192mm manila paper, black *2,500.*

718-E1

Design size: 6x7 inches
Watercolor drawing of unadopted design with 2c denomination.

718-E1 2c Drawing on thick artist's card, red *2,500.*

719-E1

Design size: 6x7 inches
Watercolor drawing of entire design similar to that eventually adopted for 5c but with 2c denomination.

719-E1 2c Drawing on thick artist's card, 150x175mm, blue *1,750.*

Engraving of vignette as adopted, within frame, but reversed from final design, without denomination or inscriptions.

742-E1 3c Die on white card, 88x69mm, black *1,750.*

786-E1

Unadopted engraving of entire design without denomination, portraits as adopted but rest of design different from accepted design, control #70027 on back of card.

786-E1 2c Die on wove, die sunk on card, 202x153mm, carmine *1,500.*

791-E1

Engravings of Decatur and MacDonough as adopted, widely spaced.

791-E1 2c Die on wove, die sunk on card, 202x153mm, carmine *1,500.*

791-E2

Engraving of incomplete design without central vignette, control #491747 (1936) on back of card.

791-E2 2c Die on wove, die sunk on card, 198x136mm, carmine *1,500.*

793-E1

Unfinished engravings of three portraits only, control #70031 or 70110 on back.

793-E1 4c Die on wove, die sunk on card, 202x153mm, red brown *2,000.*

795-E1

Design size: 36x21mm
Card size: 92x81mm
Engraving of rejected design from which only the portraits of Cutler and Putnam were carried forward to the approved design. Clear die layout lines surround image plus horizontal lines within framelines.

795-E1 3c Die on glazed card, black *1,500.*

795-E2

Design size: 36x21mm
Card size: 49x33mm
Engraving of rejected design from which only the portraits of Cutler and Putnam were carried forward to the approved design. Layout lines present but significantly muted compared to those on No. 795-E1.

795-E2 3c Die on glazed card, dark purple *1,500.*

PANAMA CANAL ISSUE

856-E1

Design size: 37x21½mm
Essay size: 99x81mm
Card size: 141x117mm
Engraving of unadopted design: "3 CENTS 3" and "25th ANNIVERSARY PANAMA CANAL" changed for final design. "W. O. Marks" at lower right corner, "Engraver's Stock Proof 594256 / Authorized by 'OML'" on reverse.

856-E1 3c Die on India, die sunk on card, deep violet *3,000.*

Unfinished engraving of adopted design, fine horizontal lines in white areas of "FOR DEFENSE" and no dash between "INDUSTRY" and "AGRICULTURE."

899-E1 1c Die on wove, die sunk on card, bright blue green *1,000.*

Engraving of entire design, lacks crosshatching in the shading of background.

899-E2 1c Die on wove, die sunk on card, 140x162mm, green *1,000.*

Engraving of frame as adopted, with "84075" at top and "United States of America" at bottom of die impression, stamped "For Approval" at top of card, signed and dated by four individuals on card.

909-921-E1 5c Die on India, die sunk on card
a. On 227x151mm card, violet *4,000.*
a. On card reduced almost to 89x74mm die size, black *1,500.*

922-E1

Incomplete engraving of entire design, sky unshaded, no smoke from engine, additional background shading missing, blue control number and "MODELING" on reverse of card.

922-E1 3c Die on India, die sunk on card, 200x148mm, violet *2,500.*

As No. 922-E1, with additional background shading added.

922-E2 3c Die on India, die sunk on card, 200x148mm, violet *2,500.*

922-E3

As No. 922-E2, with shading of sky added.

922-E3 3c Die on India, die sunk on card, 200x148mm, violet *2,500.*

922-E4

As No. 922-E3, with additional background and figure shading added.

922-E4 3c Die on India, die sunk on card, 200x148mm, violet *2,500.*

Unadopted design showing steamship under sail, without denomination or background shading, handstamp "Engraver's Stock Proof/Authorized by," initials, "Brooks" (the engraver) in pencil and control #818347A all on back of stamp.

923-E1 3c Die on wove, die sunk on card, 201x152mm, violet *1,500.*

Unfinished engraving of adopted design, lacking smoke from the smokestack and background shading. "Modeling" handstamp and control #818995A on back of card.

923-E2 3c Die on wove, die sunk on card, 201x150mm, violet *1,500.*

928-E1

Design size: 36x21mm
Photograph of rejected design model, mounted on thick card, with BEP overleaf

928-E1 5c model photo, on 100x120mm card, foldover overleaf same size *750.*

Engraved vignette as adopted, "Engraver's Stock Proof/Authorized by," initials, "Brooks" (the engraver) in pencil and control #867263A all on back of stamp.

930-933-E2 Die on wove, die sunk on card, 202x151mm, black *1,500.*

1016-E1

Engraving of adopted design, except "c" cut in design at right where cross should be printed (held in place by tape on back); "Engraver's Stock Proof, Authorized by," initials and blue "103120B" control number on back.

1016-E1 3c Die on wove, die sunk on card, 202x152mm, deep blue *2,500.*

1105-E1

Individual design sizes: 58x33mm; area of 6 designs: 213x87mm

1105-E1 3c Black charcoal on light beige laid artist's paper, irregular 343 x225mm, six hand-drawn designs, note below in blue ink, "First Roughs James Monroe Commemorartive. F. Conley 1957" —

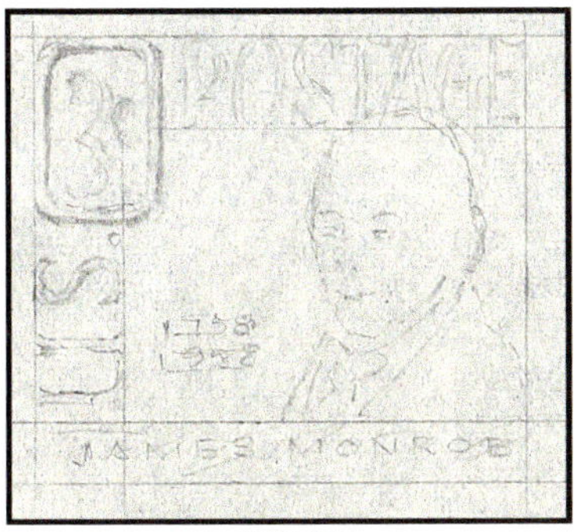

1105-E2

Design size: 43x38mm

1105-E2 3c Pencil drawing of proposed design on tracing paper, irregular 165 x127mm, notes on either side in blue ink, "Trial Layout New Size James Monroe Commemorative." and signed "Frank P. Conley Designer Dec. 1957" —

1105-E3

Design size: 32x37mm

1105-E3 3c Pencil drawing of proposed design on tracing paper, irregular 165 x120mm, notes on either side in blue ink, "Trial Layout New Size Jan. 1958 James Monroe stamp" and signed "Frank P. Conley Designer" —

1105-E4

Design size: 41x35mm

1105-E4 3c Black ink drawing of proposed design in format of issued stamp on tracing paper, 207 x133mm, notes on either side in blue ink, "Trial Layout New Size James Monroe stamp" and signed "Frank P. Conley Designer Jan. 1958" —

1128-E1

Design size: 295x178mm

1128-E1 4c Rough sketch in pencil, black pen and blue artist's crayon on tracing paper *1,500.*

1128-ER2

Design size: 158x95mm

1128-E2 4c Pencil, gray and black watercolor ink, white painted year date, "U.S. Postage," "c" and outline of "4," horizontal background lines on a premade shiny, raised sticker, very close to issued design but with small differences, on white card, signed "George Samerjan, designer of stamp ↔ 1959" beneath in black 1,500.

1139-E1

Design size (3): 135x21mm

1139-E1 3c Black charcoal and silver ink rough drawings of three proposed designs on tracing paper, 276 x166mm, no designer notes —

1139-E2

Design size (3): 165x22mm

1139-E2 4c Black and silver ink drawings of three proposed designs on tracing paper, 275x164mm, no designer notes —

E31139

Design size: 35x22mm

1139-E3 4c Dark brown, light brown, dull orange and silver ink handpainted full design on tracing paper, 110 x 92mm, "POSTAGE" on right panel, signed "Frank P. Conley 58" beneath in brown *1,000.*

1139-E4

Design size: 35x22mm

1139-E4 4c Dark brown, light brown, dull orange and silver ink handpainted full design on tracing paper, 122 x117mm, "POSTAGE" on right panel, symbol plus other small design differences from #1139-E3, signed "Frank P. Conley '58" beneath in dull orange *1,000.*

1139-E5

Design size: 35x22mm

1139-E5 4c Dark brown, dull orange and silver ink handpainted full design on tracing paper, 127x216mm, "POSTAGE" on right panel, small design differences from #1139-E3 and 1139-E4, signed "Frank P. Conley '58" beneath in dull orange *1,000.*

1139-E6

Design size: 35x22mm

1139-E6 4c Brown and silver ink handpainted full design on tracing paper, 274 x152mm, "The AMERICAN CREDO" on right panel, signed "Frank P. Conley '58" beneath in brown *1,000.*

1139-E7

Design size: 35x22mm

1139-E7 4c Dark brown, brown and silver ink handpainted full design on tracing paper, 279 x216mm, "AN AMERICAN CREDO" on right panel, signed "Frank P. Conley '58" beneath in dull orange *1,000.*

1139-E8

Design size: 35x22mm

1139-E8 4c Dark brown, brown, dull orange and silver ink handpainted full design on tracing paper, 130 x216mm, "CREDO" on right panel, signed "Frank P. Conley '58" beneath in dull orange *1,000.*

1139-E9

Design size (2): 136x22mm

1139-E9 4c Dark brown, brown, dull orange and silver ink handpainted full designs on tracing paper, 302 x234mm, each with "CREDO" on right panel each with small design differences from #1139-E8, each signed "Frank P. Conley '58" beneath in dull orange —

It is interesting to note that none of the No. 1139 essays contain the text on the center text panel that appears on the issued stamp. Likely, a last-minute change was made.

1140-E1

Design size: 32x21mm

1140-E1 4c Red, blue and silver handpainted full design on tracing paper, 129 x 81mm, similar to issued design but with different symbol at left and different Franklin signature, signed "Frank P. Conley designer" beneath in red *1,000.*

1141-E1

Design size: 125x80mm

1141-E1 4c Rough pencil drawing of proposed design on irregular-sized tracing paper, "Over the mind of man" repeated beneath, "Ervine Metzl's rough layout for copy revision of Thomas Jefferson Credo stamp. Frank P. Conley 1959" at right —

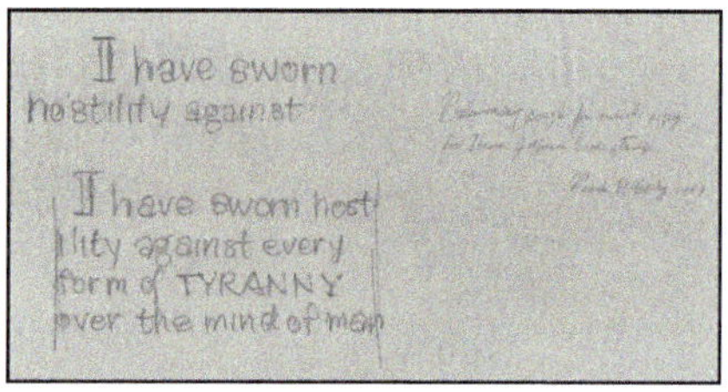

1141-E2

Design size: 90x41mm

1141-E2 4c Rough text only in pencil on irregular-sized tracing paper, part of text repeated above, "Preliminary rough for revised copy for Thomas Jefferson Credo stamp. Frank P. Conley, 1959" at right —

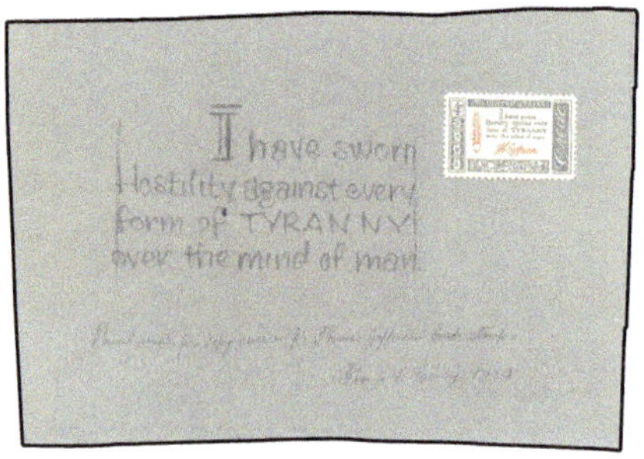

1141-E3

Design size: 98x50mm

1141-E3 4c Rough text only in pencil on tracing paper, 185 x 130mm, "Pencil rough for copy revised for Thomas Jefferson Credo stamp, Frank P. Conley, 1959" beneath —

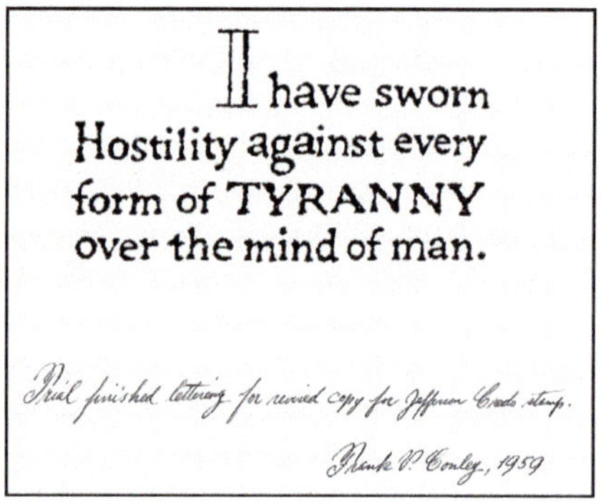

1141-E4

Design size: 69x37mm

1141-E4 4c Black India ink sketch of text only on thin wove paper, 280 x 216mm "Trial finished lettering for revised copy for Jefferson Credo stamp. Frank P. Conley, 1959" beneath —

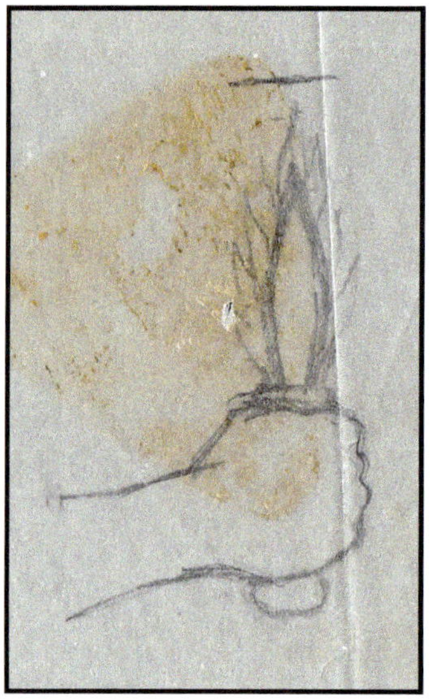

1141-E5

Design size: 33x55mm

1141-E5 4c Pencil sketch of symbol on irregular piece of tracing paper, approximately 220 x110mm, no designer notes —

1141-E6

Design size: 32x55mm

1141-E6 4c Black charcoal sketch of symbol on irregular piece of tracing paper, approximately 200 x120mm, no designer notes —

1141-E7

Design size (2): 69x68mm

1141-E7 4c Black charcoal sketches of two symbols on thin wove paper, 280 x216mm, "Symbols for Jefferson Credo stamp, Frank P. Conley, 1959" beneath, in black ink —

1141-E8

Design size (3): 147x68mm

1141-E8 4c Black charcoal sketches of three symbols on thin wove paper, 280 x216mm, "Symbols for Jefferson Credo stamp. Frank P. Conley, 1959" beneath, in black ink —

1141-E9

Design size: 37x21mm

1141-E9 4c Dark brown, vermilion and silver handpainted full design on tracing paper, 125 x108mm, signed "Frank P. Conley Designer" beneath in vermilion *1,000.*

1141-E10

Design size: 37x21mm

1141-E10 4c Dark brown, vermilion and silver handpainted full design on tracing paper, 125 x108mm, different symbol and signature than #1141-E9 or 1141-E11, signed "Frank P. Conley Designer" beneath in vermilion *1,000.*

1141-E11

Design size: 37x21mm

1141-E11 4c Dark brown, vermilion and silver handpainted full design on tracing paper, 125 x108mm, different symbol and signature than #1141-E9 or 1141-E10, signed "Frank P. Conley Designer" beneath in vermilion *1,000.*

1141-E12

Design size (4 together): 156 x121mm

1141-E12 4c Dark brown, vermilion and silver handpainted full designs on thin wove paper, 280 x 216mm, 4 similar but different essays arranged in a square, each with different symbols and signatures (and each different than those on #1141-E9, 1141-E10 and 1141-E11), each signed "Frank P. Conley Designer" beneath in dark brown —

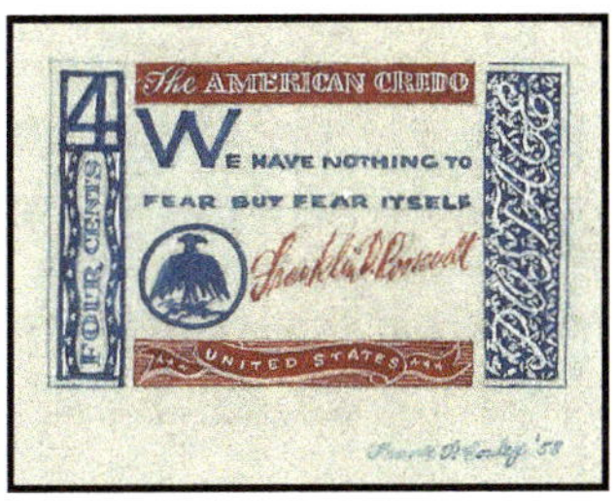

Design size: 36x22mm

1144X-E1 4c Blue, red and silver handpainted full unadopted design on thin wove paper for a proposed Franklin D. Roosevelt Credo series stamp, paper is 135x120mm, signed "Frank P. Conley 1958" beneath in blue —

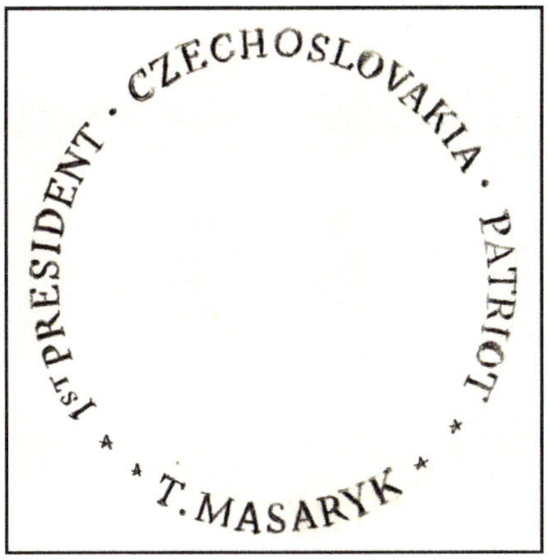

1147-E1

Design size: 157x157mm circle

1147-E1 4c Black charcoal trial design of circular text on medallion on tracing paper, approximately 260 x257mm, double stars before and after name (which does not include middle initial "G"), no dates —

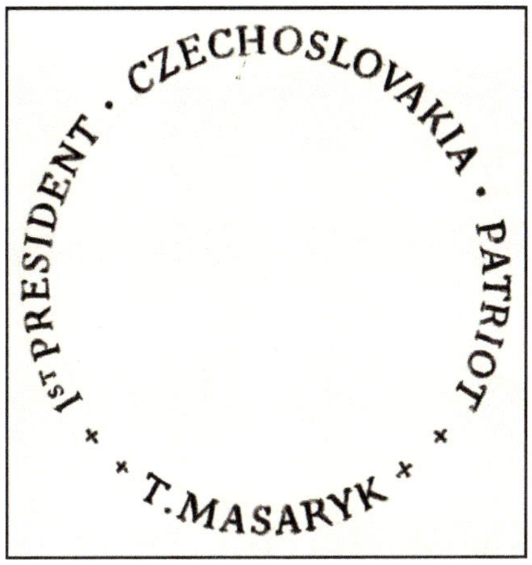

1147-E2

Design size: 159x159mm circle

1147-E2 4c Black charcoal trial design of circular text on medallion on tracing paper, approximately 268 x268mm, double crosses before and after name (which does not include middle initial "G"), no dates —

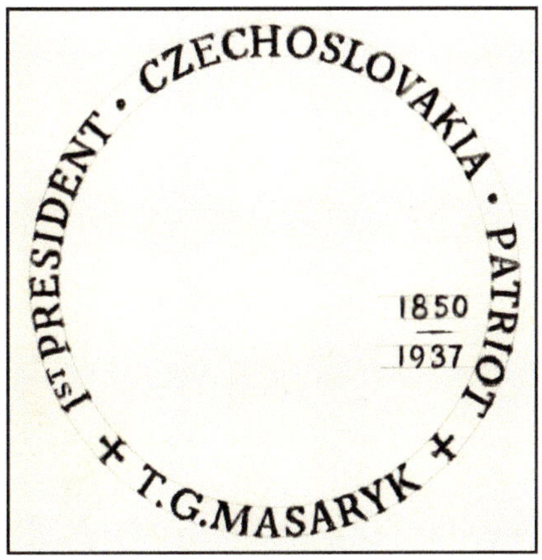

1147-E3

Design size: 159x159mm circle

1147-E3 4c Black charcoal trial design of circular text on medallion on tracing paper, 255 x255mm, large crosses before and after name, "1850/1937" dates instead of "1918/1935" as on issued stamp —

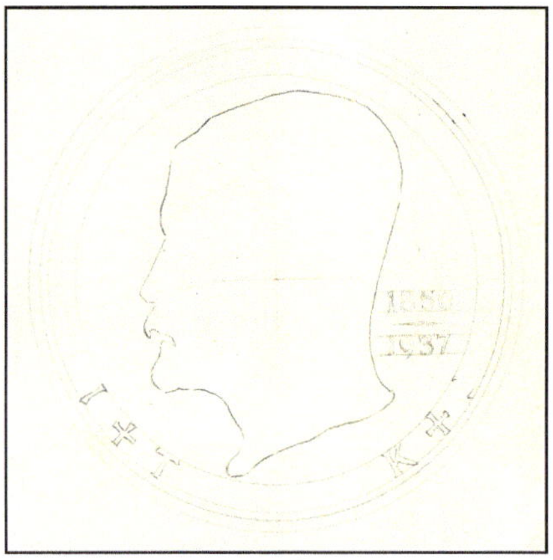

1147-E4

Design size: 173x173mm circle

1147-E4 4c Black pencil design on tracing paper, approximately 250 x290mm with uneven edges, showing circles with outline of Masaryk head, large crosses at bottom before and after name, "1830/1937" dates instead of "1918/1935" as on issued stamp —

1147-E5

Design size: 123x140mm

1147-E5 4c White, tan and black design on 160 x174mm photographic paper with complete design, section showing torch, leaves and ribbons pasted in place, vignette also pasted in place, "1850/1937" dates instead of "1918/1935" as on issued stamp —

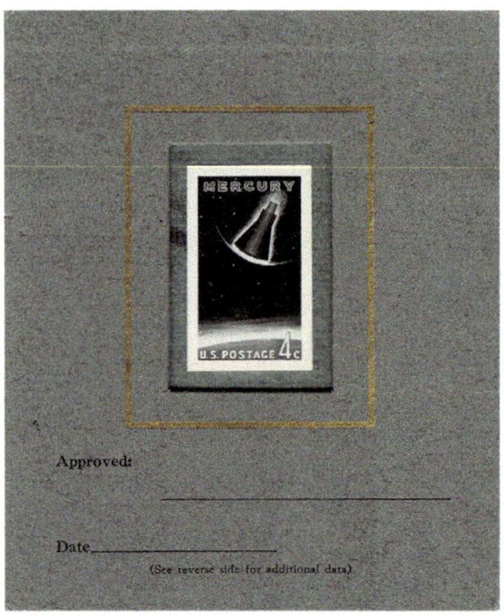

1193-E1

Design size: 21x36mm
Photograph of rejected design model, mounted on thick card, with BEP overleaf calling attention to the "Special Project."

1193-E1 4c Model photo, on 100x120mm card, fold-over overleaf same size, with printed information on back of overleaf *2,500.*

1529-E1

Design size: 183x109mm
Multicolored drawing in colored pencils similar to accepted design on 305x241 sheet of tracing paper, several ink and pencil notes above, at right and below design.

1529-E1 10c Multicolored design —

1699-E1

Design size: 166x217mm
Preliminary drawing in pencil and purple ink that matches well the final design, but without detail.

1699-E1 10c Design, text and and head outline on 203x264mm tracing paper —

1799-E1

Design size: 21x25mm
Picture of painting by Gerard David cropped and affixed on picture of simulated stamp with perfs and text, on card with covering gray thin card with cut-out in center to frame the essay; note at top left of covering card says "No (Rejected 3-6-74)," but in fact this is the design that was chosen (with painting cropped slightly differently).

1799-E1 13c Hybrid mock-up of design similar to accepted design —

1851-E1

Design size: 109x126mm
Ink drawing of 'USA,' '00' denomination and text; text at bottom.

1851-E1 No denomination, simulated perfs and text on 217x281mm white wove paper, with measurement notes at left, black —

1851-E2

Design size: 109x126mm
Ink drawing of 'USA,' '00' denomination and text; text at top as on issued stamp.

1851-E2 No denomination, simulated perfs and text on 217x281mm white wove paper, with measurement notes at left, black —

2176-E1

Design size: 133x155mm

Pencil trial design (not adopted) on 198x252mm tracing paper, text below design.

2176-E1 4c Pencil design on tracing paper, black —

Incomplete engraving of vignette, no shading or collar.

2179-E1 20c Die on wove, die sunk on card, red brown *600.*

2179-E2

Similar to No. 2179-E1, but with collar added.

2179-E2 20c Die on wove, die sunk on card, red brown *600.*

Similar to issued stamp, but with substantial differences in shading, etc.

2179-E3 20c Die on India, die sunk on thin card, black *650.*

2181-E1

Design size: 106x127mm
Pencil drawing on white board, covered by thick gray paper with center cut-out of design size taped to board at top.

2181-E1 20c Design on white board, covering gray paper marked "B," black —

2181-E2

Design size: 96x115mm
Pencil drawing on white board, covered by thick gray paper with center cut-out of design size taped to board at top.

2181-E2 20c Design on white board, covering gray paper marked "C," black —

2181-E3

Design size: 106x127mm
Pencil drawing with gray wash in hair and at right on white board, covered by thick gray paper with center cut-out of design size taped to board at top.

2181-E3 20c Design on white board, covering gray paper marked "D," black and gray —

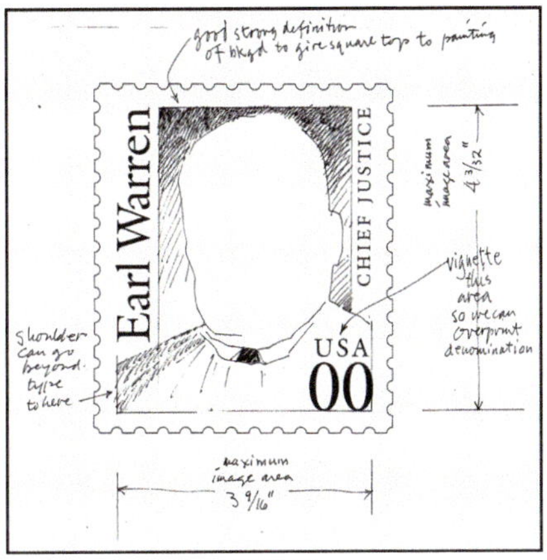

2184-E1

Design size: 108x124
Early version of design on white paper, denomination "00," "Chief Justice" at right, with many black ink notations indicating/suggesting wanted design elements.

2184-E1 No denomination, design and notes on 8½x11 inches white wove paper, black —

2184-E2

Design size: 112x127mm
Photo essay of early full design, with black felt-tip pen notation at right crossing out "United States" and suggesting it be changed to "OF THE U.S." and "Suggested by Mr. Rehnquist."

2184-E2 30c Design on 8½x11 inches photo paper with handwritten suggestion to change "United States" to "of the U.S.," which suggestion noted as coming from William Rehnquist, Chief Justice of the U.S. Supreme Court, black —

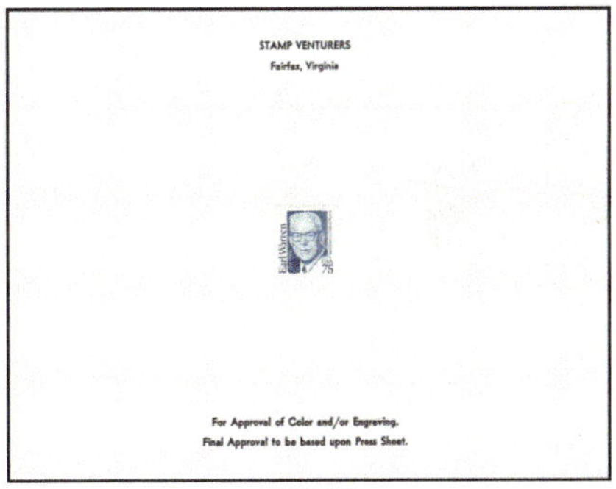

2184-E3

Design size: 18x21mm
Engraving of full design, but denomination shown as 75c and with "Chief Justice, United States" at right.

2184-E3 75c Engraved design cut to 22x24mm size and affixed to 202x152mm card with "STAMP VENTURERS / Fairfax, Virginia" at top and "For Approval of Color and/or Engraving./Final Approval to be based upon Press Sheet.," blue —

2184-E4

Design size: 115x131mm
A 176x204 piece of white wove paper with simulated perforations and 100x115mm cut-out at center inside the perforations, affixed to an 8½x11 inches sheet of white wove paper, prior essay of Warren's face added and correct text at left, dates and denomination blocks affixed, "Chief Justice of the U.S." block replaces previous text at right, signed Chris Calle on backing paper.

2184-E4 29c Photo essay with text, dates and denomination add-ons affixed, black —

2189-E1

Design size: 111x122mm
Ink drawing of "00" denomination and text.

2189-E1 No denomination, text and simulated perfs on photo paper, measurement notes at left and large image reduced to stamp size affixed below, note on covering tracing paper says "Not Used," black —

2189-E2

Design size: 111x122mm
Ink drawing of "00" denomination and text.

2189-E2 No denomination, text and simulated perfs on white wove paper, measurement notes at left and large image reduced to stamp size affixed below, 8/23/89 handwritten note at lower right, black —

2189-E3

Design size: 98x112mm
Photo of complete essay with handwritten notes indicating that the word "VICE PRESIDENT" at right must be changed to capital and lower case lettering.

2189-E3 25c Essay design on 8½x11 inches white wove paper, black —

2204-E1

Design size: 129x201mm
Mock-up of text with three corrections on white paper affixed over photo of original essay, with image of original essay reduced to stamp size shown at lower right.

2204-E1 22c Design on photopaper with corrections affixed, multicolored —

2277-E1

Design size: 108x126mm
Black charcoal unadopted trial design of eagle "E" stamp with black ink simulated perforations.

2277-E1 (25c) Design on white wove paper, affixed to 155x205mm thick black card, black —

2284-E1

Design size: each picture 63x73mm plus text underneath. Original multicolored artwork in watercolor and ink affixed to thick white card, names of birds below in black ink.

2284-E1, 2285-E1 25c Two separate designs, each on thin card, affixed to thick white card, printed sticker of artist Chuck Ripper with address at lower right of card, multicolored —

2376-E1

Design size: 108x184mm
Pencil drawing on thin white wove.

2376-E1 (22c) Design on 160x264mm wove paper, "JIM SHARPE" in black ink at lower right corner —

2376-E2

Design size: 108x184mm
Pencil drawing on thin white wove.

2376-E2 (22c) Design on 172x264mm wove paper —

2376-E3

Design size: 109x184mm
Pencil drawing on thin white wove.

2376-E3 (22c) Design on 152x264mm wove paper —

2376-E4

Design size: 109x183mm
Pencil drawing on thin white wove.

2376-E4 (22c) Design on 172x267mm wove paper —

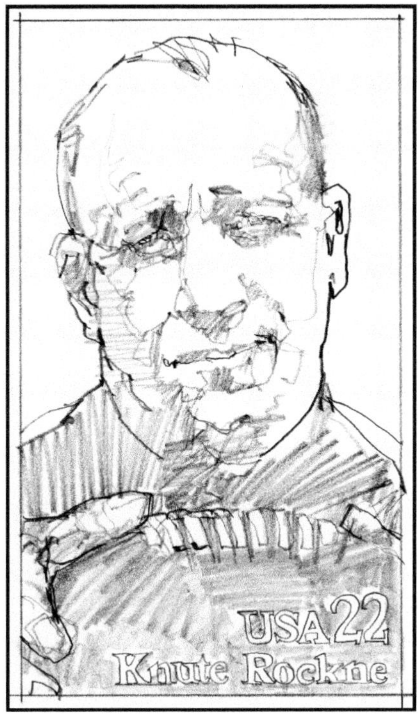

2376-E5

Design size: 113x184mm
Pencil drawing on thin white wove.

2376-E5 (22c) Design on 157x264mm wove paper —

2376-E6

Design size: 113x184mm
Pencil drawing on thin white wove.

2376-E6 (22c) Design on 160x261mm wove paper —

2376-E7

Design size: 108x181mm
Pencil drawing on thin white wove.

2376-E7 (22c) Design on 145x261mm wove paper —

2376-E8

Design size: 108x182mm
Pencil drawing on thin white wove.

2376-E8 (22c) Design on 174x261mm wove paper —

2376-E9

Design size: 115x176mm
Handpainted image on white board, reduced photo of painting mounted below.

2376-E9 (22c) Painting on 202x278mm white board with reduced photo below, small "2" in circle at lower right corner, "Dennis LUZAK" in ink on reverse at top —

2376-E10

Design size: 126-198mm
Photo of design mounted on mock-up photo of stamp perforations and lettering.

2376-E10 (22c) Design mounted beneath cutout of thin board adhering to 215x278mm thick gray board —

2403-E1

Design size: 36x21mm
Imperforate stamp image as issued except "USA 25" in black instead of white as issued.

2403-E1 25c Near-final image on gummed 211x94mm stamp paper, color bars and "A1111" at left of stamp —

2453-E1

Design size: 110x124mm
Pencil drawing of canoe with black ink lettering and simulated perforations.

2453-E1 12c Design on white wove paper, taped at corners to 207x278mm white wove sheet of paper, stamp-size photo essay of design affixed below on paper with pencil design —

2453-E2

Design size: 110-124mm
Pencil drawing of canoe with black ink lettering and pencil and black ink simulated perforations.

2453-E2 12c Design on white wove paper, taped at corners to 207x278mm white wove sheet of paper, stamp-size photo essay of design affixed below on paper with pencil design, ms. "Punch up, like other one" at top right of large sheet of paper —

Image of pine cone portion of stamp, only.

2491-E1 32c Die on India (?), affixed to card, black —

2538-E1

Design size: 109x176mm
Pencil drawing on thin tracing paper.

2538-E1 No denomination, design on approximately 190x215mm tracing paper, signed "Wolfe" at right bottom beneath design —

2538-E2

Design size: 109x176mm
Photo of No. 2538-E1 with plastic overlay bearing William Soroyan (sic) name at top.

2538-E2 No denomination, photo in black on beige, with plastic overlay in black, all mounted on 8½x11 inch sheet of white wove paper —

2538-E3

Design size: 108x174mm
Pencil drawing on thin tracing paper.

2538-E3 No denomination, design on 171x273mm tracing paper, signed "Wolfe" at right bottom beneath design —

2538-E4

Design size: 108x174mm
Photo of No. 2538-E3 with plastic overlay bearing william Soroyan (sic) name at top.

2538-E4 No denomination, photo in black and beige, with plastic overlay in black, all mounted on 8½x11 inch sheet of white wove paper —

2538-E5

Design size: 108x177mm
Pencil drawing on thin tracing paper.

2538-E5 No denomination, design on 191x215mm tracing paper, signed "Wolfe" at right bottom beneath stamp —

2538-E6

Design size: 108x177mm
Photo of No. 2538-E5 with plastic overlay bearing William Soroyan (sic) name at top.

2538-E6 No denomination, photo in black on beige, plastic overlay in black, all mounted on 8½x11 inch sheet of white wove paper —

2538-E7

Design size: 108x179mm
Pencil drawing on thin tracing paper, includes name Wm Soroyan (sic) at top.

2538-E7 22c Design on 171x260mm tracing paper, signed "Wolfe" at right bottom beneath design —

2538-E8

Design size: 108x179mm
Photo of No. 2538-E7 with plastic overlay changing name at top to William Soroyan (sic).

2538-E8 22c Photo in black on beige, plastic overlay in black, all mounted on 8½x11 inch sheet of white wove paper —

2538-E9

Design size: 109x178mm
Pencil drawing on thin tracing paper.

2538-E9 No denomination, design on tracing paper with no signature (but clearly by Wolfe) —

2538-E10

Design size: 109x178mm
Photo of No. 2538-E9 with plastic overlay bearing William Saroyan (correct spelling) at top.

2538-E10 No denomination, photo in black on beige, plastic overlay in black, all mounted on 8½x11 inch sheet of white wove paper —

2538-E11

Design size: 106x172mm
Pencil drawing on thin tracing paper, Saroyan spelled correctly.

2538-E11 25c Design on 189x250mm tracing paper —

2538-E12

Design size: 172x110mm
Photo on plastic essay of picture only, with simulated perforations, and "25/USA" and "William Saroyan" on plastic taped to photo.

2538-E12 25c Design on plastic, mounted on 284x191mm white board —

2549-E1

Design size: 73x44mm, "block" size: 161x103mm
Original multicolored art in watercolor and ink.

2545-2549-E1 25c Four separate designs, each on thin card, mounted in block of 4 format on thick brown card, sticker on reverse of "Chuck Ripper/Wildlife Art . . ." —

2551-E1

Design size: 139x216mm
Gray card glued to white card with simulated perforations, picture of service medal carefully cut and glued on gray card, with shading added, "Honoring Those Who Served" and "USA/29" handpainted on gray card in watercolors, plastic overlay taped at top bears the "Desert Shield" and "Desert Storm" wording, PMS310 color choice on tag taped at bottom of overlay, signed "A. Frank/PMG" at right bottom beneath design.

2551-E1 29c Design similar to issued stamp but different in many details —

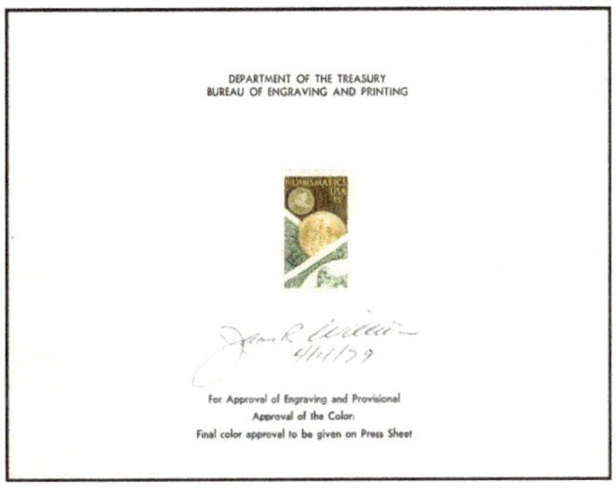

2558-E1

2558-E1 15c Large hybrid die essay, signed "Jack R Williams/ 4/11/79;" while presented in the usual form as a proof on card for approval of engraving and color, this design itself was never approved for stamp —

2602-E1

Design size: 88x97mm
Photo of original Eagle and Shield art with simulated perforations, with artist tracing paper taped overlay with photo of shield with four stars painted in taped to the overlay, reduced original artwork at right without stars.

2602-E1 (10c) Design in cutout of thin card on 280x216 thick white card —

2635-E1

Design size: 111x182mm
Original art from Library of Congress with plastic overlay taped on with "USA 30 / THE ALCAN HIGHWAY" attached to overlay.

2635-E1 30c Design on rough artist's card attached to thick black 175x282mm card, with plastic overlay, description of art beneath design —

2636-E1

Design size: 177x116mm
Design on tracing paper with enhancements in clouds done in pencil, with overlay on tracing paper with further enhancements to clouds done in pencil.

2636-E1 No denomination, 232x161 overlay taped to design of My Old Kentucky Home on 294x210mm underlay —

2636-E2

Design size: 177x116mm
Design of My Old Kentucky Home with cutouts of "30c" attached at upper right and slips of paper glued on to cover "USA" at upper left and "KENTUCKY 1792" at bottom.

2636-E2 Design on 204x191mm white wove paper taped to 290x209mm thin white card —

2646a-E1

Design size of each: 54x93mm; "block" size: 116x193mm
Original multicolored art in watercolor and ink.

2646a-E1 25c Four separate designs, each on thin card, mounted in block of 4 format on white card, mounted on blue backing —

2646a-E2

Design size: 126x199mm
Original art in watercolor and ink.

2646a-E2 25c Multicolored art in watercolor and black ink, bird slightly different than #2646a-E1 —

2646a-E3

Design size: 24x38mm
Original art in watercolor and ink.

2646a-E3 25c Multicolored bird slightly different than #2646a-E1 and #2646a-E2, done in stamp size, mounted on white card —

2646a-E4

Design size: 126x198mm
Ink drawing of 30c denomination and text.

2646a-E4 30c Simulated perfs, denomination and text on white card, with measurement notes at left, black —

2646a-E5

Design size: 126x198mm
Ink drawing of final 29c denomination and text.

2646a-E5 29c Simulated perfs, denomination and text on white card, with measurement notes at left, black —

2646a-E6

Design size: 52x129mm; overall size: 65x143mm
Original art in watercolor and black ink.

2646a-E6 25c Multicolored art for proposed booklet cover, later revised, on thin card —

2704-E1

Design size: 94x143mm
Photo of accepted design except with 30c denomination, with plastic overlay with Cabrillo name in both Spanish and Portuguese attached as a possible design alteration (not chosen thus).

2704-E1 30c multicolored, design with Spanish Cabrillo name, overlay in plastic taped at top bearing names in Spanish and Portuguese, underlay 215x278mm —

2746-E1

Design size: 115x178mm
Design in charcoal, 156x28mm slip of paper with identifying verbiage taped beneath design.

2746-E1 No denomination, design on very thin white card attached to thicker 175x229mm white card, "HIGGINS BOND, ILLUSTRATOR . . ." on reverse of card —

2746-E2

Design size: 115x178mm
Design in charcoal, "PERCY LAVON JULIAN" added by hand at top, "29" on very thin card glued on at top left, "Black Heritage USA" on black strip of paper taped to bottom across design.

2746-E2 29c Design on very thin white card attached to thicker 175x229mm white card, "HIGGINS BOND, ILLUSTRATOR . . ." on reverse of card —

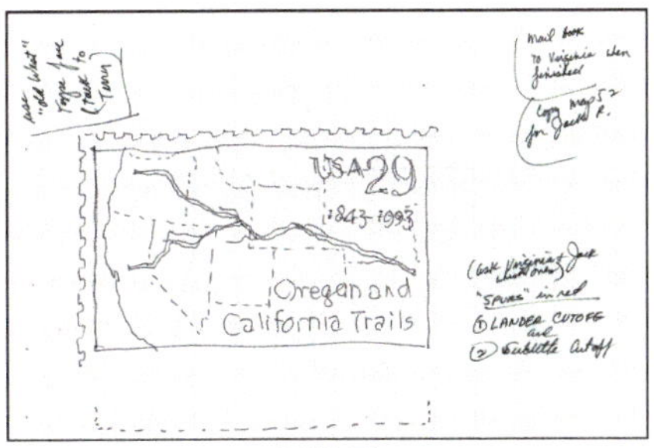

2747-E1

Design size: "stamp" only 151x100mm
Ink drawing of design for Oregon and California trails, with notes and ideas in margins of paper.

2747-E1 29c Hand drawn design on 8½x11 inch white paper from note pad with blue lines, a second very crude drawing on reverse —

2747-E2

Design size: 94x58mm
Ink drawing of design with "Oregon Trail" only text, yellow note paper on back "'Noodling' sketches by Howard Paine" which is certainly also true for No. 2747-E1.

2747-E2 29c Hand drawn design on 8½x11 inch white paper from note pad with blue lines —

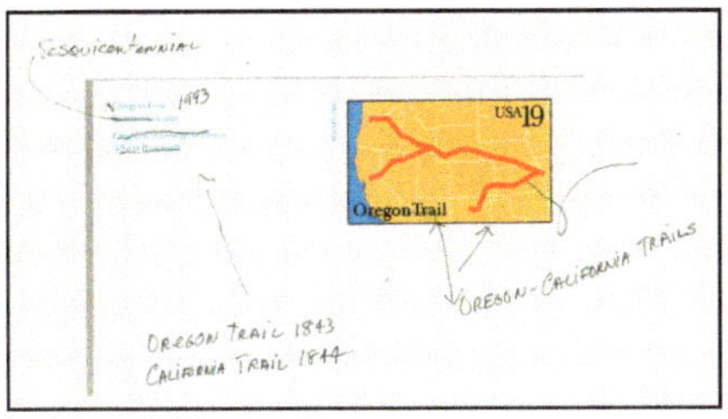

2747-E3

Design size: 57x34mm
Photo of official design showing Oregon, California and New Mexico trails with ink notes indicating New Mexico trail should be omitted and stamp text should say "Oregon-California Trails," plus note indicating this should be called the "Oregon Trail Sesquicentennial 1993."

2747-E3 19c Design and text on 215x146mm white wove paper —

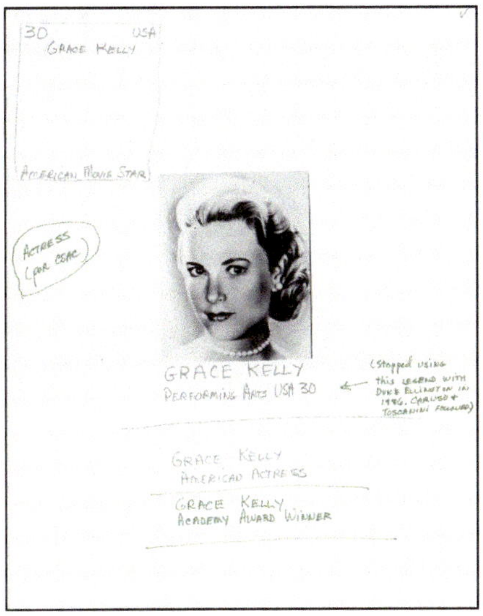

2749-E1

Design size: 69x84mm
Black on white copy of photo of Grace Kelly attached to white paper with notes for several possible texts that could be used (but all ignored on final stamp issue — except name).

2749-E1 30c Photo plus ink and pencil development notes on 8½x11 inch white wove —

Similar to issued stamp, but with noticeable differences in tie, hairline, etc.

2933-E1 32c Die on gummed paper, brown *1,000.*

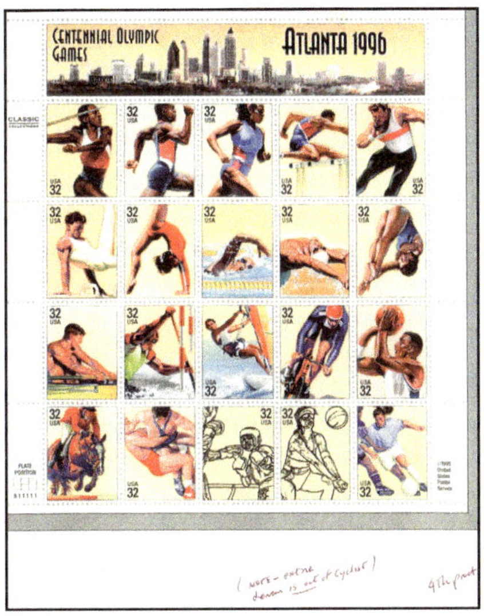

3068-E1

Design size: 185x196mm
Copy of proposed designs (some accepted, others rejected), different banner at top and designs without Olympic rings and text, copyright 1995 instead of 1996 on lower right selvage, ms. notations and "4th proof" at bottom of paper.

3068-E1 32c multicolored copy of 20-stamp pane on 8½x11 inch plain white paper —

3087-E1

Design size: 165x184mm
Copy of proposed pane of 16, 4 each of 4 different triangle designs.

3087-E1 32c multicolored copy of full pane of 16 on 8½x11 inch plain white paper —

3087-E2

Design size: 175x87mm
Copy of proposed individual design, noted as "PRELIMINARY DESIGN" and with production information including proof date "5 Sept 95" and "Second Proof" on the paper below shaded area.

3087-E2 32c green and gold blown-up copy of individual stamp on 8½x11 inch plain white paper —

3087-E3

Design size: 101x158mm

Copy of proposed individual design, noted as "PRELIMINARY DESIGN" and with production information below including proof date of "27 Sept 95" and "Second Proof" on paper bvelow shaded area.

3087-E3 32c multicolored copy of individual stamp on 8½x11 inch plain white paper —

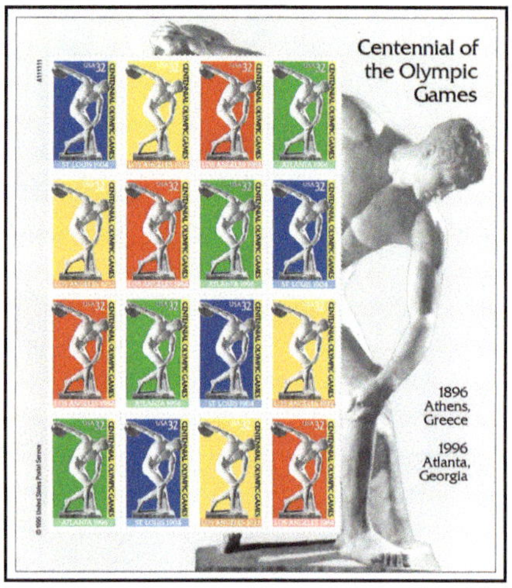

3087-E4

Design size: 165x184mm

Copy of proposed pane of 16, 4 each of 4 different designs differing by colors, ms. note below image: "from my new Kodak 8600 printer!"

3087-E4 32c multicolored copy of full pane of 16 on 8½x11 inch Kodak Electronic Imaging Paper —

3087-E5

Design size: 100x158mm

Copy of proposed individual design, extremely close to accepted design, "1996" year date beneath frameline at left bottom, with production information below including "PRELIMINARY DESIGN," proof date "9 Nov 95" and "Fourth Proof."

3087-E5 32c brown on 8½x11 inch plain white paper —

3087-E6

Design size: 125x160mm

Copy of a proposed design for a "passing the ympic] torch" from Atlanta to Sydney, Australia joint issue that was never issued in any final form, with production information below including "PRELIMINARY DESIGN," proof date "20 Sept 95" and "First Proof."

3087-E6 60c multicolored torch design on 8½x11 inch plain white paper —

3136-E1

Design size: 184x173mm

Copy of proposed 4-stamp sheet design.

3136-E1 32c multicolored preliminary artwork on 8½x11 inch plain white paper —

3136-E2

Design size: 259x193mm

Copy of proposed 10-stamp sheet design, 4-color "S1111" plus plate position of sheet in lower left selvage.

3136-E2 32c multicolored artwork and layout for 10 stamps on 8½x11 inch plain white paper —

3136-E3

Design size: 252x199mm Copy of proposed 10-stamp sheet design, denominations and dinosaur names in black, "Camarassurus" misspelling, ms. notation below sheet image says "Tried Bitmap art with color bkgrd in illustration / Prints fast, but . . ."

3136-E3 32c red, beige and black sheet design on 8½x11 inch plain white paper —

3136-E4

Design size: 252x199mm

Copy of proposed 10-stamp sheet design, as No. 3136-E3 but denominations and dinosaur names in red and in different fonts, "Comarassurus" still misspelled, ms. notation below sheet image says "Tried to rescue Bitmap version with color type / Prints fast, but . . ."

3136-E4 32c red, beige and black sheet design on 8½x11 inch plain white paper —

3136-E5

Design size: 252x199mm

Copy of proposed 10-stamp sheet design, as No. 3136-E4 but with lighter background plus denominations and dinosaur names in black, "Camarassurus" still misspelled, ms. notation below sheet image says: "lower duotone needs more yellow."

3136-E5 32c red, beige and black sheet design on 8½x11 inch plain white paper —

3136-E6

Design size: 259x199mm

Copy of proposed 10-stamp sheet design, like No. 3136-E5 but "A scene in Wyoming . . ." and "A scene in Colorado . . ." added at lower left of both top and bottom panels, plus ms. note to correct the spelling of 'Camarassurus' and ms. indications in red of where to add additional stamps.

3136-E6 32c red, light beige and black sheet design on 8½x11 inch plain white paper —

3136-E7

Design size: 257x196mm
Copy of proposed 10-stamp sheet design in multicolors, "A scene in Colorado . . ." and "A scene in Colorado . . ." replace wording in No. 3136-E6, spelling of "Camarasaurus" corrected, red ms. In lower left selvage indicates a change to a 15-stamp sheet in the works.

3136-E7 32c multicolored final 10-stamp sheet essay proposal on 8½x11inch plain white paper —

3136-E8

Design size: 259x199mm
Copy of 15-stamp sheet design, all stamp designs in single color and not all are the chosen designs, background shading extended to sheet margins, "Camarassurus" misspelled, printed value multiplier in left selvage revised to 15 stamps.

3136-E8 32c beige, red, yellow and black sheet design on 8½x11 inch plain white paper —

3136-E9

Design size: 246x134mm Copy of upper panel of 8 stamps for 15-stamp sheet design, fairly close to final designs but "Camarassus" still misspelled, etc., ms. "upper art / 3rd proof" notation below design, etc.

3136-E9 32c multicolored upper panel designs on 8½x11 inch plain white paper —

3136-E10

Design size: 257x200mm
Copy of 15-stamp sheet design, very close to issued design, panels with thin black frames, top panel background purple, banner at top blue, ms. notations concerning color of top panel sky, length of "A scene . . ." verbiage moved to beneath designs and lengthened slightly on issued sheet.

3136-E10 32c multicolored full sheet design on 8½x11inch plain white paper —

3136-E11

Design size: 257x200mm
Copy of 15-stamp sheet design, very close to issued design, as No. 3136-E10 except both panel background color and banner are blue as issued.

3136-E11 32c multicolored full sheet design on 8½x11 inch plain white paper —

AIR POST STAMPS

1918 ISSUE

Complete engraving of frame only as adopted. Backstamped "626646A ENGRAVER'S STOCK PROOF AUTHORIZED BY" (signature), plus pencil "663" and "Weeks" (?).

C3-E1 24c Die on India, die sunk on card, deep carmine *5,000.*

Incomplete engraving of entire design as adopted: unfinished plumes above value numerals and no serial number on biplane.

C3-E2 24c Die on wove, 40x37mm, black vignette, blue frame —

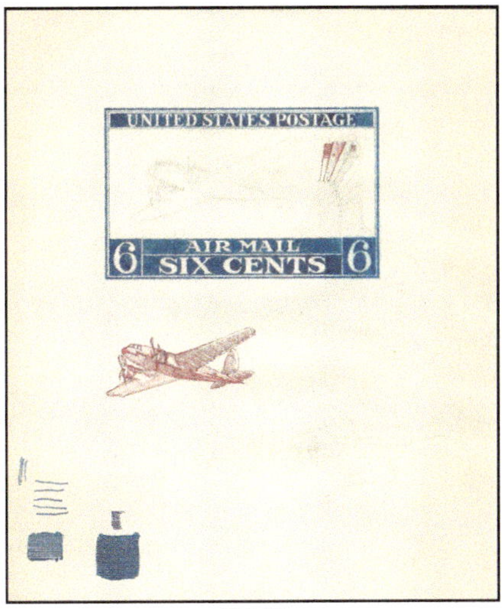

C25-E1

Original pen, ink and wash drawing on thick card for the 1941-44 Transport series of air post stamps, various elements of which were used in the creation of the final accepted design. Size of blue frame is 4⅞x3 inches.

C25-E1 Drawing on thick card, blue and red *3,000.*

Engraving of adopted design except without denomination, "C" punch where denominations go, control #722657A (1942) on back of card.

C25-C31-E2 Die on wove, die sunk on card, 201x150mm, black *5,500.*

SPECIAL DELIVERY STAMPS

1885 ISSUE
American Bank Note Co.

E1-E1

Incomplete engraving of entire design as adopted: ornaments missing at each side of "SPECIAL," line under messenger is in pencil, shading on left side of messenger tablet missing, leaves and vert. background lines unfinished (latter shaded over with pencil).

E1-E1 10c Die on India, dim dusky g-b. green *2,500.*

E2-E1

1888 ISSUE

No. E1P1 with "AT ANY OFFICE" drawn in wash on small piece of thin paper and mounted over "AT A SPECIAL / DELIVERY / OFFICE." Pencil "any post office" and ms. "At once O.K. / J.C.M. 14 Aug. 86" (?) on backing card.

E2-E1 10c Die on India, on card, black *2,500.*

1908 ISSUE
Bureau of Engraving and Printing

E7-E1

Design size: about 8½x7⅛ inches
Preliminary ink and pencil drawing of entire design somewhat similar to that adopted: ("V.S." for U.S. and other minor changes).

E7-E1 10c Drawing on vellum, black —

E7-E2

Design size: about 8 ½x7 ⅛ inches
Preliminary ink and pencil drawing of entire design nearly as adopted: ("V.S." for U.S.)

E7-E2 10c Drawing on white drawing paper, black —

E7-E3

Design size: 213 ½x179mm
Similar to No. E7-E2 but with "U.S."

E7-E3 10c Drawing on white drawing paper, black *750.*

E7-E4

Design size: 26x21 ½mm
Woodblock size: 45x42mm
Woodblock of entire design as adopted with about 5mm colorless border outside design, solid color beyond, engraved on wood by Giraldon of Paris. (One exists with ms. "Wood cut made in Paris by Mr. Whitney Warren — The cuts and the impression therefrom were turned over to the Director of the Bureau of Engraving & Printing, and by him turned over to the Custodian of Dies, Rolls and Plates and given No. 446. They are now held by the Custodian." Another has typewritten "Prints made in Paris, France, from a wood-cut engraving by an unknown engraver from a design made by Mr. Whitney Warren, architect, of New York City." with ms. "Compliments J.E. Ralph" director of B.E.P. and pencil date "9/7/1917.")

Ridgeway numbers used for colors of Nos. E7-E4 and E7-E5.

E7-E4 10c
- ***a.*** Woodcut on 19g/2 yellowish wove
  - 43k/1 dim dark green blue *450.*
  - 44m/2 dull dusky m. g-blue *450.*
  - 45j/1 dim v. dark b-g-blue *450.*
  - 45m/1 dim dusky b-g-blue *450.*
- ***b.*** Woodcut on 19f/2 dull faint y-o-yellow wove
  - 43k/1 dim dark g-blue *450.*
  - 43m/1 dim dusky g-blue *450.*
  - 44k/1 dim dark m. g-blue *450.*
  - 44k/2 dull dark m. g-blue *450.*
  - 45m/1 dim dusky b-g-blue *450.*
  - 45m/2 dull dusky b-g-blue *450.*
- ***c.*** Woodcut on 19g/2 dull v. faint y-o-yellow wove
  - 43k/1 dim dark g-blue *450.*
  - 43m/1 dim dusky g-blue *450.*

E7-E5

Design size: 26x21 ½mm
Complete engraving of entire design fairly similar to that adopted but with minor differences.

E7-E5 10c
- ***a.*** Die on India, die sunk on card, 37m/0 dusky g-b. green blue *750.*
- ***b.*** Die on soft white wove, 30x35mm, 37m/0 dusky g-blue-green *750.*

REGISTRATION STAMP

F1-E1

Design size: 19x22 ½mm
Retouched circular photo of vignette mounted on wash drawing of frame design as adopted. Ms. "Approved July 8/11 — Frank H. Hitchcock — Postmaster General" on backing card.

F1-E1 10c Model on white paper, mounted on thick gray cardboard, 81x92mm, black *1,250.*

POSTAGE DUE STAMPS

1879 ISSUE
American Bank Note Co.

J1-E1

Design size: 19 ½x25 ½mm
Die size: 54x66 ½mm
Complete engraving of entire design as adopted except "UNPAID POSTAGE" instead of "POSTAGE DUE" above vignette oval.

J1-E1 1c
- ***a.*** Die on India, die sunk on card
  - orange brown *850.*
  - slate gray *850.*
  - dark red violet *850.*
  - dull yellow *850.*
  - light orange *850.*
  - red brown *850.*
- ***b.*** Die on India, cut small (1-4mm)
  - gray black *300.*
  - dull red *300.*
  - dull brown *300.*
  - dull green *300.*
  - dull blue *300.*
- ***c.*** Die on India, cut close (0-1mm)
  - orange brown *300.*
  - slate gray *300.*
  - dark red violet *300.*
  - dull yellow *300.*
- ***d.*** Die on ivory glazed paper, die sunk
  - black *700.*
  - black brown *700.*
  - scarlet *700.*
  - blue *700.*

Design size: 19 ½x25 ½mm
Die size: 53 ½x53 ½mm
Complete engraving of entire design as adopted except "UNPAID POSTAGE" instead of "POSTAGE DUE" above vignette oval.

J2-E1 2c
- ***a.*** Die on India, die sunk on card
  - dark red violet *850.*
  - black *850.*
- ***b.*** Die on India, cut small
  - gray black *300.*
  - dull red *300.*
  - dull brown *300.*
  - dull green *300.*
  - dull blue *300.*
- ***c.*** Die on India, cut close
  - orange brown *300.*
  - dark red violet *300.*
  - slate gray *400.*
- ***d.*** Die on ivory glazed paper, die sunk
  - black *700.*
  - black brown *700.*
  - scarlet *700.*
  - blue *700.*

Design size: 19 ½x25 ½mm
Die size: 53x53mm
Complete engraving of entire design as adopted except "UNPAID POSTAGE" instead of "POSTAGE DUE" above vignette oval.

J3-E1 3c
- ***a.*** Die on India, die sunk on card, dull yellow *850.*
- ***b.*** Die on India, cut small
  - gray black *300.*
  - dull red *300.*
  - dull brown *300.*
  - dull green *300.*
  - dull blue *300.*
- ***c.*** Die on India, cut close, dull yellow *300.*
- ***d.*** Die on ivory glazed paper, die sunk
  - black *700.*
  - black brown *700.*
  - scarlet *700.*
  - blue *700.*

Design size: 19 ½x25 ½mm
Complete engraving of entire design as adopted except "UNPAID POSTAGE" instead of "POSTAGE DUE" above vignette oval.

J4-E1 5c
- ***a.*** Die on India, die sunk on card, slate gray *850.*
- ***b.*** Die on India, cut small
  - gray black *300.*
  - dull red *300.*
  - dull brown *300.*
  - dull green *300.*
  - dull blue *300.*
- ***c.*** Die on India, cut close
  - orange brown *300.*
  - slate gray *300.*
  - dark red violet *300.*
  - dull yellow *300.*
- ***d.*** Die on ivory glazed paper, die sunk
  - black *700.*
  - black brown *700.*
  - scarlet *700.*
  - blue *700.*

J4-E2

As No. J4-E1 except frame a pencil and wash drawing, vignette engraved numeral and oval lathework numeral cut to shape and pasted over lathework, with design notations.

J4-E2 5c Engraved vignette, frame pencil and wash, on thick card, 70x88mm, brown *4,500.*

1894 ISSUE
Bureau of Engraving and Printing

J31-E1

Design size: 18 ½x22 ½mm
Die size: 50x99mm
Incomplete engraving of entire design: no engraved lines on numeral, lathework unfinished on two inclined spots at each side of numeral.

J31-E1 1c Die on India, die sunk on card, deep claret *1,400.*

J31-E2

Design size: 18½x22½mm
Die size: 50x99mm
Incomplete engraving of entire design: engraved lines on numeral but lathework still unfinished on two inclined spots at each side of numeral.

J31-E2 1c Die on India, die sunk on card, claret *1,000.*

J32-E1

Design size: 18½x22½mm
Die size: unknown
Incomplete engraving of entire design: unfinished ornaments by "P" of "POSTAGE" and "E" of "DUE."

J32-E1 2c Die on India, size 26x30mm, deep claret *1,500.*

J33-E1

Incomplete engraving of entire design: blank space for numeral with "3" drawn in pencil.

J33-E1 3c Die on India, die sunk on card, black *1,100.*

J33-E2

Incomplete engraving of entire design: no engraved lines on numeral, bottom lettering in pencil only, no hand retouching of lathework around numeral.

J33-E2 3c Die on India, die sunk on card, black *1,500.*

J33-E3

Incomplete engraving of entire design: no engraved lines on numeral.

J33-E3 3c Die on India, die sunk on card, claret *1,000.*

J35-E1

Incomplete engraving of entire design: no engraved lines on numerals, signed by Lyman F. Ellis.

J35-E1 10c Die on India, die sunk on card, black *2,100.*

J36-E1

Incomplete engraving of entire design: no engraved lines on numerals.

J36-E1 30c Die on India, die sunk on card, claret *1,600.*

J37-E1

Incomplete engraving of entire design: 9x9mm blank space for numerals.

J37-E1 50c Die on India, die sunk on card
black *1,600.*
claret *1,600.*

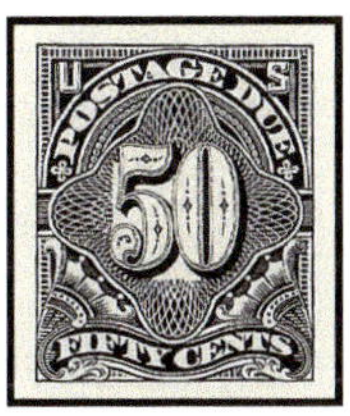

J37-E2

Incomplete engraving of entire design: numerals engraved but hand engraving to retouch lathework around numerals missing.

J37-E2 50c Die on India, die sunk on card, black *2,300.*

J67-E1

Complete engraving of unissued 1917 denomination with wash drawing in "1" and dollar sign, "Approved / Walter F. Brown (signature) / Postmaster General" below design.

J67A-E1 $1 Die on white card, mounted on gray card, black *21,000.*

OFFICIAL STAMPS

Continental Bank Note Co.
AGRICULTURE

O1-E1

Engraved Franklin vignette with 1 and value label.

O1-E1 1c Die on India, on card (1873), black *2,250.*

O2-E1

Engraved Jackson vignette with 2 and value label.

O2-E1 2c Die on glazed paper (1873), black *2,250.*

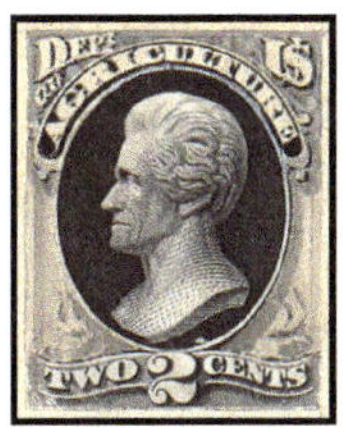

O2-E2

Design size: 20x25mm
Engraved vignette, numeral and value label from 1873 2c (No. O2-E1) mounted on pencil and wash drawing for frame design as adopted for Agriculture set. Pencil signature "J. Claxton" on backing card. Frame differs for each dept.

O2-E2 2c Model on yellowish card, 23x30mm, on 90x118mm white card, black vignette, gray black frame *6,500.*

O3-E1

Washington vignette, 3 and value label.

O3-E1 3c Die on India, card mounted (1873), black *2,250.*

O4-E1

Completed vignette with 6 and value label.

O4-E1 6c Die on India, on card (1873), black *2,400.*

O6-E1

Completed Clay vignette with 12 and value label.

O6-E1 12c Die on white glazed paper (1873), black *2,000.*

O7-E1

Vignette of Webster with 15 below.

O7-E1 15c Die on white glazed paper (1873), black *1,250.*

O9-E1

Completed vignette with 30 below.

O9-E1 30c Die on white glazed paper (1873), black *1,500.*

EXECUTIVE

O12-E1

Design size: 20x25mm
See design note for No. O2-E1.

O12-E1 3c Model on yellowish card, 23x30mm, on 90x118mm white card, black *6,000.*

O12-E2

Design size: 19½x25mm
Die size: 64x76mm
Engraving of complete design of No. O12-E1 with "DEP'T" in top label.

O12-E2 3c
- ***a.*** Die on India, die sunk on card, green *2,750.*
- ***b.*** Die on India, cut close
  - black *2,250.*
  - green *2,250.*

INTERIOR

O17-E1

Design size: 20x25mm
See design note for No. O2-E1.

O17-E1 3c Model on yellowish card, 23x30mm, on 90x118mm white card, black *9,000.*

JUSTICE

O27-E1

Design size: 20x25mm
See design note for No. O2-E1.

O27-E1 3c Model on yellowish card, 23x30mm, on 90x118mm white card, black *10,000.*

NAVY

O37-E1

Design size: 20x25mm
See design note for No. O2-E1.

O37-E1 3c Model on yellowish card, 23x30mm, on 90x118mm white card, black *4,750.*

O39-E1

Die size: 62x76mm
Completed vignette with 7 and value label.

O39-E1 7c
- ***a.*** Die on India, on card (1873), black *1,000.*
- ***b.*** Die on white glazed paper, black *1,000.*

POST OFFICE

O47-E1

Design size: 19½x25mm
Complete engraving of entire design as adopted except with Franklin vignette instead of large numeral.

O47-E1 1c
- ***a.*** Die on India, mounted on white ivory card
  - blue *1,750.*
- ***b.*** Die on proof paper
  - gray black *1,250.*
  - dull scarlet *1,250.*
  - dull brown *1,250.*
  - dull green *1,250.*
  - dull blue *1,250.*
- ***c.*** Die on ivory glazed paper
  - brown black *1,750.*
  - orange red *1,750.*
  - blue *1,750.*

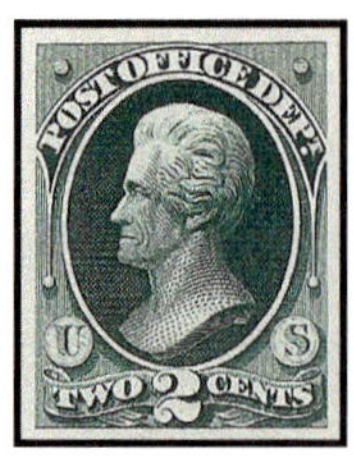

O48-E1

Design size: 19½x25mm

Complete engraving of entire design as adopted except with Jackson vignette instead of large numeral.

O48-E1 2c
- *a.* Die on India, mounted on white ivory card
  - orange brown *1,500.*
- *b.* Die on proof paper
  - gray black *1,250.*
  - dull scarlet *1,250.*
  - dull brown *1,250.*
  - dull green *1,250.*
  - dull blue *1,250.*
- *c.* Die on ivory glazed paper
  - black *1,750.*
  - brown black *1,750.*
  - orange red *1,750.*
  - blue *1,750.*

O49-E1

O49-E2

Design size: 20x25mm
Engraved vignette, numeral and value label from 1873 3c (No. 147-E10) mounted on pencil and wash drawing for frame design not adopted for Post Office set.

O49-E1 3c Model on yellowish card, 23x30mm, on 90x118mm white card, black *5,750.*

O49-E2 3c Model on yellowish card, 23x30mm, on 90x118mm white card, black *5,750.*

O49-E3

Design size: 20x25mm
See design note for No. O2-E1.

O49-E3 3c Model on yellowish card, 23x30mm, on 90x118mm white card, black *5,750.*

O49-E4

Design size: 19½x25mm
Complete engraving of entire design as adopted except with Washington vignette instead of large numeral.

O49-E4 3c
- *a.* Die on India, mounted on white ivory card
  - green *1,500.*
- *b.* Die on proof paper
  - gray black *1,250.*
  - dull scarlet *1,250.*
  - dull brown *1,250.*
  - dull green *1,250.*
  - dull blue *1,250.*
- *c.* Die on ivory glazed paper
  - brown black *1,750.*
  - orange red *1,750.*
  - blue *1,750.*

O49-E5

Design size: 19½x25mm

As No. O49-E4, but with pencil and watercolor modifications in both top corners.

O49-E5 3c Die on India, black *4,000.*

O49-E6

1870 1c stamp (No. 145) with vignette cut out, "OFFICIAL 3 STAMP" drawn in pencil on envelope on which stamp is mounted. Blue pencil notations on backing envelope "1st design of official stamp for POD" and "Design by Mr. J. Barber for P O Official."

O49-E6 1c Stamp frame mounted on envelope, ultramarine frame, black vignette *7,500.*

O49-E7

Model of engraved frame from No. O49-E4 with hollow oval engraved lathework band with "OFFICIAL / STAMP" drawn in wash mounted in place, numeral drawn in pencil and wash. Ms. "No. 1" on backing card.

O49-E7 3c Model on stiff white card, 50x75mm, green *7,500.*

O49-E8

Like No. O49-E6, Ms. "No. 3" on backing card.

O49-E8 3c Model on stiff white card, 50x75mm, green & black *17,500.*

O50-E1

Incomplete engraving of design with Lincoln vignette, without rectangular frame design.

O50-E1 6c Die on white ivory paper, black *4,250.*

O56-E1

Design size: 19½x25mm
Complete engraving of entire design as adopted except with Perry vignette instead of large numeral.

O56-E1 90c
- *a.* Die on India, mounted on white ivory card
  - brown *1,500.*
  - blue *1,500.*
  - orange red *1,500.*
- *b.* Die on proof paper
  - gray black *1,500.*
  - dull scarlet *1,500.*
  - dull brown *1,500.*
  - dull green *1,500.*
  - dull blue *1,500.*
- *c.* Die on ivory glazed paper
  - brown black *1,750.*
  - orange red *1,750.*
  - blue *1,750.*

STATE

O59-E1

Design size: 20x25mm
Engraved vignette, numeral and value label from 1873 3c (No. 147-E10) mounted on pencil and wash drawing for frame design as adopted for State set. Pencil signature "J. Claxton" on backing card.

O59-E1 3c Model on yellowish card, 23x30mm, on 90x118mm white card, black *4,750.*

O68-E1

Design size: 25½x40mm
Engraved vignette of Seward mounted in watercolor drawing of adopted frame design. Ms. signatures of J. Claxton and Chas. Skinner on backing card.

O68-E1 Two Dollars, Model on 29x43mm grayish white card, mounted on 96x120mm white card, black *7,500.*

O68-E2

Complete engraving of adopted frame only with "TWO DOLLARS." in value label at bottom. With "FIVE DOLLARS." and "TEN DOLLARS." value labels outside design at left and "TWENTY DOLLs." value tablet at right.

O68-E2 Two Dollars, Die on India, black *15,000.*

O68-E3

Plate engraved frame only (three examples in a block of four with complete bicolor plate proof of $2 at upper left in block).

O68-E3 Two Dollars, Plate essay on India, green *10,000.*

O71-E1

Plate engraving of top half of frame only, paired with $20 plate proof.

O71-E1 Die on India, mounted on card, green *9,000.*

WAR

O85-E1

Design size: 20x25mm

Engraved vignette, numeral and value label from 1873 3c (No. 147-E10) mounted on pencil and wash drawing for frame design as adopted for War set. Pencil signature "J. Claxton" on backing card.

O85-E1 3c Model on yellowish card, 23x30mm, on 90x118mm white card, black *4,750.*

NEWSPAPER AND PERIODICALS

1865 ISSUE
National Bank Note Co.

PR1-E1

Design size: 51x89mm

Typographed design somewhat similar to that adopted but with large Franklin vignette facing left, "PACKAGE" at bottom, other minor differences.

PR1-E1 5c Die on stiff white ivory paper
- deep orange red *2,000.*
- dusky g-b. blue *2,000.*
- bright blue *2,000.*

a. Die on paper with blue ruled lines
- deep orange red *2,000.*
- carmine *2,000.*

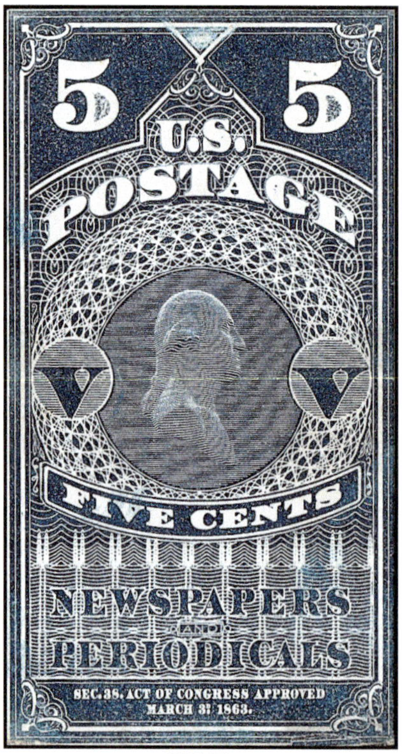

PR1-E2

Design size: 52x96½mm

Typographed design as issued but lacking "National Bank Note Company, New York" imprint at bottom.

PR1-E2 5c Die on wove paper, blue 2,250.

1875 ISSUE
Continental Bank Note Co.

PR9-E1

Design size: 19½x25mm

Engraved vignette and numerals (25's) with pencil sketch of unadopted frame design.

PR9-E1 25c Die on India, on card, black *1,500.*

PR9-E2

Design size: 19½x25mm

Engraving of unadopted design with "US" at top and "25 CENTS 25" at bottom, no ornaments above the "P" and "E" of "POSTAGE" and no crossed lines below "CENTS."

PR9-E2 25c Die on India, mounted on card, black 900.

PR9-E3

Design size: 19½x25mm

Complete engraving of unadopted design with "U S" at top and "25 CENTS 25" at bottom.

PR9-E3 25c

a. Die on India, on card
- black *900.*
- scarlet *900.*
- blue *900.*
- green *900.*

b. Die on white ivory paper
- black *900.*
- black brown *900.*
- scarlet *900.*
- blue *900.*

PR9-E4

Engraved unfinished die with final design, blank spaces for numerals and value tablets.

PR9-E4 Blank denomination, die on India, mounted on 27x45mm card, black *1,150.*

PR14-E1

Design size: 25x35mm
Wash drawing of complete design as adopted. Backing card signed by both designers, Chas. Skinner and Jos. Claxton.

PR14-E1 9c Drawing on 26x36mm card, on 56x74mm card, black *900.*

Complete engraving except value tablets blank.

PR16-E1 (12c) Die on India, mounted on 26x40mm card, black *1,700.*

PR23-E1

Design size: 24x35½mm
Wash drawing similar to that adopted, backing card signed by designers Skinner and Claxton, also has pencil "$12" and ms. "Continental Bank Note Co."

PR23-E1 96c Drawing on 88x121mm card, black *900.*

PR27-E1

Design size: 24½x35mm
Incomplete engraving of entire design: unshaded (shading pencilled in) inside left, right and bottom framelines, value label, top of "9." Upper corners unfinished.

PR27-E1 $9 Die on India, die sunk on 76x82mm card, black *1,350.*

PR28-E1

Design size: 24½x35mm
Incomplete engraving of entire design: no shading on dollar signs and numerals. No shading on frame around numerals and around value tablet.

PR28-E1 $12 Die on India, die sunk on 66x80mm card, black *1,350.*

PR28-E2

Incomplete engraving of entire design, shading pencilled in around bottom value tablet and top right and left dollar signs and numerals.

PR28-E2 $12 Die on India, die sunk on card, 75x90mm, black *850.*

PR29-E1

Design size: 24x35½mm
Wash drawing similar to that adopted but with "U S" in six-pointed stars instead of at top. Backing card signed by designers Skinner and Claxton, also pencil "31/32" and "8 13/32," pencil "Alter" with lines to stars.

PR29-E1 $24 Drawing on 88x121mm card, black *1,600.*

PR31-E1

Vignette size: 13½x26mm
Engraved vignette only as adopted.

PR31-E1 $48 Die on India, die sunk on card, black *750.*

PR31-E2

Design size: 24x36mm
Wash drawing similar to that adopted, backing card signed by designers Skinner and Claxton, also has pencil "$48" above each value numeral.

PR31-E2 $48 Drawing on 88x121mm card, black *1,600.*

PR32-E1

Design size: 24½x35½mm
Wash drawing similar to that adopted, backing card signed by designers Skinner and Claxton.

PR32-E1 $60 Drawing on 88x121mm card, black *750.*

PR32-E2

Incomplete engraving of complete design, no shading lines within "US" and around "POSTAGE" at top.

PR32-E2 $60
a. Die on India, die sunk on card

dark carmine	*1,250.*
brown rose	*1,250.*
scarlet	*1,250.*
sepia	*1,250.*
orange yellow	*1,250.*
brown orange	*1,250.*
dull orange	*1,250.*
orange brown	*1,250.*
green	*1,250.*
ultramarine	*1,250.*
purple	*1,250.*
black	*1,250.*

1885 ISSUE
American Bank Note Co.

PR81-E1

Design size: 23x25mm
Complete engraving of entire design as adopted for 12c-96c.

PR81-E1 1c
a. Die on India, die sunk on card

black	*900.*

b. Die on white ivory paper

black	*500.*
black brown	*500.*
scarlet	*500.*
blue	*500.*

1895 ISSUE
Bureau of Engraving and Printing

PR102-E2

Incomplete engraving of entire design: background at upper ends of value label, shading on side lettering and numerals missing.

PR102-E2 1c Die on India, die sunk on card
black *900.*
green *1,250.*

Incomplete engraving of entire design but further engraved than No. PR102-E2: shading on PA is light, no shading on PE of NEWSPAPERS or IO of PERIODICALS and shading on OD is light.

PR102-E3 1c Die on India, die sunk on card, black *900.*

Incomplete engraving of entire design but further engraved than No. PR102-E3: shading on PERIODICALS is finished but not on PAPE.

PR102-E4 1c Die on India, die sunk on card, black *900.*

PR103-E1

Design size: 21½x34½mm
Die size: 56x75½mm
Incomplete engraving of entire design: spaces for numerals and value label blank but with pencil outline of lettering.

PR103-E1 2c Die on India, die sunk on card, black *1,250.*

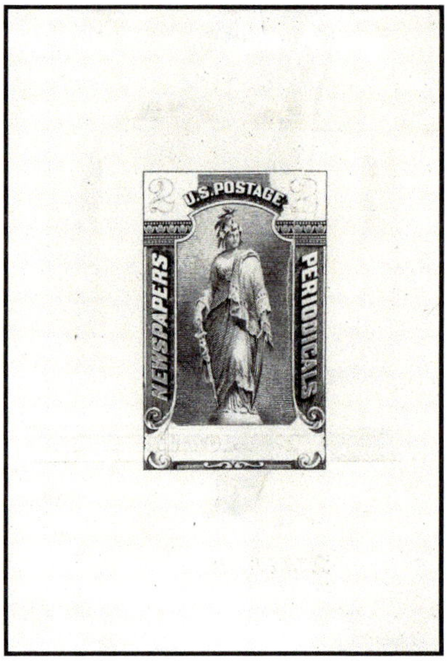

PR103-E2

Incomplete engraving of entire design similar to No. PR103-E1, no shading of "2"s in corners, ruled lines extend 10mm from left side and 15mm from right side by the penciled "TWO CENTS," neatly penciled "TWO CENTS" about 10mm below the design.

PR103-E2 2c Die on India, die sunk on card, black *1,250.*

PR103-E3

Incomplete engraving of entire design but further engraved than No. PR103-E2: shading on leaves at ends of value label unfinished, numerals unshaded, unfinished shading on APE of NEWSPAPERS and RIO of PERIODICALS.

PR103-E3 2c Die on India, black *1,250.*

Incomplete engraving of entire design but further engraved than No. PR103-E3: no shading on PE of NEWSPAPERS, unfinished shading on PA of NEWSPAPERS and RIO of PERIODICALS.

PR103-E4 2c Die on India, die sunk on card, black *1,250.*

PR104-E1

Design size: 21½x34½mm
Die size: 57x73mm
Incomplete engraving of entire design: spaces for numerals and value label blank but with pencil outline of lettering.

PR104-E1 5c Die on India, die sunk on card, black *1,500.*

PR105-E1

Design size: 21½x34½mm
Die size: 56x75mm
Incomplete engraving of entire design: spaces for numerals and value label blank but with pencil outline of lettering.

PR105-E1 10c Die on India, die sunk on card, black *1,600.*

PR105-E2

Incomplete engraving of entire design but further engraved than No. PR105-E1: numerals unfinished, lower corners blank.

PR105-E2 10c Die on India, die sunk on card, black *2,100.*

Incomplete engraving of entire design but further engraved than No. PR105-E2: lower right corner blank.

PR105-E3 10c Die on India, die sunk on card, black *1,250.*

Incomplete engraving of entire design but further engraved than No. PR105-E3: numerals blank, no inner lines.

PR105-E4 10c Die on India, die sunk on card, black *1,250.*

PR105-E5

Design size: 21½x34½mm
Die size: 56x75mm
Incomplete engraving of entire design (early state of die similar to No. PR105-E1) with "10" pencilled in upper right corner and "TEN CENTS" pencilled in at bottom. Pencil notes on India

include “Make top of 1 a little larger and put on spur,” “Work up Vignette” and “Use same scrolls as marked on 5c-.”

PR105-E5 10c Die on India, die sunk on card, black *2,750.*

PR106-E1

Vignette size: 13x25½mm
Die size: 56x72mm
Incomplete engraving of vignette only (transfer of Continental Banknote Co. die for 72c with left side cut off): eagle crest faces front and its right wing is not pointed, shading on left thigh near sword hilt incomplete, bottom of vignette straight instead of curved.

PR106-E1 25c Die on India, die sunk on card
black *2,000.*
deep red *2,000.*

PR106-E2

Design size: about 21x34½mm
Die size: 57½x75mm
Entire design with frame incompletely engraved: vert. lines around CENTS label missing, no shading on TWENTY FIVE, colorless beads under E and FI of same.

PR106-E2 25c Die on India, die sunk on card
black *2,000.*
deep red *2,000.*

PR106-E3

An impression from No. PR106-E2 with pencil shading on TWENTY FIVE and vert. ink lines in spaces around CENTS label, colorless beads also blacked out in ink. Below engraving are three diff. pencil sketches for shape and shading to be engraved.

PR106-E3 25c Die on India, die sunk on card
black *2,750.*
deep red *2,750.*

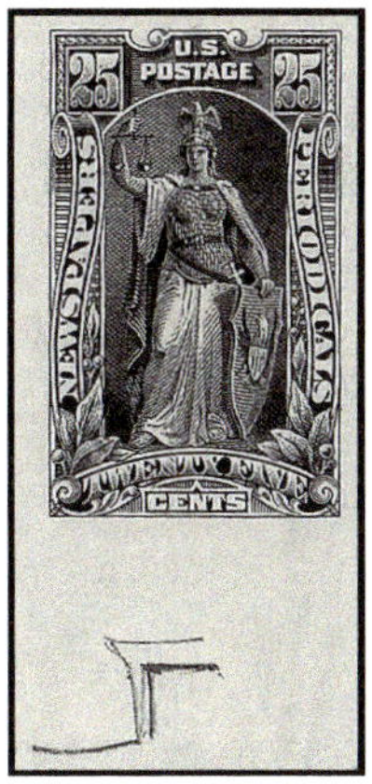

PR106-E4

An impression from No. PR106-E2 but with shading suggestions from No. PR106-E3 partly engraved except colorless beads have pencil shading only. Below engraving is pencil sketch for corner of CENTS label.

PR106-E4 25c Die on India, die sunk on card
black *2,250.*
deep red *2,000.*

PR106-E5

Design size: 21½x34½mm
Die size: 55x72mm
Large die proof of PR107 with bottom value label cut out and “TWENTY-FIVE CENTS” pencilled in on backing card.

PR106-E5 25c Die on India, die sunk on card, black *3,000.*

PR107-E1

Incomplete engraving of entire design: eagle's head and much of bottom of stamp's design unfinished, top of frame unfinished, value lettering sketched in pencil.

PR107-E1 50c Die on card, die sunk, black *3,250.*

PR107-E3

Incomplete engraving of entire design: top of frame and scrolls below FIFTY CENTS unfinished.

PR107-E3 50c Die on India, die sunk on card, black *2,500.*

PR108-E1

Design size: 24½x37mm
Die size: 75x76mm
Incomplete engraving of entire design: vignette and spaces around numerals incomplete, pencil sketch instructions for engraver at top and side for these spaces.

PR108-E1 $2 Die on India, die sunk on card, black *4,750.*

PR108-E2

Design size: 24½x37mm
Die size: 75x76mm
Incomplete engraving of entire design but further engraved than No. PR108-E1: space for ornaments under POSTAGE blank, numerals unshaded.

PR108-E2 $2 Die on India, die sunk on card, scarlet *1,500.*

Further engraved than No. PR108-E2: scrolls under POSTAGE engraved but unfinished.

PR108-E3 $2 Die on India, die sunk on card, black *1,500.*

PR110-E1

Incomplete engraving of design, no frame line under “Postage” and other small differences from final design.

PR110-E1 $10 Die on India, green *1,250.*

PR111-E1

Design size (incomplete): 24½x30mm
Die size: 75x84mm
Incomplete engraving of partial design: spaces for stars and 0s of numerals blank, design missing below bottom of vignette.

PR111-E1 $20 Die on India, die sunk on card, black *1,250.*

PR111-E2

Design size: 24½x35½mm
Incomplete lines below denomination at top, only 7 lines below right "0" of "$20" and 8 lines below left "$20" (issued design has 13 lines in both places), die no. "74" at bottom.

PR111-E2 $20 Die on India, 42x54mm, black *1,900.*

PR111-E3

Design size: 24½x35½mm
Incomplete lines below denomination at top, but with addition of pencil lines of shading to indicate further work needed, die no. "74" at bottom and signed "Smillie" in pencil.

PR111-E3 $20 Die on India, on 71x83mm card, black *1,900.*

PR112-E1

Design size: 24½x35½mm
Die size: 72½x76mm
Incomplete engraving of entire design: upper corners around value numerals unfinished, etc.

PR112-E1 $50 Die on India, on card, black *4,750.*

PR113-E1

Design size: 24½x35½mm
Die size: unknown
Incomplete engraving of entire design: spaces at lower inner corners of value shields blank, shading on numerals and letters at top unfinished.

PR113-E1 $100 Die on India, on card, black *2,600.*

PR113-E2

Design size: 24½x35½mm
Die size: 75x73mm
Further engraved than No. PR113-E1.

PR113-E2 $100 Die on India, die sunk on 80x80mm card, violet *1,500.*

PR113-E3

Further engraved than No. PR113-E2: vignette completed but numerals not shaded, shadows on frame not etched dark.

PR113-E3 $100 Die on India
black *1,750.*
red-violet *1,750.*

Further engraved than No. PR113-E3: numerals shaded, shadows on frame not finally etched, especially above POSTAGE.

PR113-E4 $100 Die on India, black *1,350.*

PARCEL POST STAMPS

Q1-E1

Design size: 35½x23mm
Photo of wash drawing of frame design with numerals, CENT and POST OFFICE CLERK in black ink, vignette in black wash. Ms. "Changed from 15c" and "Approved Nov. 15, 1912 — Frank H. Hitchcock — Postmaster General" on backing card.

Q1-E1 1c Model on thick gray card, 106x91mm, black *5,500.*

Q2-E1

Design size: 35x23½mm
Photo of wash drawing of frame only as adopted. Ms. "Approved Oct. 10, 1912, for border and size of stamps. Engraving to be ⅞ by 1⅜ inches. Frank H. Hitchcock. Postmaster General" on backing card.

Q2-E1 2c Model on thick gray cardboard, 122x110mm, black *3,500.*

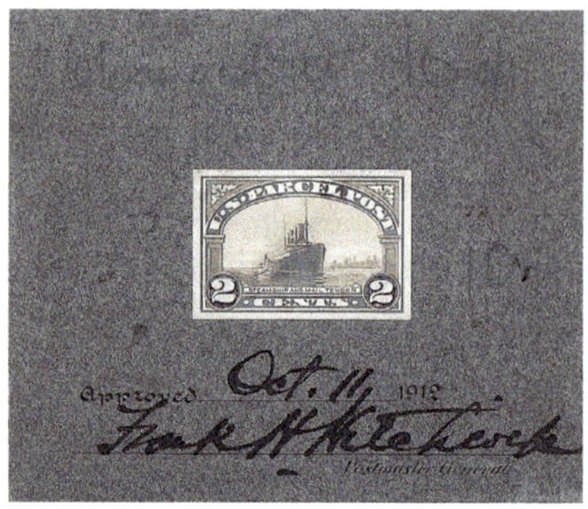

Q2-E2

Design size: 35x23mm
Photo of wash drawing of frame design and retouched photo of ship vignette as eventually used for 10c, numerals and STEAMSHIP AND MAIL TENDER in black ink. Ms. "Changed to 10c" and "Approved Oct. 11, 1912. Frank H. Hitchcock. Postmaster General" on backing card.

Q2-E2 2c Model on thick gray cardboard, 110x83mm, black *8,500.*

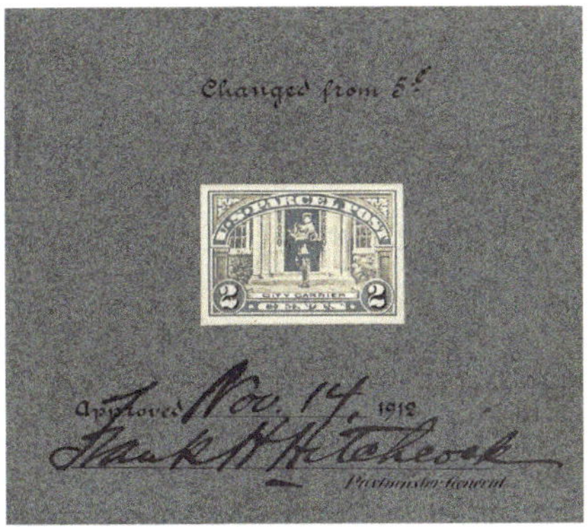

Q2-E3

Design size: 34x22mm
Photo of wash drawing of entire design with adopted vignette, numerals in white wash and CITY CARRIER in black ink. Ms. "Changed from 5c" and "Approved Nov. 14, 1912. Frank H. Hitchcock. Postmaster General" on backing card.

Q2-E3 2c Model on thick gray cardboard, 111x92mm, black *7,500.*

Design size: 34½x22mm
Engraving of adopted design with blank value tablets and "CITY CARRIER" inscription, mail carrier unfinished.

Q2-E4 2c Die on India, sunk on 118x89mm card, black —

Q3-E1

Design size: 35x23mm
Complete engraving of unadopted design: vignette shows mail truck backing up to railroad mail train with clerk about to handle pouches.

Q3-E1 3c Die on white wove, about 43x31mm, carmine *5,000.*

Q3-E2

Design size: 35x22mm
Photo of wash drawing of entire design with adopted vignette (retouched around door to mail car). Ms. "Approved Feb. 22, 1913. Frank H. Hitchcock. Postmaster General" on backing card.

Q3-E2 3c Model on thick gray cardboard, black *5,000.*

Q3-E3

Design size: 35x22mm
Almost complete engraving of adopted design with subtle differences (most evident in shading on windows), on 100x76mm card, affixed with tape to 125x98mm card, small cutout in design, blue control No. 578444 on back.

Q3-E3 3c Die sunk on card, affixed to card, carmine *4,500.*

Q4-E1

Design size: 33½x22mm
Photo of wash drawing of entire design with adopted vignette, numerals drawn in white and RURAL CARRIER in black ink. Ms. "Changed from 10c" and "Approved Nov. 14, 1912. Frank H. Hitchcock. Postmaster General" on backing card.

Q4-E1 4c Model on thick gray cardboard, 116x92mm, black *5,500.*

Q5-E1

Design size: 35x23mm
Photo of wash drawing of entire design with vignette (retouched) eventually used for 2c, numerals and CITY LETTER CARRIER in black ink and white wash. Ms. "Changed to 2c.--City Carrier" and "Approved Oct. 10, 1912. Frank H. Hitchcock. Postmaster General" on backing card.

Q5-E1 5c Model on thick gray cardboard, 110x84mm, black *5,500.*

Q5-E2

Design size: 33½x21½mm
Photo of wash drawing of entire design with numerals in gray, unadopted vignette with MAIL TRAIN in black ink, first car retouched with wash. Ms. "Approved . . . 1912 / . . . Postmaster General" on backing card.

Q5-E2 5c Model on thick gray cardboard, 104½x92mm, black *2,750.*

Q5-E3

Design size: 33½x22mm
Photo of wash drawing of entire design with numerals in gray, MAIL TRAIN in black ink, first car retouched with wash. Ms. "Approved . . . 1912 / . . . Postmaster General" on backing card.

Q5-E3 5c Model on thick gray cardboard, 104½x92mm, black *5,500.*

Q5-E4

Design size: 33½x22mm
Photo of wash drawing of entire design with numerals in white with black background, MAIL TRAIN and pouch catcher in black ink. Ms. "Approved Nov. 19, 1912 Frank H. Hitchcock Postmaster General" on backing card.

Q5-E4 5c Model on thick gray cardboard, 94x90mm, black *2,250.*

Q5-E5

Design size: 26x16mm
Complete engraving of accepted vignette (smoke from engine reworked from previous essays).

Q5-E5 5c Die on India, die sunk on card, a square of the India cut away removing the frame and leaving just the vignette *4,600.*

Q6-E1

Design size: 35½x23mm
Photo of wash drawing of entire design with vignette (retouched) eventually used for 4c, numerals and RURAL DELIVERY in black ink and white wash. Ms. "Changed to 4c."

and "Approved Oct. 10, 1912. Frank H. Hitchcock. Postmaster General" on backing card.

Q6-E1 10c Model on thick gray cardboard, 111x83mm, black *2,500.*

Q6-E2

Design size: 35x23mm
Photo of wash drawing of entire design with adopted vignette, numerals and STEAMSHIP AND MAIL TENDER in black ink and white wash. Ms. "Changed from 2c." and "Approved Nov. 8, 1912. Frank H. Hitchcock. Postmaster General" on backing card.

Q6-E2 10c Model on thick gray cardboard, 116x92mm, black *2,500.*

Q7-E1

Design size: 33½x22mm
Photo of wash drawing of entire design (redrawn in front of autocar and U S MAIL and STATION A) with AUTOMOBILE SERVICE in black ink. Ms. "Approved . . . 1912 / . . . Postmaster General" on backing card.

Q7-E1 15c Model on thick gray cardboard, 115x93mm, black *1,500.*

Q7-E2

Design size:
Complete engraving of entire design with unadopted title label "COLLECTION SERVICE" instead of the adopted "AUTOMOBILE SERVICE."

Q7-E2 15c Die on white wove, card mounted, carmine *1,500.*

Q8-E1

Design size: 35x22mm
Incomplete engraved design nearly as adopted: aviator wears football helmet, head tilted far forward and one leg dangling over edge of plane, mail bag "No. 1" at his right while another sack hangs loosely out of plane.

Q8-E1 20c Die on white wove, about 37x24mm, carmine *1,500.*

Q8-E2

Design size: 35x22mm
Photo of incomplete engraved design as adopted. Ms. "Approved Nov. 19, 1912. Frank H. Hitchcock. Postmaster General" on backing card.

Q8-E2 20c Model on thick gray cardboard, 98x95mm, black *2,500.*

Q9-E1

Design size: 34½x22½mm
Photo of wash drawing of entire design with numerals and smoke at right painted in. Ms. "Changed from $1.00." and "Approved Nov. 14, 1912. Frank H. Hitchcock. Postmaster General" on backing card.

Q9-E1 25c Model on thick gray cardboard, 112x92mm, black *3,000.*

Q10-E1

Design size: 35x23mm
Photo of drawing of entire design with vignette eventually used for 25c with roof, smokestacks and smoke drawn in. Typed label "Stamp Division / Feb / 21 / 1912 / P.O. Dept" on back of backing paper.

Q10-E1 50c Model on thick white paper, black *1,500.*

Q10-E2

Design size: 33x21½mm
Photo of wash drawing of frame design with vignette cut out, mounted over photo of wash drawing of unadopted vignette design, retouched with wash on cows, etc., with DAIRYING in black ink. Pencil "Original" and ms. "Approved . . . 1912 / . . . Postmaster General" on backing card.

Q10-E2 50c Model on thick gray cardboard, 98x93mm, black *1,500.*

Q10-E3

Design size: 35x23mm
Complete engraving of entire design with unadopted vignette: silo and barns placed closer to front of design.

Q10-E3 50c Die on white wove, about 43x31mm, carmine *3,000.*

Q10-E4

Design size: 35x22mm
Photo of incomplete engraved design: no vert. lines on frame around corner foliate spandrels or in numeral circles. Ms. "Approved Jan. 8, 1913. Frank H. Hitchcock. Postmaster General" on backing card.

Q10-E4 50c Model on thick gray cardboard, 99x94mm, black *5,500.*

Q11-E1

Design size: 33½x21½mm
Photo of wash drawing of entire design with central horses and thresher retouched. Ms. "Approved Dec. 12, 1912. Frank H. Hitchcock. Postmaster General" on backing card.

Q11-E1 75c Model on thick gray cardboard, 108x89mm, black *5,250.*

Design size: 28x16mm
Complete engraving of accepted vignette.

Q11-E2 75c Die on India, die sunk on card, a square of the India cut away removing the frame and leaving just the vignette —

Q12-E1

Photo of wash drawing of entire design with vignette much retouched in black ink, numerals, MANUFACTURING and DOLLAR drawn in black ink and white wash. Ms. "Changed to 25c" and "Approved Oct. 22, 1912. Frank H. Hitchcock. Postmaster General" on backing card.

Q12-E1 $1 Model on thick gray cardboard, 114x86mm, black *5,250.*

Q12-E2

Design size: 35x22mm
Photo of wash drawing of complete design with DOLLAR painted in white and black and FRUIT GROWING in black ink, vignette retouched with wash on fruit pickers. Ms. "Approved . . . 1912 . . . Postmaster General" on backing card.

Q12-E2 $1 Model on thick gray cardboard, 105x94mm, black *5,500.*

Q12-E3

Design size: 36x23½mm

Incomplete engraving of entire design: no shading lines in sky. This may be from a rejected die.

Q12-E3 $1 Die on white wove, about 43x31mm, carmine *4,000.*

Q12a-E1

Engraving of entire design as adopted for 1917 offset Documentary Revenues, etc., but with "U.S. PARCEL POST" around value oval.

Q12a-E1	1c Die on card, green	*1,500.*
Q12b-E1	2c Die on card, carmine	*1,500.*
Q12c-E1	3c Die on card, deep violet	*1,500.*
Q12d-E1	4c Die on card, brown	*1,500.*
Q12e-E1	5c Die on card, blue	*1,500.*
Q12f-E1	10c Die on card, orange yellow	*1,500.*
Q12g-E1	15c Die on card, gray	*1,500.*
Q12h-E1	20c Die on wove, carmine rose, affixed to card	*1,500.*

PARCEL POST POSTAGE DUE

Retouched photo of design as adopted, officially dated and approved.

QJQ5-E1a 25c Model, black *1,500.*

BOOKLETS: PANES & COVERS

BK294-E1 obverse

BK294-E1 reverse

Design size: 167x96mm, same as issued booklet
Complete essay booklet in full color, the two No. 3780b panes of 10 with simulated printed die cuts and the panes with two different stamps that were subsequently unadopted and replaced with two different stamps when issued, booklet pages with thicker card stock than normal production issues and also with many text and design differences.

BK294-E1 34c multicolored complete essay booklet —

CARRIER'S STAMPS

Essays by Toppan, Carpenter, Casilear & Co. in 1851

LO1-E1

Die size: 55x50mm
Unfinished die with outer border in a very incomplete state, pencil "For U.S. Carriers Stamp, Vignette 1851, Toppan, Carpenter Casilier & Co."

1851

LO1-E1 (1c) Die on India, die sunk on 96x76mm card, which is mounted on 101x82mm card, black *9,000.*

LO1-E1Ab

LO1-E1Ac

LO1-E1Ad

Die size: 57x50mm
Unfinished die with framelines complete at top and bottom, lathework impinging on white oval and rosettes in lower right corner, plus uncleaned horizontal and vertical layout lines.

LO1-E1A (1c)
b. Die on 34x42mm, white bond, black *11,000.*
c. Die on 60x50mm old ivory paper, die sunk, black *11,000.*
d. Die on 62x54mm, pale green bond, red *7,500.*

Essays by Schernikow in 1903 from a new soft steel die made from the original 1851 transfer roll. (See paragraph eight of the Essay section introduction)

LO1-E2

Die size: 50x50mm
Engraving of Franklin vignette only.

1903

LO1-E2 (1c)
a. Die on proof paper

black	*75.*
carmine	*75.*
red	*75.*
light red	*75.*
orange	*75.*
orange brown	*75.*
yellow	*75.*
olive	*75.*
green	*75.*
dark green	*75.*
dark blue	*75.*
violet	*75.*
violet brown	*75.*

b. Die on colored card, about 75x75mm

deep red, *pinkish white*	*175.*
yellow brown, *pale blue*	*175.*
violet brown, *pale green*	*175.*
dark green, *pale pink*	*175.*
dark blue, *pale pink*	*175.*
violet, *pale yellow*	*175.*

c. Die on green bond (die size: 49x50mm)

dull scarlet	*175.*
dull olive	*175.*
dark ultramarine	*175.*

See note above No. 63-E1.

LO1-E3

Design size: 19½x25mm
Die size: 50x50mm
Design as No. LO1-E1, but distinguished by addition of left and right inner frame lines.

1903

LO1-E3 (1c)
a. Die on proof paper

black	*100.*
carmine	*100.*
dark carmine	*100.*
scarlet	*100.*
orange	*100.*
yellow	*100.*
yellow brown	*100.*
olive	*100.*
light green	*100.*
green	*100.*
steel blue	*100.*
violet	*100.*
red violet	*100.*
violet brown	*100.*
ultramarine	*100.*

b. Die on colored card

dull carmine, *pale olive*	*175.*
brown orange, *pink*	*175.*
brown, *pale buff*	*175.*
brown, *pale blue*	*175.*
gray green, *buff*	*175.*
gray green, *yellow*	*175.*
violet, *ivory*	*175.*
dull carmine, *pale blue*	*175.*

c. Die on blue pelure

carmine	*200.*
scarlet	*200.*
orange	*200.*
brown	*200.*
dark green	*200.*

d. Die on green bond

scarlet	*250.*
orange	*250.*
green	*250.*
dull violet	*250.*

e. Die on gummed thick rose paper, cut to stamp size 6,500.

Essays by Clarence Brazer in 1952 using the Schernikow complete die with addition of two diagonal lines in upper right corner.

LO1-E4

Die size: 50x50mm

1952

LO1-E4 (1c) Die on approximately 121x125mm glazed card

scarlet	*650.*
brown	*650.*
green	*650.*
red	*650.*

POST OFFICE SEALS

Registry Seals
1872 ISSUE
National Bank Note Co.

OXF1-E1

Design size: 72x40mm
Block size: 100x56 ½mm
Design cut on a steel block intended for printing by typography from electrotyped clichés. The design is similar to the adopted design except REGISTERED obliterates other words where it touches them. Apparently only one essay block was made and was not itself altered to produce the die with the adopted image from which electrotypes were made for printing. Accordingly, it is likely that a significant proportion of the impressions from the essay die were made subsequent to the pre-production period. Listed in each category are ink colors that have been seen and are known to be from the essay die; others may exist.

The image for OXF1-E1 was pulled from the essay die as if it were a die for intaglio printing. Accordingly, where the image was intended to print in color, this image is clear; and where the image was intended to print clear, this image is colored. Depsite its appearance, it is from the same die as all OXF1 essays.

OXF1-E1

a. Die on card

chocolate	*1,250.*
black	*1,250.*

OXF1-E2

"Colorless borders." The image was pulled from the essay die as if it were for typographic printing, and the ink from the non-image portion of the die was wiped clean before printing. The images printed on card are often, but not always, on India paper impressed on the card. The images on other surfaces do not use India paper and usually do not show the die block impression.

OXF1-E2

a. Die on card

green	*1,000.*
carmine (rose)	*1,000.*
red brown	*1,000.*
orange	*1,000.*
orange brown	*1,000.*
yellow	*1,000.*
blue	*1,000.*
blue (left), green (right)	*1,200.*

b. Die on India

blue	*1,000.*
lavender	*1,000.*

c. Die on bond weight paper

green	*1,000.*
blue	*1,000.*

d. Die on glossy paper or thin card

green	*1,000.*

OXF1-E3

"Colored borders." As No. OXf1-E2 except that the non-image portion of the die was not wiped clean before printing. The colored border area is found both completely and partially colored. Most impressions on card do not use India paper.

OXF1-E3

a. Die on card

green	*1,000.*
rose	*1,000.*
blue	*1,000.*
violet	*1,000.*
brown	*1,000.*

b. Die on India

green	*1,000.*
red	*1,000.*
rose	*1,000.*
orange brown	*1,000.*
yellow	*1,000.*
blue	*1,000.*
violet	*1,000.*

c. Die on bond weight paper

blue	*1,000.*

d. Die on glossy paper or thin card

blue	*1,000.*
brown	*1,000.*

OXF1-E4

As with No. OXF1-E2 except printed on stamp paper, perforated and gummed.

OXF1-E4

a. Die on stamp paper, perf. 12, gummed

blue	*1,000.*
blue (left), green (right)	*1,000.*

Block size: 80x128mm
Engraving of entire design as adopted but in reverse for making typographed block.

OXF1-E5 Die on white wove, chocolate *1,000.*

Post Office Seals
1877 ISSUE

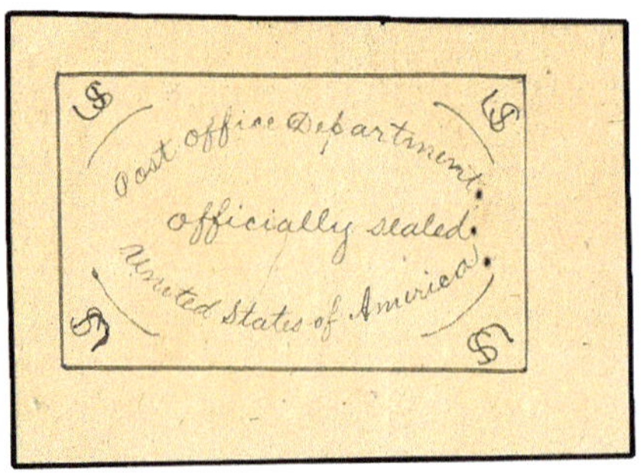

OX1-E1

Preliminary pen and ink concept design on thick light brown paper. Image size: 44x27mm.

OX1-E1 Black *5,000.*

Value based on 2011 auction realization.

OX1-E2

Design size: 44x27mm
Composite model built up from card proofs of intermediate dies; "Post Obitum," the vignette, and the National Bank Note Company imprint cut out and pasted to card. Hand drawn and water-color additions of frame and lettering, Dated Febry 21, 1877 and signed by "Thos. F. Morris" the designer.

OX1-E2 Brown *5,500.*

Value based on 2011 auction realization.

OX1-E3

Design size: 44x27mm
Progressive die essay on India paper on card. Incomplete engraving of entire design with vignette lacking the cap and background, and border lacking the vertical shading lines (probalby unique).

OX1-E3 Brown *1,900.*

OX1-E4

Design size: 44x27mm.
Progressive die essay on India paper. Lacking the vertical shading lines in the border (probably unique).

OX1-E4 Brown *1,000.*

1861 FIRST DESIGN ESSAYS AND TRIAL COLOR PROOFS

For the convenience of collectors and dealers, the Scott editors present here in one location the important 1861 First Design Essays and Trial Color Proofs. The final "stamps" produced with these designs or colors were at one time listed in the Postage section as Nos. 55-57 and 59-62. These so-called "August" issues or "Premiere Gravure" issues, printed on thin and semitransparent stamp paper, gummed and perforated, were not issued as prepared, but were either engraved further to complete the issued designs (1c, 3c, 5c, 12c and 90c) or issued in slightly revised colors (24c and 30c), and they were therefore appropriately moved to the Essay and Trial Color Proof sections of the U.S. Specialized catalogue in 1991.

The 10c denomination of this First Design series, previously No. 58, was pressed into service as an issued stamp, No. 62B, presumably because the demand for this denomination was greater than could be supplied by the plate or plates in use. Former No. 58 and current No. 62B are the same stamp, and it is listed in the Postage section as No. 62B.

The listings here duplicate the listings in the Essay and Trial Color Proof sections rather than replace them. Their listing here is for the convenience of catalogue users only.

Without Dash Below UL Ornament

Die size: 58x56mm

"Premiere Gravure" die No. 440. No dash under the right tip of the ornament at right of the numeral in upper left corner.

63-E11 1c

- ***a.*** "Premiere Gravure" die essay on India (**formerly Nos. 55P1, 55TC1**)

black	*5,500.*
indigo	*1,500.*
ultramarine	*2,250.*

- ***b.*** RA "Premiere Gravure" small die essay on white wove, 28x31mm (**formerly No. 55P2**), indigo — *325.*
- ***c.*** "Premiere Gravure" plate essay on India (**formerly Nos. 55P3, 55TC3**)

indigo	*300.*
blue	—
ultramarine	*300.*
violet ultramarine	—

- ***d.*** "Premiere Gravure" plate essay on semitransparent stamp paper (**formerly No. 55TC4**), ultramarine — *400.*

63-E11e

63-E11e 1c **indigo,** finished "Premiere Gravure" plate essay on semitransparent stamp paper, gummed, perf. 12 **(formerly No. 55)** — *55,000.*

No. 63-E11e is valued with perfs cutting slightly into design at top.

Without Corner Ornaments

65-E11

Die size: 64x76 ½mm

Incomplete engraving of Washington head only.

65-E11 3c

- ***a.*** Die on India, on card, carmine — *750.*
- ***b.*** Die on white glazed paper

black	*750.*
scarlet	*750.*
brown violet	*750.*

65-E12

Die size: 78x55mm

Incomplete engraved design, no scrolls outside framelines, no silhouette under chin, no ornaments on 3s, U and S.

65-E12 3c Die on India, die sunk on card

black	*1,000.*
blue	*1,000.*

65-E13

As No. 65-E12 but ornaments on 3s, U and S. Shows traces of first border design erased. With imprint and No. 441 below design.

65-E13 3c Die on India, card mounted

scarlet	*1,000.*
brown red	*1,000.*
ultramarine	*1,000.*

65-E14

Die size: 59x55mm

As No. 65-E13 but with ornaments outside frame.

65-E14 3c Die on India, die sunk on card

black	*750.*
scarlet	*750.*
pink	*1,250.*
brown orange	*750.*
deep orange red	*750.*
deep red	*750.*

"Premiere Gravure" design; no corner ornaments. No imprint or die number on die impression.

65-E15 3c

- ***a.*** Die on India, card mounted, deep orange red — *1,000.*
- ***b.*** "Premiere Gravure" die essay on semitransparent stamp paper, 20x25mm-30x37mm

deep orange red	*750.*
deep red orange	*750.*
dim red	*750.*
dim deep red	*750.*
dim orange red	*750.*
dull pink	*750.*
dull violet red	*750.*

- ***c.*** "Premiere Gravure" die essay on India (**formerly Nos. 56P1, 56TC1**)

red	*1,350.*
black	*1,750.*
scarlet	*1,750.*
pink	*2,850.*
orange red	*2,000.*
dark orange red	*2,000.*

- ***d.*** RA Small die essay on white wove, 28x31mm altered laydown die of complete design but with outer scrolls removed and replaced by ones similar to "Premiere Gravure" design (1903) (**formerly No. 56P2**), dim deep red — *325.*
- ***e.*** As "c," PP small die essay on pale cream soft wove, 24x29mm (1915) (**formerly No. 56P2a**), deep red — *1,250.*
- ***f.*** "Premiere Gravure" plate No. 2 essay on India (**formerly Nos. 56P3, 56TC3**)

red	*250.*
scarlet	*350.*

- ***g.*** "Premiere Gravure" plate essay on semitransparent stamp paper (**formerly Nos. 56aP4, 56TC4**)

red, pair with gum	*1,750.*
black	*400.*

65-E15h

65-E15h 3c **brown rose,** finished "Premiere Gravure" plate essay on semitransparent stamp paper, gummed, perf. 12 **(formerly No. 56)**

	600.
orange red	475.
bright orange red	475.
dark orange red	475.
dim deep red	475.
pink	475.
deep pink	475.
P# block of 8, Impt. (any shade)	*20,000.*

No Leaflets at Corners

67-E8

Incomplete impression from die No. 442, border lines and corner scrolls missing.

67-E8 5c Die on India, mounted on 34x50mm card, black — *1,750.*

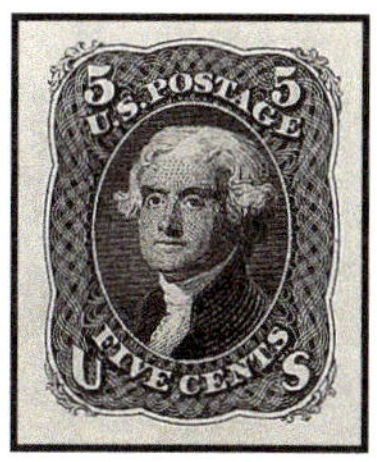

67-E9

Size of die: 58x59mm

"Premiere Gravure" design, with corner scrolls but without leaflets.

67-E9 5c

- ***a.*** "Premiere Gravure" die essay on India, card mounted (formerly No. 57TC1)

black	*2,500.*
scarlet	*2,500.*

- ***b.*** RA Small die essay on white wove, 28x31mm, altered laydown die of complete design but with scrolls removed from corners to resemble "Premiere Gravure" (1903) (**formerly No. 57P2), brown** — 325.
- ***c.*** As "b," PP die essay on pale cream soft wove, 24x29mm (1915) (**formerly No. 57P2a**), brown — *1,750.*

d. "Premiere Gravure" plate No. 3 essay on India (**formerly Nos. 57P3, 57TC3)**
brown *250.*
light brown *300.*
dark brown *300.*
red brown *300.*

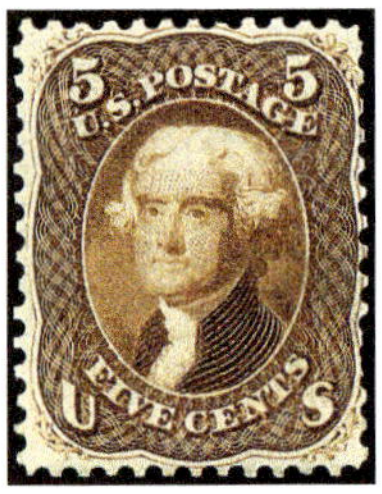
67-E9e

67-E9e 5c **brown,** finished "Premiere Gravure" plate essay on semitransparent stamp paper, gummed, perf. 12 **(formerly No. 57)** *25,000.*

One example is recorded of No. 67-E9e postally used. It has small faults and a circular datestamp in black, and it is valued thus. Value, $30,000.

Without Corner Ornaments

69-E5

Design size: 12½x16mm
Die size: about 62x65mm
Washington vignette only.

69-E5 12c
a. Die on India, die sunk on card
black *400.*
dark red *400.*
orange red *400.*
b. Die on ivory paper, about 24x28mm
black *500.*
scarlet *500.*
black brown *500.*
blue *500.*

Incomplete die No. 444, without corner ornaments.

69-E6 12c
a. "Premiere Gravure" die essay on India, mounted on card (**formerly Nos. 59P1, 59TC1**)
black *2,500.*
scarlet *2,500.*
dark green *2,500.*
b. RA Small die essay on white wove, 29x31mm, altered laydown die of complete design but with scrolls removed from corners to resemble the "Premiere Gravure" (1903) (formerly Nos. 59P2), black *450.*
c. PP "Premiere Gravure" small die essay on pale cream soft wove, 24x29mm (1915) (**formerly No. 59P2a**), black *1,750.*
d. "Premiere Gravure" plate No. 5 essay on India (**formerly No. 59P3**), black *300.*

69-E6e

69-E6e 12c **black,** finished "Premiere Gravure" plate essay on semitransparent stamp paper, gummed, perf. 12 **(formerly No. 59)** *80,000.*

70TC6

No. 70TC6 differs from the issued 1861 24c stamps by its color.

70TC6 24c **dark violet,** finished "Premiere Gravure" trial color plate proof on semitransparent stamp paper, gummed, perf. 12 **(formerly No. 60)** *15,000.*

71-E1

Die size: 46x60mm
Incomplete die (No. 446): additional ornaments at top and bottom in pencil, as later engraved.

71-E1 30c Die on India, black *1,750.*

71-E2

"Premiere Gravure" die: left side of frame and silhouette at lower right unfinished.

71-E2 30c
a. "Premiere Gravure" die essay on India, die sunk on card (**formerly No. 61TC1**)
black *1,500.*
green *1,500.*
dull gray blue *1,500.*
violet brown *1,500.*
scarlet *1,500.*
dull rose *1,500.*
b. "Premiere Gravure" plate essay on India (**formerly No. 61P3**), deep red orange *500.*
c. "Premiere Gravure" plate essay on card
black (split thin) *500.*
blue *750.*
d. "Premiere Gravure" plate essay on card, black 12x2mm SPECIMEN overprint, blue *750.*
e. "Premiere Gravure" plate essay on semitransparent stamp paper
deep red orange *1,250.*
yellow orange *1,250.*
lemon yellow *1,250.*
dark orange yellow *1,250.*
dull orange yellow *1,250.*

71TC6

No. 71TC6 differs from the issued 1861 30c stamp primarily by its color.

71TC6 30c **red orange,** finished "Premiere Gravure" trial color plate proof on semitransparent stamp paper, gummed, perf. 12 **(formerly No. 61)** *40,000.*

One example is recorded of No. 71TC6 with a quartered cork cancel and repairs. Value, $40,000.

No Dashes Between the Parallel Angled Lines Above Top Ribbon; No Point of Color at Apex of Lower Angled Line

72-E6

Die size: 54x63mm
Incomplete die: without thin lines at bottom of frame and in upper left triangle between label and frame, and without leaves at left of U and right of S.

72-E6 90c Die on India, blue (shades) *1,000.*

72-E7

Similar to 72-E6 but lines added in upper left triangle, leaves added at left of U and at right of S. Exists with and without imprint and Die No. 447 added below design.

72-E7 90c
a. Die on India, die sunk on card, black *1,750.*
b. "Premiere Gravure" die essay on India, thin line under bottom center frame (**formerly Nos. 62P1, 62TC1**)
blue *1,350.*
black *1,500.*
c. RA "Premiere Gravure" small die essay on white wove, 28x31mm (1903) (**formerly No. 62P2**), blue *500.*
d. PP "Premiere Gravure" small die essay on pale cream soft wove, 24x29mm (1915) (**formerly No. 62P2a**), blue *1,750.*
e. "Premiere Gravure" plate essay on India, blue *500.*
f. "Premiere Gravure" plate essay on card, black (split thin) *500.*
g. "Premiere Gravure" plate essay on semitransparent stamp paper (**formerly Nos. 62aP4, 62TC4**)
blue, pair, gummed *5,500.*
blue green *275.*

72-E7h

72-E7h 90c **blue,** finished "Premiere Gravure" plate essay on semitransparent stamp paper, gummed, perf. 12 **(formerly No. 62)** *40,000.*

Die size: 54x63mm
Similar to Nos. 72-E6 and 72-E7 but leaf at left of "U" only, no shading around "U" and "S," leaf and some shading missing at bottom right above "S," shading missing in top label, etc., faint ms. "8" at bottom of backing card.

72-E8 90c Die on India, die sunk on 3¼x3½-inch card, dark blue —

TRIAL COLOR, DIE AND PLATE PROOFS

PROOFS are known in many styles other than those noted in this section. For the present, however, listings are restricted to die proofs, large and small, and plate proofs on India paper and card, and occasionally on stamp paper or other types of paper. The listings of normal color proofs include several that differ somewhat from the types and/or colors of the issued stamps.

Proofs in other than accepted or approved colors exist in a large variety of shades, colors and papers produced at various times by various people for many different reasons. The field is large. Trial Color Proofs are also listed as die proofs, large and small, and plate proofs on a variety of papers. The listings of Trial Color Proofs also include several that are similar to the colors of the issued stamps.

Some Trial Color Proofs are listed out of sequence. Nos. 156TC2-166TC2, the so-called "Goodall" Small Die Proofs in five colors, follow No. 166P4. Nos. O1TC2-O93TC2, another set of "Goodall" Small Die Proofs, follow No. O123P2a. The last set of "Goodall" Small Die Proofs, Nos. PR9TC2-PR32TC2, follow No. PR113P2a. The "Atlanta" set of Plate Proofs in five colors, Nos. 3TC4-LO2TC4, are listed after QE4aP1.

Large Die Proofs are so termed because of the relatively large piece of paper on which they are printed which is about the size of the die block, 40mm by 50mm or larger. The margins of this group of proofs usually are from 15mm to 20mm in width though abnormal examples prevent the acceptance of these measurements as a complete means of identification.

These proofs were prepared in most cases by the original contracting companies and 19th century issues often show the imprint thereof and letters and numbers of identification. They are listed under Large die (P1). The India paper on which these proofs are printed is of an uneven texture and in some respects resembles hand-made paper. These large die proofs were usually mounted on cards though many are found removed from the card. Large Die Proofs autographed by the engraver or officially approved are worth much more, except for those of the 1922-29 period, which are generally approved and signed proofs.

Values for Large Die Proofs are for the full die proofs mounted on cards unless noted otherwise. Full large die proofs measure 5-6" x 7-8". Cut-down Large Die Proofs sell for less. Values for die proofs of the bicolored 1869 issue are for examples which are completely printed. Occasionally the vignette has been cut out and affixed to an impression of the border.

Die Proofs of all United States stamps of later issues exist. Only those known outside of government ownership are listed.

Hybrids are plate proofs of all issues before 1894, and some from 1989-95, which have been cut to shape, mounted and pressed on large cards to resemble large die proofs. These sell for somewhat less than the corresponding large die proofs.

Small Die Proofs are so called because of the small piece of paper on which they are printed. Proofs of stamps issued prior to 1904 are reprints and not in all cases from the same dies as the large die proofs.

Small Die Proofs (Roosevelt Album, Small die (P2)) — These 302 small die proofs are from sets prepared for 85 ("Roosevelt presentation") albums in 1903 by the Bureau of Engraving and Printing but bear no imprint to this effect. The white wove paper on which they are printed is of a fibrous nature. The margins are small, seldom being more than from 3-5mm in width. Values are for proofs affixed to the original gray card backing from the Roosevelt album. Proofs without the card backing sell for less. Small die proofs from the 1903 Roosevelt albums have "RA" as part of the listing description. Small die proofs before 1904 that do not have "RA" as part of the listing description are not from the 1903 Roosevelt albums.

Small Die Proofs (Panama-Pacific Issue, Small die (P2a)) — A special printing of 413 different small die proofs was made in 1915 for the Panama-Pacific Exposition. These have small margins (2½-3mm) and are on soft yellowish wove paper. They are extremely scarce as only 3-5 of each are known and a few exist only in this special printing. 6-10 exist of No. E6 in two slightly different colors. Panama-Pacific small die proofs have "PP" as part of the listing description.

Plate Proofs are, quite obviously, impressions taken from finished plates and differ from the stamps themselves chiefly in their excellence of impression and the paper on which they are printed. Some of the colors vary.

India Paper is a thin, soft, opaque paper which wrinkles when wet. It varies in thickness and shows particles of bamboo.

Card is a plain, clear white card of good quality, which is found in varying thicknesses for different printings. Plate proofs on card were made in five printings in 1879-94. Quantities range from 500 to 3,200 of the card proofs listed between Scott 3P and 245P.

Margin blocks with full imprint and plate number are indicated by the abbreviation "P# blk. of -."

Numbers have been assigned to all proofs consisting of the number of the regular stamp with the suffix letters "TC" to denote Trial Color or "P" to denote Proof.

Some proofs are not identical to the issued stamps. Some of these are now listed in the Essay section. Others have been left in the proof section to keep sets together at this time.

Values are for items in very fine condition. Most "Panama-Pacific" small die proofs are toned. Values are for moderately toned examples. **Plate proof pairs on stamp paper are valued with original gum unless otherwise noted.**

POSTMASTER PROVISIONAL ISSUES

New York

The die proofs are of the No. 9X1 design. All trial color plate proofs and plate proofs in black are from the small sheet of 9. These latter proofs have minutely different design dimensions.

1845

9X1TC2 5c small die on India paper
b. **dull dark violet** 300.
c. **brown violet** 300.
d. **deep rose violet** 300.
e. **deep blue** 300.
f. **dark green** 300.
g. **orange yellow** 300.
h. **brown** 300.

9X1TC5 5c plate on bond paper
a. **deep blue** 200.
b. **dk green** 200.
c. **brown** 200.
d. **scarlet** 200.

With "Scar" on Neck

9X1TC2 5c small die on India paper
i. **dull blue** 175.
j. **vermilion** 175.

With "Scar" and dot in "P" of "POST"

9X1TC1d 5c large die on thin glazed card
e. **deep ultramarine** 450.
f. **orange vermilion** 450.
g. **brown black** 450.

9X1TC2 5c small die on India paper
k. **dull gray blue** 300.
l. **deep green** 300.
m. **dull dark green** 300.
n. **dark brown red** 300.
o. **dull dark brown** 300.
p. **deep blue,** on bond paper 250.
q. **deep green,** on bond paper 250.
r. **dull brown red,** on bond paper 250.
s. **dull dark brown,** on bond paper 250.

Large die trial color proofs with additional impression of the portrait medallion are listed in the Essay section as Nos. 9X1-E1.

9X1P1 5c **black,** large die on India paper 750.
b. Dot in "P" of "POST" and scar on neck 525.
c. As "b," on Bond 525.
d. As "b," on glazed paper 525.
e. With scar on neck, on Bond 525.

9X1P2 5c **black,** small die on India paper 350.
b. With scar on neck 300.
c. Dot in "P" of "POST" and scar on neck 300.
d. As "b," on Bond 300.

9X1P3 5c **black,** plate on India paper —
9X1P4 5c As No. 9X1P2c, plate on card —

The above listed Large Die varieties have an additional impression of the portrait medallion.

9X1P5 5c **black,** plate on bond paper
a. Black on white bond 175.
b. Black on blue bond 150.
Sheet of 9, either paper *7,500.*

Providence, R.I.

10X1TC4 5c plate on card
a. **gray blue** 250.
b. **green** 250.
c. **brown carmine** 250.
d. **brown** 250.

10X2TC4 10c plate on card
a. **gray blue** 450.
b. **green** 450.
c. **brown carmine** 450.
d. **brown** 450.
Sheet of 12, any color 3,750.

10X1P4 5c **black,** plate on card 300.
10X2P4 10c **black,** plate on card 500.
Sheet of 12 3,250.

GENERAL ISSUES

1847

1TC1a 5c large die on India paper
e. **violet** 1,000.
f. **dull blue** 1,000.
g. **blue green** 1,000.
h. **dull green** 1,000.
i. **dark green** 1,000.
j. **orange yellow** 1,000.
k. **orange vermilion** 1,000.
l. **scarlet vermilion** 1,000.
m. **rose lake** 1,000.
n. **brown red** 1,000.
o. **black** 1,000.

1TC1b 5c large die on bond paper
e. **deep blue** 800.
f. **dull blue green** 800.
g. **orange yellow** 800.
h. **orange vermilion** 800.
i. **scarlet vermilion** 800.
j. **black brown** 800.
k. **black** 800.

1TC1c 5c large die on wove paper
e. **deep blue** 800.
f. **orange yellow** 800.
g. **deep yellow** 800.
h. **orange vermilion** 800.

1TC1d 5c large die on thin glazed card
e. **deep ultra** 850.
f. **scarlet vermilion** 850.
g. **black brown** 850.
h. **black** 800.

1TC2 5c small die on India paper
b. **deep blue** 625.
c. **blue green** 625.
d. **dull green,** on bond 600.
e. **yellow green** 625.
f. **orange yellow** 625.
g. **rose lake,** on bond 625.
h. **dull rose lake,** on bond 625.
i. **black** 675.

1TC3 5c plate on India paper
a. **orange** 625.
b. **black** 625.

Double transfer (80R1) —
Double transfer (90R1) —
1P1 5c **red brn,** large die on India paper 800.
a. White bond paper 800.
b. Colored bond paper 1,250.
c. White laid paper 1,000.
d. Bluish laid paper 800.
e. Yelsh wove paper 800.
f. Bluish wove paper 800.
g. White wove paper 800.
h. Card 1,000.
i. Glazed paper 1,000.
1P3 5c **red brn,** plate on India paper 600.
2TC1a 10c large die on India paper
e. **violet** 1,000.
f. **dull blue** —
g. **deep blue** 1,000.
h. **dark green** 1,000.
i. **orange yellow** 1,000.
j. **orange vermilion** 1,000.
k. **golden brown** 1,000.
l. **light brown** 1,000.
m. **dark brown** 1,000.
n. **rose lake** 1,000.
o. **yellow green,** on blue pelure paper 1,000.
2TC1b 10c large die on bond paper
e. **deep blue** 800.
f. **blue green** 800.
g. **dull blue green** 800.
h. **dull green** 800.
i. **orange vermilion** 800.
j. **golden brown** 800.
k. **dark brown** 800.
2TC1c 10c large die on wove paper
e. **deep blue** 800.
f. **dull yellow** 800.
g. **orange yellow** 800.
h. **orange vermilion** 800.
2TC1d 10c large die on thin glazed card
e. **deep blue** 850.
f. **scarlet vermilion** 850.
g. **golden brown** 850.
h. **red brown** 675.
i. **dull red** 675.
j. **black brown** 850.
2TC2 10c small die on India paper
b. **deep blue** 675.
c. **dull gray blue,** on bond paper 625.
d. **yellow green** 675.
e. **orange vermilion** 625.
f. **rose lake** 625.
2TC3 10c plate on India paper
a. **orange** 625.
b. **deep brown** 625.

Original trial color die proofs are often cut down and reduced in size; full-size trial color die proofs sell at higher prices. Reprint proofs with cross-hatching are valued as full-size; cut-down examples sell for less.

Nos. 1TC3 and 2TC3 exist with and without "specimen" overprint. Values are for examples without the overprint. Examples with the overprint are equally as scarce and sell for about the same values.

2P1 10c **black,** large die on India paper 800.
a. White bond paper 800.
b. Colored bond paper 1,250.
c. White laid paper 800.
d. Bluish laid paper 800.
e. Yelsh wove paper 800.
f. Bluish wove paper 800.
g. White wove paper 800.
h. Card 1,000.
i. Glazed paper 1,000.
2P3 10c **black,** plate on India paper 900.
Dbl. transfer (31R1) 1,750.

Original die proofs are generally found cut to stamp size; full size die proofs sell at higher prices. Reprint proofs with cross-hatching are valued as full size; cut down examples sell for less. Plate proofs overprinted "Specimen" sell for about the same as the above values.

Reproductions of 1847 Issue

Actually, official imitations made about 1875 from new dies and plates by order of the Post Office Department.

3TC1a 5c large die on India paper
e. **black** 900.
f. **green** 900.
3TC4 5c plate on card
f. **dull rose lake** 600.
3P1 5c **red brn,** large die on India paper 900.
3P2 5c **red brn,** RA sm die on white wove paper 425.
b. On bond paper 650.
3P2a 5c **red brn,** PP sm die on yelsh wove paper 2,750.
3P3 5c **red brn,** plate on India paper 375.
Block of 4 1,750.
3P4 5c **red brn,** plate on card 250.
Block of 4 1,100.
Plate scratches at UL —
4TC1a 10c large die on India paper
e. **green** 900.
f. 3TC1af and 4TC1ae, **green,** side-by-side composite proof on India paper 11,000.
4TC3 10c plate on India paper
a. **green** 750.
4P1 10c **black,** large die on India paper 1,500.
4P2 10c **black,** RA sm die on white wove paper 425.
b. On bond paper 650.
4P2a 10c **black,** PP sm die on yelsh wove paper 2,750.
4P3 10c **black,** plate on India paper 375.
Block of 4 1,750.
4P4 10c **black,** plate on card 250.
Block of 4 1,100.

1851-60

5TC1a 1c large die on India paper
e. **black** —
5P1 1c **blue,** Type I, large die on India paper *5,000.*
7TC5 1c plate on stamp paper
a. **black** *3,750.*
11TC5 3c plate on stamp paper
a. **black** *3,000.*
11P1 3c **red,** Type I, large die on India paper *5,000.*
11P3 3c **red,** Type I, plate on India paper, brush obliteration 1,000.
Block of 4 5,000.
P# block of 8 *20,000.*
12TC1a 5c large die on India paper
e. **black** *8,500.*
12TC5 5c plate on wove paper
a. **pale brown** 275.
b. **rose brown** 275.
c. **deep red brown** 800.
d. **dark olive bister** 275.
e. **olive brown** 275.
f. **olive green** 275.
g. **deep orange** 275.
h. **black** *5,000.*
12P1 5c **brn,** Type I, large die on India paper *7,000.*
12P2a 5c **brn,** Type I, PP sm die on yelsh wove paper *5,000.*
13TC1a 10c large die on India paper
e. **black** *5,000.*
13TC5 10c Plate on wove paper
a. **black** 1,500.
13P1 10c **grn,** Type I, large die on India paper *5,000.*
15TC5 10c plate on wove paper
a. **black** *5,000.*
17P1 12c **black,** large die on India paper *12,500.*
24P3 1c **blue,** Type V (pl. 9), plate on India *750.*
Pair *1,800.*
26P3 3c **red,** Type III, plate on India *750.*
Pair *1,800.*
30P3 5c **brn,** Type II, plate on India *750.*
35P3 10c **grn,** Type V, plate on India *.750*
36BP3 12c **blk,** plate III (broken frame lines), plate on India *750.*
Block of 4 *3,750.*
36BP5 12c **blk,** plate III (broken frame lines), plate on stamp paper —
Pair —
Block of 4 —
37TC1a 24c large die on India paper
e. **black** *7,000.*
37TC5 24c plate on wove paper
a. **claret brown** 600.
b. **red brown** 600.
c. **orange** 600.
d. **deep yellow** 600.
e. **yellow** 600.
f. **deep blue** 600.
g. **black** —
h. **violet black** 600.
37TC6 24c **red lilac,** on stamp paper, perf 15½, gummed (formerly No. 37b) 1,000.
Block of 4 6,000.
37P1 24c **lilac,** large die on India paper —
37P3 24c **lilac,** plate on India *750.*
Pair *1,800.*
37P5 24c **lilac,** plate on stamp paper *1,500.*
Pair *10,000.*
38TC1a 30c large die on India paper
e. **black** *5,000.*
38TC2 30c small die on India paper
b. **black** 1,250.
38TC3 30c plate on India paper
a. **black** 1,400.
Block of 4 9,000.
38TC5 30c plate on wove paper
a. **black** 1,000.
38P1 30c **org,** large die on India paper —
38P2 30c **org,** sm die on white wove paper —
38P3 30c **org,** plate on India *750.*
Pair *1,800.*
38P5 30c **org,** plate on stamp paper *1,500.*
Pair *7,750.*
39TC1a 90c large die on India paper
e. **brown orange** *6,000.*
f. **black** *6,000.*
39TC2 90c small die on India paper
b. **black** 1,250.
39TC5 90c plate on wove paper
a. **rose lake** 625.
b. **henna brown** 625.
c. **orange red** 625.
d. **brown orange** 625.
e. **sepia** 625.
f. **dark green** 625.
g. **dark violet brown** 625.
h. **black** 675.

Former Nos. 55-57, 59, 62 are now in the Essay section. Former Nos. 60-61 will be found below as Nos. 70TC3e and 71TC3b, respectively.

39P1 90c **blue,** large die on India paper —
39P2 90c **blue,** sm die on white wove paper —
39P3 90c **blue,** plate on India *750.*
Pair *1,800.*
39P5 90c **blue,** plate on stamp paper *4,500.*
Pair *37,500.*

Plate proofs of 24P to 39P are from the original plates. They may be distinguished from the 40P to 47P by the type in the case of the 1c, 3c, 10c and 12c, and by the color in the case of the 5c, 24c, 30c and 90c.

The 3c plate proofs (No. 11) are on proof paper and all known examples have a vertical brush stroke obliteration.

Die proofs of the 30c show full spear point in corners of design.

Reprints of 1857-60 Issue

40TC5 1c plate on wove paper
a. **orange vermilion** 275.
b. **orange** 275.
c. **yellow orange** 275.
d. **orange brown** 275.
e. **dark brown** 275.
f. **dull violet** 275.
g. **violet** 275.
h. **red violet** 275.
i. **gray** 275.
40P1 1c **br blue,** type I, large die on India paper 300.
40P2 1c **br blue,** type I, RA sm die on white wove paper 325.
40P2a 1c **br blue,** type I, PP sm die on yelsh wove paper *2,500.*
40P3 1c **br blue,** type I (new plate), plate on India 80.
Block of 4 475.
40P4 1c **br blue,** type I (new plate), plate on card 45.
Block of 4 200.
40P5 1c **br blue,** type I (new plate), plate on stamp paper 750.
41TC3 3c **red,** plate on India paper —
41P1 3c **scarlet,** type I, large die on India paper 300.
41P2 3c **scarlet,** type I, RA sm die on white wove paper 325.
41P2a 3c **scarlet,** type I, PP sm die on yelsh wove paper *2,500.*
41P3 3c **scarlet,** type I (new plate), plate on India 80.
Block of 4 475.
41P4 3c **scarlet,** type I (new plate), plate on card 70.
Block of 4 310.
41P5 3c **scarlet,** type I (new plate), plate on stamp paper —
42P1 5c **org brn,** type II, large die on India paper 300.
42P2 5c **org brn,** type I, RA sm die on white wove paper 80.
42P3 5c **org brn,** type II (plate II), plate on India
Block of 4 475.
P# blk. of 8 1,450.
42P4 5c **org brn,** type II (plate II), plate on card 45.
Block of 4 200.
P# blk. of 8 —
43P1 10c **grn,** type I, large die on India paper 300.
43P2 10c **grn,** type I, RA sm die on white wove paper 325.
43P2a 10c **grn,** type I, PP sm die on yelsh wove paper *2,500.*
43P3 10c **grn,** type I (new plate), plate on India 80.
Block of 4 475.
43P4 10c **grn,** type I (new plate), plate on card 45.
Block of 4 200.
43P5 10c **grn,** type I (new plate), plate on stamp paper 50.
44P1 12c **greenish blk,** (new die, frame line complete), large die on India paper 300.
44P2 12c **greenish blk,** (new die, frame line complete), RA sm die on white wove paper 325.
44P2a 12c **greenish blk,** (new die, frame line complete), PP sm die on yelsh wove paper *3,500.*
44P3 12c **greenish blk,** (new plate, frame line complete), plate on India 120.
Block of 4 525.
44P4 12c **greenish blk,** (new plate, frame line complete), plate on card 45.
Block of 4 200.
44P5 12c **greenish blk,** (new plate, frame line complete), plate on stamp paper —
45P1 24c **blksh vio,** large die on India paper 300.
45P2 24c **blksh vio,** RA sm die on white wove paper 325.
45P2a 24c **blksh vio,** PP sm die on yelsh wove paper *2,500.*
45P3 24c **blksh vio,** (plate I), plate on India 80.
Block of 4 350.
P# blk. of 8 1,050.
45P4 24c **blksh vio,** (plate I), plate on card 45.
Block of 4 200.
46P1 30c **yel org,** large die on India paper 300.
46P2 30c **yel org,** RA sm die on white wove paper 325.
46P2a 30c **yel org,** PP sm die on yelsh wove paper *2,500.*
46P3 30c **yel org,** (plate I), plate on India 80.
Block of 4 500.
P# blk. of 8 1,450.
46P4 30c **yel org,** (plate I), plate on card 45.
Block of 4 200.
P# blk. of 8 —
47P1 90c **dp blue,** large die on India paper 300.
47P2 90c **dp blue,** RA sm die on white wove paper 325.
47P2a 90c **dp blue,** PP sm die on yelsh wove paper *2,500.*
47P3 90c **dp blue,** (plate I), plate on India 120.
Block of 4 525.
P# blk. of 8 2,000.
47P4 90c **dp blue,** (plate I), plate on card 45.
Block of 4 200.
P# blk. of 8 800.
Nos. 40P4-47P4 (8) 385.00

Nos. 42P2-44P2 were printed from original dies. The 5c shows type I projections at top and bottom. The 12c was printed from a new die and shows complete frame lines.

Nos. 40P1-47P1, large die, exist only as hybrids.

SECOND DESIGNS (Regular Issue)

For "First Designs" see Essay section (former Nos. 55-57, 59, 62), Proofs and Trial Color Proofs (former No. 58) and Trial Color Proofs (former Nos. 60-61).

1861

62BTC1a 10c large die on India paper
e. **black** *2,500.*
62BTC3 10c plate on India paper
a. **green** 300.
b. **light green** 300.
62BP2 10c RA small die proof on white wove paper
b. **Dark green** *325.*
c. **Green** *325.*

Both shades of No. 62BP2 were actually printed from the No. 68 die.

62BP3 10c **dark green,** plate on India *500.*
P# blk. of 8 —
63TC1a 1c large die on India paper
e. **black** *2,500.*
63TC2 1c small die on India paper
b. **black** 750.
c. **red** 750.
d. **brown** 750.
e. **green** —
f. **orange** —
63TC5 1c plate on wove paper, imperf.
a. **rose** 40.
b. **deep orange red** 40.
c. **deep red orange** 40.
d. **dark orange** 40.
e. **yellow orange** 40.
f. **orange brown** 40.
g. **dark brown** 40.
h. **yellow green** 40.
i. **green** 40.
j. **blue green** 40.
k. **gray lilac** 40.
l. **gray black** 40.
m. **slate black** 40.
n. **blue** 40.
o. **light blue** 40.
p. **deep blue** 100.
63TC6 1c plate on wove paper, perf.
a. **rose** 50.
b. **deep orange red** 50.
c. **deep red orange** 50.
d. **dark orange** 50.
e. **yellow orange** 50.
f. **orange brown** 50.
g. **dark brown** 50.
h. **yellow green** 50.
i. **green** 50.
j. **blue green** 50.
k. **gray lilac** 50.
l. **gray black** 50.
m. **slate black** 50.
n. **blue** 50.
o. **light blue** 50.
p. **deep blue** 50.

The perforated 1861 1c trial colors are valued with perfs cutting the design on two sides. Well centered examples are extremely scarce and sell for more.

There are many trial color impressions of the issues of 1861 to 1883 made for experimentation with various patent papers, grills, etc. Some are fully perforated, gummed and with grill.

63P1 1c **blue,** large die on India paper 700.
63P2 1c **blue,** RA sm die on white wove paper 200.
63P2a 1c **blue,** PP sm die on yelsh wove paper 2,250.
b. **indigo** 2,250.
63P3 1c **blue,** plate on India 55.
Block of 4 225.
P# blk. of 8 1,750.
63P4 1c **blue,** plate on card 40.
Block of 4 250.
P# blk. of 8 —
64TC6 3c plate on thin stamp paper, perf 12, gummed
a. **carmine pink** *650.*
64P1 3c **pink,** large die on India paper 3,500.
64P2 3c **pink,** RA sm die on white wove paper —
65TC1a 3c large die on India paper
e. **black** 2,500.
f. **black,** on glazed 2,500.
g. **blue green** 2,500.
h. **orange** 2,500.
i. **brown** 2,500.
j. **dark blue** 2,500.
k. **ocher** 2,500.
l. **green** 2,500.
m. **dull red** 2,500.
n. **slate** 2,500.
o. **red brown** 2,500.
p. **deep pink** 2,500.
q. **rose pink** 2,500.
r. **dark rose** 2,500.
65TC6 3c plate on thin stamp paper, perf 12, gummed
a. **dark carmine** —
65P1 3c **rose,** large die on India paper 1,500.
65P2 3c **rose,** RA sm die on white wove paper 200.

Specialists have questioned the existence of Nos. 64P2 and 65P2. The editors would like to receive evidence of the existence of either of these proofs.

65P2a 3c **rose,** PP sm die on yelsh wove paper 2,750.
65P3 3c **rose,** plate on India 500.
Block of 4 550.
P# blk. of 8 1,750.
a. **dull red** 100.
65P4 3c **rose,** plate on card 150.
65P5 3c **rose,** plate on stamp paper, pair 1,000.
P# blk. of 8 —
67TC1a 5c large die on India paper
e. **black** 2,500.
f. **dark orange** 2,500.
g. **green** 2,500.
h. **ultramarine** 2,500.
i. **gray** 2,500.
j. **rose brown** —
67TC2 5c small die on India paper
b. **black** —
67P1 5c **buff,** large die on India paper *5,000.*
67P2a 5c **buff,** PP sm die on white wove paper *5,000.*
76P1 5c **brown,** large die on India paper 700.
76P2 5c **brown,** RA sm die on white wove paper 200.
76P2a 5c **brown,** PP sm die on yelsh wove paper *2,750.*
76P3 5c **brown,** plate on India 45.
Block of 4 200.
P# blk. of 8 1,750.
76P4 5c **brown,** plate on card 30.
Block of 4 140.
P# blk. of 8 —
68TC1a 10c large die on India paper
e. **orange** 2,500.
f. **red brown** 2,500.
g. **dull pink** 2,500.
h. **scarlet** 2,500.
i. **black** 2,500.
j. **ocher** 2,500.
k. **ultramarine** 2,500.
68TC2 10c small die on India paper
b. **black** 550.
68P1 10c **green,** large die on India paper 650.
68P2 10c **green,** RA sm die on white wove paper 200.
68P2a 10c **green,** PP sm die on yelsh wove paper 2,750.
68P3 10c **green,** plate on India 65.
Block of 4 275.
P# blk. of 8 1,500.
68P4 10c **green,** plate on card 30.
Block of 4 140.
P# blk. of 8 —
69TC1a 12c large die on India paper
e. **scarlet vermilion** 2,500.
f. **brown** 2,500.
g. **red brown** 2,500.
h. **green** 2,500.
i. **orange yellow** 2,500.
69TC2 12c small die on India paper
b. **black** 550.
69P1 12c **black,** large die on India paper 600.
69P2 12c **black,** RA sm die on white wove paper 200.
69P2a 12c **black,** PP sm die on yelsh wove paper 2,750.
69P3 12c **black,** plate on India 65.
Block of 4 275.
P# blk. of 8 1,500.
69P4 12c **black,** plate on card 30.
Block of 4 140.
P# blk. of 8 —
70TC1a 24c large die on India paper
e. **scarlet** 2,500.
f. **green** 2,500.
g. **orange** 2,500.
h. **red brown** 2,500.
i. **orange brown** 2,500.
j. **orange yellow** 2,500.
k. **rose red** 2,500.
l. **gray** 2,500.
m. **steel blue** 2,500.
n. **blue** 2,500.
o. **black** 2,500.
p. **violet** 2,500.
70TC2 24c small die on India paper
b. **violet** 375.
70TC2a 24c PP small die on yelsh wove paper
e. **violet** 2,250.
70TC3 24c plate on India paper
a. **violet** *750.*
Block of 4 *3,250.*
70TC5 24c **gray,** on bluish gray stamp paper 250.
70TC6 24c **dark violet,** semi-transparent stamp paper, perf 12, gummed **(formerly No. 60)** *15,000.*
70P1 24c **red lilac,** large die on India paper —
70P2a 24c **red lilac,** PP sm die on yelsh wove paper 2,750.
70P4 24c **red lilac,** plate on card 425.
78P2 24c **lilac,** RA sm die on white wove paper 200.
78P2a 24c **lilac,** PP sm die on yelsh wove paper 2,750.
78P3 24c **lilac,** plate on India 75.
Block of 4 350.
P# blk. of 8 1,850.
78P4 24c **lilac,** plate on card 80.
Block of 4 400.
P# blk. of 8 —
71TC1a 30c large die on India paper
e. **rose** 2,500.
f. **red orange** 2,500.
71TC2 30c small die on India paper
e. **black** 600.
f. **red orange** 375.
71TC2a 30c PP small die on yelsh wove paper
e. **red orange** 1,250.
71TC6 30c **red orange,** semi-transparent stamp paper, perf 12, gummed **(formerly No. 61)** *47,500.*

One example is recorded of No. 71TC6 with a quartered cork cancel and repairs. Value, $40,000.

71P1 30c **orange,** large die on India paper 500.
71P2 30c **orange,** RA sm die on white wove paper 200.
71P2a 30c **orange,** PP sm die on yelsh wove paper 2,750.
71P3 30c **orange,** plate on India 45.
Block of 4 300.
P# blk. of 8 2,250.
71P4 30c **orange,** plate on card 30.
Block of 4 140.
P# blk. of 8 —
72TC1a 90c large die on India paper
e. **black** 2,500.
f. **ultramarine** 2,500.
g. **bluish gray** 2,500.
h. **violet gray** 2,500.
i. **red brown** 2,500.
j. **orange** 2,500.
k. **yellow orange** 2,500.
l. **scarlet** 2,500.
m. **green** 2,500.
72P1 90c **blue,** large die on India paper 600.
72P2 90c **blue,** RA sm die on white wove paper 200.
72P2a 90c **blue,** PP sm die on yelsh wove paper 2,750.
72P3 90c **blue,** plate on India 50.
Block of 4 350.
P# blk. of 8 2,250.
72P4 90c **blue,** plate on card 30.
Block of 4 140.
P# blk. of 8 —

1861 Gummed Stamp Paper

66TC6 3c **lake,** perf. 12 *2,000.*
Pair *4,500.*
Block of 4 *9,250.*
P# strip of 4 *10,000.*
Double transfer *2,250.*
a. Imperf, pair *1,850.*
P# block of 8 —

John N. Luff recorded the plate number for No. 66TC as 34.

74TC6 3c **scarlet,** perf. 12 *7,000.* 5,000.
Block of 4 *29,000.* 5,000.
With 4 horiz. black pen strokes *5,000.*
With handstamped cancel *10,000.*
a. Imperf, pair *4,000.*

John N. Luff recorded the plate number for No. 74TC as 19.

1861

66TC2 3c **lake,** RA small die on India paper 250.
66TC2a 3c **lake,** PP small die on yelsh wove paper 1,100.
66TC3 3c **lake,** plate on India paper 150.
Block of 4 850.
P# Block of 8 2,250.
74TC1a 3c **scarlet,** large die on India paper 2,250.
74TC2 3c **scarlet,** RA small die on India paper 375.
74TC2a 3c **scarlet,** small die on yelsh wove paper 900.
74TC3 3c **scarlet,** plate on India paper 150.
Block of 4 725.
74TC4 3c **scarlet,** plate on card 150.
Block of 4 725.
P# Block of 8 —

1861-67

73TC1a 2c large die on India paper
e. **dull chalky blue** *8,000.*
f. **green** *8,000.*
g. **dull yellow** *8,000.*
h. **dark orange** *8,000.*
i. **scarlet** *8,000.*
j. **dull rose** *8,000.*
k. **brown** *8,000.*
l. **ultramarine** *8,000.*
73TC3 2c plate on India paper
a. **light blue** 250.
b. **dull chalky blue** 500.
c. **green** 250.
d. **olive green** 250.
e. **blue green** *400.*
f. **vermilion** 250.
g. **scarlet** 250.
h. **dull red** 250.
i. **dull rose** 250.
j. **gray black** 250.
Block of 4 *2,500.*
73P1 2c **black,** die I, large die on India paper 7,500.
a. Die II 2,500.
73P2 2c **black,** die II, RA sm die on white wove paper 1,300.
73P2a 2c **black,** die II, PP sm die on yelsh wove paper 8,750.
73P3 2c **black,** die I, plate on India 150.
Block of 4 650.
P# blk. of 8 2,150.
a. Die II 110.
Block of 4 550.
P# blk. of 8 1,750.
73P4 2c **black,** die I, plate on card, P# block of 8 —
a. Die II 75.
Block of 4 400.
P# blk. of 8 —
77TC1a 15c large die on India paper
e. **deep blue** 2,500.
f. **dark red** 2,500.
g. **orange red** 2,500.
h. **dark orange** 2,500.
i. **yellow orange** 2,500.
j. **dark yellow** 2,500.
k. **sepia** 2,500.
l. **orange brown** 2,500.
m. **red brown** 2,500.
n. **blue green** 2,500.
o. **dusky blue** 2,500.
p. **gray black** 2,500.

No.	Description	Value
77TC3	15c plate on India paper	
a.	**deep blue**	335.
	Block of 4	1,650.
77P1	15c **black,** large die on India paper	1,500.
77P2	15c **black,** RA sm die on white wove paper	500.
77P2a	15c **black,** PP sm die on yelsh wove paper	2,750.
77P3	15c **black,** plate on India	.50
	Block of 4	225.
	P# blk. of 8	2,750.
77P4	15c **black,** plate on card	45.
	Block of 4	200.
	P# blk. of 8	—
79P5	3c **rose,** A grill, plate on stamp paper, pair	*1,500.*
	Block of 4	*4,000.*
	P# blk. of 8	*10,000.*
83P5	3c **rose,** C grill, plate on stamp paper, pair	*2,500.*
94P5	3c **red,** F grill, plate on stamp paper, pair	*1,500.*

The listed plate proofs of the 1c (63P), 5c (76P), 10c (68P) and 12c (69P) are from the 100 subject re-issue plates of 1875. Single proofs of these denominations from the regular issue plates cannot be told apart from the reprints. As the reprint plates had wider spacing between the subjects, multiples can be differentiated. Values are for proofs from the reprint plates. The 2c Die II has a small dot on the left cheek. The 5c has a small notch at the bottom left of the design.

1869

No.	Description	Value
112TC1a	1c large die on India paper	
e.	**black**	2,500.
112P1	1c **buff,** large die on India paper	750.
112P2	1c **buff,** RA sm die on white wove paper	300.
112P2a	1c **buff,** PP sm die on yelsh wove paper	3,000.
112P3	1c **buff,** plate on India	50.
	Block of 4	225.
	P# blk. of 10	950.
112P4	1c **buff,** plate on card	60.
	Block of 4	275.
113TC1a	2c large die on India paper	
e.	**black**	2,500.
113P1	2c **brown,** large die on India paper	750.
113P2	2c **brown,** RA sm die on white wove paper	300.
113P2a	2c **brown,** PP sm die on yelsh wove paper	3,500.
113P3	2c **brown,** plate on India	35.
	Block of 4	160.
	P# blk. of 10	800.
113P4	2c **brown,** plate on card	45.
	Block of 4	200.
	P# blk. of 10	950.
114TC1a	3c large die on India paper	
e.	**black**	2,500.
114P1	3c **ultra,** large die on India paper	900.
114P2	3c **ultra,** RA sm die on white wove paper	500.
114P2a	3c **ultra,** PP sm die on yelsh wove paper	*4,000.*
114P3	3c **ultra,** plate on India	40.
	Block of 4	170.
	P# blk. of 10	1,000.
114P4	3c **ultra,** plate on card	70.
	Block of 4	325.
	P# blk. of 10	1,200.
115TC1a	6c large die on India paper	
e.	**deep dull blue**	2,500.
f.	**black**	2,500.
115P1	6c **ultra,** large die on India paper	900.
115P2	6c **ultra,** RA sm die on white wove paper	300.
115P2a	6c **ultra,** PP sm die on yelsh wove paper	3,000.
115P3	6c **ultra,** plate on India	40.
	Block of 4	170.
	P# blk. of 10	1,000.
115P4	6c **ultra,** plate on card	70.
	Block of 4	325.
	P# blk. of 10	1,200.
116TC1a	10c large die on India paper	
e.	**black**	2,500.
f.	**dull dark violet**	2,500.
g.	**deep green**	2,500.
h.	**dull dark orange**	2,500.
i.	**dull rose**	2,500.
j.	**copper red**	2,500.
k.	**chocolate**	2,500.
l.	**dark Prussian blue**	2,500.
116P1	10c **yellow,** large die on India paper	900.
116P2	10c **yellow,** RA sm die on white wove paper	300.
116P2a	10c **yellow,** PP sm die on yelsh wove paper	3,000.
116P3	10c **yellow,** plate on India	40.
	Block of 4	170.
	P# blk. of 10	2,000.
116P4	10c **yellow,** plate on card	50.
	Block of 4	225.
	P# blk. of 10	2,400.
117TC1a	12c large die on India paper	
e.	**black**	2,500.
117P1	12c **green,** large die on India paper	900.
117P2	12c **green,** RA sm die on white wove paper	300.
117P2a	12c **green,** PP sm die on yelsh wove paper	3,000.
117P3	12c **green,** plate on India	40.
	Block of 4	170.
	P# blk. of 10	2,250.
117P4	12c **green,** plate on card	50.
	Block of 4	225.
	P# blk. of 10	2,650.
118TC1a	15c large die on India paper	
e.	**dull dark violet**	2,500.
f.	**deep blue**	2,500.
g.	**dull red brown**	2,500.
h.	**black**	2,500.
i.	**dark blue gray**	2,500.
119P1	15c **brn & bl,** (type II), large die on India paper	550.
119P2	15c **brn & bl,** (type II), RA sm die on white wove paper	400.
119P2a	15c **brn & bl,** (type II), PP sm die on yelsh wove paper	3,000.
119P3	15c **brn & bl,** (type II), plate on India	110.
	Block of 4	550.
	P# blk. of 8	4,000.
129P1	15c **Reissue,** (type III), large die on India paper	550.
129P2	15c **Reissue,** (type III), RA sm die on white wove paper	400.
129P2a	15c **Reissue,** (type III), PP sm die on yelsh wove paper	3,000.
129P3	15c **Reissue,** (type III), plate on India	325.
	Block of 4	1,400.
	P# blk. of 8	4,500.
129P4	15c **Reissue,** (type III), plate on card	130.
	Block of 4	675.
	P# blk. of 8	3,750.
a.	Center inverted *(100)*	*2,400.*
	Block of 4	*14,000.*
	P# blk. of 8	*75,000.*
120TC1a	24c large die on India paper	
e.	**black**	4,500.
120TC3	24c plate on India paper	
a.	**green & reddish lilac**	400.
	Block of 4	1,750.
	P# block of 8	6,000.
120P1	24c **grn & vio,** large die on India paper	550.
120P2	24c **grn & vio,** RA sm die on white wove paper	400.
120P2a	24c **grn & vio,** PP sm die on yelsh wove paper	3,000.
120P3	24c **grn & vio,** plate on India	125.
	Block of 4	575.
	P# blk. of 8	6,000.
120P4	24c **grn & vio,** plate on card	130.
	Block of 4	650.
	P# blk. of 8	7,500.
a.	Center inverted *(100)*	*2,400.*
	Block of 4	*14,000.*
	P# blk. of 8	*75,000.*
121TC1a	30c large die on India paper	
e.	**deep blue & deep green**	3,500.
f.	**deep brown & blue**	3,500.
g.	**golden brown & carmine lake**	3,500.
h.	**carmine lake & dull violet**	3,500.
i.	**carmine lake & green**	3,500.
j.	**carmine lake & brown**	3,500.
k.	**carmine lake & black**	3,500.
l.	**dull orange red & deep green**	3,500.
m.	**deep ocher & golden brown**	3,500.
n.	**dull violet & golden brown**	3,500.
o.	**black & deep green**	3,500.
121P1	30c **ultra & car,** large die on India paper	1,250.
121P2	30c **ultra & car,** RA sm die on white wove paper	400.
121P2a	30c **ultra & car,** PP sm die on yelsh wove paper	3,000.
121P3	30c **ultra & car,** plate on India	125.
	Block of 4	575.
	P# blk. of 8	7,500.
121P4	30c **ultra & car,** plate on card	160.
	Block of 4	825.
	P# blk. of 8	—
a.	Flags inverted *(100)*	*2,400.*
	Block of 4	*14,000.*
	P# blk. of 8	*75,000.*
122TC1a	90c large die on India paper	
e.	**brown & deep green**	3,500.
122TC4	90c Plate on card	
a.	**green & black**	1,500.
122P1	90c **car & blk,** large die on India paper	550.
122P2	90c **car & blk,** RA sm die on white wove paper	400.
122P2a	90c **car & blk,** PP sm die on yelsh wove paper	5,000.
122P3	90c **car & blk,** plate on India	165.
	Block of 4	775.
	P# blk. of 8	6,500.
122P4	90c **car & blk,** plate on card	160.
	Block of 4	825.
	P# blk. of 8	8,250.
a.	Center inverted *(100)*	*2,400.*
	Block of 4	*14,000.*
	P# blk. of 8 (unique)	*87,500.*
	Nos. 112P3-117P3, 119P3-122P3 (10)	770.00
	Nos. 112P4-117P4, 120P4-122P4 (9)	795.00

Large die proofs of Nos. 119, 129, 120 and 122 exist only as hybrids.

1880

No.	Description	Value
133P1	1c **dark buff,** large die on India paper	1,000.
133P3	1c **dark buff,** plate on India	110.
	Block of 4	475.
	P# blk. of 10	1,350.

1870-71 National Bank Note Co.

No.	Description	Value
136P5	3c **green,** grill, on stamp paper, pair	*1,200.*
	P# blk. of 12	*14,000.*
145TC1a	1c large die on India paper	
e.	**yellow orange**	600.
f.	**red brown**	600.
g.	**red violet**	600.
h.	**black**	—
i.	**green**	600.
145TC3	1c plate on India paper	
a.	**black**	—
145P1	1c **ultra,** large die on India paper	250.
145P2	1c **ultra,** RA sm die on white wove paper, from new die	160.
145P2a	1c **ultra,** PP sm die on yelsh wove paper	2,500.
145P3	1c **ultra,** plate on India	20.
	Block of 4	90.
	P# blk. of 10	750.
146TC1a	2c large die on India paper	
e.	**black**	600.
146P1	2c **red brn,** large die on India paper	250.
146P3	2c **red brn,** plate on India	20.
	Block of 4	90.
	P# blk. of 12	750.
147TC1a	3c large die on India paper	
e.	**brown**	—
f.	**red brown**	—
g.	**dark red**	—
h.	**light ultramarine**	—
i.	**yellow brown**	—
j.	**dull red violet**	—
k.	**dull grayish red**	—
l.	**yellow orange**	—
m.	**red violet**	—
n.	**green**	—
147TC3	3c plate on India paper	
a.	**brown**	125.
b.	**dark brown**	125.
c.	**red brown**	125.
d.	**orange brown**	125.
e.	**dark red**	125.
f.	**light ultramarine**	125.
g.	**yellow brown**	125.
h.	**dull red violet**	125.
i.	**yellow orange**	125.
j.	**red violet**	125.
147TC5	3c plate on wove paper	
a.	**deep red brown**	125.

Former Nos. 147aTC and 147bTC are now listed in the Essay section as No. 147-E13c.

No.	Description	Value
147P1	3c **green,** large die on India paper	300.
147P3	3c **green,** plate on India	20.
	Block of 4	90.
	P# blk. of 12	750.

The former No. 147Pc4 is now listed in the Essay section as No. 147-E13e.

No.	Description	Value
148TC1a	6c large die on India paper	
e.	**deep magenta**	600.
f.	**ultramarine**	600.
g.	**carmine**	600.
h.	**maroon**	600.
148P1	6c **carmine,** large die on India paper	1,750.
148P3	6c **carmine,** plate on India	35.
	Block of 4	150.
	P# blk. of 12	1,400.
149TC1a	7c large die on India paper	
e.	**black**	550.
149P1	7c **vermilion,** large die on India paper	250.
149P3	7c **vermilion,** plate on India	15.
	Block of 4	70.
	P# blk. of 12	750.
150TC1a	10c large die on India paper	
e.	**blue**	550.
f.	**dull pale blue**	550.
g.	**ultramarine**	550.
h.	**blue green**	550.
i.	**carmine**	550.
j.	**bister**	550.
k.	**dull red**	550.
l.	**red orange**	550.
m.	**yellow brown**	550.
n.	**brown orange**	550.
150P1	10c **brown,** large die on India paper	300.
150P3	10c **brown,** plate on India	40.
	Block of 4	165.
	P# blk. of 12	2,000.
151TC1a	12c large die on India paper	
e.	**orange**	550.
f.	**orange brown**	550.
g.	**brown red**	550.
h.	**dull red**	550.
i.	**carmine**	550.
j.	**blue**	550.
k.	**light blue**	550.
l.	**ultramarine**	550.
m.	**green**	550.
151P1	12c **violet,** large die on India paper	250.
151P3	12c **violet,** plate on India	16.
	Block of 4	70.
	P# blk. of 10	750.
152P1	15c **orange,** large die on India paper	300.
152P3	15c **orange,** plate on India	30.
	Block of 4	135.
	P# blk. of 12	750.
153TC1a	24c large die on India paper	
e.	**dark brown**	550.
153P1	24c **purple,** large die on India paper	300.
153P3	24c **purple,** plate on India	30.
	Block of 4	135.
	P# blk. of 12	750.
154P1	30c **black,** large die on India paper	300.
154P3	30c **black,** plate on India	40.
	Block of 4	170.
	P# blk. of 12	2,250.
155TC1a	90c large die on India paper	
e.	**carmine**	550.
f.	**ultramarine**	550.
g.	**black**	550.
155P1	90c **carmine,** large die on India paper	300.
155P3	90c **carmine,** plate on India	45.
	Block of 4	195.
	P# blk. of 12	2,500.

Secret Marks on 24, 30 and 90c Dies of the Bank Note Issues

National 24c — Rays of lower star normal.

Continental 24c — Rays of lower star strengthened.

National 30c — Lower line does not join point of shield.

Continental and American 30c — Lower line joins point of shield and bottom line of shield thicker.

National 90c — Rays of star in upper right normal.

Continental and American 90c — Rays of star in upper right strengthened.

1873 Continental Bank Note Co.

156TC1a	1c large die on India paper	
	e. **scarlet**	*1,500.*
156TC3	1c plate on India paper	
	a. **black**	15.
	Block of 4	65.
156TC4	1c plate on card	
	a. **black**	30.
	Block of 4	140.
156P1	1c **ultra,** large die on India paper	450.
156P3	1c **ultra,** plate on India	55.
	Block of 4	250.
	P# blk. of 14	1,150.
156P4	1c **ultra,** plate on card	250.
157TC1a	2c large die on India paper	
	e. **black**	850.
	f. **dull blue**	850.
	g. **rose**	850.
	h. **deep rose**	850.
157TC3	2c plate on India paper	
	a. **black**	15.
	Block of 4	65.
157P1	2c **brown,** large die on India paper	350.
157P2	2c **brown,** RA sm die on white wove paper	160.
157P2a	2c **brown,** PP sm die on yelsh wove paper	2,500.
157P3	2c **brown,** plate on India	35.
	Block of 4	165.
	P# blk. of 14	1,150.
157P4	2c **brown,** plate on card	20.
	Block of 4	90.
	P# blk. of 14	—
157P5	2c **brown,** plate on stamp paper	—
158TC1a	3c large die on India paper	
	e. **black**	750.
	g. **orange red**	—
158TC3	3c plate on India paper	
	a. **black**	12.
	Block of 4	55.
158P1	3c **green,** large die on India paper	350.
158P2	3c **green,** RA sm die on white wove paper	160.
158P3	3c **green,** plate on India	55.
	Block of 4	220.
	P# blk. of 14	1,150.
158P4	3c **green,** plate on card	130.
158P5	3c **green,** plate on stamp paper, pair	*150.*
	a. On stamp paper, grill, pair	*650.*
158TC4	3c plate on card	
	a. **black**	15.
	Block of 4	75.
	P# block of 12	450.
159TC3	6c plate on India paper	
	a. **black**	30.
	Block of 4	150.
159P1	6c **rose,** large die on India paper	2,000.
159P2	6c **rose,** RA sm die on white wove paper	250.
159P2a	6c **rose,** PP sm die on yelsh wove paper	2,500.
159P3	6c **rose,** plate on India	110.
	Block of 4	525.
	P# blk. of 12	2,000.
159P4	6c **pink,** plate on card	250.
160TC3	7c plate on India paper	
	a. **black**	75.
	Block of 4	325.
160P1	7c **org vermilion,** large die on India paper	250.
160P2	7c **org vermilion,** RA sm die on white wove paper	160.
160P2a	7c **org vermilion,** PP sm die on yelsh wove paper	2,500.
160P3	7c **org vermilion,** plate on India	35.
	Block of 4	165.
	P# blk. of 14	1,150.
160P4	7c **org vermilion,** plate on card	20.
	Block of 4	90.
	P# blk. of 14	—
161P1	10c **brown,** large die on India paper	450.
161P2	10c **brown,** RA sm die on white wove paper	180.
161P3	10c **brown,** plate on India	60.
	Block of 4	300.
	P# blk. of 14	1,300.
161P4	10c **brown,** plate on card	250.
162P1	12c **blackish vio,** large die on India paper	200.
162P2	12c **blackish vio,** RA sm die on white wove paper	160.
162P2a	12c **blackish vio,** PP sm die on yelsh wove paper	2,500.
162P3	12c **blackish vio,** plate on India	38.
	Block of 4	190.
	P# blk. of 14	1,150.
162P4	12c **blackish vio,** plate on card	20.
	Block of 4	90.
	P# blk. of 14	—
162P5	12c **blackish vio,** plate on stamp paper	—
163P1	15c **yel org,** large die on India paper	400.
163P2	15c **yel org,** RA sm die on white wove paper	160.
163P2a	15c **yel org,** PP sm die on yelsh wove paper	2,250.
163P3	15c **yel org,** plate on India	65.
	Block of 4	250.
	P# blk. of 12	1,000.
163P4	15c **yel org,** plate on card	20.
	Block of 4	100.
	P# blk. of 12	—
164P1	24c **violet,** large die on India paper	400.
164P2	24c **violet,** RA sm die on white wove paper	175.
164P2a	24c **violet,** PP sm die on yelsh wove paper	2,500.
164P3	24c **violet,** plate on India	50.
	Block of 4	225.
	P# blk. of 12	1,150.
164P4	24c **violet,** plate on card	30.
	Block of 4	130.
165P1	30c **gray blk,** large die on India paper	400.
165P2	30c **gray blk,** RA sm die on white wove paper	160.
165P2a	30c **gray blk,** PP sm die on yelsh wove paper	2,500.
165P3	30c **gray blk,** plate on India	40.
	Block of 4	200.
	P# blk. of 12	1,150.
165P4	30c **gray blk,** plate on card	80.
	Block of 4	90.
166P1	90c **rose car,** large die on India paper	400.
166P2	90c **rose car,** RA sm die on white wove paper	160.
166P2a	90c **rose car,** PP sm die on yelsh wove paper	2,500.
166P3	90c **rose car,** plate on India	55.
	Block of 4	250.
	P# blk. of 12	1,500.
166P4	90c **rose car,** plate on card	35.
	Block of 4	160.

Die proofs of the 24c, 30c and 90c show secret marks, as illustrated, but as plates of these denominations were not made from these dies, plate proofs can be identified only by color.

Nos. 159TC2-166TC2 are so-called "Goodall" set of Small Die proofs on India Paper of Official Stamps in five colors

159TC2	6c "Goodall" small die on India paper	
	b. **black**	600.
	c. **deep green**	600.
	d. **dull gray blue**	600.
	e. **deep brown**	600.
	f. **dull red**	600.
160TC2	7c "Goodall" small die on India paper	
	b. **black**	600.
	c. **deep green**	600.
	d. **dull gray blue**	600.
	e. **deep brown**	600.
	f. **dull red**	600.
161TC2	10c "Goodall" small die on India paper	
	b. **black**	600.
	c. **deep green**	600.
	d. **dull gray blue**	600.
	e. **deep brown**	600.
	f. **dull red**	600.
162TC2	12c "Goodall" small die on India paper	
	b. **black**	600.
	c. **deep green**	600.
	d. **dull gray blue**	600.
	e. **deep brown**	600.
	f. **dull red**	600.
163TC2	15c "Goodall" small die on India paper	
	b. **black**	600.
	c. **deep green**	600.
	d. **dull gray blue**	600.
	e. **deep brown**	600.
	f. **dull red**	600.
164TC2	24c "Goodall" small die on India paper	
	b. **black**	600.
	c. **deep green**	600.
	d. **dull gray blue**	600.
	e. **deep brown**	600.
	f. **dull red**	600.
165TC2	30c "Goodall" small die on India paper	
	b. **black**	600.
	c. **deep green**	600.
	d. **dull gray blue**	600.
	e. **deep brown**	600.
	f. **dull red**	600.
166TC2	90c "Goodall" small die on India paper	
	b. **black**	600.
	c. **deep green**	600.
	d. **dull gray blue**	600.
	e. **deep brown**	600.
	f. **dull red**	600.

1875

178P5	2c **vermilion,** plate on stamp paper, pair	*600.*
	P# blk. of 12	*12,000.*
179TC1a	5c large die on India paper	
	e. **black**	650.
	f. **scarlet**	1,000.
179TC2	5c "Goodall" small die on India paper	
	b. **black**	550.
	c. **deep green**	550.
	d. **deep brown**	550.
	e. **dull red**	550.
	f. **dull gray blue**	550.
179TC3	5c plate on India paper	
	a. **black**	25.
	Block of 4	125.
179TC4	5c Plate on card	
	a. **black**	45.
	Block of 4	200.

1879 American Bank Note Co.

182TC6	1c plate on stamp paper, gummed, perf. 12	
	a. **ultramarine**	300.
	b. **green**	300.
	c. **deep green**	300.
	d. **vermilion**	300.
	e. **brown**	300.
182P1	1c **gray blue,** large die on India paper	525.
182P3	1c **gray blue,** plate on India	60.
	Block of 4	275.
	P# blk. of 12	1,000.
183TC6	2c plate on stamp paper, gummed, perf. 12	
	a. **ultramarine**	300.
	b. **blue**	300.
	c. **green**	300.
183P1	2c **vermilion,** large die on India paper	300.
183P2	2c **vermilion,** RA sm die on white wove paper	190.
183P2a	2c **vermilion,** PP sm die on yelsh wove paper	2,500.
183P3	2c **vermilion,** plate on India	35.
	Block of 4	160.
	P# blk. of 12	600.
183P4	2c **vermilion,** plate on card	22.
	Block of 4	125.
	P# blk. of 12	—
184TC6	3c plate on stamp paper, gummed, perf. 12	
	a. **ultramarine**	300.
	b. **blue**	300.
	c. **vermilion**	300.
	Block of 4	1,100.
	d. **brown**	300.
184P6	3c **green,** plate on stamp paper, pair	*500.*
	P# blk. of 12	—
185TC6	5c plate on stamp paper, gummed, perf. 12	
	a. **ultramarine**	300.
	b. **green**	300.
	c. **vermilion**	300.
185P1	5c **blue,** large die on India paper	700.
185P2	5c **blue,** RA sm die on white wove paper	225.
185P2a	5c **blue,** PP sm die on yelsh wove paper	2,500.
185P3	5c **blue,** plate on India	70.
	Block of 4	325.
	P# blk. of 12	1,300.
185P4	5c **blue,** plate on card	22.
	Block of 4	125.
	P# blk. of 12	—
186TC6	6c plate on stamp paper, gummed, perf. 12	
	a. **ultramarine**	300.
	b. **blue**	300.
	c. **vermilion**	300.
187TC6	10c plate on stamp paper, gummed, perf. 12	
	a. **ultramarine**	300.
	b. **blue**	300.
	c. **vermilion**	300.
	d. **green**	300.
189TC1a	15c large die on India paper	
	e. **orange vermilion**	800.
	f. **orange brown**	800.
	g. **chestnut brown**	800.

h. **dark brown** 800.
i. **deep green** 800.
j. **black** 800.
189TC1d 15c large die on card
e. **orange vermilion** 450.
f. **orange brown** 450.
g. **chestnut brown** 450.
h. **dark brown** 450.
i. **deep green** 450.
j. **black** 450.
189TC6 15c plate on stamp paper, gummed, perf. 12
a. **ultramarine** 300.
b. **green** 300.
c. **vermilion** 300.
d. **brown** 300.
e. **dull red** 300.
190TC1a 30c large die on India paper
e. **black** 800.
f. **orange vermilion** 800.
g. **dark brown** 800.
h. **deep green** 800.
i. **dull red brown** 800.
j. **green** 800.
190TC1d 30c large die on card
e. **orange vermilion** 450.
f. **dark brown** 450.
g. **deep green** 450.
h. **dull red brown** 450.
i. **green** 450.
190TC6 30c plate on stamp paper, gummed, perf. 12
a. **ultramarine** 300.
b. **blue** 300.
c. **green** 300.

See Specimens for No. 189 in deep blue (No. 189S L), No. 209 in green (No. 209S L), No. 210 in pale rose lake (No. 210S L).

190P3 30c **full black,** plate on India —
Block of 4 —
P# block of 10 1,000.
190P4 30c **full black,** plate on card 500.
Block of 4 2,500.
P# blk. of 12 *7,500.*
191TC1a 90c large die on India paper
e. **carmine** 800.
f. **dark brown** 800.
g. **deep dull orange** 800.
h. **indigo** 800.
i. **dull red brown** 800.
j. **black** 800.
191TC1d 90c large die on card
e. **carmine** 450.
f. **dark brown** 450.
g. **deep dull orange** 450.
h. **indigo** 450.
i. **dull red brown** 450.
j. **black** 450.
191P5 90c **car,** plate on stamp paper, pair *2,250.*
P# strip of 5 5,000.
193P4 2c **blk brown,** plate on card 400.
Block of 4 2,000.
P# blk. of 12 7,500.

1881-82 American Bank Note Co.

205TC1a 5c large die on India paper
e. **chestnut brown** 800.
f. **deep dull orange** 800.
g. **pale ultramarine** 800.
h. **deep green** 800.
i. **green** 800.
j. **carmine** 800.
k. **carmine lake** 800.
l. **blue black** 800.
205TC1d 5c large die on card
e. **chestnut brown** —
f. **pale ultramarine** —
g. **carmine** 450.
h. **black** on glazed card 1,000.
205TC3 5c plate on India paper
a. **green** 200.
b. **carmine lake** 225.
205P1 5c **yel brn,** large die on India paper 250.
205P2 5c **yel brn,** RA sm die on white wove paper 200.
205P2a 5c **yel brn,** PP sm die on yelsh wove paper 2,250.
205P3 5c **yel brn,** plate on India 40.
Block of 4 175.
P# blk. of 12 1,000.
205P4 5c **yel brn,** plate on card 15.
Block of 4 90.
P# blk. of 12 —
Bottom margin P# block of 30 *2,700.*
206TC1a 1c large die on India paper
e. **deep green** 600.
f. **black** 600.
g. **ultramarine** 600.
h. **dark yellow green** 600.
206TC2 1c small die on India paper
b. **deep green** 125.
206TC3 1c plate on India paper
a. **black** 125.
206P1 1c **blue,** large die on India paper 375.
206P2 1c **blue,** RA sm die on white wove paper 200.
206P2a 1c **blue,** PP sm die on yelsh wove paper 2,250.
206P3 1c **blue,** plate on India 40.
Block of 4 175.
P# blk. of 12 1,000.
206P4 1c **blue,** plate on card 20.
Block of 4 115.
P# blk. of 12 —
Bottom margin P# block of 30 *2,700.*
207P1 3c **blue grn,** large die on India paper 375.
207P2 3c **blue grn,** RA sm die on white wove paper 200.
207P2a 3c **blue grn,** PP sm die on yelsh wove paper 2,250.
207P3 3c **blue grn,** plate on India 40.
Block of 4 175.
P# blk. of 12 1,000.
207P4 3c **blue grn,** plate on card 20.
Block of 4 115.
P# blk. of 12 —
Bottom margin P# block of 30 *2,700.*
208TC1a 6c large die on India paper
e. **deep dull orange** 1,000.
f. **indigo** 1,250.
g. **orange vermilion** 1,100.
h. **dark violet** 1,000.
i. **chestnut brown** 1,350.
j. **carmine** 1,250.
208TC1d 6c large die on card
e. **deep dull orange** 450.
f. **orange vermilion** 450.
g. **dark violet** 450.
h. **chestnut brown** 450.
208P1 6c **deep rose,** large die on India paper 2,250.
208P2 6c **deep rose,** RA sm die on white wove paper 200.
208P2a 6c **deep rose,** PP sm die on yelsh wove paper 2,250.
b. **brown red** 2,250.
208P3 6c **deep rose,** plate on India 90.
Block of 4 425.
P# blk. of 12 —
a. **brown red** 100.
208P4 6c **deep rose,** plate on card 50.
Block of 4 225.
P# blk. of 12 —
Bottom margin P# block of 30 *2,700.*
a. **brown red** 50.
209TC1a 10c large die on India paper
e. **carmine** 1,000.
f. **orange brown** 1,000.
g. **orange** 1,000.
h. **deep dull orange** 1,000.
i. **chestnut brown** 1,000.
j. **indigo** 1,000.
k. **pale ultramarine** 1,000.
209TC1d 10c large die on card
e. **carmine** 450.
f. **orange brown** 450.
g. **deep dull orange** 450.
h. **chestnut brown** 450.
i. **indigo** 450.
j. **pale ultramarine** 450.
k. **black,** on glazed card 1,000.
209TC4 10c plate on card
a. **orange brown** 125.
b. **green** 125.
209TC6 10c plate on stamp paper, gummed, perf. 12
a. **green** 300.
b. **brownish black** 300.
209P1 10c **brn,** large die on India paper 800.
209P2 10c **brn,** RA sm die on white wove paper 200.
209P2a 10c **brn,** PP sm die on yelsh wove paper 2,250.
209P3 10c **brn,** plate on India 40.
Block of 4 170.
P# blk. of 12 1,000.
209P4 10c **brn,** plate on card 20.
Block of 4 110.
P# blk. of 12 —
Bottom margin P# block of 30 *2,700.*

1883

210TC1a 2c large die on India paper
e. **red brown** 1,000.
f. **deep dull orange** 1,000.
g. **chestnut brown** 1,000.
h. **violet rose** 1,000.
i. **indigo** 1,000.
j. **black** 1,000.
k. **pale ultramarine** 1,000.
l. **olive green** 1,000.
210TC1d 2c large die on card
e. **brown red** 450.
f. **chestnut brown** 450.
g. **violet rose** 450.
h. **indigo** 450.
i. **olive green** 450.
j. **olive brown** 450.
210TC4 2c plate on card
a. **lake** 140.
b. **rose lake** 140.
c. **deep carmine** 140.
d. **deep red** 140.
210P1 2c **red brn,** large die on India paper 400.
210P2 2c **red brn,** RA sm die on white wove paper 180.
210P2a 2c **red brn,** PP sm die on yelsh wove paper 2,500.
210P3 2c **red brn,** plate on India 35.
Block of 4 160.
P# blk. of 12 1,000.
210P4 2c **red brn,** plate on card 20.
Block of 4 110.
P# blk. of 12 —
Bottom margin P# block of 30 *2,700.*
210P5 2c **red brn,** plate on stamp paper, pair —
211TC1a 4c large die on India paper
e. **green** 1,000.
f. **chestnut brown** 1,000.
g. **orange brown** 1,000.
h. **pale ultramarine** 1,000.
i. **dark brown** 1,000.
j. **black** 1,000.
211TC1d 4c large die on card
e. **green** 450.
f. **chestnut brown** 450.
g. **orange brown** 450.
h. **pale ultramarine** 450.
i. **black** 450.
211P1 4c **grn,** large die on India paper 500.
211P2 4c **grn,** RA sm die on white wove paper 180.
211P2a 4c **grn,** PP sm die on yelsh wove paper 2,500.
211P3 4c **grn,** plate on India 35.
Block of 4 160.
P# blk. of 12 1,000.
211P4 4c **grn,** plate on card 20.
Block of 4 100.
P# blk. of 12 —
Bottom margin P# block of 30 *2,700.*
211P5 4c **green,** plate on stamp paper, pair —

1887-88

212TC1a 1c large die on India paper
e. **indigo** 1,000.
f. **carmine** 1,000.
g. **green** 1,000.
h. **deep green** 1,000.
i. **copper brown** 1,000.
j. **chestnut brown** 1,000.
212TC1d 1c large die on card
e. **green** 450.
f. **deep green** 450.
g. **copper brown** 450.
212P1 1c **ultra,** large die on India paper 650.
212P2 1c **ultra,** RA sm die on white wove paper 180.
212P2a 1c **ultra,** PP sm die on yelsh wove paper 2,500.
212P3 1c **ultra,** plate on India 110.
Block of 4 525.
P# blk. of 12 2,250.
212P4 1c **ultra,** plate on card *2,750.*
Block of 4 *12,500.*
212P5 1c **ultra,** plate on stamp paper, pair —

Examples of No. 212P3 mounted on card are frequently offered as No. 212P4.

213P1 2c **grn,** large die on India paper 500.
213P2 2c **grn,** RA sm die on white wove paper 180.
213P2a 2c **grn,** PP sm die on yelsh wove paper 2,500.
213P3 2c **grn,** plate on India 65.
Block of 4 300.
P# blk. of 12 1,150.
213P4 2c **grn,** plate on card 45.
Block of 4 210.
P# blk. of 12 —
213P5 2c **green,** plate on stamp paper, pair 2,000.
214TC1a 3c large die on India paper
e. **green** 1,000.
f. **dark green** —
g. **dark brown** 1,000.
h. **chestnut brown** 1,000.
i. **dull red brown** 1,000.
j. **deep dull orange** —
214TC1d 3c large die on card
e. **green** 450.
f. **dark green** —
g. **dark brown** 450.
h. **chestnut brown** 450.
i. **dull red brown** 450.
j. **deep dull orange** —
214TC4 3c plate on card
a. **dark green** —
b. **deep orange brown** —
c. **deep dull orange** —

All of 214TC1s above bear inscription "Worked over by new company, June 29th, 1881."

214P1 3c **vermilion,** large die on India paper 500.
214P2 3c **vermilion,** RA sm die on white wove paper 180.
214P2a 3c **vermilion,** PP sm die on yelsh wove paper 2,500.
214P3 3c **vermilion,** plate on India 65.
Block of 4 300.
P# blk. of 12 —
214P4 3c **vermilion,** plate on card 45.
Block of 4 210.
P# blk. of 12 —

Nos. 207P1 & 214P1 inscribed: "Worked over by new company, June 29th, 1881."

215P1 4c **car,** large die on India paper 650.
215P2 4c **car,** RA sm die on white wove paper 180.
215P2a 4c **car,** PP sm die on yelsh wove paper 2,500.
215P3 4c **car,** plate on India 85.
Block of 4 400.
215P4 4c **car,** plate on card 45.
Block of 4 210.
P# blk. of 12 —
216P1 5c **indigo,** large die on India paper 650.
216P2 5c **indigo,** RA sm die on white wove paper 180.
216P2a 5c **indigo,** PP sm die on yelsh wove paper 2,500.
216P3 5c **indigo,** plate on India 65.
Block of 4 300.
216P4 5c **indigo,** plate on card 45.
Block of 4 210.
P# blk. of 12 —
216P5 5c **indigo,** plate on stamp paper, pair *1,500.*
217P1 30c **org brn,** large die on India paper 750.
217P2 30c **org brn,** RA sm die on white wove paper 180.
217P2a 30c **org brn,** PP sm die on yelsh wove paper 2,500.
217P3 30c **org brn,** plate on India 65.
Block of 4 300.
217P4 30c **org brn,** plate on card 45.
Block of 4 210.
P# blk. of 10 —
217P5 30c **org brn,** plate on stamp paper, pair *1,750.*
218P1 90c **purple,** large die on India paper 1,100.
218P2 90c **purple,** RA sm die on white wove paper 180.

218P2a 90c **purple,** PP sm die on yelsh wove paper 2,500.
218P3 90c **purple,** plate on India 80.
Block of 4 350.
218P4 90c **purple,** plate on card 45.
Block of 4 210.
P# strip of 5 *1,500.*
218P5 90c **purple,** plate on stamp paper, pair —

1890-93

219TC1a 1c large die on India paper
e. **green** 600.
f. **dull violet** 600.
219P1 1c **ultra,** large die on India paper 225.
219P2 1c **ultra,** RA sm die on white wove paper 200.
219P2a 1c **ultra,** PP sm die on yelsh wove paper 2,000.
219P3 1c **ultra,** plate on India 25.
Block of 4 110.
P# blk. of 12 500.
219P4 1c **ultra,** plate on card 35.
Block of 4 160.
P# blk. of 12 600.
219P5 1c **ultra,** plate on stamp paper, pair *190.*
219DP1 2c **lake,** large die on India paper *1,000.*
219DP2 2c **lake,** RA sm die on white wove paper 190.
219DP2a 2c **lake,** PP sm die on yelsh wove paper 2,000.
219DP3 2c **lake,** plate on India 80.
Block of 4 385.
P# blk. of 12 1,650.
219DP4 2c **lake,** plate on card 165.
Block of 4 700.
P# blk. of 12 *3,250.*
219DP5 2c **lake,** plate on stamp paper, pair *80.*
P# blk. of 10 800.
220TC1a 2c large die on India paper
e. **dull violet** 600.
f. **blue green** 600.
g. **orange,** plate on stamp paper, gummed, pair 250.
220TC5 2c large die on India paper 250.
220P1 2c **car,** large die on India paper 450.
220P2 2c **car,** RA sm die on white wove paper 200.
220P3 2c **car,** plate on India 300.
Block of 4 1,250.
P# blk. of 12 *3,850.*
220P4 2c **car,** plate on card 175.
Block of 4 750.
P# blk. of 12 *2,250.*
220P5 2c **car,** plate on stamp paper, pair *125.*
As No. 220P5, without gum *60.*
P# blk. of 12 —
221P1 3c **purple,** large die on India paper 225.
221P2 3c **purple,** RA sm die on white wove paper 200.
221P2a 3c **purple,** PP sm die on yelsh wove paper 2,000.
221P3 3c **purple,** plate on India 35.
Block of 4 160.
P# blk. of 12 650.
221P4 3c **purple,** plate on card 20.
Block of 4 90.
P# blk. of 12 550.
221P5 3c **purple,** plate on stamp paper, pair *225.*
222TC1a 4c large die on India paper
e. **green** 450.
222TC5 4c plate on stamp paper
a. **orange brown** 120.
b. **yellow brown** 120.
c. **brown** (shades) 120.
222P1 4c **dk brn,** large die on India paper 550.
222P2 4c **dk brn,** RA sm die on white wove paper 225.
222P2a 4c **dk brn,** PP sm die on yelsh wove paper 2,000.
222P3 4c **dk brn,** plate on India 35.
Block of 4 160.
P# blk. of 12 650.
222P4 4c **dk brn,** plate on card 20.
Block of 4 90.
P# blk. of 12 650.
222P5 4c **dk brn,** plate on stamp paper, pair *210.*
223TC1c 5c Large die on glossy wove paper
e. **blue** 400.
f. **dark brown** 400.
223TC5 5c plate on plate on stamp paper
a. **bister** —
b. **sepia** —
c. **brown** (shades) 100.
223P1 5c **chocolate,** large die on India paper 225.
223P2 5c **chocolate,** RA sm die on white wove paper 225.
223P2a 5c **chocolate,** PP sm die on yelsh wove paper 2,000.
223P3 5c **chocolate,** plate on India 32.
Block of 4 135.
P# blk. of 12 600.
223P4 5c **chocolate,** plate on card 20.
Block of 4 90.
P# blk. of 12 600.
223P5 5c **yel brn,** plate on stamp paper, pair *225.*
224TC1a 6c large die on India paper
e. **deep orange red** 400.
224TC5 6c plate on stamp paper
a. **orange red** 120.
b. **violet black** 120.
c. **yellow** 120.
d. **olive green** 120.
e. **purple** 120.
f. **red orange** 120.
g. **brown** 120.
h. **red brown** 120.
i. **orange brown** 120.
j. **black brown** 120.
k. **slate green** 120.
l. **brown olive** 120.
224P1 6c **brn red,** large die on India paper 225.
224P2 6c **brn red,** RA sm die on white wove paper 200.
224P2a 6c **brn red,** PP sm die on yelsh wove paper 2,000.
224P3 6c **brn red,** plate on India 32.
Block of 4 135.
P# blk. of 12 600.
224P4 6c **brn red,** plate on card 18.
Block of 4 75.
P# blk. of 12 725.
224P5 6c **brn red,** plate on stamp paper, pair *225.*
225TC1a 8c large die on India paper
e. **yellow orange** —
f. **green** —
225TC1d 8c large die on card
e. **dark violet red** 450.
f. **metallic green** 450.
g. **salmon** 450.
h. **orange brown** 450.
i. **light green** 450.
j. **blue** 450.
k. **steel blue** 450.
225P1 8c **lilac,** large die on India paper 600.
225P2 8c **lilac,** RA sm die on white wove paper 200.
225P2a 8c **lilac,** PP sm die on yelsh wove paper 2,000.
225P3 8c **lilac,** plate on India 55.
Block of 4 250.
P# blk. of 12 1,100.
225P4 8c **lilac,** plate on card 100.
Block of 4 450.
P# blk. of 12 1,800.
225P5 8c **lilac,** plate on stamp paper, pair *1,000.*
226P1 10c **grn,** large die on India paper 225.
226P2 10c **grn,** RA sm die on white wove paper 200.
226P2a 10c **grn,** PP sm die on yelsh wove paper 2,000.
226P3 10c **grn,** plate on India 45.
Block of 4 200.
P# blk. of 12 700.
226P4 10c **grn,** plate on card 35.
Block of 4 160.
P# blk. of 12 700.
226P5 10c **grn,** plate on stamp paper, pair *325.*
227P1 15c **indigo,** large die on India paper 300.
227P2 15c **indigo,** RA sm die on white wove paper 200.
227P2a 15c **indigo,** PP sm die on yelsh wove paper 2,000.
227P3 15c **indigo,** plate on India 45.
Block of 4 190.
P# blk. of 12 825.
227P4 15c **indigo,** plate on card .35
Block of 4 160.
P# blk. of 12 825.
227P5 15c **indigo,** plate on stamp paper, pair *625.*
P# blk. of 12 *5,000.*
228P1 30c **black,** large die on India paper 300.
228P2 30c **black,** RA sm die on white wove paper 200.
228P2a 30c **black,** PP sm die on yelsh wove paper 2,000.
228P3 30c **black,** plate on India 45.
Block of 4 190.
P# blk. of 12 825.
228P4 30c **black,** plate on card 40.
Block of 4 175.
P# blk. of 12 800.
228P5 30c **black,** plate on stamp paper, pair *1,000.*
229P1 90c **orange,** large die on India paper 300.
229P2 90c **orange,** RA sm die on white wove paper 200.
229P2a 90c **orange,** PP sm die on yelsh wove paper 2,000.
229P3 90c **orange,** plate on India 60.
Block of 4 275.
P# blk. of 12 1,100.
229P4 90c **orange,** plate on card 45.
Block of 4 200.
P# blk. of 12 1,100.
229P5 90c **orange,** plate on stamp paper, pair *1,450.*

Columbian Issue

1893

230P1 1c **blue,** large die on India paper 900.
230P2 1c **blue,** RA sm die on white wove paper 325.
230P2a 1c **blue,** PP sm die on yelsh wove paper 2,000.
230P3 1c **blue,** plate on India 50.
Block of 4 250.
P# blk. of 8 700.
230P4 1c **blue,** plate on card 18.
Block of 4 120.
P# blk. of 8 400.
231TC1a 2c large die on India paper
e. **sepia** 850.
231TC1d 1c large die on card
e. **sepia** 850.
f. **orange brown** 850.
g. **deep orange** 850.
h. **light brown** 850.
i. **blue green** 850.
j. **bright rose red** 850.
k. **rose violet** 850.
231P1 2c **violet,** large die on India paper 1,000.
231P2 2c **violet,** RA sm die on white wove paper 350.
231P2a 2c **violet,** PP sm die on yelsh wove paper 2,500.
231P3 2c **violet,** plate on India 300.
Block of 4 1,750.
P# blk. of 8 4,500.
231P4 2c **violet,** plate on card 40.
Block of 4 225.
P# blk. of 8 700.
a. "Broken hat" variety, plate on card 130.
231P5 2c **violet,** plate on stamp paper, pair *2,000.*

Almost all examples of No. 231P5 are faulty. Value is for pair with minimal faults.

232TC1d 3c large die on card
e. **sepia** 850.
f. **blackish green** 850.
g. **black** 850.
232TC3 3c plate on India paper
a. **blackish green** 800.
232P1 3c **green,** large die on India paper 900.
232P2 3c **green,** RA sm die on white wove paper 325.
232P2a 3c **green,** PP sm die on yelsh wove paper 3,000.
232P3 3c **green,** plate on India 85.
Block of 4 500.
P# blk. of 8 1,300.
232P4 3c **green,** plate on card 60.
Block of 4 375.
P# blk. of 8 1,000.
233TC1d 4c large die on card
e. **sepia** 850.
f. **deep orange** 850.
g. **light brown** 850.
h. **blue green** 850.
i. **rose red** 850.
j. **rose violet** 850.
233P1 4c **ultra,** large die on India paper 900.
233P2 4c **ultra,** RA sm die on white wove paper 325.
233P2a 4c **ultra,** PP sm die on yelsh wove paper 3,000.
233P3 4c **ultra,** plate on India 85.
Block of 4 500.
P# blk. of 8 1,300.
233P4 4c **ultra,** plate on card 60.
Block of 4 375.
P# blk. of 8 1,150.
233aP1 4c **blue,** (error) large die on thin card *2,750.*
234TC1a 5c large die on India paper
e. **black** 850.
f. **dark violet** 850.
g. **rose violet** 850.
h. **red violet** 850.
i. **brown violet** 850.
j. **deep blue** 850.
k. **deep ultramarine** 850.
l. **black** 850.
m. **green** 850.
n. **deep green** 850.
o. **blue green** —
p. **dark olive green** 850.
q. **deep orange** 850.
r. **orange red** 850.
s. **orange brown** 850.
t. **bright rose red** 850.
u. **claret** 850.
v. **brown rose** 850.
w. **dull rose brown** 850.
x. **sepia** 850.
y. **black brown** —
234TC1d 5c large die on card
e. **dark violet** 850.
f. **rose violet** 850.
g. **blue green** 850.
h. **dark olive green** —
i. **deep orange** —
j. **orange brown** 850.
k. **claret** —
k. **sepia** 850.
m. **black brown** —

The 5c trial color proofs differ from the issued stamp.

234P1 5c **choc,** large die on India paper 900.
234P2 5c **choc,** RA sm die on white wove paper 325.
234P2a 5c **choc,** PP sm die on yelsh wove paper 3,000.
234P3 5c **choc,** plate on India 85.
Block of 4 500.
P# blk. of 8 1,300.
234P4 5c **choc,** plate on card 60.
Block of 4 375.
P# blk. of 8 1,150.
235P1 6c **purple,** large die on India paper 900.
235P2 6c **purple,** RA sm die on white wove paper 325.
235P2a 6c **purple,** PP sm die on yelsh wove paper 3,000.
235P3 6c **purple,** plate on India 85.
Block of 4 500.
P# blk. of 8 1,300.
235P4 6c **purple,** plate on card 60.
Block of 4 375.
P# blk. of 8 1,150.
236P1 8c **magenta,** large die on India paper 900.
236P2 8c **magenta,** RA sm die on white wove paper 325.
236P2a 8c **magenta,** PP sm die on yelsh wove paper 3,000.
236P3 8c **magenta,** plate on India 85.
Block of 4 500.
P# blk. of 8 1,300.
236P4 8c **magenta,** plate on card 135.
Block of 4 850.
P# blk. of 8 2,350.
237TC1a 10c large die on India paper
e. **bright rose red** 1,250.
f. **claret** 1,250.
237P1 10c **blk brn,** large die on India paper 750.
237P2 10c **blk brn,** RA sm die on white wove paper 325.
237P2a 10c **blk brn,** PP sm die on yelsh wove paper 3,000.

237P3 10c **blk brn,** plate on India 85.
Block of 4 500.
P# blk. of 8 1,300.
237P4 10c **blk brn,** plate on card 60.
Block of 4 375.
P# blk. of 8 1,150.
238P1 15c **dk grn,** large die on India paper 900.
238P2 15c **dk grn,** RA sm die on white wove paper 325.
238P2a 15c **dk grn,** PP sm die on yelsh wove paper 3,000.
238P3 15c **dk grn,** plate on India 85.
Block of 4 500.
P# blk. of 8 1,300.
238P4 15c **dk grn,** plate on card 70.
Block of 4 450.
P# blk. of 8 2,750.
239TC1d 30c large die on card
e. **sepia** 1,000.
239TC4 30c plate on card
a. **black** 300.
239P1 30c **org brn,** large die on India paper 900.
239P2 30c **org brn,** RA sm die on white wove paper 325.
239P2a 30c **org brn,** PP sm die on yelsh wove paper 3,000.
239P3 30c **org brn,** plate on India 125.
Block of 4 775.
P# blk. of 8 2,250.
239P4 30c **org brn,** plate on card 90.
Block of 4 550.
P# blk. of 8 2,300.
240TC1d 50c large die on card
e. **sepia** 1,000.
240P1 50c **slate bl,** large die on India paper 900.
240P2 50c **slate bl,** RA sm die on white wove paper 325.
240P2a 50c **slate bl,** PP sm die on yelsh wove paper 3,000.
240P3 50c **slate bl,** plate on India 200.
Block of 4 1,200.
P# blk. of 8 3,000.
240P4 50c **slate bl,** plate on card 105.
Block of 4 650.
P# blk. of 8 2,350.
241P1 $1 **salmon,** large die on India paper 1,150.
241P2 $1 **salmon,** RA sm die on white wove paper 450.
241P2a $1 **salmon,** PP sm die on yelsh wove paper 3,000.
241P3 $1 **salmon,** plate on India 225.
Block of 4 1,500.
P# blk. of 8 3,500.
241P4 $1 **salmon,** plate on card 180.
Block of 4 1,100.
242TC1a $2 large die on India paper
e. **sepia** —
f. **red brown** —
242TC3 $2 plate on India paper
a. **blackish brown** 1,000.
242P1 $2 **brn red,** large die on India paper 1,150.
242P2 $2 **brn red,** RA sm die on white wove paper 450.
242P2a $2 **brn red,** PP sm die on yelsh wove paper 3,000.
242P3 $2 **brn red,** plate on India 260.
Block of 4 1,700.
P# blk. of 8 4,000.
242P4 $2 **brn red,** plate on card 160.
Block of 4 925.
P# blk. of 8 2,800.
243P1 $3 **yel grn,** large die on India paper 1,150.
243P2 $3 **yel grn,** RA sm die on white wove paper 450.
243P2a $3 **yel grn,** PP sm die on yelsh wove paper 3,000.
243P3 $3 **yel grn,** plate on India 300.
Block of 4 1,900.
P# blk. of 8 4,750.
243P4 $3 **yel grn,** plate on card 200.
Block of 4 1,200.
P# blk. of 8 3,200.
244P1 $4 **crimson lake,** large die on India paper 1,150.
244P2 $4 **crimson lake,** RA sm die on white wove paper 450.
244P2a $4 **crimson lake,** PP sm die on yelsh wove paper 3,000.
244P3 $4 **crimson lake,** plate on India 400.
Block of 4 2,500.
P# blk. of 8 5,750.
244P4 $4 **crimson lake,** plate on card 250.
Block of 4 1,500.
P# blk. of 8 5,250.
245P1 $5 **black,** large die on India paper 1,150.
245P2 $5 **black,** RA sm die on white wove paper 450.
245P2a $5 **black,** PP sm die on yelsh wove paper 3,000.
245P3 $5 **black,** plate on India 475.
Block of 4 2,900.
P# blk. of 8 2,000.
245P4 $5 **black,** plate on card 350.
Block of 4 2,000.
P# blk. of 8 6,500.
Nos. 230P3-245P3 (16) 2,930.
Nos. 230P4-245P4 (16) 1,898.

This set also exists as Large Die proofs, not die sunk, but printed directly on thin card. Set value $7,000. 1c through 50c, $350 each; $1 through $5, $650 each.

Nos. 234P1, 234P2 differ from issued stamp.

1894 Bureau of Engraving and Printing

246TC1a 1c large die on India paper
e. **dusky blue green** 450.
f. **dark blue** 450.
246P1 1c **ultra,** large die on India paper 450.
247P1 1c **blue,** large die on India paper 250.
247P2 1c **blue,** RA sm die on white wove paper 200.
247P2a 1c **blue,** PP sm die on yelsh wove paper 2,000.
247P4 1c **blue,** plate on card 90.
Block of 4 400.
P# blk. of 6 2,150.
248P1 2c **pink,** Type I, large die on India paper —
248P4 2c **pink,** Type I, plate on card 90.
Block of 4 400.
P# blk. of 6 2,150.
250P1 2c **car,** Type I, large die on India paper 250.
250P2 2c **car,** Type I, RA sm die on white wove paper 200.
251P1 2c **car,** Type II, large die on India paper 250.
252P1 2c **car,** Type III, 15-subject die (3x5) on India *6,000.*
Single design 350.
Block of 4 1,500.
253TC1a 3c large die on India paper
e. **light red violet** 450.
f. **dark red violet** 450.
253P1 3c **purple,** Triangle I, large die on India paper 750.
253P5 3c **purple,** Triangle I, plate on stamp paper, pair *300.*
Block of 4 *625.*
P# blk. of 6 *7,500.*
253AP1 3c **purple,** Triangle II, large die on India paper 325.
253AP2 3c **purple,** Triangle II, RA sm die on white wove paper 200.
253AP2a 3c **purple,** Triangle II, PP sm die on yelsh wove paper 2,000.
254P1 4c **dk brn,** large die on India paper 600.
254P2 4c **dk brn,** RA sm die on white wove paper 200.
254P2a 4c **dk brn,** PP sm die on yelsh wove paper 2,000.
254P5 4c **dk brn,** plate on stamp paper, pair *275.*
Block of 4 *575.*
P# blk. of 6 *7,500.*
255TC1a 5c large die on India paper
e. **black** 1,250.
255P1 5c **choc,** large die on India paper 250.
255P2 5c **choc,** RA sm die on white wove paper 200.
255P2a 5c **choc,** PP sm die on yelsh wove paper 2,000.
255P5 5c **choc,** plate on stamp paper, pair *300.*
Block of 4 *625.*
P# blk. of 6 *9,500.*
256TC1a 6c large die on India paper
e. **dark brown** 1,000.
256P1 6c **brn,** large die on India paper 250.
256P2 6c **brn,** RA sm die on white wove paper 200.
256P2a 6c **brn,** PP sm die on yelsh wove paper 2,000.
256P4 6c **brn,** plate on card 400.
Block of 4 1,700.
P# blk. of 6 *5,250.*
257TC1a 8c large die on India paper
e. **black** 1,250.
257P1 8c **vio brn,** large die on India paper 250.
257P2 8c **vio brn,** RA sm die on white wove paper 200.
257P2a 8c **vio brn,** PP sm die on yelsh wove paper 2,000.
258TC1a 10c large die on India paper
e. **olive** 1,250.
258P1 10c **grn,** large die on India paper 275.
258P2 10c **grn,** RA sm die on white wove paper 200.
258P2a 10c **grn,** PP sm die on yelsh wove paper 2,000.
258P5 10c **grn,** plate on stamp paper, pair *500.*
Block of 4 *1,100.*
P# blk. of 6 *9,500.*
259TC1a 15c large die on India paper
e. **red violet** 1,250.
f. **dark red orange** 1,250.
259P1 15c **dk bl,** large die on India paper 300.
259P2 15c **dk bl,** RA sm die on white wove paper 200.
259P2a 15c **dk bl,** PP sm die on yelsh wove paper 2,000.
260TC1a 50c large die on India paper
e. **black** 1,500.
260P1 50c **org,** large die on India paper 450.
260P2 50c **org,** RA sm die on white wove paper 170.
260P2a 50c **org,** PP sm die on yelsh wove paper 2,000.
261TC1a $1 type I, large die on India paper
e. **orange** 1,500.
f. **orange** 1,500.
261P1 $1 **blk,** large die on India paper 500.
261P2 $1 **blk,** RA sm die on white wove paper 275.
261P2a $1 **blk,** PP sm die on yelsh wove paper 2,000.
261ATC1d $1 type II, large die on card
e. **lake** 1,500.
262TC1a $2 large die on India paper
e. **black** 1,500.
f. **dull violet** 1,500.
g. **violet** 1,500.
h. **turquoise blue** 1,500.
i. **orange brown** 1,500.
j. **olive green** 1,500.
k. **sepia** 1,500.
l. **greenish black** 1,500.
262P1 $2 **dk bl,** large die on India paper 500.
262P2 $2 **dk bl,** RA sm die on white wove paper 275.
262P2a $2 **dk bl,** PP sm die on yelsh wove paper 2,000.
262P4 $2 **dk bl,** plate on card 400.
Block of 4 2,250.
Margin block of 4, arrow *2,500.*
P# blk. of 6 *6,000.*
263TC1a $5 large die on India paper
e. **black** 1,500.
f. **dark yellow** 1,500.
g. **orange brown** 1,500.
h. **olive green** 1,500.
i. **dull violet** 1,500.
j. **sepia** 1,500.
k. **brown red** 1,500.
263P1 $5 **dk grn,** large die on India paper 650.
263P2 $5 **dk grn,** RA sm die on white wove paper 300.
263P2a $5 **dk grn,** PP sm die on yelsh wove paper 2,000.
263P4 $5 **dk grn,** plate on card 400.
Block of 4 2,250.
Margin block of 4, arrow *2,500.*
P# blk. of 6 *6,000.*

1895 Imperf, with gum

264P5 1c **blue,** plate on stamp paper, pair *275.*
Block of 4 *700.*
P# strip of 3 *850.*
P# blk. of 6 *1,150.*
a. Horiz. P# strip of 3, perf horiz., imperf. vert. *19,000.*
267P5 2c **car,** Type III, plate on stamp paper, pair *200.*
Block of 4 *550.*
P# strip of 3 *650.*
P# blk. of 6 *1,100.*
268P5 3c **purple,** plate on stamp paper, pair *250.*
Block of 4 *700.*
P# strip of 3 *950.*
P# blk. of 6 *2,000.*
269P5 4c **dk brn,** plate on stamp paper, pair *250.*
Block of 4 *700.*
P# strip of 3 *1,250.*
P# blk. of 6 *3,250.*
270P5 5c **choc,** plate on stamp paper, pair *250.*
Block of 4 *700.*
P# strip of 3 *950.*
271P5 6c **dull brn,** plate on stamp paper, pair *275.*
Block of 4 *825.*
P# strip of 3 *1,150.*
272P5 8c **vio brn,** plate on stamp paper, pair *400.*
Block of 4 *1,100.*
P# strip of 3 *1,500.*
P# blk. of 6 *3,100.*
273P5 10c **dk grn,** plate on stamp paper, pair *325.*
Block of 4 *900.*
P# strip of 3 *1,250.*
274P5 15c **dk bl,** plate on stamp paper, pair *1,000.*
Block of 4 *2,750.*
P# strip of 3 *3,750.*
275P5 50c **org,** plate on stamp paper, pair *1,100.*
Block of 4 *3,250.*
P# strip of 3 *4,500.*
276P5 $1 **blk,** Type I, plate on stamp paper, pair *1,450.*
Block of 4 *3,750.*
P# strip of 3 *5,250.*
277P5 $2 **brt bl,** plate on stamp paper, pair *3,250.*
Block of 4 *7,500.*
P# strip of 3 *10,500.*
278P5 $5 **dk grn,** plate on stamp paper, pair *3,250.*
Block of 4 *7,500.*
P# strip of 3 *10,500.*

No. 264P5a exists only as a bottom margin P#24 and imprint strip of 3.

1897-1903

279P1 1c **grn,** large die on India paper 700.
279P2 1c **grn,** RA sm die on white wove paper 375.
279P2a 1c **grn,** PP sm die on yelsh wove paper 2,000.
279BdP2a 2c **org red,** Type IV, PP sm die on yelsh wove paper 2,000.
279BfP1 2c **car,** Type IV, large die on India paper 400.
279BfP2a 2c **car,** Type IV, PP sm die on yelsh wove paper 2,000.
280P1 4c **rose brn,** large die on India paper 700.
280P2a 4c **rose brn,** PP sm die on yelsh wove paper 2,000.
281P1 5c **blue,** large die on India paper 700.
281P2 5c **blue,** RA sm die on white wove paper 375.
281P2a 5c **blue,** PP sm die on yelsh wove paper 2,000.
282P1 6c **lake,** large die on India paper 700.
282P2a 6c **lake,** PP sm die on yelsh wove paper 2,000.
283TC1a 10c large die on India paper
e. **orange** 1,250.
f. **sepia** 1,250.
283P1 10c **org brn,** Type II, large die on India paper 800.
283P2 10c **org brn,** Type II, RA sm die on white wove paper 375.
283P2a 10c **org brn,** Type II, PP sm die on yelsh wove paper 2,000.
283aP1 10c **brn,** Type II, large die on India paper 800.
284TC1a 15c large die on India paper
e. **yellowish olive** *1,500.*
f. **red violet** *1,750.*
g. **deep dull green** *1,750.*
284P1 15c **ol grn,** Type II, large die on India paper 800.
284P2 15c **ol grn,** Type II, RA sm die on white wove paper 375.
284P2a 15c **ol grn,** Type II, PP sm die on yelsh wove paper 2,000.

Trans-Mississippi Issue

1898

285TC1a	1c large die on India paper	
	e. **black**	—
285P1	1c **grn,** large die on India paper	850.
285P2	1c **grn,** RA sm die on white wove paper	750.
285P2a	1c **grn,** PP sm die on yelsh wove paper	3,000.
286TC1a	2c large die on India paper	
	e. **black**	—
286TC4	2c plate on card	
	a. **purple**	2,500.
	b. **black**	2,500.
	c. **blue**	2,500.
	d. **brown**	2,500.
	e. **deep carmine rose**	2,500.
286P1	2c **copper red,** large die on India paper	850.
286P2	2c **copper red,** RA sm die on white wove paper	750.
286P2a	2c **copper red,** PP sm die on yelsh wove paper	3,000.
286P4	2c **copper red,** plate on card	*10,000.*
287TC1a	4c large die on India paper	
	e. **black**	—
287P1	4c **org,** large die on India paper	850.
287P2	4c **org,** RA sm die on white wove paper	750.
287P2a	4c **org,** PP sm die on yelsh wove paper	3,000.
288TC1a	5c large die on India paper	
	e. **black**	—
	f. **orange brown**	*2,500.*
288P1	5c **dull bl,** large die on India paper	850.
288P2	5c **dull bl,** RA sm die on white wove paper	750.
288P2a	5c **dull bl,** PP sm die on yelsh wove paper	3,000.
289TC1a	8c large die on India paper	
	e. **black**	—
289P1	8c **vio brn,** large die on India paper	850.
289P2	8c **vio brn,** RA sm die on white wove paper	750.
289P2a	8c **vio brn,** PP sm die on yelsh wove paper	3,000.
290TC1a	10c large die on India paper	
	e. **black**	1,500.
290TC2	10c small die on India paper	
	b. **black**	1,250.
290P1	10c **gray vio,** large die on India paper	850.
290P2	10c **gray vio,** RA sm die on white wove paper	750.
290P2a	10c **gray vio,** PP sm die on yelsh wove paper	3,000.
291TC1a	50c large die on India paper	
	e. **black**	1,500.
291TC2	50c small die on wove paper	
	b. **black**	2,400.
291P1	50c **sage grn,** large die on India paper	850.
291P2	50c **sage grn,** RA sm die on white wove paper	750.
291P2a	50c **sage grn,** PP sm die on yelsh wove paper	3,000.
292TC1a	$1 large die on India paper	
	e. **black**	—
292P1	$1 **blk,** large die on India paper	1,000.
292P2	$1 **blk,** RA sm die on white wove paper	750.
292P2a	$1 **blk,** PP sm die on yelsh wove paper	3,000.
293TC1a	$2 large die on India paper	
	e. **black**	5,000.
293P1	$2 **org brn,** large die on India paper	1,000.
293P2	$2 **org brn,** RA sm die on white wove paper	750.
293P2a	$2 **org brn,** PP sm die on yelsh wove paper	3,000.
293P4	$2 **org brn,** plate on card	6,000.
	Block of 4	*27,500.*
	P# blk. of 6	*35,000.*

The bicolored essays commonly offered as Nos. 285-293 bicolored proofs in "original" colors can be found under the following essay listings: Nos. 285-E8, 286-E8, 287-E9, 288-E5, 289-E4, 290-E4, 291-E8, 292-E6, and 293-E7. Value, set of nine $6,550.

Pan-American Issue

1901

294P1	1c **grn & blk,** large die on India paper	575.
294P1a	1c **grn & blk,** large die on wove paper	*1,500.*
294P2	1c **grn & blk,** RA sm die on white wove paper	525.
294P2a	1c **grn & blk,** PP sm die on yelsh wove paper	3,000.
295P1	2c **car & blk,** large die on India paper	575.
295P1a	2c **car & blk,** large die on wove paper	*1,500.*
295P2	2c **car & blk,** RA sm die on white wove paper	525.
295P2a	2c **car & blk,** PP sm die on yelsh wove paper	3,000.
	b. small die proof on yelsh bond	*1,250.*
296P1	4c **choc & blk,** large die on India paper	575.
296P1a	4c **choc & blk,** large die on wove paper	*1,500.*
296P2	4c **choc & blk,** RA sm die on white wove paper	525.
296P2a	4c **choc & blk,** PP sm die on yelsh wove paper	3,000.
297P1	5c **ultra & blk,** large die on India paper	575.
297P1a	5c **ultra & blk,** large die on wove paper	*1,500.*
297P2	5c **ultra & blk,** RA sm die on white wove paper	525.
297P2a	5c **ultra & blk,** PP sm die on yelsh wove paper	3,000.
298TC2	8c small die on wove	
	b. **violet & black**	*3,250.*
298P1	8c **brn vio & blk,** large die on India paper	575.
298P1a	8c **brn vio & blk,** large die on wove paper	*1,500.*
298P2	8c **brn vio & blk,** RA sm die on white wove paper	525.
298P2a	8c **brn vio & blk,** PP sm die on yelsh wove paper	3,000.
299P1	10c **yel brn & blk,** large die on India paper	575.
299P1a	10c **yel brn & blk,** large die on wove paper	*1,500.*
299P2	10c **yel brn & blk,** RA sm die on white wove paper	525.
299P2a	10c **yel brn & blk,** PP sm die on yelsh wove paper	3,000.

1902-03

300P1	1c **grn,** large die on India paper	1,750.
300P2	1c **grn,** RA sm die on white wove paper	275.
300P2a	1c **grn,** PP sm die on yelsh wove paper	2,500.
301P1	2c **car,** large die on India paper	1,750.
301P2	2c **car,** RA sm die on white wove paper	275.
301P2a	2c **car,** PP sm die on yelsh wove paper	2,500.
302P1	3c **purple,** large die on India paper	1,750.
302P2	3c **purple,** RA sm die on white wove paper	275.
302P2a	3c **purple,** PP sm die on yelsh wove paper	2,500.
303P1	4c **org brn,** large die on India paper	1,750.
303P2	4c **org brn,** RA sm die on white wove paper	275.
303P2a	4c **org brn,** PP sm die on yelsh wove paper	2,500.
304P1	5c **blue,** large die on India paper	1,750.
304P2	5c **blue,** RA sm die on white wove paper	275.
304P2a	5c **blue,** PP sm die on yelsh wove paper	2,500.
305P1	6c **lake,** large die on India paper	1,750.
305P2	6c **lake,** RA sm die on white wove paper	275.
305P2a	6c **lake,** PP sm die on yelsh wove paper	2,500.
306P1	8c **vio blk,** large die on India paper	1,750.
306P2	8c **vio blk,** RA sm die on white wove paper	275.
306P2a	8c **vio blk,** PP sm die on yelsh wove paper	2,500.
307P1	10c **org brn,** large die on India paper	1,750.
307P2	10c **org brn,** RA sm die on white wove paper	275.
307P2a	10c **org brn,** PP sm die on yelsh wove paper	2,500.
308TC1a	13c large die on India paper	
	e. **gray violet, type I**	1,000.
308P1	13c **dp vio brn,** large die on India paper	1,750.
308P2	13c **dp vio brn,** RA sm die on white wove paper	275.
308P2a	13c **dp vio brn,** PP sm die on yelsh wove paper	2,500.
309P1	15c **ol grn,** large die on India paper	1,750.
309P2	15c **ol grn,** RA sm die on white wove paper	275.
309P2a	15c **ol grn,** PP sm die on yelsh wove paper	2,500.
310P1	50c **org,** large die on India paper	1,750.
310P2	50c **org,** RA sm die on white wove paper	275.
310P2a	50c **org,** PP sm die on yelsh wove paper	2,500.
311P1	$1 **blk,** large die on India paper	1,750.
311P2	$1 **blk,** RA sm die on white wove paper	275.
311P2a	$1 **blk,** PP sm die on yelsh wove paper	2,500.
312P1	$2 **blue,** large die on India paper	2,500.
312P2	$2 **blue,** RA sm die on white wove paper	275.
312P2a	$2 **blue,** PP sm die on yelsh wove paper	2,500.
313P1	$5 **grn,** large die on India paper	3,000.
313P2	$5 **grn,** RA sm die on white wove paper	325.
313P2a	$5 **grn,** PP sm die on yelsh wove paper	2,500.

1903

319TC1a	2c large die on India paper	
	e. **black,** type I	3,250.
	f. **lake,** type I	—
319P1	2c **car,** Type I, large die on India paper	1,500.
319FiP1	2c **car,** Type II, large die on India paper	2,750.
319FiP2	2c **car,** Type II, sm die on white wove paper	1,000.
319FiP2a	2c **car,** Type II, PP sm die on yelsh wove paper	3,500.
	b. small die proof on yelsh wove paper	*1,000.*

Louisiana Purchase Issue

1904

323P1	1c **grn,** large die on India paper	1,400.
323P2	1c **grn,** sm die on white wove paper	1,250.
323P2a	1c **grn,** PP sm die on yelsh wove paper	3,500.
324P1	2c **car,** large die on India paper	1,400.
324P2	2c **car,** sm die on white wove paper	1,250.
324P2a	2c **car,** PP sm die on yelsh wove paper	3,500.
325P1	3c **vio,** large die on India paper	1,400.
325P2	3c **vio,** sm die on white wove paper	1,250.
325P2a	3c **vio,** PP sm die on yelsh wove paper	3,500.
326TC1d	5c large die on thin glazed card	
	e. **black**	3,500.
326P1	5c **dk bl,** large die on India paper	1,400.
326P2	5c **dk bl,** sm die on white wove paper	1,250.
326P2a	5c **dk bl,** PP sm die on yelsh wove paper	3,500.
327P1	10c **brn,** large die on India paper	1,400.
327P2	10c **brn,** sm die on white wove paper	1,250.
327P2a	10c **brn,** PP sm die on yelsh wove paper	3,500.

Jamestown Exposition Issue

1907

328P1	1c **grn,** large die on India paper	2,100.
328P2	1c **grn,** sm die on white wove paper	1,000.
328P2a	1c **grn,** PP sm die on yelsh wove paper	2,200.
329P1	2c **car,** large die on India paper	2,100.
329P2	2c **car,** sm die on white wove paper	1,000.
329P2a	2c **car,** PP sm die on yelsh wove paper	2,200.
330TC1a	5c large die on India paper	
	e. **ultramarine**	1,600.
	f. **black**	1,700.
330P1	5c **dk bl,** large die on India paper	2,100.
330P2	5c **dk bl,** sm die on white wove paper	1,000.
330P2a	5c **dk bl,** PP sm die on yelsh wove paper	2,200.

1908-09

331P1	1c **grn,** large die on India paper	1,250.
331P2	1c **grn,** sm die on white wove paper	725.
331P2a	1c **grn,** PP sm die on yelsh wove paper	2,500.
332TC1a	2c large die on India paper	
	e. **dull violet**	750.
	f. **light ultramarine**	750.
	g. **bright ultramarine**	750.
	h. **light green**	750.
	i. **dark olive green**	750.
	j. **golden yellow**	750.
	k. **dull orange**	750.
	l. **rose carmine**	750.
	m. **ultramarine**	750.
	n. **black**	—
	o. **dark blue**	—
	p. **blue**	850.
	q. **lilac brown**	850.
	r. **lilac**	850.
	s. **blue black**	850.
	t. **sage green**	850.
	u. **lilac black**	850.
	v. **brown**	850.
	w. **brown black**	850.
	x. **purple**	—
	y. **orange brown**	850.
	z. **ultra,** *orange brown*	750.
	aa. **ultra,** *green*	750.
	ab. **green,** *pink*	750.
	ac. **green,** *rose*	750.
	ad. **dark green,** *green*	750.
	ae. **green,** *orange brown*	750.
	af. **purple,** *orange brown*	750.
	ag. **blue,** *yellow*	750.
	ah. **green,** *yellow*	750.
	ai. **brown,** *orange brown*	750.
	aj. **brown,** *yellow*	750.
	ak. **green,** *amber yellow*	—
332P1	2c **car,** large die on India paper	1,250.
	a. **carmine,** large die on amber paper	—
	b. **carmine,** large die on lt blue paper	—
332P2	2c **car,** sm die on white wove paper	725.
332P2a	2c **car,** PP sm die on yelsh wove paper	2,500.
333P1	3c **dp vio,** large die on India paper	1,250.
333P2	3c **dp vio,** sm die on white wove paper	725.
333P2a	3c **dp vio,** PP sm die on yelsh wove paper	2,500.
334P1	4c **brn,** large die on India paper	1,250.
334P2	4c **brn,** sm die on white wove paper	725.
334P2a	4c **brn,** PP sm die on yelsh wove paper	2,500.
335TC1a	5c large die on India paper	
	e. **green,** *pink*	—
335P1	5c **blue,** large die on India paper	1,250.
	a. **blue,** large die on salmon paper	—
335P2	5c **blue,** sm die on white wove paper	725.
335P2a	5c **blue,** PP sm die on yelsh wove paper	2,500.
336TC1a	6c large die on India paper	
	e. **brown**	—
336P1	6c **red org,** large die on India paper	1,250.
336P2	6c **red org,** sm die on white wove paper	725.
336P2a	6c **red org,** PP sm die on yelsh wove paper	2,500.
337TC1a	8c large die on India paper	
	e. **green (shades),** *yellow*	*1,000.*
	f. **orange (shades),** *yellow*	—
	g. **blue,** *buff*	—
	h. **blue,** *yellow*	—
337P1	8c **ol grn,** large die on India paper	1,250.
	a. **olive green,** large die on yellow paper	—
337P2	8c **ol grn,** sm die on white wove paper	725.
337P2a	8c **ol grn,** PP sm die on yelsh wove paper	2,500.
338TC1a	10c large die on India paper	
	e. **carmine,** *pale yellow green*	—
	f. **brown,** *yellow*	—
	g. **green,** *pink*	*1,000.*
	h. **orange,** *greenish blue*	*1,000.*
	i. **brown,** *gray lavender*	—
	j. **orange,** *orange*	—
	k. **black,** *pink*	—
	l. **orange,** *yellow*	—
	m. **brown**	—
	n. **carmine**	—
	o. **blue,** *pink*	—
	p. **brown,** *pink*	*1,000.*
	q. **black**	—
338P1	10c **yel,** large die on India paper	1,250.
338P2	10c **yel,** sm die on white wove paper	725.
338P2a	10c **yel,** PP sm die on yelsh wove paper	2,500.
339TC1a	13c large die on India paper	
	e. **blue,** *yellow*	—
	f. **sea green,** *deep yellow*	—
	g. **sea green,** *pale blue*	—
	h. **deep violet,** *yellow*	—
339P1	13c **bl grn,** large die on India paper	1,250.
339P2	13c **bl grn,** sm die on white wove paper	725.
339P2a	13c **bl grn,** PP sm die on yelsh wove paper	2,500.
340TC1a	15c large die on India paper	
	e. **blue,** *pale lilac*	1,000.
	f. **blue,** *greenish blue*	1,000.
	g. **blue,** *pink*	1,000.
	h. **blue,** *yellow*	1,000.
	i. **dark blue,** *buff*	1,000.
	j. **orange brown,** *yellow*	1,000.
	k. **dark purple,** *yellow*	1,000.
	l. **orange,** *yellow*	1,000.
	m. **violet,** *yellow*	1,000.
	n. **black,** *orange*	1,000.

340P1 15c **pale ultra,** large die on India paper 1,250.
340P2 15c **pale ultra,** sm die on white wove paper 725.
340P2a 15c **pale ultra,** PP sm die on yelsh wove paper 2,500.
341TC1a 50c large die on India paper
e. **lilac,** *light blue* *1,000.*
f. **dark violet,** *yellow* *1,000.*
g. **violet,** *yellow* —
h. **orange,** *yellow* —
i. **orange brown,** *yellow* —
341P1 50c **vio,** large die on India paper 1,250.
a. **violet,** large die on pale lilac paper —
b. **violet,** large die on yellow paper —
c. **violet,** large die on greenish paper —
341P2 50c **vio,** sm die on white wove paper 725.
341P2a 50c **vio,** PP sm die on yelsh wove paper 2,500.
342TC1a $1 large die on India paper
e. **brown,** *blue* —
f. **carmine lake** 1,200.
g. **pink** 1,200.
h. **brown,** *blue green* —
i. **violet brown,** *pink* —
j. **violet brown,** *gray* —
342TC2 $1 small die on India paper
b. **carmine lake** 1,100.
c. **pink** 1,100.
342P1 $1 **vio blk,** large die on India paper 1,500.
342P2 $1 **vio blk,** sm die on white wove paper 725.
342P2a $1 **vio blk,** PP sm die on yelsh wove paper 2,500.

Lincoln Memorial Issue

1909

367P1 2c **car,** large die on India paper 2,500.
367P2 2c **car,** sm die on white wove paper 3,350.
367P2a 2c **car,** PP sm die on yelsh wove paper 6,000.

Alaska-Yukon Issue

370P1 2c **car,** large die on India paper 1,250.
370P2 2c **car,** sm die on white wove paper 1,900.
370P2a 2c **car,** PP sm die on yelsh wove paper 3,250.

Hudson-Fulton Issue

372P1 2c **car,** large die on India paper 1,250.
372P2 2c **car,** sm die on white wove paper 1,800.
372P2a 2c **car,** PP sm die on yelsh wove paper 3,250.

Panama-Pacific Issue

1912-13

397P1 1c **grn,** large die on India paper 1,750.
397P2 1c **grn,** sm die on white wove paper 1,500.
397P2a 1c **grn,** PP sm die on yelsh wove paper 3,000.
398P1 2c **car,** large die on India paper 1,750.
398P2 2c **car,** sm die on white wove paper 1,500.
398P2a 2c **car,** PP sm die on yelsh wove paper 3,000.
399P1 5c **blue,** large die on India paper 1,750.
399P2 5c **blue,** sm die on white wove paper 1,500.
399P2a 5c **blue,** PP sm die on yelsh wove paper 3,000.
400TC1a 10c large die on India paper
e. **brown red** 1,750.
400TC2 10c small die on India paper
b. **carmine lake** 1,100.
400P1 10c **org yel,** large die on India paper 1,750.
400P2 10c **org yel,** sm die on white wove paper 1,500.
400P2a 10c **org yel,** PP sm die on yelsh wove paper 3,000.
400AP1 10c **org,** large die on India paper 1,750.
400AP2 10c **org,** sm die on white wove paper 1,500.
400AP2a 10c **org,** PP sm die on yelsh wove paper 3,000.

No. 398P inscribed "Gatun Locks" is listed in the Essay section as No. 398-E3.

1912-19

405P1 1c **grn,** large die on India paper 1,400.
405P2 1c **grn,** sm die on white wove paper 650.
405P2a 1c **grn,** PP sm die on yelsh wove paper 2,500.
406P1 2c **car,** large die on India paper 1,400.
406P1a 2c **car,** large die on white wove paper *2,750.*
406P2 2c **car,** sm die on white wove paper 650.
406P2a 2c **car,** PP sm die on yelsh wove paper 2,500.
407P1 7c **blk,** large die on India paper 1,400.
407P2 7c **blk,** sm die on white wove paper 650.
407P2a 7c **blk,** PP sm die on yelsh wove paper 2,500.
414TC1a 8c large die on India paper
e. **black** 1,750.
414P1 8c **ol grn,** large die on India paper 1,400.
414P2 8c **ol grn,** sm die on white wove paper 650.
414P2a 8c **ol grn,** PP sm die on yelsh wove paper 2,500.
415P1 9c **ol grn,** large die on India paper 1,400.
415P2 9c **ol grn,** sm die on white wove paper 650.
415P2a 9c **ol grn,** PP sm die on yelsh wove paper 2,500.
416P1 10c **org yel,** large die on India paper 1,400.
416P2 10c **org yel,** sm die on white wove paper 650.
416P2a 10c **org yel,** PP sm die on yelsh wove paper 2,500.
434P1 11c **dk grn,** large die on India paper 1,500.
417P1 12c **cl brn,** large die on India paper 1,400.
417P2 12c **cl brn,** sm die on white wove paper 650.
417P2a 12c **cl brn,** PP sm die on yelsh wove paper 2,500.
513TC1a 13c large die on India paper
e. **violet** 650.
f. **lilac** 650.
g. **violet brown** 650.
h. **light ultramarine** 650.
i. **ultramarine** 650.
j. **deep ultramarine** 650.
k. **green** 650.
l. **dark green** 650.
m. **olive green** 650.
n. **orange yellow** 650.
o. **orange** 650.
p. **red orange** 650.
q. **ocher** 650.
r. **salmon red** 650.
s. **brown carmine** 650.
t. **claret brown** 650.
u. **brown** 650.
v. **black brown** 650.
w. **gray** 650.
x. **black** 650.
513P1 13c **apple grn,** large die on India paper 1,500.
418P1 15c **gray,** large die on India paper 1,400.
418P2 15c **gray,** sm die on white wove paper 650.
418P2a 15c **gray,** PP sm die on yelsh wove paper 2,500.
419P1 20c **ultra,** large die on India paper 1,400.
419P2 20c **ultra,** sm die on white wove paper 650.
419P2a 20c **ultra,** PP sm die on yelsh wove paper 2,500.
420P1 30c **org red,** large die on India paper 1,400.
420P2 30c **org red,** sm die on white wove paper 650.
420P2a 30c **org red,** PP sm die on yelsh wove paper 2,500.
421P1 50c **violet,** large die on India paper 1,500.
421P2 50c **violet,** sm die on white wove paper 650.
421P2a 50c **violet,** PP sm die on yelsh wove paper 2,500.
423P1 $1 **vio blk,** large die on India paper 1,400.
423P2 $1 **vio blk,** sm die on white wove paper 650.
423P2a $1 **vio blk,** PP sm die on yelsh wove paper 2,500.

1917-20

502P1 3c **dk vio,** type II, 10-subject die proof (2x5) on India paper, die sunk on card *6,500.*
524TC1a $5 large die on India paper
e. **carmine & black** 1,350.
524P1 $5 **dp grn & blk,** large die on India paper 1,500.
547TC1a $2 large die on India paper
e. **green & black** 1,500.
547P1 $2 **car & blk,** large die on India paper 1,500.

Victory Issue

1919

537P1 3c **violet,** large die on India paper 1,100.
537P2 3c **violet,** sm die on white wove paper 1,500.

Pilgrim Issue

1920

548P1 1c **grn,** large die on India paper 1,250.
548P2 1c **grn,** sm die on white wove paper 1,200.
549P1 2c **car,** large die on India paper 1,250.
549P2 2c **car,** sm die on white wove paper 1,200.
550P1 5c **blue,** large die on India paper 1,250.
550P2 5c **blue,** sm die on white wove paper 1,200.

1922-26

551P1 ½c **ol brn,** large die on India paper 1,500.
551P1a ½c **ol brn,** large die on white wove paper —
551P3 ½c **ol brn,** plate on white wove paper —
551P4 ½c **ol brn,** plate on card —
552TC2 1c small die on thin glazed card
b. **black** —
552P1 1c **dp grn,** large die on India paper 1,000.
552P1a 1c **dp grn,** large die on white wove paper 700.
552P3 1c **dp grn,** plate on white wove paper —
553P1 1½c **yel brn,** large die on India paper 1,000.
553P3 1½c **yel brn,** plate on white wove paper —
554TC2 2c small die on bond paper
b. **black** 1,250.
554P1 2c **car,** large die on India paper 1,000.
554P1a 2c **car,** large die on white wove paper 700.
554P3 2c **car,** plate on white wove paper —
555P1 3c **vio,** large die on India paper 1,250.
555P1a 3c **vio,** large die on white wove paper 1,000.
555P3 3c **vio,** plate on white wove paper —
556P1 4c **yel brn,** large die on India paper 1,200.
556P1a 4c **yel brn,** large die on white wove paper 700.
556P3 4c **yel brn,** plate on white wove paper —
557P1 5c **dk bl,** large die on India paper 1,000.
557P1a 5c **dk bl,** large die on white wove paper 700.
557P3 5c **dk bl,** plate on white wove paper —
558P1 6c **red org,** large die on India paper 1,000.
558P1a 6c **red org,** large die on white wove paper 700.
558P3 6c **red org,** plate on white wove paper —
559P1 7c **blk,** large die on India paper 1,000.
559P1a 7c **blk,** large die on white wove paper 700.
559P3 7c **blk,** plate on white wove paper —
560P1 8c **ol grn,** large die on India paper 1,000.
560P1a 8c **ol grn,** large die on white wove paper 700.
560P3 8c **ol grn,** plate on white wove paper —
561TC1a 9c large die on India paper
e. **red orange** 2,250.
561P1 9c **rose,** large die on India paper 1,000.
561P1a 9c **rose,** large die on white wove paper 700.
561P3 9c **rose,** plate on white wove paper —
562P1 10c **org,** large die on India paper 1,000.
562P1a 10c **org,** large die on white wove paper 700.
562P3 10c **org,** plate on white wove paper —
563TC1a 11c large die on India paper
e. **deep green** 2,250.
563P1 11c **lt bl,** large die on India paper 1,500.
563P1a 11c **lt bl,** large die on white wove paper 700.
563P3 11c **lt bl,** plate on white wove paper —
564P1 12c **brn vio,** large die on India paper 1,000.
564P1a 12c **brn vio,** large die on white wove paper 700.
564P3 12c **brn vio,** plate on white wove paper —
622TC1a 13c large die on India paper
e. **black** 2,250.
622P1 13c **grn,** large die on India paper 1,000.
622P1a 13c **grn,** large die on white wove paper 700.
622P3 13c **grn,** plate on white wove paper —
565TC1a 14c large die on India paper
e. **dark brown** 2,250.
565P1 14c **dk bl,** large die on India paper 1,250.
565P1a 14c **dk bl,** large die on white wove paper 700.
565P3 14c **dk bl,** plate on white wove paper —
566TC1a 15c large die on India paper
e. **black** 2,250.
566P1 15c **grey,** large die on India paper 1,250.
566P1a 15c **grey,** large die on white wove paper 700.
566P3 15c **grey,** plate on white wove paper —
623P1 17c **blk,** large die on India paper 1,000.
623P3 17c **blk,** plate on white wove paper —
567P1 20c **car rose,** large die on India paper 1,000.
567P1a 20c **car rose,** large die on white wove paper 700.
567P3 20c **car rose,** plate on white wove paper —
568P1 25c **dp grn,** large die on India paper 1,000.
568P1a 25c **dp grn,** large die on white wove paper 700.
568P3 25c **dp grn,** plate on white wove paper —
569P1 30c **ol brn,** large die on India paper 1,000.
569P1a 30c **ol brn,** large die on white wove paper 700.
569P3 30c **ol brn,** plate on white wove paper —
570P1 50c **lilac,** large die on India paper 1,250.
570P1a 50c **lilac,** large die on white wove paper 700.
570P3 50c **lilac,** plate on white wove paper —
571P1 $1 **vio brn,** large die on India paper 1,500.
571P1a $1 **vio brn,** large die on white wove paper 700.
571P3 $1 **vio brn,** plate on white wove paper —
572P1 $2 **dp bl,** large die on India paper 2,500.
572P1a $2 **dp bl,** large die on white wove paper 700.
572P2 $2 **dp bl,** small die on India paper —
572P3 $2 **dp bl,** plate on white wove paper —
573P1 $5 **car & dk bl,** large die on India paper 5,000.
573P1b $5 **car & dk bl,** large die on card *1,500.*

Catalogue values for large and small proofs between Nos. 610TC1a and 1193P1 are often based on one-time auction realizations. Because these items range in scarcity from unique to just a few known, actual market prices, when available, may be higher or lower than the values shown.

Harding Memorial Issue

1923-26

610TC1a 2c large die on India paper
e. **green** *4,000.*
610P1 2c large die on India paper 3,000.
610P1a 2c large die on white wove paper 2,000.
610P2 2c small die on white or yelsh wove paper 1,500.

Huguenot Walloon Issue

614P1 1c large die on India paper 3,000.
614P1a 1c large die on white wove paper 2,000.
614P2 1c small die on white or yelsh wove paper 2,000.
615P1 2c large die on India paper 3,000.
615P1a 2c large die on white wove paper 2,000.
615P2 2c small die on white or yelsh wove paper 2,000.
616P1 5c large die on India paper 3,000.
616P1a 5c large die on white wove paper 2,000.
616P2 5c small die on white or yelsh wove paper 2,000.

Lexington Concord Issue

617P1 1c large die on India paper 2,500.
617P1a 1c large die on white wove paper 2,000.
617P2 1c small die on white or yelsh wove paper 2,000.
618TC1a 2c large die on India paper
e. **black** *3,000.*
618P1 2c large die on India paper 2,500.
618P1a 2c large die on white wove paper 2,000.
618P2 2c small die on white or yelsh wove paper 2,000.
619P1 5c large die on India paper 2,500.
619P1a 5c large die on white wove paper 2,000.
619P2 5c small die on white or yelsh wove paper 2,000.

Norse American Issue

620P1 2c large die on India paper 3,000.
620P1a 2c large die on white wove paper 2,000.
620P2 2c small die on white or yelsh wove paper 3,000.
621P1 5c large die on India paper 3,000.
621P1a 5c large die on white wove paper 2,000.
621P2 5c small die on white or yelsh wove paper 3,000.

Sesquicentennial Exposition Issue

627P1 2c large die on India paper 1,500.
627P1a 2c large die on white wove paper 1,000.
627P2 2c small die on white or yelsh wove paper 1,500.

Ericsson Memorial Issue

628TC1a 5c large die on India paper
e. **dull dusky blue** 1,500.
628TC2 5c small die on India paper
b. **gray blue** 1,000.
628P1 5c large die on India paper 1,500.
628P1a 5c large die on white wove paper 1,000.
628P2 5c small die on white or yelsh wove paper 1,500.

Battle of White Plains Issue

629P1 2c large die on India paper 1,500.
629P1a 2c large die on white wove paper 1,000.
629P2 2c small die on white or yelsh wove paper 1,500.

1927-29

Vermont Sesquicentennial Issue

643P1 2c large die on India paper 1,500.
643P1a 2c large die on white wove paper 1,000.
643P2 2c small die on white or yelsh wove paper 1,500.

Burgoyne Campaign Issue

644P1 2c large die on India paper 1,500.
644P1a 2c large die on white wove paper 1,000.
644P2 2c small die on white or yelsh wove paper 1,500.

Valley Forge Issue

645P1	2c large die on India paper	1,500.
645P1a	2c large die on white wove paper	1,000.
645P2	2c small die on white or yelsh wove paper	1,500.

Aeronautics Conference Issue

649P1	2c large die on India paper	1,500.
649P1a	2c large die on white wove paper	1,000.
649P2	2c small die on white or yelsh wove paper	1,500.
650P1	5c large die on India paper	1,500.
650P1a	5c large die on white wove paper	1,000.
650P2	5c small die on white or yelsh wove paper	1,500.

George Rogers Clark Issue

651P1	2c large die on India paper	1,500.
651P1a	2c large die on white wove paper	1,000.
651P2	2c small die on white or yelsh wove paper	1,500.

Electric Lights Golden Jubilee

654P1	2c large die on India paper	1,500.
654P1a	2c large die on white wove paper	1,000.
654P2	2c small die on white or yelsh wove paper	1,500.

John Sullivan

657P1	2c large die on India paper	1,500.
657P1a	2c large die on white wove paper	1,000.
657P2	2c small die on white or yelsh wove paper	1,500.

Battle of Fallen Timbers Issue

680P1	2c large die on India paper	1,500.
680P1a	2c large die on white wove paper	1,000.
680P2	2c small die on white or yelsh wove paper	2,500.

Ohio River Canalization Issue

681P1	2c large die on India paper	1,500.
681P1a	2c large die on white wove paper	1,500.
681P2	2c small die on white or yelsh wove paper	1,500.

1930-31

Massachusetts Bay Colony Issue

682P1	2c large die on India paper	1,500.
682P1a	2c large die on white wove paper	1,000.
682P2	2c small die on white or yelsh wove paper	1,500.

Carolina Charleston Issue

683P1	2c large die on India paper	1,500.
683P1a	2c large die on white wove paper	1,000.
683P2	2c small die on white or yelsh wove paper	1,500.

Harding & Taft

684P1	1½c **brn**, large die on India paper	1,500.
685P1	4c **brn**, large die on India paper	1,500.

Braddock's Field Issue

688P1	2c large die on India paper	1,500.
688P1a	2c large die on white wove paper	1,000.
688P2	2c small die on white or yelsh wove paper	1,500.

Von Steuben Issue

689P1	2c large die on India paper	1,500.
689P1a	2c large die on white wove paper	1,000.
689P2	2c small die on white or yelsh wove paper	1,500.

Pulaski Issue

690P1	2c large die on India paper	1,500.
690P1a	2c large die on white wove paper	1,000.
690P2	2c small die on white or yelsh wove paper	1,500.

Red Cross Issue

702P1a	2c large die on white wove paper	1,000.
702P2	2c small die on white or yelsh wove paper	1,500.

Yorktown Issue

703P1	2c large die on India paper	1,500.
703P1a	2c large die on white wove paper	1,000.
703P2	2c small die on white or yelsh wove paper	1,500.

Washington Bicentennial

1932

704P1	½c **ol brn**, large die on India paper	1,000.
704P1a	½c **ol brn**, large die on white wove paper	1,000.
704P2	½c **ol brn**, sm die on white or yelsh wove paper	1,500.
705P1	1c **grn**, large die on India paper	1,000.
705P1a	1c **grn**, large die on white wove paper	1,000.
705P2	1c **grn**, sm die on white or yelsh wove paper	1,500.
706P1	1½c **brn**, large die on India paper	1,000.
706P1a	1½c **brn**, large die on white wove paper	1,000.
706P2	1½c **brn**, sm die on white or yelsh wove paper	1,500.
707P1	2c **car rose**, large die on India paper	1,000.
707P1a	2c **car rose**, large die on white wove paper	1,000.
707P2	2c **car rose**, sm die on white or yelsh wove paper	1,500.
708P1	3c **dp vio**, large die on India paper	1,000.
708P1a	3c **dp vio**, large die on white wove paper	1,000.
708P2	3c **dp vio**, sm die on white or yelsh wove paper	1,500.
709P1	4c **lt brn**, large die on India paper	1,000.
709P1a	4c **lt brn**, large die on white wove paper	1,000.
709P2	4c **lt brn**, small die on white or yelsh wove paper	1,500.
710P1	5c **blue**, large die on India paper	1,000.
710P1a	5c **blue**, large die on white wove paper	1,000.
710P2	5c **blue**, sm die on white or yelsh wove paper	1,500.
711P1	6c **red org**, large die on India paper	1,000.
711P1a	6c **red org**, large die on white wove paper	1,000.
711P2	6c **red org**, sm die on white or yelsh wove paper	1,500.
711P3	6c **red org**, plate proof on wove paper	*2,500.*
712P1	7c **blk**, large die on India paper	1,000.
712P1a	7c **blk**, large die on white wove paper	1,000.
712P2	7c **blk**, sm die on white or yelsh wove paper	1,500.
713P1	8c **ol bis**, large die on India paper	1,000.
713P1a	8c **ol bis**, large die on white wove paper	1,000.
713P2	8c **ol bis**, sm die on white or yelsh wove paper	1,500.
714P1	9c **pale red**, large die on India paper	1,000.
714P1a	9c **pale red**, large die on white wove paper	1,000.
714P2	9c **pale red**, sm die on white or yelsh wove paper	1,500.
715P1	10c **org yel**, large die on India paper	1,000.
715P1a	10c **org yel**, large die on white wove paper	1,000.
715P2	10c **org yel**, sm die on white or yelsh wove paper	1,500.

Winter Olympic Games Issue

716P1	2c large die on India paper	1,000.
716P1a	2c large die on white wove paper	1,000.
716P2	2c small die on white or yelsh wove paper	1,500.

Arbor Day Issue

717P1	2c large die on India paper	1,000.
717P1a	2c large die on white wove paper	1,000.
717P2	2c small die on white or yelsh wove paper	1,500.

Summer Olympic Games Issue

718TC1a	3c large die on India paper	
e. **carmine**		*7,500.*
718P1	3c large die on India paper	*10,000.*
718P1a	3c large die on white wove paper	1,000.
718P2	3c small die on white or yelsh wove paper	1,500.
719P1	5c large die on India paper	*15,000.*
719P1a	5c large die on white wove paper	1,000.
719P2	5c small die on white or yelsh wove paper	1,500.

Washington Issue

720TC2	3c small die on bond paper	
b. **black**		2,750.
720P1	3c large die on India paper	2,000.

William Penn Issue

724P1	3c large die on India paper	1,000.
724P1a	3c large die on white wove paper	1,000.
724P2	3c small die on white or yelsh wove paper	1,500.

Daniel Webster Issue

725P1	3c large die on India paper	1,000.
725P1a	3c large die on white wove paper	1,000.
725P2	3c small die on white or yelsh wove paper	1,500.

Georgia Bicentennial Issue

1933-34

726P1	3c large die on India paper	1,000.
726P1a	3c large die on white wove paper	1,000.
726P2	3c small die on white or yelsh wove paper	1,500.

Peace of 1783 Issue

727P1	3c large die on India paper	1,000.
727P1a	3c large die on white wove paper	1,000.
727P2	3c small die on white or yelsh wove paper	1,500.

Century of Progress Issue

728P1	1c large die on India paper	1,000.
728P1a	1c large die on white wove paper	1,000.
728P2	1c small die on white or yelsh wove paper	1,500.
729P1	3c large die on India paper	1,000.
729P1a	3c large die on white wove paper	1,000.
729P2	3c small die on white or yelsh wove paper	1,500.

National Recovery Act Issue

732P1a	3c large die on white wove paper	1,000.
732P2	3c small die on white or yelsh wove paper	1,500.

Byrd Antarctic Issue

733P1	3c large die on India paper	*1,250.*
733P1a	3c large die on white wove paper	1,000.
733P2	3c small die on white or yelsh wove paper	1,500.

Kosciuszko Issue

734P1	5c large die on India paper	*1,250.*
734P1a	5c large die on white wove paper	1,000.
734P2	5c small die on white or yelsh wove paper	1,500.

Maryland Tercentenary Issue

736P1	3c large die on India paper	*1,250.*
736P1a	3c large die on white wove paper	1,000.
736P2	3c small die on white or yelsh wove paper	1,500.

Mothers of America Issue

737P1	3c large die on India paper	1,000.
737P1a	3c large die on white wove paper	1,000.
737P2	3c small die on white or yelsh wove paper	1,500.

Wisconsin Tercentenary Issue

739P1a	3c large die on white wove paper	1,000.
739P2	3c small die on white or yelsh wove paper	1,500.

National Parks Year

740P1a	1c large die on white wove paper	1,000.
740P2	1c small die on white or yelsh wove paper	1,500.
741P2	2c small die on white or yelsh wove paper	1,500.
742P1a	3c large die on white wove paper	1,000.
742P2	3c small die on white or yelsh wove paper	1,500.
743P2	4c small die on white or yelsh wove paper	1,500.
744P2	5c small die on white or yelsh wove paper	1,500.
745P2	6c small die on white or yelsh wove paper	1,500.
746P1a	7c large die on white wove paper	1,000.
746P2	7c small die on white or yelsh wove paper	1,500.
747P2	8c small die on white or yelsh wove paper	1,500.
748P1a	9c large die on white wove paper	1,000.
748P2	9c small die on white or yelsh wove paper	1,500.
749P2	10c small die on white or yelsh wove paper	1,500.

For imperforates of the National Parks set, plus other issues, see the lined note following No. 749 in the Postage section.

Connecticut Tercentennary Issue

1935-37

772TC1d	3c Large die on thin glazed card	
e. **black**		*1,500.*
772P1	3c large die on India paper	*1,500.*
772P2	3c small die on white or yelsh wove paper	1,500.

California Pacific Expo Issue

773TC1d	3c Large die on yellow glazed card	
e. **orange red**		*1,500.*
773P2	3c small die on white or yelsh wove paper	1,500.

Boulder Dam Issue

774P2	3c small die on white or yelsh wove paper	1,500.

Michigan Centenary Issue

775P2	3c small die on white or yelsh wove paper	1,500.

Texas Centennial Issue

776P2	3c small die on white or yelsh wove paper	1,500.

Rhode Island Tercentenary Issue

777P2	3c small die on white or yelsh wove paper	1,500.

Arkansas Centennial Issue

782P1	3c large die on India paper	1,500.
782P1a	3c large die on white wove paper	1,500.
782P2	3c small die on white or yelsh wove paper	1,500.

Oregon Territory Issue

783P1	3c large die on India paper	1,500.
783P1a	3c large die on white wove paper	1,500.
783P2	3c small die on white or yelsh wove paper	1,500.

Susan B. Anthony Issue

784TC1d	3c large die on glazed card	
a. Deep lilac		1,750.
784P2	3c small die on white or yelsh wove paper	1,500.

Army Issue

785TC2	1c small die on bond paper	
b. **black**		750.
785P1a	1c large die on white wove paper	1,500.
785P2	1c small die on white or yelsh wove paper	1,500.
786P2	2c small die on white or yelsh wove paper	1,500.
787P1	3c large die on India paper	1,500.
787P1a	3c large die on white wove paper	1,500.
787P2	3c small die on white or yelsh wove paper	1,500.
788TC1a	4c large die on India paper	
e. **dark brown**		1,500.
788P2	4c small die on white or yelsh wove paper	1,500.
789TC1a	5c large die on India paper	
e. **blue**		1,500.
789P1	5c large die on India paper	*1,500.*
789P1a	5c large die on white wove paper	1,500.
789P2	5c small die on white or yelsh wove paper	1,500.

Navy Issue

790P2	1c small die on white or yelsh wove paper	1,500.
791P1	2c large die on India paper	1,500.
791P2	2c small die on white or yelsh wove paper	1,500.
792P2	3c small die on white or yelsh wove paper	1,500.
793TC1a	4c large die on India paper	
e. **dark brown**		1,500.
793P2	4c small die on white or yelsh wove paper	1,500.
794P2	5c small die on white or yelsh wove paper	1,500.

Ordinance of 1787 Issue

795P1d	3c large die on glazed card (49x34mm)	1,500.
795P2	3c small die on white or yelsh wove paper	1,500.

Virginia Dare Issue

796P1	5c large die on India paper	1,500.
796P2	5c small die on white or yelsh wove paper	1,500.

Society of Philatelic Americans

797P2	10c small die on white or yelsh wove paper	1,500.

Constitution Sesquicentennial Issue

798TC2	3c small die on bond paper	
b. **black**		750.
798P1	3c large die on India paper	1,500.

798P2 3c small die on white or yelsh wove paper 1,500.

Territorial Issues

799TC2 3c small die on bond paper
b. **black** 750.
799P1 3c large die on India paper 1,500.
799P2 3c small die on white or yelsh wove paper 1,500.
800TC2 3c small die on India paper
b. **black** 750.
c. **black,** on bond paper 750.
800P2 3c small die on white or yelsh wove paper 1,500.
801TC1a 3c large die on India paper
e. **black** 1,500.
801TC1b 3c Large die on bond paper
e. **black** 1,500.
801TC2 3c small die on bond paper
b. **black** 750.
801P1 3c large die on India paper 1,500.
801P2 3c small die on white or yelsh wove paper 1,500.
802TC2 3c small die on bond paper
b. **black** 750.
802P1 3c large die on India paper 1,500.
802P2 3c small die on white or yelsh wove paper 1,500.

Presidential Issue

1938

803TC1a ½c large die on India paper
e. **black** *3,000.*
803P1 ½c **dp org,** large die on India paper *2,000.*
803P2 ½c **dp org,** small die on white or yelsh wove paper 3,000.
804P2 1c **grn,** small die on white or yelsh wove paper 3,000.
805P2 1½c **bis brn,** small die on white or yelsh wove paper 2,500.
806P1a 2c **rose car,** large die on white wove paper *1,800.*
806P2 2c **rose car,** small die on white or yelsh wove paper *3,000.*
807P1 3c **dp vio,** large die on glazed card —
807P2 3c **dp vio,** small die on white or yelsh wove paper 3,000.
808P2 4c **red vio,** small die on white or yelsh wove paper 3,000.
809P1 4½c **dk gray,** large die on India paper *1,500.*
809P2 4½c **dk gray,** small die on white or yelsh wove paper 3,000.
810P1 5c **brt bl,** large die on India paper *1,500.*
810P2 5c **brt bl,** small die on white or yelsh wove paper 3,000.
811P2 6c **red org,** small die on white or yelsh wove paper 3,000.
812P1 7c **sepia,** large die on India paper *1,750.*
812P2 7c **sepia,** small die on white or yelsh wove paper 3,000.
813P1a 8c **ol grn,** large die on white wove paper *1,800.*
813P2 8c **ol grn,** small die on white or yelsh wove paper 3,000.
814P1 9c **ol grn,** large die on India paper *1,800.*
814P1a 9c **ol grn,** large die on white wove paper *1,800.*
814P2 9c **ol grn,** small die on white or yelsh wove paper 3,000.
815TC1a 10c large die on India paper
e. **sepia** 1,500.
815P1 10c **brn red,** large die on India paper *2,500.*
815P2 10c **brn red,** small die on white or yelsh wove paper 3,000.
816P2 11c **ultra,** small die on white or yelsh wove paper 3,000.
817P1 12c **brt vio,** large die on India paper *1,500.*
817P2 12c **brt vio,** small die on white or yelsh wove paper 3,000.
818P2 13c **bl grn,** small die on white or yelsh wove paper 3,000.
819P2 14c **blue,** small die on white or yelsh wove paper 3,000.
820P1 15c **bl gray,** large die on India paper *1,800.*
820P1a 15c **bl gray,** large die on white wove paper *1,800.*
820P2 15c **bl gray,** small die on white or yelsh wove paper 3,000.
821P1 16c **blk,** large die on India paper *1,500.*
821P2 16c **blk,** small die on white or yelsh wove paper 3,000.
822P2 17c **rose red,** small die on white or yelsh wove paper 3,000.
823P2 18c **brn car,** small die on white or yelsh wove paper 3,000.
824P1 19c **brt vio,** large die on India paper *1,800.*
824P1a 19c **brt vio,** large die on white wove paper *1,800.*
824P2 19c **brt vio,** small die on white or yelsh wove paper 3,000.
825P1 20c **brt bl grn,** large die on India paper *1,800.*
825P1a 20c **brt bl grn,** large die on white wove paper *1,800.*
825P2 20c **brt bl grn,** small die on white or yelsh wove paper 3,000.
826TC1a 21c large die on India paper
e. **black** *2,000.*
826P2 21c **dull bl,** small die on white or yelsh wove paper 3,000.
827P2 22c **ver,** small die on white or yelsh wove paper 3,000.
828P1 24c **gray blk,** large die on India paper *1,800.*
828P2 24c **gray blk,** small die on white or yelsh wove paper 3,000.
829TC1a 25c large die on India paper
e. **green** *2,000.*
829P2 25c **dp red lilac,** small die on white or yelsh wove paper 3,000.
830P2 30c **dp ultra,** small die on white or yelsh wove paper 3,000.
831P1 50c **lt red vio,** large die on India paper *1,500.*
831P2 50c **lt red vio,** small die on white or yelsh wove paper 3,000.
832P2 $1 **pur & blk,** small die on white or yelsh wove paper 5,000.
833P2 $2 **yel grn & blk,** small die on white or yelsh wove paper 5,000.
834P2 $5 **car & blk,** small die on white or yelsh wove paper 5,000.

Constitution Ratification Issue

1938

835P1 3c large die on India paper 1,500.
835P2 3c small die on white or yelsh wove paper 1,500.

Swedish-Finnish Tercentenary Issue

836TC1a 3c large die on India paper
e. **purple** 1,500.
836P1 3c large die on India paper 1,500.
836P2 3c small die on white or yelsh wove paper 1,500.

Northwest Territory Sesquicentennial

837TC1a 3c large die on India paper
e. **dark purple** 1,500.
837P2 3c small die on white or yelsh wove paper 800.

Iowa Territory Centennial Issue

838P1 3c large die on India paper *1,500.*
838P2 3c small die on white or yelsh wove paper 1,500.

Golden Gate Intl. Exposition Issue

1939

852P1 3c large die on India paper *1,800.*
852P2 3c small die on white or yelsh wove paper 1,500.

New York World's Fair Issue

853P1 3c large die on India paper *1,500.*
853P2 3c small die on white or yelsh wove paper 1,500.

Washington Inauguration Issue

854TC1a 3c large die on India paper
e. **purple** 900.
854P1 3c large die on India paper *1,500.*
854P2 3c small die on white or yelsh wove paper 1,500.

Baseball Centennial Issue

855TC1a 3c large die on India paper
e. **red violet** *2,500.*
855P1 3c large die on India paper *5,000.*
855P1a 3c large die on white wove paper *2,000.*
855P2 3c small die on white or yelsh wove paper 2,500.

Panama Canal Issue

856P1 3c large die on white wove paper 2,250.
856P2 3c small die on white or yelsh wove paper 1,500.

Printing Trecentenary Issue

857P2 3c small die on white or yelsh wove paper 1,500.

Statehood Issue

858P2 3c small die on white or yelsh wove paper 1,500.

Famous Americans Issue

Authors

1940

859P2 1c small die on white or yelsh wove paper 1,500.
860P2 2c small die on white or yelsh wove paper 1,500.
861P2 3c small die on white or yelsh wove paper 1,500.
862TC1a 5c large die on India paper
e. **dull blue** 1,500.
862P1 5c large die on India paper 1,500.
862P2 5c small die on white or yelsh wove paper 1,500.
863P1 10c large die on India paper *2,500.*
863P2 10c small die on white or yelsh wove paper 1,500.

Poets

864P1 1c large die on India paper *1,500.*
864P2 1c small die on white or yelsh wove paper 1,500.
865P2 2c small die on white or yelsh wove paper 1,500.
866TC1a 3c large die on India paper
e. **dark blue violet** 1,500.
866P2 3c small die on white or yelsh wove paper 1,500.
867P1 5c large die on India paper 1,500.
867P2 5c small die on white or yelsh wove paper 1,500.
868P1 10c large die on India paper *1,500.*
868P2 10c small die on white or yelsh wove paper 1,500.

Educators

869P1 1c large die on India paper 1,500.
869P2 1c small die on white or yelsh wove paper 1,500.
870P2 2c small die on white or yelsh wove paper 1,500.
871P2 3c small die on white or yelsh wove paper 1,500.
872P1 5c large die on India paper 1,500.
872P2 5c small die on white or yelsh wove paper 1,500.
873P1 10c large die on India paper 1,500.
873P2 10c small die on white or yelsh wove paper 1,500.

Scientists

874P1 1c large die on India paper *1,500.*
874P2 1c small die on white or yelsh wove paper 1,500.
875P1 2c large die on India paper 1,500.
875P2 2c small die on white or yelsh wove paper 1,500.
876P1 3c large die on India paper 1,500.
876P2 3c small die on white or yelsh wove paper 1,500.
877P2 5c small die on white or yelsh wove paper 1,500.
878P1 10c large die on India paper *1,500.*
878P2 10c small die on white or yelsh wove paper 1,500.

Composers

879P2 1c small die on white or yelsh wove paper 1,500.
880P1 2c large die on India paper 1,500.
880P2 2c small die on white or yelsh wove paper 1,500.
881P2 3c small die on white or yelsh wove paper 1,500.
882P1 5c large die on India paper 1,500.
882P2 5c small die on white or yelsh wove paper 1,500.
883P2 10c small die on white or yelsh wove paper 1,500.

Artists

884P2 1c small die on white or yelsh wove paper 1,500.
885P1 2c large die on wove paper 1,500.
885P2 2c small die on white or yelsh wove paper 1,500.
886P1 3c large die on wove paper 1,500.
886P2 3c small die on white or yelsh wove paper 1,500.
887P1 5c large die on India paper 1,500.
887P2 5c small die on white or yelsh wove paper 1,500.
888P1 10c large die on India paper 1,500.
888P2 10c small die on white or yelsh wove paper 1,500.

Inventors

889P2 1c small die on white or yelsh wove paper 1,500.
890P1 2c large die on India paper *1,500.*
890P2 2c small die on white or yelsh wove paper 1,500.
891P1 3c large die on wove paper 1,500.
891P2 3c small die on white or yelsh wove paper 1,500.
892P2 5c small die on white or yelsh wove paper 1,500.
893P2 10c small die on white or yelsh wove paper 1,500.

Pony Express Issue

1940

894P1 3c large die on India paper *1,500.*
894P2 3c small die on white or yelsh wove paper 1,500.

Pan American Union Issue

895P2 3c small die on white or yelsh wove paper 1,500.

Idaho Statehood Issue

896P1 3c large die on India paper *1,500.*
896P2 3c small die on white or yelsh wove paper 1,500.

Wyoming Statehood Issue

897TC1a 3c large die on India paper
e. **red violet** 1,500.
897P2 3c small die on white or yelsh wove paper 1,500.

Coronado Expedition Issue

898P1 3c large die on India paper *1,500.*
898P2 3c small die on white or yelsh wove paper 1,500.

National Defense Issue

899P1 1c large die on India paper *1,500.*
899P2 1c small die on white or yelsh wove paper 1,500.
900P1 2c large die on India paper *1,500.*
900P2 2c small die on white or yelsh wove paper 1,500.
901P1 3c large die on India paper *1,500.*
901P2 3c small die on white or yelsh wove paper 1,500.

Thirteenth Amendment Issue

902P1 3c large die on India paper *1,500.*
902P2 3c small die on white or yelsh wove paper 1,500.

Vermont Statehood Issue

1941-44

903P1 3c large die on wove paper 1,750.
903P2 3c small die on white or yelsh wove paper 1,500.

Kentucky Statehood Issue

904P1 3c large die on India paper *1,500.*
904P2 3c small die on white or yelsh wove paper 1,500.

Win the War Issue

905P2 3c small die on white or yelsh wove paper 1,500.

China Resistance Issue

906P2 3c small die on white or yelsh wove paper 1,750.

Allied Nations Issue

907P2 2c small die on white or yelsh wove paper 1,500.

Four Freedoms Issue

908P1 1c large die on India paper *1,500.*
908P2 1c small die on white or yelsh wove paper 1,500.

Overrun Countries Issue

909P2 5c small die on wove paper *600.*
910P2 5c small die on wove paper *600.*
911P2 5c small die on wove paper *600.*
912P2 5c small die on wove paper *600.*
913P2 5c small die on wove paper *600.*
914P2 5c small die on wove paper *600.*
915P2 5c small die on wove paper *600.*
916P2 5c small die on wove paper *600.*

917P2 5c small die on wove paper 600.
918P2 5c small die on wove paper 600.
919P2 5c small die on wove paper 600.
920P2 5c small die on wove paper 600.
921P2 5c small die on wove paper 600.

Transcontinental Railroad Issue

922P1 3c large die on India paper 1,500.
922P2 3c small die on white or yelsh wove paper 1,500.

Steamship Issue

923P1 3c large die on wove paper 1,600.
923P2 3c small die on white or yelsh wove paper 1,500.

Telegraph Issue

924P1 3c large die on wove paper 1,500.
924P2 3c small die on white or yelsh wove paper 1,500.

Philippine Issue

925P1 3c large die on India paper 1,500.
925P2 3c small die on white or yelsh wove paper 1,500.

Motion Picture Issue

926P1 3c large die on India paper 1,500.
926P2 3c small die on white or yelsh wove paper 1,000.

Florida Statehood Issue

1945-46

927P1 3c large die on India paper 1,500.
927P2 3c small die on white or yelsh wove paper 1,500.

United Nations Conference Issue

928P2 5c small die on white or yelsh wove paper 1,500.

Iwo Jima (Marines) Issue

929TC1a 3c large die on India paper
e. **bright purple** 2,300.
929P2 3c small die on white or yelsh wove paper 1,500.

Franklin D. Roosevelt Issue

930P2 1c small die on white or yelsh wove paper 1,500.
931P1a 2c large die on wove paper 1,750.
931P2 2c small die on white or yelsh wove paper 1,500.
932P1a 3c large die on wove paper 1,750.
932P2 3c small die on white or yelsh wove paper 1,500.
933P1a 5c large die on wove paper 1,750.

Army & Navy Issues

934P1a 3c large die on wove paper 1,500.
934P2 3c small die on white or yelsh wove paper 1,200.
935P1a 3c large die on wove paper 1,500.
935P2 3c small die on white or yelsh wove paper 1,500.

Merchant Marine Issue

939P1a 5c large die on wove paper 1,500.

Tennessee Statehood Issue

941P1a 3c large die on wove paper 1,500.

Iowa Statehood Issue

942P1a 3c large die on white wove paper 1,500.

Kearny Expedition Issue

944P1a 3c large die on wove paper 1,500.

Thomas A. Edison Issue

1947-50

945P1a 3c large die on wove paper 1,500.

Joseph Pulitzer Issue

946P1a 3c large die on white wove paper 1,500.

Postage Stamp Centenary Issue

947P1a 3c large die on wove paper 1,500.

Doctors Issue

949P1a 3c large die on wove paper 1,500.

Utah Issue

950TC1c 3c large die on wove paper
e. **deep brown** 1,500.

U.S.S. Constitution Issue

951P1a 3c large die on wove paper 1,500.

Mississippi Territory Issue

955P1a 3c large die on white wove paper 1,500.

Four Chaplains Issue

956P1a 3c large die on wove paper 1,500.

Swedish Pioneers Issue

958P1a 5c large die on wove paper 1,500.

Progress of Women Issue

959TC1b 3c large die on wove paper
e. **bright violet** 1,750.
959P1a 3c large die on wove paper 1,500.

William Allen White Issue

960P1a 3c large die on wove paper 1,500.

U.S.-Canada Friendship Issue

961TC1b 3c large die on wove paper
e. **brown violet** 1,500.

Francis Scott Key Issue

962P1a 3c large die on wove paper 1,500.

Youth Issue

963TC1b 3c large die on white wove paper
e. **violet** 1,500.

Oregon Statehood Issue

964TC1b 3c large die on wove paper
e. **dull violet** 1,500.

Harlan Fiske Stone Issue

965P1a 3c large die on wove paper 1,500.

Clara Barton Issue

967P1a 3c large die on wove paper 2,000.

Poultry Issue

968TC1b 3c large die on wove paper
e. **red brown** 1,500.

Volunteer Firemen Issue

971P1a 3c large die on wove paper 1,500.

Indian Centennial Issue

972P1a 3c large die on wove paper 1,500.

Rough Riders Issue

973P1a 3c large die on wove paper 1,500.

Girl Scouts Issue

974P1a 3c large die on white wove paper 1,500.

Will Rogers Issue

975P1a 3c large die on wove paper 1,750.

Fort Bliss Centennial Issue

976P1a 3c large die on wove paper 1,500.

Moina Michael Issue

977P1a 3c large die on white wove paper 1,500.

Minnesota Territory Issue

981P1a 3c large die on white wove paper 1,500.

Puerto Rico Election Issue

983P1a 3c large die on wove paper 1,500.

G.A.R. Issue

985P1a 3c large die on wove paper 1,500.

American Bankers Assoc. Issue

987TC1b 3c large die on wove paper
e. **dark green** 1,500.

Samuel Gompers Issue

988P1a 3c large die on wove paper 1,500.

National Capital Sesquicentennial Issue

989P1a 3c large die on white wove paper 1,500.
991P1a 3c large die on wove paper 1,500.
992P1a 3c large die on wove paper 1,500.

Boy Scouts Issue

995P1a 3c large die on white wove paper 2,000.

Nevada Centennial Issue

1951-53

999P1a 3c large die on wove paper 1,500.

Landing of Cadillac Issue

1000P1a 3c large die on wove paper 1,500.

Colorado Statehood Issue

1001P1a 3c large die on wove paper 1,500.

American Chemical Society Issue

1002P1a 3c large die on wove paper 1,500.

Battle of Brooklyn Issue

1003P1a 3c large die on wove paper 1,500.

Betsy Ross Issue

1004P1a 3c large die on wove paper 1,500.

4-H Club Issue

1005P1a 3c large die on wove paper 1,500.

B & O Railroad Issue

1006TC1b 3c large die on wove paper
e. **deep blue** 1,500.
1006P1a 3c large die on wove paper 1,750.

A.A.A. Issue

1007P1a 3c large die on wove paper 1,500.

Grand Coulee Dam Issue

1009P1a 3c large die on wove paper 1,500.

Lafayette Issue

1010P1a 3c large die on wove paper 1,500.

Mt. Rushmore Memorial Issue

1011P1a 3c large die on wove paper 1,500.

Engineering Centennial Issue

1012P1a 3c large die on wove paper 1,500.

Service Women Issue

1013P1a 3c large die on wove paper 1,500.

Red Cross Issue

1016P1a 3c large die on wove paper 3,000.

National Guard Issue

1017P1a 3c large die on wove paper 1,500.

Ohio Statehood Issue

1018P1a 3c large die on wove paper 1,500.

Washington Territory Issue

1019P1a 3c large die on wove paper 1,500.

Louisana Purchase Issue

1020P1a 3c large die on wove paper 1,500.

Opening of Japan Centennial Issue

1021P1a 5c large die on wove paper 2,000.

American Bar Association Issue

1022P1a 3c large die on wove paper 1,500.

Trucking Industry Issue

1025P1a 3c large die on wove paper 1,500.

Gen. George S. Patton Issue

1026P1a 3c large die on wove paper 1,500.

Columbia University Issue

1954-98

1029P1a 3c large die on wove paper 1,500.

Liberty Issue

1030P1a ½c *Franklin,* large die on wove paper 2,500.
1031P1a 1c *Washington,* large die on wove paper 1,500.
1032P1a 1½c *Mt. Vernon,* large die on wove paper 1,500.
1033P1a 2c *Jefferson,* large die on wove paper 1,500.
1036P1a 4c *Lincoln,* large die on wove paper 1,500.
1038P1a 5c *Monroe,* large die on wove paper 1,500.
1039P1a 6c *Roosevelt,* large die on wove paper 1,500.
1044P1a 10c *Independence Hall,* large die on wove paper 1,500.
1047P1a 20c *Monticello,* large die on wove paper 1,500.
1049P1a 30c *Lee,* large die on wove paper 2,000.
1050P1a 40c *Marshall,* large die on wove paper 2,000.
1051P1a 50c *Anthony,* large die on wove paper 2,000.
1052P1a $1 *Henry,* large die on wove paper 2,000.
1053P1a $5 *Hamilton,* large die on wove paper 2,500.

Nebraska Territory Issue

1060P1a 3c large die on wove paper 1,500.

George Eastman Issue

1062P1a 3c large die on wove paper 1,500.

Lewis & Clark Issue

1063P1a 3c large die on wove paper 1,500.

Pennsylvania Academy of Fine Arts Issue

1064P1a 3c large die on wove paper 1,500.

Armed Forces Reserve Issue

1067P1a 3c large die on wove paper 1,500.

New Hampshire Issue

1068P1a 3c large die on wove paper 1,500.

Soo Locks Issue

1069P1a 3c large die on wove paper 1,500.

Ft. Ticonderoga Issue

1071P1a 3c large die on wove paper 1,500.

Benjamin Franklin Issue

1073P1a 3c large die on wove paper 1,500.

Booker T. Washington Issue

1074P1a 3c large die on wove paper 1,500.

FIPEX Souvenir Sheet

1076P1a large die on wove paper 1,500.

Wildlife Conservation Issue

1077P1a 3c large die on wove paper 1,500.
1078P1a 3c large die on wove paper 1,500.
1079P1a 3c large die on wove paper 1,500.

Pure Food & Drug Laws

1080P1a 3c large die on wove paper 1,500.

Wheatland Issue

1081P1a 3c large die on wove paper 1,500.

Labor Day Issue

1082P1a 3c large die on wove paper 1,500.

Nassau Hall Issue

1083P1a 3c large die on wove paper 1,500.

Children's Issue

1085P1a 3c large die on wove paper 1,500.

Alexander Hamilton Issue

1086P1a 3c large die on wove paper 1,500.

Polio Issue

1087P1a 3c large die on wove paper 1,500.

Coast & Geodetic Survey Issue

1088P1a 3c large die on wove paper 1,500.

Steel Industry Issue

1090P1a 3c large die on wove paper 1,500.

Oklahoma Statehood Issue

1092P1a 3c large die on wove paper 1,500.

Civil War Centennial Issue

1178P1 4c Ft. Sumter, large die
a. On white wove paper 1,500.
b. On stiff yellowish bond paper 1,500.

Project Mercury Issue

1193P1a 4c large die on wove paper 1,500.

Antarctic Issue

1431P1

1431P1 8c large die on white wove, mounted on card autographed by PMG Winton M. Blount *1,000.*

Olympic Games Issue

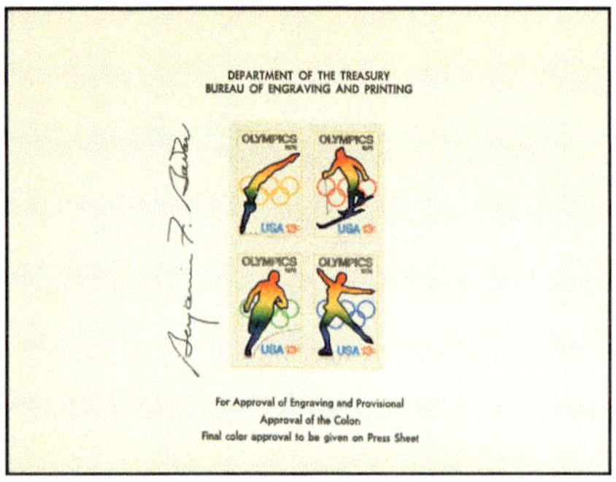

1698aP1

1698aP1 13c large hybrid die proof, mounted on large card imprinted for approval of engraving and color, signed by PMG Benjamin F. Bailar *800.*

Duck Decoy Issue

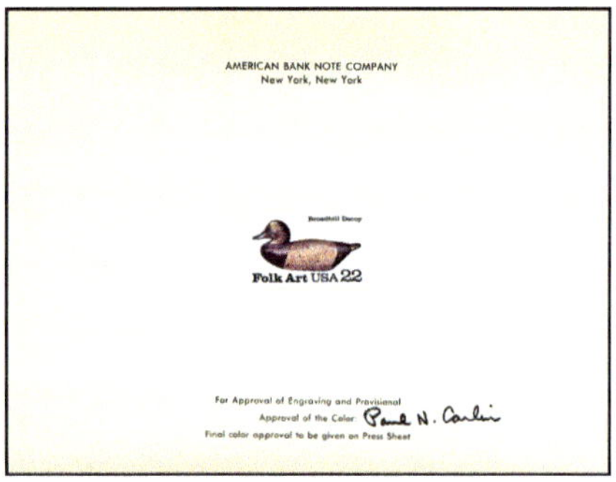

2138P1

2138P1 22c *Broadbill* decoy, large hybrid die proof, mounted on large card imprinted for approval of engraving and color, "Duck Decoys Cylinder Proof," etc. on reverse *240.*

Dennis Chavez Issue

2186P1a

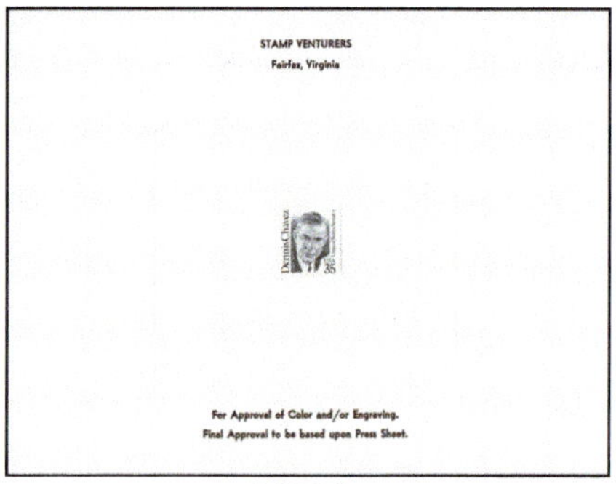

2186P1b

Design size: 13x20mm

2186P1 35c *Dennis Chavez*

a. Engraved large die impression on 114x147mm gummed stamp paper, dated in red "Jan. 30/91," black —

b. Engraved large die impression, cut to stamp size and affixed to large card imprinted for approval of color and/or engraving, black —

Statue of Liberty, 100th Anniversary

2224TC1

2224TC1e 22c **olive green,** die sunk on card *1,300.*

1988 Winter Olympics, Calgary Issue

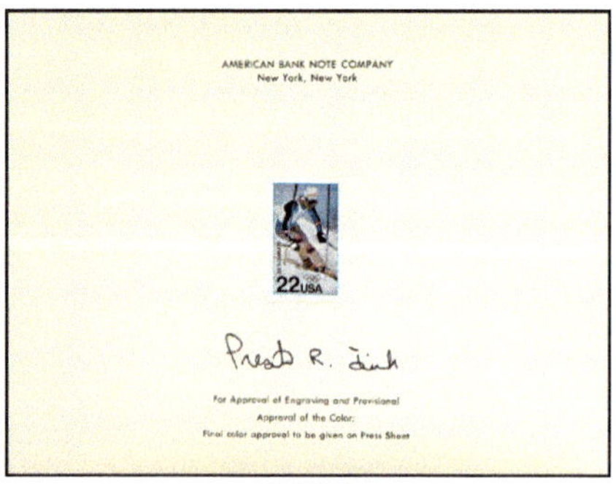

2369P1

2369P1 22c large hybrid die proof, mounted on large card imprinted for approval of engraving and color, "Winter Olympics Stamp From Approved Press Sheet," etc. on reverse *550.*

Moon Landing, 20th Anniversary

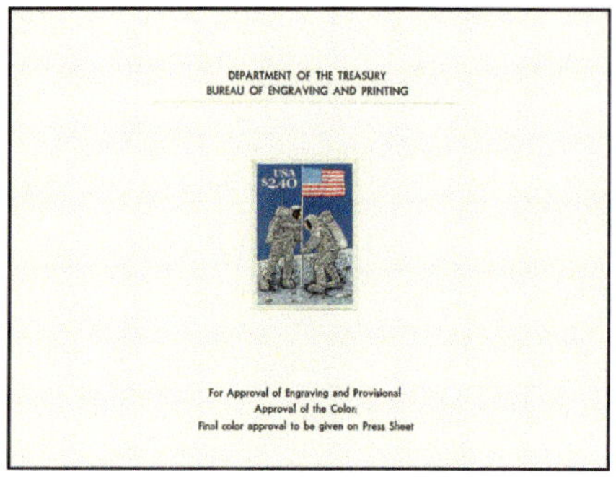

2419P1

2419P1 $2.40 large hybrid die proof, pressed on large card imprinted for approval of engraving and color *2,850.*

Flag and Olympic Rings Issue

2528P1

2528P1 29c large hybrid die proof, mounted on large card imprinted for approval of engraving and color, "Flag with Olympic Rings Stamp From Approved Press Sheet," etc. on reverse *550.*

Basketball, 100th Anniversary Issue

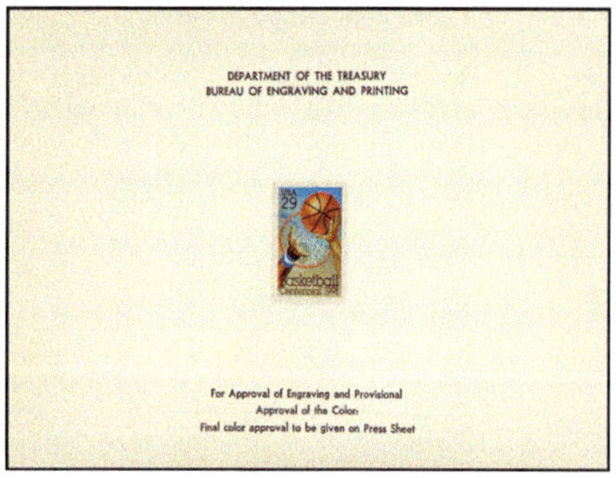

2560P1

2560P1 29c large hybrid die proof, mounted on large card imprinted for approval of engraving and color *950.*

1995

2587P1b 29c **red brown,** die proof on gummed wove paper, ms "7/17/95" and "#3" below design —

Winter Olympics Issue

2615P1

2615P1 29c *Bobsledding,* large hybrid die proof, mounted on large card imprinted for approval of engraving and color, "Winter Olympics Stamp from Approved Sheet," etc. on reverse *600.*

Summer Olympics Issue

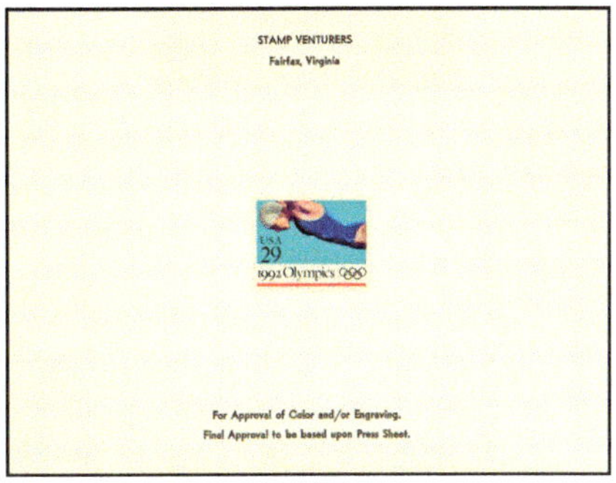

2641P1

2641P1 29c *Swimming,* large hybrid die proof, mounted on large card imprinted for approval of engraving and color, "Summer Olympics Stamp from Approved Sheet," etc. on reverse *500.*

Great Americans — Milton S. Hershey Issue

2933P1a

2933P1a 32c large die on wove, dated "7/3/95" at lower right —

Prisoners of War & Missing in Action Issue

2966P1

2966P1 32c large hybrid die proof, pressed on large card imprinted with Ashton Potter logo and approval information *300.*

World War II Issue

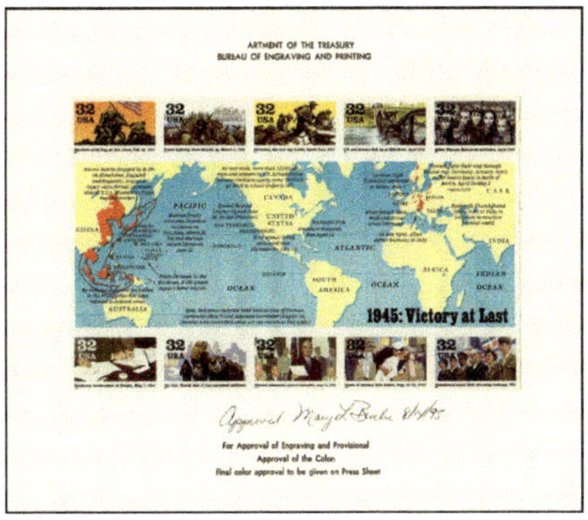

2981P1

2981P1 32c large hybrid die proof, pressed on large card, ms, approved by Mary L. Burke, USPS Production Staff *1,250.*

Space Shuttle Issues

3261P

3262P

3262Pc

3261P $3.20 **magenta** color only
- *a.* On coated paper —
- *b.* On uncoated paper *225.*

3262P $11.75 **cyan** color only
- *a.* On coated paper —
- *b.* On uncoated paper *225.*
- *c.* As "a," vertical pair, #3261P and 3262P, with full horiz. gutter between 1,150.
- *d.* As "b," vertical pair, #3261P and 3262P, with full horiz. gutter between —

Nos. 1789P through 2788aP, listed below, are all from the proof files of the American Bank Note Co. archives that were sold and are available to collectors. All items listed are on gummed stamp paper and are imperf unless otherwise noted, and they therefore have the appearance of imperf or part-perf stamps, though their source makes clear that they are, in fact, proofs. This group includes progressive proofs in the different colors, plus one variety of No. 2624P and three varieties of No. 2770aP that differ slightly from the issued designs and, therefore, are actually essays. Where single proofs are listed, pairs are worth double the values shown.

1789Pg finished design as issued, pair

1789Pd blue color only, pair

1979

1789P 15c John Paul Jones
a. Single, red color ("John Paul Jones") only 50.00
Pair with vert. gutter between —
Pair with horiz. gutter between —
Cross gutter block of four —
b. Single, yellow color only 50.00
Pair with vert. gutter between —
Pair with horiz. gutter between —
Cross gutter block of four —
c. Single, magenta color only 50.00
Pair with vert. gutter between —
Pair with horiz. gutter between —
Cross gutter block of four —
d. Single, blue color only 50.00
Pair with vert. gutter between —
Pair with horiz. gutter between —
Cross gutter block of four —
e. Single, black color only 50.00
Pair with vert. gutter between —
Pair with horiz. gutter between —
Cross gutter block of four —
f. Single, tagging blocks only 50.00
Pair with vert. gutter between —
Pair with horiz. gutter between —
Cross gutter block of four —
g. Single, finished design as issued 25.00
Pair 50.00
Pair with vert. gutter between 700.00
Pair with horiz. gutter between 600.00
Cross gutter block of four 3,000.

2418P

1989

2418P 25c Ernest Hemingway, pair 2,000.
Pair with vert. gutter between —
Pair with horiz. gutter between —
Cross gutter block of four —

2478Pa cross gutter block

Illustration reduced.

1991

2476P 1c Kestrel, pair 150.
Pair with vert. gutter between 200.
Pair with horiz. gutter between 200.
Cross gutter block of four —
a. Perforated
Pair with vert. gutter between 675.
Pair with horiz. gutter between 675.
Cross gutter block of four —

2478P 3c Bluebird, pair 150.
Pair with vert. gutter between 200.
Pair with horiz. gutter between 200.
Cross gutter block of four —
a. Se-tenants, Nos. 2476P and 2478P
Pair, one No. 2476P and one No. 2478P, with vert. gutter between —
Cross gutter block of four, two No. 2476P at left and two No. 2478P at right —
b. Perforated
Pair with vert. gutter between —
Pair with horiz. gutter between —
Cross gutter block of four —
c. Perforated se-tenants
Pair, one No. 2476Pa and one No. 2478Pb, with vert. gutter between —
Cross gutter block of four, two No. 2476Pa at left and two No. 2478Pb at right (unique) —

1990-91

2500aP 25c Olympics, horiz. strip of five 1,500.
Two strips of five with vert. gutter between —
Two strips of five with horiz. gutter between —
Cross gutter block of four strips of five —

2513P 25c Dwight D. Eisenhower, pair 875.

2517P (29c) "F" stamp, perforated
Pair with vert. gutter between —
Pair with horiz. gutter between —
Cross gutter block of four (unique) —

2540Pi with all litho. colors

2540Pf magenta, yellow and blue colors only

1991

2540P $2.90 Eagle
a. Single, magenta color only 175.
Pair with vert. gutter between —
Pair with horiz. gutter between —
Cross gutter block of four —
b. Single, yellow color only 175.
Pair with vert. gutter between —
Pair with horiz. gutter between —
Cross gutter block of four —
c. Single, blue color only 175.
Pair with vert. gutter between —
Pair with horiz. gutter between —
Cross gutter block of four —
d. Single, magenta and yellow colors only 175.
Pair with vert. gutter between —
Pair with horiz. gutter between —
Cross gutter block of four —
e. Single, yellow and blue colors only 175.
Pair with vert. gutter between —
Pair with horiz. gutter between —
Cross gutter block of four —
f. Single, magenta, yellow and blue colors only 175.
Pair with vert. gutter between —
Pair with horiz. gutter between —
Cross gutter block of four —
g. Single, black (litho.) color only 175.
Pair with vert. gutter between —
Pair with horiz. gutter between —
Cross gutter block of four —
h. Single, black (litho.) and yellow colors only 175.
Pair with vert. gutter between —
Pair with horiz. gutter between —
Cross gutter block of four —
i. Single, all litho. colors but without black engr. 175.
Pair with vert. gutter between —
Pair with horiz. gutter between —
Cross gutter block of four —
j. Single, finished design as issued 500.
Pair 1,000.
Pair with vert. gutter between —
Pair with horiz. gutter between —
Cross gutter block of four —
k. Perforated, all litho. colors but without black engr. —
Pair with vert. gutter between —
Pair with horiz. gutter between —
Cross gutter block of four —
l. Perforated, finished design as issued
Pair with vert. gutter between —
Pair with horiz. gutter between —
Cross gutter block of four —

2605P, with plate numbers

2605P 23c Flag Presorted First Class Coil, vert. pair, uncut between 250.
Vert. pair, uncut between, with P#A111 —

1992

2624P 1c, 4c and $1 Columbian souvenir sheet 750.
Pair of sheets —
a. As No. 2624P, but with background of No. 2627P (essay) —

2625P 2c, 3c and $4 Columbian souvenir sheet 750.
Pair of sheets —

2626P 5c, 30c and 50c Columbian souvenir sheet 750.
Pair of sheets —

2627P 6c, 8c and $3 Columbian souvenir sheet 750.
Pair of sheets —

2628P 10c, 15c and $2 Columbian souvenir sheet 750.
Pair of sheets —

2629P $4 Columbian souvenir sheet 750.
Pair of sheets —

2646aPi finished design as issued

2646aPe brown color only

Illustrations reduced.

2646aP 29c Hummingbirds booklet pane
b. Pane of five, yellow color only 450.
Two panes of five with vert. gutter between —
Two panes of five with horiz. gutter between —
Cross gutter block of four panes of five —
c. Pane of five, magenta color only 450.
Two panes of five with vert. gutter between —
Two panes of five with horiz. gutter between —
Cross gutter block of four panes of five —
d. Pane of five, blue color only 450.
Two panes of five with vert. gutter between —
Two panes of five with horiz. gutter between —
Cross gutter block of four panes of five —
e. Pane of five, brown color (birds) only 450.
Two panes of five with vert. gutter between —
Two panes of five with horiz. gutter between —
Cross gutter block of four panes of five —
f. Pane of five, brown color ("USA/29") only 450.
Two panes of five with vert. gutter between —
Two panes of five with horiz. gutter between —
Cross gutter block of four panes of five —
g. Pane of five, green color (frames) only 450.
Two panes of five with vert. gutter between —
Two panes of five with horiz. gutter between —
Cross gutter block of four panes of five —
h. Pane of five, orange color (frames) only 450.

Two panes of five with vert. gutter between —
Two panes of five with horiz. gutter between —
Cross gutter block of four panes of five —
i. Pane of five, finished design as issued 450.
Two panes of five with vert. gutter between —
Two panes of five with horiz. gutter between —
Cross gutter block of four panes of five —

2718aPd

2718aPe

Illustrations reduced.

2718aP 29c Christmas Toys booklet pane 600.
Horiz. pair of panes of four 1,500.
Vert. pair of panes of four 1,500.
b. As No. 2718aP, pane of four with two stamps at top from bottom row of normal pane and two stamps at bottom from top row of normal pane 1,000.
c. As No. 2718aP, perforated, pair of panes, uncut horiz. 2,000.
d. Pane of four with two stamps at top from bottom row of normal pane and two stamps at bottom from top row of normal pane, perforated 1,200.
e. Pane of four without red "Greetings" or green denominations 1,200.
f. As No. 2718aPe, two stamps at top from bottom row of "normal" pane and two stamps at bottom from top row of "normal" pane 1,500.
g. Pane of four without green denominations 1,200.
h. As No. 2718aPg, two stamps at top from bottom row of "normal" pane and two stamps at bottom from top row of "normal" pane 1,500.

1993

2737aP 29c American Music booklet pane of eight —
Pair of panes of eight —
c. As No. 2737aP, perforated horiz., uncut vert., pair of panes of eight —
2737bP 29c American Music booklet pane of four 2,000.
d. As No. 2737bP, perforated horiz., uncut vert., pair of panes of four —
e. Pair of panes, one No. 2737aP + one 2737bP —
f. Pair of panes, one No. 2737aPc + one 2737bPd —

2754Pa

2754Pb

Illustration of No. 2754Pa reduced.

2754P 29c Cherokee Strip Land Run, pair 350.
Pair with vert. gutter between 400.
Pair with horiz. gutter between 400.
Cross gutter block of four 1,500.
a. Perforated
Pair with vert. gutter between 250.
Pair with horiz. gutter between 250.
Cross gutter block of four 750.
b. As No. 2754P, without purple inscriptions and black denominations, pair —
Pair with vert. gutter between —
Pair with horiz. gutter between —
Cross gutter block of four —
c. Die proof, signed 11/25/92 for color and/or engraving —
2770aP 29c American Musicals booklet pane of four 1,250.
Pair of panes —
a. Perforated horiz., uncut vert., pair of panes of four —
b. Pane of four, blue color only, with designs slightly different from issued designs (essay) —
c. Pane of four, blue and magenta colors only, with designs slightly different from issued designs (essay) —
d. Pane of four, blue, magenta and yellow colors only, with designs slightly different from issued designs (essay) —

2778aP 29c American Music booklet pane of four
a. Pane of four, yellow color only 300.
On approval card (unique) —
b. Pane of four, pink color only 300.
On approval card (unique) —
c. Pane of four, red color only 300.
On approval card (unique) —
d. Pane of four, blue color only 300.
On approval card (unique) —
e. Pane of four, black color (frames and wording) only 300.
On approval card (unique) —
f. Pane of four, black color (Musicians) only 300.
On approval card (unique) —
g. Pane of four, finished design as issued 1,500.
On approval card (unique) —
h. Pane of four, finished design as issued, on cromalin paper, taped to approval card (unique) —
i. Booklet cover, finished design as issued, on card stock, pair of covers —
j. Booklet cover, finished design as issued, on cromalin paper, taped to approval card (unique) —
k. Perforated horiz., uncut vert., pair of panes of four 1,500.

Some of the sets of progressive proofs are in panes that are 2½ to 3½ stamps tall. These sell for somewhat less than the full panes.

About 20 percent of the examples of No. 2778aPk are split into two pieces. From these pieces come horizontal pairs or blocks of booklet stamps imperf vertically.

2788aP

2788aP 29c Classic Books, block of four 400.
Pair of blocks with vert. gutter between —
Pair of blocks with horiz. gutter between —
Cross gutter block of four blocks —

AIR POST

1918

C1P1 6c **org**, large die on India paper 8,500.
C2P1 16c **grn**, large die on India paper 7,000.
C3P1 24c **car rose & bl**, large die on India paper 8,500.

1923

C4P1 8c **dk grn**, large die on India paper 4,750.
C4P2 8c **dk grn**, small die on white wove paper 5,000.
C5TC1a 16c large die on India paper
e. **dark green** 5,000.
C5P1 16c **dk bl**, large die on India paper 4,750.
C5P2 16c **dk bl**, small die on white wove paper 5,000.
C6P1 24c **car**, large die on India paper 4,750.
C6P2 24c **car**, small die on white wove paper 5,000.

1926-27

C7P1 10c **dk bl**, large die on India paper 3,000.
C8TC1a 15c large die on India paper
e. **orange** 4,750.
C8P1 15c **ol brn**, large die on India paper 3,000.
C9P1 20c **yel grn**, large die on India paper 3,000.

Lindbergh Issue

1927

C10P1 10c **dk bl**, large die on India paper 6,000.
C10P2 10c **dk bl**, small die on white wove paper 7,000.

1928

C11P1 5c **car & bl**, large die on India paper 11,000.

1930

C12P1 5c **vio**, large die on India paper 3,000.

Zeppelin Issue

1930

C13P1 65c **grn**, large die on India paper 17,500.
a. On wove paper 15,000.
C13P2 65c **grn**, small die on white wove paper 25,000.
b. On stamp paper, imperf corner margin plate single —
C14P1 $1.30 **brn**, large die on India paper 17,500.
a. On wove paper 15,000.
C14P2 $1.30 **brn**, small die on white wove paper 25,000.
b. On stamp paper, imperf corner margin plate single —
C15P1 $2.60 **bl**, large die on India paper 17,500.
a. On wove paper 15,000.
C15P2 $2.60 **bl**, small die on white wove paper 25,000.
b. On stamp paper, imperf corner margin plate single —

1932

C17P1 8c **ol bis**, large die on India paper 4,000.

Century of Progress Issue

1933

C18P1 50c **grn**, large die on India paper 17,500.
C18P2 50c **grn**, small die on white wove paper 45,000.

1935-39

C20P2 25c **bl**, small die on white wove paper 3,250.
C21P2 20c **grn**, small die on white wove paper 3,250.
C22P2 50c **car**, small die on white wove paper 3,250.
C23P2 6c **dk bl & car**, small die on white wove paper 7,000.
C24P1 30c **dull bl**, large die on India paper 3,500.
C24P2 30c **dull bl**, small die on white wove paper 2,750.

1941-89
C25P2 6c **car,** small die on white wove paper *3,000.*
C26P2 8c **ol grn,** small die on white wove paper *3,000.*
C27P1 10c **vio,** large die on white wove paper *5,000.*
C27P2 10c **vio,** small die on white wove paper *3,000.*
C28P2 15c **brn car,** small die on white wove paper *3,000.*
C29P2 20c **brt grn,** small die on white wove paper *3,000.*
C30P2 30c **bl,** small die on white wove paper *3,000.*
C31P2 50c **org,** small die on white wove paper *3,000.*
C32TC1a 5c large die on India paper
e. **blue** 4,750.
C33P1 5c **car,** large die on white wove paper *5,500.*
C35TC1a 15c large die on India paper
e. **brown violet** 4,750.
C40P1 6c **car,** large die on white wove paper *5,000.*
C44P1 25c **rose car,** large die on white wove paper *5,000.*
C44P2 25c **rose car,** small die on white wove paper *3,500.*
C45P1 6c **mag,** large die on white wove paper *6,000.*
C45P2 6c **mag,** small die on white wove paper *5,000.*
C46P1 80c **brt red vio,** large die on white wove paper *5,000.*
C46P2 80c **brt red vio,** small die on white wove paper —
C47P1 6c **car,** large die on white wove paper *6,000.*
C48P1 4c **brt bl,** large die on white wove paper —

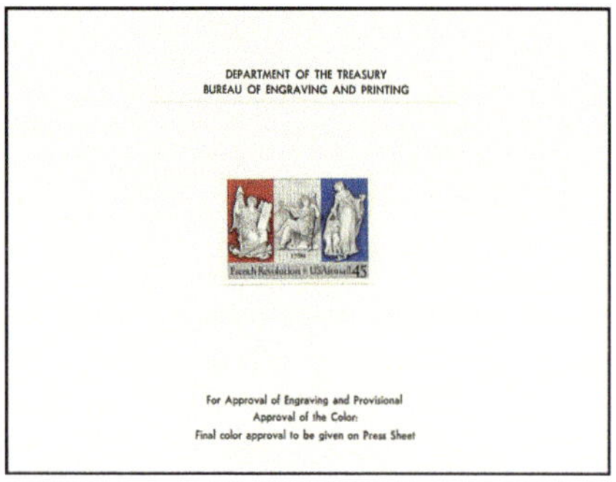

C120P1

C120P1 45c large hybrid die proof, pressed on large card imprinted for approval of engraving and color 1,250.

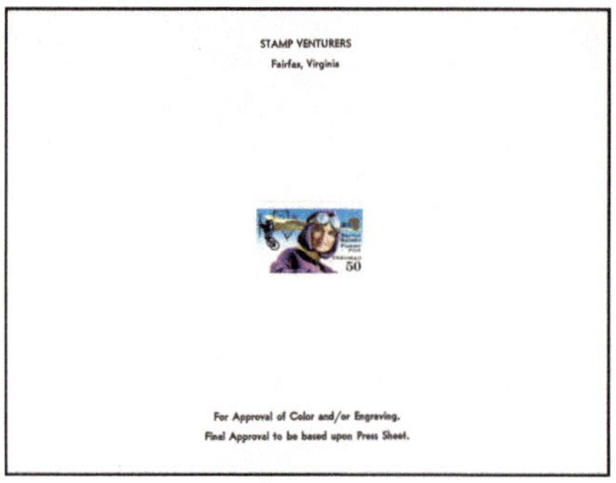

C128P1

C128P1 50c large hybrid die proof, pressed on large card imprinted for approval of engraving and color 1,250.

AIR POST SPECIAL DELIVERY

1934-36
CE1TC1a 16c large die on India paper
e. **black** 4,000.
CE1P2 16c **dk bl,** small die on white wove paper *4,000.*
CE2P2 16c **red & bl,** small die on white wove paper *4,000.*

SPECIAL DELIVERY

1885
E1TC1a 10c large die on India paper
e. **black** 3,000.
f. **dark brown** 3,000.
E1TC2 10c small die on wove paper
b. **orange yellow** *2,000.*
E1P1 10c **bl,** large die on India paper 600.
E1P2 10c **bl,** RA sm die on white wove paper 300.
E1P2a 10c **bl,** PP sm die on yelsh wove paper 2,500.
E1P3 10c **bl,** plate on India 35.
Block of 4 175.
E1P4 10c **bl,** plate on card 25.
Block of 4 125.
P# blk. of 8, Impt. *1,400.*

1888
E2TC1a 10c large die on India paper
e. **black** 3,000.
f. **green** 3,000.
E2TC2 10c small die on India paper
b. **olive yellow** 2,000.
E2P1 10c **bl,** large die on India paper 750.
E2P2 10c **bl,** RA sm die on white wove paper 300.
E2P2a 10c **bl,** PP sm die on yelsh wove paper 2,600.
E2P3 10c **bl,** plate on India 35.
Block of 4 200.
P# blk. of 8 525.
E2P4 10c **bl,** plate on card 25.
Block of 4 125.
P# blk. of 8 —

1893
E3P1 10c **org,** large die on India paper 2,500.
E3P2 10c **org,** RA sm die on white wove paper 300.
E3P2a 10c **org,** PP sm die on yelsh wove paper 4,000.
E3P3 10c **org,** plate on India 75.
Block of 4 325.
E3P4 10c **org,** plate on card 60.
Block of 4 275.
P# blk. of 8, Impt. 1,150.

1894-95
E4P1 10c **bl,** large die on India paper 550.
E4P2 10c **bl,** RA sm die on white wove paper 300.
E4P2a 10c **bl,** PP sm die on yelsh wove paper 3,000.
E4P5 10c **bl,** plate on stamp paper, pair *6,500.*
E5P5 10c **bl,** plate on stamp paper, pair *3,500.*
Block of 4 —
P# blk. of 6, Impt. *27,500.*

1902
E6TC1a 10c large die on India paper
e. **orange** 3,750.
f. **black** 3,750.
g. **rose red** *3,750.*
E6P1 10c **ultra,** large die on wove paper *3,500.*
E6P2 10c **ultra,** RA sm die on white wove paper 300.
E6P2a 10c **ultra,** PP sm die on yelsh wove paper 2,500.

1908
E7TC2 10c small die on India paper
b. **blue** *3,500.*
c. **green** *3,500.*
E7P1 10c **grn,** large die on India paper 2,750.
E7P2 10c **grn,** sm die on white wove paper 2,000.
E7P2a 10c **grn,** PP sm die on yelsh wove paper 3,000.

1922
E12TC1a 10c large die on India paper
e. **black** 3,250.
E12P1 10c **dp ultra,** large die on India paper 2,000.
E12P1a 10c **dp ultra,** large die on white wove paper 2,250.

1925-54
E13P1 15c **dp org,** large die on India paper 2,000.
E13P2 15c **dp org,** small die on white wove paper *3,000.*
E14P1 20c **blk,** large die on India paper 2,000.
E14P2 20c **black,** small die on white wove paper 1,500.
E14TC1a 20c large die on India paper
e. **purple** 4,000.
E17P2 13c **bl,** small die on white or yelsh wove paper *3,000.*
E20P1 20c **dp bl,** large die on India paper 3,000.

REGISTRATION

1911
F1TC1d 10c Large die on glazed card
e. **black** 1,500.
F1P1 10c **ultra,** large die on India paper 10,000.
F1P2 10c **ultra,** sm die on white wove paper 2,000.
F1P2a 10c **ultra,** PP sm die on yelsh wove paper 3,000.

POSTAGE DUE

1879
J1TC1a 1c large die on India paper
e. **black** 500.
f. **gray black** 500.
g. **ultramarine** 500.
h. **blue** 500.
i. **blue green** 500.
j. **orange** 500.
k. **red orange** 500.
l. **olive bister** 500.
J1TC2 1c small die on India paper
b. **orange** 100.
J1TC4 1c plate on card
a. **black** 50.
J1P1 1c **brn,** large die on India paper 250.
J1P2 1c **brn,** RA sm die on white wove paper 100.
J1P2a 1c **brn,** PP sm die on yelsh wove paper 750.
J1P3 1c **brn,** plate on India 22.
Block of 4 105.
P# blk. of 12 450.
J1P4 1c **brn,** plate on card 15.
Block of 4 90.
J2TC1a 2c large die on India paper
e. **black** 500.
f. **gray black** 500.
g. **ultramarine** 500.
h. **blue** 500.
i. **blue green** 500.
j. **orange** 500.
k. **red orange** 500.
l. **sepia** 500.
J2TC2 2c small die on India paper
b. **orange** 100.
J2P1 2c **brn,** large die on India paper 250.
a. **dk brn,** large die on India paper —
J2P2 2c **brn,** RA sm die on white wove paper 100.
J2P2a 2c **brn,** PP sm die on yelsh wove paper 750.
J2P3 2c **brn,** plate on India 20.
Block of 4 90.
P# blk. of 12 425.
J2P4 2c **brn,** plate on card 15.
Block of 4 90.
J3TC1a 3c large die on India paper
e. **black** 500.
f. **ultramarine** 500.
g. **blue** 500.
h. **blue green** 500.
i. **orange** 500.
j. **red orange** 500.
k. **light brown** 500.
l. **olive yellow** —
J3TC2 3c small die on India paper
b. **gray black** 100.
c. **orange** 500.
J3P1 3c **brn,** large die on India paper 250.
a. **dk brn,** large die on India paper —
J3P2 3c **brn,** RA sm die on white wove paper 100.
b. **dk brn,** RA sm die on India paper —
J3P2a 3c **brn,** PP sm die on yelsh wove paper 750.
J3P3 3c **brn,** plate on India 20.
Block of 4 90.
P# blk. of 12 425.
J3P4 3c **brn,** plate on card 15.
Block of 4 90.
J4TC1a 5c large die on India paper
e. **black** 500.
f. **gray black** 500.
g. **ultramarine** 500.
h. **blue** 500.
i. **blue green** 500.
j. **orange** 500.
k. **red orange** 500.
J4TC2 5c small die on India paper
b. **orange** 500.
J4P1 5c **brn,** large die on India paper 250.
a. **dk brn,** large die on India paper —
J4P2 5c **brn,** RA sm die on white wove paper 100.
J4P2a 5c **brn,** PP sm die on yelsh wove paper 750.
J4P3 5c **brn,** plate on India 20.
Block of 4 90.
P# blk. of 12 425.
J4P4 5c **brn,** plate on card 15.
Block of 4 90.
J5TC1a 10c large die on India paper
e. **black** 500.
f. **gray black** 500.
g. **blue** 500.
h. **olive yellow** 500.
i. **blue green** 500.
j. **orange** 500.
k. **red orange** 500.
l. **olive bister** 500.
m. **sepia** 500.
n. **gray** 500.
J5TC2 10c small die on India paper
b. **orange** 100.
J5P1 10c **brn,** large die on India paper 250.
a. **dk brn,** large die on India paper —
J5P2 10c **brn,** RA sm die on white wove paper 100.
J5P2a 10c **brn,** PP sm die on yelsh wove paper 750.
J5P3 10c **dk brn,** plate on India 32.
Block of 4 145.
P# blk. of 12 675.
J5P4 10c **brn,** plate on card 15.
Block of 4 90.
J6TC1a 30c large die on India paper
e. **black** 500.
f. **gray black** 500.
g. **blue** 500.
h. **blue green** 500.
i. **orange** 500.
j. **red orange** 500.
k. **olive bister** 500.
J6TC2 30c small die on India paper
b. **olive yellow** 100.
c. **orange** 100.
d. **sepia** 100.
J6P1 30c **brn,** large die on India paper 250.
a. **dk brn,** large die on India paper —
J6P2 30c **brn,** RA sm die on white wove paper 100.
J6P2a 30c **brn,** PP sm die on yelsh wove paper 750.
J6P3 30c **dk brn,** plate on India 32.
Block of 4 145.
P# blk. of 12 675.
J6P4 30c **brn,** plate on card 15.
Block of 4 90.
J7TC1a 50c large die on India paper
e. **black** 500.
f. **gray black** 500.
g. **blue** 500.
i. **blue green** 500.
j. **orange** 500.
k. **red orange** 500.
l. **olive bister** 500.
m. **sepia** 500.
n. **gray** 500.
J7TC2 50c small die on India paper
b. **blue** 100.
c. **olive yellow** 100.
d. **orange** 100.
J7P1 50c **brn,** large die on India paper 250.
a. **dk brn,** large die on India paper —
J7P2 50c **brn,** RA sm die on white wove paper 100.
J7P2a 50c **brn,** PP sm die on yelsh wove paper 750.
J7P3 50c **dk brn,** plate on India 32.
Block of 4 145.
P# blk. of 12 675.
J7P4 50c **brn,** plate on card 15.
Block of 4 90.
J1P1-J7P1 1c-50c **brown,** hybrid large die proofs on India paper, cut close and pressed on die sunk card in a "H" pattern *1,350.*
Nos. J1P3-J7P3 (7) 178.00
Nos. J1P4-J7P4 (7) 105.00

1887

J15P2a 1c **red brn,** PP sm die on yelsh wove paper 1,000.
J15P4 1c **red brn,** plate on card 15.
J16P2a 2c **red brn,** PP sm die on yelsh wove paper 1,000.
J16P4 2c **red brn,** plate on card 15.
J17P2a 3c **red brn,** PP sm die on yelsh wove paper 1,000.
J17P4 3c **red brn,** plate on card 20.
J18P2a 5c **red brn,** PP sm die on yelsh wove paper 1,000.
J18P4 5c **red brn,** plate on card 15.
J19P2a 10c **red brn,** PP sm die on yelsh wove paper 1,000.
J19P3 10c **red brn,** plate on India 19.
Block of 4 90.
P# blk. of 12 360.
J19P4 10c **red brn,** plate on card 25.
J20P2a 30c **red brn,** PP sm die on yelsh wove paper 1,000.
J20P3 30c **red brn,** plate on India 19.
Block of 4 90.
P# blk. of 12 360.
J20P4 30c **red brn,** plate on card 20.
J21P2a 50c **red brn,** PP sm die on yelsh wove paper 1,000.
J21P3 50c **red brn,** plate on India 45.
Block of 4 210.
P# blk. of 12 900.
J21P4 50c **red brn,** plate on card 25.
Nos. J15P4-J21P4 (7) 135.00

1891-93

J22P1 1c **brt cl,** large die on India paper 140.
J22P2 1c **brt cl,** RA sm die on white wove paper 100.
J22P2a 1c **brt cl,** PP sm die on yelsh wove paper 500.
J22P3 1c **brt cl,** plate on India 12.
Block of 4 65.
J22P4 1c **brt cl,** plate on card 17.
Block of 4 80.
P# blk. of 12 —
J22P5 1c **br cl,** plate on stamp paper, pair *425.*
J23P1 2c **brt cl,** large die on India paper 140.
J23P2 2c **brt cl,** RA sm die on white wove paper 100.
J23P2a 2c **brt cl,** PP sm die on yelsh wove paper 500.
J23P3 2c **brt cl,** plate on India 12.
Block of 4 65.
J23P4 2c **brt cl,** plate on card 17.
Block of 4 80.
P# blk. of 12 —
J23P5 2c **br cl,** plate on stamp paper, pair *425.*
J24P1 3c **brt cl,** large die on India paper 140.
J24P2 3c **brt cl,** RA sm die on white wove paper 100.
J24P2a 3c **brt cl,** PP sm die on yelsh wove paper 500.
J24P3 3c **brt cl,** plate on India 12.
Block of 4 65.
J24P4 3c **brt cl,** plate on card 17.
Block of 4 80.
P# blk. of 12 —
J24P5 3c **br cl,** plate on stamp paper, pair *425.*
J25P1 5c **brt cl,** large die on India paper 140.
J25P2 5c **brt cl,** RA sm die on white wove paper 100.
J25P2a 5c **brt cl,** PP sm die on yelsh wove paper 500.
J25P3 5c **brt cl,** plate on India 12.
Block of 4 65.
J25P4 5c **brt cl,** plate on card 17.
Block of 4 80.
P# blk. of 12 —
J25P5 5c **br cl,** plate on stamp paper, pair *425.*
J26P1 10c **brt cl,** large die on India paper 140.
J26P2 10c **brt cl,** RA sm die on white wove paper 100.
J26P2a 10c **brt cl,** PP sm die on yelsh wove paper 500.
J26P3 10c **brt cl,** plate on India 12.
Block of 4 65.
J26P4 10c **brt cl,** plate on card 17.
Block of 4 80.
P# blk. of 12 —
J26P5 10c **br cl,** plate on stamp paper, pair *425.*
J27P1 30c **brt cl,** large die on India paper 140.
J27P2 30c **brt cl,** RA sm die on white wove paper 100.
J27P2a 30c **brt cl,** PP sm die on yelsh wove paper 500.
J27P3 30c **brt cl,** plate on India 28.
Block of 4 140.
J27P4 30c **brt cl,** plate on card 17.
Block of 4 80.
P# blk. of 12 —
J27P5 30c **br cl,** plate on stamp paper, pair *500.*
J28P1 50c **brt cl,** large die on India paper 140.
J28P2 50c **brt cl,** RA sm die on white wove paper 100.
J28P2a 50c **brt cl,** PP sm die on yelsh wove paper 500.
J28P3 50c **brt cl,** plate on India 19.
Block of 4 90.
J28P4 50c **brt cl,** plate on card 17.
Block of 4 80.
P# blk. of 12 —
J28P5 50c **br cl,** plate on stamp paper, pair *500.*
Nos. J22P3-J28P3 (7) 107.00
Nos. J22P4-J28P4 (7) 119.00

Values for Nos. J22P5-J28P5 are for pairs with original gum and minor faults.

1894

J31P1 1c **cl,** large die on India paper 165.
J31P2 1c **cl,** RA sm die on white wove paper 120.
J31P2a 1c **cl,** PP sm die on yelsh wove paper 500.
J31P5 1c **cl,** plate on stamp paper, pair *225.*
Block of 4 *500.*
J32P1 2c **brt cl,** large die on India paper 165.
J32P2 2c **brt cl,** RA sm die on white wove paper 120.
J32P2a 2c **brt cl,** PP sm die on yelsh wove paper 500.
J32P4 2c **brt cl,** plate on card 200.
Block of 4 900.
P# blk. of 6 3,500.
J33P1 3c **brt cl,** large die on India paper 165.
J33P2 3c **brt cl,** RA sm die on white wove paper 120.
J33P2a 3c **brt cl,** PP sm die on yelsh wove paper 500.
J34P1 5c **brt cl,** large die on India paper 165.
J34P2 5c **brt cl,** RA sm die on white wove paper 120.
J34P2a 5c **brt cl,** PP sm die on yelsh wove paper 500.
J35P1 10c **brt cl,** large die on India paper 165.
J35P2 10c **brt cl,** RA sm die on white wove paper 120.
J35P2a 10c **brt cl,** PP sm die on yelsh wove paper 500.
J36P1 30c **brt cl,** large die on India paper 165.
J36P2 30c **brt cl,** RA sm die on white wove paper 120.
J36P2a 30c **brt cl,** PP sm die on yelsh wove paper 500.
J37P1 50c **brt cl,** large die on India paper 165.
J37P2 50c **brt cl,** RA sm die on white wove paper 120.
J37P2a 50c **brt cl,** PP sm die on yelsh wove paper 500.

1925

J68P1 ½c **dull red,** large die on India paper *5,750.*

1930-31

J69P1 ½c **dp cl,** large die on India paper 450.
J70P1 1c **dp cl,** large die on India paper 450.
J71P1 2c **dp cl,** large die on India paper 450.
J72P1 3c **dp cl,** large die on India paper 450.
J73P1 5c **dp cl,** large die on India paper 450.
J74P1 10c **dp cl,** large die on India paper 450.
J75P1 30c **dp cl,** large die on India paper 450.
J76P1 50c **dp cl,** large die on India paper 450.
J77P1 $1 **dp cl,** large die on India paper 1,750.
J78P1 $5 **dp cl,** large die on India paper 1,750.

PARCEL POST POSTAGE DUE

1912

JQ1P1 1c **dk grn,** large die on India paper 600.
JQ1P2 1c **dk grn,** sm die on white wove paper 500.
JQ1P2a 1c **dk grn,** PP sm die on yelsh wove paper 750.
JQ2P1 2c **dk grn,** large die on India paper 600.
JQ2P2 2c **dk grn,** sm die on white wove paper 500.
JQ2P2a 2c **dk grn,** PP sm die on yelsh wove paper 750.
JQ3P1 5c **dk grn,** large die on India paper 600.
JQ3P2 5c **dk grn,** sm die on white wove paper 500.
JQ3P2a 5c **dk grn,** PP sm die on yelsh wove paper 700.
JQ4P1 10c **dk grn,** large die on India paper 600.
JQ4P2 10c **dk grn,** sm die on white wove paper 500.
JQ4P2a 10c **dk grn,** PP sm die on yelsh wove paper 700.
JQ5P1 25c **dk grn,** large die on India paper 600.
JQ5P2 25c **dk grn,** sm die on white wove paper 500.
JQ5P2a 25c **dk grn,** PP sm die on yelsh wove paper 700.

Specialists have questioned the existence of genuine examples of Nos. JQ1P2, JQ2P2, JQ3P2, JQ4P2 and JQ5P2. The editors would like to see recent authenticated evidence of their existence.

CARRIERS

1851

LO1TC3 1c plate on India paper
a. **deep green** 250.
Block of 4 1,250.
LO1TC5 1c Plate on wove paper
a. **orange** 350.
LO1P1 1c **bl,** *(Franklin)* large die on India paper 600.
LO1P2 1c **bl,** *(Franklin)* RA sm die on white wove paper 300.
LO1P2a 1c **bl,** *(Franklin)* PP sm die on yelsh wove paper 1,500.
LO1P3 1c **bl,** *(Franklin)* plate on India 50.
Block of 4 210.
Cracked plate —
LO1P4 1c **bl,** *(Franklin)* plate on card 30.
Block of 4 125.
Cracked plate —
LO2TC3 plate on India paper
a. **deep green** 250.
Block of 4 1,250.
LO2TC5 plate on wove paper
a. **orange** 350.
LO2P1 1c **bl,** *(Eagle)* large die on India paper 600.
LO2P2 1c **bl,** *(Eagle)* RA sm die on white wove paper 300.
LO2P2a 1c **bl,** *(Eagle)* PP sm die on yelsh wove paper 1,500.
LO2P3 1c **bl,** *(Eagle)* plate on India 50.
Block of 4 210.
Pl # block of 8 675.
LO2P4 1c **bl,** *(Eagle)* plate on card 30.
Block of 4 125.

Nos. LO1P1 and LO2P1 exist only as hybrids.

LOCALS

1844

5L1P1 5c **blk,** large die on India paper *3,500.*

1855

15L18TC3 (1c) plate on India paper
a. **brown** —
b. **blue** —
c. **green** —
d. **reddish brown** —

OFFICIAL

AGRICULTURE

1873

O1TC1a 1c large die on India paper
e. **black** 500.
O1TC3 1c plate on India paper
a. **black** 75.
O1P1 1c **yel,** large die on India paper 80.
O1P2 1c **yel,** RA sm die on white wove paper 100.
O1P2a 1c **yel,** PP sm die on yelsh wove paper 700.
O1P3 1c **yel,** plate on India 20.
Block of 4 100.
O1P4 1c **yel,** plate on card 10.
Block of 4 50.
P# blk. of 12 225.
O2TC1a 2c large die on India paper
e. **black** 500.
O2TC3 2c plate on India paper
a. **black** 75.
O2P1 2c **yel,** large die on India paper 80.
O2P2 2c **yel,** RA sm die on white wove paper 100.
O2P2a 2c **yel,** PP sm die on yelsh wove paper 700.
O2P3 2c **yel,** plate on India 20.
Block of 4 100.
O2P4 2c **yel,** plate on card 10.
Block of 4 50.
P# blk. of 12 225.
O3TC1a 3c large die on India paper
e. **black** 500.
f. **deep green** 500.
g. **ultra** 500.
O3P1 3c **yel,** large die on India paper 80.
O3P2 3c **yel,** RA sm die on white wove paper 100.
O3P2a 3c **yel,** PP sm die on yelsh wove paper 700.
O3P3 3c **yel,** plate on India 20.
Block of 4 100.
O3P4 3c **yel,** plate on card 10.
Block of 4 50.
P# blk. of 12 225.
O4TC1a 6c large die on India paper
e. **black** 500.
O4TC3 6c plate on India paper
a. **black** 150.
O4P1 6c **yel,** large die on India paper 125.
O4P2 6c **yel,** RA sm die on white wove paper 100.
O4P2a 6c **yel,** PP sm die on yelsh wove paper 700.
O4P3 6c **yel,** plate on India 20.
Block of 4 100.
O4P4 6c **yel,** plate on card 10.
Block of 4 50.
P# blk. of 12 225.
O5TC1a 10c large die on India paper
e. **black** 500.
O5P1 10c **yel,** large die on India paper 80.
O5P2 10c **yel,** RA sm die on white wove paper 100.
O5P2a 10c **yel,** PP sm die on yelsh wove paper 700.
O5P3 10c **yel,** plate on India 20.
Block of 4 100.
O5P4 10c **yel,** plate on card 10.
Block of 4 50.
P# blk. of 12 225.
O6TC1a 12c large die on India paper
e. **black** 500.
O6TC3 12c plate on India paper
a. **black** 75.
O6P1 12c **yel,** large die on India paper 80.
O6P2 12c **yel,** RA sm die on white wove paper 100.
O6P2a 12c **yel,** PP sm die on yelsh wove paper 700.
O6P3 12c **yel,** plate on India 20.
Block of 4 100.
O6P4 12c **yel,** plate on card 10.
Block of 4 50.
P# blk. of 12 225.
O7P1 15c **yel,** large die on India paper 80.
O7P2 15c **yel,** RA sm die on white wove paper 100.
O7P2a 15c **yel,** PP sm die on yelsh wove paper 700.
O7P3 15c **yel,** plate on India 20.
Block of 4 100.
O7P4 15c **yel,** plate on card 10.
Block of 4 50.
P# blk. of 12 225.
O8P1 24c **yel,** large die on India paper 80.
O8P2 24c **yel,** RA sm die on white wove paper 100.
O8P2a 24c **yel,** PP sm die on yelsh wove paper 700.
O8P3 24c **yel,** plate on India 20.
Block of 4 100.
O8P4 24c **yel,** plate on card 10.
Block of 4 50.
P# blk. of 12 225.
O9TC1a 20c large die on India paper
e. **black** 500.
O9P1 30c **yel,** large die on India paper 80.
O9P2 30c **yel,** RA sm die on white wove paper 100.
O9P2a 30c **yel,** PP sm die on yelsh wove paper 700.
O9P3 30c **yel,** plate on India 20.
Block of 4 100.
O9P4 30c **yel,** plate on card 10.
Block of 4 50.
P# blk. of 12 225.
Nos. O1P3-O9P3 (9) 180.00
Nos. O1P4-O9P4 (9) 90.00

EXECUTIVE

O10P1 1c **car,** large die on India paper 100.
O10P2 1c **car,** RA sm die on white wove paper 100.
O10P2a 1c **car,** PP sm die on yelsh wove paper 700.
O10P3 1c **car,** plate on India 20.
Block of 4 100.
O10P4 1c **car,** plate on card 10.
Block of 4 50.
P# blk. of 12 225.
O11TC1a 2c large die on India paper
e. **black** 500.
f. **deep brown** 500.

No.	Description	Price
O11TC3	2c plate on India paper	
a.	**black**	75.
b.	**brown carmine**	75.
O11TC4	2c plate on card	
a.	**brown carmine**	75.
O11P1	2c **car,** large die on India paper	100.
O11P2	2c **car,** RA sm die on white wove paper	100.
O11P2a	2c **car,** PP sm die on yelsh wove paper	700.
O11P3	2c **car,** plate on India	20.
	Block of 4	100.
O11P4	2c **car,** plate on card	10.
	Block of 4	50.
	P# blk. of 12	225.
	Foreign entry of 6c Agriculture (pos. 40)	—
O12TC1a	3c large die on India paper	
e.	**black**	500.
f.	**deep green**	500.
O12TC3	3c plate on India paper	
a.	**black**	75.
O12P1	3c **car,** large die on India paper	100.
O12P2	3c **car,** RA sm die on white wove paper	100.
O12P2a	3c **car,** PP sm die on yelsh wove paper	700.
O12P3	3c **car,** plate on India	20.
	Block of 4	100.
O12P4	3c **car,** plate on card	10.
	Block of 4	50.
	P# blk. of 12	225.
O13TC3	6c plate on India paper	
a.	**black**	90.
O13P1	6c **car,** large die on India paper	100.
O13P2	6c **car,** RA sm die on white wove paper	100.
O13P2a	6c **car,** PP sm die on yelsh wove paper	700.
O13P3	6c **car,** plate on India	20.
	Block of 4	125.
O13P4	6c **car,** plate on card	10.
	Block of 4	85.
	P# blk. of 12	350.
O14TC3	10c plate on India paper	
a.	**black**	90.
O14P1	10c **car,** large die on India paper	100.
O14P2	10c **car,** RA sm die on white wove paper	100.
O14P2a	10c **car,** PP sm die on yelsh wove paper	700.
O14P3	10c **car,** plate on India	20.
	Block of 4	100.
O14P4	10c **car,** plate on card	10.
	Block of 4	50.
	P# blk. of 12	225.
	Nos. O10P3-O14P3 (5)	100.00
	Nos. O10P4-O14P4 (5)	50.00

INTERIOR

No.	Description	Price
O15P1	1c **ver,** large die on India paper	80.
O15P2	1c **ver,** RA sm die on white wove paper	100.
O15P2a	1c **ver,** PP sm die on yelsh wove paper	700.
O15P3	1c **ver,** plate on India	20.
	Block of 4	100.
O15P4	1c **ver,** plate on card	10.
	Block of 4	50.
	P# blk. of 12	225.
O16TC1a	2c large die on India paper	
e.	**black**	500.
f.	**deep brown**	500.
O16P1	2c **ver,** large die on India paper	80.
O16P2	2c **ver,** RA sm die on white wove paper	100.
O16P2a	2c **ver,** PP sm die on yelsh wove paper	700.
O16P3	2c **ver,** plate on India	20.
	Block of 4	100.
O16P4	2c **ver,** plate on card	10.
	Block of 4	50.
	P# blk. of 10	200.
O17TC1a	3c large die on India paper	
e.	**black**	500.
f.	**deep green**	500.
O17TC3	3c plate on India paper	
a.	**black**	90.
O17P1	3c **ver,** large die on India paper	80.
O17P2	3c **ver,** RA sm die on white wove paper	100.
O17P2a	3c **ver,** PP sm die on yelsh wove paper	700.
O17P3	3c **ver,** plate on India	20.
	Block of 4	100.
O17P4	3c **ver,** plate on card	10.
	Block of 4	50.
	P# blk. of 10	225.
O18P1	6c **ver,** large die on India paper	80.
O18P2	6c **ver,** RA sm die on white wove paper	100.
O18P2a	6c **ver,** PP sm die on yelsh wove paper	700.
O18P3	6c **ver,** plate on India	20.
	Block of 4	100.
O18P4	6c **ver,** plate on card	10.
	Block of 4	50.
	P# blk. of 12	250.
O19P1	10c **ver,** large die on India paper	80.
O19P2	10c **ver,** RA sm die on white wove paper	100.
O19P2a	10c **ver,** PP sm die on yelsh wove paper	700.
O19P3	10c **ver,** plate on India	20.
	Block of 4	100.
O19P4	10c **ver,** plate on card	10.
	Block of 4	50.
	P# blk. of 12	225.
O20P1	12c **ver,** large die on India paper	80.
O20P2	12c **ver,** RA sm die on white wove paper	100.
O20P2a	12c **ver,** PP sm die on yelsh wove paper	700.
O20P3	12c **ver,** plate on India	20.
	Block of 4	100.
O20P4	12c **ver,** plate on card	10.
	Block of 4	50.
	P# blk. of 12	225.
O21P1	15c **ver,** large die on India paper	80.
O21P2	15c **ver,** RA sm die on white wove paper	100.
O21P2a	15c **ver,** PP sm die on yelsh wove paper	700.
O21P3	15c **ver,** plate on India	20.
	Block of 4	100.
O21P4	15c **ver,** plate on card	10.
	Block of 4	50.
	P# blk. of 12	225.
O22P1	24c **ver,** large die on India paper	80.
O22P2	24c **ver,** RA sm die on white wove paper	100.
O22P2a	24c **ver,** PP sm die on yelsh wove paper	700.
O22P3	24c **ver,** plate on India	20.
	Block of 4	100.
O22P4	24c **ver,** plate on card	10.
	Block of 4	50.
	P# blk. of 12	225.
O23P1	30c **ver,** large die on India paper	80.
O23P2	30c **ver,** RA sm die on white wove paper	100.
O23P2a	30c **ver,** PP sm die on yelsh wove paper	700.
O23P3	30c **ver,** plate on India	20.
	Block of 4	100.
O23P4	30c **ver,** plate on card	10.
	Block of 4	50.
	P# blk. of 12	225.
O24P1	90c **ver,** large die on India paper	80.
O24P2	90c **ver,** RA sm die on white wove paper	100.
O24P2a	90c **ver,** PP sm die on yelsh wove paper	700.
O24P3	90c **ver,** plate on India	20.
	Block of 4	100.
O24P4	90c **ver,** plate on card	10.
	Block of 4	50.
	P# blk. of 12	225.
	Nos. O15P3-O24P3 (10)	200.00
	Nos. O15P4-O24P4 (10)	100.00

JUSTICE

No.	Description	Price
O25P1	1c **pur,** large die on India paper	80.
O25P2	1c **pur,** RA sm die on white wove paper	100.
O25P2a	1c **pur,** PP sm die on yelsh wove paper	700.
O25P3	1c **pur,** plate on India	20.
	Block of 4	100.
O25P4	1c **pur,** plate on card	10.
	Block of 4	50.
	P# blk. of 12	225.
O26P1	2c **pur,** large die on India paper	80.
O26P2	2c **pur,** RA sm die on white wove paper	100.
O26P2a	2c **pur,** PP sm die on yelsh wove paper	700.
O26P3	2c **pur,** plate on India	20.
	Block of 4	100.
O26P4	2c **pur,** plate on card	10.
	Block of 4	50.
	P# blk. of 12	225.
O27TC1a	3c large die on India paper	
e.	**black**	500.
f.	**deep green**	500.
O27TC3	3c plate on India paper	
a.	**black**	90.
b.	**bister yellow**	90.
c.	**dull orange**	90.
d.	**black violet**	90.
e.	**violet**	90.
f.	**pale violet**	90.
O27P1	3c **pur,** large die on India paper	80.
O27P2	3c **pur,** RA sm die on white wove paper	100.
O27P2a	3c **pur,** PP sm die on yelsh wove paper	700.
O27P3	3c **pur,** plate on India	20.
	Block of 4	100.
O27P4	3c **pur,** plate on card	10.
	Block of 4	50.
	P# blk. of 12	225.
	Plate Scratches	—
O28P1	6c **pur,** large die on India paper	80.
O28P2	6c **pur,** RA sm die on white wove paper	100.
O28P2a	6c **pur,** PP sm die on yelsh wove paper	700.
O28P3	6c **pur,** plate on India	20.
	Block of 4	100.
O28P4	6c **pur,** plate on card	10.
	Block of 4	50.
	P# blk. of 12	225.
O29P1	10c **pur,** large die on India paper	80.
O29P2	10c **pur,** RA sm die on white wove paper	100.
O29P2a	10c **pur,** PP sm die on yelsh wove paper	700.
O29P3	10c **pur,** plate on India	20.
	Block of 4	100.
O29P4	10c **pur,** plate on card	10.
	Block of 4	50.
	P# blk. of 10	225.
O30P1	12c **pur,** large die on India paper	80.
O30P2	12c **pur,** RA sm die on white wove paper	100.
O30P2a	12c **pur,** PP sm die on yelsh wove paper	700.
O30P3	12c **pur,** plate on India	20.
	Block of 4	100.
O30P4	12c **pur,** plate on card	10.
	Block of 4	50.
	P# blk. of 12	225.
O31P1	15c **pur,** large die on India paper	80.
O31P2	15c **pur,** RA sm die on white wove paper	100.
O31P2a	15c **pur,** PP sm die on yelsh wove paper	700.
O31P3	15c **pur,** plate on India	20.
	Block of 4	100.
O31P4	15c **pur,** plate on card	10.
	Block of 4	50.
	P# blk. of 10	225.
O32P1	24c **pur,** large die on India paper	80.
O32P2	24c **pur,** RA sm die on white wove paper	100.
O32P2a	24c **pur,** PP sm die on yelsh wove paper	700.
O32P3	24c **pur,** plate on India	20.
	Block of 4	100.
O32P4	24c **pur,** plate on card	10.
	Block of 4	50.
	P# blk. of 12	225.
	Short transfer (pos. 98)	—
O33P1	30c **pur,** large die on India paper	80.
O33P2	30c **pur,** RA sm die on white wove paper	100.
O33P2a	30c **pur,** PP sm die on yelsh wove paper	700.
O33P3	30c **pur,** plate on India	20.
	Block of 4	100.
O33P4	30c **pur,** plate on card	10.
	Block of 4	50.
	P# blk. of 12	225.
O34P1	90c **pur,** large die on India paper	80.
O34P2	90c **pur,** RA sm die on white wove paper	100.
O34P2a	90c **pur,** PP sm die on yelsh wove paper	700.
O34P3	90c **pur,** plate on India	20.
	Block of 4	100.
O34P4	90c **pur,** plate on card	10.
	Block of 4	50.
	P# blk. of 12	225.
	Nos. O25P3-O34P3 (10)	200.00
	Nos. O25P4-O34P4 (10)	100.00

NAVY

No.	Description	Price
O35TC3	1c plate on India paper	
a.	**black**	90.
O35P1	1c **ultra,** large die on India paper	80.
O35P2	1c **ultra,** RA sm die on white wove paper	100.
O35P2a	1c **ultra,** PP sm die on yelsh wove paper	700.
O35P3	1c **ultra,** plate on India	20.
	Block of 4	100.
O35P4	1c **ultra,** plate on card	10.
	Block of 4	50.
	P# blk. of 12	225.
O36TC1a	2c large die on India paper	
e.	**black**	500.
f.	**deep brown**	500.
O36TC5	2c plate on wove paper, imperf.	
a.	**deep green**	250.
b.	**greenish black**	250.
O36TC6	2c plate on wove paper, perf.	
a.	**deep green** on pinkish wove	250.
b.	**black**	250.
O36P1	2c **ultra,** large die on India paper	80.
O36P2	2c **ultra,** RA sm die on white wove paper	100.
O36P2a	2c **ultra,** PP sm die on yelsh wove paper	700.
O36P3	2c **ultra,** plate on India	20.
	Block of 4	100.
O36P4	2c **ultra,** plate on card	10.
	Block of 4	50.
	P# blk. of 12	225.
O37TC1a	3c large die on India paper	
e.	**black**	500.
f.	**deep green**	500.
O37TC3	3c plate on India paper	
a.	**black**	90.
O37P1	3c **ultra,** large die on India paper	80.
O37P2	3c **ultra,** RA sm die on white wove paper	100.
O37P2a	3c **ultra,** PP sm die on yelsh wove paper	700.
O37P3	3c **ultra,** plate on India	20.
	Block of 4	100.
O37P4	3c **ultra,** plate on card	10.
	Block of 4	50.
	P# blk. of 10	225.
O38P1	6c **ultra,** large die on India paper	80.
O38P2	6c **ultra,** RA sm die on white wove paper	100.
O38P2a	6c **ultra,** PP sm die on yelsh wove paper	700.
O38P3	6c **ultra,** plate on India	20.
	Block of 4	100.
O38P4	6c **ultra,** plate on card	15.
	Block of 4	75.
	P# blk. of 10	350.
O39P1	7c **ultra,** large die on India paper	80.
O39P2	7c **ultra,** RA sm die on white wove paper	100.
O39P2a	7c **ultra,** PP sm die on yelsh wove paper	700.
O39P3	7c **ultra,** plate on India	20.
	Block of 4	100.
O39P4	7c **ultra,** plate on card	10.
	Block of 4	50.
	P# blk. of 10	225.

No.	Description	Value
O40P1	10c **ultra,** large die on India paper	80.
O40P2	10c **ultra,** RA sm die on white wove paper	100.
O40P2a	10c **ultra,** PP sm die on yelsh wove paper	700.
O40P3	10c **ultra,** plate on India	20.
	Block of 4	100.
	P# blk. of 12	—
O40P4	10c **ultra,** plate on card	10.
	Block of 4	50.
	P# blk. of 12	225.
O41P1	12c **ultra,** large die on India paper	80.
O41P2	12c **ultra,** RA sm die on white wove paper	100.
O41P2a	12c **ultra,** PP sm die on yelsh wove paper	700.
O41P3	12c **ultra,** plate on India	20.
	Block of 4	100.
O41P4	12c **ultra,** plate on card	10.
	Block of 4	50.
	P# blk. of 12	225.
O42P1	15c **ultra,** large die on India paper	80.
O42P2	15c **ultra,** RA sm die on white wove paper	100.
O42P2a	15c **ultra,** PP sm die on yelsh wove paper	700.
O42P3	15c **ultra,** plate on India	20.
	Block of 4	100.
O42P4	15c **ultra,** plate on card	10.
	Block of 4	50.
	P# blk. of 12	225.
O43P1	24c **ultra,** large die on India paper	80.
O43P2	24c **ultra,** RA sm die on white wove paper	100.
O43P2a	24c **ultra,** PP sm die on yelsh wove paper	700.
O43P3	24c **ultra,** plate on India	20.
	Block of 4	100.
O43P4	24c **ultra,** plate on card	10.
	Block of 4	50.
	P# blk. of 12	225.
O44P1	30c **ultra,** large die on India paper	80.
O44P2	30c **ultra,** RA sm die on white wove paper	100.
O44P2a	30c **ultra,** PP sm die on yelsh wove paper	700.
O44P3	30c **ultra,** plate on India	20.
	Block of 4	100.
O44P4	30c **ultra,** plate on card	10.
	Block of 4	50.
	P# blk. of 12	225.
O45P1	90c **ultra,** large die on India paper	80.
O45P2	90c **ultra,** RA sm die on white wove paper	100.
O45P2a	90c **ultra,** PP sm die on yelsh wove paper	700.
O45P3	90c **ultra,** plate on India	20.
	Block of 4	100.
O45P4	90c **ultra,** plate on card	10.
	Block of 4	50.
	P# blk. of 12	225.
	Short transfer at upper left (106, pos. 1, 5)	—
	Nos. O35P3-O45P3 (11)	220.00
	Nos. O35P4-O45P4 (11)	115.00

POST OFFICE

No.	Description	Value
O47P1	1c **blk,** large die on India paper	80.
O47P2	1c **blk,** RA sm die on white wove paper	100.
O47P2a	1c **blk,** PP sm die on yelsh wove paper	700.
O47P3	1c **blk,** plate on India	20.
	Block of 4	100.
O47P4	1c **blk,** plate on card	10.
	Block of 4	50.
	P# blk. of 10	225.
O48TC1a	2c large die on India paper	
e.	**deep brown**	500.
O48P1	2c **blk,** large die on India paper	80.
O48P2	2c **blk,** RA sm die on white wove paper	100.
O48P2a	2c **blk,** PP sm die on yelsh wove paper	700.
O48P3	2c **blk,** plate on India	20.
	Block of 4	100.
O48P4	2c **blk,** plate on card	10.
	Block of 4	50.
	P# blk. of 14	225.
O49TC1a	3c large die on India paper	
e.	**deep green**	500.
O49P1	3c **blk,** large die on India paper	80.
O49P2	3c **blk,** RA sm die on white wove paper	100.
O49P2a	3c **blk,** PP sm die on yelsh wove paper	700.
O49P3	3c **blk,** plate on India	20.
	Block of 4	100.
O49P4	3c **blk,** plate on card	10.
	Block of 4	50.
	P# blk. of 12	225.
O50TC1a	6c large die on India paper	
e.	**deep brown**	500.
f.	**brown carmine**	500.
O50P1	6c **blk,** large die on India paper	80.
O50P2	6c **blk,** RA sm die on white wove paper	100.
O50P2a	6c **blk,** PP sm die on yelsh wove paper	700.
O50P3	6c **blk,** plate on India	20.
	Block of 4	100.
O50P4	6c **blk,** plate on card	10.
	Block of 4	50.
	P# blk. of 12	225.
O51P1	10c **blk,** large die on India paper	80.
O51P2	10c **blk,** RA sm die on white wove paper	100.
O51P2a	10c **blk,** PP sm die on yelsh wove paper	700.
O51P3	10c **blk,** plate on India	20.
	Block of 4	100.
O51P4	10c **blk,** plate on card	10.
	Block of 4	50.
	P# blk. of 12	225.
O52P1	12c **blk,** large die on India paper	80.
O52P2	12c **blk,** RA sm die on white wove paper	100.
O52P2a	12c **blk,** PP sm die on yelsh wove paper	700.
O52P3	12c **blk,** plate on India	20.
	Block of 4	100.
O52P4	12c **blk,** plate on card	10.
	Block of 4	50.
	P# blk. of 12	225.
O53P1	15c **blk,** large die on India paper	80.
O53P2	15c **blk,** RA sm die on white wove paper	100.
O53P2a	15c **blk,** PP sm die on yelsh wove paper	700.
O53P3	15c **blk,** plate on India	20.
	Block of 4	100.
O53P4	15c **blk,** plate on card	10.
	Block of 4	50.
	P# blk. of 12	225.
O54P1	24c **blk,** large die on India paper	80.
O54P2	24c **blk,** RA sm die on white wove paper	100.
O54P2a	24c **blk,** PP sm die on yelsh wove paper	700.
O54P3	24c **blk,** plate on India	20.
	Block of 4	100.
O54P4	24c **blk,** plate on card	10.
	Block of 4	50.
	P# blk. of 12	225.
O55P1	30c **blk,** large die on India paper	80.
O55P2	30c **blk,** RA sm die on white wove paper	100.
O55P2a	30c **blk,** PP sm die on yelsh wove paper	700.
O55P3	30c **blk,** plate on India	20.
	Block of 4	100.
O55P4	30c **blk,** plate on card	10.
	Block of 4	50.
	P# blk. of 12	225.
O56P1	90c **blk,** large die on India paper	80.
O56P2	90c **blk,** RA sm die on white wove paper	100.
O56P2a	90c **blk,** PP sm die on yelsh wove paper	700.
O56P3	90c **blk,** plate on India	20.
	Block of 4	100.
O56P4	90c **blk,** plate on card	10.
	Block of 4	50.
	P# blk. of 12	225.
	Nos. O47P3-O56P3 (10)	200.00
	Nos. O47P4-O56P4 (10)	100.00

STATE

No.	Description	Value
O57TC1a	1c large die on India paper	
e.	**black**	500.
f.	**light ultramarine**	500.
O57TC3	1c plate on India paper	
a.	**black**	90.
O57P1	1c **grn,** large die on India paper	80.
O57P2	1c **grn,** RA sm die on white wove paper	100.
O57P2a	1c **grn,** PP sm die on yelsh wove paper	700.
O57P3	1c **grn,** plate on India	20.
	Block of 4	100.
O57P4	1c **grn,** plate on card	10.
	Block of 4	50.
	P# blk. of 12	225.
O58TC1a	2c large die on India paper	
e.	**black**	500.
f.	**deep brown**	500.
O58P1	2c **grn,** large die on India paper	80.
O58P2	2c **grn,** RA sm die on white wove paper	100.
O58P2a	2c **grn,** PP sm die on yelsh wove paper	700.
O58P3	2c **grn,** plate on India	20.
	Block of 4	100.
O58P4	2c **grn,** plate on card	10.
	Block of 4	50.
	P# blk. of 10	225.
O59TC1a	3c large die on India paper	
e.	**black**	500.
O59P1	3c **grn,** large die on India paper	80.
O59P2	3c **grn,** RA sm die on white wove paper	100.
O59P2a	3c **grn,** PP sm die on yelsh wove paper	700.
O59P3	3c **grn,** plate on India	20.
	Block of 4	100.
O59P4	3c **grn,** plate on card	10.
	Block of 4	50.
	P# blk. of 10	225.
O60P1	6c **grn,** large die on India paper	80.
O60P2	6c **grn,** RA sm die on white wove paper	100.
O60P2a	6c **grn,** PP sm die on yelsh wove paper	700.
O60P3	6c **grn,** plate on India	25.
	Block of 4	125.
O60P4	6c **grn,** plate on card	16.
	Block of 4	85.
	P# blk. of 12	375.
O61P1	7c **grn,** large die on India paper	80.
O61P2	7c **grn,** RA sm die on white wove paper	100.
O61P2a	7c **grn,** PP sm die on yelsh wove paper	700.
O61P3	7c **grn,** plate on India	20.
	Block of 4	100.
O61P4	7c **grn,** plate on card	10.
	Block of 4	50.
	P# blk. of 12	225.
O61TC3	7c plate on India paper	
a.	**black**	90.
O62P1	10c **grn,** large die on India paper	80.
O62P2	10c **grn,** RA sm die on white wove paper	100.
O62P2a	10c **grn,** PP sm die on yelsh wove paper	700.
O62P3	10c **grn,** plate on India	20.
	Block of 4	100.
O62P4	10c **grn,** plate on card	10.
	Block of 4	50.
	P# blk. of 12	225.
O62TC3	10c plate on India paper	
a.	**black**	90.
O63P1	12c **grn,** large die on India paper	80.
O63P2	12c **grn,** RA sm die on white wove paper	100.
O63P2a	12c **grn,** PP sm die on yelsh wove paper	700.
O63P3	12c **grn,** plate on India	20.
	Block of 4	100.
O63P4	12c **grn,** plate on card	10.
	Block of 4	50.
	P# blk. of 12	225.
O64P1	15c **grn,** large die on India paper	80.
O64P2	15c **grn,** RA sm die on white wove paper	100.
O64P2a	15c **grn,** PP sm die on yelsh wove paper	700.
O64P3	15c **grn,** plate on India	20.
	Block of 4	100.
O64P4	15c **grn,** plate on card	10.
	Block of 4	50.
	P# blk. of 12	225.
O65P1	24c **grn,** large die on India paper	80.
O65P2	24c **grn,** RA sm die on white wove paper	100.
O65P2a	24c **grn,** PP sm die on yelsh wove paper	700.
O65P3	24c **grn,** plate on India	20.
	Block of 4	100.
O65P4	24c **grn,** plate on card	10.
	Block of 4	50.
	P# blk. of 12	225.
O66P1	30c **grn,** large die on India paper	80.
O66P2	30c **grn,** RA sm die on white wove paper	100.
O66P2a	30c **grn,** PP sm die on yelsh wove paper	700.
O66P3	30c **grn,** plate on India	20.
	Block of 4	100.
O66P4	30c **grn,** plate on card	10.
	Block of 4	50.
	P# blk. of 12	225.
O67TC1a	90c large die on India paper	
e.	**black**	500.
O67P1	90c **grn,** large die on India paper	80.
O67P2	90c **grn,** RA sm die on white wove paper	100.
O67P2a	90c **grn,** PP sm die on yelsh wove paper	700.
O67P3	90c **grn,** plate on India	20.
	Block of 4	100.
O67P4	90c **grn,** plate on card	10.
	Block of 4	50.
	P# blk. of 12	225.
O68TC1a	$2 large die on India paper	
e.	**violet & black**	2,500.
f.	**brown red & black**	2,500.
g.	**orange red & slate blue**	2,500.
O68P1	$2 **grn & blk,** large die on India paper	150.
O68P2	$2 **grn & blk,** RA sm die on white wove paper	125.
O68P2a	$2 **grn & blk,** PP sm die on yelsh wove paper	850.
O68P3	$2 **grn & blk,** plate on India	100.
	Block of 4	475.
	Sheet of 10	*4,000.*
O68P4	$2 **grn & blk,** plate on card	35.
	Block of 4	175.
	Sheet of 10	*5,000.*
a.	Invtd. center	*12,500.*
	Half sheet of 5	*70,000.*
O69P1	$5 **grn & blk,** large die on India paper	150.
O69P2	$5 **grn & blk,** RA sm die on white wove paper	125.
O69P2a	$5 **grn & blk,** PP sm die on yelsh wove paper	850.
O69P3	$5 **grn & blk,** plate on India	100.
	Block of 4	475.
	Sheet of 10	*4,000.*
O69P4	$5 **grn & blk,** plate on card	35.
	Block of 4	175.
	Sheet of 10	*5,000.*
a.	Invtd. center	*8,500.*
	Half sheet of 5	*47,500.*
	Sheet of 10	*100,000.*
O70P1	$10 **grn & blk,** large die on India paper	150.
O70P2	$10 **grn & blk,** RA sm die on white wove paper	125.
O70P2a	$10 **grn & blk,** PP sm die on yelsh wove paper	850.
O70P3	$10 **grn & blk,** plate on India	100.
	Block of 4	475.
	Sheet of 10	*4,000.*
O70P4	$10 **grn & blk,** plate on card	35.
	Block of 4	—
	Sheet of 10	*5,000.*
O71P1	$20 **grn & blk,** large die on India paper	150.
O71P2	$20 **grn & blk,** RA sm die on white wove paper	125.

O71P2a	$20 **grn & blk,** PP sm die on yelsh wove paper	900.
O71P3	$20 **grn & blk,** plate on India	100.
	Block of 4	475.
	Sheet of 10	*4,000.*
O71P4	$20 **grn & blk,** plate on card	35.
	Block of 4	175.
	Sheet of 10	*5,000.*
	a. Invtd. center	
	Block of 4	*40,000.*
	Half sheet of 5	*50,000.*
	Nos. O57P3-O71P3 (15)	625.00
	Nos. O57P4-O71P4 (15)	256.00

Nos. O68P1 to O71P1 Large Dies exist as hybrids only.

TREASURY

O72TC1a	1c large die on India paper	
	***e.* black**	500.
	***f.* light ultramarine**	500.
O72P1	1c **brn,** large die on India paper	80.
O72P2	1c **brn,** RA sm die on white wove paper	100.
O72P2a	1c **brn,** PP sm die on yelsh wove paper	700.
O72P3	1c **brn,** plate on India	20.
	Block of 4	100.
O72P4	1c **brn,** plate on card	10.
	Block of 4	50.
	P# blk. of 12	225.
O73TC1a	2c large die on India paper	
	***e.* black**	500.
O73P1	2c **brn,** large die on India paper	80.
O73P2	2c **brn,** RA sm die on white wove paper	100.
O73P2a	2c **brn,** PP sm die on yelsh wove paper	700.
O73P3	2c **brn,** plate on India	20.
	Block of 4	100.
O73P4	2c **brn,** plate on card	10.
	Block of 4	50.
	P# blk. of 12	225.
O74TC1a	3c large die on India paper	
	***e.* black**	500.
	***f.* deep green**	500.
O74P1	3c **brn,** large die on India paper	80.
O74P2	3c **brn,** RA sm die on white wove paper	100.
O74P2a	3c **brn,** PP sm die on yelsh wove paper	700.
O74P3	3c **brn,** plate on India	20.
	Block of 4	100.
O74P4	3c **brn,** plate on card	10.
	Block of 4	50.
	P# blk. of 12	225.
O75TC1a	6c large die on India paper	
	***e.* black**	500.
O75P1	6c **brn,** large die on India paper	80.
O75P2	6c **brn,** RA sm die on white wove paper	100.
O75P2a	6c **brn,** PP sm die on yelsh wove paper	700.
O75P3	6c **brn,** plate on India	20.
	Block of 4	100.
O75P4	6c **brn,** plate on card	15.
	Block of 4	75.
	P# blk. of 12	375.
O76P1	7c **brn,** large die on India paper	80.
O76P2	7c **brn,** RA sm die on white wove paper	100.
O76P2a	7c **brn,** PP sm die on yelsh wove paper	700.
O76P3	7c **brn,** plate on India	20.
	Block of 4	100.
O76P4	7c **brn,** plate on card	10.
	Block of 4	50.
	P# blk. of 12	225.
O77TC1a	10c large die on India paper	
	***e.* black**	500.
O77P1	10c **brn,** large die on India paper	80.
O77P2	10c **brn,** RA sm die on white wove paper	100.
O77P2a	10c **brn,** PP sm die on yelsh wove paper	700.
O77P3	10c **brn,** plate on India	20.
	Block of 4	100.
O77P4	10c **brn,** plate on card	10.
	Block of 4	50.
	P# blk. of 12	225.
O78TC1a	12c large die on India paper	
	***e.* black**	500.
O78P1	12c **brn,** large die on India paper	80.
O78P2	12c **brn,** RA sm die on white wove paper	100.
O78P2a	12c **brn,** PP sm die on yelsh wove paper	700.
O78P3	12c **brn,** plate on India	20.
	Block of 4	100.
O78P4	12c **brn,** plate on card	10.
	Block of 4	50.
	P# blk. of 12	225.
O79TC1a	15c large die on India paper	
	***e.* black**	500.
O79P1	15c **brn,** large die on India paper	80.
O79P2	15c **brn,** RA sm die on white wove paper	100.
O79P2a	15c **brn,** PP sm die on yelsh wove paper	700.
O79P3	15c **brn,** plate on India	20.
	Block of 4	100.
O79P4	15c **brn,** plate on card	10.
	Block of 4	50.
	P# blk. of 12	275.
O80TC1a	24c large die on India paper	
	***e.* black**	500.
O80P1	24c **brn,** large die on India paper	80.
O80P2	24c **brn,** RA sm die on white wove paper	100.
O80P2a	24c **brn,** PP sm die on yelsh wove paper	700.
O80P3	24c **brn,** plate on India	20.
	Block of 4	100.
O80P4	24c **brn,** plate on card	10.
	Block of 4	45.
	P# blk. of 12	225.
O81TC1a	30c large die on India paper	
	***e.* black**	500.
O81P1	30c **brn,** large die on India paper	80.
O81P2	30c **brn,** RA sm die on white wove paper	100.
O81P2a	30c **brn,** PP sm die on yelsh wove paper	700.
O81P3	30c **brn,** plate on India	20.
	Block of 4	100.
O81P4	30c **brn,** plate on card	10.
	Block of 4	45.
	P# blk. of 12	225.
O82TC1a	90c large die on India paper	
	***e.* black**	500.
O82P1	90c **brn,** large die on India paper	80.
O82P2	90c **brn,** RA sm die on white wove paper	100.
O82P2a	90c **brn,** PP sm die on yelsh wove paper	700.
O82P3	90c **brn,** plate on India	20.
	Block of 4	100.
O82P4	90c **brn,** plate on card	10.
	Block of 4	50.
	P# blk. of 12	225.
	Nos. O72P3-O82P3 (11)	220.00
	Nos. O72P4-O82P4 (11)	115.00

WAR

O83TC1a	1c large die on India paper	
	***e.* black**	500.
	***f.* light ultramarine**	500.
O83TC3	1c plate on India paper	
	***a.* black**	80.
O83P1	1c **rose,** large die on India paper	80.
O83P2	1c **rose,** RA sm die on white wove paper	100.
O83P2a	1c **rose,** PP sm die on yelsh wove paper	700.
O83P3	1c **rose,** plate on India	20.
	Block of 4	100.
O83P4	1c **rose,** plate on card	10.
	Block of 4	50.
	P# blk. of 12	225.
O84TC1a	2c large die on India paper	
	***e.* black**	500.
	***f.* deep brown**	500.
O84TC3	2c plate on India paper	
	***a.* black**	80.
O84TC4	2c plate on card	
	***a.* black**	75.
O84P1	2c **rose,** large die on India paper	80.
O84P2	2c **rose,** RA sm die on white wove paper	100.
O84P2a	2c **rose,** PP sm die on yelsh wove paper	700.
O84P3	2c **rose,** plate on India	20.
	Block of 4	100.
O84P4	2c **rose,** plate on card	10.
	Block of 4	50.
O85TC1a	3c large die on India paper	
	***e.* black**	500.
	***f.* deep green**	500.
	***g.* chocolate**	675.
	***h.* porcelain blue**	675.
	***i.* ultra**	675.
O85P1	3c **rose,** large die on India paper	80.
O85P2	3c **rose,** RA sm die on white wove paper	100.
O85P2a	3c **rose,** PP sm die on yelsh wove paper	700.
O85P3	3c **rose,** plate on India	20.
	Block of 4	100.
O85P4	3c **rose,** plate on card	10.
	Block of 4	50.
	Plate flaw at upper left (32R20)	—
O86TC3	6c plate on India paper	
	***a.* black**	80.
O86P1	6c **rose,** large die on India paper	80.
O86P2	6c **rose,** RA sm die on white wove paper	100.
O86P2a	6c **rose,** PP sm die on yelsh wove paper	700.
O86P3	6c **rose,** plate on India	20.
	Block of 4	100.
O86P4	6c **rose,** plate on card	10.
	Block of 4	50.
	P# blk. of 12	225.
O87P1	7c **rose,** large die on India paper	80.
O87P2	7c **rose,** RA sm die on white wove paper	100.
O87P2a	7c **rose,** PP sm die on yelsh wove paper	700.
O87P3	7c **rose,** plate on India	20.
	Block of 4	100.
O87P4	7c **rose,** plate on card	10.
	Block of 4	50.
	P# blk. of 10	225.
O88P1	10c **rose,** large die on India paper	80.
O88P2	10c **rose,** RA sm die on white wove paper	100.
O88P2a	10c **rose,** PP sm die on yelsh wove paper	700.
O88P3	10c **rose,** plate on India	20.
	Block of 4	100.
O88P4	10c **rose,** plate on card	10.
	Block of 4	50.
	P# blk. of 10	225.
O89TC3	12c plate on India paper	
	***a.* black**	80.
O89P1	12c **rose,** large die on India paper	80.
O89P2	12c **rose,** RA sm die on white wove paper	100.
O89P2a	12c **rose,** PP sm die on yelsh wove paper	700.
O89P3	12c **rose,** plate on India	20.
	Block of 4	100.
O89P4	12c **rose,** plate on card	10.
	Block of 4	50.
	P# blk. of 12	225.
O90P1	15c **rose,** large die on India paper	80.
O90P2	15c **rose,** RA sm die on white wove paper	100.
O90P2a	15c **rose,** PP sm die on yelsh wove paper	700.
O90P3	15c **rose,** plate on India	20.
	Block of 4	100.
O90P4	15c **rose,** plate on card	10.
	Block of 4	50.
	P# blk. of 12	225.
O91P1	24c **rose,** large die on India paper	80.
O91P2	24c **rose,** RA sm die on white wove paper	100.
O91P2a	24c **rose,** PP sm die on yelsh wove paper	700.
O91P3	24c **rose,** plate on India	20.
	Block of 4	100.
O91P4	24c **rose,** plate on card	10.
	Block of 4	50.
	P# blk. of 12	225.
O92P1	30c **rose,** large die on India paper	80.
O92P2	30c **rose,** RA sm die on white wove paper	100.
O92P2a	30c **rose,** PP sm die on yelsh wove paper	700.
O92P3	30c **rose,** plate on India	20.
	Block of 4	100.
O92P4	30c **rose,** plate on card	10.
	Block of 4	50.
	P# blk. of 12	225.
O93P1	90c **rose,** large die on India paper	80.
O93P2	90c **rose,** RA sm die on white wove paper	100.
O93P2a	90c **rose,** PP sm die on yelsh wove paper	700.
O93P3	90c **rose,** plate on India	20.
	Block of 4	100.
O93P4	90c **rose,** plate on card	10.
	Block of 4	50.
	P# blk. of 12	225.
	Nos. O83P3-O93P3 (11)	220.00
	Nos. O83P4-O93P4 (10)	100.00
	Nos. O1P3-O93P3 (92)	1,675.
	Nos. O1P4-O93P4 (92)	1,036.

Nos. O83P-O93P exist in a plum shade.

POSTAL SAVINGS MAIL

1911

O124P1	1c **dk vio,** large die on India paper	1,000.
O124P2	1c **dk vio,** sm die on white wove paper	275.
O124P2a	1c **dk vio,** PP sm die on yelsh wove paper	1,000.
O121TC1a	2c large die on India paper	
	***e.* lake**	500.
O121P1	2c **blk,** large die on India paper	1,000.
O121P2	2c **blk,** sm die on white wove paper	275.
O121P2a	2c **blk,** PP sm die on yelsh wove paper	1,000.
O126TC1c	10c Large die on wove paper	
	***e.* black**	*1,250.*
O126P1	10c **car,** large die on India paper	1,000.
O126P2	10c **car,** sm die on white wove paper	275.
O126P2a	10c **car,** PP sm die on yelsh wove paper	1,000.
O122P1	50c **dk grn,** large die on India paper	1,000.
O122P2	50c **dk grn,** sm die on white wove paper	275.
O122P2a	50c **dk grn,** PP sm die on yelsh wove paper	1,000.
O123P1	$1 **ultra,** large die on India paper	1,000.
O123P2	$1 **ultra,** sm die on white wove paper	275.
O123P2a	$1 **ultra,** PP sm die on yelsh wove paper	1,000.

The so-called "Goodall" set of Small Die proofs on India Paper of Official Stamps in five colors

AGRICULTURE

O1TC2	1c "Goodall" small die on India paper	
	***b.* black**	300.
	***c.* deep green**	300.
	***d.* dull gray blue**	300.
	***e.* deep brown**	300.
	***f.* dull red**	300.
O2TC2	2c "Goodall" small die on India paper	
	***b.* black**	300.
	***c.* deep green**	300.
	***d.* dull gray blue**	300.
	***e.* deep brown**	300.
	***f.* dull red**	300.
O3TC2	3c "Goodall" small die on India paper	
	***b.* black**	300.
	***c.* deep green**	300.
	***d.* dull gray blue**	300.
	***e.* deep brown**	300.
	***f.* dull red**	300.
O4TC2	6c "Goodall" small die on India paper	
	***b.* black**	300.
	***c.* deep green**	300.
	***d.* dull gray blue**	300.
	***e.* deep brown**	300.
	***f.* dull red**	300.
O5TC2	10c "Goodall" small die on India paper	
	***b.* black**	300.
	***c.* deep green**	300.
	***d.* dull gray blue**	300.

e. deep brown 300.
f. dull red 300.

O6TC2 12c "Goodall" small die on India paper
b. black 300.
c. deep green 300.
d. dull gray blue 300.
e. deep brown 300.
f. dull red 300.

O7TC2 15c "Goodall" small die on India paper
b. black 300.
c. deep green 300.
d. dull gray blue 300.
e. deep brown 300.
f. dull red 300.

O8TC2 24c "Goodall" small die on India paper
b. black 300.
c. deep green 300.
d. dull gray blue 300.
e. deep brown 300.
f. dull red 300.

O9TC2 30c "Goodall" small die on India paper
b. black 300.
c. deep green 300.
d. dull gray blue 300.
e. deep brown 300.
f. dull red 300.

EXECUTIVE

O10TC2 1c "Goodall" small die on India paper
b. black 300.
c. deep green 300.
d. dull gray blue 300.
e. deep brown 300.
f. dull red 300.

O11TC2 2c "Goodall" small die on India paper
b. black 300.
c. deep green 300.
d. dull gray blue 300.
e. deep brown 300.
f. dull red 300.

O12TC2 3c "Goodall" small die on India paper
b. black 300.
c. deep green 300.
d. dull gray blue 300.
e. deep brown 300.
f. dull red 300.

O13TC2 6c "Goodall" small die on India paper
b. black 300.
c. deep green 300.
d. dull gray blue 300.
e. deep brown 300.
f. dull red 300.

O14TC2 10c "Goodall" small die on India paper
b. black 300.
c. deep green 300.
d. dull gray blue 300.
e. deep brown 300.
f. dull red 300.

INTERIOR

O15TC2 1c "Goodall" small die on India paper
b. black 300.
c. deep green 300.
d. dull gray blue 300.
e. deep brown 300.
f. dull red 300.

O16TC2 2c "Goodall" small die on India paper
b. black 300.
c. deep green 300.
d. dull gray blue 300.
e. deep brown 300.
f. dull red 300.

O17TC2 3c "Goodall" small die on India paper
b. black 300.
c. deep green 300.
d. dull gray blue 300.
e. deep brown 300.
f. dull red 300.

O18TC2 6c "Goodall" small die on India paper
b. black 300.
c. deep green 300.
d. dull gray blue 300.
e. deep brown 300.
f. dull red 300.

O19TC2 10c "Goodall" small die on India paper
b. black 300.
c. deep green 300.
d. dull gray blue 300.
e. deep brown 300.
f. dull red 300.

O20TC2 12c "Goodall" small die on India paper
b. black 300.
c. deep green 300.
d. dull gray blue 300.
e. deep brown 300.
f. dull red 300.

O21TC2 15c "Goodall" small die on India paper
b. black 300.
c. deep green 300.
d. dull gray blue 300.
e. deep brown 300.
f. dull red 300.

O22TC2 24c "Goodall" small die on India paper
b. black 300.
c. deep green 300.
d. dull gray blue 300.
e. deep brown 300.
f. dull red 300.

O23TC2 30c "Goodall" small die on India paper
b. black 300.
c. deep green 300.
d. dull gray blue 300.
e. deep brown 300.
f. dull red 300.

O24TC2 90c "Goodall" small die on India paper
b. black 300.
c. deep green 300.
d. dull gray blue 300.
e. deep brown 300.
f. dull red 300.

JUSTICE

O25TC2 1c "Goodall" small die on India paper
b. black 300.
c. deep green 300.
d. dull gray blue 300.
e. deep brown 300.
f. dull red 300.

O26TC2 2c "Goodall" small die on India paper
b. black 300.
c. deep green 300.
d. dull gray blue 300.
e. deep brown 300.
f. dull red 300.

O27TC2 3c "Goodall" small die on India paper
b. black 300.
c. deep green 300.
d. dull gray blue 300.
e. deep brown 300.
f. dull red 300.

O28TC2 6c "Goodall" small die on India paper
b. black 300.
c. deep green 300.
d. dull gray blue 300.
e. deep brown 300.
f. dull red 300.

O29TC2 10c "Goodall" small die on India paper
b. black 300.
c. deep green 300.
d. dull gray blue 300.
e. deep brown 300.
f. dull red 300.

O30TC2 12c "Goodall" small die on India paper
b. black 300.
c. deep green 300.
d. dull gray blue 300.
e. deep brown 300.
f. dull red 300.

O31TC2 15c "Goodall" small die on India paper
b. black 300.
c. deep green 300.
d. dull gray blue 300.
e. deep brown 300.
f. dull red 300.

O32TC2 24c "Goodall" small die on India paper
b. black 300.
c. deep green 300.
d. dull gray blue 300.
e. deep brown 300.
f. dull red 300.

O33TC2 30c "Goodall" small die on India paper
b. black 300.
c. deep green 300.
d. dull gray blue 300.
e. deep brown 300.
f. dull red 300.

O34TC2 90c "Goodall" small die on India paper
b. black 300.
c. deep green 300.
d. dull gray blue 300.
e. deep brown 300.
f. dull red 300.

NAVY

O35TC2 1c "Goodall" small die on India paper
b. black 300.
c. deep green 300.
d. dull gray blue 300.
e. deep brown 300.
f. dull red 300.

O36TC2 2c "Goodall" small die on India paper
b. black 300.
c. deep green 300.
d. dull gray blue 300.
e. deep brown 300.
f. dull red 300.

O37TC2 3c "Goodall" small die on India paper
b. black 300.
c. deep green 300.
d. dull gray blue 300.
e. deep brown 300.
f. dull red 300.

O38TC2 6c "Goodall" small die on India paper
b. black 300.
c. deep green 300.
d. dull gray blue 300.
e. deep brown 300.
f. dull red 300.

O39TC2 7c "Goodall" small die on India paper
b. black 300.
c. deep green 300.
d. dull gray blue 300.
e. deep brown 300.
f. dull red 300.

O40TC2 10c "Goodall" small die on India paper
b. black 300.
c. deep green 300.
d. dull gray blue 300.
e. deep brown 300.
f. dull red 300.

O41TC2 12c "Goodall" small die on India paper
b. black 300.
c. deep green 300.
d. dull gray blue 300.
e. deep brown 300.
f. dull red 300.

O42TC2 15c "Goodall" small die on India paper
b. black 300.
c. deep green 300.
d. dull gray blue 300.
e. deep brown 300.
f. dull red 300.

O43TC2 24c "Goodall" small die on India paper
b. black 300.
c. deep green 300.
d. dull gray blue 300.
e. deep brown 300.
f. dull red 300.

O44TC2 30c "Goodall" small die on India paper
b. black 300.
c. deep green 300.
d. dull gray blue 300.
e. deep brown 300.
f. dull red 300.

O45TC2 90c "Goodall" small die on India paper
b. black 300.
c. deep green 300.
d. dull gray blue 300.
e. deep brown 300.
f. dull red 300.

POST OFFICE

O47TC2 1c "Goodall" small die on India paper
b. black 300.
c. deep green 300.
d. dull gray blue 300.
e. deep brown 300.
f. dull red 300.

O48TC2 2c "Goodall" small die on India paper
b. black 300.
c. deep green 300.
d. dull gray blue 300.
e. deep brown 300.
f. dull red 300.

O49TC2 3c "Goodall" small die on India paper
b. black 300.
c. deep green 300.
d. dull gray blue 300.
e. deep brown 300.
f. dull red 300.

O50TC2 6c "Goodall" small die on India paper
b. black 300.
c. deep green 300.
d. dull gray blue 300.
e. deep brown 300.
f. dull red 300.

O51TC2 10c "Goodall" small die on India paper
b. black 300.
c. deep green 300.
d. dull gray blue 300.
e. deep brown 300.
f. dull red 300.

O52TC2 12c "Goodall" small die on India paper
b. black 300.
c. deep green 300.
d. dull gray blue 300.
e. deep brown 300.
f. dull red 300.

O53TC2 15c "Goodall" small die on India paper
b. black 300.
c. deep green 300.
d. dull gray blue 300.
e. deep brown 300.
f. dull red 300.

O54TC2 24c "Goodall" small die on India paper
b. black 300.
c. deep green 300.
d. dull gray blue 300.
e. deep brown 300.
f. dull red 300.

O55TC2 30c "Goodall" small die on India paper
b. black 300.
c. deep green 300.
d. dull gray blue 300.
e. deep brown 300.
f. dull red 300.

O56TC2 90c "Goodall" small die on India paper
b. black 300.
c. deep green 300.
d. dull gray blue 300.
e. deep brown 300.
f. dull red 300.

STATE

O57TC2 1c "Goodall" small die on India paper
b. black 300.
c. deep green 300.
d. dull gray blue 300.
e. deep brown 300.
f. dull red 300.

O58TC2 2c "Goodall" small die on India paper
b. black 300.
c. deep green 300.
d. dull gray blue 300.
e. deep brown 300.
f. dull red 300.

O59TC2 3c "Goodall" small die on India paper
b. black 300.
c. deep green 300.
d. dull gray blue 300.
e. deep brown 300.
f. dull red 300.

O60TC2 6c "Goodall" small die on India paper
b. black 300.
c. deep green 300.
d. dull gray blue 300.
e. deep brown 300.
f. dull red 300.

O61TC2 7c "Goodall" small die on India paper
b. black 300.
c. deep green 300.
d. dull gray blue 300.
e. deep brown 300.
f. dull red 300.

O62TC2 10c "Goodall" small die on India paper
b. black 300.
c. deep green 300.
d. dull gray blue 300.
e. deep brown 300.
f. dull red 300.

O63TC2 12c "Goodall" small die on India paper
b. black 300.
c. deep green 300.
d. dull gray blue 300.
e. deep brown 300.
f. dull red 300.

No.	Description	Value
O64TC2	15c "Goodall" small die on India paper	
	b. **black**	300.
	c. **deep green**	300.
	d. **dull gray blue**	300.
	e. **deep brown**	300.
	f. **dull red**	300.
O65TC2	24c "Goodall" small die on India paper	
	b. **black**	300.
	c. **deep green**	300.
	d. **dull gray blue**	300.
	e. **deep brown**	300.
	f. **dull red**	300.
O66TC2	30c "Goodall" small die on India paper	
	b. **black**	300.
	c. **deep green**	300.
	d. **dull gray blue**	300.
	e. **deep brown**	300.
	f. **dull red**	300.
O67TC2	90c "Goodall" small die on India paper	
	b. **black**	300.
	c. **deep green**	300.
	d. **dull gray blue**	300.
	e. **deep brown**	300.
	f. **dull red**	300.
O68TC2	$2 "Goodall" small die on India paper	
	b. **scarlet frame, green center**	*3,250.*
	c. **scarlet frame, black center**	*3,250.*
	d. **scarlet frame, blue center**	*3,250.*
	e. **scarlet frame, brown center**	*3,250.*
	f. **violet frame, black center**	*3,250.*
	g. **green frame, brown center**	*3,250.*
	h. **brown frame, green center**	*3,250.*
	i. **brown frame, black center**	*3,250.*
	j. **red brown frame, green center**	*3,250.*

TREASURY

No.	Description	Value
O72TC2	1c "Goodall" small die on India paper	
	b. **black**	300.
	c. **deep green**	300.
	d. **dull gray blue**	300.
	e. **deep brown**	300.
	f. **dull red**	300.
O73TC2	2c "Goodall" small die on India paper	
	b. **black**	300.
	c. **deep green**	300.
	d. **dull gray blue**	300.
	e. **deep brown**	300.
	f. **dull red**	300.
O74TC2	3c "Goodall" small die on India paper	
	b. **black**	300.
	c. **deep green**	300.
	d. **dull gray blue**	300.
	e. **deep brown**	300.
	f. **dull red**	300.
O75TC2	6c "Goodall" small die on India paper	
	b. **black**	300.
	c. **deep green**	300.
	d. **dull gray blue**	300.
	e. **deep brown**	300.
	f. **dull red**	300.
O76TC2	7c "Goodall" small die on India paper	
	b. **black**	300.
	c. **deep green**	300.
	d. **dull gray blue**	300.
	e. **deep brown**	300.
	f. **dull red**	300.
O77TC2	10c "Goodall" small die on India paper	
	b. **black**	300.
	c. **deep green**	300.
	d. **dull gray blue**	300.
	e. **deep brown**	300.
	f. **dull red**	300.
O78TC2	12c "Goodall" small die on India paper	
	b. **black**	300.
	c. **deep green**	300.
	d. **dull gray blue**	300.
	e. **deep brown**	300.
	f. **dull red**	300.
O79TC2	15c "Goodall" small die on India paper	
	b. **black**	300.
	c. **deep green**	300.
	d. **dull gray blue**	300.
	e. **deep brown**	300.
	f. **dull red**	300.
O80TC2	24c "Goodall" small die on India paper	
	b. **black**	300.
	c. **deep green**	300.
	d. **dull gray blue**	300.
	e. **deep brown**	300.
	f. **dull red**	300.
O81TC2	30c "Goodall" small die on India paper	
	b. **black**	300.
	c. **deep green**	300.
	d. **dull gray blue**	300.
	e. **deep brown**	300.
	f. **dull red**	300.
O82TC2	90c "Goodall" small die on India paper	
	b. **black**	300.
	c. **deep green**	300.
	d. **dull gray blue**	300.
	e. **deep brown**	300.
	f. **dull red**	300.

WAR

No.	Description	Value
O83TC2	1c "Goodall" small die on India paper	
	b. **black**	300.
	c. **deep green**	300.
	d. **dull gray blue**	300.
	e. **deep brown**	300.
	f. **dull red**	300.
O84TC2	2c "Goodall" small die on India paper	
	b. **black**	300.
	c. **deep green**	300.
	d. **dull gray blue**	300.
	e. **deep brown**	300.
	f. **dull red**	300.
O85TC2	3c "Goodall" small die on India paper	
	b. **black**	300.
	c. **deep green**	300.
	d. **dull gray blue**	300.
	e. **deep brown**	300.
	f. **dull red**	300.
O86TC2	6c "Goodall" small die on India paper	
	b. **black**	300.
	c. **deep green**	300.
	d. **dull gray blue**	300.
	e. **deep brown**	300.
	f. **dull red**	300.
O87TC2	7c "Goodall" small die on India paper	
	b. **black**	300.
	c. **deep green**	300.
	d. **dull gray blue**	300.
	e. **deep brown**	300.
	f. **dull red**	300.
O88TC2	10c "Goodall" small die on India paper	
	b. **black**	300.
	c. **deep green**	300.
	d. **dull gray blue**	300.
	e. **deep brown**	300.
	f. **dull red**	300.
O89TC2	12c "Goodall" small die on India paper	
	b. **black**	300.
	c. **deep green**	300.
	d. **dull gray blue**	300.
	e. **deep brown**	300.
	f. **dull red**	300.
O90TC2	15c "Goodall" small die on India paper	
	b. **black**	300.
	c. **deep green**	300.
	d. **dull gray blue**	300.
	e. **deep brown**	300.
	f. **dull red**	300.
O91TC2	24c "Goodall" small die on India paper	
	b. **black**	300.
	c. **deep green**	300.
	d. **dull gray blue**	300.
	e. **deep brown**	300.
	f. **dull red**	300.
O92TC2	30c "Goodall" small die on India paper	
	b. **black**	300.
	c. **deep green**	300.
	d. **dull gray blue**	300.
	e. **deep brown**	300.
	f. **dull red**	300.
O93TC2	90c "Goodall" small die on India paper	
	b. **black**	300.
	c. **deep green**	300.
	d. **dull gray blue**	300.
	e. **deep brown**	300.
	f. **dull red**	300.

POST OFFICE SEALS

1872

No.	Description	Value
OXF1TC1a	large die on India paper	
	e. **ultramarine**	*1,000.*
	f. **carmine**	*1,000.*
	g. **brown**	*1,000.*
	h. **red violet**	*1,000.*
OXF1TC2	small die on glossy bond paper	
	b. **chocolate**	*1,000.*
OXF1TC2	small die on card	
	c. **blue,** colored border	*1,000.*
	d. **deep blue,** colored border	*1,000.*
	e. **green,** colored border	*1,000.*
	f. **chocolate,** colored border	*1,000.*
OXF1P1	**brn,** large die on India paper	*1,750.*
	a. Wove paper	*850.*
	b. Glazed paper	*450.*
	c. Card	*850.*
OXF1P3	**green,** plate proof on India	—
OXF1P4	**green,** plate on card	—
OXF1P5	**green,** plate proof on wove, sheet of 9 (unique)	*4,250.*

1877

No.	Description	Value
OX1TC1a	large die on India paper	
	e. **blue**	*1,250.*
	f. **green**	*1,250.*
	g. **orange**	*1,250.*
	h. **red orange**	*1,250.*
	i. **black**	*1,250.*
OX1TC5	plate on bond paper, imperf.	
	a. **green**	*750.*
OX1TC6	plate on bond paper, perforated & gummed	
	a. **green**	*400.*
OX1P1	**brn,** large die on India paper	*1,750.*
OX1P3	**brn,** plate on India paper	*125.*
	Block of 4	650.

1879

No.	Description	Value
OX2TC1a	large die on India paper	
	e. **black**	*1,250.*
OX2aP1	**brn,** large die on India paper	*1,500.*
OX2aP3	**brn,** plate on India paper	125.
	Block of 4	550.

1888-94

No.	Description	Value
OX5P1	**choc,** large die on India paper	*750.*

1901-03

No.	Description	Value
OX11P1	**red brn,** large die on India paper	*750.*

No. OX11P is a hybrid proof sunk on card.

1972

No.	Description	Value
OX41P1	Pane of 5, blue line proof	—

POSTAL NOTE STAMPS

No.	Description	Value
PN1TC5	1c **bister,** plate on white wove, imperf.	—

NEWSPAPER

1865

No.	Description	Value
PR1TCb	5c large die on thin hard wove	
	e. **bright red**	600.
	f. **deep reddish brown**	2,500.
	g. **dark orange**	2,500.
	d. **green**	2,500.
PR1P2a	5c **bl,** PP sm die on yelsh wove paper	*4,500.*
PR2TC1a	10c large die on India paper	
	e. **brown**	600.
	f. **dull red**	600.
	g. **blue**	600.
	h. **blue green**	600.
PR2TC5	10c plate on thick cream wove paper	
	a. **black**	85.
	b. **lake**	85.
	c. **blue green**	85.
	d. **blue**	85.
PR2P1	10c **grn,** large die on India paper	400.
PR2P2	10c **grn,** RA sm die on white wove paper	225.
PR2P2a	10c **grn,** PP sm die on yelsh wove paper	*4,500.*
PR2P4	10c **grn,** plate on card	75.
	Block of 4	375.
	P# blk. of 6	—
PR2P4a	10c **grn,** plate on thin card	85.
	Block of 4	425.
PR3TC1a	25c large die on India paper	
	e. **ocher**	600.
	f. **brown**	600.
	g. **brick red**	600.
PR3TC1b	25c large die on thin hard paper	
	e. **carmine**	*2,500.*
PR3TC5	25c plate on thick cream wove paper	
	a. **black**	85.
	b. **lake**	85.
	c. **blue green**	85.
	d. **blue**	85.
PR3P1	25c **org red,** large die on India paper	400.
PR3P2	25c **org red,** RA sm die on white wove paper	225.
PR3P2a	25c **org red,** PP sm die on yelsh wove paper	*4,500.*
PR3P4	25c **org red,** plate on card	75.
	Block of 4	375.
	P# blk. of 6	—
PR3P4a	25c **org red,** plate on thin card	100.
	Block of 4	500.
PR4TC5	5c plate on thick cream wove paper	
	a. **black**	85.
	b. **lake**	85.
	c. **blue green**	85.
	d. **blue**	85.
	e. **green,** green	*375.*
PR4P1	5c **bl,** large die on India paper	400.
PR4P2	5c **bl,** RA sm die on white wove paper	225.
PR4P4	5c **bl,** plate on card	75.
	Block of 4	375.
	P# blk. of 6	—
PR4P4a	5c **bl,** plate on thin card	85.
	Block of 4	425.

1875

No.	Description	Value
PR5P4	5c **dk bl,** plate on card	65.
PR6P4	10c **dp grn,** plate on card	65.
PR7P4	25c **dk car red,** plate on card	65.
PR9TC1a	2c large die on India paper	
	e. **orange brown**	*600.*
	f. **black brown**	*600.*
	g. **blue green**	*600.*
PR9TC3	2c plate on India paper	
	a. **dark carmine**	35.
	b. **brown rose**	35.
	c. **scarlet**	35.
	d. **orange brown**	35.
	e. **sepia**	35.
	f. **orange yellow**	35.
	g. **dull orange**	35.
	h. **green**	35.
	i. **light ultramarine**	35.
	j. **light blue**	35.
	k. **dark violet**	35.
	l. **violet black**	35.
PR9P1	2c **blk,** large die on India paper	100.
PR9P2	2c **blk,** RA sm die on white wove paper	50.
PR9P2a	2c **blk,** PP sm die on yelsh wove paper	575.
PR9P3	2c **blk,** plate on India paper	15.
	Block of 4	65.
	P# block of 10	—
PR9P4	2c **blk,** plate on card	12.
	Block of 4	55.
	P# blk. of 8	—
PR10TC1a	3c large die on India paper	
	e. **rose lake**	*600.*
PR10P1	3c **blk,** large die on India paper	100.
PR10P2	3c **blk,** RA sm die on white wove paper	50.
PR10P2a	3c **blk,** PP sm die on yelsh wove paper	575.
PR10P3	3c **blk,** plate on India paper	15.
	Block of 4	65.
	Margin block of 8, Impt. and "B"	—
PR10P4	3c **blk,** plate on card	12.
	Block of 4	55.
	P# blk. of 8	—
PR11P1	4c **blk,** large die on India paper	100.
PR11P2	4c **blk,** RA sm die on white wove paper	50.
PR11P2a	4c **blk,** PP sm die on yelsh wove paper	575.
PR11P3	4c **blk,** plate on India paper	15.
	Block of 4	65.
PR11P4	4c **blk,** plate on card	12.
	Block of 4	55.

No.	Description	Price
PR12P1	6c **blk,** large die on India paper	100.
PR12P2	6c **blk,** RA sm die on white wove paper	50.
PR12P2a	6c **blk,** PP sm die on yelsh wove paper	575.
PR12P3	6c **blk,** plate on India paper	15.
	Block of 4	65.
PR12P4	6c **blk,** plate on card	12.
	Block of 4	55.
PR13P1	8c **blk,** large die on India paper	100.
PR13P2	8c **blk,** RA sm die on white wove paper	50.
PR13P2a	8c **blk,** PP sm die on yelsh wove paper	575.
PR13P3	8c **blk,** plate on India paper	15.
	Block of 4	65.
PR13P4	8c **blk,** plate on card	12.
	Block of 4	55.
PR14P1	9c **blk,** large die on India paper	100.
PR14P2	9c **blk,** RA sm die on white wove paper	50.
PR14P2a	9c **blk,** PP sm die on yelsh wove paper	575.
PR14P3	9c **blk,** plate on India paper	15.
	Block of 4	65.
PR14P4	9c **blk,** plate on card	12.
	Block of 4	55.
PR15P1	10c **blk,** large die on India paper	100.
PR15P2	10c **blk,** RA sm die on white wove paper	50.
PR15P2a	10c **blk,** PP sm die on yelsh wove paper	575.
PR15P3	10c **blk,** plate on India paper	15.
	Block of 4	65.
PR15P4	10c **blk,** plate on card	12.
	Block of 4	55.
PR16TC1a	12c large die on India paper	
e.	**brown rose**	*600.*
f.	**scarlet**	*600.*
g.	**sepia**	*600.*
h.	**green**	*600.*
i.	**light ultramarine**	*600.*
j.	**dark violet**	*600.*
k.	**violet black**	*600.*
l.	**black**	*600.*
PR16TC3	12c plate on India paper	
a.	**dark carmine**	35.
b.	**brown rose**	35.
c.	**scarlet**	35.
d.	**orange brown**	35.
e.	**sepia**	35.
f.	**orange yellow**	35.
g.	**dull orange**	35.
h.	**green**	35.
i.	**light ultramarine**	35.
j.	**light blue**	35.
k.	**dark violet**	35.
l.	**violet black**	35.
m.	**black**	35.
PR16P1	12c **rose,** large die on India paper	100.
PR16P2	12c **rose,** RA sm die on white wove paper	50.
PR16P2a	12c **rose,** PP sm die on yelsh wove paper	575.
PR16P3	12c **rose,** plate on India paper	15.
	Block of 4	65.
PR16P4	12c **rose,** plate on card	12.
	Block of 4	55.
PR17TC1a	24c large die on India paper	
e.	**green**	*600.*
f.	**black**	*600.*
PR17TC3	24c plate on India paper	
a.	**black**	35.
PR17P1	24c **rose,** large die on India paper	100.
PR17P2	24c **rose,** RA sm die on white wove paper	50.
PR17P2a	24c **rose,** PP sm die on yelsh wove paper	575.
PR17P3	24c **rose,** plate on India paper	15.
	Block of 4	65.
PR17P4	24c **rose,** plate on card	12.
	Block of 4	55.
PR18TC1a	36c large die on India paper	
e.	**green**	*600.*
f.	**black**	*600.*
g.	**sepia**	*600.*
PR18TC3	36c plate on India paper	
a.	**black**	35.
PR18P1	36c **rose,** large die on India paper	100.
PR18P2	36c **rose,** RA sm die on white wove paper	50.
PR18P2a	36c **rose,** PP sm die on yelsh wove paper	575.
PR18P3	36c **rose,** plate on India paper	15.
	Block of 4	65.
PR18P4	36c **rose,** plate on card	12.
	Block of 4	55.
PR19TC1a	48c large die on India paper	
e.	**green**	*600.*
f.	**black**	*600.*
g.	**sepia**	*600.*
PR19TC3	48c plate on India paper	
a.	**black**	35.
PR19P1	48c **rose,** large die on India paper	100.
PR19P2	48c **rose,** RA sm die on white wove paper	50.
PR19P2a	48c **rose,** PP sm die on yelsh wove paper	575.
PR19P3	48c **rose,** plate on India paper	15.
	Block of 4	65.
PR19P4	48c **rose,** plate on card	12.
	Block of 4	55.
PR20TC1a	60c large die on India paper	
e.	**black**	*600.*
PR20TC3	60c plate on India paper	
a.	**black**	35.
PR20P1	60c **rose,** large die on India paper	100.
PR20P2	60c **rose,** RA sm die on white wove paper	50.
PR20P2a	60c **rose,** PP sm die on yelsh wove paper	575.
PR20P3	60c **rose,** plate on India paper	15.
	Block of 4	65.
PR20P4	60c **rose,** plate on card	12.
	Block of 4	55.
PR21TC1a	72c large die on India paper	
e.	**black**	*600.*
PR21TC3	72c plate on India paper	
a.	**black**	35.
PR21P1	72c **rose,** large die on India paper	100.
PR21P2	72c **rose,** RA sm die on white wove paper	50.
PR21P2a	72c **rose,** PP sm die on yelsh wove paper	575.
PR21P3	72c **rose,** plate on India paper	15.
	Block of 4	65.
PR21P4	72c **rose,** plate on card	12.
	Block of 4	55.
PR22TC1a	84c large die on India paper	
e.	**black**	*600.*
PR22TC3	84c plate on India paper	
a.	**black**	35.
PR22P1	84c **rose,** large die on India paper	100.
PR22P2	84c **rose,** RA sm die on white wove paper	50.
PR22P2a	84c **rose,** PP sm die on yelsh wove paper	575.
PR22P3	84c **rose,** plate on India paper	15.
	Block of 4	65.
PR22P4	84c **rose,** plate on card	12.
	Block of 4	55.
PR23TC1a	96c Large die on India paper	
e.	**black**	*600.*
PR23TC3	96c plate on India paper	
a.	**black**	35.
PR23P1	96c **rose,** large die on India paper	100.
PR23P2	96c **rose,** RA sm die on white wove paper	50.
PR23P2a	96c **rose,** PP sm die on yelsh wove paper	575.
PR23P3	96c **rose,** plate on India paper	15.
	Block of 4	65.
PR23P4	96c **rose,** plate on card	12.
	Block of 4	55.
PR24TC1a	$1.92 large die on India paper	
e.	**orange brown**	*600.*
f.	**green**	*600.*
PR24TC3	$1.92 plate on India paper	
a.	**dark carmine**	35.
b.	**brown rose**	35.
c.	**scarlet**	35.
d.	**orange brown**	35.
e.	**sepia**	35.
f.	**orange yellow**	35.
g.	**dull orange**	35.
h.	**green**	35.
i.	**light ultramarine**	35.
j.	**dark violet**	35.
k.	**violet black**	35.
l.	**black**	35.
PR24P1	$1.92 **dk brn,** large die on India paper	100.
PR24P2	$1.92 **dk brn,** RA sm die on white wove paper	50.
PR24P2a	$1.92 **dk brn,** PP sm die on yelsh wove paper	575.
PR24P3	$1.92 **dk brn,** plate on India paper	18.
	Block of 4	80.
PR24P4	$1.92 **dk brn,** plate on card	15.
	Block of 4	70.
PR25TC1a	$3 large die on India paper	
e.	**dark carmine**	*600.*
f.	**orange yellow**	*600.*
g.	**dull orange**	*600.*
h.	**green**	*600.*
i.	**light ultramarine**	*600.*
j.	**dark violet**	*600.*
k.	**violet black**	*600.*
l.	**black**	*600.*
m.	**brown**	—
PR25TC3	$3 plate on India paper	
a.	**dark carmine**	35.
b.	**brown rose**	35.
c.	**scarlet**	35.
d.	**orange brown**	35.
e.	**sepia**	35.
f.	**orange yellow**	35.
g.	**dull orange**	35.
h.	**green**	35.
i.	**light ultramarine**	35.
j.	**light blue**	35.
k.	**dark violet**	35.
l.	**violet black**	35.
m.	**black**	35.
PR25P1	$3 **ver,** large die on India paper	100.
PR25P2	$3 **ver,** RA sm die on white wove paper	50.
PR25P2a	$3 **ver,** PP sm die on yelsh wove paper	575.
PR25P3	$3 **ver,** plate on India paper	18.
	Block of 4	80.
PR25P4	$3 **ver,** plate on card	15.
	Block of 4	70.
PR26TC1a	$6 large die on India paper	
e.	**dark carmine**	*600.*
f.	**brown rose**	*600.*
g.	**scarlet**	*600.*
h.	**sepia**	*600.*
i.	**orange yellow**	*600.*
j.	**dull orange**	*600.*
k.	**green**	*600.*
l.	**light blue**	*600.*
m.	**dark violet**	*600.*
n.	**violet black**	*600.*
o.	**black**	*600.*
PR26TC3	$6 plate on India paper	
a.	**dark carmine**	35.
b.	**brown rose**	35.
c.	**scarlet**	35.
d.	**orange brown**	35.
e.	**dark brown**	35.
f.	**sepia**	35.
g.	**orange yellow**	35.
h.	**dull orange**	35.
i.	**green**	35.
j.	**light ultramarine**	35.
k.	**light blue**	35.
l.	**dark violet**	35.
m.	**violet black**	35.
n.	**black**	35.
PR26P1	$6 **ultra,** large die on India paper	100.
PR26P2	$6 **ultra,** RA sm die on white wove paper	50.
PR26P2a	$6 **ultra,** PP sm die on yelsh wove paper	575.
PR26P3	$6 **ultra,** plate on India paper	18.
	Block of 4	80.
PR26P4	$6 **ultra,** plate on card	15.
	Block of 4	70.
PR27TC1a	$9 large die on India paper	
e.	**dark carmine**	*600.*
f.	**brown rose**	*600.*
g.	**scarlet**	*600.*
h.	**sepia**	*600.*
i.	**orange yellow**	*600.*
j.	**dull orange**	*600.*
k.	**green**	*600.*
l.	**light ultramarine**	*600.*
m.	**dark violet**	*600.*
n.	**violet black**	*600.*
o.	**black**	*600.*
PR27TC3	$9 plate on India paper	
a.	**dark carmine**	35.
b.	**brown rose**	35.
c.	**scarlet**	35.
d.	**orange brown**	35.
e.	**sepia**	35.
f.	**orange yellow**	35.
g.	**dull orange**	35.
h.	**green**	35.
i.	**light ultramarine**	35.
j.	**light blue**	35.
k.	**dark violet**	35.
l.	**violet black**	35.
m.	**black**	35.
PR27P1	$9 **yel,** large die on India paper	100.
PR27P2	$9 **yel,** RA sm die on white wove paper	50.
PR27P2a	$9 **yel,** PP sm die on yelsh wove paper	575.
PR27P3	$9 **yel,** plate on India paper	18.
	Block of 4	80.
PR27P4	$9 **yel,** plate on card	15.
	Block of 4	70.
PR28TC1a	$12 large die on India paper	
e.	**black**	*600.*
f.	**sepia**	*600.*
g.	**orange brown**	*600.*
PR28P1	$12 **bl grn,** large die on India paper	100.
PR28P2	$12 **bl grn,** RA sm die on white wove paper	50.
PR28P2a	$12 **bl grn,** PP sm die on yelsh wove paper	575.
PR28P3	$12 **bl grn,** plate on India paper	18.
	Block of 4	80.
PR28P4	$12 **bl grn,** plate on card	15.
	Block of 4	70.
PR29TC1a	$24 large die on India paper	
e.	**black**	*600.*
f.	**black brown**	*600.*
g.	**orange brown**	*600.*
h.	**green**	*600.*
PR29TC3	$24 plate on India paper	
a.	**black**	35.
PR29P1	$24 **dk gray vio,** large die on India paper	100.
PR29P2	$24 **dk gray vio,** RA sm die on white wove paper	50.
PR29P2a	$24 **dk gray vio,** PP sm die on yelsh wove paper	575.
PR29P3	$24 **dk gray vio,** plate on India paper	18.
	Block of 4	80.
PR29P4	$24 **dk gray vio,** plate on card	15.
	Block of 4	70.
PR30TC1a	$36 large die on India paper	
e.	**dark carmine**	*600.*
f.	**black**	*600.*
g.	**black brown**	*600.*
h.	**orange brown**	*600.*
i.	**sepia**	*600.*
j.	**violet**	*600.*
k.	**green**	*600.*
PR30TC3	$36 plate on India paper	
a.	**black**	35.
PR30P1	$36 **brn rose,** large die on India paper	100.
PR30P2	$36 **brn rose,** RA sm die on white wove paper	50.
PR30P2a	$36 **brn rose,** PP sm die on yelsh wove paper	575.
PR30P3	$36 **brn rose,** plate on India paper	18.
	Block of 4	90.
PR30P4	$36 **brn rose,** plate on card	15.
	Block of 4	70.
PR31TC1a	$48 large die on India paper	
e.	**violet brown**	*600.*
f.	**black**	*600.*
g.	**sepia**	*600.*
h.	**green**	*600.*
PR31TC3	$48 plate on India paper	
a.	**black**	35.
b.	**violet brown**	35.
PR31P1	$48 **red brn,** large die on India paper	100.
PR31P2	$48 **red brn,** RA sm die on white wove paper	50.

PR31P2a $48 **red brn,** PP sm die on yelsh wove paper 575.
PR31P3 $48 **red brn,** plate on India paper 23.
Block of 4 100.
PR31P4 $48 **red brn,** plate on card 15.
Block of 4 70.
PR32TC1a $60 large die on India paper
e. **dark carmine** *600.*
f. **brown rose** *600.*
g. **scarlet** *600.*
h. **sepia** *600.*
i. **orange yellow** *600.*
j. **dull orange** *600.*
k. **green** *600.*
l. **light ultramarine** *600.*
m. **orange brown** *600.*
n. **violet black** *600.*
o. **black** *600.*
PR32TC3 $60 plate on India paper
a. **dark carmine** 35.
b. **brown rose** 35.
c. **scarlet** 35.
d. **sepia** 35.
e. **orange yellow** 35.
f. **dull orange** 35.
g. **green** 35.
h. **light ultramarine** 35.
i. **orange brown** 35.
j. **violet black** 35.
k. **black** 35.
PR32P1 $60 **vio,** large die on India paper 100.
PR32P2 $60 **vio,** RA sm die on white wove paper 50.
PR32P2a $60 **vio,** PP sm die on yelsh wove paper 575.
PR32P3 $60 **vio,** plate on India paper 25.
Block of 4 110.
PR32P4 $60 **vio,** plate on card 18.
Block of 4 85.
Nos. PR9P3-PR32P3 (24) 399.00
Nos. PR9P4-PR32P4 (24) 318.00

1879

PR57P1 2c **dp blk,** large die on India paper 100.
PR57P3 2c **dp blk,** plate on India paper 25.
Block of 4 125.
P# block of 10, Impt. —
PR57P4 2c **dp blk,** plate on card 15.
Block of 4 90.
PR58P1 3c **dp blk,** large die on India paper 100.
PR58P3 3c **dp blk,** plate on India paper 25.
Block of 4 125.
PR58P4 3c **dp blk,** plate on card 15.
Block of 4 90.
PR59P1 4c **dp blk,** large die on India paper 100.
PR59P3 4c **dp blk,** plate on India paper 25.
Block of 4 125.
PR59P4 4c **dp blk,** plate on card 15.
Block of 4 90.
PR60P1 6c **dp blk,** large die on India paper 100.
PR60P3 6c **dp blk,** plate on India paper 25.
Block of 4 125.
PR60P4 6c **dp blk,** plate on card 15.
Block of 4 90.
PR61P1 8c **dp blk,** large die on India paper 100.
PR61P3 8c **dp blk,** plate on India paper 25.
Block of 4 125.
PR61P4 8c **dp blk,** plate on card 15.
Block of 4 90.
PR62P1 10c **dp blk,** large die on India paper 100.
PR62P3 10c **dp blk,** plate on India paper 25.
Block of 4 125.
PR62P4 10c **dp blk,** plate on card 15.
Block of 4 90.
PR63P1 12c **red,** large die on India paper 100.
PR63P3 12c **red,** plate on India paper 25.
Block of 4 125.
PR63P4 12c **red,** plate on card 15.
Block of 4 90.
PR64P1 24c **red,** large die on India paper 100.
PR64P3 24c **red,** plate on India paper 25.
Block of 4 125.
PR64P4 24c **red,** plate on card 15.
Block of 4 90.
PR65P1 36c **red,** large die on India paper 100.
PR65P3 36c **red,** plate on India paper 25.
Block of 4 125.
PR65P4 36c **red,** plate on card 15.
Block of 4 90.
PR66P1 48c **red,** large die on India paper 100.
PR66P3 48c **red,** plate on India paper 25.
Block of 4 125.
PR66P4 48c **red,** plate on card 15.
Block of 4 90.
PR67P1 60c **red,** large die on India paper 100.
PR67P3 60c **red,** plate on India paper 25.
Block of 4 125.
PR67P4 60c **red,** plate on card 15.
Block of 4 90.
PR68P1 72c **red,** large die on India paper 100.
PR68P3 72c **red,** plate on India paper 25.
Block of 4 125.
PR68P4 72c **red,** plate on card 15.
Block of 4 90.
PR69P1 84c **red,** large die on India paper 100.
PR69P3 84c **red,** plate on India paper 25.
Block of 4 125.
PR69P4 84c **red,** plate on card 15.
Block of 4 90.
PR70P1 96c **red,** large die on India paper 100.
PR70P3 96c **red,** plate on India paper 25.
Block of 4 125.
PR70P4 96c **red,** plate on card 15.
Block of 4 90.
PR71P1 $1.92 **pale brn,** large die on India paper 100.
PR71P3 $1.92 **pale brn,** plate on India paper 25.
Block of 4 125.
PR71P4 $1.92 **pale brn,** plate on card 15.
Block of 4 90.
PR72P1 $3 **red ver,** large die on India paper 100.
PR72P3 $3 **red ver,** plate on India paper 25.
Block of 4 125.
PR72P4 $3 **red ver,** plate on card 15.
Block of 4 90.
PR73P1 $6 **bl,** large die on India paper 100.
PR73P3 $6 **bl,** plate on India paper 25.
Block of 4 125.
PR73P4 $6 **bl,** plate on card 15.
Block of 4 90.
PR74P1 $9 **org,** large die on India paper 100.
PR74P3 $9 **org,** plate on India paper 25.
Block of 4 125.
PR74P4 $9 **org,** plate on card 15.
Block of 4 90.
PR75P1 $12 **yel grn,** large die on India paper 100.
PR75P3 $12 **yel grn,** plate on India paper 25.
Block of 4 125.
PR75P4 $12 **yel grn,** plate on card 15.
Block of 4 90.
PR76P1 $24 **dk vio,** large die on India paper 100.
PR76P3 $24 **dk vio,** plate on India paper 25.
Block of 4 125.
PR76P4 $24 **dk vio,** plate on card 15.
Block of 4 90.
PR77P1 $36 **Indian red,** large die on India paper 100.
PR77P3 $36 **Indian red,** plate on India paper 25.
Block of 4 125.
PR77P4 $36 **Indian red,** plate on card 15.
Block of 4 90.
PR78P1 $48 **yel brn,** large die on India paper 100.
PR78P3 $48 **yel brn,** plate on India paper 25.
Block of 4 125.
PR78P4 $48 **yel brn,** plate on card 15.
Block of 4 90.
PR79P1 $60 **pur,** large die on India paper 100.
PR79P3 $60 **pur,** plate on India paper 25.
Block of 4 125.
PR79P4 $60 **pur,** plate on card 15.
Block of 4 90.
Nos. PR57P3-PR79P3 (23) 575.00
Nos. PR57P4-PR79P4 (23) 345.00

1885

PR81TC1a 1c large die on India paper
e. **salmon** *600.*
PR81TC3 1c plate on India paper
a. **scarlet** 225.
b. **dark brown** 225.
c. **violet brown** 225.
d. **dull orange** 225.
e. **green** 225.
f. **light blue** 225.
PR81P1 1c **blk,** large die on India paper 100.
PR81P2 1c **blk,** RA sm die on white wove paper 60.
PR81P2a 1c **blk,** PP sm die on yelsh wove paper 1,100.
PR81P3 1c **blk,** plate on India paper 25.
Block of 4 125.
P# blk. of 8 —
PR81P4 1c **blk,** plate on card 15.
Block of 4 90.
P# blk. of 8 425.
PR82P2a 12c **car,** PP sm die on yelsh wove paper 1,100.
PR82P3 12c **car,** plate on India paper 25.
Block of 4 125.
PR82P4 12c **car,** plate on card 15.
PR83P2a 24c **car,** PP sm die on yelsh wove paper 1,100.
PR83P3 24c **car,** plate on India paper 25.
Block of 4 125.
PR83P4 24c **car,** plate on card 15.
PR84P2a 36c **car,** PP sm die on yelsh wove paper 1,100.
PR84P3 36c **car,** plate on India paper 25.
Block of 4 125.
PR84P4 36c **car,** plate on card 15.
PR85P2a 48c **car,** PP sm die on yelsh wove paper 1,100.
PR85P3 48c **car,** plate on India paper 25.
Block of 4 125.
PR85P4 48c **car,** plate on card 15.
PR86P2a 60c **car,** PP sm die on yelsh wove paper 1,100.
PR86P3 60c **car,** plate on India paper 25.
Block of 4 125.
PR86P4 60c **car,** plate on card 15.
PR87P2a 72c **car,** PP sm die on yelsh wove paper 1,100.
PR87P3 72c **car,** plate on India paper 25.
Block of 4 125.
PR87P4 72c **car,** plate on card 15.
PR88P2a 84c **car,** PP sm die on yelsh wove paper 1,100.
PR88P3 84c **car,** plate on India paper 25.
Block of 4 125.
PR88P4 84c **car,** plate on card 15.
PR89P2a 96c **car,** PP sm die on yelsh wove paper 1,100.
PR89P3 96c **car,** plate on India paper 25.
Block of 4 125.
PR89P4 96c **car,** plate on card 15.
Nos. PR81P3-PR89P3 (9) 225.00
Nos. PR81P4-PR89P4 (9) 135.00

1895

PR102TC1a 1c large die on India paper
e. **deep scarlet** *675.*
PR102P1 1c **blk,** large die on India paper 110.
PR102P2 1c **blk,** RA sm die on white wove paper 100.
PR102P2a 1c **blk,** PP sm die on yelsh wove paper 1,100.
PR103P1 2c **blk,** large die on India paper 110.
PR103P2 2c **blk,** RA sm die on white wove paper 100.
PR103P2a 2c **blk,** PP sm die on yelsh wove paper 1,100.
PR104P1 5c **blk,** large die on India paper 110.
PR104P2 5c **blk,** RA sm die on white wove paper 100.
PR104P2a 5c **blk,** PP sm die on yelsh wove paper 1,100.
PR105P1 10c **blk,** large die on India paper 110.
PR105P2 10c **blk,** RA sm die on white wove paper 100.
PR105P2a 10c **blk,** PP sm die on yelsh wove paper 1,100.
PR106TC1a 25c large die on India paper
e. **deep carmine** *675.*
f. **dark carmine** *675.*
PR106P1 25c **car,** large die on India paper 110.
PR106P2 25c **car,** RA sm die on white wove paper 100.
PR106P2a 25c **car,** PP sm die on yelsh wove paper 1,100.
PR107TC1a 50c large die on India paper
e. **black** *675.*
f. **deep carmine** *675.*
PR107P1 50c **car,** large die on India paper 110.
PR107P2 50c **car,** RA sm die on white wove paper 100.
PR107P2a 50c **car,** PP sm die on yelsh wove paper 1,100.
PR108TC1a $2 large die on India paper
e. **deep scarlet** *675.*
f. **dark scarlet** *675.*
PR108P1 $2 **scar,** large die on India paper 110.
PR108P2 $2 **scar,** RA sm die on white wove paper 100.
PR108P2a $2 **scar,** PP sm die on yelsh wove paper 1,100.
PR109TC1a $5 large die on India paper
e. **light ultramarine** *675.*
f. **dark ultramarine** *675.*
PR109P1 $5 **bl,** large die on India paper 110.
PR109P2 $5 **bl,** RA sm die on white wove paper 100.
PR109P2a $5 **bl,** PP sm die on yelsh wove paper 1,100.
PR110TC1a $10 large die on India paper
e. **black** *675.*
PR110P1 $10 **grn,** large die on India paper 110.
PR110P2 $10 **grn,** RA sm die on white wove paper 100.
PR110P2a $10 **grn,** PP sm die on yelsh wove paper 1,100.
PR111P1 $20 **slate,** large die on India paper 110.
PR111P2 $20 **slate,** RA sm die on white wove paper 100.
PR111P2a $20 **slate,** PP sm die on yelsh wove paper 1,100.
PR112TC1a $50 large die on India paper
e. **black** *675.*
f. **deep rose** *675.*
g. **dark rose** *675.*
PR112P1 $50 **car,** large die on India paper 110.
PR112P2 $50 **car,** RA sm die on white wove paper 100.
PR112P2a $50 **car,** PP sm die on yelsh wove paper 1,100.
PR113TC1a $100 large die on India paper
e. **black** *675.*
PR113P1 $100 **pur,** large die on India paper 110.
PR113P2 $100 **pur,** RA sm die on white wove paper 100.
PR113P2a $100 **pur,** PP sm die on yelsh wove paper 1,100.

The so-called "Goodall" set of Small Die proofs on India Paper of Newspaper Stamps in five colors

PR9TC2 2c "Goodall" small die on India paper
b. **black** 150.
d. **deep green** 125.
d. **dull gray blue** 125.
e. **deep brown** 125.
f. **dull red** 125.
PR10TC2 3c "Goodall" small die on India paper
b. **black** 150.
c. **deep green** 125.
d. **dull gray blue** 125.
e. **deep brown** 125.
f. **dull red** 125.
PR11TC2 4c "Goodall" small die on India paper
b. **black** 150.
c. **deep green** 125.
d. **dull gray blue** 125.
e. **deep brown** 125.
f. **dull red** 125.
PR12TC2 6c "Goodall" small die on India paper
b. **black** 150.
c. **deep green** 125.
d. **dull gray blue** 125.
e. **deep brown** 125.
f. **dull red** 125.
PR13TC2 8c "Goodall" small die on India paper
b. **black** 150.
c. **deep green** 125.
d. **dull gray blue** 125.
e. **deep brown** 125.
f. **dull red** 125.
PR14TC2 9c "Goodall" small die on India paper
b. **black** 150.
c. **deep green** 125.
d. **dull gray blue** 125.
e. **deep brown** 125.
f. **dull red** 125.

PR15TC2 10c "Goodall" small die on India paper
b. **black** 150.
c. **deep green** 125.
d. **dull gray blue** 125.
e. **deep brown** 125.
f. **dull red** 125.

PR16TC2 12c "Goodall" small die on India paper
b. **black** 150.
c. **deep green** 125.
d. **dull gray blue** 125.
e. **deep brown** 125.
f. **dull red** 125.

PR17TC2 24c "Goodall" small die on India paper
b. **black** 150.
c. **deep green** 125.
d. **dull gray blue** 125.
e. **deep brown** 125.
f. **dull red** 125.

PR18TC2 36c "Goodall" small die on India paper
b. **black** 150.
c. **deep green** 125.
d. **dull gray blue** 125.
e. **deep brown** 125.
f. **dull red** 125.

PR19TC2 48c "Goodall" small die on India paper
b. **black** 150.
c. **deep green** 125.
d. **dull gray blue** 125.
e. **deep brown** 125.
f. **dull red** 125.

PR20TC2 60c "Goodall" small die on India paper
b. **black** 150.
c. **deep green** 125.
d. **dull gray blue** 125.
e. **deep brown** 125.
f. **dull red** 125.

PR21TC2 72c "Goodall" small die on India paper
b. **black** 150.
c. **deep green** 125.
d. **dull gray blue** 125.
e. **deep brown** 125.
f. **dull red** 125.

PR22TC2 84c "Goodall" small die on India paper
b. **black** 150.
c. **deep green** 125.
d. **dull gray blue** 125.
e. **deep brown** 125.
f. **dull red** 125.

PR23TC2 96c "Goodall" small die on India paper
b. **black** 150.
c. **deep green** 125.
d. **dull gray blue** 125.
e. **deep brown** 125.
f. **dull red** 125.

PR24TC2 $1.92 "Goodall" small die on India paper
b. **black** 150.
c. **deep green** 125.
d. **dull gray blue** 125.
e. **deep brown** 125.
f. **dull red** 125.

PR25TC2 $3 "Goodall" small die on India paper
b. **black** 150.
c. **deep green** 125.
d. **dull gray blue** 125.
e. **deep brown** 125.
f. **dull red** 125.

PR26TC2 $6 "Goodall" small die on India paper
b. **black** 150.
c. **deep green** 125.
d. **dull gray blue** 125.
e. **deep brown** 125.
f. **dull red** 125.

PR27TC2 $9 "Goodall" small die on India paper
b. **black** 150.
c. **deep green** 125.
d. **dull gray blue** 125.
e. **deep brown** 125.
f. **dull red** 125.

PR28TC2 $12 "Goodall" small die on India paper
b. **black** 150.
c. **deep green** 125.
d. **dull gray blue** 125.
e. **deep brown** 125.
f. **dull red** 125.

PR29TC2 $24 "Goodall" small die on India paper
b. **black** 150.
c. **deep green** 125.
d. **dull gray blue** 125.
e. **deep brown** 125.
f. **dull red** 125.

PR30TC2 $36 "Goodall" small die on India paper
b. **black** 150.
c. **deep green** 125.
d. **dull gray blue** 125.
e. **deep brown** 125.
f. **dull red** 125.

PR31TC2 $48 "Goodall" small die on India paper
b. **black** 150.
c. **deep green** 125.
d. **dull gray blue** 125.
e. **deep brown** 125.
f. **dull red** 125.

PR32TC2 $60 "Goodall" small die on India paper
b. **black** 150.
c. **deep green** 125.
d. **dull gray blue** 125.
e. **deep brown** 125.
f. **dull red** 125.

PARCEL POST

1912-13

Q1P1 1c **car rose,** large die on India paper 1,400.
Q1P2 1c **car rose,** sm die on India paper 1,200.
Q1P2a 1c **car rose,** PP sm die on yelsh wove paper 2,500.
Q2P1 2c **car rose,** large die on India paper 1,400.
Q2P2 2c **car rose,** sm die on India paper 1,200.
Q2P2a 2c **car rose,** PP sm die on yelsh wove paper 2,500.
Q3P1 3c **car rose,** large die on India paper 1,400.
Q3P2 3c **car rose,** sm die on India paper 1,200.
Q3P2a 3c **car rose,** PP sm die on yelsh wove paper 2,500.
Q4P1 4c **car rose,** large die on India paper 1,400.
Q4P2 4c **car rose,** sm die on India paper 1,200.
Q4P2a 4c **car rose,** PP sm die on yelsh wove paper 2,500.
Q5P1 5c **car rose,** large die on India paper 1,400.
Q5P2 5c **car rose,** sm die on India paper 1,200.
Q5P2a 5c **car rose,** PP sm die on yelsh wove paper 2,500.
Q6P1 10c **car rose,** large die on India paper 1,400.
Q6P2 10c **car rose,** sm die on India paper 1,200.
Q6P2a 10c **car rose,** PP sm die on yelsh wove paper 2,500.
Q7P1 15c **car rose,** large die on India paper 1,400.
Q7P2 15c **car rose,** sm die on India paper 1,200.
Q7P2a 15c **car rose,** PP sm die on yelsh wove paper 2,500.
Q8P1 20c **car rose,** large die on India paper 1,400.
Q8P2 20c **car rose,** sm die on India paper 1,200.
Q8P2a 20c **car rose,** PP sm die on yelsh wove paper 2,500.
Q9P1 25c **car rose,** large die on India paper 1,400.
Q9P2 25c **car rose,** sm die on India paper 1,200.
Q9P2a 25c **car rose,** PP sm die on yelsh wove paper 2,500.
Q10P1 50c **car rose,** large die on India paper 1,400.
Q10P2 50c **car rose,** sm die on India paper 1,200.
Q10P2a 50c **car rose,** PP sm die on yelsh wove paper 2,500.
Q11P1 75c **car rose,** large die on India paper 1,400.
Q11P2 75c **car rose,** sm die on India paper 1,200.
Q11P2a 75c **car rose,** PP sm die on yelsh wove paper 2,500.
Q12P1 $1 **car rose,** large die on India paper 1,400.
Q12P2 $1 **car rose,** sm die on India paper 1,200.
Q12P2a $1 **car rose,** PP sm die on yelsh wove paper 2,500.

SPECIAL HANDLING

1925-28

QE1P1 10c **yel grn,** large die on India paper *2,500.*
QE2P1 15c **yel grn,** large die on India paper *2,500.*
QE3P1 20c **yel grn,** large die on India paper *2,500.*
QE4TC1a 25c large die on India paper
e. **apple green** *3,250.*
f. **olive green** *3,250.*
g. **light blue green** *3,250.*
h. **blue** *3,250.*
i. **dark blue** *3,250.*
j. **orange yellow** *3,250.*
k. **orange** *3,250.*
l. **dull rose** *3,250.*
m. **carmine lake** *3,250.*
n. **carmine rose** *3,250.*
o. **brown** *3,250.*
p. **gray brown** *3,250.*
q. **dark violet brown** *3,250.*
r. **gray black** *3,250.*
s. **black** *3,250.*
QE4P1 25c **dp grn,** large die on India paper *2,500.*
QE4aP1 25c **yel grn,** large die on India paper *3,250.*

THE "ATLANTA" SET OF PLATE PROOFS

A set in five colors on thin card reprinted in 1881 for display at the International Cotton Exhibition in Atlanta, Ga. Blocks exist; they are very rare.

1847 Designs (Reproductions)

3TC4 5c Atlanta plate on card
a. **black** 450.
b. **scarlet** 450.
c. **brown** 450.
d. **green** 450.
e. **blue** 450.

4TC4 10c Atlanta plate on card
a. **black** 450.
b. **scarlet** 450.
c. **brown** 450.
d. **green** 450.
e. **blue** 450.

1851-60 Designs

40TC4 1c Atlanta plate on card
a. **black** 100.
b. **scarlet** 80.
c. **brown** 80.
d. **green** 80.
e. **blue** 80.

41TC4 3c Atlanta plate on card
a. **black** 100.
b. **scarlet** 80.
c. **brown** 80.
d. **green** 80.
e. **blue** 80.

42TC4 5c Atlanta plate on card
a. **black** 100.
b. **scarlet** 80.
c. **brown** 80.
d. **green** 80.
e. **blue** 80.

43TC4 10c Atlanta plate on card
a. **black** 100.
b. **scarlet** 80.
c. **brown** 80.
d. **green** 80.
e. **blue** 80.

44TC4 12c Atlanta plate on card
a. **black** 100.
b. **scarlet** 80.
c. **brown** 80.
d. **green** 80.
e. **blue** 80.

45TC4 24c Atlanta plate on card
a. **black** 100.
b. **scarlet** 80.
c. **brown** 80.
d. **green** 80.
e. **blue** 80.

46TC4 30c Atlanta plate on card
a. **black** 100.
b. **scarlet** 80.
c. **brown** 80.
d. **green** 80.
e. **blue** 80.

47TC4 90c Atlanta plate on card
a. **black** 100.
b. **scarlet** 80.
c. **brown** 80.
d. **green** 80.
e. **blue** 80.

1861-66 Designs

102TC4 1c Atlanta plate on card
a. **black** 100.
b. **scarlet** 90.
c. **brown** 90.
d. **green** 90.
e. **blue** 90.

103TC4 2c Atlanta plate on card
a. **black** 175.
b. **scarlet** 175.
c. **brown** 175.
d. **green** 175.
e. **blue** 175.

104TC4 3c Atlanta plate on card
a. **black** 100.
b. **scarlet** 90.
c. **brown** 90.
d. **green** 90.
e. **blue** 90.

105TC4 5c Atlanta plate on card
a. **black** 100.
b. **scarlet** 90.
c. **brown** 90.
d. **green** 90.
e. **blue** 90.

106TC4 10c Atlanta plate on card
a. **black** 100.
b. **scarlet** 90.
c. **brown** 90.
d. **green** 90.
e. **blue** 90.

107TC4 12c Atlanta plate on card
a. **black** 100.
b. **scarlet** 90.
c. **brown** 90.
d. **green** 90.
e. **blue** 90.

108TC4 15c Atlanta plate on card
a. **black** 100.
b. **scarlet** 90.
c. **brown** 90.
d. **green** 90.
e. **blue** 90.

109TC4 24c Atlanta plate on card
a. **black** 100.
b. **scarlet** 90.
c. **brown** 90.
d. **green** 90.
e. **blue** 90.

110TC4 30c Atlanta plate on card
a. **black** 100.
b. **scarlet** 90.
c. **brown** 90.
d. **green** 90.
e. **blue** 90.

111TC4 90c Atlanta plate on card
a. **black** 100.
b. **scarlet** 90.
c. **brown** 90.
d. **green** 90.
e. **blue** 90.

1869 Designs

123TC4 1c Atlanta plate on card
a. **black** 150.
b. **scarlet** 125.
c. **brown** 125.
d. **green** 125.
e. **blue** 125.

124TC4 2c Atlanta plate on card
a. **black** 150.
b. **scarlet** 125.
c. **brown** 125.
d. **green** 125.
e. **blue** 125.

125TC4 3c Atlanta plate on card
a. **black** 150.
b. **scarlet** 125.
c. **brown** 125.
d. **green** 125.
e. **blue** 125.

126TC4 6c Atlanta plate on card
a. **black** 150.
b. **scarlet** 125.
c. **brown** 125.
d. **green** 125.
e. **blue** 125.

127TC4 10c Atlanta plate on card
a. **black** 150.
b. **scarlet** 125.
c. **brown** 125.
d. **green** 125.
e. **blue** 125.

128TC4 12c Atlanta plate on card
a. **black** 150.
b. **scarlet** 125.
c. **brown** 125.
d. **green** 125.
e. **blue** 125.

129TC4	15c Atlanta plate on card	
a.	black frame, scarlet center	325.
b.	black frame, green center	325.
c.	scarlet frame, black center	325.
d.	scarlet frame, blue center	325.
e.	brown frame, black center	325.
f.	brown frame, green center	325.
g.	brown frame, blue center	325.
h.	green frame, black center	325.
i.	green frame, blue center	325.
j.	blue frame, black center	325.
k.	blue frame, brown center	325.
l.	blue frame, green center	325.
130TC4	24c Atlanta plate on card	
a.	black frame, scarlet center	325.
b.	black frame, green center	325.
c.	black frame, blue center	325.
d.	scarlet frame, black center	325.
e.	scarlet frame, blue center	325.
f.	brown frame, black center	325.
g.	brown frame, blue center	325.
h.	green frame, black center	325.
i.	green frame, brown center	325.
j.	green frame, blue center	325.
k.	blue frame, brown center	325.
l.	blue frame, green center	325.
131TC4	30c Atlanta plate on card	
a.	black frame, scarlet center	325.
b.	black frame, green center	325.
c.	black frame, blue center	325.
d.	scarlet frame, black center	325.
e.	scarlet frame, green center	325.
f.	scarlet frame, blue center	325.
g.	brown frame, black center	325.
h.	brown frame, scarlet center	325.
i.	brown frame, blue center	325.
j.	green frame, black center	325.
k.	green frame, brown center	325.
l.	blue frame, scarlet center	325.
m.	blue frame, brown center	325.
n.	blue frame, green center	325.
132TC4	90c Atlanta plate on card	
a.	black frame, scarlet center	500.
b.	black frame, brown center	500.
c.	black frame, green center	500.
d.	scarlet frame, blue center	500.
e.	brown frame, black center	500.
f.	brown frame, blue center	500.
g.	green frame, black center	*10,000.*
h.	green frame, brown center	500.
i.	green frame, blue center	500.
j.	blue frame, brown center	500.
k.	blue frame, green center	500.

1873-75 Designs

156TC4	1c Atlanta plate on card	
a.	black	80.
b.	scarlet	75.
c.	brown	75.
d.	green	75.
e.	blue	75.
157TC4	2c Atlanta plate on card	
a.	black	80.
b.	scarlet	75.
c.	brown	75.
d.	green	75.
e.	blue	75.
158TC4	3c Atlanta plate on card	
a.	black	90.
b.	scarlet	85.
c.	brown	85.
d.	green	85.
e.	blue	85.
159TC4	6c Atlanta plate on card	
a.	black	90.
b.	scarlet	85.
c.	brown	85.
d.	green	85.
e.	blue	85.
160TC4	7c Atlanta plate on card	
a.	black	80.
b.	scarlet	75.
c.	brown	75.
d.	green	75.
e.	blue	75.
161TC4	10c Atlanta plate on card	
a.	black	80.
b.	scarlet	75.
c.	brown	75.
d.	green	75.
e.	blue	75.
162TC4	12c Atlanta plate on card	
a.	black	80.
b.	scarlet	75.
c.	brown	75.
d.	green	75.
e.	blue	75.
163TC4	15c Atlanta plate on card	
a.	black	80.
b.	scarlet	75.
c.	brown	75.
d.	green	75.
e.	blue	75.
164TC4	24c Atlanta plate on card	
a.	black	80.
b.	scarlet	75.
c.	brown	75.
d.	green	75.
e.	blue	75.
165TC4	30c Atlanta plate on card	
a.	black	80.
b.	scarlet	75.
c.	brown	75.
d.	green	75.
e.	blue	75.
166TC4	90c Atlanta plate on card	
a.	black	80.
b.	scarlet	75.
c.	brown	75.
d.	green	75.
e.	blue	75.
179TC4	5c Atlanta plate on card	
a.	black	80.
b.	scarlet	75.
c.	brown	75.
d.	green	75.
e.	blue	75.

POSTAGE DUE

J1TC4	1c Atlanta plate on card	
a.	black	55.
b.	scarlet	50.
c.	brown	50.
d.	green	50.
e.	blue	50.
J2TC4	2c Atlanta plate on card	
a.	black	55.
b.	scarlet	50.
c.	brown	50.
d.	green	50.
e.	blue	50.
J3TC4	3c Atlanta plate on card	
a.	black	55.
b.	scarlet	50.
c.	brown	50.
d.	green	50.
e.	blue	50.
J4TC4	5c Atlanta plate on card	
a.	black	55.
b.	scarlet	50.
c.	brown	50.
d.	green	50.
e.	blue	50.
J5TC4	10c Atlanta plate on card	
a.	black	55.
b.	scarlet	50.
c.	brown	50.
d.	green	50.
e.	blue	50.
J6TC4	30c Atlanta plate on card	
a.	black	55.
b.	scarlet	50.
c.	brown	50.
d.	green	50.
e.	blue	50.
J7TC4	50c Atlanta plate on card	
a.	black	55.
b.	scarlet	50.
c.	brown	50.
d.	green	50.
e.	blue	50.

OFFICIALS

Agriculture

O1TC4	1c Atlanta plate on card	
a.	black	43.
b.	scarlet	37.
c.	brown	37.
d.	green	37.
e.	blue	37.
O2TC4	2c Atlanta plate on card	
a.	black	43.
b.	scarlet	37.
c.	brown	37.
d.	green	37.
e.	blue	37.
O3TC4	3c Atlanta plate on card	
a.	black	43.
b.	scarlet	37.
c.	brown	37.
d.	green	37.
e.	blue	37.
O4TC4	6c Atlanta plate on card	
a.	black	55.
b.	scarlet	50.
c.	brown	50.
d.	green	50.
e.	blue	50.
O5TC4	10c Atlanta plate on card	
a.	black	43.
b.	scarlet	37.
c.	brown	37.
d.	green	37.
e.	blue	37.
O6TC4	12c Atlanta plate on card	
a.	black	43.
b.	scarlet	37.
c.	brown	37.
d.	green	37.
e.	blue	37.
O7TC4	15c Atlanta plate on card	
a.	black	43.
b.	scarlet	37.
c.	brown	37.
d.	green	37.
e.	blue	37.
O8TC4	24c Atlanta plate on card	
a.	black	43.
b.	scarlet	37.
c.	brown	37.
d.	green	37.
e.	blue	37.
O9TC4	30c Atlanta plate on card	
a.	black	43.
b.	scarlet	37.
c.	brown	37.
d.	green	37.
e.	blue	37.

Executive

O10TC4	1c Atlanta plate on card	
a.	black	43.
b.	scarlet	37.
c.	brown	37.
d.	green	37.
e.	blue	37.
O11TC4	2c Atlanta plate on card	
a.	black	43.
b.	scarlet	37.
c.	brown	37.
d.	green	37.
e.	blue	37.
O12TC4	3c Atlanta plate on card	
a.	black	43.
b.	scarlet	37.
c.	brown	37.
d.	green	37.
e.	blue	37.
O13TC4	6c Atlanta plate on card	
a.	black	43.
b.	scarlet	37.
c.	brown	37.
d.	green	37.
e.	blue	37.
O14TC4	10c Atlanta plate on card	
a.	black	43.
b.	scarlet	37.
c.	brown	37.
d.	green	37.
e.	blue	37.

Interior

O15TC4	1c Atlanta plate on card	
a.	black	43.
b.	scarlet	37.
c.	brown	37.
d.	green	37.
e.	blue	37.
O16TC4	2c Atlanta plate on card	
a.	black	43.
b.	scarlet	37.
c.	brown	37.
d.	green	37.
e.	blue	37.
O17TC4	3c Atlanta plate on card	
a.	black	43.
b.	scarlet	37.
c.	brown	37.
d.	green	37.
e.	blue	37.
O18TC4	6c Atlanta plate on card	
a.	black	55.
b.	scarlet	50.
c.	brown	50.
d.	green	50.
e.	blue	50.
O19TC4	10c Atlanta plate on card	
a.	black	43.
b.	scarlet	37.
c.	brown	37.
d.	green	37.
e.	blue	37.
O20TC4	12c Atlanta plate on card	
a.	black	43.
b.	scarlet	37.
c.	brown	37.
d.	green	37.
e.	blue	37.
O21TC4	15c Atlanta plate on card	
a.	black	43.
b.	scarlet	37.
c.	brown	37.
d.	green	37.
e.	blue	37.
O22TC4	24c Atlanta plate on card	
a.	black	43.
b.	scarlet	37.
c.	brown	37.
d.	green	37.
e.	blue	37.
O23TC4	30c Atlanta plate on card	
a.	black	60.
b.	scarlet	55.
c.	brown	55.
d.	green	55.
e.	blue	55.
O24TC4	90c Atlanta plate on card	
a.	black	43.
b.	scarlet	37.
c.	brown	37.
d.	green	37.
e.	blue	37.

Justice

O25TC4	1c Atlanta plate on card	
a.	black	43.
b.	scarlet	37.
c.	brown	37.
d.	green	37.
e.	blue	37.
O26TC4	2c Atlanta plate on card	
a.	black	43.
b.	scarlet	37.
c.	brown	37.
d.	green	37.
e.	blue	37.
O27TC4	3c Atlanta plate on card	
a.	black	43.
b.	scarlet	37.
c.	brown	37.
d.	green	37.
e.	blue	37.
O28TC4	6c Atlanta plate on card	
a.	black	55.
b.	scarlet	50.
c.	brown	50.
d.	green	50.
e.	blue	50.
O29TC4	10c Atlanta plate on card	
a.	black	43.
b.	scarlet	37.
c.	brown	37.
d.	green	37.
e.	blue	37.

O30TC4 12c Atlanta plate on card
a. **black** 43.
b. **scarlet** 37.
c. **brown** 37.
d. **green** 37.
e. **blue** 37.
O31TC4 15c Atlanta plate on card
a. **black** 43.
b. **scarlet** 37.
c. **brown** 37.
d. **green** 37.
e. **blue** 37.
O32TC4 24c Atlanta plate on card
a. **black** 43.
b. **scarlet** 37.
c. **brown** 37.
d. **green** 37.
e. **blue** 37.
O33TC4 30c Atlanta plate on card
a. **black** 60.
b. **scarlet** 55.
c. **brown** 55.
d. **green** 55.
e. **blue** 55.
O34TC4 90c Atlanta plate on card
a. **black** 43.
b. **scarlet** 37.
c. **brown** 37.
d. **green** 37.
e. **blue** 37.

Navy

O35TC4 1c Atlanta plate on card
a. **black** 43.
b. **scarlet** 37.
c. **brown** 37.
d. **green** 37.
e. **blue** 37.
O36TC4 2c Atlanta plate on card
a. **black** 43.
b. **scarlet** 37.
c. **brown** 37.
d. **green** 37.
e. **blue** 37.
O37TC4 3c Atlanta plate on card
a. **black** 43.
b. **scarlet** 37.
c. **brown** 37.
d. **green** 37.
e. **blue** 37.
O38TC4 6c Atlanta plate on card
a. **black** 55.
b. **scarlet** 50.
c. **brown** 50.
d. **green** 50.
e. **blue** 50.
O39TC4 7c Atlanta plate on card
a. **black** 43.
b. **scarlet** 37.
c. **brown** 37.
d. **green** 37.
e. **blue** 37.
O40TC4 10c Atlanta plate on card
a. **black** 43.
b. **scarlet** 37.
c. **brown** 37.
d. **green** 37.
e. **blue** 37.
O41TC4 12c Atlanta plate on card
a. **black** 43.
b. **scarlet** 37.
c. **brown** 37.
d. **green** 37.
e. **blue** 37.
O42TC4 15c Atlanta plate on card
a. **black** 43.
b. **scarlet** 37.
c. **brown** 37.
d. **green** 37.
e. **blue** 37.
O43TC4 24c Atlanta plate on card
a. **black** 43.
b. **scarlet** 37.
c. **brown** 37.
d. **green** 37.
e. **blue** 37.
O44TC4 30c Atlanta plate on card
a. **black** 60.
b. **scarlet** 55.
c. **brown** 55.
d. **green** 55.
e. **blue** 55.
O45TC4 90c Atlanta plate on card
a. **black** 43.
b. **scarlet** 37.
c. **brown** 37.
d. **green** 37.
e. **blue** 37.

Post Office

O48TC4 2c Atlanta plate on card
a. **black** 43.
b. **scarlet** 37.
c. **brown** 37.
d. **green** 37.
e. **blue** 37.
O49TC4 3c Atlanta plate on card
a. **black** 43.
b. **scarlet** 37.
c. **brown** 37.
d. **green** 37.
e. **blue** 37.
O50TC4 6c Atlanta plate on card
a. **black** 43.
b. **scarlet** 37.
c. **brown** 37.
d. **green** 37.
e. **blue** 37.
O51TC4 10c Atlanta plate on card
a. **black** 43.
b. **scarlet** 37.
c. **brown** 37.
d. **green** 37.
e. **blue** 37.
O52TC4 12c Atlanta plate on card
a. **black** 43.
b. **scarlet** 37.
c. **brown** 37.
d. **green** 37.
e. **blue** 37.
O53TC4 15c Atlanta plate on card
a. **black** 43.
b. **scarlet** 37.
c. **brown** 37.
d. **green** 37.
e. **blue** 37.
O54TC4 24c Atlanta plate on card
a. **black** 43.
b. **scarlet** 37.
c. **brown** 37.
d. **green** 37.
e. **blue** 37.
O55TC4 30c Atlanta plate on card
a. **black** 43.
b. **scarlet** 37.
c. **brown** 37.
d. **green** 37.
e. **blue** 37.
O56TC4 90c Atlanta plate on card
a. **black** 43.
b. **scarlet** 37.
c. **brown** 37.
d. **green** 37.
e. **blue** 37.

State

O57TC4 1c Atlanta plate on card
a. **black** 43.
b. **scarlet** 37.
c. **brown** 37.
d. **green** 37.
e. **blue** 37.
O58TC4 2c Atlanta plate on card
a. **black** 43.
b. **scarlet** 37.
c. **brown** 37.
d. **green** 37.
e. **blue** 37.
O59TC4 3c Atlanta plate on card
a. **black** 43.
b. **scarlet** 37.
c. **brown** 37.
d. **green** 37.
e. **blue** 37.
O60TC4 6c Atlanta plate on card
a. **black** 55.
b. **scarlet** 50.
c. **brown** 50.
d. **green** 50.
e. **blue** 50.
O61TC4 7c Atlanta plate on card
a. **black** 43.
b. **scarlet** 37.
c. **brown** 37.
d. **green** 37.
e. **blue** 37.
O62TC4 10c Atlanta plate on card
a. **black** 43.
b. **scarlet** 37.
c. **brown** 37.
d. **green** 37.
e. **blue** 37.
O63TC4 12c Atlanta plate on card
a. **black** 43.
b. **scarlet** 37.
c. **brown** 37.
d. **green** 37.
e. **blue** 37.
O64TC4 15c Atlanta plate on card
a. **black** 43.
b. **scarlet** 37.
c. **brown** 37.
d. **green** 37.
e. **blue** 37.
O65TC4 24c Atlanta plate on card
a. **black** 43.
b. **scarlet** 37.
c. **brown** 37.
d. **green** 37.
e. **blue** 37.
O66TC4 30c Atlanta plate on card
a. **black** 60.
b. **scarlet** 55.
c. **brown** 55.
d. **green** 55.
e. **blue** 55.
O67TC4 90c Atlanta plate on card
a. **black** 43.
b. **scarlet** 37.
c. **brown** 37.
d. **green** 37.
e. **blue** 37.
O68TC4 $2 Atlanta plate on card
a. **scarlet frame, black center** 1,000.
b. **scarlet frame, blue center** 1,000.
c. **brown frame, black center** 1,000.
d. **brown frame, blue center** 1,000.
e. **green frame, brown center** 1,000.
f. **blue frame, brown center** 1,000.
g. **blue frame, green center** 1,000.
O69TC4 $5 Atlanta plate on card
a. **scarlet frame, black center** 1,000.
b. **scarlet frame, blue center** 1,000.
c. **brown frame, black center** 1,000.
d. **brown frame, blue center** 1,000.
e. **green frame, brown center** 1,000.
f. **blue frame, brown center** 1,000.
g. **blue frame, green center** 1,000.
O70TC4 $10 Atlanta plate on card
a. **scarlet frame, black center** 1,000.
b. **scarlet frame, blue center** 1,000.
c. **brown frame, black center** 1,000.
d. **brown frame, blue center** 1,000.
e. **green frame, brown center** 1,000.
f. **blue frame, brown center** 1,000.
g. **blue frame, green center** 1,000.
O71TC4 $20 Atlanta plate on card
a. **scarlet frame, black center** 1,000.
b. **scarlet frame, blue center** 1,000.
c. **brown frame, black center** 1,000.
d. **brown frame, blue center** 1,000.
e. **green frame, brown center** 1,000.
f. **blue frame, brown center** 1,000.
g. **blue frame, green center** 1,000.

Treasury

O72TC4 1c Atlanta plate on card
a. **black** 43.
b. **scarlet** 37.
c. **brown** 37.
d. **green** 37.
e. **blue** 37.
O73TC4 2c Atlanta plate on card
a. **black** 43.
b. **scarlet** 37.
c. **brown** 37.
d. **green** 37.
e. **blue** 37.
O74TC4 3c Atlanta plate on card
a. **black** 43.
b. **scarlet** 37.
c. **brown** 37.
d. **green** 37.
e. **blue** 37.
O75TC4 6c Atlanta plate on card
a. **black** 55.
b. **scarlet** 50.
c. **brown** 50.
d. **green** 50.
e. **blue** 50.
O76TC4 7c Atlanta plate on card
a. **black** 43.
b. **scarlet** 37.
c. **brown** 37.
d. **green** 37.
e. **blue** 37.
O77TC4 10c Atlanta plate on card
a. **black** 43.
b. **scarlet** 37.
c. **brown** 37.
d. **green** 37.
e. **blue** 37.
O78TC4 12c Atlanta plate on card
a. **black** 43.
b. **scarlet** 37.
c. **brown** 37.
d. **green** 37.
e. **blue** 37.
O79TC4 15c Atlanta plate on card
a. **black** 43.
b. **scarlet** 37.
c. **brown** 37.
d. **green** 37.
e. **blue** 37.
O80TC4 24c Atlanta plate on card
a. **black** 43.
b. **scarlet** 37.
c. **brown** 37.
d. **green** 37.
e. **blue** 37.
O81TC4 30c Atlanta plate on card
a. **black** 60.
b. **scarlet** 55.
c. **brown** 55.
d. **green** 55.
e. **blue** 55.
O82TC4 90c Atlanta plate on card
a. **black** 43.
b. **scarlet** 37.
c. **brown** 37.
d. **green** 37.
e. **blue** 37.

War

O83TC4 1c Atlanta plate on card
a. **black** 43.
b. **scarlet** 37.
c. **brown** 37.
d. **green** 37.
e. **blue** 37.
O84TC4 2c Atlanta plate on card
a. **black** 43.
b. **scarlet** 37.
c. **brown** 37.
d. **green** 37.
e. **blue** 37.
O85TC4 3c Atlanta plate on card
a. **black** 43.
b. **scarlet** 37.
c. **brown** 37.
Plate flaw at upper left (32R20) —
d. **green** 37.
e. **blue** 37.
O86TC4 6c Atlanta plate on card
a. **black** 55.
b. **scarlet** 50.
c. **brown** 50.
d. **green** 50.
e. **blue** 50.
O87TC4 7c Atlanta plate on card
a. **black** 43.
b. **scarlet** 37.
c. **brown** 37.
d. **green** 37.
e. **blue** 37.

O88TC4 10c Atlanta plate on card
a. **black** 43.
b. **scarlet** 37.
c. **brown** 37.
d. **green** 37.
e. **blue** 37.
O89TC4 12c Atlanta plate on card
a. **black** 43.
b. **scarlet** 37.
c. **brown** 37.
d. **green** 37.
e. **blue** 37.
O90TC4 15c Atlanta plate on card
a. **black** 43.
b. **scarlet** 37.
c. **brown** 37.
d. **green** 37.
e. **blue** 37.
O91TC4 24c Atlanta plate on card
a. **black** 43.
b. **scarlet** 37.
c. **brown** 37.
d. **green** 37.
e. **blue** 37.
O92TC4 30c Atlanta plate on card
a. **black** 60.
b. **scarlet** 55.
c. **brown** 55.
d. **green** 55.
e. **blue** 55.
O93TC4 90c Atlanta plate on card
a. **black** 43.
b. **scarlet** 37.
c. **brown** 37.
d. **green** 37.
e. **blue** 37.

NEWSPAPERS

PR9TC4 2c Atlanta plate on card
a. **black** 55.
b. **scarlet** 40.
c. **brown** 40.
d. **green** 40.
e. **blue** 40.
PR10TC4 3c Atlanta plate on card
a. **black** 55.
b. **scarlet** 40.
c. **brown** 40.
d. **green** 40.
e. **blue** 40.
PR11TC4 4c Atlanta plate on card
a. **black** 55.
b. **scarlet** 40.
c. **brown** 40.
d. **green** 40.
e. **blue** 40.
PR12TC4 6c Atlanta plate on card
a. **black** 55.
b. **scarlet** 40.
c. **brown** 40.
d. **green** 40.
e. **blue** 40.
PR13TC4 8c Atlanta plate on card
a. **black** 55.
b. **scarlet** 40.
c. **brown** 40.
d. **green** 40.
e. **blue** 40.
PR14TC4 9c Atlanta plate on card
a. **black** 55.
b. **scarlet** 40.
c. **brown** 40.
d. **green** 40.
e. **blue** 40.
PR15TC4 10c Atlanta plate on card
a. **black** 55.
b. **scarlet** 40.
c. **brown** 40.
d. **green** 40.
e. **blue** 40.
PR16TC4 12c Atlanta plate on card
a. **black** 55.
b. **scarlet** 40.
c. **brown** 40.
d. **green** 40.
e. **blue** 40.
PR17TC4 24c Atlanta plate on card
a. **black** 55.
b. **scarlet** 40.
c. **brown** 40.
d. **green** 40.
e. **blue** 40.
PR18TC4 36c Atlanta plate on card
a. **black** 55.
b. **scarlet** 40.
c. **brown** 40.
d. **green** 40.
e. **blue** 40.
PR19TC4 48c Atlanta plate on card
a. **black** 55.
b. **scarlet** 40.
c. **brown** 40.
d. **green** 40.
e. **blue** 40.
PR20TC4 60c Atlanta plate on card
a. **black** 55.
b. **scarlet** 40.
c. **brown** 40.
d. **green** 40.
e. **blue** 40.
PR21TC4 72c Atlanta plate on card
a. **black** 55.
b. **scarlet** 40.
c. **brown** 40.
d. **green** 40.
e. **blue** 40.
PR22TC4 84c Atlanta plate on card
a. **black** 55.
b. **scarlet** 40.
c. **brown** 40.
d. **green** 40.
e. **blue** 40.
PR23TC4 96c Atlanta plate on card
a. **black** 55.
b. **scarlet** 40.
c. **brown** 40.
d. **green** 40.
e. **blue** 40.
PR24TC4 $1.92 Atlanta plate on card
a. **black** 55.
b. **scarlet** 40.
c. **brown** 40.
d. **green** 40.
e. **blue** 40.
PR25TC4 $3 Atlanta plate on card
a. **black** 55.
b. **scarlet** 40.
c. **brown** 40.
d. **green** 40.
e. **blue** 40.
PR26TC4 $6 Atlanta plate on card
a. **black** 55.
b. **scarlet** 40.
c. **brown** 40.
d. **green** 40.
e. **blue** 40.
PR27TC4 $9 Atlanta plate on card
a. **black** 55.
b. **scarlet** 40.
c. **brown** 40.
d. **green** 40.
e. **blue** 40.
PR28TC4 $12 Atlanta plate on card
a. **black** 55.
b. **scarlet** 40.
c. **brown** 40.
d. **green** 40.
e. **blue** 40.
PR29TC4 $24 Atlanta plate on card
a. **black** 55.
b. **scarlet** 40.
c. **brown** 40.
d. **green** 40.
e. **blue** 40.
PR30TC4 $36 Atlanta plate on card
a. **black** 55.
b. **scarlet** 40.
c. **brown** 40.
d. **green** 40.
e. **blue** 40.
PR31TC4 $48 Atlanta plate on card
a. **black** 55.
b. **scarlet** 40.
c. **brown** 40.
d. **green** 40.
e. **blue** 40.
PR32TC4 $60 Atlanta plate on card
a. **black** 55.
b. **scarlet** 40.
c. **brown** 40.
d. **green** 40.
e. **blue** 40.

CARRIERS

LO1TC4 1c Franklin, Atlanta plate on card
a. **black** 120.
b. **scarlet** 110.
c. **brown** 110.
d. **green** 110.
e. **blue** 110.
LO2TC4 1c Eagle, Atlanta plate on card
a. **black** 120.
b. **scarlet** 110.
c. **brown** 110.
d. **green** 110.
e. **blue** 110.

TELEGRAPH

1881 American Rapid Telegraph Co.

1T1TC2 1c small die on India paper
b. **green** 55.
c. **brown** 55.
d. **red** 55.
e. **blue** 55.
f. **bluish green** 55.
1T1P2 1c **blk,** sm die on India paper 80.
1T1P3 1c **blk,** plate on India paper 32.
Pair 68.
1T2P3 3c **org,** plate on India paper 32.
Pair 68.
1T3TC2 5c small die on India paper
b. **green** 55.
c. **black** 55.
d. **red** 55.
e. **blue** 55.
f. **bluish green** 55.
1T3P2 5c **bis brn,** sm die on India paper 80.
1T3P3 5c **bis brn,** plate on India paper 32.
Pair 68.
1T4P1 10c **pur,** large die on India paper *850.*
1T4P3 10c **pur,** plate on India paper 32.
Pair 68.
1T5TC2 15c small die on India paper
b. **red** 55.
c. **black** 55.
d. **brown** 55.
e. **bluish green** 55.
1T5P2 15c **grn,** sm die on India paper 80.
1T5P3 15c **grn,** plate on India paper 32.
Pair 68.
1T6TC2 20c small die on India paper
b. **green** 55.
c. **black** 55.
d. **brown** 55.
e. **blue** 55.
f. **bluish green** 55.
1T6P2 20c **red,** sm die on India paper 80.
1T6P3 20c **red,** plate on India paper 32.
Pair 68.
1T7P2 25c **rose,** sm die on India paper 80.
1T7P3 25c **rose,** plate on India paper 32.
Pair 68.
1T8P3 50c **bl,** plate on India paper 32.
Pair 68.

"Collect"

1T9P3 1c **brn,** plate on India paper 32.
1T10TC2 5c small die on India paper
b. **red** 55.
c. **black** 55.
d. **brown** 55.
e. **green** 55.
f. **bluish green** 55.
1T10P3 5c **bl,** plate on India paper 32.
1T11TC2 15c small die on India paper
b. **red** 55.
c. **black** 55.
d. **brown** 55.
e. **green** 55.
f. **blue** 55.
g. **bluish green** 55.
1T11P3 15c **red brn,** plate on India paper 32.
1T12P1 20c **ol grn,** large die on India paper *850.*
1T12P3 20c **ol grn,** plate on India paper 32.

Office Coupon

1T13P3 1c **brn,** plate on India paper 32.
a. Pair Nos. 1T9P3, 1T13P3 68.
Same, block of 4 145.
1T14TC2 5c small die on India paper
b. **red** 55.
c. **black** 55.
d. **brown** 55.
e. **green** 55.
f. **bluish green** 55.
1T14P3 5c **bl,** plate on India paper 32.
a. Pair Nos. 1T10P3, 1T14P3 68.
Same, block of 4 145.
1T15TC2 15c small die on India paper
b. **red** 55.
c. **black** 55.
d. **brown** 55.
e. **green** 55.
f. **blue** 55.
g. **bluish green** 55.
1T15P3 15c **red brn,** plate on India paper 32.
a. Pair Nos. 1T11P3, 1T15P3 68.
Same, block of 4 145.
1T16P1 20c **ol grn,** large die on India paper *850.*
1T16P3 20c **ol grn,** plate on India paper 32.
a. Pair Nos. 1T12P3, 1T16P3 68.
Same, block of 4 145.

1885 Baltimore & Ohio Telegraph Co.

3T1P3 1c **ver,** plate on India paper 32.
Pair 68.
3T2TC2 5c small die on India paper
b. **dark olive** 65.
3T2P3 5c **bl,** plate on India paper 32.
Pair 68.
3T3P1 10c **red brn,** large die on India paper *900.*
3T3P3 10c **red brn,** plate on India paper 32.
Pair 68.
3T4TC2 25c small die on India paper
b. **dark olive** 65.
3T4P3 25c **org,** plate on India paper 32.
Pair 68.

1886

3T6P3 **blk,** plate on India paper 32.
Pair 68.
3T7P3 1c **grn,** plate on India paper 32.
3T8P3 5c **bl,** plate on India paper 32.
3T9P3 10c **brn,** plate on India paper 32.
3T10P3 25c **org,** plate on India paper 32.

1894-95 Northern New York Telegraph Co.

12T1P4 **green,** plate on card 125.
12T2P4 **red,** plate on card 125.
12T3P4 1c **yellow,** plate on card 40.
12T4P4 10c **blue,** plate on card 40.

1885 Postal Telegraph Co.

15T1TC1a 10c large die on India paper
e. **red** 65.
f. **blue** 65.
g. **black** 65.
15T1TC2 10c small die on India paper
b. **brown red** 65.
15T1TC3 10c plate on India paper
a. **orange** 65.
15T1P2 10c **grn,** sm die on India paper 55.
15T1P3 10c **grn,** plate on India paper 32.
15T2TC1a 15c large die on India paper
e. **red** 65.
f. **blue** 65.
g. **black** 65.
15T2TC2 15c small die on India paper
b. **red** 55.
c. **blue** 55.
15T2TC3 15c plate on India paper
a. **black** 55.
15T2P3 15c **org red,** plate on India paper 32.
15T3TC1a 25c large die on India paper
e. **red** 65.
f. **black** 65.
15T3TC2 25c small die on India paper
b. **brown red** 65.
c. **brown** 55.

15T3TC3 25c plate on India paper
a. **ultramarine** 40.
b. **brown** 40.
15T3P1 25c **bl,** large die on India paper 65.
15T3P3 25c **bl,** plate on India paper 32.
15T4TC1a 50c large die on India paper
e. **red** 65.
f. **blue** 65.
g. **black** 65.
15T4TC2 50c small die on India paper
b. **dull blue** 65.
15T4TC3 50c plate on India paper
a. **black** 40.
15T4P2 50c **brn,** sm die on India paper 65.
15T4P3 50c **brn,** plate on India paper 32.
15T6TC3 plate on India paper
a. **red brown** 40.

Western Union Telegraph Co.

16T1TC3 (1871) plate on India paper
a. **lilac** 20.
Pair 45.
b. **orange** 20.
Pair 45.
c. **black** 20.
Pair 45.
16T1TC4 (1871) plate on card
a. **lilac** 20.
Pair 45.
b. **orange** 20.
Pair 45.
c. **black** 20.
Pair 45.
d. **violet brown** 20.
Pair 45.
e. **light olive** 20.
Pair 45.
f. **brown** 20.
Pair 45.
g. **orange brown** 20.
Pair 45.
h. **blue green** 20.
Pair 45.
16T1P3 (1871) **brn,** plate on India paper 17.
Pair 35.
16T2P3 (1872) **red,** plate on India paper 17.
Pair 35.
16T3P3 (1873) **bl,** plate on India paper 17.
Pair 35.
16T4P3 (1874) **brn,** plate on India paper 17.
Pair 35.
16T5P3 (1875) **dp grn,** plate on India paper 17.
16T6TC3 (1876) plate on India paper
a. **violet blue** 20.
16T6TC4 (1876) plate on card
a. **violet blue** 20.
16T6P3 (1876) **red,** plate on India paper 17.
16T7TC4 (1877) plate on card
a. **orange yellow** 20.
Pair 45.
b. **dark brown** 20.
Pair 45.
c. **black** 20.
Pane of 4 —
16T7P3 (1877) **vio,** plate on India paper —
16T8TC4 (1878) plate on card
a. **dark brown** —
16T8P3 (1878) **gray brn,** plate on India paper 20.
16T9TC4 (1879) plate on card
a. **blue** —
16T9P3 (1879) **bl,** plate on India paper 14.
16T10TC4 (1880) plate on card
a. **violet brown** —
b. **rose** —
16T10P3 (1880) **lil rose,** plate on India paper 16.
16T11P3 (1881) **grn,** plate on India paper 16.
16T12TC3 (1882) plate on India paper
a. **green** —
16T12P3 (1882) **bl,** plate on India paper 20.
16T13P3 (1883) **yel brn,** plate on India paper 16.
16T14P1 (1884) **gray vio,** large die on India paper 250.
16T14P3 (1884) **gray vio,** plate on India paper 20.
16T15P3 (1885) **grn,** plate on India paper 20.
16T16P3 (1886) **brn vio,** plate on India paper 13.
Pair 28.
16T17P3 (1887) **red brn,** plate on India paper 13.
Pair 28.
16T18P3 (1888) **bl,** plate on India paper 13.
Pair 28.
16T19P3 (1889) **ol grn,** plate on India paper 16.
16T22TC4 (1892) plate on card
a. **black** —
16T22P3 (1892) **ver,** plate on India paper 16.
16T30P3 (1900) **red vio,** plate on India paper 28.
16T44TC1a large die on India paper
e. **deep rose** —
f. **carmine lake** —
g. **rose lake** —
h. **deep ultramarine** —
16T44TC1d Large die printed directly on card
e. **dull red** —
f. **orange** —
g. **rose red** —
h. **orange brown** —
i. **ocher** —
j. **dark blue** —
k. **dark ultramarine** —
l. **green** —
m. **brown lake** —
n. **reddish brown** —
o. **sepia** —
p. **sepia,** unsurfaced card —
q. **dull violet** —
r. **slate green** —
s. **slate blue** —
t. **black** —
u. **black,** unsurfaced card —

16T44TC3 Plate on India paper, sheet of 16
a. **deep rose** —
b. **orange** —
c. **dark blue** —
d. **slate green** —
e. **rose lake** —
16T44TC5 Plate on bond paper, sheet of 16
a. **deep rose** —
b. **orange** —
c. **dark blue** —
d. **slate green** —
e. **rose lake** —
f. **sepia** —
16T44P1 (1913) **brn,** large die on India paper —
16T44P2 (1913) **brn,** sm die on India paper —
16T44P3 (1913) **brn,** plate on India paper —
16T99P5 1c **yel grn,** plate on bond 100.
16T100P5 2c **chestnut,** plate on bond 100.
16T101P5 5c **dp bl,** plate on bond 100.
16T102P5 10c **org,** plate on bond 100.
16T103P5 25c **brt car,** plate on bond 100.

REVENUE

1862-68 by Butler & Carpenter, Philadelphia.
1868-75 by Joseph R. Carpenter, Philadelphia.

Several lists of revenue proofs in trial colors have been published, but the accuracy of some of them is questionable. The following listings are limited to items seen by the editors. The list is not complete.

In the following listing the so-called small die proofs on India paper may be, in fact probably are, plate proofs. The editors shall consider them die proofs, however, until they see them in pairs or blocks. Many revenue proofs on India are mounted on card.

First Issue

1862-71

R1P3 1c Express, **red,** plate on India paper 70.
R1P4 1c Express, **red,** plate on card 65.
Block of 4 275.
R2P1 1c Playing Cards, **red,** large die on India paper 600.
R2P3 1c Playing Cards, **red,** plate on India paper 60.
Block of 4 250.
R2P4 1c Playing Cards, **red,** plate on card 65.
Block of 4 275.
R3TC1a 1c **Proprietary,** die on India paper
e. **black** *950.*
R3TC3 1c **Proprietary,** plate on India paper
a. **black** 80.
R3TC4 1c **Proprietary,** plate on card
a. **carmine** 80.
R3TC5 1c **Proprietary,** plate on bond paper
a. **dull red** 125.
b. **orange red** 125.
c. **dull yellow** 125.
d. **violet rose** 125.
e. **deep blue** 125.
f. **red,** *blue* 125.
g. **blue,** perf. & gum 125.
R3TC5 1c **Proprietary,** plate on wove paper
h. **green,** *buff* —
R3P3 1c Proprietary, **red,** plate on India paper 140.
R3P4 1c Proprietary, **red,** plate on card 45.
Block of 4 200.
R4P4 1c Telegraph, **red,** plate on card 28.
Block of 4 125.
R5P2 2c Bank Check, **bl,** sm die on India paper 525.
R5P4 2c Bank Check, **bl,** plate on card 33.
Block of 4 140.
R6P3 2c Bank Check, **org,** plate on India paper 60.
Block of 4 250.
R7TC4 2c **Certificate,** plate on card
a. **ultramarine** 65.
R7P4 2c Certificate, **bl,** plate on card 28.
Block of 4 125.
R8P3 2c Certificate, **org,** plate on India paper 82.
Block of 4 350.
R9P4 2c Express, **bl,** plate on card 28.
Block of 4 125.
R10P1 2c Express, **org,** large die on India paper 600.
R10P3 2c Express, **org,** plate on India paper 60.
Block of 4 250.
R11TC1a 2c **Playing Cards,** die on India paper
e. **black** 500.
R11P4 2c Playing Cards, **bl,** plate on card 38.
Block of 4 160.
R13TC1a 2c **Proprietary,** die on India paper
e. **black** 650.
f. **carmine** 650.
R13TC3 2c **Proprietary,** plate on India paper
a. **black** 75.
R13P2 2c Proprietary, **bl,** sm die on India paper 400.
R13P4 2c Proprietary, **bl,** plate on card 28.
Block of 4 125.
R15TC3 2c **U.S.I.R.,** plate on India paper
a. **black** 110.
R15TC5 2c **U.S.I.R.,** plate on bond paper
a. **violet rose** 110.
b. **light green** 110.
c. **pale blue** 110.
d. **pale rose** 200.
e. **orange,** *blue* —
f. **pale orange,** perf. & gum 110.
R15P3 2c U.S.I.R., **org,** plate on India paper *1,250.*
R16TC5 3c **Foreign Exchange,** plate on bond paper
a. **green,** *blue* 140.
R16TC7 3c **Foreign Exchange,** plate on goldbeater's skin
a. **blue** 110.
R16P1 3c Foreign Exchange, **grn,** large die on India paper 600.
a. R16P1 + R19P1 composite —
R16P3 3c Foreign Exchange, **grn,** plate on India paper 225.

R16P4 3c Foreign Exchange, **grn,** plate on card 38.
Block of 4 160.
R17P1 3c Playing Cards, **grn,** large die on India paper 700.
R17P2 3c Playing Cards, **grn,** sm die on India paper 400.
R17P4 3c Playing Cards, **grn,** plate on card 100.
Block of 4 425.
R18TC1a 3c **Proprietary,** die on India paper
e. **black** 300.
R18P3 3c Proprietary, **grn,** plate on India paper 60.
Block of 4 250.
R18P4 3c Proprietary, **grn,** plate on card 28.
Block of 4 125.
R19P1 3c Telegraph, **grn,** large die on India paper 600.
R19P3 3c Telegraph, **grn,** plate on India paper 225.
R19P4 3c Telegraph, **grn,** plate on card 28.
Block of 4 125.
R20P3 4c Inland Exchange, **brn,** plate on India paper 225.
R20P4 4c Inland Exchange, **brn,** plate on card 28.
Block of 4 125.
R21TC1a 4c **Playing Cards,** die (?) on India paper
e. **black** 300.
R21P2 4c Playing Cards, **vio,** sm die on India paper 400.
R21P4 4c Playing Cards, **vio,** plate on card 95.
Block of 4 400.
R22TC1a 4c **Proprietary,** die on India paper
e. **black** 350.
f. **deep red lilac** 400.
R22TC3 4c **Proprietary,** plate on India paper
a. **black** 110.
R22TC4 4c **Proprietary,** plate on card
a. **red lilac** 110.
R22P1 4c Proprietary, **vio,** large die on India paper 600.
R22P3 4c Proprietary, **vio,** plate on India paper 110.
Block of 4 475.
R22P4 4c Proprietary, **vio,** plate on card 60.
Block of 4 250.
R23P4 5c Agreement, **red,** plate on card 33.
Block of 4 140.
R24TC3 5c **Certificate,** plate on India paper
a. **carmine** 110.
R24P1a 5c R24P1 + R25P1 composite, large die on India paper —
R24P3 5c Certificate, **red,** plate on India paper 95.
Block of 4 400.
R24P4 5c Certificate, **red,** plate on card 110.
R25TC6 5c **Express,** plate on wove paper
a. **pale olive** —
R25P2 5c Express, **red,** sm die on India paper 250.
R25P4 5c Express, **red,** plate on card 33.
Block of 4 145.
R26TC3 5c **Foreign Exchange,** plate on India paper
a. **orange** 110.
R26P4 5c Foreign Exchange, **red,** plate on card 300.
R27P2 5c Inland Exchange, **red,** sm die on India paper 250.
R27P4 5c Inland Exchange, **red,** plate on card 28.
Block of 4 125.
R28TC1a 5c **Playing Cards,** die (?) on India paper
e. **black** 300.
R28P2 5c Playing Cards, **red,** sm die on India paper —
R28P3 5c Playing Cards, **red,** plate on India paper 105.
Block of 4 440.
R28P4 5c Playing Cards, **red,** plate on card 325.
R29TC5 5c **Proprietary,** plate on bond paper
a. **red,** *blue* —
R29P5 5c Proprietary, **red,** plate on blue wove, gummed —
R30TC1a 6c **Inland Exchange,** die on India paper
e. **black** 350.
R30P3 6c Inland Exchange, **org,** plate on India paper 60.
Block of 4 250.
R30P4 6c Inland Exchange, **org,** plate on card 33.
Block of 4 140.
R31TC1a 6c **Proprietary,** die on India paper
e. **black** —
R32TC1a 10c **Bill of Lading,** die on India paper
e. **greenish blue** 350.
f. **dark green,** R32TC1a+R37TC1a composite —
R32P4 10c Bill of Lading, **bl,** plate on card 33.
Block of 4 140.
R33P3 10c Certificate, **bl,** plate on India paper 140.
R33P4 10c Certificate, **bl,** plate on card 33.
Block of 4 140.
R34P4 10c Contract, **bl,** plate on card 33.
Block of 4 140.
R35TC1a 10c **Foreign Exchange,** die (?) on India paper
e. **black** 350.
R35P4 10c Foreign Exchange, **bl,** plate on card 33.
Block of 4 140.
R36P4 10c Inland Exchange, **bl,** plate on card 33.
Block of 4 140.
R37TC1a 10c **Power of Attorney,** die on India paper
e. **greenish blue** 350.
R37P4 10c Power of Attorney, **bl,** plate on card 33.
Block of 4 140.
R38TC1a 10c **Proprietary,** die on India paper
e. **black** 350.
R38P1 10c Proprietary, **bl,** large die on India paper *700.*
R38P3 10c Proprietary, **bl,** plate on India paper 70.
Block of 4 300.
R39P3 15c Foreign Exchange, **brn,** plate on India paper 90.
Block of 4 375.
R39P4 15c Foreign Exchange, **brn,** plate on card 325.
Block of 4 1,600.

No.	Description	Price
R40P3	15c Inland Exchange, **brn,** plate on India paper	120.
R40P4	15c Inland Exchange, **brn,** plate on card	33.
	Block of 4	140.
R41P1	20c Foreign Exchange, **red,** large die on India paper	600.
a.	R41P1 + R42P1 composite	—
R41P3	20c Foreign Exchange, **red,** plate on India paper	90.
	Block of 4	375.
R41P4	20c Foreign Exchange, **red,** plate on card	100.
	Block of 4	425.
R42P1	20c Inland Exchange, **red,** large die on India paper	600.
R42P2	20c Inland Exchange, **red,** sm die on India paper	250.
R42P3	20c Inland Exchange, **red,** plate on India paper	260.
R42P4	20c Inland Exchange, **red,** plate on card	33.
	Block of 4	140.
R43TC4	25c **Bond,** plate on card	
a.	**carmine**	90.
R43P4	25c Bond, **red,** plate on card	500.
	Block of 4	2,500.
R44TC5	25c **Certificate,** plate on bond paper	
a.	**blue**	300.
b.	**green**	300.
c.	**orange**	300.
R44P4	25c Certificate, **red,** plate on card	33.
	Block of 4	140.
R45TC1a	25c **Entry of Goods,** hybrid die on India paper	
e.	**black**	—
R45P4	25c Entry of Goods, **red,** plate on card	550.
R46TC5	25c **Insurance,** plate on bond paper	
a.	**dull red**	150.
b.	**vermilion**	170.
c.	**blue**	170.
d.	**dark blue**	155.
R46TC7	25c **Insurance,** plate on goldbeater's skin	
a.	**dull red**	210.
b.	**vermilion**	210.
c.	**blue**	215.
d.	**dark blue**	215.
e.	**green**	215.
R46P3	25c Insurance, **red,** plate on India paper	60.
	Block of 4	250.
R46P4	25c Insurance, **red,** plate on card	33.
	Block of 4	140.
R47P4	25c Life Insurance, **red,** plate on card	33.
	Block of 4	140.
R48P4	25c Power of Attorney, **red,** plate on card	33.
	Block of 4	140.
R49P4	25c Protest, **red,** plate on card	33.
	Block of 4	140.
R50P4	25c Warehouse Receipt, **red,** plate on card	33.
	Block of 4	140.
R51TC3	30c **Foreign Exchange,** plate on India paper	
a.	**violet**	130.
b.	**violet gray**	130.
c.	**deep red lilac**	155.
d.	**slate blue**	155.
e.	**black**	155.
f.	**red**	155.
R51P3	30c Foreign Exchange, **lil,** plate on India paper	110.
	Block of 4	475.
R51P4	30c Foreign Exchange, **lil,** plate on card	100.
	Block of 4	425.
R52TC3	30c **Inland Exchange,** plate on India paper	
a.	**deep red lilac**	155.
R52P3	30c Inland Exchange, **lil,** plate on India paper	65.
	Block of 4	275.
R52P4	30c Inland Exchange, **lil,** plate on card	55.
	Block of 4	230.
R53TC1a	40c **Inland Exchange,** hybrid die on India paper	
e.	**black**	—
R53P3	40c Inland Exchange, **brn,** plate on India paper	150.
R53P4	40c Inland Exchange, **brn,** plate on card	75.
	Block of 4	325.
R54P2	50c Conveyance, **bl,** sm die on India paper	250.
R54P4	50c Conveyance, **bl,** plate on card	33.
	Block of 4	140.
R55TC5	50c **Entry of Goods,** plate on bond paper	
a.	**orange**	275.
b.	**green**	275.
c.	**red**	340.
d.	**deep blue**	—
R55P3	50c Entry of Goods, **bl,** plate on India paper	65.
	Block of 4	275.
R55P4	50c Entry of Goods, **bl,** plate on card	45.
	Block of 4	190.
R56P3	50c Foreign Exchange, **bl,** plate on India paper	65.
	Block of 4	275.
R56P4	50c Foreign Exchange, **bl,** plate on card	45.
	Block of 4	190.
R57P3	50c Lease, **bl,** plate on India paper	65.
	Block of 4	275.
R57P4	50c Lease, **bl,** plate on card	38.
	Block of 4	160.
R58TC3	50c **Life Insurance,** plate on India paper	
a.	**ultramarine**	85.
R58P3	50c Life Insurance, **bl,** plate on India paper	65.
	Block of 4	275.
R58P4	50c Life Insurance, **bl,** plate on card	38.
	Block of 4	160.
R59P4	50c Mortgage, **bl,** plate on card	110.
	Block of 4	475.
R60TC1a	50c **Original Process,** die (?) on India paper	
e.	**black**	280.
R60P3	50c Original Process, **bl,** plate on India paper	65.
	Block of 4	275.
R60P4	50c Original Process, **bl,** plate on card	38.
	Block of 4	160.
R61P4	50c Passage Ticket, **bl,** plate on card	55.
	Block of 4	230.
R62P3	50c Probate of Will, **bl,** plate on India paper	65.
	Block of 4	275.
R62P4	50c Probate of Will, **bl,** plate on card	55.
	Block of 4	230.
R63P4	50c Surety Bond, **bl,** plate on card	55.
	Block of 4	230.
R64TC1a	60c **Inland Exchange,** die (?) on India paper	
e.	**green**	—
R64P3	60c Inland Exchange, **org,** plate on India paper	55.
R64P4	60c Inland Exchange, **org,** plate on card	38.
	Block of 4	160.
R65TC1a	70c **Foreign Exchange,** die (?) on India paper	
e.	**orange**	—
f.	**black**	285.
R65P3	70c Foreign Exchange, **grn,** plate on India paper	120.
R65P4	70c Foreign Exchange, **grn,** plate on card	55.
	Block of 4	230.
R66TC3	$1 **Conveyance,** plate on India paper	
a.	**carmine**	85.
R66P4	$1 Conveyance, **red,** plate on card	45.
	Block of 4	190.
R67TC3	$1 **Entry of Goods,** plate on India paper	
a.	**carmine**	60.
R67P1	$1 Entry of Goods, **red,** large die on India paper	525.
R67P4	$1 Entry of Goods, **red,** plate on card	45.
	Block of 4	190.
R68TC3	$1 **Foreign Exchange,** plate on India paper	
a.	**carmine**	60.
R68P4	$1 Foreign Exchange, **red,** plate on card	33.
	Block of 4	140.
R69TC3	$1 **Inland Exchange,** plate on India paper	
a.	**carmine**	60.
R69P4	$1 Inland Exchange, **red,** plate on card	55.
	Block of 4	230.
R70TC3	$1 **Lease,** plate on India paper	
a.	**carmine**	130.
R70P4	$1 Lease, **red,** plate on card	*425.*
R71TC3	$1 **Life Insurance,** plate on India paper	
a.	**carmine**	75.
R71P4	$1 Life Insurance, **red,** plate on card	33.
	Block of 4	140.
R72TC3	$1 **Manifest,** plate on India paper	
a.	**carmine**	80.
R72P3	$1 Manifest, **red,** plate on India paper	55.
	Block of 4	—
R72P4	$1 Manifest, **red,** plate on card	33.
	Block of 4	140.
R73TC1a	$1 **Mortgage,** hybrid die on India paper	
e.	**black**	—
R73TC3	$1 **Mortgage,** plate on India paper	
a.	**carmine**	85.
R73P4	$1 Mortgage, **red,** plate on card	55.
	Block of 4	230.
R74TC3	$1 **Passage Ticket,** plate on India paper	
a.	**carmine**	120.
R74P4	$1 Passage Ticket, **red,** plate on card	*425.*
	Block of 4	*1,850.*
R75TC3	$1 **Power of Attorney,** plate on India paper	
a.	**carmine**	120.
R75P4	$1 Power of Attorney, **red,** plate on card	100.
	Block of 4	425.
R76TC3	$1 **Probate of Will,** plate on India paper	
a.	**carmine**	60.
R76P4	$1 Probate of Will, **red,** plate on card	33.
	Block of 4	140.
R77P1	$1.30 Foreign Exchange, **org,** large die on India paper	*700.*
R77P3	$1.30 Foreign Exchange, **org,** plate on India paper	140.
	Block of 4	575.
R77P4	$1.30 Foreign Exchange, **org,** plate on card	100.
	Block of 4	425.
R78TC1a	$1.50 **Inland Exchange,** die on India paper	
e.	**black**	475.
R78P3	$1.50 Inland Exchange, **bl,** plate on India paper	110.
	Block of 4	475.
R78P4	$1.50 Inland Exchange, **bl,** plate on card	45.
	Block of 4	190.
R79P3	$1.60 Foreign Exchange, **grn,** plate on India paper	140.
R79P4	$1.60 Foreign Exchange, **grn,** plate on card	100.
	Block of 4	425.
R80TC3	$1.90 **Foreign Exchange,** plate on India paper	
a.	**black**	155.
R80P3	$1.90 Foreign Exchange, **vio,** plate on India paper	140.
	Block of 4	575.
R80P4	$1.90 Foreign Exchange, **vio,** plate on card	100.
	Block of 4	425.
R81TC4	$2 **Conveyance,** plate on card	
a.	**carmine**	85.
R81P3	$2 Conveyance, **red,** plate on India paper	120.
R81P4	$2 Conveyance, **red,** plate on card	33.
	Block of 4	140.
R82TC4	$2 **Mortgage,** plate on card	
a.	**carmine**	85.
R82P3	$2 Mortgage, **red,** plate on India paper	120.
	Block of 4	—
R82P4	$2 Mortgage, **red,** plate on card	33.
	Block of 4	140.
R83TC1a	$2 **Probate of Will,** hybrid die on India paper	
e.	**black**	—
R83P4	$2 Probate of Will, **red,** plate on card	110.
	Block of 4	—
R84TC1a	$2.50 **Inland Exchange,** die (?) on India paper	
e.	**black**	120.
R84P3	$2.50 Inland Exchange, **vio,** plate on India paper	250.
R84P4	$2.50 Inland Exchange, **vio,** plate on card	250.
	Block of 4	—
R85TC4	$3 **Charter Party,** plate on thin card	
a.	**dark green**	—
R85P3	$3 Charter Party, **grn,** plate on India paper	120.
	Block of 4	500.
R85P4	$3 Charter Party, **grn,** plate on card	65.
	Block of 4	275.
R86P1	$3 Manifest, **grn,** large die on India paper	—
R86P2	$3 Manifest, **grn,** sm die on India paper	350.
R86P3	$3 Manifest, **grn,** plate on India paper	180.
R86P4	$3 Manifest, **grn,** plate on card	65.
	Block of 4	275.
R87TC1a	$3.50 **Inland Exchange,** die on India paper	
e.	**black**	400.
R87P3	$3.50 Inland Exchange, **bl,** plate on India paper	180.
R87P4	$3.50 Inland Exchange, **bl,** plate on card	140.
	Block of 4	575.
R88TC1a	$5 **Charter Party,** hybrid die on India paper	
e.	**black**	—
R88TC3	$5 **Charter Party,** plate on India paper	
a.	**carmine**	85.
R88P3	$5 Charter Party, **red,** plate on India paper	70.
	Block of 4	300.
R88P4	$5 Charter Party, **red,** plate on card	55.
	Block of 4	230.
R89TC3	$5 **Conveyance,** plate on India paper	
a.	**carmine**	90.
R89P3	$5 Conveyance, **red,** plate on India paper	450.
R89P4	$5 Conveyance, **red,** plate on card	55.
	Block of 4	230.
R90P2	$5 Manifest, **red,** sm die on India paper	300.
R90P4	$5 Manifest, **red,** plate on card	55.
	Block of 4	230.
R91TC3	$5 **Mortgage,** plate on India paper	
a.	**carmine**	90.
R91P3	$5 Mortgage, **red,** plate on India paper	650.
R91P4	$5 Mortgage, **red,** plate on card	55.
	Block of 4	230.
R92P2	$5 Probate of Will, **red,** sm die on India paper	300.
R92P4	$5 Probate of Will, **red,** plate on card	55.
	Block of 4	230.
R93P3	$10 Charter Party, **grn,** plate on India paper	120.
R93P4	$10 Charter Party, **grn,** plate on card	55.
	Block of 4	230.
R94P4	$10 Conveyance, **grn,** plate on card	55.
	Block of 4	230.
R95TC4	$10 **Mortgage,** plate on thin card	
a.	**yellow green**	—
R95P4	$10 Mortgage, **grn,** plate on card	55.
	Block of 4	230.
R96P1	$10 Probate of Will, **grn,** large die on India paper	*700.*
R96P2	$10 Probate of Will, **grn,** sm die on India paper	300.
R96P4	$10 Probate of Will, **grn,** plate on card	75.
	Block of 4	325.
R97P2	$15 Mortgage, **dk bl,** sm die on India paper	—
R97P3	$15 Mortgage, **dk bl,** plate on India paper	350.
R97P4	$15 Mortgage, **dk bl,** plate on card	180.
	Block of 4	800.
R97eP2	$15 Mortgage, **ultra,** sm die on India paper	—
R97eP4	$15 Mortgage, **ultra,** plate on card	350.
	Block of 4	—
R97fP3	$15 Mortgage, **milky bl,** plate on India paper	290.
R98TC3	$20 **Conveyance,** plate on India paper	
a.	**red orange**	220.
R98TC4	$20 **Conveyance,** plate on card	
a.	**red orange**	120.
R98P3	$20 Conveyance, **org,** plate on India paper	220.
	Block of 4	900.
R98P4	$20 Conveyance, **org,** plate on card	100.
	Block of 4	425.
R99TC4	$20 **Probate of Will,** plate on card	
a.	**red orange**	275.
b.	**black**	275.
R99P4	$20 Probate of Will, **org,** plate on card	220.
	Block of 4	—
R100P3	$25 Mortgage, **red,** plate on India paper	220.
R100P4	$25 Mortgage, **red,** plate on card	160.
	Block of 4	675.
R101TC1a	$50 **U.S.I.R.,** hybrid die on India paper	
e.	**black**	—
R101TC5	$50 **U.S.I.R.,** plate on bond paper	
a.	**orange**	275.
b.	**deep blue**	275.
R101P3	$50 U.S.I.R., **grn,** plate on India paper	220.
R101P4	$50 U.S.I.R., **grn,** plate on card	230.
	Block of 4	950.

R102TC3 $200**U.S.I.R.**, plate on India paper
a. **black** —
b. **green & brown red** 2,000.
R102TC4 $200**U.S.I.R.**, plate on card
a. **black & red** 1,600.
R102TC5 $200**U.S.I.R.**, plate on bond paper
a. **gray brown & red** 1,600.
R102P3 $200U.S.I.R., **grn & org red,** plate on India paper 1,400.

Second Issue

1871-72

R104TC5 2c plate on bond paper
a. **pale blue & black** 60.
R105P3 3c **bl & blk,** plate on India paper 20.
Block of 4 90.
R105P4 3c **bl & blk,** plate on card 15.
Block of 4 65.
P# block of 10 —
R109P3 10c **bl & blk,** plate on India paper 20.
Block of 4 90.
R109P4 10c **bl & blk,** plate on card 15.
Block of 4 65.
P# block of 10 —
R111P3 20c **bl & blk,** plate on India paper 20.
Block of 4 90.
R111P4 20c **bl & blk,** plate on card 15.
Block of 4 65.
P# block of 10 —
R112P3 25c **bl & blk,** plate on India paper 20.
Block of 4 90.
R112P4 25c **bl & blk,** plate on card 15.
Block of 4 65.
P# block of 10 —
R115P3 50c **bl & blk,** plate on India paper 50.
Block of 4 225.
R115P4 50c **bl & blk,** plate on card 15.
Block of 4 65.
P# block of 10 —
R119P3 $1.30 **bl & blk,** plate on India paper 50.
Block of 4 225.
R119P4 $1.30 **bl & blk,** plate on card 38.
Block of 4 160.
P# block of 10 —
R120P3 $1.50 **bl & blk,** plate on India paper 28.
Block of 4 120.
R120P4 $1.50 **bl & blk,** plate on card 22.
Block of 4 100.
Double transfer, design of $1 —
R121P3 $1.60 **bl & blk,** plate on India paper 60.
Block of 4 260.
R121P4 $1.60 **bl & blk,** plate on card 60.
Block of 4 260.
P# block of 10 —
R122P3 $1.90 **bl & blk,** plate on India paper 50.
Block of 4 225.
R122P4 $1.90 **bl & blk,** plate on card 38.
Block of 4 170.
P# block of 10 —
R126P3 $3.50 **bl & blk,** plate on India paper 90.
Block of 4 400.
R126P4 $3.50 **bl & blk,** plate on card 100.
Block of 4 425.
P# block of 8 —
R130P3 $25 **bl & blk,** plate on India paper 150.
Block of 4 650.
R130P4 $25 **bl & blk,** plate on card 110.
Block of 4 500.
P# block of 4 —
R131P3 $50 **bl & blk,** plate on India paper 160.
Block of 4 700.
R131P4 $50 **bl & blk,** plate on card 140.
Block of 4 625.
P# block of 4 —

The "small die proofs" formerly listed under Nos. R103P-R131P are plate proofs from the sheets listed under "Trial Color Proofs."

R132TC1a $200 die on India paper
e. **red, green & black** 2,500.
f. **orange,** master die 2,500.
g. **blue,** master die 2,500.
h. **green,** master die 2,500.
R132P1 $200 **red, bl & blk,** large die on India paper 3,500.
R132P2 $200 **red, bl & blk,** sm die on India paper 2,750.
R132P3 $200 **red, bl & blk,** plate on India paper 2,500.
Red (frame) inverted —
R133TC1a $500 die on India paper
e. **yellow, green & black** *5,000.*
f. **bright green, orange brown & black** *5,000.*
g. **black,** master die *10,000.*
R133TC1b $500 die on bond paper
e. **red, green & black** *5,000.*
f. **light green, light brown & black** *5,000.*
g. **blue, scarlet & black** *5,000.*
R133TC1d $500 die on card
e. **light green, light brown & black** *14,500.*
R133P1 $500 **red, org, grn & blk,** large die on India paper *5,500.*
R133ATC1a $5000 die on India paper
e. **yellow orange, green & black** *20,000.*
f. **olive brown, green & black** *20,000.*
g. **orange red, dark green & black** *20,000.*
h. **orange red, dark blue & black** *20,000.*

The master die is the completed stamp design prior to its division into separate color dies.

Full-size die proofs on full-size card bring substantial premiums above the catalogue values listed for R132TC1a, R133TC1a-R133TC1d, R133ATC1a.

R133AP1 $5000 **red org, dk grn & blk,** large die on India paper *7,500.*

No. R133AP was approved in these colors but never issued. Shade differences of the red orange and dark green colors will be found. It comes both with and without manufacturer's imprints to the left and right of the design. One example exists on bond paper mounted on card with "853½" printed on the lower right card margin.

Due to the unusual manufacturing process of printing these tri-color stamps from single impression plates, proofs with imprints could also be considered to be plate proofs. All are extremely scarce or unique, and are valued in the grade, condition and scarcity in which they exist. For other colors see the trial color proofs listings under No. R133ATC.

Third Issue

1871-72

R134TC4 1c plate on card
a. **brown & black** 60.
R134P4 1c **cl & blk,** plate on card 15.
Block of 4 70.
P# block of 10 —
R135P3 2c **org & blk,** plate on India paper 28.
Block of 4 120.
R135P4 2c **org & blk,** plate on card 15.
Block of 4 70.
P# block of 10 —
R136P3 4c **brn & blk,** plate on India paper 33.
Block of 4 140.
R136P4 4c **brn & blk,** plate on card 15.
Block of 4 70.
P# block of 10 —
R137P3 5c **org & blk,** plate on India paper 33.
Block of 4 140.
R137P4 5c **org & blk,** plate on card 15.
Block of 4 70.
P# block of 10 —
R138P3 6c **org & blk,** plate on India paper 33.
Block of 4 140.
R138P4 6c **org & blk,** plate on card 15.
Block of 4 70.
P# block of 10 —
R139P3 15c **brn & blk,** plate on India paper 33.
Block of 4 140.
R139P4 15c **brn & blk,** plate on card 15.
Block of 4 70.
P# block of 10 —
R140P3 30c **brn & blk,** plate on India paper 38.
Block of 4 160.
R140P4 30c **brn & blk,** plate on card 18.
Block of 4 80.
P# block of 10 —
R141P3 40c **brn & blk,** plate on India paper 38.
Block of 4 160.
R141P4 40c **brn & blk,** plate on card 18.
Block of 4 80.
P# block of 12 —
R142P3 60c **org & blk,** plate on India paper 85.
Block of 4 360.
Foreign entry, design of 70c 225.
R142P4 60c **org & blk,** plate on card 50.
Block of 4 225.
P# block of 10 —
Foreign entry, design of 70c 150.
a. Center inverted *2,250.*
Block of 4 *10,000.*
Foreign entry, design of 70c —
R143P3 70c **grn & blk,** plate on India paper 55.
Block of 4 230.
R143P4 70c **grn & blk,** plate on card 38.
Block of 4 170.
P# block of 10 —
R144P3 $1 **grn & blk,** plate on India paper 50.
Block of 4 210.
R144P4 $1 **grn & blk,** plate on card 38.
Block of 4 170.
P# block of 10 —
R145P3 $2 **ver & blk,** plate on India paper 105.
Block of 4 450.
R145P4 $2 **ver & blk,** plate on card 105.
Block of 4 450.
P# block of 8 —
R146P3 $2.50 **cl & blk,** plate on India paper 65.
Block of 4 260.
R146P4 $2.50 **cl & blk,** plate on card 40.
Block of 4 170.
P# block of 8 —
R147P3 $3 **grn & blk,** plate on India paper 85.
Block of 4 360.
R147P4 $3 **grn & blk,** plate on card 70.
Block of 4 300.
P# block of 8 —
R148P3 $5 **ver & blk,** plate on India paper 85.
Block of 4 360.
R148P4 $5 **ver & blk,** plate on card 55.
Block of 4 240.
P# block of 4 —
R149P3 $10 **grn & blk,** plate on India paper 105.
Block of 4 440.
R149P4 $10 **grn & blk,** plate on card 55.
Block of 4 240.
P# block of 4 —
R150P3 $20 **org & blk,** plate on India paper 150.
Block of 4 650.
R150P4 $20 **org & blk,** plate on card 150.
Block of 4 635.
P# block of 4 —

1875 National Bank Note Co., New York City

R152TC1a 2c Liberty, die on India paper
e. **green** 600.
f. **brown** 600.
g. **black** 600.
R152P1 2c **bl,** (Liberty) large die on India paper 450.
R152P3 2c **bl,** (Liberty) plate on India paper 110.
Block of 4 475.

Documentary

1898

R161TC1a ½c large die on India paper
e. **green** 750.
R163TC1a 1c large die on India paper
e. **green** 750.
f. **black** 750.
R165TC2 1c small die on India paper
b. **green** 650.
R169TC1a 25c large die on India paper
e. **green** 650.
R170TC1a 40c large die on India paper
e. **black** 650.
R172TC1a 80c large die on India paper
e. **green** 1,100.
R173P1 $1 **dk grn,** large die on India paper *600.*
R174TC1a $3 die on India paper
e. **black** 650.
R174P1 $3 **dk brn,** large die on India paper *600.*
R175P1 $5 **org red,** large die on India paper *600.*
R176TC1a $10 die on India paper
e. **green** 650.
R176P1 $10 **blk,** large die on India paper *600.*
R177P1 $30 **red,** large die on India paper *600.*
R178P1 $50 **gray brn,** large die on India paper *600.*

1899

R179TC1a $100 die on India paper
e. **dark green & black** 1,250.
R180P1 $500 **car lake & blk,** large die on India paper *1,650.*
R181TC1a $1000 die on India paper
e. **dark blue & black** 1,250.

1914

R195TC2 ½c small die on wove
b. **black** —
R196TC2 1c small die on wove
b. **blue green** —
R197P2 2c **rose,** sm die on India paper —
R198TC2 3c small die on wove
b. **ultramarine** —
R199TC2 4c small die on wove
b. **brown** —
R200TC2 5c small die on wove
b. **blue** —
R201TC2 10c small die on wove
b. **yellow** —
R202TC2 25c small die on wove
b. **dull violet** —
R203TC2 40c small die on wove
b. **blue green** —
R204TC2 50c small die on wove
b. **red brown** —
R205TC2 80c small die on wove
b. **orange** —

1914-15

R226P1 $500 **bl,** large die on India paper *675.*

1917

R246P1 $30 **dp org,** (without serial No.) large die on India paper *650.*

1940

R298P1 50c **car,** (without ovpt.) large die on India paper *700.*
R305P1 $10 **car,** large die on India paper *825.*
Without overprint —
R306AP1 $50 **car,** large die on India paper *825.*
Without overprint —

1952

R597P1 55c **car,** large die on India paper *675.*

Proprietary

1871-75 Joseph R. Carpenter, Philadelphia

RB1TC5 1c plate on bond paper
a. **blue & black** 70.
b. **scarlet & black** 70.
c. **orange & black** 70.
d. **orange & ultramarine,** on granite bond 60.
RB1P3 1c **grn & blk,** plate on India paper —
RB1P4 1c **grn & blk,** plate on card 12.
Block of 4 50.
P# block of 10 *250.*
RB1P5 1c **grn & blk,** plate on bond 12.
Block of 4 50.
P# block of 10 175.
RB2P3 2c **grn & blk,** plate on India paper 175.
RB2P4 2c **grn & blk,** plate on card 12.
Block of 4 50.
RB2P5 2c **grn & blk,** plate on bond, P# block of 10 175.
RB3TC5 3c Plate on bond paper
a. **blue & black,** with gum 60.
b. **blue & black,** *gray* 60.
RB3TC6 3c plate on wove paper
a. **blue & black** —
RB3P3 3c **grn & blk,** plate on India paper 22.
Block of 4 100.
RB3P4 3c **grn & blk,** plate on card 12.
Block of 4 50.
RB3P5 3c **grn & blk,** plate on bond, P# block of 10 175.
RB4P3 4c **grn & blk,** plate on India paper 22.
Block of 4 100.
RB4P4 4c **grn & blk,** plate on card 12.
Block of 4 50.
RB4P5 4c **grn & blk,** plate on bond, P# block of 10 175.
RB5P3 5c **grn & blk,** plate on India paper 22.
Block of 4 100.

No.	Description	Price
RB5P4	5c **grn & blk,** plate on card	12.
	Block of 4	50.
RB5P5	5c **grn & blk,** plate on bond, P# block of 10	175.
RB6P3	6c **grn & blk,** plate on India paper	22.
	Block of 4	100.
RB6P4	6c **grn & blk,** plate on card	12.
	Block of 4	50.
RB6P5	6c **grn & blk,** plate on bond, P# block of 10	175.
RB7P3	10c **grn & blk,** plate on India paper	22.
	Block of 4	100.
RB7P4	10c **grn & blk,** plate on card	12.
	Block of 4	50.
RB7P5	10c **grn & blk,** plate on bond, P# block of 10	175.
RB8TC1a	50c Die on India paper	
	e. **green & brown**	675.
	f. **green & purple**	675.
	g. **green & brown red**	675.
	h. **green & violet**	675.
	i. **green & dark carmine**	675.
	j. **ultramarine & red**	675.
RB8P2	50c **grn & blk,** sm die on India paper	1,400.
RB8P4	50c **grn & blk,** plate on card	1,000.
RB9TC1a	$1 die on India paper	
	e. **green & brown**	675.
	f. **green & purple**	675.
	g. **green & violet brown**	675.
	h. **green & brown red**	675.
	i. **green & violet**	675.
	j. **green & dark carmine**	675.
RB9P2	$1 **grn & blk,** sm die on India paper	1,600.
RB9P4	$1 **grn & blk,** plate on card	1,250.
RB10P2	$5 **grn & blk,** sm die on India paper	6,000.
RB10P3	$5 **grn & blk,** plate on India paper	4,500.
RB10P4	$5 **grn & blk,** plate on card	2,750.

1875-83 National Bank Note Co., New York City

No.	Description	Price
RB11TC1a	1c die on India paper	
	e. **brown**	500.
	f. **red brown**	500.
	g. **blue**	500.
	h. **black**	500.
RB11P1	1c **grn,** lg die on India paper	500.
RB11P3	1c **grn,** plate on India paper	65.
	Block of 4	325.
RB11P4	1c **grn,** plate on card	—
RB12TC1a	2c die on India paper	
	e. **green**	500.
	f. **black**	500.
	g. **brown**	500.
	h. **orange brown**	500.
	i. **blue**	500.
RB12P1	2c **brn,** lg die on India paper	500.
RB12P3	2c **brn,** plate on India paper	65.
	Pair	160.
RB12P4	2c **brn,** plate on card	—
RB13TC1a	3c die on India paper	
	e. **brown**	500.
	f. **green**	500.
	g. **blue**	500.
RB13TC3	3c plate on India paper	
	a. **black**	150.
RB13P1	3c **org,** lg die on India paper	500.
RB13P3	3c **org,** plate on India paper	65.
	Pair	160.
RB13P4	3c **org,** plate on card	—
	Pair	—
	Block of 4	—
RB14TC1a	4c die on India paper	
	e. **green**	450.
	f. **black**	450.
	g. **dark brown**	450.
	h. **blue**	450.
RB14TC3	4c plate on India paper	
	a. **black**	150.
RB14P1	4c **red brn,** lg die on India paper	500.
RB14P3	4c **red brn,** plate on India paper	65.
	Pair	160.
RB14P4	4c **red brn,** plate on card	—
	Pair	—
	Block of 4	—
RB15P1	4c **red,** lg die on India paper	500.
RB16TC1a	5c die on India paper	
	e. **green**	450.
	f. **dark slate**	450.
	g. **blue**	450.
RB16P1	5c **blk,** lg die on India paper	500.
RB16P3	5c **blk,** plate on India paper	65.
	Pair	160.
RB16P4	5c **blk,** plate on card	—
	Pair	—
	Block of 4	—
RB17TC1a	6c die on India paper	
	e. **black**	500.
	f. **blue**	500.
	g. **purple**	500.
	h. **dull violet**	500.
	i. **violet**	500.
	j. **violet brown**	500.
	k. **dark brown**	500.
RB17TC3	6c plate on India paper	
	a. **green**	150.
	b. **black**	150.
RB17P1	6c **vio bl,** lg die on India paper	500.
RB17P3	6c **vio bl,** plate on India paper	65.
	Pair	160.
RB18P1	6c **bl,** lg die on India paper	500.
RB18P3	6c **bl,** plate on India paper	175.
	Pair	400.
RB19TC1a	10c die on India paper	
	e. **black**	550.
RB19P1	10c **bl,** lg die on India paper	500.

No. RB19P1 was produced by the Bureau of Engraving and Printing.

SECOND, THIRD AND PROPRIETARY ISSUES

Stamps Nos. R103 to R131, R134 to R150 and RB1 to RB7.

A special composite plate was made and impressions taken in various colors and shades. Although all varieties in all colors must have been made, only those seen by the editors are listed.

CENTERS IN BLACK

1871-75

No.	Description	Price
R103TC3	1c plate on India paper	
	a. **dark purple**	60.
	b. **dull purple**	60.
	d. **brown**	60.
	e. **black brown**	60.
	g. **light blue**	60.
	h. **dark blue**	70.
	i. **ultramarine**	70.
	k. **yellow green**	70.
	n. **green**	65.
	o. **dark green**	65.
	p. **blue green**	65.
	q. **light orange**	65.
	r. **dark orange**	65.
	s. **deep orange**	65.
	t. **scarlet**	65.
	u. **carmine**	65.
	x. **dark brown red**	65.
R103TC7	1c plate on goldbeater's skin	
	a. **dark brown orange**	90.
R104TC3	2c plate on India paper	
	a. **dark purple**	60.
	b. **dull purple**	60.
	d. **brown**	60.
	e. **black brown**	60.
	g. **light blue**	60.
	h. **dark blue**	70.
	i. **ultramarine**	70.
	k. **yellow green**	70.
	l. **dark yellow green**	70.
	n. **green**	65.
	o. **dark green**	65.
	p. **blue green**	65.
	q. **light orange**	65.
	r. **dark orange**	65.
	s. **deep orange**	65.
	t. **scarlet**	65.
	u. **carmine**	65.
	x. **dark brown red**	65.
R104TC7	2c plate on goldbeater's skin	
	a. **dark brown orange**	90.
R105TC3	3c plate on India paper	
	a. **dark purple**	60.
	b. **dull purple**	60.
	d. **brown**	60.
	e. **black brown**	60.
	g. **light blue**	60.
	h. **dark blue**	70.
	i. **ultramarine**	70.
	k. **yellow green**	70.
	n. **green**	65.
	o. **dark green**	65.
	p. **blue green**	65.
	q. **light orange**	65.
	r. **dark orange**	65.
	s. **deep orange**	65.
	t. **scarlet**	65.
	u. **carmine**	65.
	x. **dark brown red**	65.
R105TC7	3c plate on goldbeater's skin	
	a. **dark brown orange**	90.
R106TC3	4c plate on India paper	
	a. **dark purple**	60.
	b. **dull purple**	60.
	d. **brown**	60.
	e. **black brown**	60.
	f. **orange brown**	65.
	g. **light blue**	60.
	h. **dark blue**	70.
	i. **ultramarine**	70.
	k. **yellow green**	70.
	n. **green**	65.
	o. **dark green**	65.
	p. **blue green**	65.
	q. **light orange**	65.
	r. **dark orange**	65.
	s. **deep orange**	65.
	t. **scarlet**	65.
	u. **carmine**	65.
	x. **dark brown red**	65.
R106TC7	4c plate on goldbeater's skin	
	a. **dark brown orange**	90.
R107TC3	5c plate on India paper	
	a. **dark purple**	60.
	b. **dull purple**	60.
	d. **brown**	60.
	e. **black brown**	60.
	f. **orange brown**	65.
	g. **light blue**	60.
	h. **dark blue**	70.
	i. **ultramarine**	70.
	k. **yellow green**	70.
	n. **green**	65.
	o. **dark green**	65.
	p. **blue green**	65.
	q. **light orange**	65.
	r. **dark orange**	65.
	s. **deep orange**	65.
	t. **scarlet**	65.
	u. **carmine**	65.
	v. **dark carmine**	65.
	w. **purplish carmine**	65.
	x. **dark brown red**	65.
R107TC7	5c plate on goldbeater's skin	
	a. **dark brown orange**	90.
R108TC3	6c plate on India paper	
	a. **dark purple**	60.
	b. **dull purple**	60.
	d. **brown**	60.
	e. **black brown**	60.
	f. **orange brown**	65.
	g. **light blue**	60.
	h. **dark blue**	70.
	i. **ultramarine**	70.
	k. **yellow green**	70.
	n. **green**	65.
	o. **dark green**	65.
	p. **blue green**	65.
	q. **light orange**	65.
	r. **dark orange**	65.
	s. **deep orange**	65.
	t. **scarlet**	65.
	u. **carmine**	65.
	v. **dark carmine**	65.
	w. **purplish carmine**	65.
	x. **dark brown red**	65.
R108TC7	6c plate on goldbeater's skin	
	a. **dark brown orange**	90.
R109TC3	10c plate on India paper	
	a. **dark purple**	60.
	b. **dull purple**	60.
	d. **brown**	60.
	e. **black brown**	60.
	g. **light blue**	60.
	h. **dark blue**	70.
	i. **ultramarine**	70.
	k. **yellow green**	70.
	n. **green**	65.
	o. **dark green**	65.
	p. **blue green**	65.
	q. **light orange**	65.
	r. **dark orange**	65.
	s. **deep orange**	65.
	t. **scarlet**	65.
	u. **carmine**	65.
	x. **dark brown red**	65.
R110TC3	15c plate on India paper	
	a. **dark purple**	60.
	b. **dull purple**	60.
	d. **brown**	60.
	e. **black brown**	60.
	f. **orange brown**	65.
	g. **light blue**	60.
	h. **dark blue**	70.
	i. **ultramarine**	70.
	k. **yellow green**	70.
	n. **green**	65.
	o. dark green	65.
	p. **blue green**	65.
	q. **light orange**	65.
	r. **dark orange**	65.
	s. **deep orange**	65.
	t. **scarlet**	65.
	u. **carmine**	65.
	w. **purplish carmine**	65.
	x. **dark brown red**	65.
R111TC3	20c plate on India paper	
	a. **dark purple**	60.
	b. **dull purple**	60.
	d. **brown**	60.
	e. **black brown**	60.
	g. **light blue**	60.
	h. **dark blue**	70.
	i. **ultramarine**	70.
	k. **yellow green**	70.
	n. **green**	65.
	o. **dark green**	65.
	p. **blue green**	65.
	q. **light orange**	65.
	r. **dark orange**	65.
	s. **deep orange**	65.
	t. **scarlet**	65.
	u. **carmine**	65.
	w. **purplish carmine**	65.
	x. **dark brown red**	65.
R111TC7	20c plate on goldbeater's skin	
	a. **dark brown orange**	90.
R112TC3	25c plate on India paper	
	a. **dark purple**	60.
	b. **dull purple**	60.
	d. **brown**	60.
	e. **black brown**	60.
	g. **light blue**	60.
	h. **dark blue**	70.
	i. **ultramarine**	70.
	k. **yellow green**	70.
	l. **dark yellow green**	70.
	n. **green**	65.
	o. **dark green**	65.
	p. **blue green**	65.
	q. **light orange**	65.
	r. **dark orange**	65.
	s. **deep orange**	65.
	t. **scarlet**	65.
	u. **carmine**	65.
	x. **dark brown red**	65.
R112TC7	25c plate on goldbeater's skin	
	a. **dark brown orange**	90.
R113TC3	30c plate on India paper	
	a. **dark purple**	60.
	b. **dull purple**	60.
	d. **brown**	60.
	e. **black brown**	60.
	g. **light blue**	60.
	h. **dark blue**	70.
	i. **ultramarine**	70.
	k. **yellow green**	70.
	n. **green**	65.
	o. **dark green**	65.
	p. **blue green**	65.
	q. **light orange**	65.
	r. **dark orange**	65.
	s. **deep orange**	65.
	t. **scarlet**	65.
	u. **carmine**	65.
	v. **dark carmine**	65.

w. purplish carmine 65.
x. dark brown red 65.
R113TC7 30c plate on goldbeater's skin
a. dark brown orange 90.
R114TC3 40c plate on India paper
a. dark purple 60.
b. dull purple 60.
d. brown 60.
e. black brown 60.
f. orange brown 65.
g. light blue 60.
h. dark blue 70.
i. ultramarine 70.
k. yellow green 70.
n. green 65.
o. dark green 65.
p. blue green 65.
q. light orange 65.
r. dark orange 65.
s. deep orange 65.
t. scarlet 65.
u. carmine 65.
x. dark brown red 65.
R115TC3 50c plate on India paper
a. dark purple 60.
b. dull purple 60.
d. brown 60.
e. black brown 60.
g. light blue 60.
h. dark blue 70.
i. ultramarine 70.
k. yellow green 70.
n. green 65.
o. dark green 65.
p. blue green 65.
q. light orange 65.
r. dark orange 65.
s. deep orange 65.
t. scarlet 65.
u. carmine 65.
x. dark brown red 65.
R116TC3 60c plate on India paper
a. dark purple 60.
b. dull purple 60.
d. brown 60.
e. black brown 60.
g. light blue 60.
h. dark blue 70.
i. ultramarine 70.
k. yellow green 70.
n. green 65.
o. dark green 65.
p. blue green 65.
q. light orange 65.
r. dark orange 65.
s. deep orange 65.
t. scarlet 65.
u. carmine 65.
v. dark carmine 65.
x. dark brown red 65.
R116TC7 60c plate on goldbeater's skin
a. dark brown orange 90.
R117TC3 70c plate on India paper
a. dark purple 60.
b. dull purple 60.
d. brown 60.
e. black brown 60.
g. light blue 60.
h. dark blue 70.
i. ultramarine 70.
k. yellow green 70.
n. green 65.
o. dark green 65.
p. blue green 65.
q. light orange 65.
r. dark orange 65.
s. deep orange 65.
t. scarlet 65.
u. carmine 65.
x. dark brown red 65.
R118TC3 $1 plate on India paper
a. dark purple 70.
b. dull purple 70.
d. brown 70.
e. black brown 70.
g. light blue 80.
h. dark blue 85.
i. ultramarine 85.
k. yellow green 80.
n. green 75.
o. dark green 75.
p. blue green 75.
q. light orange 75.
r. dark orange 75.
s. deep orange 75.
t. scarlet 80.
u. carmine 80.
w. purplish carmine 80.
x. dark brown red 80.
R118TC7 $1 plate on goldbeater's skin
a. dark brown orange 90.
R119TC3 $1.30 plate on India paper
a. dark purple 70.
b. dull purple 70.
d. brown 70.
e. black brown 70.
g. light blue 80.
h. dark blue 85.
i. ultramarine 85.
k. yellow green 80.
n. green 75.
o. dark green 75.
p. blue green 75.
q. light orange 75.
r. dark orange 75.
s. deep orange 75.
t. scarlet 80.
u. carmine 80.
x. dark brown red 80.

R120TC3 $1.50 plate on India paper
a. dark purple 70.
b. dull purple 70.
d. brown 70.
e. black brown 70.
g. light blue 80.
h. dark blue 85.
i. ultramarine 85.
k. yellow green 80.
n. green 75.
o. dark green 75.
p. blue green 75.
q. light orange 75.
r. dark orange 75.
s. deep orange 75.
t. scarlet 80.
u. carmine 80.
x. dark brown red 80.
R120TC4 $1.50 plate on card
a. bright yellow green 75.
R121TC3 $1.60 plate on India paper
a. dark purple 70.
b. dull purple 70.
d. brown 70.
e. black brown 70.
g. light blue 80.
h. dark blue 85.
i. ultramarine 85.
k. yellow green 80.
n. green 75.
o. dark green 75.
p. blue green 75.
q. light orange 75.
r. dark orange 75.
s. deep orange 75.
t. scarlet 80.
u. carmine 80.
x. dark brown red 80.
R122TC3 $1.90 plate on India paper
a. dark purple 70.
b. dull purple 70.
d. brown 70.
e. black brown 70.
g. light blue 80.
h. dark blue 85.
i. ultramarine 85.
k. yellow green 80.
n. green 75.
o. dark green 75.
p. blue green 75.
q. light orange 75.
r. dark orange 75.
s. deep orange 75.
t. scarlet 80.
u. carmine 80.
x. dark brown red 80.
R122TC4 $1.90 plate on card
a. bright yellow green 75.
R123TC3 $2 plate on India paper
a. dark purple 70.
b. dull purple 70.
d. brown 70.
e. black brown 70.
g. light blue 80.
h. dark blue 85.
i. ultramarine 85.
k. yellow green 80.
n. green 75.
o. dark green 75.
p. blue green 75.
q. light orange 75.
r. dark orange 75.
s. deep orange 75.
t. scarlet 80.
u. carmine 80.
w. purplish carmine 80.
x. dark brown red 80.
R123TC4 $2 plate on card
a. bright yellow green 75.
R123TC7 $2 plate on goldbeater's skin
a. dark brown orange 90.
R124TC3 $2.50 plate on India paper
a. dark purple 70.
b. dull purple 70.
d. brown 70.
e. black brown 70.
g. light blue 80.
h. dark blue 85.
i. ultramarine 85.
k. yellow green 80.
n. green 75.
o. dark green 75.
p. blue green 75.
q. light orange 75.
r. dark orange 75.
s. deep orange 75.
t. scarlet 80.
u. carmine 80.
v. dark carmine 80.
x. dark brown red 80.
R125TC3 $3 plate on India paper
a. dark purple 70.
b. dull purple 70.
d. brown 70.
e. black brown 70.
g. light blue 80.
h. dark blue 85.
i. ultramarine 85.
k. yellow green 80.
n. green 75.
o. dark green 75.
p. blue green 75.
q. light orange 75.
r. dark orange 75.
s. deep orange 75.
t. scarlet 80.
u. carmine 80.
x. dark brown red 80.

R125TC4 $3 plate on card
a. bright yellow green 75.
R126TC3 $3.50 plate on India paper
a. dark purple 70.
b. dull purple 70.
c. red purple 75.
d. brown 70.
e. black brown 70.
g. light blue 80.
h. dark blue 85.
i. ultramarine 85.
k. yellow green 80.
n. green 75.
o. dark green 75.
p. blue green 75.
q. light orange 75.
r. dark orange 75.
s. deep orange 75.
t. scarlet 90.
u. carmine 80.
x. dark brown red 80.
R127TC3 $5 plate on India paper
a. dark purple 70.
b. dull purple 70.
d. brown 70.
e. black brown 70.
g. light blue 80.
h. dark blue 85.
i. ultramarine 85.
k. yellow green 80.
n. green 75.
o. dark green 75.
p. blue green 75.
q. light orange 75.
r. dark orange 75.
s. deep orange 75.
t. scarlet 75.
u. carmine 75.
w. purplish carmine 75.
x. dark brown red 80.
R127TC7 $5 plate on goldbeater's skin
a. dark brown orange 100.
R128TC $10 plate on India paper
a. dark purple 70.
b. dull purple 70.
d. brown 70.
e. black brown 70.
g. light blue 80.
h. dark blue 85.
i. ultramarine 85.
k. yellow green 75.
n. green 75.
o. dark green 75.
p. blue green 75.
q. light orange 75.
r. dark orange 75.
s. deep orange 75.
t. scarlet 75.
u. carmine 80.
x. dark brown red 80.
R128TC4 $10 plate on card
a. bright yellow green 75.
R129TC3 $20 plate on India paper
a. dark purple 95.
b. dull purple 95.
d. brown 95.
e. black brown 95.
g. light blue 90.
h. dark blue 90.
i. ultramarine 90.
k. yellow green 85.
m. emerald green 85.
n. green 75.
o. dark green 75.
p. blue green 75.
q. light orange 75.
r. dark orange 85.
s. deep orange 85.
t. scarlet 90.
u. carmine 80.
v. dark carmine 90.
x. dark brown red 80.
R130TC3 $25 plate on India paper
a. dark purple 100.
b. dull purple 100.
d. brown 100.
e. black brown 100.
g. light blue 90.
h. dark blue 90.
i. ultramarine 90.
k. yellow green 85.
m. emerald green 85.
n. green 75.
o. dark green 75.
p. blue green 75.
q. light orange 75.
r. dark orange 85.
s. deep orange 85.
t. scarlet 90.
u. carmine 80.
w. purplish carmine 90.
x. dark brown red 300.
R130TC7 $5 plate on goldbeater's skin
a. dark brown orange 100.
R131TC3 $50 plate on India paper
a. dark purple 95.
b. dull purple 95.
d. brown 95.
e. black brown 95.
g. light blue 90.
h. dark blue 90.
i. ultramarine 90.
k. yellow green 85.
m. emerald green 85.
n. green 75.
o. dark green 75.
p. blue green 75.
q. light orange 75.
r. dark orange 85.

s. **deep orange** 85.
t. **scarlet** 90.
u. **carmine** 80.
x. **dark brown red** 80.
R131TC4 $50 plate on card
a. **bright yellow green** 85.
RB1TC3 1c plate on India paper
a. **dark purple** 70.
b. **dull purple** 70.
d. **brown** 65.
e. **black brown** 65.
g. **light blue** 75.
h. **dark blue** 75.
i. **ultramarine** 70.
k. **yellow green** 70.
l. **dark yellow green** 70.
n. **green** 65.
o. **dark green** 65.
p. **blue green** 65.
q. **light orange** 65.
r. **dark orange** 65.
s. **deep orange** 65.
t. **scarlet** 65.
u. **carmine** 65.
x. **dark brown red** 65.
RB2TC3 2c plate on India paper
a. **dark purple** 70.
b. **dull purple** 70.
d. **brown** 65.
e. **black brown** 65.
g. **light blue** 70.
h. **dark blue** 70.
i. **ultramarine** 70.
k. **yellow green** 70.
n. **green** 65.
o. **dark green** 65.
p. **blue green** 65.
q. **light orange** 65.
r. **dark orange** 65.
s. **deep orange** 65.
t. **scarlet** 65.
u. **carmine** 65.
x. **dark brown red** 65.
RB2TC4 2c plate on card
a. **bright yellow green** 70.
RB3TC3 3c plate on India paper
a. **dark purple** 70.
b. **dull purple** 70.
d. **brown** 65.
e. **black brown** 65.
g. **light blue** 70.
h. **dark blue** 70.
i. **ultramarine** 70.
k. **yellow green** 70.
l. **dark yellow green** 70.
n. **green** 65.
o. **dark green** 65.
p. **blue green** 65.
q. **light orange** 65.
r. **dark orange** 65.
s. **deep orange** 65.
t. **scarlet** 65.
u. **carmine** 65.
x. **dark brown red** 65.
RB4TC3 4c plate on India paper
a. **dark purple** 70.
b. **dull purple** 70.
d. **brown** 65.
e. **black brown** 65.
g. **light blue** 70.
h. **dark blue** 70.
i. **ultramarine** 70.
k. **yellow green** 70.
n. **green** 65.
o. **dark green** 65.
p. **blue green** 65.
q. **light orange** 65.
r. **dark orange** 65.
s. **deep orange** 65.
t. **scarlet** 65.
u. **carmine** 65.
x. **dark brown red** 65.
RB5TC3 5c plate on India paper
a. **dark purple** 70.
b. **dull purple** 70.
d. **brown** 65.
e. **black brown** 65.
g. **light blue** 70.
h. **dark blue** 70.
i. **ultramarine** 70.
k. **yellow green** 70.
l. **dark yellow green** 70.
n. **green** 65.
o. **dark green** 65.
p. **blue green** 65.
q. **light orange** 65.
r. **dark orange** 65.
s. **deep orange** 65.
t. **scarlet** 65.
u. **carmine** 65.
x. **dark brown red** 65.
RB5TC4 5c plate on card
a. **bright yellow green** 70.
RB6TC3 6c plate on India paper
a. **dark purple** 70.
b. **dull purple** 70.
d. **brown** 65.
e. **black brown** 65.
g. **light blue** 70.
h. **dark blue** 70.
i. **ultramarine** 70.
k. **yellow green** 70.
l. **dark yellow green** 70.
n. **green** 65.
o. **dark green** 65.
p. **blue green** 65.
q. **light orange** 65.
r. **dark orange** 65.
s. **deep orange** 65.
t. **scarlet** 65.
u. **carmine** 65.
x. **dark brown red** 65.
RB7TC3 10c plate on India paper
a. **dark purple** 70.
b. **dull purple** 70.
d. **brown** 65.
e. **black brown** 65.
g. **light blue** 70.
h. **dark blue** 70.
i. **ultramarine** 70.
k. **yellow green** 70.
l. **dark yellow green** 70.
n. **green** 65.
o. **dark green** 65.
p. **blue green** 65.
q. **light orange** 65.
r. **dark orange** 65.
s. **deep orange** 65.
t. **scarlet** 65.
u. **carmine** 65.
x. **dark brown red** 65.

Battleship Type

1898
RB20TC1d ⅛c large die on card
e. **light blue** *1,000.*
RB20P1 ⅛c **yel grn,** lg die on India paper *2,000.*
RB21TC1a ¼c large die on India paper
e. **dull green** 1,300.
RB21P1 ¼c **brn,** lg die on India paper *2,000.*
RB22TC1a ⅜c large die on India paper
e. **dull green** 750.
RB22P1 ⅜c **dp org,** lg die on India paper *2,000.*
RB23P1 ⅝c **dp ultra,** lg die on India paper *2,000.*
RB24TC1a 1c large die on India paper
e. **dull green** 750.
RB24P1 1c **dk grn,** lg die on India paper *2,000.*
RB25P1 1¼c **vio,** lg die on India paper *2,000.*
RB26TC1a 1⅞c large die on India paper
e. **dull green** 750.
f. **black** 750.
RB26P1 1⅞c **dull bl,** lg die on India paper *2,000.*
RB27TC1a 2c large die on India paper
e. **dull green** 500.
RB27P1 2c **vio brn,** lg die on India paper *2,000.*
RB28P1 2½c **lake,** lg die on India paper *2,000.*
RB29P1 3¾c **ol gray,** lg die on India paper *2,000.*
RB30P1 4c **pur,** lg die on India paper *2,000.*
RB31TC1a 5c large die on India paper
e. **dull green** 500.
RB31P1 5c **brn org,** lg die on India paper *2,000.*

Stock Transfer

1918-29
RD20TC1a $50 large die on India paper
e. **black** *2,250.*
f. **blue** *2,250.*

Wines

1916
RE33P1 3c **grn,** with "c" punch cancel, lg die on India paper —
RE34P1 4c **grn,** with "c" punch cancel, lg die on India paper —
RE41P1 20c **grn,** with "c" punch cancel, lg die on India paper —
RE42TC1a 24c large die on India paper
e. **blue** —
RE48P1 80c **grn,** with "c" punch cancel, lg die on India paper —
RE51TC1a $1.60 large die on India paper
e. **bister** —
RE56P1 $20 **grn,** lg die on India paper *5,000.*

Playing Cards

1896 **Bureau of Engraving & Printing**
RF1TC1a 2c large die on India paper
e. **black,** (On hand) *1,500.*
RF2TC1a 2c large die on India paper
e. **lake,** (Act of) *1,000.*
RF2P1 2c **ultra,** lg die on India paper *550.*
a. **blue** *1,100.*
RF23P1 10c **light blue,** large die on India paper *4,500.*

Silver Tax

1941
RG60P1 3c **gray,** without overprint, with "c" punch cancel, lg die on India paper *1,500.*
RG61P1 4c **gray,** without overprint, with "c" punch cancel, lg die on India paper *1,500.*
RG66P1 25c **gray,** without overprint, with "c" punch cancel, lg die on India paper *1,500.*
RG72P1 $3 **gray,** without overprint, lg die on India paper *1,500.*
RG77P5 $30 **gray,** plate on stamp paper, imperf., serial #0000 *900.*

Consular Service Fee

1952
RK40P1a $20 **violet,** large die on wove, on card —

PRIVATE DIE PROPRIETARY

The editors are indebted to Eric Jackson and Philip T. Bansner for the compilation of the following listing of Private Die Proprietary die and plate proofs as well as the corrresponding trial color proofs. The large die proofs range in size and format from die impressions on India die sunk on cards generally up to 6x9 inches, through die impressions on India on or off card in medium to stamp size. Many individual listings are known in more than one size and format. Values reflect the size and format most commonly seen.

Private Die Match Stamps

1864
RO1TC1a 1c large die on India paper
e. **black** 210.
f. **green** 360.
RO1P1 1c **bl,** lg die on India paper 270.
RO2TC1a 1c large die on India paper
e. **black** 270.
f. **green** 360.
RO2P1 1c **org,** lg die on India paper 600.
RO2P3 1c **org,** plate on India paper 90.
RO3P1 1c **bl,** lg die on India paper 270.
RO4P1 1c **bl,** lg die on India paper 600.
RO5TC1a 1c large die on India paper
e. **black** 330.
f. **blue** 600.
RO5P1 1c **grn,** lg die on India paper 600.
RO6TC1a 1c large die on India paper
e. **black** 360.
f. **green** 600.
RO6P1 1c **bl,** lg die on India paper 210.
RO7TC1a 1c large die on India paper
e. **black** 360.
f. **green** 360.
g. **dull green** 600.
RO7P1 1c **bl,** lg die on India paper 210.
RO7P3 1c **bl,** plate on India paper 210.
RO9TC1a 1c large die on India paper 100.
e. **blue** 270.
f. **brown** 330.
g. **dark green** 600.
h. **green** 360.
RO9P1 1c **blk,** lg die on India paper 210.
RO10TC1a 1c large die on India paper
e. **blue** 360.
f. **green** 600.
RO10P1 1c **blk,** lg die on India paper 220.
RO11TC1a 3c large die on India paper
e. **blue** 600.
f. **green** 600.
RO11P1 3c **blk,** lg die on India paper 300.
RO12TC1a 1c large die on India paper
e. **blue** 270.
f. **green** 600.
RO12P1 1c **blk,** lg die on India paper 270.
RO13TC1a 3c large die on India paper
e. **black** 600.
f. **blue** 1,200.
RO13P1 3c **grn,** lg die on India paper 1,200.
RO14TC1a 1c large die on India paper
e. **blue** 270.
f. **green** 600.
RO14P1 1c **blk,** lg die on India paper 210.
RO15TC1a 1c large die on India paper
e. **black** 270.
f. **blue** 270.
RO15P1 1c **grn,** lg die on India paper 360.
RO16TC1a 1c large die on India paper
e. **black** 270.
f. **green** 360.
RO16P1 1c **bl,** lg die on India paper 270.
RO16P3 1c **bl,** plate on India paper 60.
RO17TC1a 1c large die on India paper
e. **black** 270.
f. **green** 600.
g. **green,** composite RO17TC+RO19TC 1,500.
RO17P1 1c **bl,** lg die on India paper 210.
a. 1c+3c **bl,** RO17P1+RO19TC1e composite 1,200.
b. 1c+3c **blk,** RO17TC1e+RO19P1 composite 900.
RO19TC1a 3c large die on India paper
e. **blue** 300.
f. **green** 125.
RO19P1 3c **blk,** lg die on India paper 450.
RO20TC1a 1c large die on India paper
e. **black** 210.
f. **green** 600.
RO20P1 1c **bl,** lg die on India paper 210.
RO21TC1a 3c large die on India paper
e. **blue** 450.
f. **green** 450.
RO21P1 3c **blk,** lg die on India paper 300.
RO22TC1a 1c large die on India paper
e. **black** 360.
RO23TC1a 1c large die on India paper
e. **black** 270.
f. **blue** 270.
g. **green** 600.
RO23P1 1c **org,** lg die on India paper 270.
RO24TC1a 1c large die on India paper
e. **black** 270.
f. **blue** 270.
g. **green** 600.
RO24P1 1c **brn,** lg die on India paper 270.
RO25TC1a 12c large die on India paper
e. **black** 475.
f. **blue** 900.
g. **green** 900.
RO26TC1a 1c large die on India paper
e. **black** 270.
f. **blue** 270.
g. **dark brown** 270.
h. **green** 360.
i. **light brown** 360.
RO27TC1a 12c large die on India paper
e. **black** 475.
f. **blue** 600.
g. **green** 900.
RO28TC1a 1c large die on India paper
e. **black** 210.
f. **brown** 360.
g. **green** 360.
RO28P1 1c **bl,** lg die on India paper 360.
RO28P3 1c **bl,** plate on India paper 90.
RO29TC1a 1c large die on India paper
e. **blue** 360.
f. **green** 360.

Number	Description	Value
RO29P1	1c **blk,** lg die on India paper	210.
RO30TC1a	1c large die on India paper	
	e. **black**	210.
	f. **blue**	270.
	g. **green**	360.
	h. **red**	600.
RO30P1	1c **grn,** lg die on India paper	210.
RO31TC1a	1c large die on India paper	
	e. **blue**	360.
	f. **green**	270.
	g. **red**	600.
RO31P1	1c **blk,** lg die on India paper	210.
RO32TC1a	4c large die on India paper	
	e. **blue**	600.
	f. **brown**	600.
	g. **orange**	600.
	h. **vermilion**	600.
RO32P1	4c **blk,** lg die on India paper	360.
RO33P1	4c **grn,** lg die on India paper	270.
RO35TC1a	1c large die on India paper	
	e. **blue**	360.
	f. **green**	600.
RO35P1	1c **blk,** lg die on India paper	210.
RO37TC1a	3c large die on India paper	
	e. **blue**	475.
	f. **green**	475.
RO37P1	3c **blk,** lg die on India paper	270.
RO38TC1a	1c large die on India paper	
	e. **blue**	425.
	f. **dark blue**	600.
	g. **green**	450.
	h. **red**	725.
RO38P1	1c **blk,** lg die on India paper	425.
RO39TC1a	1c large die on India paper	
	e. **black**	360.
RO39P1	1c **grn,** lg die on India paper	600.
RO40P1	1c **bl,** lg die on India paper	210.
RO41TC1a	1c large die on India paper	
	e. **black**	270.
	f. **green**	360.
RO41P1	1c **lake,** lg die on India paper	270.
RO42TC1a	1c large die on India paper	
	e. **black**	360.
	f. **blue**	360.
	g. **green**	600.
RO42P1	1c **lake,** lg die on India paper	270.
RO43TC1a	1c large die on India paper	
	e. **blue**	600.
RO43P1	1c **blk,** lg die on India paper	270.
RO44P1	1c **grn,** lg die on India paper	270.
RO45TC1a	1c large die on India paper	
	e. **blue**	425.
	f. **green**	900.
RO45P1	1c **blk,** lg die on India paper	270.
RO46TC1a	1c large die on India paper	
	e. **blue**	425.
	f. **dark blue**	600.
	g. **green**	600.
	h. **orange**	360.
RO46P1	1c **blk,** lg die on India paper	360.
RO47TC1a	1c large die on India paper	
	e. **blue**	360.
	f. **green**	600.
RO47P1	1c **blk,** lg die on India paper	270.
RO47P3	1c **blk,** plate on India paper	90.
RO47P4	1c **blk,** plate on card	75.
RO48P1	1c **blk,** lg die on India paper	600.
RO49TC1a	1c large die on India paper	
	e. **blue**	270.
	f. **brown**	600.
	g. **brown red**	360.
	h. **dark blue**	600.
	i. **green**	600.
	j. **red brown**	600.
RO49P1	1c **blk,** lg die on India paper	210.
RO50P1	1c **blk,** lg die on India paper	450.
RO55TC1a	1c large die on India paper	
	e. **blue**	450.
RO55P1	1c **blk,** lg die on India paper	300.
RO56TC1a	1c large die on India paper	
	e. **blue**	900.
	f. **green**	360.
RO56P1	1c **blk,** lg die on India paper	300.
RO57TC1a	1c large die on India paper	
	e. **black**	210.
	f. **blue**	270.
RO57P1	1c **grn,** lg die on India paper	360.
RO58TC1a	1c large die on India paper	
	e. **black**	360.
	f. **blue**	270.
	g. **dark rose**	600.
	h. **green**	600.
	i. **rose**	360.
RO58P1	1c **lake,** lg die on India paper	270.
RO58P3	1c **lake,** plate on India paper	75.
RO59TC1a	1c large die on India paper	
	e. **black**	270.
RO60TC1a	3c large die on India paper	
	e. **blue**	600.
	f. **green**	600.
RO60P1	3c **blk,** lg die on India paper	360.
RO61TC1a	1c large die on India paper	
	e. **black**	210.
	f. **blue**	360.
RO61P1	1c **grn,** lg die on India paper	360.
RO62TC1a	1c large die on India paper	
	e. **black**	210.
	f. **blue**	210.
RO62P1	1c **grn,** lg die on India paper	210.
RO64TC1a	1c large die on India paper	
	e. **black**	270.
	f. **blue**	360.
	g. **green**	360.
RO64P1	1c **lake,** lg die on India paper	270.
RO65TC1a	1c large die on India paper	
	e. **green**	360.
RO65P1	1c **blk,** lg die on India paper	270.
RO66P1	1c **bl,** lg die on India paper	210.

Number	Description	Value
RO67TC1a	1c large die on India paper	
	e. **blue**	270.
	f. **green**	360.
	g. **red**	600.
	h. **rose**	600.
RO67P1	1c **blk,** lg die on India paper	210.
RO68TC1a	1c large die on India paper	
	e. **black**	270.
	f. **blue**	270.
RO68P1	1c **grn,** lg die on India paper	270.
RO69TC1a	1c large die on India paper	
	e. **blue**	360.
	f. **green**	600.
RO69P1	1c **blk,** lg die on India paper	210.
RO71TC1a	1c large die on India paper	
	e. **black**	300.
	f. **green**	475.
RO72TC1a	1c large die on India paper	
	e. **black**	600.
RO72P1	1c **grn,** lg die on India paper	600.
RO73TC1a	1c large die on India paper	
	e. **blue**	270.
	f. **green**	360.
	g. **red**	600.
	h. **red brown**	270.
RO73P1	1c **blk,** lg die on India paper	210.
RO75P1	1c **car,** lg die on India paper	540.
RO76TC1a	1c large die on India paper	
	e. **blue**	600.
	f. **green**	360.
RO76P1	1c **blk,** lg die on India paper	210.
RO77TC1a	1c large die on India paper	
	e. **black**	270.
	f. **green**	360.
RO77P1	1c **bl,** lg die on India paper	270.
RO78TC1a	1c large die on India paper	
	e. **black**	270.
	f. **dark blue**	600.
	g. **green**	600.
RO78P1	1c **bl,** lg die on India paper	270.
RO80TC1a	1c large die on India paper	
	e. **black**	270.
	f. **green**	600.
RO80P1	1c **bl,** lg die on India paper	600.
RO81TC1a	1c large die on India paper	
	e. **blue**	210.
	f. **dark green**	600.
	g. **green**	270.
	h. **lake**	600.
	i. **red**	360.
RO81P1	1c **blk,** lg die on India paper	210.
RO82TC1a	1c large die on India paper	
	e. **blue**	210.
	f. **green**	600.
RO82P1	1c **blk,** lg die on India paper	210.
RO83TC1a	1c large die on India paper	
	e. **black**	210.
	f. **green**	360.
	g. **red**	600.
RO83P1	1c **bl,** lg die on India paper	210.
RO84TC1a	1c large die on India paper	
	e. **blue**	360.
	f. **green**	600.
RO84P1	1c **blk,** lg die on India paper	210.
RO85TC1a	1c large die on India paper	
	e. **black**	300.
	f. **blue**	360.
	g. **green**	425.
	h. **orange**	600.
	i. **vermilion**	600.
RO85P1	1c **brn,** lg die on India paper	360.
RO85P3	1c **brn,** plate on India paper	100.
RO86TC1a	1c large die on India paper	
	e. **blue**	600.
	f. **brown**	600.
	g. **green**	475.
	h. **orange**	600.
	i. **red**	600.
RO86P1	1c **blk,** lg die on India paper	300.
RO86P3	1c **blk,** plate on India paper	125.
RO87TC1a	1c large die on India paper	
	e. **dull rose**	600.
	f. **orange**	600.
RO87P1	1c **blk,** lg die on India paper	600.
RO87P3	1c **blk,** plate on India paper	50.
RO88TC1a	1c large die on India paper	
	e. **blue**	360.
	f. **green**	600.
RO88P1	1c **blk,** lg die on India paper	210.
RO89TC1a	3c large die on India paper	
	e. **blue**	360.
	f. **green**	360.
RO89P1	3c **blk,** lg die on India paper	210.
RO90TC1a	6c large die on India paper	
	e. **blue**	270.
	f. **brown**	600.
	g. **green**	600.
	h. **orange**	600.
RO90P1	6c **blk,** lg die on India paper	210.
RO90P3	6c **blk,** plate on India paper	125.
RO91TC1a	3c large die on India paper	
	e. **blue**	270.
	f. **brown**	600.
	g. **green**	600.
	h. **orange**	600.
	i. **red**	600.
RO91P1	3c **blk,** lg die on India paper	270.
RO91P3	3c **blk,** plate on India paper	125.
RO92TC1a	1c large die on India paper	
	e. **blue**	360.
	f. **green**	600.
RO92P1	1c **blk,** lg die on India paper	210.
RO94TC1a	3c large die on India paper	
	e. **blue**	270.
	f. **brown**	360.
	g. **green**	270.
	h. **orange**	360.
	i. **red**	600.
	j. **vermilion**	600.

Number	Description	Value
RO94P1	3c **blk,** lg die on India paper	210.
RO94P3	3c **blk,** plate on India paper	175.
RO95TC1a	1c large die on India paper	
	e. **black**	210.
	f. **blue**	210.
	g. **brown**	270.
	h. **dark blue**	600.
RO95P1	1c **grn,** lg die on India paper	270.
RO96TC1a	1c large die on India paper	
	e. **black**	210.
	f. **blue**	270.
RO96P1	1c **grn,** lg die on India paper	360.
RO97TC1a	1c large die on India paper	
	e. **blue**	360.
RO97P1	1c **blk,** lg die on India paper	210.
RO98P1	1c **grn,** lg die on India paper	270.
RO99TC1a	1c large die on India paper	
	e. **black**	210.
	f. **blue**	600.
RO99P1	1c **grn,** lg die on India paper	600.
RO100TC1a	1c large die on India paper	
	e. **blue**	600.
RO100P1	1c **grn,** lg die on India paper	270.
RO100P3	1c **grn,** plate on India paper	65.
RO101TC1a	3c large die on India paper	
	e. **black**	210.
	f. **green**	360.
RO101TC3	3c Plate on India paper	
	a. **orange**	75.
RO101P3	3c **car,** plate on India paper	75.
RO102TC1a	1c large die on India paper	
	e. **black**	210.
	f. **blue**	600.
	g. **green**	600.
RO102P3	5c **org,** plate on India paper	75.
RO103TC1a	1c large die on India paper	
	e. **blue**	270.
	f. **rose**	360.
RO103P1	1c **blk,** lg die on India paper	210.
RO104P1	1c **grn,** lg die on India paper	210.
RO105TC1a	1c large die on India paper	
	e. **blue**	360.
	f. **green**	600.
RO105P1	1c **blk,** lg die on India paper	210.
RO105P3	1c **blk,** plate on India paper	100.
RO106TC1a	1c large die on India paper	
	e. **black**	210.
	f. **blue**	270.
RO106P1	1c **grn,** lg die on India paper	360.
RO107TC1a	1c large die on India paper	
	e. **black**	210.
	f. **green**	360.
RO107P1	1c **bl,** lg die on India paper	270.
RO108P1	1c **red,** lg die on India paper	900.
RO109P1	1c **blk,** lg die on India paper	360.
RO110TC1a	1c large die on India paper	
	e. **black**	210.
	f. **blue**	210.
	g. **orange**	600.
	h. **red**	270.
RO110P1	1c **grn,** lg die on India paper	210.
RO112TC1a	1c large die on India paper	
	e. **black**	210.
	f. **green**	600.
RO112P1	1c **bl,** lg die on India paper	270.
RO112P3	1c **bl,** plate on India paper	100.
RO113TC1a	1c large die on India paper	
	e. **blue**	360.
	f. **green**	600.
	g. **orange**	600.
RO113P1	1c **blk,** lg die on India paper	210.
RO114TC1a	1c large die on India paper	
	e. **black**	900.
RO114P1	1c **lake,** lg die on India paper	900.
RO115TC1a	1c large die on India paper	
	e. **black**	210.
	f. **green**	600.
RO115P1	1c **bl,** lg die on India paper	210.
RO116TC1a	1c large die on India paper	
	e. **black**	270.
	f. **green**	360.
RO116P1	1c **bl,** lg die on India paper	210.
RO118TC1a	8c large die on India paper	
	e. **black**	270.
	f. **dark blue**	600.
	g. **green**	600.
RO118P1	8c **bl,** lg die on India paper	600.
RO119TC1a	1c large die on India paper	
	e. **black**	270.
	f. **blue**	270.
RO119P1	1c **grn,** lg die on India paper	360.
RO120TC1a	1c large die on India paper	
	e. **black**	600.
RO120P1	1c+2c **grn,** RO120P1+RS29P1 composite, lg die on India paper	1,500.
RO121TC1a	1c large die on India paper	
	e. **black**	210.
	f. **blue**	360.
RO121P1	1c **grn,** lg die on India paper	600.
RO122TC1a	1c large die on India paper	
	e. **blue**	360.
	f. **green**	600.
RO122P1	1c **blk,** lg die on India paper	210.
RO123TC1a	1c large die on India paper	
	e. **blue**	600.
	f. **green**	600.
RO123P1	1c **blk,** lg die on India paper	210.
RO124P1	1c **grn,** lg die on India paper	900.
RO125TC1a	1c large die on India paper	
	e. **black**	270.
RO125P1	1c **bl,** lg die on India paper	360.
RO126P1	1c **blk,** lg die on India paper	210.
RO127TC1a	1c large die on India paper	
	e. **black**	360.
	f. **green**	270.
RO127P1	1c **bl,** lg die on India paper	210.
RO128TC1a	1c large die on India paper	
	e. **black**	270.
	f. **green**	600.

RO128P1 1c **bl,** lg die on India paper 270.
RO130TC1a 1c large die on India paper
e. **black** 270.
f. **green** 360.
RO130P1 1c **bl,** lg die on India paper 600.
RO130P4 1c **bl,** plate on thin card —
RO131TC1a 1c large die on India paper
e. **black** 210.
f. **green** 270.
g. **red** 270.
RO131P1 1c **bl,** lg die on India paper 360.
RO132TC1a 1c large die on India paper
e. **black** 270.
f. **green** 600.
RO132P1 1c **bl,** lg die on India paper 270.
RO132P3 1c **bl,** plate on India paper 125.
RO133TC1a 1c large die on India paper
e. **blue** 600.
f. **green** 360.
RO133P1 1c **blk,** lg die on India paper 270.
RO134TC1a 1c large die on India paper
e. **black** 360.
f. **green** 360.
RO134TC3 1c plate on India paper
a. **black** 150.
RO134P1 1c **bl,** lg die on India paper 210.
RO134P3 1c **bl,** plate on India paper 75.
RO135TC1a 1c large die on India paper
e. **black** 600.
f. **blue** 360.
g. **green** 360.
h. **rose** 270.
RO135P1 1c **lake,** lg die on India paper 600.
RO136TC1a 1c large die on India paper
e. **black** 270.
f. **green** 360.
RO136P1 1c **bl,** lg die on India paper 210.
RO137TC1a 1c large die on India paper
e. **black** 210.
f. **blue** 210.
g. **green** 600.
RO138TC1a 1c large die on India paper
e. **black** 210.
f. **blue** 600.
RO138P1 1c **grn,** lg die on India paper 210.
RO139TC1a 5c large die on India paper
e. **black** 210.
f. **green** 600.
RO139P1 5c **bl,** lg die on India paper 270.
RO140TC1a 4c large die on India paper
e. **black** 270.
f. **blue** 360.
RO140P1 4c **grn,** lg die on India paper 270.
RO141TC1a 1c large die on India paper
e. **black** 210.
f. **dark blue** 360.
g. **green** 600.
h. **yellow green** 360.
RO141P1 1c **bl,** lg die on India paper 210.
RO142TC1a 1c large die on India paper
e. **black** 210.
f. **blue** 270.
RO142P1 1c **grn,** lg die on India paper 270.
RO143TC1a 3c large die on India paper
e. **black** 210.
f. **blue** 270.
g. **green** 360.
RO143P1 3c **org,** lg die on India paper 270.
RO144TC1a 1c large die on India paper
e. **black** 600.
RO144P1 1c **bl,** lg die on India paper 475.
RO145TC1a 1c large die on India paper
e. **black** 600.
f. **blue** 600.
RO146TC1a 1c large die on India paper
e. **blue** 600.
f. **green** 360.
RO146P1 1c **blk,** lg die on India paper 210.
RO148TC1a 1c large die on India paper
e. **black** 210.
f. **green** 360.
g. **red** 360.
RO148P1 1c **bl,** lg die on India paper 270.
RO148P3 1c **bl,** plate on India paper 100.
RO152TC1a 1c large die on India paper
e. **blue** 360.
f. **green** 360.
RO152P1 1c **blk,** lg die on India paper 210.
RO152P3 1c **blk,** plate on India paper 75.
RO153TC1a 1c large die on India paper
e. **blue** 270.
f. **brown** 360.
g. **green** 270.
h. **orange** 360.
i. **red** 360.
RO153P1 1c **blk,** lg die on India paper 210.
RO153P3 1c **blk,** plate on India paper 75.
RO155TC1a 1c large die on India paper
e. **blue** 270.
f. **green** 600.
RO155P1 1c **blk,** lg die on India paper 210.
RO155P3 1c **blk,** plate on India paper 65.
RO157TC1a 3c large die on India paper
e. **black** 210.
f. **green** 360.
RO157P1 3c **bl,** lg die on India paper 270.
RO157P3 3c **bl,** plate on India paper 80.
RO158TC1a 1c large die on India paper
e. **blue** 360.
f. **green** 600.
RO158P1 1c **blk,** lg die on India paper 210.
RO159TC1a 3c large die on India paper
e. **black** 270.
f. **green** 600.
RO159P1 3c **bl,** lg die on India paper 210.
RO160TC1a 1c large die on India paper
e. **black** 270.
f. **brown** 600.
g. **green** 360.
RO160P1 1c **bl,** lg die on India paper 210.
RO161TC1a 1c large die on India paper
e. **black** 270.
f. **green** 360.
RO161P1 1c **bl,** lg die on India paper 600.
RO163TC1a 1c large die on India paper
e. **blue** 360.
f. **green** 600.
RO163P1 1c **blk,** lg die on India paper 210.
RO164TC1a 1c large die on India paper
e. **black** 600.
RO164P1 1c **lake,** lg die on India paper 600.
RO165TC1a 12c large die on India paper
e. **black** 900.
f. **green** 1,200.
g. **red** 1,200.
RO165P1 12c **bl,** lg die on India paper 900.
RO166TC1a 1c large die on India paper
e. **black** 360.
f. **blue** 270.
g. **green** 600.
h. **red** 210.
RO166P1 1c **ver,** lg die on India paper 270.
RO167TC1a 3c large die on India paper
e. **black** 210.
f. **green** 360.
g. **red** 360.
h. **ultramarine** 360.
RO167P1 3c **bl,** lg die on India paper 210.
RO168TC1a 1c large die on India paper
e. **black** 600.
f. **green** 360.
RO168P1 1c **bl,** lg die on India paper 210.
RO170P1 1c **blk,** lg die on India paper 550.
RO171TC1a 1c large die on India paper
e. **blue** 360.
f. **green** 360.
RO171P1 1c **blk,** lg die on India paper 210.
RO172TC1a 1c large die on India paper
e. **blue** 270.
f. **green** 600.
RO172P1 1c **blk,** lg die on India paper 210.
RO173TC1a 1c large die on India paper
e. **black** 270.
f. **green** 360.
RO173P1 1c **bl,** lg die on India paper 270.
RO173P3 1c **bl,** plate on India paper 75.
RO174TC1a 1c large die on India paper
e. **black** 360.
f. **green** 360.
RO174P1 1c **bl,** lg die on India paper 210.
RO175TC1a 1c large die on India paper
e. **blue** 325.
f. **green** 425.
g. **red** 600.
RO175P1 1c **blk,** lg die on India paper 270.
RO176P1 1c **bl,** lg die on India paper 600.
RO177TC1a 1c large die on India paper
e. **black** 210.
f. **blue** 270.
g. **green** 600.
RO177P1 1c **grn,** lg die on India paper 210.
RO178TC1a 1c large die on India paper
e. **black** 210.
f. **blue** 360.
RO178P1 1c **grn,** lg die on India paper 600.
RO179TC1a 1c large die on India paper
e. **blue** 600.
f. **green** 600.
RO179P1 1c **blk,** lg die on India paper 210.
RO179P3 1c **blk,** plate on India paper 75.
RO179P4 1c **blk,** plate on card 50.
RO180TC1a 1c large die on India paper
e. **blue** 270.
f. **green** 600.
RO180P1 1c **blk,** lg die on India paper 210.
RO180P3 1c **blk,** plate on India paper 80.
RO181TC1a 1c large die on India paper
e. **blue** 600.
f. **green** 360.
RO181P1 1c **blk,** lg die on India paper 210.
RO182TC1a 1c large die on India paper
e. **blue** 360.
f. **green** 360.
RO182P1 1c **blk,** lg die on India paper 210.
RO183TC1a 1c large die on India paper
e. **blue** 775.
f. **green** 775.
RO183P1 1c **blk,** lg die on India paper 600.
RO184TC1a 1c large die on India paper
e. **blue** 270.
f. **brown** 360.
g. **green** 270.
h. **orange** 360.
i. **red** 360.
RO184P1 1c **blk,** lg die on India paper 210.
RO184P3 1c **blk,** plate on India paper 75.
RO185P1 1c+1c **blk,** RO185P1+RO12P1 composite, lg die on India paper 900.
RO186TC1a 1c large die on India paper
e. **black** 210.
RO186P1 1c **bl,** lg die on India paper 270.

Private Die Canned Fruit Stamp

RP1TC1a 1c large die on India paper
e. **black** 475.
RP1P1 1c **grn,** lg die on India paper 475.

Private Die Medicine Stamps

RS1TC1a 1c large die on India paper
e. **blue** 360.
RS1P1 1c **blk,** lg die on India paper 210.
RS1P3 1c **blk,** plate on India paper —
RS4TC1a 1c large die on India paper
e. **green** 600.
RS4P1 1c **blk,** lg die on India paper 270.
RS4P3 1c **blk,** plate on India paper 125.
RS4P4 1c **blk,** plate on card 150.
RS5P1 1c **bl,** lg die on India paper 600.
RS10TC1a 4c large die on India paper
e. **black** 360.
RS10P1 4c **bl,** lg die on India paper 270.
RS10P3 4c **bl,** plate on India paper 125.
RS10P4 4c **bl,** plate on card 150.
RS14TC1a 4c large die on India paper
e. **black** 360.
f. **blue** 360.
RS14P1 4c **grn,** lg die on India paper 600.
RS14P3 4c **grn,** plate on India paper 100.
RS16TC1a 2c large die on India paper
e. **green** 600.
RS16P1 2c **ver,** lg die on India paper 600.
RS18P1 1c **blk,** lg die on India paper 600.
RS18P4 1c **blk,** plate on card 125.
RS19P4 2c **blk,** plate on card 125.
RS20P4 4c **blk,** plate on card 125.
RS21TC1a 1c large die on India paper
e. **blue** 600.
f. **green** 600.
RS21P1 1c **blk,** lg die on India paper 210.
RS21P3 1c **blk,** plate on India paper 125.
RS22TC1a 2c large die on India paper
e. **blue** 600.
f. **green** 600.
RS22P1 2c **blk,** lg die on India paper 270.
RS22P3 2c **blk,** plate on India paper 125.
RS23TC1a 4c large die on India paper
e. **green** 600.
RS23P1 4c **blk,** lg die on India paper 270.
RS23P3 4c **blk,** plate on India paper 125.
RS24TC1a 1c large die on India paper
e. **blue** 600.
f. **green** 600.
RS24P1 1c **blk,** lg die on India paper 210.
RS25TC1a 2c large die on India paper
e. **blue** 600.
f. **green** 600.
RS25P1 2c **blk,** lg die on India paper 210.
RS26TC1a 4c large die on India paper
e. **blue** 600.
f. **green** 600.
RS26P1 4c **blk,** lg die on India paper 210.
RS27TC1a 4c large die on India paper
e. **blue** 270.
f. **green** 600.
RS27P1 4c **blk,** lg die on India paper 210.
RS28TC1a 2c large die on India paper
e. **black** 270.
f. **blue** 270.
RS28P1 2c **grn,** lg die on India paper 210.
RS29TC1a 2c large die on India paper
e. **black,** composite RS29TC + unissued Eugene Jones & Co. essay with "B.J. & Co." added 900.
f. **black** 210.
g. **blue** 210.
h. **dark blue** 600.
i. **green** 600.
j. **red** 360.
RS29P1 2c **grn,** lg die on India paper 270.

For composite proof RO120P1 + RS29P1, see No. RO120P1.

RS30TC1a 1c large die on India paper
e. **black** 210.
f. **blue** 600.
g. **green** 600.
h. **red** 600.
RS30P1 1c **lake,** lg die on India paper 360.
RS31TC1a 1c large die on India paper
e. **black** 600.
f. **blue** 270.
g. **red** 600.
RS31P1 1c **grn,** lg die on India paper 210.
RS31P3 1c **grn,** plate on India paper 100.
RS31P4 1c **grn,** plate on card 100.
RS33P1 1c **blk,** lg die on India paper 210.
RS33P3 1c **blk,** plate on India paper 50.
RS33P4 1c **blk,** plate on card 50.
RS34TC1a 1c large die on India paper
e. **blue** 210.
f. **green** 270.
g. **red** 600.
RS34P1 1c **blk,** lg die on India paper 270.
RS35TC1a 1c large die on India paper
e. **blue** 360.
f. **green** 600.
RS35P1 1c **blk,** lg die on India paper 210.
RS36TC1a 1c large die on India paper
e. **black** 600.
f. **dark blue** 600.
g. **green** 600.
h. **ultramarine** 600.
i. **yellow green** 270.
RS36P1 1c **bl,** lg die on India paper 210.
RS37P1 2c **blk,** lg die on India paper 550.
RS38TC1a 2c large die on India paper
e. **blue** 900.
f. **green** 900.
RS38P1 2c **blk,** lg die on India paper 360.
RS39TC1a 1c large die on India paper
e. **blue** 360.
f. **green** 360.
g. **orange** 600.
RS39P1 1c **blk,** lg die on India paper 210.
RS39P3 1c **blk,** plate on India paper 100.
RS39P4 1c **blk,** plate on card 100.
RS40TC1a 2c large die on India paper
e. **black** 270.
f. **blue** 360.
RS40P1 2c **grn,** lg die on India paper 600.
RS40P3 2c **grn,** plate on India paper 100.
RS40P4 2c **grn,** plate on card 100.
RS41TC1a 4c large die on India paper
e. **black** 270.
f. **blue** 600.
g. **green** 600.

No.	Description	Price
RS41P3	4c **brn,** plate on India paper	125.
RS41P4	4c **brn,** plate on card	125.
RS42TC1a	1c large die on India paper	
	e. **green**	600.
	f. **blue**	600.
RS42P1	1c **blk,** lg die on India paper	210.
RS43TC1a	4c large die on India paper	
	e. **black**	270.
	f. **green**	600.
RS43P1	4c **bl,** lg die on India paper	270.
RS44TC1a	1c large die on India paper	
	e. **green**	900.
RS44P1	1c **blk,** lg die on India paper	725.
RS46TC1a	4c large die on India paper	
	e. **blue**	270.
	f. **green**	360.
RS46P1	4c **blk,** lg die on India paper	210.
RS47TC1a	4c large die on India paper	
	e. **blue**	360.
	f. **brown**	600.
	g. **green**	360.
	h. **orange**	600.
	i. **red**	600.
RS47P1	4c **blk,** lg die on India paper	210.
RS47P3	4c **blk,** plate on India paper	125.
RS49TC1a	4c large die on India paper	
	e. **black**	270.
	f. **blue**	360.
RS49P1	4c **grn,** lg die on India paper	210.
RS50TC1a	1c large die on India paper	
	e. **black**	360.
	f. **blue**	360.
	g. **green**	600.
RS50P1	1c **ver,** lg die on India paper	270.
RS51TC1a	2c large die on India paper	
	e. **blue**	600.
	f. **green**	600.
RS51P1	2c **blk,** lg die on India paper	210.
RS52TC1a	4c large die on India paper	
	e. **blue**	600.
	f. **green**	600.
RS52P1	4c **blk,** lg die on India paper	210.
RS53TC1a	1c large die on India paper	
	e. **blue**	270.
	f. **brown**	360.
	g. **green**	270.
	h. **orange**	360.
	i. **red**	360.
RS53P1	1c **blk,** lg die on India paper	210.
RS53P3	1c **blk,** plate on India paper	125.
RS54TC1a	2c large die on India paper	
	e. **blue**	270.
	f. **brown**	360.
	g. **green**	270.
	h. **orange**	360.
	i. **red**	600.
RS54P1	2c **blk,** lg die on India paper	210.
RS54P3	2c **blk,** plate on India paper	125.
RS55TC1a	4c large die on India paper	
	e. **blue**	270.
	f. **green**	270.
	g. **orange**	270.
	h. **red**	600.
RS55P1	4c **blk,** lg die on India paper	210.
RS55P3	4c **blk,** plate on India paper	125.
RS56TC1a	3c large die on India paper	
	e. **black**	425.
	f. **green**	600.
RS56P1	3c **bl,** lg die on India paper	425.
RS56P3	3c **bl,** plate on India paper	125.
RS57TC1a	6c large die on India paper	
	e. **blue**	270.
	f. **brown**	360.
	g. **green**	270.
	h. **orange**	360.
	i. **red**	360.
RS57P1	6c **blk,** lg die on India paper	210.
RS57P3	6c **blk,** plate on India paper	100.
RS58TC1a	4c large die on India paper	
	e. **blue**	270.
	f. **blue green**	600.
	g. **dark blue**	600.
	h. **green**	270.
	i. **light blue**	600.
	j. **red**	270.
RS58P1	4c **blk,** lg die on India paper	210.
RS59TC1a	1c large die on India paper	
	e. **blue**	360.
	f. **green**	600.
RS59P1	1c **blk,** lg die on India paper	210.
RS60TC1a	1c large die on India paper	
	e. **blue**	600.
RS60P1	1c **blk,** lg die on India paper	210.
RS60P3	1c **blk,** plate on India paper	65.
RS61P1	4c **bl,** lg die on India paper	600.
RS62TC1a	1c large die on India paper	
	e. **brown**	360.
	f. **green**	270.
	g. **orange**	360.
	h. **red**	600.
	i. **vermilion**	600.
RS62P1	1c **blk,** lg die on India paper	270.
RS62P3	1c **blk,** plate on India paper	125.
RS63P1	1c **bl,** lg die on India paper	210.
RS64TC1a	2c large die on India paper	
	e. **blue**	270.
	f. **brown**	300.
	g. **green**	270.
	h. **orange**	360.
	i. **red**	600.
	j. **vermilion**	600.
RS64P1	2c **blk,** lg die on India paper	210.
RS64P3	2c **blk,** plate on India paper	125.
RS65TC1a	4c large die on India paper	
	e. **blue**	600.
	f. **green**	600.
RS65P1	4c **blk,** lg die on India paper	210.
RS66TC1a	1c large die on India paper	
	e. **blue**	360.
	f. **green**	600.
	g. **light green**	600.
	h. **orange**	600.
	i. **rose red**	600.
RS66P1	1c **blk,** lg die on India paper	600.
RS66P4	1c **blk,** plate on card	85.
RS67TC1a	1c large die on India paper	
	e. **green**	600.
RS67P1	1c **blk,** lg die on India paper	210.
RS68P1	2c **blk,** lg die on India paper	210.
RS68P3	2c **blk,** plate on India paper	90.
RS69TC1a	1c large die on India paper	
	e. **blue**	600.
	f. **green**	600.
RS69P1	1c **blk,** lg die on India paper	210.
RS70TC1a	2c large die on India paper	
	e. **blue**	600.
	f. **green**	600.
RS70P1	2c **blk,** lg die on India paper	270.
RS71TC1a	1c large die on India paper	
	e. **blue**	600.
	f. **green**	600.
RS71P1	1c **blk,** lg die on India paper	210.
RS72TC1a	2c large die on India paper	
	e. **blue**	600.
	f. **green**	600.
RS72P1	2c **blk,** lg die on India paper	210.
RS73TC1a	2c large die on India paper	
	e. **black**	600.
	f. **blue**	900.
	g. **red**	1,200.
RS73P1	2c **grn,** lg die on India paper	600.
RS74TC1a	1c large die on India paper	
	e. **blue**	600.
	f. **green**	600.
RS74hTC1a	$100 large die on India paper	
	e. **blue**	600.
	f. **green**	600.
RS74P1	1c **blk,** lg die on India paper	270.
	h. **blk,** $100 instead of $1.00 (error), lg die on India paper	210.
RS75TC1a	1c large die on India paper	
	e. **black**	360.
	f. **green**	600.
RS75P1	1c **bl,** lg die on India paper	210.
RS76TC1a	2c large die on India paper	
	e. **blue**	360.
	f. **green**	360.
RS77P1	2c **blk,** lg die on India paper	270.
RS78P1	2c **dull pur,** lg die on India paper	900.
RS81TC1a	4c large die on India paper	
	e. **black**	270.
	f. **blue**	600.
	g. **green**	600.
RS81P1	4c **brn,** lg die on India paper	270.
RS82P1	2c **blk,** lg die on India paper	210.
RS83TC1a	4c large die on India paper	
	e. **blue**	600.
	f. **green**	600.
RS83P1	4c **blk,** lg die on India paper	270.
RS84TC1a	1c large die on India paper	
	e. **black**	300.
	f. **blue**	425.
	g. **green**	300.
	h. **orange**	775.
	i. **red**	775.
	j. **slate**	775.
RS84P1	1c **lake,** lg die on India paper	600.
RS84P3	1c **lake,** plate on India paper	—
RS84P4	1c **lake,** plate on card	110.
RS85TC1a	4c large die on India paper	
	e. **blue**	330.
	f. **brown**	330.
	g. **green**	360.
	h. **orange**	450.
RS85P1	4c **blk,** lg die on India paper	300.
RS85P3	4c **blk,** plate on India paper	—
RS86TC1a	1c large die on India paper	
	e. **black**	270.
	f. **blue**	270.
RS86P1	1c **grn,** lg die on India paper	210.
RS88TC1a	1c large die on India paper	
	e. **blue**	600.
	f. **green**	600.
RS88P1	1c **blk,** lg die on India paper	270.
RS88P3	1c **blk,** plate on India paper	100.
RS88P4	1c **blk,** plate on card	100.
RS89TC1a	1c large die on India paper	
	e. **green**	360.
RS89P1	1c **blk,** lg die on India paper	600.
RS90P1	1c **bl,** lg die on India paper	270.
RS90P3	1c **bl,** plate on India paper	125.
RS90P4	1c **bl,** plate on card	125.
RS91TC1a	4c large die on India paper	
	e. **blue**	270.
	f. **green**	600.
RS91P1	4c **blk,** lg die on India paper	210.
RS92TC1a	3c large die on India paper	
	e. **blue**	270.
	f. **brown**	360.
	g. **green**	270.
	h. **orange**	360.
	i. **red**	600.
	j. **vermilion**	600.
RS92P1	3c **blk,** lg die on India paper	210.
RS92P3	3c **blk,** plate on India paper	—
RS94TC1a	4c large die on India paper	
	e. **blue**	600.
	f. **green**	600.
RS94P1	4c **blk,** lg die on India paper	210.
RS95TC1a	1c large die on India paper	
	e. **black**	360.
	f. **blue**	270.
RS95TC3	1c plate on India paper	
	a. **dark blue**	90.
RS95P1	1c **grn,** lg die on India paper	270.
RS95P3	1c **grn,** plate on India paper	90.
RS96TC1a	3c large die on India paper	
	e. **blue**	270.
	f. **green**	600.
RS96P1	3c **blk,** lg die on India paper	210.
RS96P3	3c **blk,** plate on India paper	50.
RS97TC1a	1c large die on India paper	
	e. **blue**	360.
	f. **green**	600.
RS97P1	1c **blk,** lg die on India paper	210.
RS98TC1a	1c large die on India paper	
	e. **blue**	270.
	f. **green**	210.
	g. **red**	600.
RS98P1	1c **blk,** lg die on India paper	210.
RS99TC1a	4c large die on India paper	
	e. **blue**	600.
RS99P1	4c **blk,** lg die on India paper	210.
RS100TC1a	6c large die on India paper	
	e. **green**	600.
RS100P1	6c **blk,** lg die on India paper	210.
RS101TC1a	1c large die on India paper	
	e. **blue**	600.
	f. **green**	600.
RS101P1	1c **blk,** lg die on India paper	210.
RS102TC1a	2c large die on India paper	
	e. **black**	210.
	f. **green**	270.
	g. **rose**	270.
RS102P1	2c **bl,** lg die on India paper	210.
RS103TC1a	4c large die on India paper	
	e. **blue**	600.
	f. **green**	600.
RS103P1	4c **blk,** lg die on India paper	210.
RS104P1	3c **blk,** lg die on India paper	900.
RS105P1	3c **brn,** lg die on India paper	725.
RS106TC1a	2c large die on India paper	
	e. **black**	600.
	f. **green**	360.
RS106P1	2c **bl,** lg die on India paper	270.
RS106P3	2c **bl,** plate on India paper	60.
RS107TC1a	3c large die on India paper	
	e. **green,** composite RS107TC+RS109TC	1,500.
	f. **blue**	360.
RS107P1	3c **blk,** lg die on India paper	270.
	a. 3c+6c **blk,** RS107P1+RS109P1 composite, lg die on India paper	1,200.
RS108TC1a	4c large die on India paper	
	e. **blue**	360.
	f. **green**	600.
RS108P1	4c **blk,** lg die on India paper	210.
RS108P3	4c **blk,** plate on India paper	45.
RS109TC1a	6c large die on India paper	
	e. **blue**	360.
RS109P1	6c **blk,** lg die on India paper	270.
RS110TC1a	2c large die on India paper	
	e. **black**	360.
	f. **green**	360.
RS110P1	2c **bl,** lg die on India paper	210.
RS111TC1a	4c large die on India paper	
	e. **blue**	360.
	f. **green**	600.
RS111P1	4c **blk,** lg die on India paper	210.
RS114TC1a	1c large die on India paper	
	e. **green**	360.
RS114P1	1c **blk,** lg die on India paper	270.
	a. 1c+2c **blk,** RS114P1+RS115P1 composite, lg die on India paper	1,200.
RS115P1	2c **bl,** lg die on India paper	270.
RS116TC1a	4c large die on India paper	
	e. **black**	270.
	f. **blue**	360.
	g. **brown**	600.
	h. **green**	600.
	i. **vermilion**	600.
RS116P1	4c **red,** lg die on India paper	270.
RS117TC1a	1c large die on India paper	
	e. **blue**	425.
	f. **green**	900.
RS117P1	1c **blk,** lg die on India paper	300.
RS118TC1a	1c large die on India paper	
	e. **black**	210.
	f. **blue**	270.
	g. **brown red**	360.
	h. **green**	360.
RS118P1	1c **red,** lg die on India paper	360.
RS118P3	1c **red,** plate on India paper	55.
RS118P4	1c **red,** plate on card	50.
RS119P1	1c **blk,** lg die on India paper	270.
RS120TC1a	2c large die on India paper	
	e. **blue**	270.
	f. **brown**	360.
	g. **green**	270.
	h. **orange**	360.
	i. **red**	600.
	j. **vermilion**	600.
RS120P1	2c **blk,** lg die on India paper	210.
RS121TC1a	3c large die on India paper	
	e. **blue**	600.
	f. **green**	600.
RS121P1	3c **blk,** lg die on India paper	270.
RS121P3	3c **blk,** plate on India paper	75.
RS122TC1a	2c large die on India paper	
	e. **blue**	600.
	f. **green**	600.
RS122P1	2c **blk,** lg die on India paper	210.
RS122P3	2c **blk,** plate on India paper	100.
RS123TC1a	4c large die on India paper	
	e. **blue**	270.
	f. **brown**	360.
	g. **green**	270.
	h. **orange**	360.
	i. **red**	600.
	j. **vermilion**	600.
RS123P1	4c **blk,** lg die on India paper	210.
RS123P3	4c **blk,** plate on India paper	125.

RS124TC1a 1c large die on India paper
e. **black** 210.
f. **blue green** 360.
g. **green** 600.
h. **orange** 600.
i. **red** 270.
RS124P1 1c **bl,** lg die on India paper 360.
RS124P3 1c **bl,** plate on India paper 90.
RS124P4 1c **bl,** plate on card 65.
RS126TC1a 1c large die on India paper
e. **black** 270.
f. **blue** 270.
g. **brown** 360.
h. **orange** 360.
i. **red** 600.
j. **vermilion** 600.
RS126P1 1c **grn,** lg die on India paper 210.
RS127TC1a 4c large die on India paper
e. **black** 270.
f. **blue** 270.
g. **brown** 270.
h. **orange** 360.
i. **red** 600.
j. **vermilion** 600.
RS127P1 4c **grn,** lg die on India paper 210.
RS127P3 4c **grn,** plate on India paper 65.
RS128TC1a 2c large die on India paper
e. **black** 725.
f. **green** 475.
g. **pale blue** 600.
RS128P1 2c **bl,** lg die on India paper 330.
RS128P3 2c **bl,** plate on India paper 150.
RS130TC1a 4c large die on India paper
e. **black** 330.
f. **blue** 425.
RS130P1 4c **grn,** lg die on India paper 330.
RS131TC1a 4c large die on India paper
e. **blue** 270.
f. **brown** 600.
g. **green** 360.
h. **orange** 360.
i. **red** 600.
j. **vermilion** 600.
RS131P1 4c **blk,** lg die on India paper 210.
RS131P3 4c **blk,** plate on India paper 75.
RS132TC1a 4c large die on India paper
e. **blue** 600.
f. **orange** 600.
RS132P4 4c **blk,** plate on card 75.
RS133TC1a 6c large die on India paper
e. **blue** 600.
f. **green** 600.
RS133P1 6c **blk,** lg die on India paper 210.
RS133P3 6c **blk,** plate on India paper 125.
RS134TC1a 4c large die on India paper
e. **black** 360.
f. **green** 360.
g. **red** 600.
RS134P1 4c **bl,** lg die on India paper 270.
RS137P1 4c **bl,** lg die on India paper 600.
RS138TC1a 1c large die on India paper
e. **blue** 360.
f. **green** 600.
g. **red** 600.
h. **yellow green** 600.
RS138P1 1c **blk,** lg die on India paper 210.
RS139TC1a 2c large die on India paper
e. **black** 270.
f. **blue** 600.
g. **green** 600.
h. **red** 270.
i. **rose** 600.
RS139TC4 2c plate on card
a. **blackish violet** 90.
RS141TC1a 4c large die on India paper
e. **black** 270.
f. **blue** 360.
RS141P1 4c **grn,** lg die on India paper 360.
RS141P3 4c **grn,** plate on India paper 125.
RS142TC1a 1c large die on India paper
e. **blue** 270.
f. **brown** 360.
g. **green** 270.
h. **orange** 360.
i. **red** 600.
j. **vermilion** 600.
RS142P1 1c **blk,** lg die on India paper 210.
RS143TC1a 4c large die on India paper
e. **black** 270.
f. **blue** 270.
RS143P1 4c **grn,** lg die on India paper 270.
RS144TC1a 1c large die on India paper
e. **black** 600.
f. **green** 600.
RS144P1 1c **bl,** lg die on India paper 210.
RS144P3 1c **bl,** plate on India paper 100.
RS144P4 1c **bl,** plate on card 100.
RS145TC1a 2c large die on India paper
e. **blue** 500.
RS145P1 2c **blk,** lg die on India paper 175.
RS145P3 2c **blk,** plate on India paper 100.
RS145P4 2c **blk,** plate on card 100.
RS146TC1a 4c large die on India paper
e. **black** 360.
f. **blue** 360.
RS146P1 4c **grn,** lg die on India paper 270.
RS146P3 4c **grn,** plate on India paper 100.
RS146P4 4c **grn,** plate on card 100.
RS150TC1a 1c large die on India paper
e. **black** 360.
f. **blue** 210.
g. **carmine** 600.
h. **green** 270.
RS150P1 1c **ver,** lg die on India paper 270.
RS150P3 1c **ver,** plate on India paper 100.
RS151TC1a 1c large die on India paper
e. **blue** 600.
f. **carmine** 600.
RS151P1 1c **blk,** lg die on India paper 210.
RS152TC1a 2c large die on India paper
e. **black** 210.
f. **blue** 360.
RS152P1 2c **grn,** lg die on India paper 210.
RS153TC1a 4c large die on India paper
e. **blue** 900.
f. **green** 900.
RS153P1 4c **blk,** lg die on India paper 550.
RS153P3 4c **blk,** plate on India paper 175.
RS153P4 4c **blk,** plate on card 150.
RS154TC1a 4c large die on India paper
e. **black** 600.
RS154P1 4c **bl,** lg die on India paper 600.
RS155TC1a 2c large die on India paper
e. **black** 360.
f. **blue** 270.
g. **red** 600.
RS155P1 2c **grn,** lg die on India paper 210.
RS156TC1a 6c large die on India paper
e. **blue** 270.
f. **green** 270.
g. **red** 270.
RS156P1 6c **blk,** lg die on India paper 210.
RS157TC1a 2c large die on India paper
e. **blue** 270.
f. **green** 270.
g. **red** 600.
h. **vermilion** 360.
RS157P1 2c **blk,** lg die on India paper 210.
RS158TC1a 1c large die on India paper
e. **black** 600.
RS158P1 1c **grn,** lg die on India paper 600.
RS159TC1a 4c large die on India paper
e. **black** 450.
RS159P1 4c **bl,** lg die on India paper 270.
RS160TC1a 6c large die on India paper
e. **blue** 360.
f. **green** 600.
RS160P1 6c **blk,** lg die on India paper 270.
RS161TC1a 4c large die on India paper
e. **blue** 600.
f. **green** 900.
RS161P1 4c **blk,** lg die on India paper 360.
RS161P3 4c **blk,** plate on India paper 150.
RS162TC1a 1c large die on India paper
e. **black** 210.
f. **green** 360.
g. **red** 600.
RS162P1 1c **bl,** lg die on India paper 360.
RS163TC1a 4c large die on India paper
e. **black** 360.
f. **green** 725.
g. **yellow green** 725.
RS163P1 4c **bl,** lg die on India paper 725.
RS164TC1a 1c large die on India paper
e. **blue** 270.
f. **green** 600.
RS164P1 1c **blk,** lg die on India paper 210.
RS165TC1a 4c large die on India paper
e. **black** 210.
f. **blue** 270.
RS165P1 4c **grn,** lg die on India paper 600.
RS166TC1a 1c large die on India paper
e. **blue** 360.
f. **green** 600.
RS166P1 1c **blk,** lg die on India paper 210.
RS169TC1a 4c large die on India paper
e. **blue** 270.
f. **green** 600.
g. **red** 270.
RS169P1 4c **blk,** lg die on India paper 210.
RS170TC1a 1c large die on India paper
e. **blue** 360.
f. **green** 600.
RS170P1 1c **blk,** lg die on India paper 210.
RS171TC1a 1c large die on India paper
e. **black** 270.
f. **blue** 270.
g. **brown** 360.
h. **dull blue** 600.
i. **green** 270.
j. **orange** 360.
k. **red** 600.
l. **vermilion** 600.
RS171P1 1c **vio,** lg die on India paper 210.
u. **pur,** lg die on India paper 600.
RS172TC1a 2c large die on India paper
e. **blue** 270.
f. **brown** 360.
g. **green** 270.
h. **orange** 270.
i. **red** 600.
j. **vermilion** 600.
RS172P1 2c **blk,** lg die on India paper 210.
RS172P3 2c **blk,** plate on India paper 100.
RS173TC1a 1c large die on India paper
e. **black** 270.
f. **green** 270.
g. **red** 360.
RS173P1 1c **bl,** lg die on India paper 210.
RS174TC1a 1c large die on India paper
e. **black** 360.
f. **dark blue** 600.
g. **green** 360.
RS174P1 1c **bl,** lg die on India paper 210.
RS175TC1a 2c large die on India paper
e. **black** 300.
f. **blue** 600.
g. **green** 600.
RS176TC1a 4c large die on India paper
e. **blue** 450.
f. **green** 600.
RS176P1 4c **blk,** lg die on India paper 300.
RS177TC1a 2c large die on India paper
e. **blue** 900.
f. **green** 1,200.
RS177P1 2c **blk,** lg die on India paper 425.
RS178TC1a 6c large die on India paper
e. **blue** 360.
f. **green** 600.
RS178P1 1c **blk,** lg die on India paper 270.
RS179TC1a 2c large die on India paper
e. **black** 360.
f. **blue** 450.
RS179P1 2c **grn,** lg die on India paper 270.
RS180TC1a 3c large die on India paper
e. **blue** 360.
f. **green** 360.
RS180P1 3c **blk,** lg die on India paper 325.
RS180P3 3c **blk,** plate on India paper 125.
RS181TC1a 4c large die on India paper
e. **blue** 270.
f. **green** 600.
RS181P1 4c **blk,** lg die on India paper 270.
RS182TC1a 4c large die on India paper
e. **blue** 270.
f. **green** 270.
g. **rose** 360.
RS182P1 4c **blk,** lg die on India paper 210.
RS183TC1a 1c large die on India paper
e. **black** 600.
f. **blue** 360.
g. **green** 600.
h. **red** 270.
RS183P1 1c **ver,** lg die on India paper 270.
RS183P3 1c **ver,** plate on India paper 85.
RS184TC1a 2c large die on India paper
e. **blue** 360.
f. **brown** 270.
g. **green** 270.
h. **orange** 360.
i. **vermilion** 360.
RS184P1 2c **blk,** lg die on India paper 210.
RS184P3 2c **blk,** plate on India paper 100.
RS185TC1a 1c large die on India paper
e. **blue** 360.
RS185P1 1c **blk,** lg die on India paper 210.
RS185P3 1c **blk,** plate on India paper 100.
RS186TC1a 4c large die on India paper
e. **blue** 270.
f. **green** 600.
RS186P1 4c **blk,** lg die on India paper 210.
RS187TC1a 4c large die on India paper
e. **blue** 270.
f. **brown** 360.
g. **green** 360.
h. **orange** 600.
i. **red** 600.
j. **vermilion** 600.
RS187P1 4c **blk,** lg die on India paper 210.
RS187P3 4c **blk,** plate on India paper 100.
RS188TC1a 1c large die on India paper
e. **blue** 600.
f. **green** 600.
RS188P1 6c **blk,** lg die on India paper 360.
RS189TC1a 1c large die on India paper
e. **black** 210.
f. **blue** 270.
g. **red** 270.
RS189P1 1c **grn,** lg die on India paper 270.
RS190TC1a 2c large die on India paper
e. **blue** 600.
f. **green** 600.
RS190P1 2c **blk,** lg die on India paper 210.
RS191TC1a 4c large die on India paper
e. **blue** 475.
f. **green** 475.
RS191P1 4c **blk,** lg die on India paper 300.
RS192TC1a 6c large die on India paper
e. **blue** 475.
f. **green** 475.
g. **rose** 600.
RS192P1 6c **blk,** lg die on India paper 300.
RS192P3 6c **blk,** plate on India paper 125.
RS193TC1a 2c large die on India paper
e. **blue** 600.
f. **green** 600.
RS193P1 2c **blk,** lg die on India paper 210.
RS194TC1a 1c large die on India paper
e. **green** 210.
RS194P1 1c **bl,** lg die on India paper 210.
RS195TC1a 2c large die on India paper
e. **blue** 600.
f. **green** 600.
RS195P1 2c **blk,** lg die on India paper 210.
RS196TC1a 1c large die on India paper
e. **black** 600.
f. **green** 270.
RS196P1 1c **bl,** lg die on India paper 210.
RS197TC1a 2c large die on India paper
e. **blue** 360.
RS197P1 2c **blk,** lg die on India paper 210.
RS198TC1a 1c large die on India paper
e. **green** 360.
f. **red** 600.
RS198P1 1c **bl,** lg die on India paper 270.
RS199TC1a 2c large die on India paper
e. **green** 600.
RS199P1 2c **bl,** lg die on India paper 300.
RS200P1 4c **blk,** lg die on India paper 210.
RS204TC1a 2c large die on India paper
e. **blue** 600.
f. **green** 600.
RS204P1 2c **blk,** lg die on India paper 210.
RS205TC1a 4c large die on India paper
e. **blue** 270.
f. **green** 600.
RS205P1 4c **blk,** lg die on India paper 210.
RS208TC1a 1c large die on India paper
e. **black** 270.
f. **blue** 270.
g. **orange** 360.
RS208P1 1c **grn,** lg die on India paper 210.
RS208P3 1c **grn,** plate on India paper 100.
RS208P4 1c **grn,** plate on card 95.

No.	Description	Value
RS209TC1a	2c large die on India paper	
	e. **black**	600.
	f. **blue**	600.
RS209P1	2c **grn,** lg die on India paper	270.
RS210TC1a	4c large die on India paper	
	e. **blue**	270.
	f. **green**	270.
	g. **red**	270.
RS210P1	4c **blk,** lg die on India paper	270.
RS212TC1a	1c large die on India paper	
	e. **black**	270.
	f. **blue**	360.
	g. **green**	600.
RS212P1	1c **grn,** lg die on India paper	270.
RS212P3	1c **grn,** plate on India paper	100.
RS213TC1a	6c large die on India paper	
	e. **blue**	600.
	f. **green**	600.
RS213P1	6c **blk,** lg die on India paper	210.
RS213P3	6c **blk,** plate on India paper	100.
RS213P4	6c **blk,** plate on card	150.
RS214TC1a	4c large die on India paper	
	e. **blue**	360.
	f. **brown**	360.
	g. **green**	270.
	h. **orange**	360.
	i. **red**	600.
	j. **vermilion**	600.
RS214P1	4c **blk,** lg die on India paper	210.
RS214P3	4c **blk,** plate on India paper	65.
RS215TC1a	1c large die on India paper	
	e. **black**	360.
	f. **blue**	550.
	g. **dark red**	600.
	h. **green**	600.
RS215P1	1c **lake,** lg die on India paper	360.
RS216TC1a	1c large die on India paper	
	e. **blue**	600.
	f. **green**	600.
RS216P1	1c **blk,** lg die on India paper	210.
RS216P3	1c **blk,** plate on India paper	75.
RS219P1	4c **bl,** lg die on India paper	360.
RS220TC1a	1c large die on India paper	
	e. **blue**	360.
RS220P1	1c **blk,** lg die on India paper	210.
RS220P3	1c **blk,** plate on India paper	50.
RS221TC1a	4c large die on India paper	
	e. **black**	210.
	f. **blue**	270.
RS221P1	4c **grn,** lg die on India paper	270.
RS221P3	4c **grn,** plate on India paper	50.
RS222TC1a	8c large die on India paper	
	e. **green**	600.
RS222P1	8c **blk,** lg die on India paper	210.
RS223TC1a	1c large die on India paper	
	e. **blue**	360.
	f. **brown**	360.
	g. **green**	270.
	h. **orange**	360.
	i. **vermilion**	360.
RS223P1	1c **blk,** lg die on India paper	210.
RS223P3	1c **blk,** plate on India paper	—
RS224TC1a	1c large die on India paper	
	e. **blue**	600.
	f. **brown**	360.
	g. **green**	270.
	h. **orange**	360.
	i. **red**	600.
RS224P1	1c **blk,** lg die on India paper	210.
RS224P3	1c **blk,** plate on India paper	—
RS225P1	4c **blk,** lg die on India paper	210.
RS226TC1a	1c large die on India paper	
	e. **black**	425.
RS226P3	1c **bl,** plate on India paper	350.
RS228TC1a	1c large die on India paper	
	e. **black**	210.
	f. **blue**	270.
	g. **brown**	600.
	h. **green**	270.
	i. **orange**	600.
	j. **red**	600.
	k. **vermilion**	600.
RS228P1	1c **brn,** lg die on India paper	270.
RS228P3	1c **brn,** plate on India paper	—
RS229TC1a	2c large die on India paper	
	e. **black**	270.
	f. **blue**	270.
	g. **brown**	360.
	h. **green**	270.
	i. **orange**	270.
	j. **red**	360.
	k. **vermilion**	600.
RS229P1	1c **choc,** lg die on India paper	210.
RS229P3	1c **choc,** plate on India paper	75.
RS230TC1a	6c large die on India paper	
	e. **blue**	270.
	f. **brown**	360.
	g. **green**	270.
	h. **orange**	360.
	i. **vermilion**	270.
RS230P1	6c **blk,** lg die on India paper	210.
RS230P3	6c **blk,** plate on India paper	—
RS231TC1a	6c large die on India paper	
	e. **black**	1,200.
	f. **blue**	1,200.
	g. **green**	1,200.
	h. **red**	900.
RS231P1	6c **org,** lg die on India paper	900.
RS231P4	6c **org,** plate on card	750.
RS232P1	8c **org,** lg die on India paper	900.
RS236TC1a	4c large die on India paper	
	e. **blue**	600.
RS236P1	4c **blk,** lg die on India paper	210.
RS239TC1a	2c large die on India paper	
	e. **black**	270.
	f. **blue**	360.
	g. **brown**	600.
	h. **green**	270.
	i. **orange**	360.
	j. **vermilion**	600.
RS239P1	2c **ver,** lg die on India paper	270.
RS239P3	2c **ver,** plate on India paper	100.
RS240TC1a	4c large die on India paper	
	e. **blue**	210.
	f. **blue green**	600.
	g. **brown**	600.
	h. **green**	270.
	i. **orange**	270.
	j. **red**	600.
	k. **vermilion**	270.
RS240P1	4c **blk,** lg die on India paper	210.
RS240P3	4c **blk,** plate on India paper	125.

Proofs of Nos. RS239 and RS240 exist in black on card with the denominations and "USIR" obliterated. These most likely are proofs made in preparation of private die facsimile labels, not proofs of or in preparation of revenue stamps.

No.	Description	Value
RS241TC1a	4c large die on India paper	
	e. **green**	600.
RS241P1	4c **red,** lg die on India paper	270.
RS242TC1a	1c large die on India paper	
	e. **blue**	270.
	f. **green**	600.
RS242P1	4c **blk,** lg die on India paper	210.
RS242P3	4c **blk,** plate on India paper	80.
RS242P4	4c **blk,** plate on card	75.
RS243TC1a	4c large die on India paper	
	e. **blue**	600.
	f. **green**	600.
RS243P1	4c **blk,** lg die on India paper	210.
RS244TC1a	6c large die on India paper	
	e. **blue**	600.
	f. **green**	600.
RS244P1	6c **blk,** lg die on India paper	210.
RS245TC1a	1c large die on India paper	
	e. **blue**	600.
RS245P1	1c **blk,** lg die on India paper	300.
RS250TC1a	6c large die on India paper	
	e. **blue**	600.
	f. **green**	600.
RS250P1	6c **blk,** lg die on India paper	210.
RS250P3	6c **blk,** plate on India paper	100.
RS251TC1a	1c large die on India paper	
	e. **blue**	270.
	f. **brown**	270.
	g. **green**	270.
RS251P1	1c **blk,** lg die on India paper	210.
RS252TC1a	1c large die on India paper	
	e. **black**	270.
	f. **blue**	270.
	g. **brown**	360.
	h. **green**	270.
	i. **orange**	600.
	j. **red**	600.
	k. **rose**	270.
RS252P1	1c **ver,** lg die on India paper	210.
RS252P3	1c **ver,** plate on India paper	100.
RS253TC1a	4c large die on India paper	
	e. **blue**	600.
	f. **green**	600.
RS253P1	4c **blk,** lg die on India paper	210.
RS258TC1a	6c large die on India paper	
	e. **black**	600.
RS258P1	6c **brn,** lg die on India paper	210.
RS259TC1a	1c large die on India paper	
	e. **blue**	270.
	f. **brown**	360.
	g. **green**	270.
	h. **orange**	360.
	i. **red**	600.
	j. **vermilion**	600.
RS259P1	1c **blk,** lg die on India paper	210.
RS259P3	1c **blk,** plate on India paper	90.
RS260TC1a	2c large die on India paper	
	e. **blue**	210.
	f. **brown**	360.
	g. **green**	270.
	h. **orange**	360.
	i. **red**	600.
	j. **rose**	600.
	k. **vermilion**	270.
RS260P1	2c **blk,** lg die on India paper	270.
RS260P3	2c **blk,** plate on India paper	90.
RS261TC1a	4c large die on India paper	
	e. **blue**	270.
	f. **brown**	360.
	g. **green**	270.
	h. **orange**	360.
	i. **red**	600.
	j. **vermilion**	600.
RS261P1	4c **blk,** lg die on India paper	210.
RS261P3	4c **blk,** plate on India paper	100.
RS262TC1a	2c large die on India paper	
	e. **blue**	600.
	f. **green**	600.
RS262P1	2c **blk,** lg die on India paper	210.
RS263P1	4c **blk,** lg die on India paper	270.
RS263P3	4c **blk,** plate on India paper	90.
RS264TC1a	4c large die on India paper	
	e. **blue**	360.
	f. **green**	360.
RS264P1	4c **blk,** lg die on India paper	270.
RS264AP1	4c **blk,** lg die on India paper	360.
RS265TC1a	1c large die on India paper	
	e. **black**	270.
	f. **blue**	600.
RS265P1	1c **grn,** lg die on India paper	270.
RS267TC1a	4c large die on India paper	
	e. **black**	270.
	f. **blue**	600.
	g. **green**	360.
RS267P1	4c **lake,** lg die on India paper	270.
RS270TC1a	12c large die on India paper	
	e. **black**	360.
	f. **blue**	600.
	g. **green**	360.
	h. **red**	270.
RS270P1	12c **bl,** lg die on India paper	210.
RS271TC1a	4c large die on India paper	
	e. **blue**	3,000.
RS271P1	4c **blk,** lg die on India paper	3,000.
RS272TC1a	1c large die on India paper	
	e. **black**	360.
	f. **blue**	360.
RS272P1	1c **grn,** lg die on India paper	270.
RS273TC1a	2c large die on India paper	
	e. **blue**	600.
RS273P1	2c **blk,** lg die on India paper	210.
RS274TC1a	1c large die on India paper	
	e. **black**	270.
RS274P1	1c **grn,** lg die on India paper	270.
RS274P3	1c **grn,** plate on India paper	65.
RS274P4	1c **grn,** plate on card	60.
RS275TC1a	2c large die on India paper	
	e. **black**	270.
	f. **blue**	360.
RS276P1	2c **grn,** lg die on India paper	210.
RS278TC1a	2½c large die on India paper	
	e. **black**	*1,200.*
RS280TC1a	¼c large die on India paper	
	e. **black**	*1,200.*
RS300P1	4⅜c **blk,** lg die on India paper	*1,200.*
RS302TC1a	2½c large die on India paper	
	e. **black**	*1,200.*
RS303TC1a	⅝c large die on India paper	
	e. **black**	*1,200.*
RS306P1	1¼c **pink,** lg die on India paper	*1,200.*

Private Die Perfumery Stamps

No.	Description	Value
RT1P3	2c **bl,** plate on India paper	125.
RT1P4	2c **bl,** plate on card	125.
RT2TC1a	1c large die on India paper	
	e. **brown**	475.
	f. **green**	475.
	g. **orange**	360.
	h. **red**	600.
RT2P1	1c **blk,** lg die on India paper	270.
RT2P3	1c **blk,** plate on India paper	95.
RT4P1	1c **bl,** lg die on India paper	270.
RT5TC1a	2c large die on India paper	
	e. **black**	210.
	f. **blue**	270.
	g. **green**	600.
	h. **orange**	600.
RT5TC3	2c plate on India paper	
	a. **orange**	125.
RT5P3	2c **ver,** plate on India paper	100.
RT6TC1a	1c large die on India paper	
	e. **blue**	450.
	f. **brown**	600.
	g. **green**	450.
	h. **orange**	600.
	i. **red**	600.
RT6P1	1c **blk,** lg die on India paper	300.
RT6P3	1c **blk,** plate on India paper	150.
RT8P1	2c **blk,** lg die on India paper	600.
RT10TC1a	4c large die on India paper	
	e. **blue**	450.
	f. **brown**	600.
	g. **green**	475.
	h. **orange**	600.
	i. **red**	600.
RT10P1	4c **blk,** lg die on India paper	300.
RT10P3	4c **blk,** plate on India paper	150.
RT12TC1a	1c large die on India paper	
	e. **black**	270.
	f. **blue**	270.
	g. **green**	600.
RT12TC4	1c plate on card	
	a. **black**	90.
RT12P1	1c **ver,** lg die on India paper	270.
RT12P3	1c **ver,** plate on India paper	—
RT13TC1a	2c large die on India paper	
	e. **black**	270.
	f. **blue**	360.
	g. **green**	360.
	h. **red**	270.
RT13TC3	2c plate on India paper	
	a. **black**	75.
RT14TC1a	3c large die on India paper	
	e. **blue**	1,200.
RT14P1	3c **blk,** lg die on India paper	600.
RT16TC1a	1c large die on India paper	
	e. **blue**	210.
	f. **green**	270.
RT16P1	1c **blk,** lg die on India paper	210.
RT17TC1a	2c large die on India paper	
	e. **black**	360.
	f. **blue**	360.
	g. **green**	360.
	h. **orange**	600.
RT17P1	2c **brn,** lg die on India paper	210.
RT18TC1a	3c large die on India paper	
	e. **black**	210.
	f. **blue**	210.
	g. **green**	600.
	h. **orange**	600.
	i. **red**	360.
RT18P1	3c **grn,** lg die on India paper	210.
RT19TC1a	1c large die on India paper	
	e. **black**	600.
RT19P1	1c **ver,** lg die on India paper	270.
RT20TC1a	1c large die on India paper	
	e. **black**	270.
	f. **blue**	360.
	g. **green**	210.
RT20P1	1c **grn,** lg die on India paper	270.
RT21TC1a	2c large die on India paper	
	e. **black**	600.
	f. **green**	600.
RT21P1	2c **bl,** lg die on India paper	210.
RT22TC1a	1c large die on India paper	
	e. **black**	210.
	f. **blue**	360.
	g. **green**	360.

	h. **red brown**	360.
	i. **ultramarine**	600.
RT22P1	1c **bl,** lg die on India paper	270.
RT23TC1a	2c large die on India paper	
	e. **blue**	270.
	f. **green**	600.
RT23P1	2c **blk,** lg die on India paper	210.
RT24TC1a	3c large die on India paper	
	e. **black**	210.
	f. **blue**	270.
	g. **green**	360.
	h. **red**	270.
RT25TC1a	4c large die on India paper	
	e. **black**	210.
	f. **blue**	270.
RT25P1	4c **grn,** lg die on India paper	210.
RT26TC1a	1c large die on India paper	
	e. **black**	210.
	f. **blue**	270.
	g. **brown**	360.
	h. **green**	600.
	i. **orange**	360.
	j. **red**	600.
RT26P1	1c **grn,** lg die on India paper	210.
RT27P3	1c **grn,** plate on India paper	100.
RT28TC1a	2c large die on India paper	
	e. **black**	270.
	f. **brown**	360.
	g. **green**	270.
	h. **orange**	360.
	i. **red**	360.
RT28P1	2c **bl,** lg die on India paper	210.
RT30TC1a	3c large die on India paper	
	e. **black**	270.
	f. **blue**	270.
	g. **brown**	360.
	h. **green**	270.
	i. **orange**	360.
	j. **red**	210.
RT30P1	3c **ver,** lg die on India paper	270.
RT32TC1a	4c large die on India paper	
	e. **black**	270.
	f. **blue**	270.
	g. **brown**	600.
	h. **green**	270.
	i. **orange**	270.
	j. **red**	360.
RT32P1	4c **brn,** lg die on India paper	210.

Private Die Playing Card Stamps

RU1P1	5c **blk,** lg die on India paper	*4,000.*
RU2TC1a	2c large die on India paper	
	e. **black**	210.
	f. **blue**	270.
	g. **green**	360.
RU3TC1a	2c large die on India paper	
	e. **blue**	270.
	f. **green**	270.
RU3P1	4c **blk,** lg die on India paper	210.
RU3P3	4c **blk,** plate on India paper	100.
RU4TC1a	5c large die on India paper	
	e. **black**	270.
	f. **green**	360.
RU4P1	5c **bl,** lg die on India paper	210.
RU5TC1a	5c large die on India paper	
	e. **black**	270.
	f. **brown**	360.
	g. **green**	360.
	h. **light brown**	600.
	i. **orange**	600.
	j. **red**	600.
RU5P1	5c **bl,** lg die on India paper	210.
RU6TC1a	10c large die on India paper	
	e. **black**	210.
	f. **green**	360.
RU6P1	10c **bl,** lg die on India paper	600.
RU6P3	10c **bl,** plate on India paper	100.
RU7TC1a	5c large die on India paper	
	e. **blue**	450.
	f. **green**	450.
RU7P1	5c **blk,** lg die on India paper	300.
RU7P3	5c **blk,** plate on India paper	100.
RU7P4	5c **blk,** plate on card	—
RU8TC1a	5c large die on India paper	
	e. **blue**	270.
	f. **green**	270.
	g. **orange**	360.
RU8P1	5c **blk,** lg die on India paper	210.
RU9TC1a	5c large die on India paper	
	e. **blue**	270.
	f. **green**	600.
RU9P1	5c **blk,** lg die on India paper	300.
RU10TC1a	2c large die on India paper	
	e. **black**	240.
	f. **brown**	600.
	g. **green**	600.
RU10P1	2c **bl,** lg die on India paper	210.
RU11TC1a	5c large die on India paper	
	e. **black**	270.
	f. **blue**	270.
	g. **brown**	360.
RU11P1	5c **grn,** lg die on India paper	270.
RU12TC1a	5c large die on India paper	
	e. **blue**	360.
	f. **green**	360.
RU12P1	5c **blk,** lg die on India paper	210.
RU13TC1a	5c large die on India paper	
	e. **green**	210.
RU13P1	5c **bl,** lg die on India paper	360.
RU14TC1a	5c large die on India paper	
	e. **blue**	270.
	f. **brown**	360.
	g. **green**	360.
	h. **light brown**	600.
	i. **orange**	600.
	j. **red**	360.
RU14P1	5c **blk,** lg die on India paper	210.
RU14P3	5c **blk,** plate on India paper	—
RU15TC1a	5c large die on India paper	
	e. **blue**	360.
	f. **green**	360.
RU15P1	5c **blk,** lg die on India paper	400.
RU16P1	5c **blk,** lg die on India paper	600.

Hunting Permit

RW1P1	1934	$1	**bl,** lg die on wove paper	—
RW1P2	1934	$1	**bl,** small die on wove paper	*22,500.*
RW2P2	1935	$1	**rose lake,** small die on wove paper	*12,500.*
RW3P1	1936	$1	**brn blk,** lg die on wove paper	*8,500.*
RW3P2	1936	$1	**brn blk,** small die on wove paper	*8,500.*
RW4TC1a		$1	large die on India paper	
	e.		**light violet**	*5,500.*
RW4P1	1937	$1	**lt grn,** lg die on wove paper	—
RW4P2	1937	$1	**lt grn,** small die on wove paper	*8,500.*
RW5P1	1938	$1	**lt vio,** lg die on wove paper	—
RW5P2	1938	$1	**lt vio,** small die on wove paper	*8,500.*
RW6P2	1939	$1	**choc,** small die on wove paper	*7,500.*
RW7P2	1940	$1	**sepia,** small die on wove paper	*7,500.*
RW8P1	1941	$1	**brn car,** lg die on wove paper	*7,500.*
RW8P2	1941	$1	**brn car,** small die on wove paper	*7,500.*
RW9P2	1942	$1	**vio brn,** small die on wove paper	*7,500.*
RW10P1	1943	$1	**dp rose,** lg die on wove paper	*7,500.*
RW10P2	1943	$1	**dp rose,** small die on wove paper	*7,500.*
RW11P2	1944	$1	**red org,** small die on wove paper	*7,500.*
RW12TC1a		$1	large die on India paper	
	e.		**light violet**	*20,000.*
RW12P1	1945	$1	**blk,** lg die on wove paper	*7,500.*
RW12P2	1945	$1	**blk,** small die on wove paper	*7,500.*
RW13P1	1946	$1	**red brn,** lg die on wove paper	*7,500.*
RW13P2	1946	$1	**red brn,** small die on wove paper	*7,500.*
RW14P1	1947	$1	**blk,** lg die on wove paper	*7,500.*
RW14P2	1947	$1	**blk,** small die on wove paper	*7,500.*
RW15P1	1948	$1	**brt bl,** lg die on wove paper	*9,500.*
RW15P2	1948	$1	**brt bl,** small die on wove paper	*7,500.*
RW16P2	1949	$2	**brt grn,** small die on wove paper	*7,500.*
RW17P2	1950	$2	**vio,** small die on wove paper	*7,500.*
RW18P2	1951	$2	**gray blk,** small die on wove paper	*7,500.*
RW19P1	1952	$2	**dp ultra,** lg die on wove paper	*7,500.*
RW20P2	1953	$2	**dp brn rose,** small die on wove paper	*7,500.*
RW21P2	1954	$2	**blk,** small die on wove paper	*7,500.*
RW22P2	1955	$2	**dk bl,** small die on wove paper	*7,500.*
RW23P1	1956	$2	**blk,** lg die on wove paper	*12,500.*
RW23P2	1956	$2	**blk,** small die on wove paper	*7,500.*
RW24P2	1957	$2	**emerald,** small die on wove paper	*7,500.*
RW25P2	1958	$2	**blk,** small die on wove paper	*7,500.*
RW26P5	1959	$3	**multi,** plate on stamp paper	*3,000.*
RW27P5	1960	$3	**multi,** plate on stamp paper	*3,000.*
RW28P5	1961	$3	**multi,** plate on stamp paper	*3,000.*
RW29P5	1962	$3	**multi,** plate on stamp paper	*3,000.*
RW30P5	1963	$3	**multi,** plate on stamp paper	*3,000.*
RW32P5	1965	$3	**multi,** plate on stamp paper	*3,000.*
RW33P5	1966	$3	**multi,** plate on stamp paper	*3,000.*
RW34P5	1967	$3	**multi,** plate on stamp paper	*3,000.*
RW35P5	1968	$3	**multi,** plate on stamp paper	*3,000.*
RW36P5	1969	$3	**multi,** plate on stamp paper	*3,000.*
RW37P5	1970	$3	**multi,** plate on stamp paper	*3,000.*
RW38P5	1971	$3	**multi,** plate on stamp paper	*3,000.*
RW39P5	1972	$5	**multi,** plate on stamp paper	*3,000.*
RW40P5	1973	$5	**multi,** plate on stamp paper	*3,000.*
RW41P5	1974	$5	**multi,** plate on stamp paper	*3,000.*
RW42P5	1975	$5	**multi,** plate on stamp paper	*3,000.*
RW43P5	1976	$5	**grn & blk,** plate on stamp paper	*3,000.*
RW44P5	1977	$5	**multi,** plate on stamp paper	*3,000.*
RW45P5	1978	$5	**multi,** plate on stamp paper	*3,000.*
RW46P5	1979	$7.50	**multi,** plate on stamp paper	*3,000.*
RW47P5	1980	$7.50	**multi,** plate on stamp paper	*3,000.*
RW48P5	1981	$7.50	**multi,** plate on stamp paper	*3,000.*
RW49P5	1982	$7.50	**multi,** plate on stamp paper	*3,000.*
RW50P5	1983	$7.50	**multi,** plate on stamp paper	*3,000.*

Firearms Transfer

RY3P1	$1 **grn,** with "c" punch cancel, lg die on wove paper	*2,000.*

POSTAL SAVINGS

1911

PS1P1	10c **org,** large die on India paper	1,000.
PS1P2a	10c **org,** PP sm die on yelsh wove paper	750.
PS4P2a	10c **dp bl,** PP sm die on yelsh wove paper	750.

1940

PS7TC1	10c **black,** large die on India paper, die sunk on 97x110mm card	—
PS7P2	10c **dp ultra,** sm die on wove paper	1,200.
PS8P2	25c **dk car rose,** sm die on wove paper	1,200.
PS9TC1	50c **black,** large die on India paper	—
PS9P2	50c **dk bl grn,** sm die on wove paper	1,200.
PS10P2	$1 **gray blk,** sm die on wove paper	1,200.

1941

PS11P2	10c **rose red,** sm die on wove paper	1,000.
PS12P2	25c **bl grn,** sm die on wove paper	1,000.
PS13P2	50c **ultra,** sm die on wove paper	1,000.
PS14P2	$1 **gray blk,** sm die on wove paper	1,000.
PS15P1	$5 **sepia,** large die on wove paper	*4,000.*
PS15P2	$5 **sepia,** sm die on wove paper	1,000.

WAR SAVINGS STAMP

1942

WS7P1	10c **rose red,** large die on India paper	1,400.